HATIM'S TALES

INDIAN TEXTS SERIES

HATIM'S TALES

KASHMIRI STORIES AND SONGS

RECORDED WITH THE ASSISTANCE OF

PANDIT GOVIND KAUL

BY SIR AUREL STENY, K. C. I. E.

AND EDITED WITH A TRA.NSLATION, LINGUISTIC ANALYSIS, VOCABULARY, INDEXES, ETC.

BY SIR GEORGE A. GRIERSON, K.C.I.E.

WITH A NOTE ON THE FOLKLORE OF THE TALES

BY W. CROOKE, C.LE.

GYAN

ISBN : 978-81-212-0136-0

Published, 2018

Published by

Gyan Publishing House
5, Ansari Road
Daryaganj, New Delhi-110002
Phone: 011-47034999, 9811692060
www.gyanbooks.com
E-mail: books@gyanbooks.com

Printed at: G. Print Process, Delhi.

TO THE MEMORY OF

PANDIT GOVIND KAUL

WHOSE SCHOLARSHIP AND FRIENDLY DEVOTION

EVER FURTHERED KASHMIRIAN RESEARCHES

DEDICATED

IN SINCERE AFFECTION AND GRATITUDE.

CONTENTS

PREFACE

THESE pages have to be written many years after the Kāshmīrī texts here presented were collected, and amidst urgent tasks concerning the results gathered in a wholly different field of work, that of my Central-Asian explorations. These conditions make me feel particularly grateful for the fact that Sir George Grierson in his Introduction has dealt so exhaustively with the manner in which those texts were originally recorded, and with all aspects of the linguistic interest which may be claimed for them. It has thus become possible for me to confine the preface he has asked for to a brief account of the circumstances which enabled me to gather these materials, and to some personal notes concerning that cherished Indian scholar friend, the late PAṆḌIT GŌVIND KAUL, whose devoted assistance was largely instrumental in rendering them of value for linguistic research, and whose memory this volume is intended to honour.

My interest in the language and folklore of Kashmīr directly arose from the labours which, during the years 1888–98, I devoted, mainly in the country itself, to the preparation of my critical edition of Kalhaṇa's *Chronicle of the Kings of Kashmīr* and of my commentated translation of it.[1] The elucidation of the manifold antiquarian questions which these tasks implied, and which in various ways constituted their chief attraction for me, was possible only in close touch with Kashmīr scholars, and needed constant reference to the traditional lore of their alpine land. In addition it was necessary for me to effect extensive archæological researches on the spot. What leisure I could spare from onerous and exacting official duties at Lahore for the purely philological portion of those tasks was far too scanty to permit

[1] See *Kalhaṇa's Rājataraṅginī, or Chronicle of the Kings of Kashmīr*, edited by M. A. Stein, Bombay, 1892, fol.; *Kalhaṇa's Rājataraṅginī, a Chronicle of the Kings of Kaśmīr*, translated with an Introduction, Commentary, etc., by M. A. Stein, Westminster, 1900, 2 vols., 4to.

of any serious study of Kāshmīrī. But during the eight summer vacations which I was privileged to devote in Kashmīr to my cherished labours, and particularly during those between 1891 and 1894, which I spent mostly on archæological tours elucidating the historical topography of the country and tracing its ancient remains, I had opportunities for acquiring some colloquial familiarity with the language. I should probably have been able to make more systematic use of these opportunities had not convenience and conservative attachment to the classical medium of Kashmīr scholarship made me prefer the use of Sanskrit conversation with my Paṇḍit friends and assistants at Śrīnagar and wherever they shared my tours and campings.

Meanwhile, Sir George Grierson had commenced his expert linguistic researches concerning Kāshmīrī. They were, for the first time, to demonstrate the full interest of the tongue and the true character of its relationship on the one hand to the Indo-Aryan vernaculars and on the other to the language group, called by him "Dardic" or "Piśāca", the separate existence of which, within the Aryan branch, he has the merit of having clearly established. His Kāshmīrī studies were at the start directed mainly towards the publication of the remarkable works by which the late Paṇḍit Īśvara Kaul had endeavoured to fix the phonetic, grammatical, and lexicographical standards for what he conceived to be the literary form of Kāshmīrī. There was every prospect that these standards, through the exhaustive labours bestowed by Sir George Grierson upon their record and interpretation, would establish themselves for a language which so far had remained free from the systematizing influence of Paṇḍit grammarians. Paṇḍit Gōvind Kaul, though a close personal friend of Paṇḍit Īśvara Kaul, and fully appreciative of his scholarly zeal and ingenuity, was inclined to doubt at times the thoroughgoing regularity in the application of all the phonetic distinctions, inflectional rules, etc., laid down by this Kashmirian epiphany of Pāṇini.

I should in no way have felt qualified to decide between the conflicting authorities, even if I could have spared time for the close investigation of the differences of detail concerned. But I realized the value which might attach to an unbiassed phonetic record of specimens of the language taken down at this stage from the mouth of speakers wholly unaffected by quasi-literary influences and grammatical theories. In the course of my Kashmīr tours I had been more than once impressed by the clearness of utterance to be met with in the speech of intelligent villagers, very different from the Protean inconstancy which certain phonetic features of Kāshmīrī seemed to present in the mouth of the townsfolk of Śrīnagar, whether Brahmans or Muhammadans. In addition, my interest had been aroused from the first by the rich store of popular lore which Kāshmīrī presents in its folk tales, songs, proverbs, and the like.

So in the course of the second summer season, that of 1896, which I was enabled through a kind dispensation to devote to my *Rājataraṅgiṇī* labours in the alpine seclusion of my cherished mountain camp, Mohand Marg, high up on a spur of the great Haramukh peaks, I endeavoured to use the chance which had opportunely offered itself for securing specimens both of the language spoken in the Sind Valley below me (the important *Lahara* tract of old Kashmīr) and of folklore texts. Hātim Til^{a}wōn^{u} had been mentioned to me as a professional story-teller in particular esteem throughout that fertile tract. He was a cultivator settled in the little hamlet of Paṇzil, at the confluence of the Sind River and the stream draining the eastern Haramukh glaciers, and owed his surname to the possession of an oil press. When he had been induced to climb up to my mountain height and had favoured Paṇḍit Gōvind Kaul and myself with his first recitation, we were both much struck by his intelligence, remarkable memory, and clear enunciation. His répertoire of stories and songs was a large one. Though wholly illiterate, he was able to recite them all at any desired rate of speed which might suit our ears or pens; to articulate each word separate from the context, and to repeat it, if necessary, without any change in pronunciation. Nor did the order of his words or phrases ever vary after however long an interval he might be called upon to recite a certain passage again. The indication of two or three initial words repeated from my written record would be quite sufficient to set the disk moving in this living phonographic machine.

It did not take me long to appreciate fully Hātim's value for the purpose I had in view. He did not at first take kindly to the cold of our airy camping-place nor to its loneliness, being himself of a very sociable disposition, such as befitted his professional calling exercised mostly at weddings and other festive village gatherings. But it was the cultivators' busy season in the rice fields, some 5,000 feet below us, and his ministrations were not needed by them for the time being. So I managed, with appropriate treatment and adequate douceurs, to retain him for over six weeks. Owing to the pressure of my work on Kalhaṇa's *Chronicle* it was impossible to spare for Hātim more than an hour in the evening, after a climb, usually in his company, had refreshed me from the strain of labours which had begun by daybreak.

Progress was necessarily made slow by the care which I endeavoured to bestow upon the exact phonetic record of Hātim's recitation and the consequent need of having each word where I did not feel sure of it, repeated, eventually several times. Whenever a story was completed I used to read it out to Hātim, who never failed to notice and correct whatever deviation from his text might have crept in through inadvertence or defective hearing. Though able to follow the context in general, I purposely avoided troubling Hātim with queries about particular words or sentences which I could not readily understand. I felt that the object in view would be best served by concentrating my attention upon the functions of a phonographic recorder and discharging them as accurately as the limitations of my ear and phonetic training would permit.

I could not have adopted this safe restriction of my own task, and might well have hesitated about attempting the record of these materials at all, if I had not been assured from the start of Paṇḍit Gōvind Kaul's most competent and painstaking collaboration. The intimate knowledge which long years of scholarly work carried on in constant close contact had given me of his methods and standards, enabled me to leave certain essential portions of the work entirely to his share and with fullest confidence in the result. I could feel completely assured that with that rare thoroughness and conscientious precision which distinguished all his work on the lines of the traditional Sanskrit scholar, his record of Hātim's text written down in Devanāgarī characters simultaneously with my own would be as exact as the system, or want of system, of Kāshmīrī spelling current among Śrīnagar Paṇḍits would permit. I was equally certain that he would spare no trouble to make his interpretation of it, both in the form of an interlinear word-for-word version and of an idiomatic Sanskrit translation, as accurate as possible.

Sir George Grierson's remarks upon the advantages which he derived from Paṇḍit Gōvind Kaul's labours make it unnecessary for me to explain here the special value attaching to them. It will suffice to state that Paṇḍit Gōvind Kaul's text as written down at the time of dictation was always revised simultaneously with my own. The interlinear translation was then added in the course of the following day, after reference to Hātim wherever doubts arose about the meaning of particular words or phrases. The preparation of the fair copy of both, with the idiomatic Sanskrit rendering added, was a task which helped to keep Paṇḍit Govind Kaul occupied during my absence in Europe for part of 1897. During the summer of the next year I enjoyed once more the benefit of his devoted assistance in labours dear to us both, and in the peaceful seclusion of my alpine camp. But my big *Rājataraṅgiṇī* task, then nearing completion, claimed all my energy and time. Thus the lacuna left in Paṇḍit Gōvind Kaul's record of Hātim's last tale, due to the accidental loss of the concluding few pages of his original manuscript, escaped attention at the time.

When it was brought to my notice by Sir George Grierson fully fourteen years later, I was encamped once more at the very spot where we had recorded those stories. But, alas, Paṇḍit Gōvind Kaul was no longer among the living to give aid; and, what with years of Central-Asian exploration and long labours on their results intervening, those records seemed to me as if gathered in a former birth. Fortunately, Hātim was still alive and quite equal to the stiff climb which his renewed visit demanded—the photograph reproduced here shows him as he looked then. His recollection of the story was as fresh as ever, though increasing years and prosperity had made him give up his peregrinations as a public story-teller. So it was easy for another old retainer, Paṇḍit Kāśī Rām, to take down from Hātim's dictation the missing end of the story; it ran exactly as my own record showed it.

During the years which followed the completion of my main Kashmīr labours the efforts needed to carry out successive Central-Asian expeditions and to assure the elaboration of their abundant results, kept me from making definite arrangements for the publication of those linguistic materials. They had meanwhile, together with my collection of Sanskrit manuscripts from Kashmīr, found a safe place of deposit in the Indian Institute's Library at Oxford. But it filled me with grateful relief when my old friend Sir George Grierson, after a preliminary examination, kindly agreed in the autumn of 1910 to publish these texts, and thus enabled me to leave them in the hands most competent for the task.

It was the solution I had hoped for all along, and realizing how much more difficult this task was than the original collection of the materials, I feel deep gratification at the fact that a kindly Fate has allowed him to complete it amidst all his great labours. In view of all the progress which Indian linguistic research for more than a generation past owes to Sir George Grierson's exceptional qualifications and powers of critical work, it would be presumption on my part to appraise how much of the value which may be claimed for this publication is derived solely from the wide range and precision of the scholarly knowledge he has brought to bear upon it.

It is the greatness of his own share in the work which makes me feel particularly grateful to Sir George Grierson for his ready consent to its dedication to the memory of Paṇḍit Gōvind Kaul. It affords me an appropriate opportunity for recording some data about the life of a cherished friend and helpmate whose memory deserves to be honoured for the nobility of his character quite as much as for his scholarly gifts and labours. The association of Paṇḍit Gōvind Kaul during close on ten years with my own efforts bearing on the history and antiquities of Kashmīr has always been appreciated by me as a special favour of Fortune, or—to name the goddess under her own Kashmirian form—of Śāradā, who is the protectress of learning as well as of the alpine land which claims to be her home; for he seemed to embody in his person all the best characteristics of that small but important class among the Brahmans of Kashmīr to which the far-off and secluded mountain territory owes its pre-eminent position in the history of Indian learning and literature.

I cannot attempt to indicate here the evidence to be gathered both from the Sanskrit literary products of Kashmīr and from surviving local tradition, which makes me believe that high scholarly attainments and a special facility of elegant rhetorical or poetic expression were to be found among the truly learned in Kashmīr more frequently combined than elsewhere in India with a keen eye for the realities of life, power of humorous observation, and distinct interest in the practical affairs of the country. Kalhaṇa himself, the author of the *Rājataraṅgiṇī*, with whose personality, I felt, I was becoming so familiar across the gap of long centuries, seemed aptly to illustrate this typical combination of features.[1] In Paṇḍit Gōvind Kaul I found them all again and united with a high sense of honour, a bearing of true innate nobility, and a capacity for faithful attachment which from the first made me cherish him greatly as a friend, not merely as an accomplished mentor in most things appertaining to Kashmīr and its traditional past. A brief account of his descent and early associations will best explain the growth of these strongly-marked characteristics.[2]

Paṇḍit Gōvind Kaul was born in 1846 as the eldest son of Paṇḍit Balabhadra Kaul (1819–96), who, by reason of his personal qualities, great scholarly attainments, and social position, was universally respected among the Brahman community of Śrīnagar. Paṇḍit Balabhadra's own father, Paṇḍit Taba Kaul, had been a Sanskrit scholar of great reputation in the closing period of Afghān rule in Kashmīr. Being connected as hereditary 'Guru' with the important Brahman family of the Dars he had enjoyed a substantial Jāgīr, and this was allowed to continue when Mahārāja Raṇjit Singh's conquest in 1819 established Sikh dominion over Kashmīr. Paṇḍit Bīrbal Dar, his patron, had held an influential administrative position already under the Afghān régime. But he incurred the suspicion of 'Aẓīm Khān, the last governor from Kābul, and persecuted by him, he was obliged to flee from Kashmīr to the Panjāb. Of the adventurous escape which he made with

[1] Cf. the sketch I have given of the information to be gathered from the *Rājataraṅgiṇī* about the personal character of its author in the Introduction to my translation, i, pp. 21 sqq.

[2] For the account here presented I have been able to utilize a series of notes which Paṇḍit Gōvind Kaul's son, Paṇḍit Nīlakaṇṭh, collected at my request among the elder members of his family and also among the surviving representatives of the Dar family, their hereditary patrons. In addition my recollection of data verbally communicated to me by Paṇḍit Gōvind Kaul has proved useful.

his young son Paṇḍit Rājakāk, in mid-winter 1818–19, across the snow-covered mountains, and of the cruel treatment endured by those of his family he was obliged to leave behind, Paṇḍit Gōvind Kaul told me interesting traditions. The experienced advice which Paṇḍit Bīrbal supplied to Mahārāja Ranjit Singh is believed to have contributed greatly to the success of the campaign, which, in the following summer, placed Kashmīr in the power of the great Sikh ruler.[1]

The high administrative posts which Paṇḍit Bīrbal, and after his death his equally capable son Paṇḍit Rājakāk, held during the period of Sikh rule in Kashmīr (1819–46), necessarily assured a prominent social position and relative affluence also for Paṇḍit Taba Kaul and his son Paṇḍit Balabhadra Kaul. The latter was thus enabled to devote himself during his youth solely to Sanskrit studies, and to lay the foundations of a scholarly renown which made him, from an early date, a prominent figure among the Paṇḍits of Kashmīr. But the far-reaching political changes which followed the accession of Mahārāja Gulāb Singh of Jammu to the rule of Kashmīr at the close of the First Sikh War, in 1846, led to the loss of the family's Jāgīr and threw a heavy strain upon Paṇḍit Balabhadra's resources. Though restricted to what income his functions as hereditary Guru and as a teacher of Śāstras could secure, and maintaining throughout his long life a dignified retirement,[2] Paṇḍit Balabhadra succeeded not only in giving his

[1] Paṇḍit Bīrbal is said to have been personally present at the fight on the Divᵃsar Karēwa in which the Afghāns were finally defeated by Diwān Chand Misar and Sardār Hari Singh, Ranjit Singh's generals, and to have decided the issue by pointing out Jabar Khān, 'Aẓīm Khān's brother and ablest commander, as the chief objective for the attack. I may mention as an interesting relic connected with this event that in the palace-like mansion of the Dar family, a monument of departed glory, I found a number of fine Persian carpets and elaborate felt rugs which according to family tradition Paṇḍit Bīrbal had been allowed to appropriate from the defeated Afghān governor's camp in recognition of the help he had rendered towards the Sikh success on that field of battle.

[2] During the latter half of his life he never left the house he occupied within the precincts of the Dar family mansion, though receiving frequent visitors from among those whom office or intellectual attainments placed high in the social world of Śrīnagar.

three sons an excellent education, but in accumulating also an important collection of Sanskrit manuscripts.

His tasks were, no doubt, facilitated by the support he derived from his close connexion with the remarkably able men who succeeded Paṇḍit Bīrbal as heads of the Dar family. Paṇḍit Rājakāk, the latter's son (1805–66), had distinguished himself as an administrator already during the troubled times of the closing Sikh régime, and quelled a rebellion in the hill tract of Drāva. When conditions had become more settled under the Dogrā rule he rose high in Mahārāja Gulāb Singh's favour by greatly developing the shawl industry of Kashmīr, then a monopoly and financial mainstay of the State. Endowed with a genuine love of knowledge and with that intellectual adaptability which has distinguished the best brains of Kashmīr through successive historical periods, he had taken care to secure for his son, Paṇḍit Rāmjīv Dar (*circ.* 1850–83), not only a sound training in Persian and Sanskrit, but also some familiarity with English and with Western ways. It was no easy departure in days when close relations with Europeans were apt to be looked at askance as infringing upon the traditional policy of seclusion and the security it was meant to assure.

It was in intimate association with Paṇḍit Rāmjīv Dar that Paṇḍit Gōvind Kaul spent most of his early manhood. The experience he thus gained of the world of affairs, of rulers and ruled alike, did much to widen the horizon of his thoughts and interests beyond that of the traditional student of Śāstras. Paṇḍit Rāmjīv seems to have been a man of an unusually active mind and of considerable practical energy. During his short but fruitful life he had the good fortune to serve a ruler so well qualified as the late Mahārāja Raṇbīr Singh to appreciate his varied mental gifts and activities. It was the cherished aim of the late Mahārāja to combine the preservation of inherited systems of Indian thought and knowledge with the development of his country's economic resources along the lines of modern

Western progress. Having proved his ability as an administrator of Kashmīr districts, Paṇḍit Rāmjīv gradually became the Mahārāja's trusted adviser in a variety of departments which were created to further that policy, including those of education, agriculture, sericulture, etc. The manifold administrative duties entrusted to Paṇḍit Rāmjīv did not divert his attention from scholarly interests, and consequently he kept Paṇḍit Gōvind Kaul as much as possible by his side wherever his tours of inspection, etc., took him. Thus, Paṇḍit Gōvind Kaul was able to acquire a great deal of first-hand knowledge of Kashmīr and the neighbouring territories in all their varied aspects.

Paṇḍit Gōvind Kaul had, from his earliest youth, received a very thorough literary training in Sanskrit under his father's direct guidance. In accordance with the traditions of Kashmīr learning he had devoted particular efforts to the study of the Alaṁkāra-śāstra and the poetic literature which is bound up with it. His stock of quotations from the latter seemed inexhaustible. He was thoroughly at home also in Vyākaraṇa, Nyāya and the Śaiva-śāstra, and he read widely in the Epics and Purāṇas. As far as Sanskrit literary qualifications were concerned, he was well equipped for the charge of the "Translation Department", to which he was appointed in 1874. By creating it together with a State Press it was the Mahārāja's intention to diffuse a knowledge of Sanskrit works on law, philosophy, etc., among wider classes of his subjects through the medium of Hindī. Other branches of the same department were intended to secure the same object with regard to selected works in English and Persian. It is needless to discuss here the practical utility of the scheme or the causes which, owing to the lingering illness of the Mahārāja, hampered its execution during the closing years of his reign. It is enough to remember that it provided suitable employments for such highly deserving scholars as Paṇḍit Gōvind Kaul and the late Paṇḍit Sahajabhaṭṭa, who was to become another of my Kashmīr assistants, and that among the works undertaken, but never finished, there was also a Hindī translation of the *Sanskrit Chronicles of Kashmīr*.

In 1883 Paṇḍit Rāmjīv Dar was carried off by a premature death. Soon after, the Translation Department ceased to exist, together with several other institutions which had owed their creation to his stimulating influence. The last years preceding Mahārāja Raṇbīr Singh's death in 1886 and the first of the reign of his son and successor were for Kashmīr a period of transition. Traditional methods of administration and economic conditions bequeathed by long centuries of practical seclusion were giving way without there being the machinery as yet available to effect needful reforms on the lines developed in British India. It was in various ways a trying time for all those representing the intellectual inheritance of the valley, and after a short spell of work as a teacher in the Sanskrit Pāṭhaśālā, maintained by the Darbār at Śrīnagar, on scant pay—and that often in arrears—Paṇḍit Gōvind Kaul found himself without official employment.

His learning and sound methods of scholarly work had already, in 1875, attracted the attention of Professor George Bühler, when that great Indologist had paid his memorable visit to Kashmīr in search of Sanskrit MSS. The very commendatory mention which Professor Bühler's report made of Paṇḍit Gōvind Kaul's attainments and of the help he had rendered,[1] directed my attention to him from the start. The personal impression gained within the first few days of my arrival at Srīnagar at the close of August, 1888, was quite sufficient to convince me how amply deserved that praise was. I was quick to notice Paṇḍit Gōvind Kaul's special interest in antiquarian subjects, such as made me then already form the plan of a critical edition

[1] Cf. Bühler, "Detailed Report of a Tour in search of Sanskrit MSS. made in Kaśmīr, Rajputana, and Central India," Extra Number of the *Journal Bombay Branch, R.A.S.*, 1877, pp. 7, 17, 27. In the last-quoted passage Professor Bühler mentions Paṇḍit Gōvind Kaul's shrewd identification of the old local name of Leh (*Loḥ* in the *Rājat.*), and rightly states: "His proceeding showed that he was possessed of a truly scientific spirit of enquiry."

and commentary of Kalhaṇa's *Chronicle of Kashmīr*. I was equally impressed by his dignified personality, which combined the best qualities of the Indian scholar and gentleman. A short archæological tour which we made in company to sites round the Ḍal Lake helped to draw us together in mutual sympathy and regard. So it was to me a great source of satisfaction when, before my departure for the plains, Paṇḍit Gōvind Kaul, with his revered father's full approval, accepted my offer of personal employment and agreed to follow me to Lahore for the cold weather season.

It was the beginning of a long period of close association between us in scholarly interests and work. It continued practically unbroken for nearly eleven years, throughout my official employment in the Panjab University at Lahore, and down to Paṇḍit Gōvind Kaul's lamented death in June, 1899. Neither my visits on leave to Europe nor an interval in 1892–3, when he was tempted to accept employment at the Court of Jammu on H.H. the Mahārāja's private staff, implied any real interruption. It was, in the first place, my labours concerning the critical publication and elucidation of Kalhaṇa's *Chronicle of Kashmīr*, for which Paṇḍit Gōvind Kaul's multifarious and ever devoted assistance proved of the greatest value. As to the character and extent of this help it is unnecessary here to give details. They have been recorded at length, and with due expression of my gratitude, both in the Introduction to my text edition of the *Rājataraṅgiṇī*, published in 1892, and in the Preface to the commentated translation of it, with which, in 1900, on the eve of departure for my first Central-Asian expedition, I completed my labours bearing on the early history and antiquities of Kashmīr.[1]

Nor need I give here details regarding the large share taken by Paṇḍit Gōvind Kaul in another important if not equally

[1] Cf. *Kalhaṇa's Rājataraṅgiṇī*, ed. Stein, p. xvii ; *Kalhaṇa's Rājataraṅgiṇī*, transl. Stein, i, pp. xvii, xxii sq.

attractive task. I mean the preparation of a classified catalogue of the great collection of Sanskrit MSS., over 5,000 in number, which, through Mahārāja Raṇbīr Singh's enlightened care, had been formed at the Raghunāth Temple Library at Jammu. The support I received from successive British residents in Kashmīr, including the late Colonels R. Parry Nisbet and N. F. Prideaux, and from my old friend the late Rāja Paṇḍit Sūraj Kaul, then Member of the Kashmīr State Council, furnished me with the means for organizing the labours by which, in the course of 1889-94, this very valuable collection was saved from the risk of dispersion and rendered accessible to research. They were effected mainly through Paṇḍit Gōvind Kaul and our common friend the late Paṇḍit Sahajabhaṭṭa. A full acknowledgment of their devoted services will be found in the Introduction to the volume which contains the descriptive catalogue, together with the plentiful and accurate extracts prepared by them from previously unknown or otherwise interesting Sanskrit texts.[1]

It would have been quite impossible for me, burdened as I was all through my years at Lahore with heavy and exacting official duties, to undertake the big tasks referred to, had not a kindly Fortune provided me in Paṇḍit Gōvind Kaul with a coadjutor of exceptional qualities. With a wide range of thorough traditional knowledge of the Śāstras and a keen sense of literary form he combined a standard of accuracy and a capacity for taking pains over details which would have done high credit to any European scholar trained on modern philological lines. Though he was no longer young when he joined me, he adapted himself with instinctive comprehension to the needs of Western critical methods, such as I was bound to apply to all my tasks. With infinite and never-failing care he would record and collate the readings of the manuscripts upon which I depended for the critical constitution of the *Rājataraṅgiṇī*

[1] See Stein, *Catalogue of the Sanskrit Manuscripts in the Raghunātha Temple Library of H.H. the Mahārāja of Jammu and Kashmīr*, Bombay, 1894, pp. vi sq., xi.

text, and also those of other Kashmirian works, almost all unpublished, reference to which was constantly needed for its interpretation. Yet I knew that scrupulously careful as he was about the formal correctness of his Sanskrit writing and speech, the exact reproduction of all the blunders, etc., to be met in the work of often ignorant copyists caused him a kind of physical pain.

It was the same with the labours he had to devote to the collection and sifting of all the multifarious materials needed for the elucidation of antiquarian problems. However much wanting in style and other literary attractions the Kashmirian texts such as Māhātmyas, later Chronicles, etc., might be which had to be searched, I could always feel sure that none of their contents which might be of interest by their bearing on the realities of ancient Kashmīr would be allowed by Paṇḍit Gōvind Kaul to escape his Index slips. The value of the help he could give me in regard to the latter labours was greatly increased by the familiarity he had gained with most parts of the country and its varied population during the years spent by the side of his old patron Paṇḍit Rāmjīv Dar. Though for various practical reasons I had but little occasion to use Paṇḍit Gōvind Kaul in that rôle of travelling camp *literatus* which made his worthy Chinese epiphany, excellent Chiang Ssŭ-yeh, so invaluable to me during my Central-Asian explorations of 1906–8, he was yet exceptionally well able to visualize topographical and other practical facts bearing on archæological questions.

But, perhaps, the greatest advantage I derived from his long association with my labours was the chance it gave me to study in close contact those peculiarities of traditional Indian thought, belief, and conduct which separate Hindu civilization so deeply both from the West and the East, and which no amount of book knowledge could ever fully reveal to a 'Mleccha'. Paṇḍit Gōvind Kaul's personality seemed to embody in a particularly clear fashion some of the most characteristic and puzzling features which constitute the inherited mentality of India, traceable through all changes of the ages. Attached with unquestioning faith to the principles and practices of his Brahman caste, he would make no concessions whatsoever in his own person to altered conditions of life. Yet he was ever ready to explain to me how the slow adaptation in others was reconcilable with traditional tenets. His meticulous observance of religious rites shrank from no personal hardship or sacrifice; he would, e.g., keep the fast days enjoined by the three different systems of worship traditional in his family, even when the chance of the calendar would bring them together in most embarrassing succession. Yet, in the privacy of my study or in the solitude of my mountain camp he was fully prepared to brush aside in my case most of the outward restrictions to which the *profanum vulgus* might attach importance.

His strongly conservative notions were the clearest reflex of those which have governed the administration of Kashmīr throughout its historical past. Their instinctive application by Paṇḍit Gōvind Kaul to the modern conditions of his country helped me greatly in comprehending how limited in reality were the changes undergone by its social fabric in the course of long centuries, notwithstanding all foreign conquests from the north and south. In his unfailing grave politeness and courtly dignity I could recognize, as it were, the patina which generations of influential employment and social distinction have deposited on the best representatives of the true ruling class of Kashmīr. Whenever Paṇḍit Gōvind Kaul was by my side, whether in the alpine peace of my beloved Kashmīr mountains or in the dusty toil of our Lahore exile, I always felt in living touch with past ages full of interest for the historical student of India.

A kindly Fate had allowed me, notwithstanding constant struggles for leisure, to carry my labours on the oldest historical records of Kashmīr close to their completion by the time when in the spring of 1899 my appointment to the charge of the Calcutta

Madrasa and the far more encouraging prospect of freedom for my first Central-Asian journey necessitated what seemed merely a temporary change in our personal association. In view of the new field of work which was soon to call me to the 'Sea of Sand' and its ruins far away in the north, I felt anxious to assure to Paṇḍit Gōvind Kaul scholarly employment in his own home, worthy of his learning and likely to benefit research. By what appeared at the time a special piece of good fortune, my friend Sir George Grierson was then anxious to avail himself of Paṇḍit Gōvind Kaul's methodical help for completing and editing Paṇḍit Īśvara Kaul's great dictionary of Kāshmīrī. It was a philological task of considerable importance, and for more than one reason I rejoiced when, before my departure from Lahore, this collaboration of the best Kashmirian scholar of his time with the leading authority in the field of Indian linguistic research had been satisfactorily arranged for.

But Fate, with that inscrutable irony on which Paṇḍit Gōvind Kaul, like another Kalhaṇa,[1] loved to expatiate with appropriate poetic quotations, had decreed otherwise. The farewell I took at Lahore from my ever devoted helpmate was destined to be the last. From a rapid visit to Simla to see Sir George Grierson he brought back an attack of fever which, after his return to Kashmīr, proved to be of a serious type and ultimately was recognized as typhoid. For weeks his strong constitution held out, supported by the loving care of his family and such proper medical attendance as I endeavoured to assure from afar. But in the end he succumbed, and separated by thousands of miles at the time in the strange mountains of Sikkim, I learned early in June, 1899, the grievous news that my best Indian friend had departed beyond all hope of reunion in this *janman*.

Paṇḍit Gōvind Kaul left behind a widow, who, after years of pious devotion to his memory, has since followed him, and a young son, Paṇḍit Nilakaṇṭh Kaul, who, while prevented by

[1] Cf. *Kalhaṇa's Rājataraṅgiṇī*, transl. Stein, i, Introduction, p. 36.

indifferent health in early youth from following a scholar's career, has grown up worthily to maintain the family's reputation for high character and unswerving devotion to duty.

The prolonged stays I was subsequently able to make in Kashmīr before and after my successive Central-Asian expeditions had to be spent on work relating to regions far away, and wholly different in character, from what I have come to look upon as my Indian alpine home. But my love for Kashmīr has remained unchanged, and so also my gratitude for the great boon it had given me in Paṇḍit Gōvind Kaul's friendship and help. That I was enabled to prefix a record of his life to this volume and thus to do something to preserve his memory, is a privilege I appreciate greatly. I owe it solely to the scholarly zeal of Sir George Grierson, who has rescued and elaborated the materials which we had collected, in a previous common birth, as it were. For the personal service thus rendered the expression of my warmest thanks is due here in conclusion.

AUREL STEIN.

23, MERTON STREET,
OXFORD.
September 21, 1917.

INTRODUCTION

THE stories and songs in the following pages were recited to Sir Aurel Stein in June and July, 1896, at Mōhand Marg, in Kashmīr, by Hātim Tilawôñ^{u}, of Panzil, in the Sind Valley, a cultivator and professional story-teller. They were taken down at his dictation by Sir Aurel Stein himself, and, simultaneously, by Paṇḍit Gōvinda Kaula, and were read again by Sir Aurel with Hātim in August, 1912. Sir Aurel Stein wrote the text phonetically in the Roman character, as he heard it, and Gōvinda Kaula recorded it in the Nāgarī character, not phonetically, but spelling the words in the manner customary among Kashmīr Paṇḍits of Śrīnagar. While there are necessarily considerable differences in the representation of Hātim's words, the two texts are in verbatim agreement. Only in very rare instances are unimportant words found in one omitted in the other. To the copy made by him from Hātim's dictation Gōvinda Kaula added an interlinear, word for word, translation into Sanskrit, and, from this, he subsequently made a fair copy of the greater part of the text with a translation into idiomatic Sanskrit.

All these materials were handed over to me by Sir Aurel Stein in November, 1910, and a perusal of them at once showed their great importance. They were a first-hand record of a collection of folklore taken straight from the mouth of one to whom they had been handed down with verbal accuracy from generation to generation of professional Rāwīs or reciters, and, in addition, they formed an invaluable example of a little-known language recorded in two ways, viz.: (1) as it sounded to an experienced scholar, and (2) as it was written down in the literary style of spelling. Moreover, Hātim's language was not the literary language of Kāshmīrī Paṇḍits, but was in a village dialect, and Sir Aurel Stein's phonetic record of the patois, placed alongside of the standard spelling of Kāshmīrī Paṇḍits, gives what is perhaps the only opportunity in existence for comparing the literary form of an Oriental speech with the actual pronunciation of a fairly educated villager. I, therefore, gratefully undertook the task of editing these tales with a view to their publication.

As I progressed, various difficulties asserted themselves, and Sir Aurel Stein took advantage of a stay in Kashmīr in August, 1912, to interview Hātim once more, to read through the text with him again, and, by inquiry from the fount of inspiration, to obtain a solution of the puzzles. The result was a remarkable proof of the accuracy of Hātim's memory. As already intimated, he belonged to a family of Rāwīs, and delivered the stories as he had received them. After sixteen years, the text that he recited in 1912 was the same as that which had been copied down in 1896. It even contained one or two words or phrases of which he did not know the meaning. They were "old words" no longer in use, but he still recited them as he had received them from his predecessor.

In the course of my examination of the papers, I found that Gōvinda Kaula's transcript was not quite complete. It extended only to the middle of paragraph 18 of Story xii. In the interval between 1896 and 1912 had occurred the lamented death of that excellent scholar, and his help was no longer available to supply the missing portion. This was, therefore, written down in August, 1912, from Hātim's dictation, and supplied with a Hindī translation by Paṇḍit Kāśī Rāma.

The method employed by me in editing the text is as follows: Sir Aurel Stein's phonetic text is first printed with a free English translation. This is followed by a careful transliteration of Gōvinda Kaula's text, with an interlinear, word for word, translation into English. As this latter text is based on the Paṇḍit's system of spelling, every word is spelt the same way every time that it occurs, and I was able to compile from it a very full vocabulary, which also served as an Index Verborum. As Hātim's pronunciation, like the pronunciation of all spoken words in any language, varied slightly almost every time that the same word was uttered, Sir Aurel Stein's phonetic transcript has necessarily no fixed system of spelling any particular word, each word being recorded as it sounded on the particular occasion of its being uttered, without reference to its pronunciation on other occasions.[1] Each word, therefore, appears under varying forms, all of which are, of course, of inestimable value for the study of the growth of dialect, but which render the text unsuitable as the basis of a vocabulary. For this reason, as stated above, my vocabulary is based on Gōvinda Kaula's text; but, to make comparison easy, two further indexes have been added. The first is an index of all the words in Sir Aurel's phonetic text, showing in each case the corresponding word in Gōvinda Kaula's text. The second index takes the words in the latter text, but arranges them in the order of their final letters, it being the letters towards the end of a word that are most liable to change in the processes of declension or conjugation. For each word in this text the corresponding word or words in Sir Aurel's text are also given.

The tales and songs are recorded in the order in which they were taken down by Sir Aurel Stein. They include six excellent folk-tales, three songs, and three tales partly in prose and partly in verse. The folk-tales speak for themselves. Of the songs, one (No. i) is a poetical account of an adventure of the famous Sulṭān Maḥmūd of Ghaznī with a fisherman; another (No. iv) purports to give a résumé of the origins of the Musalmān religion; and the third (No. xi) is an amusing account of the turmoil created in Kashmīr by Sir Douglas Forsyth's mission to Yarkand in 1873–4. The tales partly in prose and partly in verse are, first, the well-known story of Yūsuf and Zulaikhā, told by Wahāb Khār[2] (No. vi). The

[1] In regard to this point we may compare Noldeke's words in a review of Prym & Socin's account of the Dialect of Ṭūr 'Abdīn (ZDMG. xxxv, 221): "Die ungemeine Genauigkeit in der Wiedergabe der Laute zeigt ubrigens wieder besonders deutlich, wie verschieden oft ein und dasselbe Wort sogar im selben Zusammenhange, ja im selben Satze gesprochen wird: ein auch durch sonstige Niederschrift aus dem Volksmunde bestatigtes Resultat, durch welches allein schon das jetzt so beliebte Dogma von der 'unbedingten Wirkung der Lautgesetze' als eine arge Uebertreibung erwiesen wird. Man bedenke, dass diese Texte sämmtlich aus dem Munde eines einzigen, völlig illiteraten Mannes aufgezeichnet sind."

[2] It is, of course, quite different from the long Kāshmīrī *Yūsuf Zulaikhā*, of Maḥmūd Gāmī, published by K. F. Burkhard in ZDMG. xlix, liii.

second is the lamentation of a reed, torn from its forest, and tortured by a carpenter till it becomes a flute (No. vii). The author is one Subḥān. The third, which is anonymous, is a curious conversation between a bee and a farmer's wife (No. ix), in which the former complains of tyranny done to it by a bear and by a farmer who robbed it of its honey, while the latter complains of the tyranny done to her by grasping revenue officials.

Three notes are appended to this Introduction. For the first we are indebted to the kindness of Mr. Crooke. In this note he has placed at the disposal of the readers of the following pages his great experience in the science of comparative folklore, and has discussed the relationships of Hātim's tales to similar stories current in other parts of the world. In the second note I have dealt with the natures of the two texts and with the philological lessons that may be drawn from them. In the third, Sir Aurel Stein discusses the metre of the songs.

I

ON THE FOLKLORE IN THE STORIES

By Mr. W. CROOKE

THIS collection of folk-tales and ballads from Kashmīr presents many features of interest. In the following notes I have not attempted to discuss the general question of their value and of the sources from which they may have been derived. I have confined myself to collecting a series of parallels to the motifs and incidents of the stories, largely drawn from oriental sources. For several of these parallels I am indebted to notes prepared by Sir G. Grierson, Dr. E. Sidney Hartland, and Canon J. A. MacCulloch. These have been specially acknowledged.

I. MAḤMŪD OF GHAZNĪ AND THE FISHERMAN

In this story the Sulṭān Maḥmūd, famous for his series of raids in Northern India, like the Khalīfah Hārūn-al-Rashīd, is described as wandering through the city in the disguise of a Faqīr in search of information. The tale, in fact, is possibly a reminiscence of one of the most interesting stories in "The Arabian Nights", "Khalīfah, the Fisherman of Baghdad,"[1] where the Caliph becomes the partner of Khalīfah, the fisherman. In the same collection there is a similar incident in the tale of "Nūr al-Dīn 'Alī and the Damsel Anis al-Jalis", where the Caliph becomes partner of Karīm, the fisherman.[2]

II. THE TALE OF A PARROT

Sir G. Grierson compares with the tale the well-known story of Vikramāditya in the *Pancatantra*, of which numerous variants have been collected by M. E. Cosquin.[3] Dr. E. Sidney Hartland writes: "In addition to the variants cited by M. E. Cosquin at the reference given, see *The History of the Forty Vezirs*, translated by Mr. E. J. W. Gibb,[4] in which a king learns a charm from a Darvesh and communicates it to his Wazīr, who practises it upon him at the first opportunity. The king is forced to enter and re-animate a dead parrot, which persuades the gardener to sell it to a courtesan. She claims a thousand sequins as her fee for a visit which she alleges she had paid to a merchant. She had, however, seen this incident only in a dream. The parrot judges between the parties, and is then sold to the king's chief wife. The Wazīr, who has meanwhile succeeded in occupying the vacant body of the king, boasts to the queen of his knowledge of the charm. She persuades him to try it. The parrot, who is present, watching his opportunity, gets possession of his own body and kills the Wazīr." The tale is an illustration of the folk-tale cycle, "The Separable Soul." In a tale from the Panjāb, while a man was asleep, his soul went wandering about. By and by the soul felt thirsty and went into a pitcher of water to get a drink. While it was inside the pitcher someone put on the lid and imprisoned the soul. When the soul of the man did not return he was believed to be dead, and his corpse was

[1] Sir R. Burton, *The Book of a Thousand Nights and a Night*, ed. 1893, vi, 296 ff.

[2] Ibid., i, 356 ff.

[3] *Les Mongols*, pp. 25-6; cf. C. H. Tawney, *Kathā-Sarit-Sāgara* of Sōmadēva, i. 21.

[4] London, 1886, p. 313.

carried out for cremation. By chance someone took the lid off the pitcher and released the soul, which at once returned to its proper owner's body. He revived amidst general rejoicings.[1] The parrot in the tale under consideration is what has been called "The Life-Index" of the king.[2]

III. THE TALE OF A MERCHANT

The plot turns on the intrigue of a dissolute woman with a beggarman. Sir G. Grierson quotes a variant from the *Linguistic Survey of India.*[3] In the *Jātaka*[4] the Queen Kinnarā falls in love with "a loathsome, misshapen cripple". The king, when she is detected in this intrigue, orders that her hand should be chopped off. But his chaplain dissuades him: "Sire! be not angry with the queen; all women are just the same." In the collection of Sōmadēva, "The Story of the Wife of Śaśin," the lady, in the absence of her husband, visits a man whose hands and feet are eaten away by leprosy; and in another tale from the same collection, "The Story of the Wife of King Simhākṣa, and the Wives of his Principal Courtiers," the ladies fall in love with the hump-backed, the blind, and the lame.[5] The stock example of this form of tale, the tragedy of which is admirably enhanced by the contrast between a beautiful woman and her loathsome paramour, is the tale from "The Arabian Nights", "The Tale of the Ensorcelled Prince."[6] Here the vicious wife visits a hideous negro slave, a person who, in oriental tales, is often selected as a paramour by dissolute women. He lives in a hole amidst the rubbish-heaps of the city. "Uncover this basin," he says in a grumbling tone, "and thou shalt find at the bottom the boiled bones of some rats we dined on; pick at these, and then go to

[1] *Panjab Notes and Queries*, iii, 166. On the question generally, see W. Crooke, *Popular Religion and Folklore of Northern India*, 2nd ed., i, 231 ff.

[2] Sir R. Temple and Mrs. F. A. Steel, *Wideawake Stories*, ed. 1884, 404.

[3] Vol. ix, pt. iii ("Bhil Languages and Khandēsī"), pp. 304 ff. (specimen of Labānī from Kangra).

[4] Cambridge translation, v, 234.

[5] *Kathā-Sarit-Sāgara*, ii, 97, 116 ff.

[6] Sir R. Burton, op. cit., i, 66 ff.

the slop-pot, where thou shalt find some leavings of beer which thou mayest drink."

The tale then diverges into the common motif of the love of a mortal for fairies, who live in a world of their own to which there is access by a spring, the moral being that the merchant is no better than his erring wife. In the story of "The Queen of the Fairies", the hero in this way finds Ratnamañjarī, daughter of the king of the Vidhyādharas, marries her by the Gāndharva rite, and loses her in consequence of the violation of a taboo, a common incident in this cycle of stories.[1] With this may be compared Sōmadēva's stories: "The King who married his dependent to the Nereid," and "Yaśaḥ Kētu, the Vidhyādharī Wife, and his Faithful Minister"; and in "The Arabian Nights", "The Second Kalandar's Tale", and "Julnār the Seaborn and her Son, King Badr Bāsim of Persia".[2]

V. THE TALE OF THE GOLDSMITH

This is based on a familiar folk-tale incident — the Language of Signs. In the tale of "The Prince and the Vizier's Son",[3] the princess "pointed to her breast, then to her head, and, lastly, she laid her hand upon a vessel which stood beside her". This is interpreted to mean: When she put her hand on her forehead she showed that she was Cashma Rānī, or "Eye Queen"; when she touched her breast, "my heart shall be thine"; when she touched the bowl, "my home is Lōtā, or the bowl." The closest analogy to the present tale will, however, be found in the tale in "The Arabian Nights" of "'Azīz and 'Azīzah",[4] in which, like the wife in this story, the love-lorn cousin of the contemptible hero interprets for her husband the signs of her rival. In the present tale, when the hero goes to the assignation and falls asleep while he is waiting for the girl, he

[1] W. A. Clouston, *The Book of Sindibād*, 309 ff.

[2] *Kathā-Sarit-Sāgara*, ii, 267, 292, and cf. ii, 288 ff.; i, 220 ff.; Burton, op. cit., i, 106 f.; vi, 54 ff.

[3] C. Swynnerton, *Indian Nights Entertainment*, 167 ff.

[4] Burton, op. cit., ii, 196 ff.

is advised, when he goes a second time, to cut his finger, so that the pain may keep him awake. A good parallel to this incident occurs in "Gul-i-Bakāwalī", when the prince, who is determined to keep awake in order that he may not fail to meet Bakāwalī, cuts his finger and rubs salt into the wound.[1]

The final test of the faithful wife is that she is ready to risk her honour in order to save that of her faithless husband and his paramour. Sir G. Grierson remarks that another version of the episodes in the garden, of the arrest of the lovers, and of the defeat of the Chief Constable, will be found in J. Hertel, *Der Kluge Vizier, ein Kaschmīrischen Volksroman.*[2] This episode assumes various forms. In Sōmadēva's "Story of Saktimatī",[3] Samudradatta is arrested with another man's wife in the temple of the Yakṣa, Maṇibhadra, and both are placed in confinement. The wife of Samudragupta, Śaktimatī, exchanges clothes with the paramour of her husband, and allows them to escape. Similar to this is the tale of "Mohammad the Shalabī, and his Minister, and his Wife" in "The Arabian Nights", in which Mohammad takes the Qāẓī's daughter to a place outside the city, where they are caught and imprisoned. Mohammad's wife dresses herself as a youth, enters the prison, and gives her clothes to the girl, who effects her escape. When Mohammad and his wife protest that they have been wrongfully arrested, the king orders that the unfortunate Chief of the Police shall be executed, his house plundered, and his women enslaved.[4]

VI. THE STORY OF YUSUF AND ZULAIKHA

This is the famous tale of Joseph and Potiphar's wife, one of the cycles of great oriental love stories, represented by

[1] W. A. Clouston, *A Group of Eastern Romances and Stories*, 318.

[2] *Zeitschrift des Vereins fur Volkskunde*, Berlin, 1908, pp. 169 ff., 379 ff.

[3] *Kathā-Sarit-Sāgara*, i, 90 ff. In his note to this tale Mr. Tawney compares a story in the *Bahār Dānish*, Nov. vii, pt. iv of Bandello, *Novelle*; H. H. Wilson, *Essays*, i, 224; and Miss R. H. Busk, *Sagas from the Far East*, 320.

[4] Burton, op. cit., xi, 384.

"Yūsuf and Zulaikha" by Abū'r-Raḥmān Jāmī; "Khusrau and Shirīn" by Niẓāmu'd-Dīn, who was the author also of "Majnūn and Laila". In the Qur'ān[1] Zulaikha is wife of Qiṭfir, or Potiphar, the ultimate source whence this tale and that of the dream of Pharaoh are derived.[2] In the story under consideration we have the familiar incident of the Selection of a New King by an Elephant, for which, as Sir G. Grierson points out, we have several parallels from Kashmīr.[3] In some of the Kashmīr tales the hawk shares the power of selection with the elephant. The fullest discussion of the widespread incident is that by Dr. E. Sidney Hartland.[4] Dr. Hartland adds: "I have also given examples showing that in various places the choice of a king actually depended on omens from animals. Thus, Bāpā, the hero of the Guhilots of Mewār, was selected as heir to the throne by an elephant which put a garland round his neck, not once, but thrice."[5] Selection of the heir by a cobra, which shields the child from the sun by its extended hood, is common. Colonel Tod gives several instances from Rājput traditions.[6] The Nagasiās and Khariās of the Central Provinces tell similar legends.[7] A legend from the French colony of Senegal-Niger tells of a bird, a metamorphosed hero, who decides the succession to the post of Chief Griot by taking up his abode with the Griot who is to obtain promotion.[8] In a Nubian story a blackbird decides the choice of a queen by settling on her head.[9] We have a good example in Sōmadēva: "In that country there was an immemorial custom that an auspicious elephant was driven about by the citizens, and anyone that he took up with his trunk and placed on his back was anointed king."[10]

[1] Surāh xii, 23–5.
[2] Genesis xli.
[3] J. H. Knowles, *Folk-tales of Kashmir*, 17, 159, 169 f, 309.
[4] *Ritual and Belief*, 1914, 30 ff.
[5] R. V. Russell, *Tribes and Castes of the Central Provinces*, 1916, iv, 462: quoting D. R. Bhandarkar, Journal Asiatic Society of Bengal, v, p. 167, 1909.
[6] *Annals of Rajasthan*, Calcutta reprint, 1884, i, 313; ii, 282, 384.
[7] Russell, op. cit., iv, 258; iii, 445.
[8] De Zeltner, *Contes du Sénégal et du Niger*, Paris, 1913, p. 36.
[9] Journal Royal Asiatic Society, xliv, 410.
[10] *Kathā-Sarit-Sāgara*, ii, 102.

VII. THE TALE OF THE REED-FLUTE

There is a close resemblance, which we may suppose can hardly be accidental, between this personification of the flute and one of the most poetical passages in the "Arabian Nights" in the tale of "'Alī Nūr-al-Dīn and Miriam, the Girdle Girl".[1] "The girl took the bag from him and opening it shook it, whereupon there fell thereout two-and-thirty pieces of wood, which she fitted one into another, male into female and female into male, till they became a polished lute of Indian workmanship. Then she uncovered her wrists, and laying the lute on her lap bent over it with the bending of mother over babe and swept the strings with her finger-tips, whereupon it moaned and resounded, and after its old home yearned, and it remembered the water that gave it drink, and the earth whence it sprang, and wherein it grew, and it minded the carpenter who cut it and the polisher who polished it, and the merchants who made it their merchandise, and the ship that shipped it; and it cried and called aloud, and moaned and groaned; and it was as if she asked it of all these things, and it answered her with the tongue of the case, reciting these couplets"—for which reference must be made to Sir R. Burton's version, which, though it may be accurate, can retain little of the music of the original poetry.

VIII. THE TALE OF A KING

For the main story Sir G. Grierson refers to the Kashmīr stories of "The Two Brothers" and "The Four Princes".[2] The basis of the story is a moral apologue, enforcing the need of caution, which is a commonplace in folk-tales, as in the cycle of "The Seven Wazīrs", "Haste in killing is a vile thing, for 'tis a grave matter: the quick we can kill, but the killed we cannot quicken, and needs must we look to the end of affairs".[3] "Often procrastination serves to avert an inauspicious measure," says Sōmadēva.[4]

[1] Burton, op. cit., vii. 16 f.; cf. xi, 267.
[2] Knowles, op. cit., 166, 423.
[3] Burton, op. cit., ix, 54.
[4] *Kathā-Sarit-Sāgara*, i, 279.

The tale diverges in various ways.

First, we have the "Potiphar's Wife" cycle, and that of Phædra and Hippolytus, with their numberless variants, in which a vicious woman fabricates a false charge against her continent stepson, or some other equally innocent person who has the ill-luck to come into contact with her. In Buddhist literature this appears in the tale of the love of Asōka's queen for Kunāla, son of her co-queen, Padmāvatī. On his refusal to accept her advances, the queen, to whom her husband, the emperor, had offered any boon she chose, asked to be allowed to assume royal power for seven days. During this time she sent officers to Takṣaśila and had Kunāla blinded. He appeared before his father in the guise of a lute-player, was recognized, and the queen was burnt to death.[1] The same authority refers to the [illegible] of Sārangdhara, who rejected the advances of his stepmother, and when she complained to the king, it was ordered that his limbs should be cut off, and that he should be exposed to wild beasts, a fate from which he was saved only by a miraculous Voice from Heaven.[2]

Then comes the incident of the king who slays his favourite falcon who dashes the cup out of his hand as he is about to drink the poisoned water. Canon J. A. MacCulloch kindly informs me that there is a version in the Persian Bidpai literature, in the Anwār-i-Suheli,[3] the reference to which has been traced by Sir G. Grierson.

Sir G. Grierson also refers to two similar tales from Bengal, one of the tale of a snake in the room of a wedded couple; the other, a full story, with tales of the three guardians, in one of which a horse is substituted for the hawk.[4]

Next, we have the well-known tale of the "Faithful Dog", best known in the story of Beddgelert. Sir G. Grierson notes

[1] W. A. Clouston, *The Book of Sindibād*, Intro., xxix f.; quoting *Orient and Occident*, iii, 177.

[2] Ibid., xxx f.; quoting H. H. Wilson, *Catalogue of the MacKenzie Manuscripts*.

[3] vi, 3, Jarrett's edition (Calcutta, 1880). 402–5; Eastwick's translation (Hertford, 1854), 413–16; Wollaston's translation (London, 1904), 320–2.

[4] Lal Bihari Day, *Folk-tales of Bengal*, ed. 1912, pp. 43, 141, 146.

that it occurs in the Kashmīr tale, "A Lach of Rupees for a Bit of Advice"[1]; and he quotes the following parallel from Baluchistan:[2] "A shrine dedicated to a dog would be a bit of an oddity anywhere, and something more than an oddity in a Musalmān country. Yet such a shrine is to be found in the Kīrthar hills. And this is the pious legend that clings to it. Once upon a time there was a dog that changed masters in a pledge for a loan. Now he had not spent many days with his new master before thieves came at dead of night and took off ever so much treasure. But he slunk after the rogues and never let them out of his sight till he had marked down the spot where they had buried the spoil. And, on the morrow, he barked and he barked and made such a to-do, there was nothing for it but for the master of his house to follow him till he came to the spot where the treasure was buried. Well, the owner was pleased enough to get his goods back, as you may guess. And round the dog's neck he tied a label whereon was writ in plain large letters that the debt was discharged, and with that he sent him packing to his old master. So the dog bounded off home, as pleased as pleased could be. But his master was mighty angry to see him, for he was an honest fellow, and much as he loved his dog, he set more store on being a man of his word. And as a warning to all breakers of pledges he hacked him limb from limb. But when in the end he saw the label round his neck, and heard all that he had done, he was exceedingly sorry. So he gathered up the limbs and buried them in a grave. Had the limbs been the limbs of a true believer, and not the limbs of an unclean beast, he could not have made more pother over the burial. And to the grave of the faithful dog Jhalawān folk resort to this day. And there they sacrifice sheep, and distribute the flesh in alms, in the certain belief that whatsoever they seek, that they will surely find."

In Western folklore the tale assumes various forms, the

[1] Knowles, op. cit., 36 ff.
[2] *Baluchistan Census Report*, 1911, p. 63, § 107.

earliest version appearing in Pausanias.[1] It appears in the *Gesta Romanorum,* No. 26 (Herrtage, p. 98). In the *Book of Sindibād* it appears as the story of "The Snake and the Cat", the faithful cat killing the snake in the baby's cradle.[2] In the *Pancatantra*[3] and *Hitopadēśa*[4] it is a mungoose which attacks the snake, and in *Kalilah and Dimna* a weasel. Sōmadēva tells it in the form of the "Story of the Brāhman and the Mungoose".[5]

The account of the shrine erected to the faithful dog in Baluchistān already quoted is not the only instance of worship of this kind in India. In the Central Provinces the tale is told of a Banjārā who, after he killed his dog, "built a temple to the dog's memory, which is called the Kukurra Maṇḍhī. And in this temple is the image of a dog. This temple is in the Drūg District, four miles from Bālōd. A similar story is told of the temple of Kukurra Maṭh in Mandlā."[6] A similar tale has been localized at Rōhisā in Kāṭhiāwār. When his master learned how basely he had treated the faithful animal, "he wept bitterly and caused the Chitrāsar lake to be excavated, and built round at the spot where the dog fell dead, and on the little island in the lake he built a temple in which he placed his dog's image, which is there to this day."[7] The tale has migrated as far west as Ireland and as far east as China.[8]

X. THE TALE OF RĀJĀ VIKRAMĀDITYA

The episode of the princess beset by a serpent is, in a slightly different form, found in the tale in the Book

[1] Pausanias, x, 33, 9, with the note of Sir J. G. Frazer, v, 421 f. See the references in Clouston, *The Book of Sindibād*, 236–41, 329, 359. But there is a much fuller account in Clouston, *Popular Tales and Fictions*, ii, 166 ff., 177, n. A complete bibliography of the tale and its analogues will be found in *The Seven Sages of Rome*, edited by K. Campbell, New York, 1907, pp. lxviii–lxxxii. In the Welsh *Fables of Cattwg the Wise* the story is given and located at Abergarwan (Iolo MSS., 154, 561). There must, therefore, have apparently been more than one version current in Wales.

[2] Clouston, 56 f.

[3] Book v, Fab. 2.

[4] Book iv, Fab. 13.

[5] *Kathā-Sarit-Sāgara*, ii, 90 f.

[6] R. V. Russell, *Tribes and Castes of the Central Provinces*, ii, 189 f.

[7] *Bombay Gazetteer*, viii, 641.

[8] W. C. Borlase, *The Dolmens of Ireland*, iii, 881 f.; H. A. Giles, *Strange Stories from a Chinese Studio*, ii, 261.

of Tobit,[1] in which, by the advice of Raphael, the devil is scared by the stench of the burnt heart and liver of a fish. Sir G. Grierson quotes a story from Bengal in which we have a princess from whose body a snake issues.[2] It is unnecessary to discuss this tale at length, because, as Dr. E. Sidney Hartland reminds me, it has been examined, with a full collection of parallels, by Mr. F. H. Groome.[3]

XII. THE TALE OF THE ĀKHŪN

Sir G. Grierson remarks that there is a somewhat similar story in the Linguistic Survey of India,[4] of which the following is a copy: "There was a Ṭhākur who had nothing to eat in his house, so he said to himself, 'Brother, I'm going to look for service.' There was also a bird of omen, but though he went every day she never gave him one. One day she went out to pick up some food, and before she started she told her children on no account to give an omen to anyone. While she was away the Ṭhākur came as usual, and the chicks gave him the looked-for indication; so he saddled his camel, mounted, and set off.

Back came the omen-bird, and overtook the Ṭhākur on his way. She assumed the form of a woman. 'Who are you?' said he. 'I'm your wife.' 'Come along; one has become two.' So he took her up on his camel. They came to a tank full of water, and he was compelled to descend for a certain purpose. 'I'll be back in a moment,' said he. 'All right,' said she. On the bank of the tank he saw a snake pursuing a frog. 'It's a shame to let the poor thing be killed,' said he. So he took out his pen-knife and cut bits of flesh out of his thigh with which he fed the snake till it could eat no more. Then he got up and went back to his camel. His thigh was all bloody. 'What's happened?' said the omen-bird. 'A snake was going to eat a frog, so I threw it lumps of flesh from my thigh instead.'[5] Straightway, the omen-bird passed her hand

[1] Chaps. vi–viii.
[2] Lal Behari Day, op. cit., 96.
[3] *Folk-lore*, ix, 226.
[4] Vol. ix, pt. i, 351.
[5] Obviously a reminiscence of the well-known tale of Buddha giving his flesh to the tiger-cubs.

over the wound, and it healed as it was before. Then they got up on the camel and went on their way."

Sir G. Grierson remarks: "This is the end of the extract. The entire story, a long one, will be found on pp. 82 ff. of Mr. Macalister's *Specimens.*[1] The frog takes the form of a barber and overtakes the Ṭhākur. The three then go on. The snake, out of gratitude for his good meal, also joins the company as a Brāhman. The four settle in a city, where the omen-bird gets the Ṭhākur service under the king, on a salary of a lākh of rupees. The king's barber persuades the king to set the Ṭhākur three apparently impossible tasks (to get a snake's jewel, to find a ring thrown into a well, and to get news of his dead and gone ancestors), all of which the Ṭhākur performs with the aid of the snake, the frog, and the omen-bird. To carry out the third task, the omen-bird assumes the form of the Ṭhākur, and gets the king to make a huge funeral pyre, on which she sits. It is lighted, and she flies away in the smoke. She then sends the Ṭhākur to the king with the news that he has come back from the king's ancestors and that they are all well, but want a barber. So the king makes another pyre, and sets his barber on it to go off to his ancestors. The pyre is lighted, and the barber is, of course, burned to death, and the king and the Ṭhākur live happy ever afterwards." The tale belongs to the cycle of Friendly Animals represented in the West by Perraults' famous version of "Puss in Boots". In this cycle the performance of seemingly impossible tasks by the aid of helping animals is common.[2]

The tasks set in the tale now under consideration deserve fuller treatment.

The incident of the ruby with a worm inside it appears in three forms in the "Arabian Nights". In the story of "Ma'arūf the Cobbler and his wife Fātimah", Ma'arūf, when called on to examine a jewel, squeezes it between his thumb

[1] G. Macalister, *Specimens of the Dialects spoken in the State of Jeypore*, Allahabad, 1898.

[2] J. A. MacCulloch, *The Childhood of Fiction*, 225 ff., and other references in the Index.

and forefinger, and shows that it is "only a bittock of mineral worth a thousand dinars. 'Why dost thou style it a jewel?'"[1] Again, in the "Tale of the King who kenned the Quintessence of Things", the old man examines the jewels brought for sale. He decides that one of them is of small value, and the merchant asks: "How can this, which is bigger of bulk and worthier for water and righter in rondure, be of less value than that?" The Shaikh decides that "in its interior is a teredo, a boring worm; but the other jewel is sound and secure against breakage".[2] Lastly, in the "Story of Three Sharpers", the sharper says, "An thou determine upon the killing of yonder man, first break the gem, and if thou find therein a worm, thou wilt know the wight's word to have been veridical." The king smashes the gem with his mace and finds a worm within it.[3]

Further on, in the episode when the jeweller seizes the garment of one of the girls as she is bạthing, we have a version of the Swan Maiden cycle, of which an early form appears in the legend of Kṛishṇa when he takes the garments of the Gōpīs as they are bathing in the Jumna. In many cases of tales of this cycle the Swan Maiden is captured to be eventually married to the hero. Sometimes, as in the present case, she is held to ransom. It is unnecessary to discuss at length a cycle of tales which has been fully investigated by Dr. E. Sidney Hartland and by others.[4] Again, we have the incident of the ruby emitting a brilliant light, a *lieu commun* in Eastern and Western folk-tales. In one of Sōmadēva's stories, "The Brave King Vikramāditya," the King Hēmaprabha gives his daughter, Ratnaprabhā, to Naravāhanadatta, with "glittering heaps of jewels, gleaming like innumerable wedding fires".[5]

[1] Burton, op. cit., viii, 16.
[2] Ibid., ix, 139.
[3] Ibid., x, 364.
[4] *The Science of Fairy Tales*, 255 ff. Cf. in the "Arabian Nights", "The Story of Jānshāh", and "Hassan of Bassorah" (Burton, op. cit., iv, 291 ff.; vi, 188 ff.), and "The Swan Children" in "Dolopathos and the Seven Sages (Clouston, *The Book of Sindibād*, 372 ff.).
[5] *Kathā-Sarit-Sāgara*, i, 327.

At every word the fairy Lālmāl speaks a ruby drops, or seven rubies fall daily from her mouth. In one of Sōmadēva's tales Marubhūti eats two grains of rice from food in which a child had been cooked, and thus gains the power of spitting gold. On this Mr. Tawney remarks: "In 'Sagas from the Far East' there is a story of a gold-spitting prince. In Gonzenbach's 'Sicilianische Märchen' Quaddaruni's sister drops pearls and precious stones from her hair when she combs it —Dr. Köhler in his note on this tale gives many European parallels. In a Swedish story a gold ring falls from the heroine's mouth whenever she speaks, and in a Norwegian story gold coins. I may add to the parallels quoted by Dr. Köhler, No. 36 in Coelho's 'Contos Portuguezes', in which tale pearls drop from the heroine's mouth."[1]

Lālmāl, the fairy, gave the Lapidary her ring and said: "Go thou again into the spring. Close by the side of it thou wilt find a great rock. Show thou my ring unto that rock, and it will arise and stand upright." We are reminded of the wonder-working ring of Aladdin in the "Arabian Nights". In a Kashmir tale, "The Charmed Ring," the merchant's son speaks to the ring, and immediately a beautiful house and a lovely woman with golden hair appeared.[2] Sulaimān, or Solomon, entrusts his seal ring, on which his kingdom depends, to his concubine, Amīnah. Sakhr, the Jinnī, transformed into the king's likeness, takes it, after which Sulaimān is reduced to beggary. But after forty days the Jinnī fled, throwing the ring into the sea, where it was swallowed by a fish, and eventually restored to its owner. The tale is Talmudic, and there is a hint of it in the Qur'ān.[3]

In the tale of "Vinītamati who became a Holy Man", in Sōmadēva's Collection, the Yakṣa gives the hero a ring which averts all calamities known as *īti*, that is to say, excessive rain, drought, locusts, birds, and injury by foreign invaders;[4]

[1] Ibid., ii, 453.
[2] Knowles, op. cit., 23.
[3] Sūrah xxxviii; cf. the ring of Polycrates, Herodotus, iii, 41, 2.
[4] *Kathā-Sarit-Sāgara*, ii, 173.

and in another tale, "Śrīdatta and Mṛgāṅkavatī," we have a magic ring which counteracts the effects of poison.[1]

The Lady of the Rock turns the Lapidary into a pebble. Then her mother says: "Aha! my girl, I smell the smell of a mortal man"—the "Fee faw fum" of "Jack, the Giant Killer", common in Märchen. The Italian demon, the Orco, has "a demonic acuteness of scent; he can tell, like a sea-monster, the approach of human flesh".[2] The technical phrase in folk-tales from the Indian plains is *manush-gandha*, "the smell of man's flesh." In a Panjāb story, the tale of "Lāl Bādshāh, the Red King", the ogre cries, "I smell man's flesh, I smell man's blood."[3] In a Bengal story the Rākṣasas cry: "How, mow, khow! A human being I smell," or "Hye, mye, khye!" with the same meaning.[4]

This tale, it may be remarked, contains a version of the Letter of Death. I have discussed this incident in connexion with the story of Bellerophon. In the Homeric version:[5] "To Bellerophon the gods granted beauty and lovely manhood; but Proitos, in his heart, devised evil for him, and being mightier far drove him from the land of the Argives, whom Zeus had made subject to his sceptre. Now Proitos' wife, goodly Anteia, lusted after him, to have converse in secret love, but no whit prevailed she, for the uprightness of his heart, on wise Bellerophon. Then spake she lyingly to King Proitos: 'Die, Proitos, or else slay Bellerophon, that would have converse in love with me against my will.' So spake she, and anger got hold upon the king at that he heard. To slay him he forbare, for his soul had shame at that; but he sent him to Lykia, and gave him tokens of woe, graving in a folded tablet many deadly things, and bade him show these to Anteia's father, that he might be slain." So the king of Lykia imposed tasks upon him, and when he accomplished

[1] Ibid., i, 61.
[2] J. Grimm, *Teutonic Mythology*, ii, 486.
[3] Swynnerton, op. cit., 335.
[4] Lal Bihari Day, op. cit., 72, 79; for other examples see MacCulloch, op. cit., 305, n.
[5] Iliad, vi, 155 ff., trans. A. Lang, W. Leaf, E. Myers. In my paper (*Folklore*, xix, 156) I have collected several parallels.

them the king gave him his daughter in marriage and half of all the honour of his kingdom. Dr. Sidney Hartland writes: "Thucydides gives a similar story of Pausanias, Regent of Sparta. The episode of Uriah the Hittite (2 Samuel xi, 14) is another case. Shakespeare, drawing from Saxo Grammaticus (lib. iii), employs it in 'Hamlet'. Walter Map (*De Nugis Curialium*, v, 4) recounts it of Count and Earl Godwin, but leaves the tale half told. It may almost be said to be a commonplace of folk-tales. It generally makes its appearance in tales belonging to the cycle of 'The Man born to be a King'." To this some oriental examples may be added. In Sōmadēva's "Story of Śivavarman" the king writes a letter to a neighbouring chief, asking him to slay his minister, Śivavarman. He escapes by announcing that God will not send rain for twelve years on that land in which he is slain.[1] In the Kashmīr story of "The Ogress Queen" the queen writes a letter to her grandmother, a Rākṣasī, telling her to kill the lad, but a faqīr reads it and tears it up.[2] In the Panjāb story of "The Son of Seven Mothers" the queen gives the lad a piece of a broken potsherd, with these words inscribed on it: "Kill the bearer at once, and sprinkle his blood like water." It is read and altered by the hero's wife.[3] In the Bengal story of "The Boy whom Seven Mothers suckled", the Rākṣasī queen sends the boy to her mother with a letter requesting her to devour him the moment he delivers the letter.[4] We have the same incident in "Brave Hīralālbāsē" and in "The Demon and the King's Son" in the collection of Miss Maive Stokes.[5] Similar to this is the action of the Sultān in the story of "Ahmed the Orphan".[6] In Arabic folklore such letters are so common that they are known as "the letters of Mutalammis", one of the intended victims of the trick.[7]

Sir G. Grierson reminds me that there is a good version of

[1] *Kathā-Sarit-Sāgara*, i, 27 f.; cf. the tale of Parityāgasēna (ibid., i, 353).
[2] Knowles, op. cit., 48.
[3] Temple-Steel, *Wideawake Stories*, 103.
[4] Lal Bihari Day, op. cit., 116.
[5] *Indian Fairy Tales*, 53, 184.
[6] Clouston, *The Book of Sindibād*, 138.
[7] Burton, op. cit., xii, 68.

the "Letter of Death" tale in the *Bhakta-māla*,[1] in which Dhṛṣṭabuddhi gives a letter to Candrahāsa, saying, "Take thou this to my house and give this letter into the hands of my son Madana, and say unto him, 'Prithee carry out what is written therein.'" But Candrahāsa falls asleep in a garden where comes to sport with her damsels and her fellow-maidens the daughter of Dhṛṣṭabuddhi. "By chance she saw Candrahāsa as he slept, and love for him entered her heart. So she led her companions away, and then leaving them she returned by another path and gazed enraptured at his beauty. In her yearning she saw by him a letter, with her brother's name upon it. She took it up and read it, and therein was written, 'At once give thou poison (*viṣa*) to the one that beareth this letter. Delay thou not in this, or dread my anger.' When she read these words, wroth was she with her father, and filled with pity was she for the youth. Now the damsel's name was Viṣayā. Ink made she with the collyrium of her eyes, and after the word *viṣa*, poison, added she but one little syllable *yā*, so that *viṣa* became *viṣayā*." So Viṣayā was married to Candrahāsa, and the plot laid by the vile Dhṛṣṭabuddhi came to naught.

We have here also a version of "Jack and the Beanstalk", fully discussed by Canon J. A. MacCulloch, who points out the connexion between mythology and folklore, where "a primitive mythological way of regarding the universe has suggested and given rise to the chief incident of one of our well-known nursery tales".[2]

On the question of eating the leathern peas, Dr. Sidney Hartland writes: "It may be suspected that the real reason why the hero is forbidden to eat the leathern peas is, not that they are indigestible, but that to do so would be to eat the food of supernatural beings, and so unite himself with them permanently; he might not be able to return; he would become one of them. I have considered elsewhere similar incidents.[3]

[1] See his article, "Gleanings from the Bhakta-māla": JRAS. April, 1910, p. 295.

[2] *The Childhood of Fiction*, 432 ff.

[3] *Science of Fairy Tales*, 40 ff.

A full discussion of the matter would be very lengthy, and would lead to inquiries into the rights of hospitality, magical belief, and so forth."

When the hero marries the lady, she directs him to ask only for the skin mat, known as the Flying Couch. We may compare this with the flying horses of the "Arabian Nights".[1] In the Bengali tales the heroine is carried through the air by two birds, and a club and rope carry people across the ocean.[2]

Brahmā, in the Hindu mythology, gives Kuvēra the great self-moving car, called Puspaka.[3] We met with flying chariots and similar magical vehicles in the tales of Sōmadēva.[4] The closest parallel to the incident under consideration is the Flying Carpet of the tale of "Prince Ahmad and the Fairy Peri-Banou" of the "Arabian Nights".[5]

W. Crooke.

II

ON THE LANGUAGE USED IN THE TALES

As regards the text of these tales recorded by Gōvinda Kaula, it is, so far as its contents and wording go, in every way worthy of the reputation of that excellent scholar. But the spelling of the words is that customary among Kāshmīrī Paṇḍits, and is based on no fixed system. These persons have no certain rules for representing the broken vowel sounds that form a prominent feature of the language, and Gōvinda Kaula, each time that a word containing one of these sounds recurred, spelt it as the spirit moved him at the time. A few examples will suffice. The word *poda*, manifest, is written पंद in ii, 1, and पांद in iii, 8; *korun*, he made, is written करुन् in iv, 6, but कुरुन् in vii, 4, although he writes करुन् in the very next line; *ōs*ᵘ, he was, is written ऑसु in ii, 4, but आस् and ऑसु in ii, 5. It is evident that to reproduce such spelling would render this work of little

1 Burton, op. cit., i. 147; iii, 415 ff.
2 Lal Bihari Day, op. cit., 130, 116.
3 J. Dowson, *Classical Dictionary*. 174.
4 *Kathā-Sarit-Sāgara*, i. 259, 392; ii, 258, 553.
5 Burton, op. cit., x. 249, who gives parallels.

use to any person not perfectly familiar with the language, and would greatly complicate the preparation of any index or vocabulary.

A uniform system of spelling Kāshmīrī in the Nāgarī character was devised by the late Paṇḍit Īśvara Kaula, and was used by him in his *Kaśmīraśabdâmṛta*, or Kāshmīrī Grammar in the Sanskrit language, which has been published by the Asiatic Society of Bengal. Although not perfect, this system has the merit of being an attempt to represent each sound in the language by one character, and by one character only. With a few minor alterations, it has been followed by me in various works on Kāshmīrī, such as my *Essays on Kāçmīrī Grammar*, my *Manual of the Kāshmīrī Language*, and the Kāshmīrī–English Dictionary in course of publication by the Asiatic Society of Bengal, and it is now, I believe, generally accepted by European scholars.

In preparing the transliterated version of Gōvinda Kaula's text I have therefore first copied the latter, spelling the words according to Īśvara Kaula's system, and have then rigidly transliterated that into the Roman character. It must be clearly understood that this process has in no way altered the real text in any way. If Īśvara Kaula were to read out the text written according to his system, and if Govinda Kaula were to read out what he himself had written, the resultant sounds would in every case be identical. The change has been one of spelling, and of nothing else; in other words, it has been merely a change from unsystematic to systematic spelling.

My text in the Roman character can at once be mechanically converted into the Nāgarī character according to Īśvara Kaula's system of spelling by the aid of the following table and appended instructions:—

अ *a*, आ *ā*, इ *i*, ई *ī*, उ *u*, ऊ *ū*. ए *ē*, ऐ *ai*, ओ *ō*, औ *au*.

क *ka*, ख *kha*, ग *ga*, ङ *na*.

च *ca*, छ *cha*, ज *ja*. ञ *ñĕ*.

च़ *tsa*, छ़ *tsha*, ज़ *za*.

ट *ṭa*, ठ *ṭha*, ड *ḍa*, ण *na*.

त *ta*, थ *tha*, द *da*, न *na*.

प *pa*, फ *pha*, ब *ba*, म *ma*.
य *yĕ*, र *ra*, ल *la*, व *va*, *wa*.
श *shĕ*, स *sa*, ह *ha*.

It will be observed that the above agrees with the ordinary system of transliterating Nāgarī, with the following exceptions :—

(1) Kāshmīrī possesses no sonant aspirates.

(2) The letters ङ and ण are each used only as a member of a conjunct consonant before a letter of its own class, as in ङ्क *nka*, ङ्ख *nkha*, ङ्ग *nga*, ण्ट *nṭa*, ण्ठ *nṭha*, ण्ड *nḍa*. Under these circumstances I have not thought it necessary to add in either case a diacritical mark to the *n*, more especially because, in the Persian character, ङ्, ण्, and न् are all represented by ن.

(3) After the letters ञ, य, and श, the letter *a* is always pronounced *ĕ*. Hence, I have transliterated them *ñĕ*, *yĕ*, and *shĕ* respectively. For श I use *shĕ* instead of *śĕ*; as in Kāshmīrī the sound of this letter is the same as that of the Persian ش. The letter not only represents a Persian ش, but also the Indian श and ष, the sound of all three having been conflated into one sound, that of the English *sh* in "shell". Kāshmīrī possesses no cerebral sibilant, although in Kāshmīrī MSS. we sometimes find the letter ष. This, however, is only Paṇḍits' affectation, who pretend that they ought to write पोष्, not पोश्, a flower, because there is a ष in the Sanskrit पुष्पम्.

(4) Attention may be called to the affricative letters च़ *tsa*, छ़ *tsha*, and ज़ *za*. The letter *tsha* is the aspirate of *tsa*, i.e. it is pronounced as in "cat's head" and not as in "cat-shark".

(5) The short vowels *ĕ* (except in the cases of *ñĕ*, *yĕ*, and *shĕ*) and *ŏ* are represented by य and व respectively. They never commence a syllable. In other words, when य and व follow a consonant they are pronounced *ĕ* and *ŏ* respectively. Thus क्य is *kĕ*, not *kyĕ*, and क्व is *kŏ*, not *kwa*. Some Kāshmīrīs, especially Hindūs, always sound *ĕ* and *ē* as if there were a half-pronounced *y* before them, so that in their mouths क्य sounds as k^y*ĕ* and के as k^y*ē*. The vowel *ĕ* is generally sounded like the *e* in "met" and the vowel *ŏ* like the *o* in "hot".

The various mātrā-vowels are represented as follows. For particulars in regard to them the reader is referred to the present writer's *Essays* and *Manual*.

कक् $k^{a}k$.
कि k^{i}.
कु k^{u}.
कू $k^{ü}$.
क्यक् $k^{ĕ}k$.

The vowels ^{a} and ^{ĕ} can never end a syllable.

The various modified, or *aprasiddha*, vowels are represented and sounded as follows :—

^{a}	written as in	कक्	$k^{a}k$,	and sounded like a very short *a*.	
ȧ	,,	क॑कि	$k^{ȧ}k^{i}$,	,,	,, ,, *ȧ*.
o	,,	क॑कु	$k^{o}k^{u}$,	,,	,, ,, *o*.
ü	,,	क॑कू	$k^{ü}k^{ü}$,	,,	,, ,, *u*.
ạ	,,	अ॑कक्	$ạk^{a}k$,	,,	something between *a* and *o*.
ȧ	,,	अ॑कि	$ȧk^{i}$,	,,	like a^{i} in $a^{i}k^{i}$.
o	,,	अ॑कु	ok^{u},	,,	,, the first *o* in "promote".
ü	,,	अ॑कू	$ük^{ü}$,	,,	,, a German *u*.
ö	,,	आ॑कक्	$ök^{a}k$,	,,	,, prolonged German *ö*.
,,	,,	आ॑कि	$ök^{i}$,	,,	,, ,,
,,	,,	आ॑कू	$ök^{ü}$,	,,	,, ,,
yu	,,	किकु	$kyuk^{u}$,	,,	as written in the Roman character.
yū	,,	कीकु	$kyūk^{u}$,	,,	as written in the Roman character.
ẹ̆	,,	क्य॑कक्	$kẹ̆k^{a}k$,	,,	like *ĕ*.
ĕ	,,	क्य॑कि	$kĕk^{i}$,	,,	,,
yo	,,	क्य॑कु	$kyok^{u}$,	,,	as written.
ě	,,	क्य॑कू	$kěk^{ü}$	,,	something like ^{y}u.
ọ̆	,,	क्व॑कक्	$kọ̆k^{a}k$,	,,	nearly the same as *o*.
ŏ	,,	क्व॑कि	$kŏk^{i}$,	,,	like an ordinary *ŏ*.
ọ̆	,,	क्व॑कु	$kọ̆k^{u}$,	,,	nearly the same as *o*.
ȯ̆	,,	क्व॑कू	$kȯ̆k^{ü}$,	,,	nearly the same as *ü*.
ô	,,	कोकु	$kôk^{u}$ (for कांकु),		sounded like the *aw* in "awful".
ŭ	,,	कॖ	*kŭ*,		sounded something like a much prolonged German *u*, approaching a long *ī*.

As explained in the *Kāshmīrī Manual*, the sounds of *ĕ* and *ŏ* are not affected by *i*-mātrā, and hence, in this case, no diacritical marks are given to them in the Roman character, although they are marked as *aprasiddha* in the Nāgarī character.

As regards Sir Aurel Stein's system of presenting the sounds uttered by Hātim, it is, of course, consistent with itself. Each letter employed by him represents one sound and one sound only, and each sound is represented by one letter and by one letter only. His system, however, is not the same as mine, and he authorized me, in preparing his materials for the press, to alter it to agree with mine, so long as the alteration was consistent. For instance, I was authorized to alter his *â* to my *ó*, provided that this was always done, that *â* was never altered to any other letter, and that no other of his letters was also altered to *ó*.

His system of arranging consonants presented no difficulty. It is practically the same as mine, and only one or two changes were necessary. These are as follows. The fricative sound resembling that of an English *ts* is represented in my system by *ts* and in his by *t̠s*. The sound which corresponds to that of the Persian ش, and which in Nāgarī is written ष़, is written *ṣ* by Sir Aurel Stein and *sh* by me. I have throughout altered his *t̠s* to *ts* and *ṣ* to *sh*. Similarly, the sound represented by the Persian ژ is written *ẓ* by Sir Aurel Stein, and, for the sake of uniformity, I have altered it to *zh*, although the sound is not heard in Srīnagar Kāshmīrī or, consequently, found in Gōvinda Kaula's transcript.

The labial semi-vowel in Kāshmīrī is a pure bi-labial, and not a dento-labial. Its sound is neither that of *v* or that of *w*, but something between both, sometimes, especially before palatal vowels, tending towards a *v*-sound, and sometimes, especially before *a* and before labial vowels, tending towards a *w*-sound. In my system I use both *v* and *w* for its representation, endeavouring so far as was possible to indicate the shade of sound to which, in my experience, it approximates. Sir Aurel Stein represents the labial semi-vowel uniformly by *v*, without regard to its exact shade of sound. I have not ventured to interfere with this, and have left his *v*'s unchanged throughout.

Possibly his *i̯* and *u̯* are also semi-vowels, but the matter is doubtful, and will be referred to again under the head of vowels.

It thus follows that, so far as the representation of consonants is concerned, the systems of transcription employed in the printed version of Sir Aurel Stein's copy of Hātim's text and in my copy of Gōvinda Kaula's text are, with the exception of the representation of the labial semi-vowel, identical.

Turning to the representation of vowel-sounds, it might appear that the matter is equally simple. I thought so myself at first, and commenced transcribing his text with the alterations necessary to make it agree with my system. But before long I found that this was an impossible task. The range of vowel-sounds used by Hātim is not the same as that used in the Śrīnagar Kāshmīrī, with which alone I am familiar. Hātim has sounds, such as the *a* in "cancelled" (Sir Aurel's *a̯*, my *ă*), which so far as I am aware occurs only rarely in Śrīnagar Kāshmīrī, and then only in monosyllables ending in an aspirated surd—e.g. in the Hindū pronunciation of *krăkh*, a noise, but not in the plural *kraka*. Again, on the other hand, Śrīnagar Kāshmīrī has two short *o*'s—one, the first *o* in the English word "promote", which I represent by *o*, and the other the *o* in "hot", which I represent by *ŏ*. Sir Aurel Stein's system knows only the latter of these, which he represents by *o*. There are numerous other differences and cross divisions in the two systems, and a thorough examination of the whole of Hātim's text gives the following results:—

On the one hand, some of Hātim's sounds have their exact equivalent in the Śrīnagar Kāshmīrī known to me. These are the *a* in "America", the *ā* in "father", the *ai* in "aisle", the *e* in "met", the *ē* like the *a* in "vale", the *ō* in "open", the *u* in "put", the *ū* in "rule", the *ü* in the German "Kürze", and the peculiar Kāshmīrī *ǖ*, for which, so far as I am aware, there is no equivalent in any European language. In all these our transcriptions agree, except that Sir Aurel represents the *e* in "met" by *e*, while I use *ĕ*. On the other hand, there is the greatest confusion between the two systems in their representation of the broken vowels, which play so important a rôle in Kāshmīrī pronunciation. One example will suffice. There is a modified *ā*, which Sir Aurel Stein represents by *ạ̄*, and which he says is sounded like the *u* in "rut" prolonged. In Śrīnagar Kāshmīrī the sound strikes my ear rather as a prolonged German *ö*, although many Paṇḍits, in certain words, sound it almost like the *o* in "note",[1] and I represent it by *ö*. So far the matter is comparatively simple, and it might be possible to solve the problem of the two competing transcriptions; but the case is complicated by the fact that this same modified *ā* almost equally often has an altogether different sound—that of the *aw* in "awful"—which Sir Aurel represents by *â*, and which I represent by *ô*. This may occur in the same word when it occurs more than once. For instance, the word which I always transliterate as *pöda*, and which means "manifest", was sounded by Hātim as *pâda* in ii, 1, and as *pạ̄da* in iii, 8. At other times it was sounded as *ō*, here following the example of the Paṇḍits to which I have just alluded. Thus my *möj*^{u}, a mother, is Hātim's *mōj* in viii, 3, but *mạ̄j* in viii, 1. It is evident that it would be impossible to arrange any system of transcription such as mine, which is based on the Nāgarī spelling of Kāshmīrī Paṇḍits, so as to agree with a pronunciation varying so greatly as in the above examples. I have therefore decided to leave Sir Aurel Stein's representation of the vowel-sounds untouched, and to print it exactly as it stands. This will give rise to inconvenience in comparing the two texts, but it is better that this inconvenience should occur than that any attempted alterations of mine should obscure the niceties of Hātim's pronunciation.

The following is the system employed by Sir Aurel Stein in representing the vowel-sounds used by Hātim :—

LIST OF VOWEL-SOUNDS, AS USED BY SIR AUREL STEIN IN HIS TRANSCRIPTION

a as in "*A*merica".

^{a} a very short *a*, but quite audible.

ā as in "l*a*rge".

[1] e.g. most Paṇḍits pronounce the word *kom*^{u}, work, as if it rhymed with "home".

a̤ as in "c*a*ncelled".

ª̤ a very short *a̤*, having the quality of the *u* in "h*u*t".

ā̤ has the sound of the *u* in "h*u*t", but long.

ā̤ as the *aw* in "*aw*ful".

ai as in "*ai*sle".

ā̤u̯ practically equal to the diphthong *au*, like the *ou* in "s*ou*nd", but sometimes heard as *ā* with a semiliquid *r*.

e as in "m*e*t".

ē as the *a* in "v*a*le".

i as in "p*i*n".

ⁱ a very short *i*, but quite audible.

ī as the *i* in "p*i*que".

o as in "hot".

ō as the *o* in "*o*pen".

u as in "p*u*t".

ᵘ a very short *u*, but quite audible.

ū as the *u* in "r*u*le".

u as in German "K*u*rze", Hungarian "*ü*res".

ū a peculiar long vowel difficult to pronounce. See *Kāshmīrī Manual*, p. 17 (*e*).

A few remarks may be made upon the above.

The so-called *mātrā*-vowels are, as in my system, represented by small letters above the line. Thus ª, ⁱ, ᵘ. Sir Aurel Stein remarks about each of them that it is "very short, but quite audible". As a rule, in Śrīnagar Kāshmīrī, this is true of ª and ⁱ, but to my ear a final ᵘ is hardly audible, if audible at all. Paṇḍits tell me that they can hear it, but I have only occasionally been able to do so. This seems also to have been Sir Aurel Stein's experience. It is evident that what is meant by his statement that ᵘ is quite audible is that he has written it when it was audible and has not written it when it was not audible. A reference to the index of words arranged according to their final letters will show that there are hundreds of words ending in ᵘ in which he did not hear that letter, and consequently did not write it. The cases in which he did hear it are comparatively few. Such are *bāgukᵘ* (iii, 9) and *votᵘmot* (vii, 29). The inaudibility of this letter is well illustrated by words such as my *amyuk*^{u}, which becomes in Hātim's mouth *ạm*^{y}*uk* or *ạmyuk* in iii, 4, and *a*^{i}*m*^{y}*uk* in xii, 17 ; and my *dop*^{u}, which is represented not only by *dop*^{u} (ii, 4 ; xi, 12), but also by *dop* (v, 9 ; viii, 1, 13 ; etc.), *dup* (xi, 2, 14 ; xii, 4), and even *dup*^{a} (xi, 11). It is unnecessary to multiply examples. Many more will be found in the indexes, and it is sufficient to state here that, like me, Sir Aurel Stein has found that *u*-mātrā is very rarely audible.

Regarding the sound represented by *āu̯*, Sir Aurel Stein says that it is practically a diphthong *au*, like the *ou* in "sound", but is sometimes heard as *ā* with a semi-liquid *v*. As it struck me that possibly this *u̯* might be the equivalent of my *w*, I referred the point to Sir Aurel, and he wrote as follows in reply :—

"As regards *gau̯*, I am now certain that I do not mean *w* by the special *u̯*, but merely wished to indicate that the sound was not a usual diphthong. Hātim always keeps the preceding long *ā* [in *āu̯*] quite clear of the *u̯*. This is all I wish to indicate by the marks I employed. It may be the semivowel *v*, but, in that case, it is exceedingly liquid." It will be observed that, as in *gau̯* above quoted, the *u̯* does not necessarily follow a long *ā*. Sir Aurel also occasionally writes an *i̯*, to which the same remarks apply.

The Kāshmīrī of these tales, as recorded by Paṇḍit Gōvinda Kaula, is practically the same as that described by Paṇḍit Īśvara Kaula in his Kāshmīrī grammar entitled the *Kaśmīra-śabdāmṛta*,[1] and by the present writer in his *Essays on Kāçmīrī Grammar* and in his *Kāshmīrī Manual*. There are, however, a few instances in which there occur forms not authorized by any of these works. Some of these are described as "village forms", i.e. as not used in the city of Śrīnagar, and hence by purists banned from literary Kāshmīrī. Others are idioms peculiar to the Musalmān dialect, Hātim, the narrator, being, of course, a follower of Islām; while a few

[1] Published by the Asiatic Society of Bengal in the *Bibliotheca Indica*.

others are additional forms allowed in Śrīnagar, but not recorded by Īśvara Kaula.

As regards vocabulary, there are two unusual words which I have not met elsewhere. One of these is *rāṭun,* to cause to seize, which is not in Īśvara Kaula's very full Dhātupāṭha. It is the causal of the verb *raṭun,* which is of frequent occurrence. The other is the word *gwāsh,* instead of *gāsh,* the light of dawn, which occurs three times, and is therefore not a slip of the transcriber. The usual negative particle is the standard *na,* not; but *nu* occurs once, and a poetical equivalent is *nau.*

In Persian the words *shāh* and *pādshāh,* a king, sometimes appear with the *ā* of the final syllable shortened, so that we also find *shah* and *pādshah.* The same is the case when these words are borrowed in the language of these tales, though, under the ordinary Kāshmīrī rule, a short *a* after *sh* becomes *ĕ,* so that we get both *shāh* and *shĕh* (in *shāhmār* or *shĕhmār,* a python) and *pātashāh* and *pātashĕh.* In the second word it will be observed that, as is frequent in borrowed words, the Paiśācī Prakrit rule of hardening the sonant *d* to *t* is followed. On the other hand, Sir Aurel Stein always writes the word *pādshāh* or *pādshah* with a *d.* From this we gather that while Hātim, like a good Musalmān, adhered to the original borrowed form of the word, Gōvinda Kaula wrote the word as he was accustomed to hear it in the standard Hindū Kāshmīrī of Śrīnagar.

As regards the vowel-sounds, Gōvinda Kaula almost always indicates the same sounds as those recorded by Īśvara Kaula. According to the latter there is an important group of nouns ending in ^{a}*r* which indicate professions (iv, 99), such as *rang*^{a}*r,* a dyer; *sŏn*^{a}*r,* a goldsmith; *man*^{a}*r,* a lapidary, and so on. The only noun of this group occurring in the Tales is *sŏn*^{a}*r,* a goldsmith, and this G.K. persistently writes *sŏnar,* with a full *a.* In Kāshmīrī, when the vowel of a monosyllable is *a* followed by an aspirated surd consonant, the *a* takes the sound of the *a* in the English word "hat" (*Essays,* p. 6). Gōvinda Kaula attempts to represent this sound in the word *krakh*, outcry, by *ē*, and writes *krēkh*. Possibly this represents a real variation of pronunciation. In villages *ä* followed by *i*-mātrā is often pronounced *i*. G.K. has reproduced this in one instance in the word *panän*ⁱ (iv, 7), which he here writes *panin*, and which Sir Aurel Stein represents by *pan*ʸ*en*. Another instance of village pronunciation recorded by G.K. is the substitution of *a* for *u* in *tshananāwun* for *tshunanāwun*, to cause to cast (x, 13).

In the Kāshmīrī of Īśvara Kaula the sound represented by *ö* is changed to *ü* before *i*-mātrā, *i*, or *y*. Thus from *köd*, imprisonment, we have *küd*ⁱ, a prisoner, with a dative singular *küdis*. G.K. never indicates this last change. Thus he writes *köd*ⁱ, *ködis*; *söty* or *sötin* for *süty* or *sütin*, with; *pöntsyum*ᵘ for *püntsyum*ᵘ, fifth.

As regards consonants we may first note that in the villages the letters *ḍ* and *r* are frequently interchanged. This *r* is a dental letter, as elsewhere on the North-West Frontier. We see this clearly in words like *khālun* or *khārun*, to mount; *wālun* or *wārun*, to bring down, in which *r* is in standard Kāshmīrī interchangeable with a dental *l*. We thus find that in the villages there is free interchange between a cerebral *ḍ* and a dental *r*, which could not take place were it not that, as in all Dardic languages, in the common village talk of Kashmīr there is a weak feeling of the difference between cerebrals and dentals. We shall see that in Hātim's pronunciation this want of differentiation between these two classes of sounds is remarkably evident. Gōvinda Kaula's spelling is more influenced by his literary training and familiarity with Sanskrit, but even he reproduces the interchange of *ḍ* and *r* in several instances, such as *lārun* or *lāḍun*, to pursue; *kūr*ᵘ or *kūḍ*ᵘ, a daughter; *mor*ᵘ or *moḍ*ᵘ, the body; *thūr*ᵘ*-kani* or *thūḍ*ᵘ*-kani*, backwards; *tshāḍun* or *tshārun*, to seek. In all these the standard form sanctioned by Īśvara Kaula is the first of each pair. The examples *mor*ᵘ and *moḍ*ᵘ are very instructive. G.K. gives both forms, and so does Sir Aurel Stein in his transcription, but the two do not always agree. Where G.K. has *ḍ* Sir Aurel often has *r*, and vice versa. This illustrates how nearly akin these two letters were as they issued from Hātim's mouth.

The pronunciation of the Persian letter ذ *z̤āl* in borrowed words varies. Sometimes we have *z* as *kākaz*, paper, and sometimes *d* as in *kākad*, paper, and *gudarun*, to happen.

There are two occurrences of the aspiration of a non-final consonant, viz. *bātha* for *bāta*, words (xii, 25), and *ṭhôṭhᵘ* for *ṭôṭhᵘ*, beloved (vii, 4). There are no other instances of such aspiration or disaspiration, although Sir Aurel's transcription teems with both. We have a solitary instance of the insertion of *w* in the word *gwāsh* for *gāsh*, already mentioned. It is probably connected with the Sanskrit *kāśa-*.

In the declension of nouns there are a few examples of departure from the rules laid down by Īśvara Kaula. According to him the suffix of the indefinite article is *āh*, as in *kālāh*, a time. Musalmāns drop the *h* and write *kālā*. G.K. writes the article in each way with about equal frequency. A list of occurrences will be found in the vocabulary under the article *āh*, *ā*. This is, however, rather a matter of spelling than one of pronunciation, as the *h* of *āh* is *hā-ĕ mukhtafī*.

The singular agent of the first declension ends in *-an*, as in *tsūran*, by a thief. The word *sŏnar* (for *sŏnᵃr*), a goldsmith, belongs to this declension, but in the one instance in which the agent of this word occurs (v, 4) it is *sŏnar*, i.e. the same as the nominative. Sir Aurel Stein's transcription shows that this is not a slip on the part of Gōvinda Kaula, and there can be no doubt that the mistake (if mistake it be and not a dialectic form) was made by Hātim.

According to the rule laid down by Ī.K. the suffix *unᵘ* of the genitive can be used only with nouns that are masculine proper names. But in poetry its use is more extended, and hence in xi, 13 we have *sapharunᵘ*, of a journey. More directly contrary to the rule is the phrase *ạshᵉkunᵘ tab*, the fever of love, in v, 10, a prose passage.

According to Ī.K. the plural agent of the first and fourth declensions ends in *-au*, and of the second and third declensions in *-yau*. G.K. very often writes these *-av* and *-iv* respectively. In my opinion these are merely two different ways of recording the same sound, one that it is difficult to represent in the Nāgarī character. Elsewhere in Kāshmīrī the diphthong *au* is at the present day pronounced exactly like *ō*, and is, in fact, a superfluous letter. But in the plural agent the *u* of *au* is almost consonantal. Perhaps *w* would represent its sound better than *u*, but *aw* could not represent the sound of the *au*. Sir Aurel Stein generally writes this diphthong *au̯*, and this is probably the best way of representing the sound. In Kāshmīrī the sound of व़ is something between a labial (not a dento-labial) *v* and a labial *w*, sometimes tending more to one and sometimes tending more to the other, and accordingly I myself sometimes transliterate it *v* and sometimes *w*, a confessedly inaccurate, if convenient, method. The following are examples of the use of *-av* by G.K.: *asmānav, dŏyav, khabardārav, malakav, nawav, nazarbāzav, phakīrav, pīrav, satav, t͟sōrav, t͟sūrav, yimav, zamīnav.* These all belong to the first or fourth declension. For the third declension we have *mŏdariv, zaniv.* In one instance (x, 1) G.K. gives, in a conversation in the colloquial style, *yimōv* for what Ī.K. would write as *yimau*, and this probably represents the pronunciation as nearly as the Nāgarī character (यिमोव़) will permit. The above list is not complete, but on the other hand it must be understood that there are numerous examples of the more usual spelling with *au* and *yau*.

The postpositions used are those commonly employed. Reference has already been made to the use of *söty* and *sötin* for *süty* and *sütin*. The word *pĕṭh* means "on", and *pĕṭha* "from on", but in x, 3 and x, 10 *pĕṭha* is exceptionally employed with the meaning of *pĕṭh*.

As regards pronouns, the proximate demonstrative pronoun *yih*, this, has a masculine form in the nominative singular, *yuh* (xii, 5) or *yüh* (ii, 9, 11; x, 12). In xii, 5 *yuh*, as masculine, is opposed to *yih* as feminine. *Yih*, of course, is also used in the masculine. These masculine forms *yuh* and *yüh* are not mentioned by Ī.K. There are a number of emphatic forms, viz. *yihōy, yihuy, yuhuy, yŏhay, yuhay* (all masc.); *yihay* (fem.); and various inanimate emphatic forms such as *yiy*, *yīy*, and *yī*. None of these are mentioned by Ī.K.

The defective pronoun *nŏth*, *nŏmis*, appears under the form *nĕmis* for the animate dative singular (v, 9; xii, 15). The other forms used (*nŏm*, *nŏman*, *nŏmav*) all have *ŏ*. The relative pronoun has its nom. sing. fem. *yĕsa* instead of Ī.K.'s *yŏssa*. Similarly the interrogative pronoun has its nom. sing. fem. *kusa* instead of *kŏssa*. Its inanimate dative singular is the regular form *kath*, with a colloquial form *kathō* (xi, 11).

The indefinite pronoun *kēh*, anything, is pronounced *kĕh* by Musalmāns, and this is followed by Hātim. Similarly we have the Musalmān *kĕntshāh* for *kēntshāh*, anything. There is a nom. plur. masc. *kĕh*[i] which is not given by Ī.K.

The verb substantive is conjugated regularly. In two cases, apparently under the influence of a neighbouring *y*, *u* has been changed to *ĕ*, so that a masculine form appears under a feminine guise. These are *chĕyĕy* for *chuyĕy*, if there is to thee (ix, 6), and *chĕy* for *chuy*, he is verily (xii, 6). In one case *ös*[i], they were, is changed to *ösī*, metri gratia.

In the standard dialect the 2nd person singular of the imperative is the same in form as the root. Thus *kar*, make thou. But if a pronominal suffix is added, *u* is inserted as a junction-vowel, as in *karu-n*, make thou him. The explanation of this is that the 2nd singular imperative originally ended in *u* (as in **karu*), and that this *u* has been dropped in the modern language. We have a survival of the old form in *gatshu*, go thou (xi, 11). To this also must be referred the forms *khyuh* (x, 5) and *khyō* (x, 12), eat thou. These represent the modern *khĕh* and an older **khĕhu*. The 2nd person plural imperative of *trāwun*, to let go, is *tröviv*. In x, 5 we have a variant *trövyuv*. This is hardly more than a variation of spelling.

In the past conditional the Hindū Śrīnagar dialect makes the 1st person singular end in *hö* (e.g. *karahö*) and the 3rd person singular in *hē* (*karihē*). Musalmāns shorten these final syllables to *ha* and *hĕ* respectively. G.K.'s transcription generally, but not always, follows the Musalmān idiom. Thus, while we have *karahö* (viii, 11), we have also *wuchaha* (viii, 10), I should have seen; *māraha-th* (ii, 11), I should kill thee; *wuchaha-n* (ii, 5), I would see it. So, for the 3rd person, we have *tsārihĕ* (vi, 14), he might pick out; and *shūbihĕh* (xii, 5), she would have been beautiful. The final *h* in the last is *hā-ĕ mukhtafī*.

In the past tenses we have, for the first past, the irregular *pūrun*, he put on (clothes), from *pairun*. For the second past and other pasts in *ōv* there is a strong tendency to weaken the *ōv* by the substitution of a short vowel. Thus *gudariv* (v, 9), it happened, for *guzaryōv*; *gav* (iii, 1), he went, for *gauv*; *khĕv* (ii, 2), eaten, for *khyauv*; *pĕv* (viii, 9), he fell, for *pyauv*. Similarly, for the plural, we have *khĕy* (x, 2), they were eaten, for *khyēy*; *niy* (v, 9), they were taken, for *nīy*. In *h*^{a}*rēyĕkh* (x, 5), for *h*^{a}*ryēyĕkh*, it (fem.) remained over and above for them, the omission of the first *y* is merely a matter of spelling, as a long *ē* is commonly pronounced as if a *y* preceded it.

There is a similar shortening in the perfect participle, as in *gamot*^{u} (viii, 1, etc.), gone, for *gōmot*^{u}; *mumot*^{u} (ii, 4, etc.), dead, for *mūmot*^{u}; *pĕmot*^{u} (viii, 9), fallen, for *pyōmot*^{u}.

In the extremely village style of story xi we find the suffix of the *k*^{u} genitive, instead of the usual suffix *mot*^{u}, added to the past participle in order to convert it into an adjective. This is quite common in the Western Pahāṛī language spoken immediately to the south-east. The examples are *thöv*^{i}*k*^{i}, stationed, and *nyöv*^{i}*k*^{i}, dispatched (both nom. plur. masc.) (xi, 6), for *thöv*^{i}*-mat*^{i} and *nyöv*^{i}*-mat*^{i} respectively.

There is an irregular form of the conjunctive participle in the same poem. It is *kä r*^{i}*than* (xi, 10), having made, in place of the standard *karith*.

There are several variations in the forms of the pronominal suffixes added to verbs. Thus we have *mŏkalāwahun* (x, 1) for *mŏkalāwōn* (*mŏkalāwaw* + *n*), we shall complete it. The suffix *wa* of the 2nd person plural very often drops the final *a*, as in *khĕyĕv* for *khĕyĕwa*, it (fem.) was eaten by you (x, 12); *karĕmav* for *karĕm*^{a}*wa*, they (fem.) were made by me for you (x, 6). This suffix is sometimes used in a very idiomatic sense, like the corresponding Panjābī singular suffix *jē*. It adds no meaning directly to the verb, but, as it were, adds the idea of "I say to you" to the whole sentence. Thus *bani*, it will become, *bani-v*, (I say to you) it will become (ii, 7); *dima-v*, (I say to you) I will give (ii, 8); *t̲sali-v*, (I say to you) he will escape (ii, 8). Village forms using the suffix of this person in its full form are *wanamōwa* for *wana-wa*, I will say to you (x, 1, 2), and *wañĕmōwa* for *wañĕm*ᵃ*wa*, they (fem.) were said by me to you (x, 1). I am informed that an alternative village form for *wanamōwa* (*wanawa*) is *wanōwa*.

Instead of *karukh*, make thou them, we have (xii, 19) *karuhukh*.

Before discussing the details of Hātim's pronunciation as illustrated by Sir Aurel Stein's transcription, it will be well to mention a few general facts.

Words are frequently wrongly divided. Thus the word *amis*ᵘ̈*y*—which is *amis*, to him, combined with the emphatic suffix *y*, to which *ü*-mātrā has been added as a junction-vowel —is invariably divided before the *s*, so that we get *am*ⁱ *suy*, *ạm*ⁱ *süy*, or some such form. So *añĕhas*, they brought (*añĕkh*) to him (*as*), is written *añye has*; the corrupt Arabic *aslāma-laikum*, may the peace be upon you, is written *aslā malaikum*; *bög*ᵃ*rēmay*, I divided (*bög*ᵃ*rēm*) verily (*ay*), is written *bāge rēmai*; and so on for hundreds of examples. On the other hand, two words are sometimes contracted into one, as in *boh*ᵃ*sạ* for *bŏh hasa*, I, Sir; *bebindạ*ⁱ*r*ⁱ for *bĕbi andar*ᵘ̈*y*, within the breastcloth; and *chetal* for *chĕh tal*, she is below. In reproducing Sir Aurel Stein's text I have carefully allowed these seeming irregularities to stand. The frequency with which they occur, and the systematic way in which they are recorded, show that they are not slips of the pen, but represent the actual manner in which Hātim, who, of course, knew nothing of Kāshmīrī grammar, pronounced the words. To him *amis*ᵘ̈*y* was two words—*ami* and *s*ᵘ̈*y*—and so on for the others. We thus have a valuable illustration of how languages change in the mouths of their speakers, and how dialectic variations and different stages of language take their rise.

Reference may also be made to one particular word—that for "king", which Sir Aurel Stein invariably records as *pādshāh*, with a *d*, while Gōvinda Kaula equally invariably records it as *pātashāh*, with a *t*. Hātim was a follower of Islām, and apparently pronounced this borrowed Persian word in the form in which it was delivered to his language, while Gōvinda Kaula, a Brāhmaṇ affected by no Musalmān prejudices, wrote the word as it is pronounced in Śrīnagar, with the typical Piśāca change of *d* to *t*.

Turning to the vowel *a*, we find that it is occasionally interchanged with *a*-mātrā in an unaccented syllable. Thus we have both *bē bahā* and *bēb^a^hā*, priceless, and *mahala̤ kān* and *mah^a^la̤khān*, for G.K.'s *mahalakhān*, the harem of a palace. Much more common is the interchange of *a* and *a̤*, as in *bāgas* and *bāga̤s*, G.K. *bāgas*, to a garden; *dalīla* and *dalīla̤*, G.K. *dalīlā*, a story; *dar* and *da̤r*, G.K. *dar*, in; *saudāgar* and *saudāga̤r*, G.K. *-gar*, a merchant; *zanāna̤* and *za̤nāna̤*, G.K. *zanāna*, a woman; and many others. Very similarly we have the interchange of *a* or *a̤* with *a̤*-mātrā, as in *jāna̤vār* and *jān^a̤^vār*, G.K. *jānāwār*, a bird; *khabar* and *khab^a̤^r*, G.K. *khabar*, news; *kāvandas*, *kāvanda̤s*, *kāva̤ndas*, *khāv^a̤^ndas*, and *khāva̤ndas*, G.K. *khāwandas*, to a husband; *halamas* and *hal^a̤^mas*, G.K. *halumas*, to a skirt; and *māre-vāta̤lan* and *māra̤vāt^a^lan*, to executioners.

The sounds *a̤* and *e* seem to be absolutely convertible. Thus we have *ad^a^*, *ada̤*, *ad^e^*, and *ade* for G.K.'s *ada*, then; *āna̤* and *âne* for G.K.'s *ŏna*, a mirror; *cha̤* and *che* for G.K.'s *chĕh*, she is; *cha̤s* and *ches* for G.K.'s *chĕs*, I (fem.) am; *dakhe nāvān* for G.K.'s *ḍakhanāwān*, leaning upon; *guḍ^a^*, *guḍ^a^*, *guḍa*, and *guḍe* for G.K.'s *gŏḍa*, at first; *hasa̤* and *hase* for G.K.'s *hasa*, Sir; *hāv^a^nam* (G.K. *hāwanam*), they will show to me, and *vāle nam* (G.K. *wālanam*), they will cause me to descend, both in the same line; *hazrat*, *hazra̤t^i^*, *hazra̤^i^t^i^*, *hazret*, and *hazret^i^*, all for G.K.'s *hazrat-i*, a certain title; *jāya̤* and *jāye*, G.K. *jāyĕ*, in a place, in two consecutive lines, also *jai* and *jāy^e^*; *kata̤*, *katha̤*, and *kathe*, G.K. *katha*, words; 1st persons singular future, such as *parạ*, I shall recite; but *behe*, I shall sit, *kare*, I shall do; *kal*^{a}, *kalạ*, and *kale*, G.K. *kala*, a head; *kartạ* and *karte*, G.K. *karta*, please do; *mār*^{a}*vātạlan*, *mār*^{a}*vātelan*, *mārạvāt*^{a}*lan*, *māre-vāt*^{a}*lan*, *mārevātạlan*, etc., G.K. *mārawātalan*, to executioners; *peṭạ*, *pyeṭe*, etc., G.K. *pĕṭha*, from on; *yil*^{a}, *yelạ*, and *yele*, G.K. *yĕla*, from restraint; and hundreds of others.

When *a* precedes *i* it is usually written *ạ*, as in *rạṭit*, G.K. *raṭith*, having seized. Sometimes it is written *ạ*^{i}, as in *ạm*^{i} or *ạ*^{i}*m*^{i}, G.K. *àm*^{i}, by him. It becomes *ạ̄*^{i} in *lạ̄*^{i}*r*^{i}, G.K. *lari*, at the side, and in one instance we have *o*, in *mạris* or *moḍis*, to a body. The change of *a* to *o*, but without a following *i*, occurs in *doh*, *doha*, *dohạ*, *doh*^{o}, or *doho*, G.K. *dŏha*, on a day.

Other less common changes are the following. We have in one case *a* lengthened to *ā*, in *khābạrdārau*, by the watchmen (elsewhere *kha-*). Cf. *lạ̄*^{i}*r*^{i} above. We have unaccented *ạ*-mātrā becoming *i*-mātrā in *ās*^{a}*nas* or *ās*^{i}*nas*, G.K. *āsanas*, for being. In the word *tulạri*, for G.K. *t*^{a}*l*^{a}*ri*, by a bee, *a*-mātrā appears as *u*.

In standard Kāshmīrī, after *sh*, *a* is pronounced as *ĕ*, and I have in such a case transliterated it by that letter. Thus the Persian *shahr*, a city, is in my transliteration of G.K.'s text shown as *shĕhar*. As a rule Hātim preserves the *a*, but there are also several instances of the change to *e*. Thus—

My transliteration of G.K.	Sir Aurel Stein's transcription of Hātim.
shĕh, six,	*she*,
shĕhara, from a city,	*shah*^{a}*rạ* and *sheherạ*,
shĕharāh, a city,	*shehra*,
shĕrīkh, a partner,	*sherīk*,

and others. The number would be increased if we included several words that Hātim pronounced with *ạ* (it being remembered that *ạ* and *e* are with him interchangeable), as in *shạhạn* for G.K. *shĕhan*, to the six; *shạhmārạs*, G.K. *shĕh-māras*, to the python.

A final short *a* is sometimes dropped, as in *gar*, *gar*^{a}, and *garạ*, G.K. *gara*, a house; *doh*, *doha*, etc., G.K. *dŏha*, on a day; *sar*, *sar*ᵃ̣, *sare*, and *serạ*, G.K. *sara*, investigation.

In standard Kāshmīrī a borrowed word ending in a consonant preceded by a long *ā* often adds a final short *a*. Thus *jahāz*, a ship, becomes *jahāza*; *nishān*, a sign, becomes *nishāna*, and so on. Sir Aurel Stein gives three words of this kind to which G.K. does not add a final *a*. These are *chālāna*, G.K. *cālān*, an invoice; *lāl* and *lāl*ᵃ̣, G.K. *lāl*, a ruby; *māl*ᵃ̣, G.K. *māl*, property. We have also *ạ* added in *dopusạ*, G.K. *dopus*, said to him, and *chukạ*, G.K. *chukh*, thou art.

In the standard dialect, when *a* is followed by *ü*-mātrā it becomes *ü*. Sir Aurel Stein usually represents this sound by *ạ*. A good example is the feminine genitive postposition which G.K. writes *sünz*ᵘ, and which Sir Aurel usually writes *sạnz*. Occasionally he represents it by *u*. Thus we have also *sunz*; *ås̊us*, G.K. *ös*ᵘ*s*, she was to him. For G.K.'s *thüḍ*ᵘ or *thür*ᵘ, on the back, we have *tạḍ*, *tor*, *tạr*, and *tür*. The syllable ᵘ*y* is represented by *uy*, *üy*, and *ai*. Thus G.K.'s *tamis*ᵘ*y*, to him verily, becomes *tạm*ⁱ *suy* or *tạm*ⁱ *süy*, while *timan*ᵘ*y*, to them verily, becomes *tim*ᵃ̣*nai*. Another example of the representation of *ü* by *u* is G.K.'s *wütsh*ᵘ, she descended, which becomes *vuts* (iii, 2), and the same word also represents G.K.'s *wŏtsh*ᵘ, she went up (iii, 1, 3).

The letter *ā* or *āh*, when final and representing the indefinite article, is usually shortened to *a* or *ạ*, as in *doha*, G.K. *dŏhā*, a day; *dalīla* and *dalīlạ*, G.K. *dalīlāh*, a story; *zālạ* and *zālā*, G.K. *zālāh*, a net. Similarly, although there is no suffix of the indefinite article, *shōrạ ga* and *shōrạgā*, G.K. *shōra-gāh*, an outcry. Often, however, as, for instance, in some of the above examples, the long *ā* is retained.

When *ā* is followed in G.K.'s dialect by *ü*-mātrā, by *i*-mātrā, or by *i* it becomes *ö*, and this same *ö* also usually represents the pronunciation of the diphthong *ai*. Sir Aurel Stein sometimes represents this *ö* by *ạ̄*, which according to his phonetic system represents approximately the same sound. Thus—

G.K.	Hātim.
böy^{i}, brothers,	*bạ̄y*,
död^{i}*laday*, suffering,	*dạ̄*^{i}*d*^{ye} *ladai*,
dón^{ü}, a pomegranate,	*dạ̄n*,
dör^{i}, holding,	*dạ̄r*,
gòj^{ü}*nas*, he caused me to waste away,	*gạ̄j*^{a}*nas*,
khöris, for a khār weight,	*khạ̄ris*,
kötyāh, how many?	*kạ̄*^{i}*t*^{y}*a*,
mòj^{ü}, a mother,	*mạ̄j*, *mōj*,

and others.

For original *ai* we have—

pöda, manifest,	*pạ̄da*, *pâda*,
göb, hidden,	*gạ̄b*,
köd, imprisonment,	*kạ̄d*,
gör, different,	*gạ̄*^{i}*ri*, *gār*.

About equally often this *ö* is represented by *å*, corresponding to my *ó*, and therefore sounded something like the *aw* in "awful". Thus—

ölis, to a nest,	*ålis*,
ör^{ü}, a shoemaker's awl,	*år*,
özīz, poor,	*åzīz*,
ös^{ü}*s*, she was to him,	*åsus*,
bōlbösh^{ü}, chirping,	*bōlbåsh*,
gum-röyī, losing one's way,	*gum*^{a}*rå yiy*,
āsh^{e}*nāv*, relations,	*åshnāụ̂*, *āsh*^{i} *nāv*, as if for *ösh*^{i}*nāv*,

and others. For original *ai* we have—

öna, a mirror,	*åne*, *ānạ*,
pöda, manifest,	*påda*, *pạ̄da*,

and others.

Very often this *ö* is represented by a simple *ā*, as in—

b̃öd^{i}*hāl*, a prison,	*bānd*^{i}*hāl*,
dazön^{i}, verily burning,	*dazān*^{i},
gös, they went for him,	*gās*,
judöyi, separation,	*zhudāī*,

G.K.	Hātim.
köshir[i], Kāshmīrīs,	*kāshir*[i],
zölith, having burnt,	*zālit*,

and others. For original *ai* we have—

gör, different,	*gār*, *gạ̄*[i]*ri*,
khörāth, alms,	*khārāt*,
sölas, for an excursion,	*sālạs*,

and others.

The word *myöñ*[u], mine (fem.), appears in various forms, viz. *mēñy*, *myē̃*, *m*[y]*ēn*, *myēn*, and *m*[y]*ēñy*, in all of which the *ö* is represented by *ē*; whereas for the corresponding *cyöñ*[u], thy (fem.), we have *ch*[i]*ān*, *ch*[y]*ān*[i], and *ch*[y]*ạ̄n*[y].

We have seen that G.K. usually represents *ṻ* by *ö*, as in *köd*[i] for *kūd*[i], *söty* for *sūty*. Sir Aurel Stein writes for these words *kạ̄*[i]*d*, *kạ̄*[i]*d*[i], and *kūd*[i], and *sạ̄it*, *sạ̄t*[y], etc., respectively.

When *ā* is followed in G.K.'s dialect by *u*-mātrā it becomes *ô*, and Sir Aurel Stein almost always gives for it his sign *ā̊*, which represents the same sound. Thus—

G.K.	Hātim.
ôkhun, a teacher,	*ā̊khun*, *ākhun*,
ôl[u], a nest,	*ā̊l*,
ôs[u], he was,	*ā̊s*, *ā̊s*[u], *ās*, *ōs*,
ôy, he came to thee,	*ā̊y*, *ạ̄y*,
bôwun, he explained,	*bā̊vun*,

and many others. It will be seen from the above that *ā*, *ạ̄*, and *ō* are also used to represent this sound. So, for *khôtūni*, to the lady, we have *khā̊tūni* and *khātūni*; for *lôyun*, he struck, *lā̊yun* and *lạ̄yun*; for *sôruy*, all, *sā̊ruy*, *sạ̄ruy*, *sō*[i]*ri*, and *soirạ*; for *bôw*[u], manifested, *bōụ*. There are many other similar examples, and from the above it will be seen that G.K.'s *ö* and *ô* are represented indiscriminately by *ạ̄*, *ā̊*, and *ā*.

The vowel *e* is, we have seen, interchangeable with *ạ*. It is also liable to be shortened to *e*-mātrā when final, as in *bāye*, *bāy*[e], or even *bai*, for G.K.'s *bāyĕ*, to a wife.

We have already noticed that in Kāshmīrī *a* after *sh* becomes *ĕ* (i.e. Sir Aurel Stein's *e*). In one instance Hātim has ō for this ĕ, G.K.'s *shĕkh*, hesitation, being represented by *shak* or *shōk*.

It is well known that the average Kāshmīrī is unable to distinguish between the letters *e* and *i*, whether long or short. In this way Hātim gives *ē* instead of G.K.'s *ī* in the following—

G.K.	Hātim.
bīṭh^{i}, seated (m. pl.),	*b*^{y}*ēth*^{i}, *bēth*^{y}, and *bạṭ*^{i},
grīst^{i}-*bāy*, a farmer's wife,	*grēst bāy*,
phīrith, having returned,	*phērith*, *phē*^{i}*rith*, or *phīrit*,

and others. It will be observed that, in the case of *bạṭ*^{i}, *ī* has become *ạ*. Similarly, G.K.'s *rīnz*^{i}, balls, is represented by *rīnz*, *rēnz*, or *rạnz*; and his *trēsh*, thirst, by *trēsh* or *trạ̄s*. Owing to the confusion of *ạ* and *e* and of *i* and *ĕ* (Stein's *e*), we sometimes have *ạ* for *i*. Thus G.K.'s *grīst*^{i}-*bāyĕ*, to a farmer's wife, becomes *grēst*^{ạ} *bāye*, *grēstạ bāye*, or *grēst bāye*. Similarly, G.K.'s *dàp*^{i}*zihĕkh*, thou must say to them, is represented by *dabzi hek* or *dabzạ hek*; G.K.'s *wás*^{i}*zi*, you should descend, by *vaz*^{i}*zạ*; and *yith*, to this, by *yet*, *yath*, *yạt*, and *yat*.

As regards *u*, we occasionally observe hesitation as to quantity. Thus G.K.'s *dop*^{u}*nas*, he said to him, is represented by both *dop*^{u}*nas* and *dopunas*; and his *yūsuph*, Joseph, by *yūsuf*, *yusūf*, and *yūsūf*.

Just as in the case of *e* and *i*, so ordinary Kāshmīrīs are unable to distinguish between *o* and *u*. There are numerous examples of this in Hātim's language. A few will suffice here—

G.K.	Hātim.
borun, he filled,	*borun* and *burun*,
koḍun, he brought out,	*koḍun*, *kuḍun*,
kuṭ^{a}*wālan*, by the policeman,	*koṭvālạn*, *kuṭvālen*,
noṭ^{u}, a pitcher,	*nut*,
byūṭh^{u}, he sat,	*byōṭh*, *byūṭh*,
pūrun, he put on,	*pōrun*, *purun*.

The Persian *k͟h͟ūbṣūrat*, beautiful, becomes *khōbsūrath* in G.K., for which Hātim has *khōb sūrat* and *khâb sūrat*.

Once or twice we find *u* interchanged with other vowels. Thus we have *che* for *chuh*, he is; and (once each) *chiy* or *chi*^{y}

for *chuy*, he is verily. The imperative *ṭshun*, cast thou, is represented by *ṭsün*, but elsewhere the *u* of this word is preserved. After *y*, *u* or *o* has a tendency to become *ü*, as in *d^{y}utuk*, *dyutuk*, *d^{y}ütuk*, or *d^{y}üthuk*, for *dyutukh*, they gave; *h^{y}ütun* or *hyütun*, for *hyotun*, he began.

An initial *u* in Kāshmīrī is always pronounced *wu*. This is not usually the case with an initial *ō*, but G.K.'s *ōra*, thence, is represented not only by *åra* and similar forms, but also by *vōḍa*.

It is well known that *ĕ* and *ē* are usually pronounced in Kāshmīrī with a short *y* before them. Thus ^{y}*ĕ*, ^{y}*ē*. This ^{y} is not usually written in G.K.'s transcription, but it is everywhere to be presumed. Sir Aurel Stein as a rule writes this ^{y} either as a small letter above the line or as a full *y*. Examples will be found on every page of his text. A few are given here—

G.K.	Stein.
khĕkh, thou wilt eat,	*kyek*,
khĕwān, eating,	*khyavān*, *khyevān*, *k^{y}avān*,
kĕth, in,	*kh^{y}ạth*, *khyạth*, *k^{y}et*, *kyet*,
pĕṭha, from,	*peṭạ*, *pyeṭe*, *p^{y}eṭh*, *p^{y}eṭhạ*.

It will be observed that *yạ* is sometimes used instead of *ĕ*. Other similar cases are—

kĕtha, how?	*kyatạ*, *k^{y}eta*, *k^{y}etạ*, *k^{y}ita*, *kh^{y}ạthạ*
khŏni, on the haunch,	*kun^{y}ạ*,
nēza, railings,	*n^{y}ạ̄zạ*,
zēni, he will conquer,	*za^{i}ni*, *z^{y}ạ̄ni*.

Turning to consonants, we first draw attention to the well-known fact that, as in all Dardic languages, Kāshmīrī possesses no sonant aspirates. Original sonant aspirates are always disaspirated. This is fully borne out by Hātim's pronunciation. There is only one occurrence of an aspirated sonant consonant in the whole of Sir Aurel Stein's transcription. This is in the word *ghāsh* (viii, 9), for *gwāsh* or *gāsh*, light, which Sir Aurel writes elsewhere as *gāsh* (five times).

But Hātim's pronunciation goes further. The aspiration of surd consonants is most irregular, many such sounds that are written by G.K. and elsewhere as aspirated surds are disaspirated, and many unaspirated surds are aspirated. In some cases this runs uniformly through every occurrence of a word or letter. Thus the verb *gatshun*, to go, is always written *gatsun*, and the letter *c* is almost invariably written *ch*. In other cases the aspiration or disaspiration is more capricious.

In the Kāshmīrī of Īśvara Kaula and other Hindūs a final surd is always, with a few specified exceptions, aspirated, while Musalmāns retain the unaspirated sound. Thus we have—

Musalmān.	Hindū.
krak, outcry,	*krakh*.
thap, seizing,	*thaph*.
rat, blood,	*rath*.
naṭ, palsy,	*naṭh*.
kāts, glass,	*kātsh*.

The transcript of these tales by Gōvinda Kaula follows the Hindū custom and aspirates final surds. With Hātim it is, curiously enough, almost a question of date. The recording of Sir Aurel Stein's transcription commenced on June 16, and continued, with intervals, till July 31, 1896. In the earlier parts of this transcription final surds were not aspirated, but in recording the recitation of July 24, Sir Aurel wrote the word *thaph* (xii, 11), seizing, previously recorded as *thap* or *tap*, and makes a special note on the margin that in this instance the *ph* is a true aspirate. An examination of the rest of the text recorded on that day and on the following and final recitation of July 31, shows that the final surds are here much more consistently aspirated than had been the case previously. It is out of the question to assume that the non-recording of this aspiration in the earlier tales was due to faulty audition on the part of Sir Aurel Stein. He was, I know, perfectly aware at the time of this distinction between Musalmān and Hindū pronunciation, and had previously corresponded with me on the subject.

The following are examples of Hātim's disaspiration :—

For the letter *b* we may take the Arabic borrowed word *sub^ahan*, at dawn, for which H. has *suban*; but how inconsistent he is in this is shown by the following cognate forms: *subu* for *subuh*; *subahanas* for *sub*^{a}*hanas*; and *subhas* for *sub*^{a}*has*.

We have said that the letter *c* is almost always aspirated to *ch*. Similarly, the aspiration of *ch* (very common in the auxiliary verb *chuh*, he is) is generally retained. But, in one instance (i, 13), *cüy* is written for *chuy*, he is indeed. Another similar case is that of the verb *wuchun*, to see. In this the *ch* is usually retained; but we have *vucehun* (ii, 5) for *wuchahun*, *vucuk* (ii, 4) for *wuchukh*, and *vucun* (ii, 8) for *wuchun*.

Of more frequent occurrence is the aspirate *kh*, and of this disaspiration is frequent. Thus—

Initial.—While the borrowed Persian word *khūb*, well, always preserves its aspiration, *khāb*, a dream, becomes *kāb* and *kāv*; *khabar*, news, is spelt *kabar*, etc., in the first five stories, and *khabar*, etc., afterwards; and *Khŏdā*, God, becomes *Kudā*, etc., in i–vi, and *Khudā*, etc., afterwards. Similarly—

khalat-ĕ-shohi, a royal robe, becomes *kal*^{a}*ti shāhi*.
khām, unripe, „ *khām* and *kām*.
khumār, languishment, „ *kumār*.
khān, N.P., „ *khān* (ii, 1) and *kān* (ii, 12).
khŏni, on the haunch, „ *kun*^{y}*ạ*.
khar, an ass, „ *khar* (iii) and *kar* (v).
khōran, to the feet, „ *kurạn*.
khash, a cut, „ *kash*.

The verb *khasun*, to ascend, retains the aspirate, except in forms derived from the past participle *khot*^{u}, in which the aspiration sometimes persists and is sometimes lost, giving forms such as *khot*^{u}, *khut*, and *kut*; *khat*^{i} and *kạ*^{i}*ty*; *kạtis*; *khats* and *kạts*.

khŏta, than, becomes *khotạ*, *khuṭạ*, and *kuṭạ*.
khôtūna, a lady, „ *kōtūna* (v) and *khâtūn* (x, xii).
khatith, secretly, „ *kạ*^{i}*tith*.
khāwand, a husband, „ *kāvand* (i–viii) and *khāvand* (x–xii).

The verb *khyon*^{u}, to eat, as a rule has *k* in the earlier tales and *kh* in the later, but this is not universal. Thus we have *khyāu* for *khĕv*, eaten, in ii, 2. Occasionally also the cognate Shiṇā language disaspirates in this word.

Khazmath or *khizmath*, service, becomes *khismat* (ii, 3) and *kismat* (xii, 3), and so many others.

It will be observed that the disaspiration occurs whether the *kh* represents the Indian aspirate or whether it represents a Persian خ. It will also be noticed that, generally speaking, but not universally, when there are two forms, one with and the other without the aspiration, the disaspirated forms occur in the earlier stories and the aspirated forms in the later stories. The same is true for the other instances of disaspiration, and I shall not trouble to refer to it again. It will, however, be understood that numerous, though not so numerous, instances of disaspiration occur also in the later stories.

Medial *kh* is not so common, but we can quote *pakạ* for *pakha*, wings; *tākhīt* (x, 12) and *tākīt* (xi, 13) for *tāhkhīth*, certainly; *vutamak*^{i} for *wŏtamukh*^{i}, upside down.

Final *kh* occurs in *akh*, one, which is represented both by *ak* and *akh* in all parts of the tales, though *akh* occurs only in i, 4, and four times in xii. For *phakh*, a stink, we have only *phak*.

Initial *ph* is preserved in the *phak* just quoted. For *phamb*, cotton wool, we have *phamb* and *pamb*, both in viii. For *phardā*, on the morrow, we have *parda*; while the verb *phērun*, to regret, loses its aspiration twice and preserves it once in viii.

Medial *ph* occurs in *naphtsas*, for the belly, which H. pronounced *naptsas* (x, 3).

Final *ph* occurs in the word *thaph*, grasping. It appears under the forms *thaph*, *thap*, and *tap*.

Although not strictly an aspirate, we may here quote the *shh* in the borrowed Arabic word *mashhūr*, celebrated, which H. (xi, 3) pronounced *maushūr*.

Initial *th* occurs in the following: in *thud* (*thod*^{u}), erect, it is preserved. For *thūr*^{u}, a shrub, we have *tūr*, and for *thūr*^{u} or *thūḍ*^{u}, on the back, we have *tạd*, *tạr*, and *tor*; *thūñ*^{u}*ā*, butter, preserves the *th*; but for *thaph*, grasping, we have *thaph*, *thap*, and *tap*. The common verb *thăwun*, to place, generally preserves the *th*, but we have *thāvum* and *tāvum*, and, for *thàv*^{i}*taw*, *tạivtau*.

Medial *th* occurs in the following: *atha*, a hand, becomes both *athạ*, etc., and *ata*, etc., the aspirated forms occurring most frequently in the later tales; *buth*^{u}, a face, is always *but*; so, for *ạth*^{ü}*r*^{ü}, the woodworm, *ạtạr*; for *katha*, stories, *kathạ*, etc., and *katạ*; *nĕth*^{a}*r*, a wedding, *nĕth*^{ạ}*r* (xii) and *n*^{y}*ĕtar* (viii); *pathar*, downward, *pathar* and *patar*, etc.; *woth*^{u}, descended, *vut* and *vuth*, and similarly in derived forms; and similarly *wọth*^{u}, ascended, also becomes *vut* or *vuth*. Other examples are *vatạ*^{i}*rith* for *watharith*, having spread out, but this verb fluctuates as regards the aspirate in other forms; *wọthus*, arose to him, becomes *vothus*, etc., or *votus*; and *wŏthith*, having arisen, *vuthit* and *vutit*. *Sāthāh*, a moment, becomes *sātha* or *sātạ*.

For final *th* the pronoun *ath* generally becomes *at*, except that we have both *at* and *ath* in xii. Conjunctive participles, such as *wŏthith* just cited, almost always end in *t*, the *th*-termination being frequent only in xii; the postposition *kĕth*, in, becomes *k*^{y}*et*, etc., except in xii, where we have *kh*^{y}*ạth*, etc., with exceptional aspiration of the *k*. The distributive particle *prath* always becomes *prat*. Pronominal datives, such as *tath*, *kath*, etc., follow *ath* in sometimes dropping the aspiration and sometimes (in the later stories) keeping it.

For initial *ṭh* the only real example is *ṭhahărān*, awaiting, for which H. has *tah*^{ạ}*rān*.

There are more examples of medial *ṭh*, such as *bōnṭha*, in front, which always has the dental *t*, as in *bōnt*^{a}, etc.; *byūṭh*^{u}, seated, and its derivatives also generally disaspirate the *ṭh*, except in xii, which also retains the aspiration. *Kuṭh*^{u}, a room, also disaspirates except once in x, 7, where we have the dative *kuṭhis*, while in x, 8 we have *kutis* and *kuṭis*; the ablative postposition *pĕṭha* occurs in several forms, *peṭạ*, *pyeṭe*, *p*^{y}*ethạ*, *p*^{y}*eṭh*, and *p*^{y}*eṭhạ*, the aspirated forms occurring chiefly in the later stories. Similar is the treatment of *pöṭh*^{i} or *pòṭhin*, like, for which we have *pā̤ʹṭʹ*, etc., and *pā̤ʹṭhʹ*, etc., and *pā̤tin* and *pāthin*. The common word *sĕṭhāh*, very, much, appears as *seṭā*, etc., and *seṭhā*, etc., it being noted that both forms occur in xii; *ṭôṭhᵘ* or *ṭhôṭhᵘ*, beloved, is always *ṭōṭ*, and *zīṭhʹ*, long (m.pl.), becomes *zīṭʹ*.

Initial *tsh* is always disaspirated by H. Thus the word *tshunun*, to throw, is always *tsunun*, and so for all others.

As for medial *tsh*, in the verb *gatshun*, to go, to be proper, it is always disaspirated by H. The same applies to the indefinite pronoun *kĕntshāh*, something, which appears under many forms, in none of which does an aspirated *tsh* appear. Similarly, we have *matsa̤* and *matsʸe* for *matshi*, on the shoulder; *ratsehᵃna* for *ratshi-hanā*, a little; *vuts* for *wŏtshᵘ*, she went up, and also for *wütshᵘ*, she went down, and others.

Turning now to aspiration, we may commence with the general statement that every *c* is aspirated by H. The solitary exception is the word *cĕshma*, an eye (i, 3), which appears as *ceshma̤*. Thus we have—

G.K.	H.
cĕnda, a pocket,	*chanda̤*.
ciṭhʹ, a letter,	*chit*.
bacĕ, young ones,	*bache*.
bacāwüñᵘ, to be released (fem.),	*bachāviny*.
nayistānücᵘ, of the canebrake,	*na̤yis tān na̤ch*.
racĕn, she took them (fem.),	*rachen*.
zacĕ, rags,	*zache*.

Reference has already been made to the aspiration of *g* in *ghāsh*, for *gāsh*, light.

Examples of the aspiration of *k* are:—

G.K.	Hātim.
kūrᵘ, a daughter,	*kūḍ*, *khūḍ*.
kŏmbakas, for help,	*khumba khas*.
kĕtha, how?	*kʸeta*, *khʸa̤tha̤*.
kĕntshāh, something,	*kyẽ tsa*, etc., or *khyẽ tsa*.
kāsun, to shave (xii),	*khāsun*.
koṭᵘ, a son (xii),	*khuṭh*.

For the aspiration of *p*, we have *put*, *puth*, *phot*, or *phut*, for *pot*^{u}, back again. Shiṇā has *phot* for this word.

For the aspiration of initial *t*, we have *tal* or *thal*, for *tal* below; *tot*, *tut*, or *thuth*, for *tot*^{u}, thither; and *thāu̯* for *tāv*, exhaustion.

Medial *t* is also sometimes aspirated. The termination *ta* of the polite imperative often becomes *thạ*, etc., as in *kartạ* or *kar the*, for *karta*, please to do; *ts̄unthạ* for *ts̄hunta*, please to throw. So also the termination *mot*^{u} of the perfect participle becomes *muth* in *on muth*, for *on*^{u}*mot*^{u}, brought; *vot*^{u}*mut* or *vōt*^{u}*muth*, for *wôt*^{u}*mot*^{u}, arrived. The *t* in *dyut*^{u}, given, is aspirated in *dyut* or *dyuth*, for *dyut*^{u}; *d*^{y}*ü̆tuk* or *d*^{y}*ü̆thuk*, for *dyutukh*, they gave; *dithin*, for *ditin*, he gave them. Similarly—

G.K.	Hātim.
kyut^{u}, for,	*kh*^{y}*ut*, *k*^{y}*ut*, *kyut*, *khyuth*, *kyuth*.
rụt^{a}*na*, a jewel (in composition),	*rotun*^{a}, *rothunạ*, *roṭhunạ*.
sāta, at a moment,	*sūt*^{a}, *sāthạ*.
söty, with,	*sạ̄it*, *sạ̄ʿth*, *sạ̄ʿth*^{y}, etc.
tot^{u}, thither,	*tot*, *tut*, *thuth*.
wôt^{u}, arrived,	*vōt*, etc., or *vōth*.

The above is in no way a complete list of all the instances of disaspiration and aspiration. It is merely a selection of typical examples.

The Dardic languages as a rule have no cerebral letters. Literary Kāshmīrī, however, preserves the distinction between cerebral and dental almost as carefully as is the case in India. There are, nevertheless, a few striking examples to the contrary, as in *ḍuṭakh* or *duṭakh*, cutting in two; *ḍal* or *dal*, a leaf; and *wŏthun*, to arise, as compared with the Hindī *uṭhnā*. But even in the literary language the pronunciation of cerebral letters cannot be so definitely cerebral as in India, for in Kāshmīrī poetry cerebral consonants are permitted to rhyme with dentals, a thing which is impossible in Indian verse. Thus, in the *Rāmâvatāracarita*, the proper name *Yindrazīth*, Indrajita, rhymes with *ḍīṭh*^{ü}, seen, in verse 699, and with *bīṭh*^{ü}, seated, in verse 872.

In the village Kāshmīrī of Hātim, the state of affairs is altogether different. Here the utmost confusion exists, dentals being used for cerebrals, and cerebrals for dentals, almost at random. From the numerous examples that follow it is evident that Hātim used an intermediate sound that at one time struck Sir Aurel Stein's ears as cerebral and at another as dental. If Hātim had pronounced real cerebral sounds, it is impossible to suppose that Sir Aurel, with his long familiarity with Indian languages, could have failed to notice them, more especially as some of the words written with dental letters, such as *ḍāk*, a stage, are words that are in everyday use in India both in colloquial speech and in literature. It might be thought that here and there Sir Aurel may have omitted a subscript dot by a slip of the pen; but the omissions are too frequent and too regular to permit this assumption to be taken as a general explanation, and, moreover, it will not account for those cases in which he has marked as cerebrals, letters which in the corresponding Hindī or Sanskrit are always dental. The following are examples of this confusion. The list is in no way complete :—

A. Dentals where we should expect cerebrals—

Literary Dialect.	Hātim.
t for *ṭ*.	
gāṭ^{ü}*j*^{ü}, skilful (f. sg.),	*gātij.*
gāṭ$^{\dot{a}}$*l*^{i}, skilful (m. pl.),	*gātily.*
haṭis, to the throat,	*hatis.*
khaṭith, secretly,	*kạ*^{i}*tith.*
noṭ^{u}, a jar,	*nut.*
phaṭun, to be broken.	
phüṭ^{ü}	*phut.*
phüṭ^{ü}*wa*	*phutu.*
phuṭ^{a}*run*, to break,	
phuṭ^{o}*r*^{u}*has*	*phut*^{ạ}*rhas.*
phuṭ^{o}*rukh*	*phut*^{ạ}*ruk.*
but *phuṭ*^{a}*ryūn*	*phuṭạ r*^{y}*ūn.*
raṭun, to seize.	
räṭ^{i}	*rạṭ*^{i}.

Literary Dialect.	Hātim.
rōṭ^{u}	*rōt, rut.*
rüṭ^{ü}	*rạt.*
roṭ^{u}*mot*^{u}	*ruṭmut.*
but (causal) *rôṭ*^{u}*mot*^{u}	*rot*^{a}*mut.*
roṭun	*rotun, rutun.*
rüṭ^{ü}*nakh*	*rut*^{a}*nak.*
raṭith	*rạtit, rạṭit.*
roṭ^{u}*wa*	*rutu.*
ṭahàl^{i}, servants,	*ṭạhạl, ṭạhạl*^{i}, *ṭạhạl*^{v}.
troṭ^{u}, a necklace,	*truṭ.*
but *traṭis* (sg. dat.)	*trạtis.*
tsāṭahāl, a school,	*tsāt*^{a}*hāl.*
tsaṭun, to cut.	
tsoṭ^{u}	*tsot.*
tsaṭàn^{i}	*tsaten*^{i}.
tsaṭun^{u}	*tsatun.*
tsàṭ^{i}*nam*	*tset*^{i}*nam.*
tsaṭanas	*tsatanas.*
but *tsaṭanasa*	*tsaṭan*^{a}*sạ.*
tsaṭith	*tsạ*^{i}*tith.*
th or *t* for *ṭh.*	
ọth, eight,	*ạ̄th.*
bĕhun, to sit down.	
bīṭh^{i}	*bạ̄ṭ*^{i}, *beth*^{v}, *b*^{v}*ēth*^{i}.
byūṭh^{u}	*byūt, byūṭ, byōth, byōṭh, byūṭh.*
byūṭhus	*b*^{v}*uthus.*
bōnṭha, before,	*bōnt*^{a}, *bōnt*^{a}, *bontạ.*
but *bōnṭh*	*bōnṭ.*
ḍēshun, to see.	
ḍyūṭh^{u}	*dyūt, ḍyūṭ.*
ḍyūṭhum	*ḍyūṭhum.*
ḍyūṭh^{u}*may*	*dyōt mai.*
ḍyūṭh^{u}*mot*^{u}	*dyūtmut.*
ḍyūṭhuth	*ḍyūṭhut.*

Literary Dialect.	Hātim.
kuṭh^{u}, a room.	
kuṭh^{i}	*kuṭi.*
kuṭh^{u}	*kut.*
kuṭh^{u}*āh*	*kuṭhā.*
kuṭhis	*kuṭhis, kutis, kuṭis.*
myūṭh^{u}, sweet,	*myūt.*
pĕṭh, on,	*p*^{y}*et, p*^{y}*eṭ, pyet, pyeṭ, p*^{y}*eṭh.*
pĕṭha, from on,	*peṭạ, pyeṭe, p*^{y}*eṭh, p*^{y}*ethạ, p*^{y}*eṭhạ.*
pöṭh^{i}, like,	*pạ̄*^{i}*ṭ*$^{'}$*, pạ̄*^{i}*th*^{i}*, pạ̄*^{i}*ṭh*^{i}*, pạ̄*^{i}*th*^{y}*, pạ̄*^{i}*ṭh*^{y}*, pạ̄*^{i}*t*^{y}*, pạ̄*$^{'}$*ty.*
poṭhin, like,	*pāthin, pạ̄tin.*
raṭun, to seize.	
raṭh	*rat.*
raṭhta	*rath ta.*
sĕṭhāh, very,	*setā, seṭā, sethā, seṭhā.*
ṭhaharān, stopping,	*tah*^{a}*rān.*
d for *ḍ*.	
ḍakhanāwān, leaning on,	*dakhe nāvān.*
ḍākas, for a stage,	*dākas.*
ḍēshun, to see.	
ḍēshān	*dēshān.*
ḍēshun^{u}	*dēshun.*
ḍīshith	*ḍēshit.*
ganḍun, to tie.	
ganḍ	*gand.*
gȧnḍ^{i}	*gand*^{i}*, ganḍi.*
gȧnḍ^{i}*mȧt*^{i}	*gand*^{a}*mạty*$^{'}$*.*
gȧnḍin	*gandin.*
gonḍun	*gundun.*
gonḍ^{u}*nas*	*gund*^{a}*nas.*
ganḍith	*ganḍit.*
gȧnḍ^{i}*zĕs*	*gand*^{i} *zyes.*

This last change occurs only when *ḍ* is initial or protected by a preceding *n*. A medial *ḍ* is interchangeable with a dental *r*. See below.

B. Cerebrals where we should expect dentals—

Literary Dialect.	Hātim.
ṭ for *t*.	
bata, boiled rice,	*bat*^{a}, *baṭa*, *baṭṭa*.
mĕ ti, me also,	*m*^{u}*eti*, *maṭ*^{i}.
raṭ^a*na*, a jewel (in composition)	*rothuna*, *roṭhuna*, *rotun*^{a}, *rutun*^{a}, etc.
tati, there,	*tat*^{i}, *ta*^{i}*ti*, *ta*^{i}*ṭ*^{i}, *tat*^{u}.
yĕtāt^i, where,	*ye ṭa*^{i}*ṭ*^{i}.
ṭh for *th*.	
bātha, words,	*bāṭha*.
hĕth, having taken,	*het*, *hit*, *h*^{u}*et*, *h*^{u}*eth*, *h*^{u}*eṭh*.

Compare *rothuna* and *roṭhuna*, for *raṭ*^{a}*na*, a jewel, above.

ḍ for *d*.	
ad^a*la*, from justice,	*aḍal*.
mūd^u, he died,	*mōd*, *mūḍ*.

In Kāshmīrī the letter *r* is a dental letter, not a cerebral as in the Indian Madhyadēśa. We see this in the frequent interchange with a dental *l*, as in Hātim's *mōl* or *mōr*, for literary *môl*^{u}, father. The same is the case in the North-Western languages, Sindhī and Lahndā. The village confusion between cerebrals and dentals hence explains the frequent interchange in Hātim's dialect, between medial *ḍ* and medial *r*. Thus we have—

A. *ḍ* where we should expect *r*—

Literary.	Hātim.
ōra, thence,	*å̄r*, etc., *vōḍa*, and even *å̄ḍa*.
garun (G.K. *gaḍun*), to make.	
garūn	*garūn*.
gorun	*guḍun*.
kor^u, a bracelet,	*kar*, *kur*, *kur*^{i}, *kuḍ*.
kūr^ü (G.K. also *kūḍ*^{u}), a daughter,	*kūḍ*, *khūḍ*, *kūr*.

kōrĕ	*kōḍ^{i}, kōḍ^{y}e, kōḍye, kōḍ^{y}i, kūḍ^{y}e, kōr^{y}e, kōr^{y}i.*
kōri	*kōḍ^{y}e, kōḍ^{ye}, kōḍ^{y}i, kōr^{y}e.*
kūr^{i}	*kūḍ^{i}.*
lārun (G.K., also *lāḍun*), to pursue.	
lārān	*lārān, lāḍān.*
lāryōmot^{u}	*lāḍ^{y}ōmut.*
lāryāv	*lā^{i}ryau, lạ̄^{i}ḍyau.*
lāryēyĕs	*lāḍēyes.*
môr^{u}, he was killed,	*mōr, mōḍ.*
parun, to read, recite.	
porukh	*paḍuk.*
parān	*parān, paḍān.*
porun	*pạḍun.*
thar (G.K. also *thaḍ*), the back.	
thür^{ü}	*tạr, tor, tür, tạḍ.*
tōra, thence,	*tōr^{a}, tōrạ, tōre, tōḍ^{a}.*

B. *r* where we should expect *ḍ*—

Literary.	Hātim.
kaḍun (G.K. also *karun*), to extract.	
kăḍ^{i}	*ka^{i}r^{y}.*
koḍ^{u}	*kur.*
kăḍikh	*kạ^{i}ḍik, karik, ka^{i}rik.*
koḍukh	*kuruk.*
küḍ^{ü}kh	*kạḍuk.*
kaḍan	*karạn.*
kaḍān	*kaḍān, karān.*
kaḍōn	*korōn^{y}.*
kaḍun	*kạrun.*
kaḍun^{u}	*kaḍun.*
koḍun	*koḍun, kuḍun, korun, kurun.*
küḍ^{ü}n	*kạḍin.*
kăḍ^{i}nas	*kạr^{y}inas.*
koḍ^{u}nas	*kurạnas.*
kaḍith	*kạ^{i}rit, ka^{i}rith.*

tshāḍun (G.K. also *tshārun*), to search.	
tshāḍān	*tsārān.*
tshāḍav	*tsārau.*
yĕḍāh, a belly,	*yerū.*

While Dardic languages show a general tendency to harden sonant consonants, Hātim shows occasional instances of the softening of surds. In every case except one the softened consonant is immediately followed by *z*. In the one exception, it is *s* that is softened to *z*. The examples are—

G.K.	Hātim.
dàp^{i}zihĕkh, thou shouldst have said to them,	*dabzạ hek, dabzi hek.*
dàp^{i}zĕkh, thou shouldst say to them,	*dạbzik.*
but *dàp^{i}zĕm*, thou shouldst say to me,	*dap^{a}zim.*
wàs^{i}zi, thou shouldst descend,	*vạz^{i}zạ.*
but *wàs^{i}zi-na*, thou shouldst not descend,	*vạ^{i}s^{i} zinạ*
pēs, they fell on him,	*p^{y}ēz.*

On the other hand, Hātim gives occasional instances of the Dardic hardening of sonants. Such are—

G.K.	Hātim.
tab, fever,	*tap.*
rasad, assembly,	*rasat.*
mōv lāg, do not fix,	*maulāk.*
khazmath, service,	*kismat.*
khizmath, service,	*khismat.*

In this connexion we may again refer to G.K.'s *pātashāh* H.'s *pādshāh*, a king.

Turning to individual consonants, we note—

(1) We have prothesis of *h* before *y* in—

G.K.	Hātim.
yun^{u}, to come,	*yün, h^{y}ün.*
yuthuy, as verily,	*yüthuy, h^{y}üthuy.*

(2) *kh* becomes *h* in—

shĕkhtsū, a certain person,	*shahtsa.*

Possibly *shahtsa* is a slip of the pen, for elsewhere Hātim has *shakhtsạn*, *shakhtsas*, and so on.

(3) The affricative *ts* sometimes becomes *s*, as in—

G.K.	Hātim.
tsŏcĕ, loaves,	*suche*, *su cho*, *tsuche*.
tsŏpŏr[i], in four directions,	*so pạ̄*[i]*ri*, *tso pạ̄*[i]*r*[i].

It becomes *z* in—

pānts, five,	*pānts*, *pānz*.

The representation of G.K.'s *adālüts*[u]*-pĕṭh*, in court, by *adālat-p*[y]*eṭh*, is probably a slip of the pen.

With these changes of *ts* we may compare the interchange of *ch* and *sh* in Hātim's *măch-tulạr*, a bee, with the *măsh-tulari* of the title of Story IX. Similarly, we have *zh* for *j* in *zhāmạ* for *jāma*, a coat.

(4) *ny* and *ñy* are interchangeable, as in Hātim's *kanye-phul* and *kañye phul*, a pebble. This is hardly more than a variation of spelling.

(5) Hātim usually preserves a Persian *f*, while G.K. has *ph* instead. Thus, Hātim *fakīr*, G.K. *phakīr*, a mendicant. For "thought" Hātim has both *fikir* and *phikir*.

(6) The letter *sh* is sometimes represented by *s*. Sir Aurel Stein's MS. represents the sound of *sh* by *ṣ*, and the occasional apparent change of *sh* to *s* is probably due to the accidental omission of the subscript dot. An example is the word *shĕmshēr*, a sword, for which we have *shamshēr*, *shamsēr*, and *samshēr*.

(7) Vocalization of the semi-vowels *y* and *v* is frequent, as in *gai* for *gay*, they went; *gau* or *gau̯* for *gav*, he went; *mạ̄*[i]*ryu* for *māriwa*, (he who) may kill; *tsalau* for *tsaliv*, flee ye; *dimau* for *dimav*, we shall give; and many others.

(8) An example of metathesis is *tsōrastạ* for *tsōratsh*, a leather-cutter.

(9) H. uses initial *v* for *b* in *Vikarmājit-* for G.K.'s *Bikarmājit-*, Vikramāditya. Cf. *kāb* or *kāv*, for *khāb*, a dream.

(10) Three miscellaneous words are—

G.K.	Hātim.
bakh^{a}*cöyish*, a present,	*bakcāyish*, *bakhshāyish*.
jalwa, glory,	*jal*^{a}*va*.
but *jĕlōy*, even glory,	*yalạ vai*.
sak^{a}*th*, hard,	*sak*, *sakh*.

The processes of declension and conjugation employed by Hātim are on the whole the same as those employed by Gōvinda Kaula. The principal differences relate to the pronunciation of the forms, and to the representation of that pronunciation by Sir Aurel Stein's transcription. A few additional points may here be noticed.

In the declension of nouns, Gōvinda Kaula, like Īśvara Kaula, makes the dative singular of nouns of the first declension end in *as*, as in *bāgas*, to a garden. Hātim sometimes has the termination *as*, and sometimes *ạs*. Examples of both will be found on almost every page. As a specimen, it will suffice to quote the two forms *bāgas* and *bāgạs* both occurring close together in ii, 1. Similarly, in the genitive of the same declension, H. has *sunasand*^{i} (v. 3) and *sunạsand*^{ı} (v. 4), both for G.K.'s *sŏna-sünd*^{i}, of gold (m. pl.). In these genitives, also, H. sometimes drops the final *a* of the stem, as in *sunạr sạnz*, for G.K.'s *sŏnara-sünz*^{u}, of the goldsmith (fem. sing.) (v. 1); *pādshāh sund*, for G.K.'s *pātashāha-sond*^{u}, of the king (vi. 11). There is a curious example of a feminine noun declined as if it were masculine in *kūḍis-sā*^{i}*th* (possibly a slip for *kūḍi sā*^{i}*th*), for G.K.'s *kōrĕ-süty*, with the girl (v. 10); and in xii, 15, we have the masculine form *ku*^{i}*niy*, used instead of the feminine *kuñ*^{u}*y*, only one. Instances like *rĩnz*, *rạnz*, and *rēnz*, for *rĩnz*^{i}, balls; *soirạ*, *sō*^{i}*ri*, *sạruy*, and *sâruy* for *sôruy*, all; *zạ*, *ze*, and *z*^{y}*i*, for *z*^{a}*h*, two, belong rather to phonetics than to declension.

Similarly, the variations in pronominal forms are really matters of spelling or pronunciation. *Bŏh*, I, is represented by *bo*, *bu*; for *myön*^{ı}, my (m. pl. masc.), we have *mẽn*^{y}, *myẽ*, and *m*^{y}*ēn*, and for the fem. sing. *myöñ*^{u} we have *mẽñy*, *myẽ*, *m*^{y}*ēn*, *myēn*, and *m*^{y}*ẽñy*. For *ts*^{a}*h*, thou, we have *su*, *tsa*, *tsạ*, *tsi*, and *tsu*, and for *cyôn*^{u}, thy, *chun*, *ch*^{y}*un*, *chōn*, *chōn*^{y}, *chōny*, and *ch*^{y}*ōn*, all with the aspirated *ch*.

The proximate demonstrative pronoun *yih*, this, and the relative *yih*, what, appear under the forms *yi* and *yü*, and the emphatic forms *yihuy*, etc., appear under quite a number of variant spellings. The relative m. sg. nom. *yus* appears as *yis*, *yus*, and *yüs*, and its fem. *yĕsa* as *yesạ* (x, 1) and *yạsi* (x, 6). In viii, 1, for *yihünz*^{u}, of these (fem. sg. nom.), we have *yihas*. As for the remote demonstrative pronoun, its emphatic fem. sg. nom. *say* or *sŏy*, she verily, appears as *sai*, *sạ̄i*, *sụy*, and *sạ̄y*. The indefinite pronoun *kĕ̃h*, with its various case-forms, appears under a great variety of spellings. The principal of these have been dealt with under the head of phonetics.

The representation of the various forms of the verb substantive is very irregular. A few examples will suffice.

For *chuh*, he is, we have *che* (v. 4); for *chuy*, he is verily, *chi*, *chī*, *chi*^{y}, *chiy*, and *cüy* (sic); for *chwā*, is he ?, *cha*; for *chĕh*, she is, *chạ*, *che*, *chu*; for *chĕy*, she is to thee, *che* and *chạy*; for *chiwa*, ye are, *chu*; for *chiway*, if ye are, *chu voi* and *chu vai*; and for *chih*, they are, *che*, *chi*, *chu*, and *ch*^{y}*ạ*.

As regards the conjugation of the active verb, there are numerous departures from G.K.'s spelling, nearly all of which fall under the head of phonetics. Here we may mention the following, which really appear to indicate difference of form :—

G.K.	Hātim.
shōlān, burning,	*shōlan*. This form of the present participle is old, and nowadays appears only in poetry and dialects.
yikh-nā, wilt thou not come,	*yihna*.
dis, give to her,	*disạ*.
kaḍōn, we shall pass over it,	*karōn*^{y}.

III

ON THE METRES OF HĀTIM'S SONGS

By SIR AUREL STEIN

On my return to Kashmir at the close of 1917 Sir George Grierson asked me to inquire into the system of metrification followed in certain old Kashmīrī poems of the Bhakti type in which he is interested. I have tried to comply with his request as far as it lay in me, i.e. in full consciousness of the fact that my philological training had never comprised any special study of metrics. After examining portions from a number of these compositions as recited by professional *cyat-gürⁱ*, I arrived at the conclusion that the metre of these poems is based solely on the number of stress accent syllables counted in each line or *pāda*. No regard is paid to quantity, even where the structure of the verses is apparently modelled on the pattern of Hindī metres dependent on quantity. Pandit Nityânanda Śāstrī, of the Śrī-Pratāp College, Srīnagar, a very competent Kashmīrī scholar, to whom I submitted this view, has endorsed it.

In order to test this conclusion with reference to the metres of Hātim's songs I secured a visit of the old storyteller. now in his 62nd year, in June, 1918, when my summer camp was once more pitched on Mohand Marg. I had him recite again the metrified story of Sultām Maḥmūd Ghaznavī, the one which of those heard from his lips in 1896 I had best in my recollection. He also gave me the benefit of several songs of lyrical contents (*ghazal*), some of his own composition, which used to be favourite numbers in his répertoire, showing more elaborate versification.

In recording these with special regard to their metre I convinced myself that their verses, whether simple couplets, as in the case of the metrified story just referred to, or built up in more intricate stanzas, have for their constructive principle solely the number of syllables bearing the stress accent of the present colloquial speech. The system is based mainly on the counting of the primary stress accent of each word, but permits also the counting of secondary stress accents for the sake of metrical convenience. This latitude, which reference to the last words in verses 1, 11, 12, 13 of Maḥmūd Ghaznavī's story may help to illustrate, has its parallel in the rudeness of the rhyme. In this, as verses 3 and 8 show, the vowel sounds of the closing syllables need not agree, as long as the final consonant is the same.

The general rule is that throughout a song the lines, usually rhymed, composing a couplet or stanza, should have a certain fixed number of stress-accented syllables, in conformity with the scheme determining the length of each line. But this simple rule is on occasion ignored through "poetical license", i.e. whenever the rustic poet's skill would be taxed too severely by strict adherence to his metrical scheme. The second line of verse 4 in Maḥmūd Ghaznavī's story with its seven accented syllables instead of the regular six is an illustration.

The lilt of the musical air which, as in the case of Indian poetical compositions generally, is an essential concomitant of the recital, helps, no doubt, to smooth over such irregularities for the not very fastidious ears of the village audience. I regret that my total want of musical knowledge has precluded my ever noting down any of these popular Kashmir airs, often far more attractive to the untrained European ear than the melodies of India proper.

In order to illustrate Hātim's metrical system, the stress-accents in the Maḥmūd Ghaznavī story have been indicated by appropriate marks.

SIR AUREL STEIN'S TRANSCRIPTION

WITH

SIR GEORGE GRIERSON'S TRANSLATION

I

[The marks of accentuation, acute and grave, indicate the stress-accents on which the metre is based.]

Shā́hạnshāh Súltān^{i} Máhmūd^{i} Gáznavī́ ।
ā̊́s^{u} kárān pā́ne múlken pā̊́ravī́ ॥ 1
fákīr lā́git ā̊́s^{u} phḗrān vā́n^{a}vā́n ।
myā́ni áh^{a}dai ā́si mā́ kah nṓt^{u}vā́n ॥ 2
jā́ye ákis ā̊́s^{i} kárān dv^{ó}y^{u} kā́r ।
ádạl tạ́m^{i} sạndi sā́t^{y} ā́sak céshmạ sḗr ॥ 3
jā́yạ ákis vúcun^{a} hā̊́nzạ ákh alī́l ।
múhimma sạ́itin ā̊́s gómmut súy zalī́l ॥ 4
múhimma sā̊́itin ā̊́s trā́vān áh tavṓsh ।
múhimma sā̊́itin tásnạ rū́d^{a}mut káhti hṓsh ॥ 5
yṓrạ zā́lā ā̊́s lā́yān gā́tạ sā́n ।
tṓrạ zā́las ā̊́sus nạ kyā̊́ khásā̀n ॥ 6
dópusạ shạ́hạn kárme sā̊́itin bā̊́j^{a}vát ।
lā́y zā́lạ yā́di Ạ́lla dílas rát ॥ 7
lā̊́yun zā́lạ tṓr^{a} khútas gā̊́dạ hát ।
pā́d^{i}shā́hạs bṓnṭ kun súy ā́u̯ hít ॥ 8
gā́dạ hátạs bádal dyútạnạs móhrạ dyā́r ।
lā́l^{a} nígīn mā́l^{a} múht^{ay} vúntạ bā́r ॥ 9
rā́t bárit pā́d^{i}shạhạn dyútus nā́d ।
tsū́y chúkạ myṓn sherī́k nā́ murā́d ॥ 10
múhim kā́s^{u}vun hékạmáti Párvardigā̀r ।
tā́p shúhul sárde gárm nṓu̯ bahā́r ॥ 11
vánạ yéy zan bánde mā̊́nzūr zā́s^{a}núy ।
kā́ts^{a} hékạmats múhim tági kā́s^{a}núy ॥ 12
ạ́t^{i} ándar cū́y vustā́dạ vánān zā́r ।
júmạlạ ā́lam bánde Áhmạd vúmedvā́r ॥ 13

I. MAḤMŪD OF GHAZNĪ AND THE FISHERMAN

Sulṭān Maḥmūd of Ghaznī, the king of kings, used himself to watch over the protection of his kingdom.

Disguised as a Faqīr, he used to wander from bazaar to bazaar, to see if any of his subjects were in distress.

In one place were the people making prayers for his welfare, and their eyes were satisfied by his justice.

In another place, he saw a wretched fisherman, brought low by poverty.

5. In his poverty he was uttering sighs and groans. In his poverty even his sense had deserted him.

Even where he skilfully cast his net, even there naught came into it.

Said the King to him, "Make me thy partner, and fling one more cast of the net, keeping firm within thy heart the memory of God."

So he flung one more cast and, behold, within his net he caught a hundred fish, and brought them all before the King.

In exchange for the hundred fish the King gave him wealth of money, rubies and jewels, possessions and pearls in camel-loads.[1]

10. After he had passed the night, the King called for him and said, "Verily thou becamest my partner without hope or expectation of result (and yet thou hast thereby acquired great wealth).

"It is the power of Providence alone that removeth poverty, (and giveth) sunshine and shade, heat and cold, and the new spring.

"Verily I would say to thee, 'Know this, O slave—accept thou (these as coming from the Almighty), for by how much power wouldst thou thyself have been able to remove thy poverty?'"

Concerning this hath a certain teacher uttered this prayer, "The hope of this slave, Aḥmad, is (on Him from whom proceedeth) all the universe."

[1] The King rewarded him because instead of bringing him the worst fifty fish, he brought the whole hundred from which the King might choose his share. As a reward the King bought also the fisherman's share of the hundred for a very high price.

II. TOTAS ÜNZ KAT

1. Dapān ustād shahar ak gāu̯ shehri Īrān tat^{i} ā̒s pādshāh tạm^{i}süy chu nāv Bah^{a}dūr Khān. tạm^{i} ā̊s kurmut bāg zạnānạn kyut tat ā̒s nạ vat gārzānas tạt^{y} bāgas manz gau̯ pā̒da fakīra nazar bāzau kạr nazar kabardārau niy kabar ạmis pādshāhạs dopuk fakīra tsāu̯ bāgạs manz bōzun pādshạhạn hyütun sạit vazīr gai tat bāgas manz vucun a^{i}ti fakīr

2. lache nā̊u̯ chiy har va^{i}t^{i} bīnā ı
bōz vuphā dạ^{i}rī ankā ॥
hā fakīrō yōr kōr tsākhu ı
kati kōchuk katye peṭạ ākhu ॥

fakīr dạpān

kurme sālạ tuhund khyāu me kya ı
bōz vupha dạirī anka ॥

3. pādshahạs bōnt^{a} kan^{i} pōsh^{a} tür at^{i} tal momut bulbula yeli yimau ạmis fakīrạs khashim kur til^{i} pyau fakīr patar vasit momut bulbul gau thud vutit pādshahạs hōvun yi vir^{i}d gau nērit phīrit beye āu̯ bulbul mōd beye fakīr gau beye zindạ hyütun nērun yimchis karān zārạ pār dapān chis

hā fakīrạ khismat kare^{y} ı
dud^{a} harik khạsihō bare^{y} ॥
khās^{a} pulāu̯ macāmạ kyek nā ı
bōz vupha dạiri anka ॥

4. yus vir^{i}d fakīrạs ā̒s suy bā̊vun ạmis pādshahạs ạm^{i} pādshạhạn bōu̯ vazīrạs

II. THE TALE OF A PARROT

1. This is what my Master told me :—

There was a certain country, the land of Persia, and it was ruled by a king named Bahādur Khān. He had made a garden for his womenfolk, into which no stranger was allowed to enter ; but once there came into it a Faqīr. The discerners then discerned him, and the newsmen gave the news to the King. Said they, "A Faqīr has come into the garden." The King heard, and took with him his Vizier. To the garden they went, and there he saw the Faqīr.

2. The Almighty, who hath a hundred thousand names, watcheth over every path.
Hark ye, loyalty is monstrous rare.[1]
"O Faqīr, how didst thou enter ?
Where dost thou belong ? whence art thou come ?"
Quoth the Faqīr :—
I came but for a stroll. What of yours have I eaten ?"
Hark ye, loyalty is monstrous rare.

3. It chanced that before the King there was a flowering plant, and at its foot a dead nightingale. As soon as they spoke angrily to the Faqīr, he fell flat, lifeless to the ground, and as he did so the nightingale arose alive. Such magic power did he show the King. The nightingale flew out of the garden, and returned. Then it fell dead and the Faqīr again became alive. He began to depart, but they entreated him, saying :—

"O Faqīr, let me be thy servant !
Cups of the cream of milk will I fill for thee.
Special *pilaos* and dainties wilt thou not eat ?"
Hark ye, loyalty is monstrous rare.

4. So the Faqīr confided the secret of his magic power to the King, and the King confided it to his Vizier.

[1] Literally a phœnix, a *rara avis*, the Arabic *'anqā*. In the original, the imperative "hark ye" is in the singular ; I have put it into the plural, as more consonant with English idiom.

kạr tạrạ byat pādshahạn vazīrạs ı
suti mạhᵃram kurun ati sīrạs ॥
gai sālạs shikārạs yeg ja ı
bōz vupha dạiri anka ॥

tōtu momut vucuk dạr biyā bān ı
hā vaziro āsi he shubān ॥
zu ạmis manz thāvutan sātha ı
bōz vupha dạiri anka ॥

dopu vazīrạn pādshạhạm yiᵗsᵃ kōl momut ı
phak chus yivān kabar kar chu gomut. ॥
chus nạ tahᵃrān vantạ sạ kare kyā ı
bōz vupha dạiri anka ॥

5. pādshāh karān zārᵃ pār vazīrạs ạmi bāpat bo vucehan tōtạ kyut āsihe shūbān ạmʸ bōzus nạ vazīrạn kyē dạpān vustād ạmis ås dilas manz dagāi. vunʸ tsāu pādᵃshāh ạmis tōtạs manz panun muḍ tsunun trȧvit tōtu vut thud chu phērān vazīrạn kạr kōm tsāv at pādshāhᵃ sạndis moḍis manz yiʸ ås ạmis dar dil.

pyau pitarun pādshahạs pānạs ı
bōr ludun vazīrạs nā dānạs ॥
åsus dagāye zāgān dād kha ı
bōz vupha dạiri anka ॥

6. tōtu chu havāye asmān vazīr chu pādshahạs sạndis mạris manz vut thud.

khut guris khalᵃkan manz gau ı
dopu nak vazīr mūḍ guri pyeṭe vasit pyau ॥
kabar dārau niyᵉ sạy kabara ı
bōz vupha dạiri anka ॥

The King gave instructions to the Vizier,
  And he thus became proficient in the secret.
They went out hunting together.
  Hark ye, loyalty is monstrous rare.

In the forest they saw a parrot lying dead.
"O Vizier, how beautiful this must have been.
Put thou, I beseech thee, thy life into it for but a moment."
  Hark ye, loyalty is monstrous rare.

Said the Vizier:—
  "My King, for long hath it been dead.
    A stink cometh from it; who knoweth when it died?
  Stay here I cannot; Sir, what am I to do?"
    Hark ye, loyalty is monstrous rare.

5. For this did the King make urgent entreaty to the Vizier. "Fain would I see how beautiful the parrot was," but the Vizier refused to listen to him.

And, further, my Master told me:—

In his heart there was treachery. At length the King himself abandoned his own body and entered into the parrot. Up rose the parrot, and flew about. Then the Vizier did a deed: he himself entered into the King's body. That was what had all along been in his heart.

The burden which had been the King's to bear,
  That became laid upon the foolish Vizier.
Treachery was watching in him like a petitioner.
  Hark ye, loyalty is monstrous rare.

6. The parrot is flying in the air, and the Vizier is in the body of the King. He stood up.

He mounted the (King's) horse and went into the army.

He said to them:—

"The Vizier fell from his horse and is dead."
  That was the news that the newsman brought.
  Hark ye, loyalty is monstrous rare.

7. ạm^{i} vazīrạn yel^{i} kạr kōm ʦāu̯ pādshaha sạndis mạris manz tujy^{e}n atas kyet shamshēr at panạnis mạris korun rēzạ at lashkạrạ dopun nē^{i}ryu tīran dāz beye bạndūk bāz yus mạ̄^{i}ryu tōtạ tạmis bañyau bakcāyish ạm^{i} tōtan yel^{i} bōz tạ ʦul gau tas fakīrạs nish yus tat bāgạs manz ā̊s tam^{i} doho.

hukum dyutanay tīrạn dāzạn ।
kan tạ̄ivtau myānen nāzan ॥
tōtạ mārạnas dyutạnak photu va ।
bōz vupha dạ̄^{i}ri anka ॥

8. yus asạl ā̊s pādshāh su chu tōtas manz fakīrạs nisạn su tōtạ ka^{i}sī mōr na doho aki drāu̯ yi pādshāh sā̊lạs shikārạs vōt jāye akis at^{i} vucum sunạ sạnz ming^{e} mạr ạm^{i} süy kạruk lār ạñyik lashkạr^{i} manz dopunak ạm^{i} pādshahạn yas kạn^{i} yi ʦalau tas dimau gardan.

9. dopān vustād ạm^{i} ming^{ye} mạri tuj vuṭ pādshahạsạndi kalạ pyet ʦiñyen vuṭ ʦạ^{i}jy lāris patạ yus su tōtạ ā̊s fakīr ā̊s sāhib^{i} āga dopun ạmis tōtạs yas manz yi pādshāh ā̊s dopunạs gaʦ^{i} sa nēr az labak panun muḍ yim che ạmis ming^{ye} mạri patạ lārān nakh^{a} rōzān chek nạ.

10. dopān vustād at^{i} ā̊s momut hāput pādshāh ʦāu̯ ạmis hāpạtas manz lạ̄^{i}ryau yus yi pādshāh^{a}sund muḍ ā̊s yi trā̊vun at^{i}.

shod bōzun tōtạn lạ̄^{i}ryau ।
kul^{i} dad^{a}ri manz ho prạ̄^{i}ryau ॥
muḍ lobun kạr^{i} tōs marhaba ।
bōz vupha dạ̄^{i}ri anka ॥

7. When this Vizier had done the deed, and when he had entered into the King's body, in his hand he raised his sword, and into small pieces did he cut his own dead body. Then said he to his army, "Go forth, ye archers, and ye gunmen. Whoever of you killeth a parrot, to him will be given a reward." When the parrot heard this order he fled afar, and went to the Faqīr, who on that day had been in the garden.

He gave the order to the archers,
"Pay ye heed, I pray, to my coaxing."
He gave an order that the parrot should be killed.
Hark ye, loyalty is monstrous rare.

8. Now, as for the real king, he was in the parrot, and had taken refuge with the Faqīr; so that parrot was not killed by anyone. One day the Vizier-King sallied forth to hunt; and when he had reached a certain place he descried a hind. After it they made pursuit. They brought it into the army, and he said to them, "I will cut off the head of him who letteth her escape."

9. And, further, my Master told me:—
But the hind gave a sudden spring and leaped over the head of the Vizier-King himself. They pursued her. Now the parrot-King was with the Faqīr,[1] and that Faqīr was a magician clairvoyant. Quoth he to the parrot-King, "Go forth, your Majesty, to-day wilt thou regain thine own body." Meanwhile the hind had far outdistanced her pursuers.

10. Furthermore, my Master told me:—
There there lay a dead bear. The Vizier-King entered into the bear and pursued the hind, leaving the real King's body lying on the ground.

The news of the Vizier-King's coming was heard by the parrot.
Thither did he run.
He waited, watching from a tree-hole.
He again entered into his own body; wish ye him all good luck!
Hark ye, loyalty is monstrous rare.

[1] A few words are here missing in Sir Aurel Stein's text.

11. tōtạ pyau at^i patạr yi ʦāụ pādshāh panạnis mạris manz yus yi vazīr å̄s su chu hāpạtas manz khut pād^a shāh asạl yus å̄s su khut guris pyeṭ dopun yiman lōkan mạ̄^i ryūn hāput lōy^a has bạndūk phut^a rhas zang ạnuk rạtit pādshahạs nish dopunạs pādshahạn ʦik^a r tam dagạ̄y bo mār^a hat nạ kya kare ha lōk dạpạnam hāput chus vazīr ʦye chi^y panun mụḍ gå̄lmut vuma thāvat ʦạ hāput vazīr boha se mārat.

12. dạpān vustād ạnuk zyūn zå̄luk hāput.

hat vạ̄^i nsi gau kam ya zhāday ı
āụ Bạh^a dūr Kānas pyāday ıı
kạr Vahab Kāre Allạh Allạh ı
bōz vuph dạ̄^i r^i anka ıı

11. Down fell the parrot dead, and the King entered his own body, but he who had been the Vizier was now in the bear. The real King mounted his horse, and said to his men, "Shoot ye that bear." They fired with their guns at him, and brake his leg. They seized him and brought him before the King. Said the King, "Treachery was done by thee to me. What can I do but kill thee? Otherwise people will say of me, 'He hath a bear for a Vizier.' Thou hast destroyed thine own body. Now no longer can I keep a bear like thee as a Vizier. Sir, I am about to kill thee."

12. And my Master further said :—

They brought firewood, and they burnt the Vizier to ashes.
A hundred years passed, less or more.
And then came the messenger of Death to Bahādur Khān.
O Wahb, the blacksmith,[1] cry "Allāh, Allāh!"
Hark ye, loyalty is monstrous rare.

[1] The name of the author of the story.

III. SAUDĀGARẠSŪNZ KAT

1. Saudāgar gau sōdahạs ga^{i}ri ā̊sus zanānạ sạ̄y gaye mushtāk fakīrạs akis vāryahạs kālạs doh^{o} aki āu̯ saudāgar gar panun māl het pādshahạs gay^{e} kabar saudāgạr vōt pādshāh drāu̯ sālạs rāt kyut vōt saudāgạrạ sund chu at^{i} vud^{a}nye pahar chu gomut rāʦ hund yi saudāgạr bāi vuʦ voḍye pyet h^{y}eten batạ trōm pādshāh chu vuchān ʦūri pạ̄tin saudāgạr bāi drāye bro-bro pādshāh chu pakān patạ patạ vạ̄t^{i} maidānạs akis manz at^{i} ā̊s fakīr nār^{a}hạn zālit kạris ạm^{i} salām batạ thōu̯nas bōnt^{a} kan^{i} dop̱unas k^{y}e ạmi tul ʦōṭ^{a} lạ̄yun ạmis saudāgạr bāye dop^{u}nas ʦīr^{y} kyāzi āyak dop^{u}nas ạ^{i}m^{i} phīrit az ā̊sum āmut panun kāvand tạm^{i} gōm ʦēr k^{y}e tam vuñy batạ dop^{u}nas ạm^{i} fakīrạn bo k^{y}emāy na guḍa^{i}ny dim ạnit ạmis saudāgārạsund kal^{a} ad^{e} k^{y}emai bat^{a} pādshāh ā̊s vuchān yi k^{y}ēnʦa yimau doyau katạ ka^{i}ri ti bōz pādshahạn sạruy.

2. dapān vustād drāye saudāgạr bāi vạ̄ʦ panun gar^{a} khaʦ hyūr pādshāh chu bun^{a} kan^{i} ạm^{i} ʦōt ạmis saudāgārạs kale vuʦ h^{y}et rumāli k^{y}et che pakān bro-bro pādshāh chu patạ patạ vạ̄ʦ ạmis fakīrạs nish tulun ʦōṭ^{a} lạ̄yun ạmis saudāgạr bāy^{e} dop^{u}nas ʦạ sap^{a}zạk nạ ạmis panạnis kāvandạsunz vuñy sap^{a}dak^{a} mēñy.

3. pādshāh drāu̯ vōt panun gar^{a} trạvun arām gāsh phul vuʦ krạ̄k dopān che saudāgạr vạʦau panun gar^{a} suy mōr ʦūrau vạ̄ʦ ạtuy saudāgạr bāi dapān che pādshahạs kāvand āyām suy mōrham ʦūrau pādshāhạs che kabar yi saudāgạr kạm^{i} mōr

III. THE TALE OF A MERCHANT

1. A Merchant once went forth to trade, leaving his wife at home, and she for long became filled with love for a beggarman—a Faqīr. One day the Merchant came home with the chattels he had bought, and to the King came the news that "the Merchant hath returned". At night the King went forth to wander through the city, and he reached the Merchant's house. While he was standing there, at the end of the first watch of the night, the Merchant's wife got up and went forth carrying a dish of cooked rice upon her head. The King watched her in secret. On ahead went she, and along after her followed the King. They arrived at a certain open space where the beggarman was seated over a little fire. She made salutation to him, and laid the dish of rice before him. Quoth she: "Eat!" But straightway he raised a cudgel and with it struck the Merchant's wife. He said unto her, "Why hast thou come so late?" She made reply to him, "My husband came home to-day, and hence was I delayed. Eat now, prithee, this dish of rice." But the beggarman said to her, "I will not eat. First bring me that Merchant's head. Then, and not till then, will I sup." Now all this time the King was watching, and he heard all this talk that passed between them.

2. Furthermore, my Master told me:—

The Merchant's wife went off, and came to her own home. She went upstairs, while the King stayed down below. She cut off her husband's head, and came down with it wrapped in a handkerchief. On ahead went she, and along after her went the King. She came to the beggarman. He raised his stick and struck the Merchant's wife. Said he to her, "Thou wast not true to thine own husband. Now wilt thou be true to me?"

3. The King departed. He returned to his palace and went to his bed. Morning blossomed forth, and there was raised a cry. They say: "The Merchant came home and thieves have killed him." To the palace came the Merchant's wife. She saith unto the King, "My husband came home to me, and he hath been killed by thieves." The King knoweth well who killed the Merchant, while

tsārān che pai saudāgạr kạm^{i} mōr kạ̄^{i}si chu nạ khasān zimạ.

4. dapān vustād kuruk yi saudāgạr zạ̄luk ạtuy drāṷ pādshāh bạy^{i} sạ̄^{i}ri chu vuchān āyạ ạmisạnz kulai yi che karān gat dapān che bot^{ye} zālạ pān āye hitsạn vut tsạneñy nārạs manz pādshāh gōs kạr^{a}nạs tap dapān chus pādshah yey tạ ti kya? t^{y}ey tạ yi kya dopunas m^{y}e trāṷ yil^{a} bo zālạ pān dopunạs nāgạs ạkis p^{y}et chai m^{y}ēn dod^{a} bạñye sạ̄i vanē ạmyuk mā^{i}nye trạ̄vun yile zōl ạm^{i} pān panạnis kāvandạs sạ̄it gay^{e} khalās pag^{a} drāṷ pādshah vōt ạt nāgạs p^{y}et vuchin ạt^{i} zạnānạ ạm^{i} sạy zạnānạ chu dapān pādshah t^{y}ey tạ yi kya yey tạ ti kya dop^{u}nạs ạm^{i} zạnānạ åth^{i} duh^{y} dapāi bo ạm^{y}uk javāb.

5. dapān vustād åth doh gai pat^{a} kun pādshahạs pyau yād lạ̄^{i}dyau pādshah tat nāgạs p^{y}et vuchin sạ zạnānạ dop^{u}nas vanum tạm^{i} kat^{y}ehund mā^{i}ni dopunas gats an tsāvul beye nut ạnun tsāvul tạ nut dop^{u}nas vasyạt nāgạs manz nut tsün phirit dop^{u}nas beye ạnun tsāvul kanạ rạtit thāvus nạtis p^{y}eṭ kal^{a} dop^{u}nas lāyus shamsēri hạnz tsunḍ.

6. dapān lạ̄^{i}yinas samshēri hạnz tsunḍ ạm^{i} sāt^{a} gatsān pādshāh gạ̄b hangạt^{a} mangạ gạ̄b.

7. dapān vustād yi che vātān bāgạs ạkis manz at^{i} chu vuchān palạng pạ̄^{i}rit ạt^{i} p^{y}eṭ pādshāh trā̊vun arām ạt^{i} åsa pạ^{i}riye yim^{a} vuy nyu tulit pādshāh tså̄nuk akis jāye manz sapud bēdār vuchān

the people are seeking for a clue to find the murderers. But on no one can they fix the guilt.

4. And, further, my Master said :—

They brought out the Merchant's body and burnt it. The King went forth to the place of cremation and watched everything that should come to pass. There came up the widow, on her way to burn herself upon her husband's pyre. She was saying : "I also will burn my body." She came and prepared to leap into the flames ; but the King went near unto her, and caught her by the hand. He said unto her, "If this, then why that ? If that, then why this ?" Said she to him, "Let me go free, I will burn my body." Again said she to him, "By such and such a spring dwelleth my milk-sister. She will tell thee the meaning of this." So he let her go, and she was burnt beside her husband, and became released from the sorrows of the world. Next day went forth the King, and came to that spring. There saw he a certain woman, and to her he said, "If that, then why this ? If this, then why that ?" The woman made reply, "After eight days will I give to thee the answer."

5. Said my Master :—

Eight days passed, and then the King called to mind the woman's words. He ran to the spring. There saw he her and again asked he of her the meaning of those words. Quoth she, "Go thou, and bring hither a goat and a jar." He brought the goat and the jar, and then said she, "Descend thou into this spring and therein set thou the jar upside-down." And further said she to him, "Lead thou down the goat by the ear, and put its head upon the jar." (He did so), and she cried, "Strike thou it a blow with the sword."

6. And my Master said :—

He struck it a blow with his sword, and on the instant did the King of a sudden disappear.

7. And furthermore my Master told me :—

He found himself in a garden, and there was there spread a bed. On the bed he climbed and lay down and fell asleep. Now there were fairies there. They lifted him up and carried him off into a certain place. There he awoke, and seeth all round him

chu janạṭạch jāy^{e} at^{i} lạ̄gimat^{y} nagmạ pādshāh chu mushtāk at^{i} tamāshạs kun.

8. dapān gạy^{e} yima pạ^{i}riye pānạs ạmis diʦuk kunz dop^{u}has yet kutis thāu̯ kulup vut aʦ andar ʦāu̯ andar at^{i} vuchun gur zīn ka^{i}rit koḍun nebạr tap ka^{i}rit nebạr yeli korun chu vud^{a}ñye tap kạ^{i}rit dop^{u}has khas yemis guris khot^{u} ạmis guris yi chu vuchān satau zemīnau tạ̄^{i}lti navau asmānau p^{y}eti yi kēʦā Kudā sābạn pādạ kurmut ti vuch pādshahạn tat sạ̄^{i}th^{y} gau mushtāk gōs pạ̄dạ Shētān dop^{u}nas kya chuk vuchān dop^{u}nas pādshahạn yi keñ^{y}ʦā Kudā sābạn pạ̄dạ kur ti chus vuchān dop^{u}nas Shētānạn phīrit ạm^{i} kutạ hāvai bo yi chạ̄y mēñy kunz yat kutis thāu̯ kulup vut aʦ andar ʦau̯ pādshāh andar vuch^{u}n at^{i} khar ganḍit dop^{u}nas karun nebạr khas ạm^{i} sạy yi kēñ^{y}ʦa Kudā sābạn pạ̄dạ kur tạm^{i} p^{y}eṭh kan^{i} vuchak beye kyĕ kut pādshah ạmis kharas.

9. dapān vustād barābạr vatạnå̄vun panun gar kut hyür phīrit vut vuchun at^{i} na khar pādshahas āu̯ armān tam^{i} bāguk^{u} voh k^{y}eta pạ̄^{i}ṭh^{y} vāt^{ye} tut dapān gau at^{i} nāgas p^{y}eṭh dopun tạmis zạnānạ m^{y}e vante yey tạ ti kya t^{y}ey tạ yi kya dop^{u}nas ami zạnānạ anun panun n^{y}echu beye an nut beye an shamshēr dop^{u}nas vasyat nāgas manz vālun panun n^{y}echu pāvun pathar thāvus nạtis p^{y}eṭh kale kanas kạr^{a}nas thap ạm^{i} pādshahạn tuh jin shamshēr lāye ạmis n^{y}ech^{a}vis kạris ạm^{i} zạnānạ thap at shamshēr^{i} dop^{u}nas yih gau ti ti gau yi ʦa gå̄k mushtāk bāgas beñye mēñy gaye mushtāk fakiras.

a region of paradise. Fair women were dancing there, and smitten with love for the entrancing spectacle did the King become.

8. And further saith my Master :—

Departed these fairies and left him all alone, but before they went gave they him a key. Said they to him, "Unlock thou this room. Arise, and go within." He went within, and there he saw a horse ready saddled. He led it without, and stood there holding it by the bridle. Said they to him, "Mount this horse." He mounted it, and, lo! at once he seeth everything that God, the Master, hath made both below the seven earths and above the seven heavens. All that did the King see, and for it did he become smitten with love. Then before him appeared Satan; and Satan asked him saying, "What is it thou dost see?" Quoth the King, "Whatever God, the Master, hath created, that do I see." And Satan said to him in answer, "More than this will I show thee. Behold, here is my key. With it unlock thou this door. Arise and go within." The King went within and there saw he an ass tied. Said Satan to him, "Bring thou it forth, and mount it, and thou shalt see something more even than all that God, the Master, hath created." Thereupon did the King mount that ass.

9. Furthermore said my Master :—

Straightway the ass carried the King back unto his palace. He dismounted and went upstairs, and when he came down again, behold, he saw no ass there. Great longing for that garden of paradise came unto the King, but how was he to reach it? They tell me that he went at once unto the spring and asked the woman, "Tell me, prithee, 'If that, then why this? If this, then why that?'" And that woman said unto him, "Bring thou thine own son, and bring also a pitcher, and also bring thy sword." Said she to him, "Descend thou into this spring, and take down with thee thy son. Cast him down, and upon the pitcher lay thou his head." So the King took the lad by the ear, and drew his sword. With it would he have struck his son had not the woman seized it. Cried she, "This it is that is that; and that it is that is this. Thou becamest smitten with love for the garden, and my sister became smitten with love for the beggarman."

IV.—LĀLA MAL^{I}KUN UNMUT G^{Y}AVUN

Dapān chu :—

Daye zār van^{u}mai Kudāye bōz tam tạ̄i ।
samsār bāzi gār ॥ 1
hazraṭ^{i} Ādam guḍe lud^{a}nam tạ̄y ।
mal^{i}kau kur hai taiyār ॥
phurtas Yib^{a}līs tat^{i} kur^{u} nam tạ̄i ।
samsār bāzi gār ॥ 2
hazraṭ^{i} Nu chi vulādi Ādam tạ̄i ।
phīrit gās kuphār ॥
ah tạm^{i} kur nay^{i} sạr^{i}gau ālam tạ̄i ।
samsār bāzi gār ॥ 3
hazraṭ^{i} Īsā k^{y}ē chu nạ kam tạ̄i ।
Sāhib^{a}sund ṭōṭ yār ॥
tsun as^{a}mānạn p^{y}eṭh tạm^{i} sabak dopu nam tạ̄i ।
samsār bāzi gār ॥ 4
hazraṭ^{i} Musāi trå̄vuy kadạm tạ̄i ।
Sāhib^{a}sund kare dīdār ॥
Koh^{y}e Tūrạ p^{y}eṭhạ tạm^{i} kathe ka^{i}ri nam tạ̄i ।
samsār bāzi gār ॥ 5
hazraṭ^{i} Ibrāhim k^{y}ē chu nạ kam tạ̄i ।
puṭalin kurun nakār ॥
tạm^{i} kur dīn^{i} Mahamad mahkam tạ̄i ।
samsār bāzi gār ॥ 6
mạrit kab^{a}rạ yeli vāle nam tạ̄i ।
pan^{y}en bạ̄i kya yār ॥
tat^{i} Lālạ Mal^{i}kas kya hāv^{a}nam tạ̄i ।
samsār bāzi gār ॥ 7

IV. A SONG OF LĀL MALIK

1. He saith :—

O God, supplication make I unto thee. Ah! hear Thou me! For this world is a deluder.

2. First sent He the holy Adam; yea, by the Angels was he made complete. Then Iblis ruined him, and thence (i.e. from Paradise) was he thrust forth. This world is a deluder.

3. From Adam was sprung the holy Noah, and from him the infidels became estranged. A sigh he uttered, and the whole universe was flooded in his tears. This world is a deluder.

4. In no way less than him was the holy Jesus. He was the beloved friend of God, the Master. Seated upon the four heavens did He utter His teaching. This world is a deluder.

5. The holy Moses stepped forward, crying, "I would see the Master with mine own eyes." He gave forth (the ten) words from Mount Sinai. This world is a deluder.

6. In no way less than him was the holy Abraham, who forbad the worship of idols. He it was who established the faith of Muḥammad. This world is a deluder.

7. When I shall die, and my brethren and friends will lower me into the grave, then what can they show to me, Lāl Malik, but that this world is a deluder.

V. SUNERẠSŪNZ KAT

1. Vustād dapān Shehra ak chu åsmut tat^{i} chu sunạr suy ås tsatạs bahan hatan hund zyuṭ yūhạy ås garān vast pādshahạs sạnzi kōḍye kit^{i} tot ås gatsān sunạr sạnz zạnānạ h^{y}et ak^{i} doho dopus am^{i} pādshāh kōḍ^{ye} sōzun gatse panun kāvand doho aki drāu̯ sunạr sunạsạnz vāj^{y} h^{y}et pādshāh sạnzi kōḍ^{y}i kits am^{i} pasand kạrus nạ dop^{u}nas yat chi vaḍ āu̯ put phīrit vōt panun gar^{ạ} pyau bimār.

2. ạmis ås pādshāhasạnzi kōḍ^{i} hund ạshik gomut pādshāh kōḍ^{y}i ås gomut ạmis sunạrsund ạshik dod^{ạ}māj^{i} kun vanān pādshāh kūḍ :—

zargạr nichuva pūr kumār ı
ḍēshit log^{ạ}mai dod^{ạ}mạj muthai amār ıı

dod^{ạ}mạj ches vanān phīrit :—

mai kar kūḍye shūri bāshe ı
lagak ashkanye vāle vāshe ıı
å^{u}re kane dithai kūḍ^{i} kane dạ^{i}li ı
år mā lag^{ạ}ham vu bạ^{i}lī ıı

3. sunạr chu bimār ạmis chu ạskun tap ạmis sunạrsạnz kulai che gātij ạmis tug bōzun ạmisund dōd dapān ches tsạ hech lāyin rīnz beye gar sunạsand^{i} rạnz ze.

4. dapān vustād gar^{i} am^{i} sunạsandi rạnz ze drāu̯ atas k^{y}et hitsạn rạnz lāyān che apạ^{i}r^{i} tạ yipạ^{i}r^{i} lāyān kañyev^{i} tạ shastrev^{i} vōt ot pādshāhasạnzi dạ^{i}ri tal lāyin at^{i} sunạsand^{i} rēnz ze pādshahasạnzi kōd^{ye} halamas manz ami hå̆vus åre phīrit tạḍ kan^{i} ānạ beye trāvun dā^{i}ri kan^{i} āb beye trå̄vun pōshe gund beye trå̄vun kih beye tujen shast^{ạ}ro salai

V. THE TALE OF THE GOLDSMITH

1. Now this is what my Master saith :—

In days of yore there was a certain city, wherein there lived a goldsmith. He was head of his guild with twelve hundred guildsmen under him. He used to make articles for the King's daughter, and these his wife would take to her. One day the princess told the goldsmith's wife that in future her husband must himself bring the things, so one day he set out to her with a ring. When the princess saw it she took exception to it. "It is crooked," said she. So he took it back and went home, and there fell sick.

2. The truth was that he had fallen in love with the princess, and she too had become enamoured of him. She cried to her foster-mother :—

"Full of sweet languishment is that son of a goldsmith.
I have seen him, O nurse, and mad is my longing for him."

But the foster-mother replied :—

"Utter not, O daughter, childish talk,
Or thou wilt be caught within the net of love.
Close thine ear, O daughter, to such words,
Or else thou wilt find thyself a mark for blame."

3. The goldsmith lay sick of the fever of love, and his wife was a clever woman. She understood the cause of his pain, and said to him, "Practise thou pitching balls, and make two balls of gold."

4. Saith my Master :—

So he made two balls of gold and went out holding (them and other) balls in his hand. Hither and thither he pitched balls of stone and balls of iron as he went along, till he came below the princess's window, and through it he flung into her lap-cloth the two balls of gold. On this she turned her back towards him and showed him a mirror. Then she threw some water out of the window. Then she threw out a posy of flowers, and again a hair.

d^{y}utun at^{i} dạ̄^{i}ri hạndis dāsas kash am^{i} sunạr vuch āṷ phīrit vōt panun garạ dop^{u}nas paneñye zạnānạ dop^{u}nas kyạho kạrut ạm^{i} vununas phīrit rēnz hai lạ̄y^{a}mas tim hai gå̄s hal^{a} mas manz tōre hai haunam phīrit tor kan^{i} å̄ne beye hai trāunam då̄^{i}ri kan^{i} āb beye traunam pōshe gund beye trāṷnam kih beye dyutun shīt^{a}rạvi salạyạ sạ̄^{i}th dāsas pash dop^{u} nas am^{i} phīrit tạr kan^{i} hau hāṷnai ānạ kustāny å̄smut chus vupar āb hau trå̄ṷ nai āb davạ kan^{i} gatse atsun pōshe gund trå̄ṷnai bāgas manz salạyạ sạ̄^{i}th hå̄ṷnai anun gatse pahre vāv tat chiy polādev^{y} n^{y}ạ̄zạ tim gatsan tsaten^{i} kih trå̄ṷnai ches vālān kangạñ^{y}.

5. dapān vustād drāṷ ye sunạr shāman bạ̄^{i}g^{i} tsāvat bāgas manz vuchun at^{i} palang kut at^{i} palangas p^{y}eṭh shikasta sạ̄^{i}th p^{y}eyes nindạr āyes yi pādshāh kūḍ shāndạ ches karān khur khurachạs karān shānd yi k^{y}e hushār gå̄s nạ yutāñy gāsh lug phulen^{i} pādshāh kūḍ tsạj gar^{a} panun patkun gāu hushār sunạr yivān chu yit^{i} panun gar^{a} vanān ches panen kulai k^{y}ạho kạrut yichus dapān phīrit sạnai k^{y}ē āyem dopunas am^{i} zạnānạ talau yūr^{i} hund vulạ gau vuchus ami paneñ^{y}e zạnānạ vuchus chandạs vuchān at^{i} rēnz ze sunạsand^{i} timai yim tam^{i} doho lāyānas hal^{a}mas manz dop^{u}nas sa chai āmuts su chuk nạ gomut hushār vo beye yeli gatsak kāl^{a}chen teli dapai bo sabak.

6. dapān vustād nam da tulinas athan hạnd^{i} akis å̄s nas dyutmut sun kash dop^{u}nas mōr thas am^{i} dop^{u}nas phīrit mạ^{i}l māji che sa tsuñye muts nāyid

Finally she lifted up an iron stiletto and with it scratched the sill of the window. When the goldsmith had seen all this he returned home, and his wife said to him, "Well, dear, what did you do?" Said he to her, "I flung, my dear, the balls to her, and they fell, my dear, into her lap-cloth. Then, my dear, she turned her back to me and showed me a mirror. Then, my dear, she threw some water out of the window. Then she threw out a posy of flowers, and then a hair. Then she made a scratch upon the window-sill with an iron stiletto." Replied she, "When she turned her back and showed the mirror, she meant that someone else was there; when she threw out water, she meant that you must come in by the water-drain; when she threw the posy of flowers, she meant that it was the garden into which you must come; when she showed the stiletto, she meant that you must bring a file, as there are iron railings to be cut through; and when she threw a hair, she meant that she was combing her locks."

5. Moreover the Master said:—

At eventide the goldsmith went forth, and entered the garden. There he found a bed and got up on to it. He was weak from illness, and fell asleep. While he so slept, there came the princess. From the pillow she walked to the foot of the bed, and from the foot back again to the pillow, but he never awoke to welcome her. By that time the dawn began to blossom forth, and the princess ran off home. Thereafter the goldsmith awoke, and returned to his house. Says his wife to him, "What, dear, did you do?" Says he in reply, "She never came to me." Says she to him, "Come here, my dear." He went up to her, and she looked into his pocket, and found there the two golden balls that on the day before he had thrown into the princess's lap-cloth. Says she to him, "She did come to you, but you never stayed awake. Now, when you go again this evening, I will tell you what to do."

6. And the Master further told me:—

She set to work paring the ten nails of his hands, and as she did so, she gave to one of them a deep gash. Cried he, "You've been and killed me!" But she replied, "I was never taught barber's

sabakas vu yeli gatsak teli dimai davāhan am^{i} dyut^{a}nas martsevāngan ratseh^{a}na beye nuna ratse h^{a}na dop^{u}nas beye yeli tat palaṅgas p^{y}eṭh khasak teli yeyiy nindạr yi dava ratsạ hạn gand^{i} zyes adạ p^{y}eyiy nindạr shạhij drāu̯ at^{i} yi sunạr davā rats^{a} hạn hitsun sạ̄^{i}th vōt at bāgas manz kut at palaṅgas p^{y}eṭh chu prārān tsēr tāñy yi kuni yivān ches na hitsanas yiny nindạr atas chus dōd at chu karit tap dopun vuñy āyinạ yetsanạ ha bo dạ̄^{i}dis davā shạhij karạha nindạr yüthuy at dạ̄^{i}dis tsunun davā tithuy pyōs vāliñj^{i} v^{y}e chu lalạvān thud vuthit.

7. dapān vustād āyiye pādshāh sạnz kūḍ ạmis mut sårhuy dōd kạrun ạmis sạ̄^{i}th yi karun guts p^{y}eyak nindạr yutāñy gāsh lug pholen^{i} kuṭvāl chu vasān apạ̄^{i}r kan^{i} āgạye. vuchun at^{i} pādshāhasạnz kūḍ beye sunạr rạṭ^{i} ạm^{i} koṭvālạn niñy rạṭit kạrin havālạ tsrālin kạrik kạ̄d at^{i} ås pakāṇ vat^{i} akha ami süy dopuk yimau kạ̄dyau doyau tsahasạ dīzi krēk sunạr aṭa p^{y}eṭhạ dạbzik pādshahas kar pyau kuṅg^{a}vār^{i} kabar cha loṭ tsaṭan^{a}sạ k^{y}inna hot tsatanas.

pādshahas kar pyau kuṅg^{a}vār^{y}ē ı
  pakān dil gōm tạt^{i} tārē ıı
vir het vātun gōts sulli gār^{y}ē ı
  natatas pādshāh tat^{i} mārē ıı

bōz sunạrsạnzạ zạnānạ ḍrāye bāzar hitsan tsuche lazan krañj^{e} drāye h^{y}et.

shen kād kānạn su cho bāge rēmai ı
  satyạmis atsayo Bār Kodāyu hāy ıı

work by my father and mother. When you go to-day, I'll give you a little remedy." So she gave him some red-pepper and salt, saying, "Next time you get up on to that bed and you feel sleepy, apply a little of this medicine to your cut finger and your sleep will become cool."[1]

So the goldsmith went out, taking with him the medicine, and came to the garden, and got up on to the bed. He waited a long time, yet no one ever came. At length he began to feel sleepy, but his hand was too sore, and he caught hold of it (to relieve the pain). He said to himself, "She hasn't come. If I had only put some of that medicine on my sore finger I should have had a cool and refreshing sleep." So he put some of the medicine on the cut, and the smart was like a fiery poison in his heart. He jumped up, nursing his aching hand.

7. And my Master went on to say:—

Just then came the princess, and all his pain was forgotten. He did with her what was proper to the occasion, and they fell asleep in each other's arms. Meantime the dawn began to blossom forth. The chief constable came by on his rounds of inspection, and found there the princess and the goldsmith. He arrested them, making them over to his henchmen, and put them into jail. Just then a man happened to be passing along the road, and they called out to him, "Please, sir, make an outcry in the goldsmiths' market. You must say, 'The King's ass has trespassed in the saffron field, and who knows whether they will cut off its tail or cut its throat.'"

"The King's ass was caught in the saffron field,
And as I went there, my heart became all full of anxiety.
Thou must come at dawn with money to pay the fine,
Otherwise the King will kill it there and then."

The goldsmith's wife heard this outcry. She went out into the market and bought some loaves. She put these into a deep basket, and went off (to the jail), crying:—

"In six prisons have I distributed loaves.
Now, O God, would I enter a seventh."

[1] She means that the desire for sleep would become cool, and he would remain awake. But the silly fellow misunderstands her, and imagines that the medicine would bring him cool and refreshing sleep.

8. dapān vustād bāg^{a}ren yimạ suche dopunak kāvand chum bīmār at^{i}kyā dop ham pīrau fakīrau suche gatsan bāg^{a}ranye satan kādkhānen yi k^{y}ētsa dapun chu ti dap^{a}zim yōrạ ats^{a}vunuy årạ nēravun k^{y}ē dap^{a}zim na me gatse shak dop^{u}nak beye mā chu kạ^{i}d^{i} yeti dop has yimau pat^{y}ạmi paharạ ani mot^{i} kuṭvālen ze kạ^{i}d^{i} tim che patkun våts yiman nish dopun ạmis panạnis kāvandạs vony k^{y}ita pạ^{i}ṭ^{i} mokli yeti pādshāh kūḍ tag^{y}e mokalāvañy yi pādshāh kūḍ dop^{u}nas ạm^{i} phīrit ti yeli tag^{y}ehạm ade kyāzi lagaha kād.

9. dapān vustād kuḍun nālạ panun poshāk tsunun pādshāh kōḍ^{y}e pādshāh kōḍ^{y}e hund kuḍun tsunun pānes k^{a}rạnd ditsạnas vutamak^{i} drāye nebạr pādshāh kūḍ gaye panun gar kuṭvālen d^{y}ut rapạṭ pādshahạs dop^{u}nas pādshāh kūḍ beye ås sunạr bāgas manz timai kyā karim kād pādshāh drāụ̂ ạdālat p^{y}eṭh anik yim rātik kūḍ^{i} ze vuchuk yim bạts ze sunạr sanzi kulạye gand^{i} gul^{i} ze pādshahas dop^{u}nas pādshahạm as^{i}kya ạs^{i} gamat^{i} sālas tōre kyā āị̂ tạ vāt^{i} yat ch^{y}ānis shehạras manz gau tsēr adạ tsāị̂ ch^{y}ānis bāgas manz at^{i} vuch palang khat^{i} at^{i} p^{y}eṭh kur arām āre āụ̂ chōn kuṭ^{a}vāl am^{i} kya niy rạṭit kạrin kåd vut kuṭvāl dopun pādshahas pādshahạm ch^{i}ān kūḍ kạrnam kasam vigñya nāge p^{y}eṭhạ dapān yus at^{i} apuz kasam karehe su vutehenạ tat^{i} thud su ås tat^{i} marān dop am^{i} sunạr sanzi zạnānạ ạmis sunạras tag^{i}ye yi pādshāh kūḍ bachāviny dop^{u}nas

8. And my Master said :—

She went about distributing these loaves, saying, "My husband is sick. And what did holy men and medicants say to me but to distribute loaves in seven jails. If ye have ought to say to me, say it to me as I go in; but say not ought to me as I go out, for that will risk the fulfilment of my vow." And then she continued, "I wonder if ye have any prisoners herein." They replied, "At the last watch of the night the chief constable brought hither two prisoners. They are in there at the back." So she came up to them, and said to her husband, "How can we now get the princess free? Have you any plan for releasing her?" Said he, "If I had any plan, would I now be in prison?"

9. Said my Master :—

She took off her clothes and put them on the princess, and took off the princess's clothes and put them on herself. Then she turned the basket upside down (over the princess's head, so as to conceal it) and the princess went straight out of the jail, and came home. In the meantime the chief constable reported to the King that the princess and goldsmith had been found in the garden, and, of course, had been put in prison. The King went forth into the judgment hall. They brought the two prisoners before him, and, lo and behold, they were the husband and wife! The goldsmith's wife respectfully folded her arms and said to the King, "Your Majesty, we had gone to a marriage feast, and on our way back happened to pass through this city of yours. It was then late, so we went into your garden. There we chanced to see a bed, and got on to it and went to sleep. Well, your chief constable came along, and, as you see, arrested us and put us into prison." Then the chief constable got up and said to the King, "Your Majesty, let your Majesty's daughter make oath at the Vigiñāh Nāg.[1] People say that if anyone make a false oath there, he never rises up again, but falls down dead on the spot."

Said the goldsmith's wife to the goldsmith, "Have you any plan for saving the princess?" Said he to her, "Please tell me how?"

[1] Vigiñāh or Vigiñ^u is the name of the tutelary goddess of the Kāshmīr forests. In the good old times she was often seen as she roamed over the mountains, but nowadays she is always invisible. A Vigiñāh Nāg is a Nāg, or spring, sacred to her.

hāvtam vat dop^{u}nas ak trāu̯ såruy poshāk kurạn tsün krāu̯ beye mat sūr lāg gosōny yeli ut vāt^{a}nāvan ạmis pādshāh kūḍ^{y}e chōn gatse gatsun ạmis pādshāh kūḍ^{y}e gatse karin^{y} tap dāmānas dopun gatses mạ dittạ guḍe khārāt sa kya hāi̯vi adạ kasam chōnuy mokrạṭit dạpi yāhaz^{i} vigñya nāge nạmis mạtis siva kya kạrüm nạ kāsi dāmānas tap.

vigñya nāgas vatsāyạs srānas ı
kuv^{a} zānạ maṭ^{i}ma ludnam ra ıı
mat^{i} tap lạyinam doili dāmānas ı
kuṭ^{a}vāl gānạs gud^{a}ryau kya ıı
sạ^{i}ri yār^{a} goi pānas pānas ı
kuṭ^{a}vāl gānas gud^{a}ryau kya ıı

10. pādshāh küḍ gaye gar kuṭ^{a}vāl d^{y}utuk phahi sunạrsandi båts ze che gar^{i} panạn^{i} yi gau sunạr bimār kurnas yạhoi ạshkun tap yi ås sunạrsạnz zạnānạ gātij guḍun moh^{a}rạ hathas akis rush yi gundun panạnis kāvandas pānạ lōgun sạnnyās ạmis pạrạn gupāl^{i} våtạnāvun pādshāhạ sund garạ dopun ạmis pādshahạs yi chạm bạy kākin^{y} yi chai tse havālạ mye chiy gatsun bạyis nish su chum gōmus (*sic*) sōdahas yi chai myĕ gupāl^{i} havālạ yu tāñy as^{i} yimōy yi chai pāk yi thāi̯vzin panạn^{y}e kūḍis sạ^{i}th āye phīrit panen gar^{a} k^{y}ĕ kāla gau āu̯ yi sunạr beye gar^{a} punun.

11. dapān vustād lōgun sōdāgār am^{i} zạnānạ våt^{i} at^{i} pādshaha sandis shehạras manz lōg ami beye sạnyās kāvand thåvun ḍēras p^{y}eṭh saudāgār lāgit

Said she, "In the first place, pull off all your clothes, and put wooden pattens on your feet. In the second place, rub ashes over your whole body, and pretend to be a mendicant devotee. As soon as they shall bring the princess to the Nāg, you must go up to her and catch hold of her skirt, saying, "First of all, pray give me alms." She can then safely take oath and say, "O holy Vigiñāh Nāg, save and except this mad fellow no one hath ever seized my skirt."[1]

She went down to bathe in the Vigiñāh Nāg.
"I know not why this charge was brought against me.
Only this mad one hath caught the skirt of my garment."
Then what happened to the vile chief constable?
All the folk took their several ways to their homes.
Then what happened to the vile chief constable?

10. So the princess went home in peace, and they took the chief constable and impaled him. The goldsmith and his wife also returned to their own house, and there he fell sick. He was sick with the fever of love for the princess. But the goldsmith's wife was very clever. She made a necklace worth a hundred *dīnārs* and put it on her husband. She dressed herself as a mendicant ascetic, and him as a dancing girl, and brought him to the King's palace. Said she to the King, "Here is my brother's wife, and I am putting her in thy charge. I must be off to my brother who has gone away on a trading expedition. So here is my dancing girl placed in thy charge until I return. She is yet a virgin and thou must keep her with thine own daughter." Saying this she (left the goldsmith there disguised as the girl and) returned to her own house. Shortly afterwards the goldsmith himself slipped away, and also went home.

11. And again my Master said:—

The goldsmith's wife dresses her husband up as a merchant, and arrives as if from a journey at the King's city. She herself is again made up as the mendicant ascetic. She leaves the pretended

[1] "To seize the skirt" has also a metaphorical meaning, which can be imagined. Hence, the princess was quite safe in saying it.

pāne gaye pādshahis gund^{a}nas dāvā dim gupāl^{i} divān achạn dü dapān ches dim gupāl^{i}.

> prārān doh gau me bāl^{y}ē ।
> sạnyās āmut gupāl^{y}ē ॥

yi chus dapān pādshāh phīrit.

> sạnyās^{a} maulāk jande lolo ।
> kōtūna ak dimai danḍa lōlō ॥

sạnyās chus dapān chus phīrit.

> sạnyās chusai bē vāstu lōlō ।
> danḍ himai dukhtarē khās lōlō ॥

12. dapān vustād moh^{a}rạ hatạs guḍun rush gundun paneñye kūḍ^{y}e karạn havālạ sạnyāsas.

> tānnạnạ tannana tanā nai ।
> yim kār che karān zạnānai ॥

niyantạ karạn havālē panạnis kāvandas dop^{u}nas ṭsu zān tạ yi zān.

merchant in the tent, and herself goes to the King. She makes her petition to him. "Give me," said she, "my dancing girl." The King replies with abuse, and throws curses at her eyes, but she reiterates, "Give me my dancing girl":—

"Longing have I been for my girl as the days went by.
The mendicant has come for his dancing girl."

And the King replies to her:—

"O mendicant, fix not the banner of thy claim, tol-lol-lay.
I will give thee another lady in compensation, tol-lol-lay."

But the mendicant answers:—

"An ascetic I am without worldly ties, tol-lol-lay.
In compensation I'll take thine own daughter, tol-lol-lay."

12. And finally said my Master:—

He made a necklace worth a hundred *dīnārs*, and putting it on his own daughter, made her over to the mendicant ascetic.

Taradiddle, taradiddle, tol-lol-lay,
It is only womenfolk who can act this way.

She took the princess and made her over to her husband. And she said to them, "You must learn, and she must learn."[1]

[1] i.e. learn the truth of the verse just quoted. They two must learn and know the power of women's wiles. There is perhaps an indication that the wiles would continue, and that the life of the husband and of the second wife might not be happy as they expected.

VI. SHĀHĪ YŪSUF ZALĪKHĀ

1. Shāhī Yūsuf Zulīkhā yār^a bōzak nā ||

Z. 2. Sālas yihna polāu̯ k^{y}eknā |
Yitam gah begā yār^a bōzak nā ||

3. Sat kuṭ^i larichim chān^{y}e lō larichim |
Beh tam sātha yār^a bōzak nā ||

4. Puṭal khānas b^{i}yun b^{i}yun pānas |
Kurnak parda yār^a bōzak nā ||

Y. 5. At^i kya thā̊vut as^i kōna hā̊vut |
Z. Dop^{u}nas chum Kūdā yār^a bōzak na ||

Y. 6. Kūdā gau suy mane paneñye kās duy |
Shōlan chu shamā yār^a bōzak nā ||

7. Kūdā chu kunuy jal^{a}va dit drāu̯ nunnuy |
Kanye manz chā mudā yār^a bōzak nā ||

8. Hazrat Yūsuf tsul pat^a lāḍēyes Zalīkhā ||
Z. Yūsūf tsalān Zalīkhā lārān |
Dop^{u}nas yi pazyā yār^a bōzak nā ||

9. Nālas tap kạrit nyūn hā tsā kạrit |
Gai pēshe pādshāh yār^a bōzak nā ||

VI. THE STORY OF YŪSUF AND ZULAIKHĀ[1]

1. Wilt thou not hear, O beloved, (the tale of) Yūsuf and Zulaikhā ?

2. (Zulaikhā) " To the feast wilt thou not come ? Dainty meats wilt thou not eat ?
In season or out of season, come thou to me. Wilt thou not hear, O beloved ?

3. " Seven rooms have I in the palace; in my longing for thee have I prepared them.
Sit thou, I pray, for but a moment. Wilt thou not hear, O beloved ? "

4. One by one she herself in the idol-house
Covereth (each idol) with a veil.[2] Wilt thou not hear, O beloved ?

5. (Yūsuf) " On what hast thou put a veil ? What hast thou displayed to us ? "
(Zulaikhā) " It is my god (that I have veiled). Wilt thou not hear, O beloved ? "

6. (Yūsuf) " There is but one God. Cast from thy mind the belief in dualism.[3]
He is burning bright as a lamp. Wilt thou not hear, O beloved ?

7. " There is but one God, who hath manifested Himself in glory.
What purpose can there be in a stone ? Wilt thou not hear, O beloved ? "

8. The holy Yūsuf fled, and after him ran Zulaikhā.
Yūsuf fleeing, Zulaikhā pursuing.
Cried she, " Is it thus that thou shouldest act ? Wilt thou not hear, O beloved ? "

9. She caught him by the neck. She made an accusation against him.
They went before the King. Wilt thou not hear, O beloved ?

[1] Yūsuf is Joseph, and Zulaikhā is Potiphar's wife.

[2] When Zulaikhā tempts Joseph she puts a veil before the image of her household idol, that it may not become aware of her unchastity. This arouses Joseph's suspicions.

[3] *Dŏy*, duality, is a technical term of Kāshmīrī Śaiva monotheism, and is here borrowed by Musalmān theology.

10. Azīza Misạr ås pādshāh ạmis ås zid Hazret^{i} Yūsūf^{ạ} sund.

Yūsūf kạ̄d khān kahchus na bōzān ।
  Mukli az Kūdā yār^{ạ} bōzak nā ॥

11. Yeli Yūsūf lug kạ̄d at^{i} ås prāñy kạ̄d timau dyūt kāb akis kurun tạ^{i}bīr tsimạ^{i}ri pādshāh mōḍ pādshahạn beyis kurun tạ^{i}bīr tsạ sapadạk pādshāh sund pēshkār mạṭ^{i} hasa pạ^{i}vzi yād.

Kạ^{i}dyau kāv dyūt tạ^{i}bīr drāk myūt ।
  Moklai parda yār^{ạ} bōzak nā ॥

12. Pādshāh Azīzạ Misạr dēshān kāb.

Azīzạ Misạr kāb^{ạ}nish ābtạr gau bedār ।
  Vut shōrạ ga yār^{ạ} bōzak nā ॥

13. Kam^{y}ük vut shōrạgā ?

Malan bāban pīran fakīran ।
  Banina hakīma yār^{ạ} bōzak nā ॥

14. Kam^{y}ük hakīm at^{i} kābus yus mānye tsārihe yus am^{i} Azīzạ Misren kāb ås dyūtmut dop^{u}nas gulāman kābuk tạ^{i}bīr zāne Hāzret Yūsūf.

Kābuk tạ^{i}bīr Yūsufas chu vāphīr ।
  Dāden chiy davā yār^{ạ} bōzak nā ॥

15. Unuk Hazret Yūsūf dop^{u}nas pādshahạn me ḍyūṭ kāb at^{i} vanum tạ^{i}bīr dop^{u}nas Yusūfan kya ḍyūṭhut dop^{u}nas pādshahạn ak ḍyūṭhum huk^{i} nāg

10. Azīz-ĕ Misr was the King, and he had enmity against Yūsuf.
Yūsuf is in prison, no one heareth his complaint.
But he will be released by the power of God. Wilt thou not hear, O beloved ?

11. When Yūsuf was put in prison there were there old prisoners. They each saw a dream. To one he interpreted it, saying, "Of a surety the King will kill thee," and the King did kill him. To the other he made interpretation saying, "Thou wilt become the King's chief clerk. Then, sir, I beseech thee, bear thou me in mind."
The prisoners saw a dream. The interpretation turned out true[1] for them.
On the morrow they were released from jail. Wilt thou not hear, O beloved ?

12. King Azīz-ĕ Misr saw a dream.
Azīz-ĕ Misr became terrified by the dream.
He awoke, and there was made proclamation. Wilt thou not hear, O beloved ?

13. What was the purport of the proclamation ?
Among the priests, among the calendars, among the saints, among the mendicants.
Can there not be found one learned man ? Wilt thou not hear, O beloved ?

14. Of what science was a learned man required ? One who could interpret this dream that had been seen by Azīz-ĕ Misr. His servant said to him, "The holy Yūsuf knoweth how to interpret a dream."
"Mighty is Yūsuf in interpretation of dreams.
Verily he is the remedy of all pains. Wilt thou not hear, O beloved ?"

15. They brought the holy Yūsuf, and the King said to him, "I have seen a certain dream. Tell thou me the interpretation thereof." Said Yūsuf, "What didst thou see ?" Replied the King, "In the first place saw I seven dry water-springs drinking

[1] Literally, "sweet."

sat yivān bartʸen nāgan satan chʸavān beye ḍyūṭhum kām sat hil vuchun pukhtan satan helen ningᵃlān beye vuchun lāgar gāu̯ sat yivān mast satan gåvun ningᵃlān amⁱ kuy vanum tạⁱbīr dopᵘnas Yusūfan drāg vuthi.

16. Dapān vustād Yusūfan moklau tạⁱbīr vanit pādshahạs gāu asar lajis boche dopᵘnak dīyūm batạ amⁱ vaktạ pādshah kʸavān ås nạ amⁱ asrᵊ sạⁱth dopᵘnak jal ạñyūm dapān gai tạ ạnuk batạ yi kyōn dopᵘnak bey ạñyūm añye has dēgạ vokᵊvit ạnhas tạ kyōn taslīkạ ås nạ dapān atⁱ bo che sạⁱthi gau mạrit dapān pagā dits vazirau vurdī pagā vasʸu sạⁱrē īdgāh yas host namⁱ pạz behe nyeche suy sapạdⁱ pādshāh dapān votⁱ īdgāh āu̯ host namʸau Yusūfas pạz āu̯ bʸūthus nʸeche banāu Yūsūf pādshāh.

Yalạ vai håvun hostᵘ mange nåvun ।
Yūsūf pādshāh yārᵊ bōzak nā ॥

17. Tạⁱrīf-i Yūsūf par Wahab Kārạ khūb ।
Gats parān lā illāh yārᵊ bōzak nā ॥

up seven full water-springs. In the second place saw I seven unripe ears of corn swallowing up seven ripe ears. Again I saw coming seven lean kine, and they were swallowing up seven fat kine. Tell thou me the interpretation of this." And Yūsuf said unto him, " A famine will arise."

16. And my Master said :—

Yūsuf finished telling the interpretation, and as he did so the power of the famine seized the King. He felt hunger, and cried out, " Give me food," although that was not his time for eating. Through the power of the famine he cried to them, " Speedily bring ye it to me." And people say that they hastened forth and brought him food. He ate it, and cried, " Bring ye more ! " They hauled it to him in cauldrons, and he ate it but could not be satisfied. And people say that (for all he ate) he died of starvation. They say that next day the Viziers gave forth this command, " Let all ye citizens descend to-morrow to the 'Īd-plain, and he to whom the royal elephant will bow, and on whose thumb-ring the royal hawk will alight, shall become King. They say that they went down to the 'Īd-plain. The elephant came and bowed to Yūsuf, and the hawk came and alighted on his thumb-ring. So Yūsuf became King.

Majesty he displayed, he sent for the elephant.
Yūsuf became King. Wilt thou not hear, O beloved ?

17. O Wahb, the blacksmith, well recite thou the praise of Yūsuf.
Ever as thou goest recite the creed. Wilt thou not hear, O beloved ?

VII. NAYE HAṆZ KAT

1. Banạ yas dōd tas chu pānạs tīnanān ।
Naye hund dōd nay che pānai tī vanān ॥

2. Nai che dapān Bār Sāhib chi kunuy ।
Diyạ tạ tsakh^{y}e nishi pānai chī b^{y}ünuy ॥

3. Nāi che dapān Bār Sāhib mun^{a} zāt ।
Pāne suy kun chi mushtāk dokht^{a}rāt ॥

4. Hamud gatsyu tas Khudāyạs kun parān ।
Pạd^{a} kurun ṭōṭ Muhammad mēz^{a}mān ॥

5. Bār Sāhiban sạ^{i}th dit^{a}nas sāmān ।
Tsōr yār chạs sạ^{i}th sạ^{i}th shōbān ॥

6. Nūr^{a} tạm^{i}sandi pạda kurun Ādam ।
Ād^{a}mas sạ^{i}th pạda kurun īdam ॥

7. Nai che dapān lodun Ādam bē navā ।
Ås mashīyat lạ^{i}r^{i} tala drạyas Havā ॥

8. Nai che dapān kya zabar ås suy sāth ।
Yam^{i} sāthai pạd^{a} kạrun zur yāt ॥

9. Nai che dapān hāl myō nuy bōz tuy̭ ।
Dạ^{i}d^{ye} ladai ch^{y}ūtạ sātạ rōz^{i} tuy̭ ॥

10. Nai che dapān pat vanan åsus pin hām ।
Shāk^{a} burgau sạ^{i}th^{i} åsus shōbān ॥

11. Nai che dapān thud me åsum bālạ pān ।
Sune kanạnuy grāye dūran ches divān ॥

12. Gai mạ gum^{a}rå yiy tạ tam^{i} kuy gōm badal ।
Pyōm^{i} guṭ^{i}lā lạ^{i}ni tsūr våtit azal ॥

VII. THE TALE OF THE REED-FLUTE

1. Only to him is the burden of woe manifested who suffereth woe himself.
The reed-flute herself is telling the reed-flute's woe.

2. Quoth the reed-flute, "The Almighty is one and only one.
God alone is of His own will devoid of wrath."

3. Quoth the reed-flute, "Pure is the Almighty;
(As He alone is free from imperfection) only towards Himself can he yearn day and night.

4. "Ever go ye giving forth praise to that God,
In that He created Muḥammad, the Beloved Guest.

5. "The Almighty gave him instruments to be with him.
Four friends[1] are illustrious as his companions.

6. "By His glory He created Adam,
And with Adam was created this world."[2]

7. Quoth the reed-flute, "Adam was sent forth into the world all alone,
And at his wish Eve issued from his side."

8. Quoth the reed-flute, "How excellent was that moment,
In which the world with all its offspring was created!"

9. Quoth the reed-flute, "Hear ye, I pray, the tale of my woe.
If ye suffer pain, remain, I pray, a moment by me."

10. Quoth the reed-flute, "At the back of the forest was I hidden,
Beautiful with my branches and my leaves."

11. Quoth the reed-flute, "Upright was my youthful form,
As (in the breeze) I waved the pendants of my golden ears.

12. "I went astray, and thus happened that change of my estate.
A woodcutter chanced upon me, a doom, a thief of my destiny."

[1] Muhammad's four friends were Abū Bakr, 'Umar, 'Uthmān, and 'Alī. The last two were his sons-in-law, and the first two his dearest friends.

[2] The word *yīdam* is a corruption of the Sanskrit *idam*, and comes curiously in a Musalmān poem.

13. **Nai che dapān sakhme gōm au suy kosūr ।**
Naz^{a}ri tạm^{i} sanzi sạ^{i}th^{i} sạpạnum tok^{a} sūr ॥

14. **Nai che dapān tsakh^{i} hut mak chum^{a} divān ।**
Phal^{a} b^{y}ūn b^{y}ūn chale māzas chum tulān ॥

15. **Mad^{a} me âsum had^{a} pānạs ches karān ।**
Bāl^{a} pānạs vāle nai kåts chum karān ॥

16. **Gay^{e} zhudā sai zhudāī chai vanān ।**
Ås vadān al vida ås suy karān ॥

17. **Tat^{i} vålit vat^{i} vat^{i} tam chum divān ।**
Vāle vunuy turke ch^{y}ānạs chum^{u} kạnān ॥

18. **Nai che dapān lạ^{i}r^{i} phīr^{i} phīr^{i} chum vuchān ।**
Dūri rōz^{i} rōz tō^{i}ri dab sak chum divān ॥

19. **Nai che dapān lit^{a}ri sạ^{i}th yeli gạj^{a}nas ।**
Ạtạr peyem yeli char kas khạj^{i}nas ॥

20. Dalīl :—

Yeli charkas kạts ạmis turke ch^{y}ānạs nishi ạmis p^{y}evān panen ham nishīn yād yim^{a}nuy kun che vanān k^{y}ētsa tạ kya vane.

Nai che dapān ham nishīn mēn^{y} rōd^{i} kat^{y}e ।
Vạn^{y} bo dim^{a} hak tūri mā rōd^{i} aḍ vat^{y}e ॥

21. **Ham nishīnạn sīr panunuy bāvạ ha ।**
Sīn^{a} muts^{a}rit dōd panunuy hāv^{a} ha ॥

22. **Nai che dapān kya ban^{y}âm kūt ches rivān ।**
Dạ^{i}de panạne nāl^{a} pharyād ches divān ॥

13. Quoth the reed-flute, "Terrible was the fault (i.e. calamity) that befel me.
At once on his seeing me, I became crushed to dust."

14. Quoth the reed-flute, "Wrathfully he striketh me blows with his axe,
Bits of my flesh in splinters is he raising.

15. "I had been full of pride, I had looked upon myself as the limit (of beauty),
And how much humiliation doth he cast upon my fair young form!"

16. Far from the forest was she sundered, and of that sundering she tells.
Lamenting was she, as she made her last farewell.

17. "Down from the mountain forest he bringeth me, and wearieth me with the long, long road.
And when he is come down, he selleth me to a carpenter." [1]

18. Quoth the reed-flute, "He turneth me round and round sideways and inspecteth me.
He standeth apart and giveth me terrible blows with an axe."

19. Quoth the reed-flute, "When he melted my flesh with a saw,
When he set me on his lathe, 'twas as though a wood-worm had attacked me."

20. When she was set on the lathe in that carpenter's shop, the memory of her friends and companions comes to her. She says some words to them. What is it she would say?

Quoth the reed-flute, "Where stayed my friends and companions?
Messages would I send them. Would that I knew if they stayed half way.

21. "I would tell my secret to my friends and neighbours,
I would open my bosom, and display my grief."

22. Quoth the reed-flute, "What hath befallen me! How much do I lament!
In my woe, I pour forth cries and calls for help."

[1] A *tŏrka-chān* is a carpenter who works on his own account in his own workshop, and who is not a village servant.

23. Nai che dapān nālạ dim^{a} ha mār^{a}kan ı
    Banạnạ rust^{a}nau kah ti rōzān mardạ zan ॥

24. Dapān vustād kya vanạhe yiman ham nishīnan yiman vanạhe yiy :—

    Narạm kạr kạr barạm pānas chum karān ı
    Vāre vuch tōm māz kōta chum harān ॥

25. Vade nā bo zade pānas tạ^{i}ri nam ı
    Khām pạ̃sạn zīṭ^{i} atạ kạt^{i} dạ^{i}ri nam ॥

26. Dapān vustad vu yeli khām pạ̃san āyi kạnanạ vuchus p^{y}ivān panun nạyis tān^{y} yād at^{i} nạyis tānạs kun che vanān k^{y}ẽtsa kya vane :—

    Nai che dapān nạyis tānuk chum tamā ı
    Gar ze panạne tsān^{y} jām arzo samā ॥

27. Nai che dapān nạyis tān myå̄n kyah chu jān ı
    Zāne kyah tat māne bōzit gạ^{i}ri zān ॥

28. Nai che dapān nạyis tān myå̄n kyah zabạr ı
    Zāne kyah tat māne bōzit bē khabar ॥

29. Nai che dapān nạyis tān nạch yas che zān ı
    Zānạ suyyus ās^{i} vot^{u}mut Lā Makān ॥

30. Nai che dapān kyah che vun^{y}muts masnavī ı
    Zāne suyyas ās^{i} p^{y}imats ashkạ chī ॥

31. Nai che dapān mudur mas kạ^{i}tya ch^{y}avān ı
    Sudạr balai nāye Subhān chiy vanān ॥

23. Quoth the reed-flute, "In the assemblies cries would I give forth.
No man or woman ever liveth free from his fated sorrow."

24. And my Master saith :—

What would she have said to her friends and companions ? To them verily would she have said this :—

"He planed me and he made me smooth, and with an auger bored he my body.
Prithee, behold me well. How much of my flesh is dropping from me !

25. "Shall I not weep ? Holes hath he made all o'er my body.
For a petty farthing how often hath he stretched his arms upon me."

26. Moreover my Master saith :—

When she had been sold for petty farthings there came to her the memory of the canebrake where she was born. She addresses some words to it. What is it she would say ?

Quoth the reed-flute, "Yearning have I for my canebrake,
For this purpose searched I earth and heaven."

27. Quoth the reed-flute, "How fair is my canebrake !
Can one who knoweth it not, understand its meaning, if he hear thereof ?"

28. Quoth the reed-flute, "How excellent is my canebrake !
Can an ignorant man understand its meaning, if he hear thereof ?"

29. Quoth the reed-flute, "He only will have knowledge of my canebrake
Who hath arrived at the true knowledge of God the Omnipresent."

30. Quoth the reed-flute, "What hath been said in these verses ?
Only he will understand on whom hath fallen a particle of love."

31. Quoth the reed-flute, "Many are they who drink sweet wine,
But only on Sŏdarbal doth Subḥān sing the tale of the reed-flute."

VIII. PĀDSHĀH SŪNZ KAT

1. Dapān vustād suy pādshāh ås nērān prat doho at^{i} zün^{a} dabi p^{y}eṭh at^{i} ås p^{y}eṭh kani ål janavāran hund yim ås^{i} prat doho yihas bōlbåsh bōzān yim ās^{i} pādshah^{a} sạnd setā khush gatsān doho aki ås na bōlbåsh k^{y}ē gatsān dop am^{i} pādshāh bāye pādshahạs az kōne che gatsān bōlbåsh dapān vuchuk at^{i} ålis at^{i} manz bache ze momut^{y} vālik bun setā p^{y}ūr yiman pādshahas sạndyan don bātsạn anik vazīr gātily gātily. dophak noman vuch tuy kya chu gomut vuch hak yiman rot^{a}mut kund hatis dānạ vazīrạn ak^{i} dop^{u} nak yi che yiman panen^{y} mạj momuts ạm^{i} narạn kurmuts b^{y}ēk vurudz am^{i} chu nak dyutmut åmpa kane dyut^{a}mut kund ami chi yim momut^{y} pādshāh vanān pādshāh bāye buy marai tsạ kar^{i}zạnạ kun^{i} pādshāh bai vanān pādshahạs buy marai tsạ kar^{i}zạnạ kun^{i} kur yimau driy kasm pāne vāny yi kyā ze kuruk driy kasm dopuk as^{i} che gabạr ze timan kya ka^{i}rē vur mạj yā mōl yiy.

2. kyē kāla gau pādshāh bai moye pādshāh kun^{i} karān chu nạ ti kyā zi pāne vān^{y} åsuk doyau bātsau driy kasm kurmut vāryạ kāla gau āy vazīr dopuk pādshahạs pādshahạm n^{y}ētar gatse karun vārya kāl bōzān chuk na kur has zōr vazīrau kurun n^{y}ētar.

3. yim pādshāh zāde ze ås tim^{i} ås paḍān sabak doh ak^{i} kạr yimau pāne vāñy bār^{a}nyau doyau muslahat māji gatsau salām h^{y}et bar^{a}k trạm^{y} lālau nigīnau gai h^{y}et salāmi māje trạm^{y} rut^{a}nak vuchuna

VIII. THE TALE OF A KING

1. Once upon a time there was a certain King, and my Master tells me that every day he used to go out to take the air in the roof summer-house of his palace. Now some birds had built their nests in its thatch, and each day the King and Queen used to listen to the chirping of the chicks, and much joy did the two derive therefrom. One day they heard none, and said the Queen to the King, "Why is there to-day no chirping?" And my Master tells me that they looked into the nest, and that they found therein only two dead chicks. They took them out and full of grief brought them down into the palace. There they summoned all their wise Viziers, and commanded them to inspect the dead chicks, and to say what had happened to them. So the Viziers inspected them, and found that a thorn had been stuck into the throat of each. Then said a very sage among the Viziers, "It is evident that the mother of these chicks died, and that the cock sought another mate and wedded her. She has been giving each of them a thorn to eat for food, and that is why they are dead." Said the King to the Queen, "If I die, thou must not wed again," and said the Queen to the King, "If *I* die, *thou* must not wed again." And so they mutually made vow and oath. Now, why was it that they made this vow and oath? "Because," said they, "we have two sons, and who knoweth but a stepmother or a stepfather may do this very thing to them."

2. In the course of time the Queen died, and the King wedded not again, because of the mutual vow and oath that the Queen and he had made. A long time passed, and at length his Viziers came to him and said, "Verily, your Majesty should once more make espousal," but for a long time he paid no heed to them. Then at last his Viziers became urgent, and he took to himself a new Queen.

3. Now, as we have heard, there were two young princes, and they were occupied in their lessons. One day the two brethren took advice of each other and decided to bring a complimentary present to their stepmother. So they filled a tray with rubies and other jewels and offered it to her. She accepted the tray, and as she did so her glance fell upon them. The princes then went off

kurnak gai yim pādshāh zāde ze sabakas yim che doha doha ithai pāthin karān dohạ aki gau ạmis pādshāh bāye khātir yiman vurạ n^{y}ech^{a} vin hund yimàn dopun tuh thạ^{i}vyu mạ sạ^{i}th^{i} salā yimau dop^{u}has tsạ chak mōj as^{i} chi gabạr tsạ tạ as^{i} vāt^{i} na gai pānạs sabakas āu̯ pādshāh panun mah^{a}lạkhān pādshah bāye trop^{u}nas kut dop^{u}nas bar kyā^{i}z^{i} kurut band yi ches dapān pādshāh bai bu chạsạ ch^{y}ạn^{y} kulai k^{y}in na ch^{y}āñyen nech^{a}vin hunz pādshāh chus dapān ti kya gau dop^{u}nas tim ām lekan guḍ^{a} dim ti hạnzạ vālinje ze adạ muts^{a}rai bar.

4. dyutun hukum vazīrạn tim ās^{i} sabak parān tsat^{a}hāl dop^{u}nak māre vāt^{a}lạn kạrūk havāla timai mārenak dapān vōt vazīr yiman pādshāhzādạn nishạn setā gōs yin sāf dop^{u}nak vasyu bun tsāt^{a}hāl^{a} dop^{u}nak tsạl^{y}u yemi shah^{a}rạ tim^{y} tsạl^{y} vazīrạn kạr kōm dopun māre vāt^{a}lan mā^{i}ryūk hōni ze karik yiman vāliñje ze lazak tạ^{i}kis gai h^{y}et pādshāh bai dop^{u}has añyai nomạ pādshāh zādạn hạnza vāliñje ze thāu̯ darvāza tạ rat thāvnak darvāza rachen yimạ vāliñje ze dop^{u}has yim^{a} chai pādshāh zādạn don hạnzạ byūṭ at^{i} pādshāhī karnạ.

5. yim bại bārạn ze vāt^{i} biyạs pādshahạs akis nish dop^{u}nak pādshahạn tuh chu sh^{a}hzādạ me yivān bōz^{a}ne tuh vạn^{i} tōy̯ tuh k^{y}etạ pạ^{i}t^{y} chu yōr lạg^{i}mat^{i} kya sabab chu yimau dop^{u}has yi panun gud^{a}run dop^{u}nak bihu m^{y}enish nōk^{a}rī dapān bēth^{y} hazūri naukar ạmis ås pādshahạs prān^{y} gulām ze yim z^{y}i ti gai tsōr tsun zanen kạrin zima rātsạs tsōr pahạr

to their lessons, and after that, day by day, they brought her a similar offering. One day, there arose in the heart of the Queen a passionate desire for the two youths, and she made proposals to them for an unlawful intrigue; but they replied, "Thou art our mother! We are thy children! Between thee and us such may not be," and went off again to their lessons. In the evening the King came to the harem, but the Queen locked the door of her room and refused to allow him to enter. Said he, "Why hast thou shut the door?" and she replied to him, "Is it of thee that I am the wife, or am I the wife of thy two sons?" Said the King, "What is it that hath happened?" Replied she, "They came to me and asked of me indecent things. Nor will I open the door to thee till thou give me their two hearts."

4. And my Master saith:—

He gave an order to his Viziers while the boys were studying their lessons in the school. Said he to the Viziers, "Make the princes over to the executioners, and let the executioners kill them." And my Master tells me that a Vizier went to the princes, and became filled with pity for them. Said he to them, "Come ye down from the school." Then he said, "Flee ye from this city." So they fled, and then the Vizier did a deed. He told the executioners to kill two dogs. So they killed two dogs, and tore out their hearts. These they put upon a charger and took to the Queen. Said they to her, "Here are the two hearts of those princes. Open thou the door and take them." So she opened the door and took the two hearts, as they said to her, "Here are they for thee straight from the bodies of the two princes." And thereafter the King lived on with her to sway the sceptre.

5. The two brothers sought refuge with another king, and he said to them, "Ye appear unto me to be princes. Prithee tell ye me how are ye come hither, and what is the cause thereof." So they told him all their happenings, and he thereupon took them into his service. And my Master tells me that they were entered into the King's bodyguard. The King had already two old servants in his bodyguard, and with these two princes they made four. Each had to guard the king during one of the four watches of the

guḍ nyukuy pahạr chu lagān ạmis pādshāh zādạs z^{y}ithis hihis dapān pād^{a}shahạ sandyau doyau bātsau tråvuk arām.

6. dapān gulām chu vud^{a}nye nazar ches pādshahạ sạndin don bātsen kun yim^{a} vuy syud log vasạni shahmār tāl^{a} va kane. gulām chu vuchān yeli yi shahmār log vātạne amis pādshāh bāye hạndis badanạs n^{y}ēzik āu̯ lārān gulām lạyin shamshēr ạmis shah mārạs hani hani karinas tukrạ tsunun palangas thal shamshēr^{i} hạndis t^{y}ēgas vulun phamb log ạmis pādshāh bāye hạndis badạnas vutherạni dopun ạmis ās^{i} shahmār^{a} sund zehar lāḍ^{y}ōmut ami mōjūb ås yi vutherān pādshāh gau bēdār vuchun gulām āmut nēzīk shamshēr h^{y}et nañyi ạm^{i}sund pahar muk^{a}lyau āu̯ duyạmis gulāmạsund pahar āu̯ n^{y}ēzīk dop^{u}nas pādshahạn ại gulām yus akha āgạs p^{y}eṭh bēvophāī ka^{i}re tas kya vāt^{i} karun yi vuthus gulām phīrit pādshahạn tas gatsi kale tsatun beye bastạ vālạñy pādshahạm bo vanāi dalīlạ tsạ thāv tam tat kan.

7. dop^{u} nas gulāmạn su ås pādshahạ ak suy gau dohạ aki sālạs shikārạs kunuy zun sạ^{i}th åsus pạz vōt jāyạ akis lajis trạs banān ches nạ kuni vuchun jāye akis āb^{a} sreha hyu at^{i} dyutun barshạ sạ^{i}th dob^{a}hạnạ kurun bag^{a}lạ manzạ pyālạ lodun at pyālạs āb h^{y}ütun chun ās pạz tsununas trạ^{i}vit beye borun yi āb^{a} pyālạ h^{y}ütun ch^{y}un ås beye yi pạz tsununạs trạ^{i}vit doye laṭ^{i} tsununạs trạ^{i}vit pādshahạs khut zahạr treyimi laṭ^{i} burun dach^{i}nạ athạ chu at pyālạs tap kạ^{i}rit khåvur athạ thåvun nebạr yüthuy h^{y}ütun chun t^{y}uthuy āu̯ pạz tsununas trạ^{i}vit dithas am^{i} tap

night. Now the first watch of the night fell to the elder of the two princes, and my Master tells me that at this time the King and Queen went to their bed.

6. Furthermore, my Master tells me :—

The guard stood by, watching and warding the royal pair, and straight in front of them he saw a great python begin to lower itself from the ceiling. He fixed his eyes upon it, and as it approached the body of the Queen he ran up and struck at it with his sword. He hacked it into little pieces and thrust them under the bed. He then wrapped the blade of his sword in cotton-wool, and some of this he used to wipe the body of the Queen, "For," said he to himself, "haply some of the python's poison may have touched her." This, you must understand, was his sole and only reason for wiping her. But just then the King awoke, and he saw that his guard had come near him with a naked sword in his hand. By this time the period of his watch had passed, and the watch of the second guard was due. He approached, and the King said to him, "O guard, what should be done to the man who is traitor to his lord?" Replied the guard, "Sire, his head should be cut off, and he should be flayed alive. But, your Majesty, I would tell to thee a story. Prithee, lend thou me thine ear."

7. Said the guardsman :—

"Once upon a time there was a King. One day he went a-hunting all alone. He took with him his falcon, and when he had come to a certain spot he fell athirst, but could find no means of alleviation. A length he saw in one place a little moisture (on the face of a cliff). He thrust in his spear to make a hole, and pulled forth a cup from his pocket, which he filled with the water as it trickled forth. As he began to take it up to drink his falcon flew at him and upset it. So he filled the cup again, and was about to drink when again the falcon upset it. Poisonous anger rose in the heart of the King. The third time he filled the cup, holding it with his right hand, leaving his left arm free. Just as he began to drink, again came the falcon

pādshahạn rutun latan thal hitsạnas pakạ ze kạr^{y}inas tān yi yeli mōrun pat^{a} p^{y}ūrus atạt^{y} vuny trēsh chayen na gau vuch^{i} ne at ābas āsi na kunạ āgur pakān chu pādshāh vōt^{i} jai akis vuchun at^{i} shah māra ak shungit am^{i} suy nērān ā̊s^{u} kạn^{i} lāl yi āb ā̊s zahạr yi chus vanān ạmis pādshahạs har ga kyēy su pādshāh sa trēsh ch^{y}aye h^{y}e su marih^{y}e vun^{y}ai sargēh kari h^{y}e su pādshāh tas pạzus mā mārihe pādshahạm sạy che dalīl sargi gatsē kariñy.

8. muk^{a}lyau ạmisund pahạr t^{y}e āu̯ treyimi sund pahar ze gai pānạs b^{y}ēth^{i} pādshāh chu bēdār dapān chu ạmis treyimis pah^{a}rạ vālis dapān chus ại gulām yus akha āgạs p^{y}eṭh dagāi ka^{i}ri tas kya vāt^{ye} karun dop^{u}nas phīrit ạm^{i} gulāmạn su gatsē pādshahạm sang sār karun pādshahạm sargī gatse kariñy bu vanāi dalīla tsạ thāvum pādshahạm kan.

9. dapān chus su ā̊s sōdāgār^{a} ak su sōdāgạr ā̊s setā bakhtāvār tạm^{i} süy pyau muh^{y}im tạm^{i} süy ā̊s hūn byāk sōdāgārạ ās dop^{u}nas yi hūn mā kạn^{a}han dop^{u}nas kạnan dop^{u}nas karus mul kurạnas mul rupia hat nyū sōdāgārạn yi hūn drāu̯ sōdā h^{y}et vōt jāye akis lajis rāt rāt^{a}li p^{y}ēz tsūr nyū has yi māl hūn chu vuchān am^{i} kur^{i} nạ k^{y}ē ti sadau phul ghāsh sodāgạr gau bēdār vuchun tạ māl nạ kuni dapān chu yat kya gōm āu̯ yi hūn am^{i} kạr nas tap pushākas chus lamān hūn drāu̯ bro-bro patạ-patạ chus sōdāgār vāte nō vun maidānas akis manz vuchun at^{i} tsūrau thāu̯ mut am^{i} sund māl parze āu̯ vun ạnun panun māl yi ā̊sus tạ ti beye ā̊s yimau tsūrau beyen sōdāgārạn hund nyumut titi ạnun vāt^{a}nā̊vun panạnạs ḍērạs gau setā khush dopun

and upset it. The King grasped the bird, and holding it under his feet tore off both its wings. As soon as he had killed it he was filled with regret, and could not drink the water. He went to look for the source of the spring, and when he had found it he saw there a huge python lying asleep, and from its mouth spittle was dripping into the streamlet. The water was poisonous." And, added the guard to His Majesty, "If that King had drunk that water he would have died, and if he had only inquired into the matter beforehand he would not have killed the falcon. Sire, that is my story. Thou shouldst scrutinize before deciding."

8. His watch also came to an end, and there came the third watch. The first two sat down to rest themselves, but the King was still wakeful, and he spoke to his third guard, saying, "O guard, what should be done to him who showeth faithlessness to his lord?" Said he in answer, "He should be stoned to death, but first, sire, investigation should be made. I would tell to thee a story. Lend thou me, sire, thine ear."

9. Said the third guardsman :—

"There was once upon a time a merchant blessed with all prosperity. But evil times befell him, so that he had naught left of his possessions but a dog. Another merchant asked him if he would sell it, and thereto did he agree. 'What is the price?' and they fixed it at a hundred rupees. So the second merchant paid the price and took away the dog. Shortly afterwards he went on a journey with some goods to do merchanting, and halted for the night at a certain place. In the night-time there came thieves and took away all his property. The dog watched them, but made no sound. When the morn blossomed forth the merchant awoke, and could not find his goods. While he was wondering what had befallen him, the dog came up and caught hold of his coat and pulled it. The dog led him out, going in front, while the merchant followed along behind. He brought him to a certain plain, and there he saw the spot where the thieves had stored his goods. He recognized them, and brought back to his lodging not only what had been taken from him, but all that these thieves had stolen from other merchants. He was filled with joy, and said to himself, 'That

tạmis saudāgārạs tōg^{u}nạ ạmis hūnis mul karun tạmis å̊s pyümut muhim tami mukhe togus nạ.

10. dapān vustād ạmis hūnis kurun mul rupiạs pānz hạt lichin chit yi hāy ṭsin^{y}an ạmis hūnis nāl dop^{u}nas ṭsạ gaṭs panạnis kāvạndas nishin yi chit h^{y}et gau hūn vōt nazdīk ạmis sōdāgārạs sōdāgarạn vuch parze nā̂ vun yi hūn dopun panenen bāṭsen dop^{u}nak hūn āụ phīrit ạm^{i} kur^{i} k^{y}ạ tāñy tahsīr ami ṭsunuk ka^{i}rit balki chus chālānạ nāl sōdāgār gau phikri dopun vun kya kare rupia hat gōm kharj koḍun bạndūk lāy^{a}nas tạ mārun yeli mårun tạ adạ ph^{y}ūrus gōs nazdīk bo vuch^{a} ha ạmis kya kākad chu nāl^{i} yohāy kurạnas nālạ muṭs^{a}run tạ vuchun at^{i} lyükhmut rupias pānz hat ad^{a} ph^{y}ūrus setā pādshahạm sāy che dalīl sargī gaṭse karin^{y} hargạ hāy su sōdāgār guḍen^{y}i vuch^{a}he ạmis hūnis kyah chu nāl su hūn ma mạrihe gau ạmisund pahạr.

11. āu ṭsūrimis gulāmạsạnz dalīl ṭsūrimis gulāmạs vanān pādshah ai gulām yüs akha āgạs p^{y}eṭh bē vuphāī ka^{i}ri tas kya vāt^{i} karun dop^{u}nas gulāman pādshạhạm tas gaṭsi sar ṭsatun shehera manzạ dūr kaḍun pādshạhạm bu vanai dalīla ṭsạ tāvum kan dopān chus gulām su å̊s pādshahạ ak ạmis suy å̊s nechiv zạ timạnai moye panen^{i} mōj pādshạhạn kạr vuruḍz zạnānạ sa gaye pādshāh zādạn don vur^{a}mōj pādshāh zādạ zạ å̊s^{i} sabạkas tōrạ āy ạmis vurạ māj^{i} niyak salām lālaụ nigīnau trå̊m thå̊vuk ạmis bōnt^{a} kan^{i} yim gai beye sabạkas doha doha che karān pādshāh bāye dạj panen^{y} rāy kya dạjis bo karạha yiman pādshāh zādạn sạ^{i}th guna dohạ aki vunun yimạn pādshāhzādạn don me sạ^{i}th ka^{i}r^{y}u guna

merchant was not able to put the true value on his dog. Hard times had fallen on him, and he had to take what he could get."

10. Moreover my Master said:—

"He put the value of the dog at five hundred rupees, and wrote a note of hand to that amount. This he tied to the dog's neck, and told him to go home with it to his old master. The dog set forth and arrived at his old master's house. The latter saw him and recognized him. He said to his people, 'Here is this dog come back. No doubt he hath done some fault. Moreover, there is an invoice to that effect tied to his neck.' So he became filled with anxiety. 'What,' cried he, 'am I to do? For I have spent the hundred rupees.' So he went and got a gun, fired it at the dog, and killed it. When he had killed it, he felt sorry and went up to look at the paper that was tied to its neck. When he took it off and opened it he saw written on it an order for five hundred rupees. Then, indeed, he felt very sorry. Your Majesty, that is my story. One should always scrutinize. If that merchant had first looked to see what was tied to the dog's neck he would not have killed it."

With that the term of his watch expired.

11. Now came the watch of the fourth guard, and this is his story. The King said to the fourth guard, "O guard, what should be done to the man who is a traitor to his lord?" Replied the guard, "Your Majesty, his head should be cut off, and he should be banished from the city. But, sire, I would tell thee a story. Lend thou me thine ear."

And the fourth guardsman said:—

"Once upon a time there was a King who had two sons. Their mother died, and the King made a second marriage, and thus gave the two princes a stepmother. While they were still at their lessons they brought her a tray filled with rubies and other jewels as a complimentary present. They laid it before her, and then went back to their lessons. They passed each day in this manner, and at length a design was aroused in the Queen. And this was her design. She said to herself, 'I would do sin with these young princes.' One day she said to them, 'Come ye and do sin with

yimau duphas ʦạ chak sāñ^{y} mọ̄j ʦ^{y}eta asi vāt^{i} na pādshāh zādạ gai sabạkas pādshāh āu̯ dạrbār murkhas kạ^{i}rit vōt mahalạ kān pādshāh bāyạ trup^{a}nas dạrvāzạ dạrvāzạ ches na thāvān dop^{u}nas yi kyāzi vuʦus pādshah bāy dop^{u}nas bu chạsạ ch^{y}ān^{i} kulai kinạ chān^{y}en nechevin hạnz dopunas pādshạhan ti kya gau dop^{u}nas tim ām l^{y}ekan pādshāh chus dạpān vun^{y} kya chu salā pādshāh bāy ches dạpān me gaʦe tạ hanzạ vālinjạ zạ timạ kh^{y}ema bo adạ kya thāvai dạrvāzạ pādshạhạn dyut hukm vazīrạs dop^{u}nas yim shahzādạ zạ dik marạvāt^{a}lan at^{i} yiman karạn vālinjạ zạ gau vazīr vōt ʦāt^{a}hāl yet^{i} yim shahzādạ zạ å̄s yiman kun kạrạn nazar setā gạ̄s yim pādshah zādạ zạ khush dilas pyōs insāf dop^{u}nak ʦal^{y}u yạmi shah^{a}ra dūr ʦạl^{y}.

12. dapān vustād mārevātạlan dyut hukạm vazīrạn mār^{y}ūk hūn zạ mārạvāt^{a}lau mạ^{i}r^{y} hūn zạ ka^{i}rik yimạn vālïñjạ zạ lazak ṭạkis manz gai h^{y}et pādshāh bāye thå̄u̯ dạrvāzạ pādshah chu karān pādshāhi tạt^{i}.

13. shahzādạ zạ āy ʦalān biyis pādshahạs nish pādshahạn rạ^{i}ṭ^{y} yim gulām guḍeñyuk pahạr āu̯ ạmis bạḍis hihis shahzādạs chu shạmā dazān pād^{a}shāhạ sand^{i} zạ bạ̄ʦ che palạngas p^{y}eṭh arāmas yimạniy s^{y}ud vasān chu shạhmār yi gulām chu kaḍān shamshēr ạmis shạhmārạs chu karān tukrạ ami patạ chu shamshēr^{i} hạndis t^{y}ēgas valān pamb ạmis pādshah bāye hạndis badạnas å̄s vutherān yi zahạr ạmis shahmārạ sund dopun ạmis mā āsim shahmārạ sund zahạr å̄s vuthạrān^{y} tạ pādshah gau bēdār

me'; but they replied, 'Thou art our mother, between thee and us such may not be,' and then went off to their lessons. After this the King came home, when he had dismissed his court, and went to the harem; but the Queen locked the door against him and refused to open it. Said he, 'What meaneth this?' Then up and answered she, 'Is it of thee that I am the wife, or am I the wife of thy two sons?' Said the King, 'What is it that hath happened?' Said she, 'They came to me and asked of me indecent things.' Said he, 'What wouldest thou have me to do?' and she replied, 'I must have their two hearts, that I may eat them. Then, and then only, will I open for thee the door.' So the King gave the command to his Vizier, and said to him, 'Make these two princes over to the executioners, that they may tear out both their hearts.' So the Vizier took his leave and came to the school where the princes were doing their lessons. He took one look at them and saw that they were both exceeding fair to behold, and pity filled his soul. He said to them, 'Flee ye far from this city.' So they fled."

12. And moreover my Master said:—

"The Vizier told the executioners to kill two dogs. They did so, and tore out their hearts, which they placed upon a charger and carried to the Queen. Then she opened the door, and the King went in, and there did he sway his sceptre.

13. "The two princes in their flight came to another King, who appointed them to be his bodyguards. The first watch of the night falls to the elder prince. A lamp is burning, and shows the King and Queen asleep upon their bed. Straight in front of them is descending a huge python. The guard draws his sword, and hacks it into little pieces. After this he wraps up the blade of his sword in cotton-wool, and some of this he uses to wipe off the python's poison from the body of the Queen. 'For,' said he to himself, 'haply some of the python's poison may be on her.' While he was still wiping her the King awoke. Said the King to himself, 'he hath

dop pādshạhạn yi ām mārạni pādshạhạm sạy che dalīl har^{a}gāk^{y}ēy su pād^{a}shāh sar^{a} ka^{i}rihe panen^{y}en nechevin p^{y}eṭh mā diyehe hukm mār^{a}vāṭạlan tuh^{y} mār^{y}ūk adạ gai tim hūnạ zạ mārạ pādshạhạm agar bāvar karak na su pād^{a}shāh ås sōnuy mōr yi pādshāh gåk tsạ yi kya che shamshēr at^{i} kya chiy palạngas thal shạhmār gan^{y}i ka^{i}rit.

14. setā gåk pādshah khush ak bōy thåvun vazīr byāk boy banåvun pādshah.

come to kill me.' Sire, that is my story. If that King had made inquiry he would not have ordered the executioners to kill his own sons, nor would those dogs have gone to death. Sire, if you believe not my story, then know that that King was our father, and this King wast thou. So, here is the sword, and there under the bed is the python cut to pieces."

14. The King became mightily pleased on hearing this explanation. And one brother he made his Vizier, while the other he made a Pasha.

IX. GRĒST BĀYE HAṆZ TA̩ MÅSH TULA̩RI-HAṆZ KAT

1. Dapān vustād yi grēst bāy ås ʦa̩ja̩ma̩ʦ kami bāpat kārdāran muka̩ daman åsus kurmut zulm ami bāpat che ʦa̩jma̩ʦ vā̩ʦ vanas akis manz otuy vā̩ʦus māch tula̩r amis āyi zabān dapān che amis grēsta̩ bāye ʦa̩ kyāzi chak ʦa̩jma̩ʦ dopᵘnas grēstᵃ bāye mʸe chu ga̩mut zulm ami dopᵘnas phērit mā̃ch tula̩ri mʸe ti chu ga̩mut zulm bo ches vadān ʦa̩ thāu̯tam kan vanān māch tula̩r grēst bāye kun.

yi tai vesī paran pʸimōs karōs zārᵃpār ı
budai che sai māch tula̩r vanuk jāna̩vār ॥

2. kohᵃ kohā̩y yūra añyām åsus ayāl bār ı
balai pʸiyen hāpat gānas vanān ʦāny nam lār ॥

3. pōtʸen tasa̩nden ālⁱnāsh kurun sāhībō āyna ār ı
budai che sai māch tula̩r vanuk jānᵃvār ॥

4. dapān amis grēsta̩ bāye yi māch tula̩r dopᵘnas yi hāl kur nam vana̩ manza̩ hāpa̩tan vunʸ ʦajēs vaʦās grēsta̩ gara̩s dapʸām kare rahat vuch ta̩ vuny kya kairim yi grost thāu̯ ta̩ kan bu kya vanai.

thanyā matit ku̩tha thāu̯nam mōteny chem bāndⁱhāl ı
bāgenⁱ āya̩s grēst gara̩s sā̩i mʸe gayem gāl ॥

5. drātis sā̩ⁱtin kashᵃ yeli ʦetⁱnam kā̩ⁱtya ka̩tis mār ı
budai che sai māch tula̩r vanuk jāna̩vār ॥

IX. THE TALE OF THE FARMER'S WIFE AND THE HONEY-BEE

1. Saith my Master :—

Here was a farmer's wife who had fled from her home. And why had she done this ? It was because the village overseer and the headman had shown her tyranny, and so she had fled. She reached a forest, and there there came a honey-bee. Behold, speech came to the honey-bee, and she saith to the farmer's wife, "Why hast thou fled ?" And she replied that tyranny had been shown to her. Then answered her the honey-bee, "I also have suffered tyranny, and therefore do I lament. Prithee, lend thou me thine ear." And thus speaketh the honey-bee to the farmer's wife :—

Prithee hither come, my friend. Let us fall at God's feet, and make our prayers to Him.

Lo, I am thy honey-bee, a poor winged creature of the forest.

2. From hill to hill did I collect my flower-nectar, and become possessed of manifold progeny.

May ruin seize that ruthless bear, for he it was that drove me to the forests.

3. He utterly destroyed my little ones. O God, why came there no pity to Thee ?

Lo, I am thy honey-bee, a poor winged creature of the forest.

4. Quoth the honey-bee to the farmer's wife, "Thus and thus was I driven from the forest by the bear, and now I fled. Then alighted I at a farmer's house, and he said unto me, 'I will give thee peace and comfort.' Behold what that farmer did unto me. Prithee, lend thou me thine ear. What shall I say unto thee ?"

He made ready a hive as an abode for me, and rubbed it o'er with fresh butter. It became a prison of death for me.

It was my fate that brought me to the farmer's house, and, of a truth, that fate was humiliation.

5. With a sickle he cut off my honey-combs, and thereby there rose upon him the guilt of countless murders.

Lo, I am thy honey-bee, a poor winged creature of the forest.

6. moklau ạmi māch tulạri vanit panun då̄d vu che dapān ạmis grēst^{a} bāye chiyai kyē gạmut tsạti van vanān che vo vanān grēst^{a} bāy dapān ches bōz m^{y}e kya zulm chu gạmut.

azạl chāvun chu samsāras chetal vasạn^{i} jāi ।
budai chesai grēst^{a} bāy yōr nai rōzạn^{i} āy ॥

7. sōntạ yeli mut^{a}sạ̄^{i}th^{i} grēst^{y}en dīlāsạ dinạ hai āy ।
mudr^{y}au kathau yerā bạrạk zālạs valenạ āy ॥

8. harde vizē dard motuk lāyine tim hai āy ।
budai chesai grēst^{a} bāy yōr nai rōzạn^{i} āy ॥

9. yim phal vavim māje zemīni tim hai papit āy ।
sumbrit sā^{i}rit kalạs ka^{i}rim hatạ bud^{i} khạ̄ris drāy ॥

10. chaklạ chaklạ mukadam tạ paṭ^{a}vār^{i} tōlạni tim hai āy ।
budai chesai grēst^{a} bāy yōr nai rōzạn^{i} āy ॥

11. å̄zīz tạ miskīn kạ̄i t^{y}a visyạ̄i halam dạ̄r dạ̄r āy ।
halam dit^{a}mak mebar bari suy chu muklan pāy ॥

12. kalạma sạ̄^{i}tin savāb likhan yit^{a}nai lagik grāy ।
budai chesai grēst^{a} bāy yōr nai rōzạn^{i} āy ॥

6. So finished that honey-bee the story of her pain, and now saith she to that farmer's wife, "If aught hath happened unto thee, do thou also tell it." Then speaketh the farmer's wife and saith to her, "Hear what hath happened unto me."

Each soul must dree its weird, and there is a place below to which it must descend.
Lo, I am thy farmer's wife. We came not to this world as an abiding place.

7. In the spring the tax-gatherers came to the farmers with soft encouragement.
With sweet words did they fill their bellies, and enclosed them as in a net.

8. In the autumn they forgot all their kindness. They it was who came to beat us.
Lo, I am thy farmer's wife. We came not to this world as an abiding place.

9. Crops sowed I in mother earth, and they it was that sprung up and ripened.
I collected and piled them on the threshing-floor, hundreds of *kharwārs* [1] in weight.

10. From village-circuit to village-circuit to weigh the produce came the headman and the accountant.
Lo, I am thy farmer's wife. We came not to this world as an abiding place.

11. How many of the poor and needy, O friend, came as beggars holding out their lap-cloths!
Their skirts I filled and filled, for that giveth an assurance of salvation.

12. The recording angels will write down with their pens the reward of these good actions, so that they may ne'er be shaken.
Lo, I am thy farmer's wife. We came not to this world as an abiding place.

[1] A *kharwār* weighs about a hundredweight and a half.

X. RĀJA VIKẠRMĀJITEÑY KAT

1. dapān vustād mahñyiu̯ ʦōr ạ̄s^{i} pakān vat^{i} āk broho maidān ạt^{i} maidānas yeli h^{y}ütuk pakun lạg^{i} vaneni pānevāñy talau van^{i}tō dalīlạ yim maidān karōn^{y} patạ kan^{i} āk byāk shahʦa ạmis dopuk ʦạ vantạ dalīla yi maidān muk^{a}lāvạ hun ạm^{i} dop^{u}nak phērit boh^{a}sạ vanemo^{v} dalīl dalīl hasạ vanemau kathe pānʦ pānʦen kathen gaʦe nam din^{i} rupias pānʦ hat yimau dop^{u} has phērit ʦōr hat dimoi ʦōr zan^{i} pānʦ^{y}ūm hat gai panenuy vanse kathe pānʦ dop^{u}nak.

dyār hase chu saf^{a}ras ।
yār hase chu na ās^{a}nas ॥
āsh^{i}nāv hasạ chu ās^{a}nas ।

gaye tre kathe beye ze kathe hasạ ch^{y}au

sạ zạnānạ ch^{y}auvna paneñy ।
yesạ nạ āsi pānes sạ̄^{i}th ॥

beye hasạ

yus rātạs bēdār rōzi ।
suy hasạ za^{i}ni rāje Vikarmājiteñy kūr ॥

vañye nak yimạ kathe pānʦ yim chus dapān van sạ dalīl yi chuk dapān me hasạ vañye mōv kathe pānʦ mil^{e}vuk laḍāi yim chus dapān rupias ʦōr hat n^{y}it dalīl k^{y}e vañyit na ma^{i}dān chu vuñye pakenai ạmis lå̄yuk yimau ʦōrau zạ^{i}nyau ạm^{i} dop^{u} nak pakyu sa yeti kis pādshahạs nish yisu dapi ti karau.

X. THE TALE OF RĀJĀ VIKRAMÂDITYA[1]

1. This is what my Master saith to me :—

Four men were once going along the road, and they came to a wide open plain. As they entered it they began to say to each other, "Come, let us tell a story to while away the journey across the plain." After a time they were joined by another man, and they asked him to tell a story to help the journey along. Said he, "Sirs, I will tell you a story. Moreover, sirs, as a story I will tell you five things,[2] but for the five things you must pay me five hundred rupees." Replied they, "We are four, and will give thee four hundred. The fifth hundred must be paid by thee as the fifth of us. So tell us, prithee, sir, the five things." Said he to them :—

"Money, sirs, is for a journey.
A friend, sirs, is for when there is no money.
A near relation, sirs, is for when there is money.

That makes three things, and, sirs, there are two others :—

Thou canst only call thy wife thine own so long as she be with thee.

And, again, sirs :—

He only will win Rājā Vikramâditya's daughter
Who keepeth awake by night."

When he told them these five things, they say to him, "Now, sir, tell a story." But he replies, "I have told you, sirs, the five things." At this they began to quarrel. Cry they, "You have taken our four hundred rupees; but, sir, you have not told us any story. We have not yet got across the plain." So the four gave him a drubbing. Then he made this proposal, "Come, sirs, to the King of this country, and let us abide by what he says."

[1] The Indian monarch of glorious, pious, and immortal memory. He is throughout entitled "Rājā", as opposed to the Musalman word "Pādshāh" used for the real hero of the story. In translating I retain "Rājā" unchanged, and translate "Pādshāh" by "King".

[2] The whole of the subsequent quarrel depends on the double meaning of the word *kath*, which like the Hindi *bāt* means not only "story" but also "statement" and "thing". The four thought they were buying five stories, but the fifth was only selling five statements. I translate *kath* by "thing", as the nearest English word with a similar indefinite meaning. On the other hand I translate *dalīl* by "story". Its meaning is not indefinite.

2. dapān vustād vāt^{i} pādshahas nish d^{y}ut pheryād tsorau zạ^{i}nyau dop^{u}has pādshahạm yim shakhtsạn kh^{y}aiy asi rupias tsōr hat dopun vanemō^{u} kathe pānts pādshahạn dop ạmis shakhtsas van^{a}sạ kya vunthak yi votus phērịt pādshahạm bo vanai kathe pānts rupias pānts hat gatse nam din^{y} adạ vanai bo kathe pānts pādshahạn ka^{i}r^{y} rupias pānts hat dithin ạmis shakhtsas yim ka^{i}rin yim band pāne ka^{i}rin kāma ạm^{i} pādshahan pādshāhīhund poshāk trā̊vun gadoi yiye hund poshāk pōrun beye gandin lāl^{a}sat gandin mats^{y}e drāu̯ yimạ kathe pānts sar kar^{a}ni.

3. dapān vustād gudeñy drāu̯ beñye hạndis shah^{a}ras kun gur chus khasun vōt^{i} yeli n^{y}ạzīk at beñye hạndis shah^{a}ras lazun shech^{y} ạmis beñye me kyā chu p^{y}ümut mohim bo kya yimạha tōr^{i} ạmi lazạnas beñye phut phērit shech^{y} me kya rōzan pāmạ vạr^{a}vis manz phut phērit laz^{a}nas beye shech^{y} me yeli nạ bani tōr^{i} yün tōt^{y}i gats^{y}em ladun naptsas k^{y}ētsā lade hamai tat gatse gand karun p^{y}ethạ gats^{y}es mohạr kareñy paneñy ami kạr beñye kāma lodun paneñye kyenzi batạ hana yā ts^{y}uṭ yā shūts p^{y}eṭhạ kar^{a}nas paneñy mohạr korun revānạ ạmis bạyis tạm^{i} yeli vuch beñye hạnz mohạr rotun ạt^{i} thā̊vun dạbāvit.

4. drāu̯ yārisạnzi vat^{i} yeli vōt n^{y}ạzīk sōzun ạmis mahñyu yār hasạ ạy pādshāhī chesna so hasạ chiy mohim zad yārạn yeli bōz drāu̯ vōt ạmis yārạs nish dapān chus hā yārạ kat^{y}i gōhạm yōr pạ^{i}dạ pakān chi dunuvai. ạmis ā̊s miskīnī hund poshāk nāl^{y} dapān chus yār yi kal^{a}ti shāhī dittạ m^{y}e yi myōn

2. Saith my Master :—

They went to the King and the four laid their complaint before him. "This fellow," said they, "hath cheated us to the tune of four hundred rupees, for he promised to tell us five things." The King asked him, "What was it that thou saidst to them?" And he up and replied, "Sire, I will tell thee the five things, but thou must pay me for them rupees five hundred. Then, and only then, can I tell these five things to thee." So the King sent for five hundred rupees, and gave them to him. (After he had told them) he tied up the money in his pouch, and the King did a deed. He doffed his royal garments, and donned those of beggary. Then he tied seven rubies under his arm and went forth to test these five things.

3. Moreover my Master said :—

First of all he went to the city where dwelt his sister. He mounted his horse, and when he arrived there he sent her this message, "I am fallen into poverty; so what else could I do but come to thee." And this was the word which she sent back, "Verily, I shall be put to shame in my father-in-law's house (if thou come to me)." Again he sent her these words in answer, "If it be not possible for me to come to thee, thou shouldst at least send me somewhat wherewith to fill my belly; and if thou send it, fasten thou it up carefully, and set thine own seal upon it." So this sister did a deed. She sent him a little rice in her bowl—it may have been orts, or it may have been fresh food. Upon it she set her own seal, and despatched it to her brother. As soon as he saw his sister's seal he accepted it, and there and then he buried it and hid it in the ground.

4. Then he set forth upon the road to his friend. When he came near he sent a man on to say, "My friend, I am come to thee. I have no more royal state, for I have been struck by the blow of poverty." And when his friend heard this he went forth and came to his friend, and cried, "Ah, my friend! Wherefore hast thou come to show thyself here (so far from my door)?" So together the two walk on. As they walked the friend seeth that the King is clothed in the weeds of poverty, and saith to him, "My

poshāk tsunthạ tsạ yi ās^{a}nạ bōz^{a}nạ yi chu ạmis miskīnī hund poshāk yi ās bōz^{a}nạ kal^{a}ti shāhī kami mukhạ mahabat sạ̄^{i}th gau vā^{i}t^{i} yārạsund garạ yārạn kür^{a}nas ziāfat lāy^{a}kạ pādshāh sap^{a}ñyes ottāñy zạ kathạ sar.

5. drāu̯ vuñy zạnānạ hạndis shah^{a}ras kun vōt at shehạras and kun at^{i} å̄s buḍ zạnānạ byūṭ ạmisạndi ga^{i}ri dopun ạmis buje zạnānạ ditam drōt bu anạ yạmis guris kh^{y}ut gāsạ drāu̯ gāsạ anạni vuchun at^{i} gāsạ maidānạ ạt^{y} chu lōnān yi å̄s rakh pādshahạsunz å̄s lāḍān tạhạl^{y} nyūk rạtit panạnis mējeras nish koruk kạ̄d rāt āye ạmis chu gatsān pạ̄^{i}dạ zạnānạ ak ạmis mējeras ziāfat h^{y}et yi chu bihit palangas p^{y}eth ziāfat thāu̯nas bōnt^{a} kan^{i} ạt^{i} vat^{i} khyeni don^{a} vai hana h^{a}rēyek yi dyutuk ạmis kạ̄^{i}dis kurhas ālau hatō kạ̄^{i}dyau yi khyau sạ̄^{i}ñy tseṭhan kạ̄^{i}d rut khyå̄n ạt^{i} chu panạni jāye behit yimau doyau kạr tamis kuri at palangas phut tạr kuruk ālau ạmis kạ̄^{i}dis tsạ vuch tạ yat palangas phut tạr tsima tạgi ạm^{i} dop^{u}nak phīrit āñy tagimna hamsai ch^{y}um ch^{y}ān dophas vulạ vōt ot ạmis zạnānạ parzạ nå̄u̯ panun khāvand ạm^{i} å̄s parzạ nå̄u̯ muts brōnt yeli yi battạhạn dits^{a} has yi zạnānạ che dapān ạmis mējeras vuñy kya karau yi chu myōn khāvand yi gatse mārun rātas rāt hukm d^{y}ütun mārạvāt^{a}lan dop^{u}nak nīyūn yi kạ̄^{i}d gatse mārun vālinje gatsyes yūr^{i} anạn^{y} nyūk yi kạ̄^{i}d shah^{a}ras nebar ạm^{i} dyut^{a}nak savāl m^{y}e trạ̄v^{i}toh yelạ bo chạlạha atạ but Khudāyạs kun karạha zārạ pār trå̄vuk yelạ vuchạn āb^{a} hạnā cholun atih atạ but

friend, prithee present me with this royal robe that thou dost wear, and put on my poor garment instead thereof." For he looked upon the King's garb not as the garb of beggary, but thought of it as a royal robe. And wherefore that? It was because of the love he bare him. They went on and reached the friend's house, and there the friend made him a feast—such a feast as one should lay before a King.

In this way the King had tested two of the things.

5. Then went he forth to the city where dwelt his wife. When he had reached the outskirts he made his lodging in the house of an old woman, and asked of her a sickle that he might cut grass for his horse. So he went out to fetch the fodder, and came to a mead where he began to cut the grass. Now this mead was in the home farm of the king of that land, and the grooms ran up and seized him, and carried him to their officer, the Master of the Horse. They shut him up in prison, and when night fell he seeth a woman coming along with a dish of dainty meats for the Master of the Horse. He was sitting on a bedstead. She laid the dish before him, and they both sat down upon the floor to eat it. A few scraps remained over, and these they gave the prisoner. They called to him, "Ho, thou prisoner, eat thou these scraps and orts of ours." The prisoner accepted them and ate. And while he remained sitting by himself the two clipped and toyed together till the joint of the bedstead broke. Again they called to the prisoner, "Prithee see, the joint of this bed hath broken. Haply thou hast wit enough to mend it." He answered, "Yea, why should I not have wit therefor? My neighbours are carpenters." Said they, "Come hither." So he came, and then the woman recognized him as her own husband; though he had recognized her before when they gave him the scraps of food. So saith she to the Master of the Horse, "What now are we to do? This is my husband, he must be killed this very night of nights." So the Master of the Horse gave his command to the executioners, "Take ye away this prisoner. He must be slain. Bring ye us back his heart." So they led him forth outside the city, and to them made he a petition. "Let me free," quoth he, "that I may wash my hands and face and make my prayers to God before I die. So they loosed his bonds, and he

Khudā sābạs kun korun zārạ pār atạ p^{y}ōs yiman lālạn satạn p^{y}eṭh yim tat^{y} åsis gand^{a}mạty^{i} matsạ yimạn dopun mārạvāt^{a}lan tsun hatạ sạ m^{y}e trạvyu yelạ nom chu lāl sat tsōr chu toh^{y}i tsun zan^{y}en tre chu m^{y}ēn tohi nish.

6. ot^{u}tāñy ka^{i}rin tsōr kathe sare påntsim kath gayạs mạshit āụ̂ vōt panen garạ beye vanān chu timạn pāntsen zanen vạnyu sạ kya van^{y}au toh^{y}i pānts kathe yi votus phot phērit pādshạhạm katse kathe ka^{i}rit sare dop^{u}nak pādshạhạn tsōr kathe yimau dophas kusạ kusạ dop^{u}nak pādshạhạn.

ås^{i} nāv ch^{y}ạ pạz^{i} pạ^{i}th^{y} ās^{i}nas |
yār chu na ās^{i}nas titi puzuy ||
zạnānạ sạ chenạ paneñy yạsinạ pānas sā^{i}th che titi puzuy |
dyār che bakār safạras titi puzuy ||

yimạ tsōr kathe karimau sar vuñy vạn^{y}ūm pạnts^{y}um kath dop^{u}nas ạm^{i} shakhtsạn phut phērit rup^{i}yạ hat gats^{y}em dyun dyutạnas pādshạhạn dop^{u}nas.

yüs rātạs bēdār rōzi |
suy z^{y}ạni rāje Vikarmājiteñy kūr ||

7. pādshạhạn kạr kåm lågun fakīr gau vōt rājạ Vikarmājitun garạ nazạr bāzau kạr nazạr khabạr dārau niye khabạr ạmis rājas dop^{u}has rājạ sābạ fakirạ ak gomut pạ^{i}dạ yohoi dapān bu z^{y}ēnan rājạsạnz kūr rājạ vanān chuk phut phērit az tāñy kạ^{i}tya rājạ zādạ gạmạt^{y} at^{y}e māre vun gau yi fakīr havālạ^{y} Khudā adạ yā lasạ yā mạri gats^{y}u khạ^{i}lyūn kuṭhis manz yạt^{i} yi rājạsunz kūr ås palang trạvhas shērit khut fakīr palangas p^{y}eṭh ạmis khåtūni ditsạn z^{y}ēr

found a little water, wherein he washed his hands and face, and made his prayers to God, the Master. As he thus did his hands fell upon the seven rubies that he had tied beneath his arm when setting forth upon his journey. Then said he to the executioners, "O sirs, let ye me go free. Here be these seven rubies. Keep ye four of them, one for each of you four, and keep the remaining three for me."

6. In this way he had tested four of the things, but the fifth he had forgotten. So he returned home, and asketh the five men, "Sirs, tell ye me what those five things were." Then up and answered that man, "Sire, how many of these things hast thou tested?" Quoth he, "Four." "Which ones?" they asked. Said the King:—

"True is it—a near relation is for when there is money.
True also is it—a friend is for when there is no money.
True also is it—thou canst only call thy wife thine own so long as she be with thee.
True also is it—money is useful on a journey.

These four things that ye told me have I tested. Now tell ye me the fifth." Replied that man to him, "A hundred rupees must thou give me." The King gave it, and he said:—

"He only will win Rājā Vikramâditya's daughter
Who keepeth awake by night."

7. And the King did a deed. He put on the garb of a mendicant faqīr. He went forth and reached Rājā Vikramâditya's palace. The discerners then discerned him, and the newsmen gave the news to the Rājā. Said they, "Your Majesty, there hath appeared a faqīr, and he saith, 'The Rājā's daughter I would win,'" And the Rājā said to them in answer, "Up to to-day, how many princes have gone to their death! Now hath this faqīr committed himself to God, that He may decide whether he live or die. Go ye, and lead ye him up to the chamber." And in the chamber where was the Rājā's daughter, a bed was ready spread. The faqīr climbed up upon it, and gave the lady a push. He conversed with her, and

kạ^{i}rin ạmis sạ̄^{i}th kathe kathe ka^{i}rit kạrun kåm at poshākas korun shakạl insān hish pāne drāu̯ dūr pahạn byūt naz^{ə}ri shamā chu dazān ạmis khåtūni hạndi shik^{ə}mạ manzạ drāu̯ ạzhda ʦāu̯ at poshākas manz yat yi ạm^{i} fakīrạn yinsān h^{y}u kurmut ås yiy chu dōnān ʦạp^{y} h^{y}evān at^{i} yelinạ insān ås beye ʦāu̯ yi ạzhda ạmis khåtūni shikmas manz ạm^{i} fakīrạn kạr sargī balai che ạmis khåtūnī hạndis shikmas manz nebạr k^{y}ē che nạ āu̯ fakīr vōt beye at palangas nishi khåtūnī diʦan zēr kathe ka^{i}rin ạmis sạ̄^{i}th at poshākas korun beye insān h^{y}u gau beye fakīr byūt dūri pahan. shamā chu dazān^{i} athas k^{y}et kạḍin shamshēr ạmis khåtūnī handi shikma manzạ log nạ̄^{i}rini yi ạzhda log at poshākas manz aʦạni tujen shamshēr chu ạmis ạzhdạhas kat^{e}rān mōrun ka^{i}rinas gañye ʦunun ạt^{i} palangas tal khut pāne at palangas p^{y}eṭh shamshēr diʦan shānd tạ shung.

8. rāt gaye āda subu log yini rājạ Vikarmājitan dop mār^{ə}vātelan gaʦ^{y}u yi fakīr āsi momut yohoi vālyūn az tāñy kạ̄^{i}tya rājạ zādạ gạmạt^{y} mārạ tạ yi ti āsi momut kạ̄^{i}t^{y} at kutis manz vuchuk fakīr vāre kāre zindai nazạr bāzau kạr nazạr khabạr dārau niye khabạr rājas dop has rājạ sạ fakīr chu zindai rājạ såb khut pāne at kuṭis manz karān chu mubārak ạmis fakīras dapān chus fakīrạ ʦạ vante k^{y}etạ pạ̄^{i}t^{y} bachōk dapān chus fakīr bēdār rōzạnạ sạ̄^{i}th rājạ sạ kar nazạr palangas tal rājạn kạr nazạr vuchun palangas tal balāyạ ak trau muʦ fakīrạn mạ̄^{i}rit dapān chu fakīr ạmis rājạs zabān kyah che kạrmuʦ rājạ chus dapān puz chu Khudā chu kunuy fakīr

when they had finished conversing he did a deed. He folded his garments into the shape of a man, and went a short way off and sat down to watch. A lamp was burning, and by its light he saw a python issue from the lady's mouth.[1] It entered the garments which he had folded into the shape of a man. It shook them, and bit them over and over again, but when it found that there was no man within them, it retreated and again entered the lady's mouth. In this way did the faqīr satisfy himself by his perscrutation that it was within the lady that there was an evil calamity dwelling, and that there was nought else outside her. Up came the faqīr to the bed. He gave the lady a push, and held converse with her. He made his garments again into the shape of a man, and again went away a short distance to sit and watch. A lamp was burning, and in his hand he held his drawn sword. The python issued from the lady's mouth, and began to enter the garments. He raised his sword and smote it to pieces and slew it. He cut it into gobbets and thrust them under the bed. Then he climbed himself upon the bed, laid the sword beneath the pillow, and fell asleep.

8. The night came to an end, and dawn began to come, and to the executioners said Rājā Vikramâditya, "Go ye. This faqīr is surely dead. Bring him too down, as ye did the others. Up to to-day how many princes have gone to their death, and he, too, must have died!" They went up into the chamber, and saw the faqīr alive and safe and sound. The discerners then discerned him, and the newsmen gave the news to the Rājā. Said they, "Your Majesty, that faqīr is of truth alive." His Majesty, the Rājā, himself ascended to the chamber, and made him gratulations, crying, "O faqīr, tell me, prithee, how thou didst escape." Quoth the faqīr, "By remaining awake. Your Majesty, cast thou a glance below the bed." The Rājā looked, and there saw he the calamity as the faqīr had thrust it after he had killed it. Said the faqīr to the Rājā, "What was the promise made by thee?" And quoth the Rājā, "True it is. There is no God but the one God." Then

[1] Literally, "belly," but as the python certainly came out viâ the mouth I use a word more suitable for Western ears when dealing with a lady.

chus dapān yi hasạ chạy at^i paneñy kūr mạ disạ panun nishānạ diťsạnas vạ̄j ạmis fakīrạs fakīrạsạnz vāj rạt ạm^i rājạn.

9. drāụ fakīr vōt panun shahar fakīri hund zhāmạ ťsunun kạ^irit pādshāhī hund poshāk purun dyütun hukum lashkạ^iri nēru sạ m^ye sạ̄^ith.

10. dapān vustād gudẹñyī gau at beñye hạndis shahạras yi pādshah ti å̄s bājạ tārān ạmi suy pādshahạs ạnyin beñye paniñy thāụnas bōnt^a ka^ini sa tami dohuch ziāfat yat tami beñye mohạr å̄sus p^yethạ kạrmuťs dapān chus yi ch^yā mohur chāny dop^unas phērit myeñyīy che dapān chus yi pādshah buy kya gå̄s tami dohuk miskīn pạz pạ̄^ity chu å̄shnāụ ās^anas.

11. hiťsan ạmis pādshahạs ti lashkar dyütun kadam yārạsund kun vōt yāras nish yārạn kạr ziāfat yiman don pādshahiyạn kiťs. rāt kạduk ạt^y suban drạ̄y.

12. dyütun kadam at h^yạhạrạ sạndis shah^aras kun anān nād dit ạmis pādshahạs dapān chus anuk sạ tạhạl^y timau chu ch^yāñye rakh^ye manzạ ťsūr rutmut su kati chuk thå̄ụmut anik tạhạl^i dop hak yus tohi ťsūr rutu rakhi manzạ su kati chu thāụmut yimau vun pādshahạm asi chu kurmut havāle panenis afsạrạs mējạras ạnuk mējạr dop has nomau tạhạlyau kuruy havālạ ťsūr su kati thå̄vut yi chuk dapān m^ye dyūṭ na tạhạl chus karān gavạ̄i pādshahạm asi kur tākhīt ạmis havālạ dop^unak ạm^i pādshạhạn yus tami doho fakīr lāgit å̄s suy chuk dapān ạnyūk mārạvātal ťsōr tim vanạn pānai ạnik tim dapān

said the faqīr to him, "Here, sire, is this thy daughter. Sire, give thou me the token (that I may claim her as my wife)." Then gave the Rājā his ring to the faqīr, and took in exchange the faqīr's ring from him.

9. Then departed the faqīr and came to his own city. He put off his mendicant's weeds and clothed himself in royal robes. He gave the command to his army to set forth with him.

10. And my Master said :—

First of all went he to his sister's city. The king, her husband, was one of those that paid him tribute. He had his sister brought to him, and put before her the bowl of food that she had sent to him on that day, and on which she had set her seal. Quoth he to her, "Is this thy seal?" Replied she, "Mine it is." Then said to her the King, "It is I who was the beggar-man of that day. True it is that a near relation is for when there is money."

11. He took the army of that king also with him, and turned his footsteps towards his friend. And the friend made a feast in honour of the royalty of both these kings. The night they passed there, and at dawn they again set forth.

12. He turned his footsteps towards the city of his father-in-law. He sent for that king and said to him, "Prithee, send thou for thy grooms. They have caught a thief in the mead of thy home farm. Where have they put him?" They brought the grooms. Quoth he to them, "Where did ye put that thief whom ye seized in the mead of the home farm?" Said they, "Sire, we made him over into the hands of our officer, the Master of the Horse." They brought before him the Master of the Horse. They said to him, "These grooms made over to thy custody a certain thief. Where hast thou put him?" But he denied that he had seen him. Then the grooms gave testimony, "Sire, of a surety, we did make him over to this man's custody." Then quoth the King—the one who formerly had been dressed as a faqīr—"bring ye the four executioners. They themselves will say what happened."

chuk yi pādshah tohi nish chu ạmānat tas fakīrạsund su dīyu yūr^{y} yimau mārạvātạlau kạr kā̊m kạ^{i}ḍik yim lāl sat thạvik pādshahạs bōnt^{ạ} kani satau manzạ tulin tsōr kạ^{i}rinak havālạ dop^{u}nak yim kạm^{i} å̄syu d^{y}itạmạty dop^{u}has fakīran ak^{i} tạm^{i} kami ʽbāpat su å̄s dyüt^{ạ}mut yem^{i} mējạran mārạnạ bāpat dapān chu pādshāh ạmis mējạras kun me chuk na parzenāvān buy kya gōs su fakīr yus kạ̄^{i}d ōstan kurmut guḍeny āyī sạ khā̊tūn ziāfat h^{y}et kheyau yek jā h^{ạ}r^{y}au ts^{y}ut kuru me ālau dopūm volo kạ̄^{i}dyau yi kh^{y}au sōn tsuṭ tam^{i} patạ ās bo rōt m^{y}e khyau tam^{i} patạ kạru murde māzạ̄^{i}ry phutu palangas tạr kurū me ālau tsạ ma zānak yat palangas vāṭ kạ^{i}rit me dop^{u}mau āñy zānenā ham sāye chum ch^{y}ān palangas dyüt^{u}mau vāṭ kạ^{i}rit am^{i} paneñ^{y}e zạnānạ parzạnāvus dop^{u}nai ts^{y}e yü chu myōn khāvand yi chu āmut fakīr lāgit yi gatse rātas rāt mārun kur thas havālạ noman mārevāt^{ạ}lan yiman āu̯ ār myōn yimau trāu̯ has yele yiman ditim lāl sat tsōr ditim tsun zanen tre thạ̄ymak amānat yạ^{i}t^{y} kya chyum tim lāl tre tsōr chim d^{y}ütmat noman tsuan zanen ye^{i}ty kya chüy tim ti kōlnas zimạ tahsīr.

13. dapān vustād dyütun hukum paneñye lashkạ^{i}ri koḍun yi mējạr ti paneñy zạnānạ ti khanenå̄vun khoḍ tsạnạnāvin don^{u}vai at khuḍas kar nāviñy kañye kan at^{i} chu lekhān sāhibi kitāb

shrāk sạrp makhri zan bēvophā ।

14. drāu̯ at^{i} phīrit yi pādshāh vōt at^{i} rājạ Vikarmājitun garạ divān che rājas khabạr pādshāh chu āmut paneneñy bātsan rājạ chuk dapān sạ chạ

They brought them, and the King said to them, "Ye have in trust a deposit made by that faqīr, give ye it here and now." Then those executioners did a deed. They brought forth those seven rubies and laid them before the King. He took up four of them, and gave them to them, as he said, "Who gave you these?" Quoth they, "A certain faqīr." "And for what purpose?" "This Master of the Horse had made him over to us to be slain." Then said the King to the Master of the Horse, "Dost thou not recognize me? It is I who am that faqīr whom thou didst imprison. At first came that lady to thee with a dish of dainty meats. Ye ate together, and some scraps and orts remained over and above. You gave a shout and called to me, 'Come, thou prisoner, eat thou these scraps and orts of ours.' So I came and took and ate. After that you clipped and toyed together, till the joint of the bed became broken. You gave a shout and called to me, 'Haply, dost thou know how to mend this bed?' and I replied to you, 'Yea, why should I not know? My neighbours are carpenters.' I mended for you the bed, and my wife saw that it was I. Said she to thee, 'This is my husband, he must be killed this very night of nights.' Thou gavest me into the hands of these executioners, and to them came compassion for me, and they let me go free. I gave them seven rubies. Four gave I, one for each of the four, and three I left with them in deposit for me. Now, here I have these three rubies, and four have I just now given to these four men. There, in their hands, are they also for thee to see." And in this way was his guilt proved against him.

13. And moreover my Master told me :—

He gave the order to his army. He dragged forth the Master of the Horse and his own wife. He had dug a pit and had them both cast into it, and had them stoned with stones until they died. On this subject verily a master of books hath written :—

Treacherous are a knife, a serpent, and the coquetry of a woman.

14. Thenceforth went again the King and came again to Rājā Vikramâditya's palace. Then gave they the news to the Rājā, "A king hath come and asketh for his wife." Then said the Rājā,

fakīrạsunz pādshahạsunz che ne pādshāh chus dapān buy gōs su fakīr m^ye nish chu ch^yōn nishānạ ts^ye nishi chu myōn nishānạ dapān chus rājạ tam^i dohuch fakīrī kya gaye azich pādshāhī kyah gaye dapān chus pādshāh me å̊sạ hetsạmatsạ kathe pānts timai å̊sus sar karān tam^i å̊sum lå̊g^u mut fakīr rājạn kạr kå̊m ditinas sạ̄^ith paneñy bạ̄ts drāu̯ vōt panenis sheh^ạras manz chu karān rāj.—vu sạlāmạ vu ikrām.

" Of a faqīr she is the wife, not of a king." Quoth the King to him, " Verily, I am no other than that faqīr. I have with me thy token, and thou hast with thee mine." Quoth the Rājā to him, " What meant the faqīrhood of those days, and what meaneth the royalty of to-day ? " Said the King to him, " I had bought five things, and them was I testing, and therefore dressed I myself as a faqīr." Then the Rājā did a deed. He gave the King his wife to be with him. The King went forth and came to his own city, and there he swayed the sceptre of his rule. This is the end, and may peace and honour attend ye all.

XI. FORSYTH SĀHIBAN SHĀR YELI YARKAND ZĒNENI GAU

Yi m^{y}e dyōt mai tih gats tạ bozān ।
Yārkand anōn zēnān ॥ 1

guḍeny dup malkānye kus ka^{i}ri yohoi kār
Fōrsat chu zōrāvār ।
rāje be Yārkand bāj^{a} gats tārān
Yārkand anōn zēnān ॥ 2

Landạnạ p^{y}eṭhạ Yārkand yimau kur tai
maushūr hā tsopōr gai ।
guḍeñy Son^{a} margạ chāvān posha mādān
Yārkand° ॥ 3

huk^{u}mạ mah^{a}rāj Buṭṭạnis brō drāu̯
Balti tum age jāo ।
pīche jāo Kashmīr nāle chālān
Yārkand° ॥ 4

rasat sai tsopōr kạrhai tarfan
guḍa lug Mạrāj pargan ।
tim vadān ās^{i} koṭ lag^{i} gār zān
Yārkand° ॥ 5

timan Buṭṭa garạn Kāshir^{i} thāvik
Buṭṭạ bāy broh n^{y}āvik ।
gur bạṭ^{i} dākas zumbạ che gāsạ sārān
Yārkand° ॥ 6

XI. THE SONG OF FORSYTH SĀHIB WHEN HE WENT TO CONQUER YĀRKAND.

The Mission of Sir Douglas Forsyth across the Hindūkush to Kashgar took place in 1873–4. *It passed through Kashmīr, where people were collected to serve in the camp. Sābir, the author of this poem, describes the events attending the impressment of these camp-followers. He evidently believes that it was a military expedition to conquer Yārkand.*

1. What I have seen, to that attend and thou shalt hear. "Yārkand will we conquer for ourselves."

2. First, said the Queen of England, "Who can do this work? A mighty man is Forsyth." To him she gave the order, "Seat thyself upon the throne of Yārkand as its king, and from it levy thou tribute. Yārkand will we conquer for ourselves."

3. They who wielded the sceptre of authority from London unto Yārkand became famous over all the world. First halted they in Sŏnamarg [1] to enjoy the delight of the flower-meads. "Yārkand will we conquer for ourselves."

4. Ahead went the order of the Mahārāj of Kashmīr to Tibet.[2] "Ye Baltīs, advance ye and then hasten ye to Kashmīr bringing passports with ye. Yārkand will we conquer for ourselves."

5. The order for their assembling issued forth on all sides, and at first the people were collected in Marāz.[3] Lamenting were they and crying "Poor ignorant souls, whither are we come?" "Yārkand will we conquer for ourselves."

6. In houses of these Tibetans were Kāshmīrīs quartered, and the brothers of Tibet were sent forward in advance. Horses were stationed for the post, and yaks for collecting and piling grass. "Yārkand will we conquer for ourselves."

[1] A celebrated upland in the Sindh Valley of Kashmīr, famous for the beauty of its wild flowers.

[2] i.e. Little Tibet or Baltistān. The people of this country are excellent carriers. They are represented as being despatched in droves to the rendezvous in Kashmīr. They are furnished with passports or certificates of dispatch.

[3] One of the two divisions—Marāz and Kamrāz—of the Valley of Kashmīr. Marāz is the southern part of the valley, on both sides of the River Vĕth above Srīnagar.

ba rai khumba khas zạnānạn che sumb^{a}rān
z^{y}ünte gāse vartāvān ı
ajạ āse pyāv^{a}lạ kyĕ āse dujān
Yārkand^{o} ‖ 7

gur^{i} mangạ nāv^{i}hai kukạr gāman
chuh karun yimnạ zānan ı
hạri hạri karān å̄si timan pak^{a}nāvān
Yārkand^{o} ‖ 8

kal^{a} kạn^{i} dumbij ches lạṭi kạn^{y} lākam
gāsạ raz kanyek mah kam ı
gāsạ gaṇḍi tạ zache zīn pạ^{i}rit soirạ sāmān
Yārkand^{o} ‖ 9

rasat kạ^{i}rtạn ạn^{y}hai nān gār
mat^{i} chuk pan paneñy kār ı
g^{y}ạjạ kạ^{i}rik krālan guḍeñy l^{y}ejạ sārān
Yārkand^{o} ‖ 10

krāje dup^{a} khāvạndas nā dānạ krālau
kathu kit kōndạ vālau ı
kå̄m hau che pak^{a}vañy ạ̄^{i}mi gatsu trāvān
Yārkand^{o} ‖ 11

gūr dop^{u} gūr bāye donovai nērau
gaṷ kits jāy shērau ı
vuḍ^{y}e p^{y}eṭh h^{y}e gāsu lāṷ gau gātsan lārān
Yārkand^{o} ‖ 12

kun^{y}ạ k^{y}et dudạ nut vāri h^{y}et bā^{i}ri drāṷ
lōkan chu safarun thāṷ ı
tākīt dudạ gūr jan^{a}tuk bāgvān
Yārkand^{o} ‖ 13

7. Women were collected to help in distributing straw and firewood. Some of them were fresh from childbed, and others were heavy with child. "Yārkand will we conquer for ourselves."

8. Horses were demanded from villages that had naught but fowls. Their drivers knew not how to say "tchk", and could say only "hårⁱ hårⁱ,"[1] as they urged them along. "Yārkand will we conquer for ourselves."

9. When they harnessed a horse they turned the crupper towards its head, and hung the bridle by its tail. Grass ropes did they use for strong binding-straps.[2] All the appliances that they had were pack-saddles[3] of straw and saddles made of rags. "Yārkand will we conquer for ourselves."

10. Menial cultivators were impressed in proportion to the size of each village, and on the shoulder of each was laid the burden of some special duty. Like bundles of grass were they crowded together, as they carried cooking pots for the potters. "Yārkand will we conquer for ourselves."

11. Said the potter's wife to the potter, "O potter, thou art a fool. What need have we to put pots into the kiln? The business, dear, is a travelling one, and we must leave all uncooked food behind us (and bring with us our food ready cooked)." "Yārkand will we conquer for ourselves."

12. Said the cow-herd to his wife, "Let us both go forth and arrange a place for the cows. If we carry a wisp of grass upon our heads, the cows will follow at a run." "Yārkand will we conquer for ourselves."

13. He went forth, milk-pail on haunch, and carrying his load of pots. The people all were exhausted by their march, and to them the kindly milkman seemed as blessed as a garden-watcher of Paradise. "Yārkand will we conquer for ourselves."

[1] "Tchk" is the click made to encourage a horse, "hårⁱ hårⁱ" is what is said for the same purpose to a cow. The impressed drivers were unaccustomed to horses, and knew only the bovine expletive.

[2] The *kaññĕkh* is the term used for the two straps or ropes attached at the back of a Kāshmīrī saddle to secure blankets, etc. (Stein).

[3] The *gàndⁱ* is the term used for the Turkistān pack-saddle, which consists of two straw-filled pommels joined in front (Stein).

vātạl^{i} dup vātüjạ bunai serạ za
chim mangān dāle muy tạ ka ।
tsōrastạ å̊r h^{y}et m^{y}eti hai pak^{a}nāvān
Yārkand^{o} ॥ 14
(vātij vanān phērit)
phērit dabzạ hek vātạl gānau
dabzi hek ạs^{i}nau zānau ।
dap^{y}āmak vātạj k^{y}ĕ nai chum bōzān
Yārkand^{o} ॥ 15
shumār bōz hai tạ^{i}fạdārạn
mang^{a}lạj ahengārạn ।
vōḍ^{y}e p^{y}eṭh yiran h^{y}et shrānz dakhe nāvān
Yārkand^{o} ॥ 16
kārau ditti bārau yingar kat^{i} tsārau
vān kat^{i} jān shērau ।
hāl kya kur hak nāl garạ nāvān
Yārkand^{o} ॥ 17
khush kya gōsai amōb gau jān
patạ nyūk nāyid chān ।
baṭṭạ daje at^{i} h^{y}et patə chuk lārān
Yārkand^{o} ॥ 18
muslạ hat karān tim^{a} å̊sạ pānevāñy
kusuy kạ^{i}ri nāyiz tạ chān^{y} ।
katạ vạn^{y} kạ^{i}rit hai karau guzrān
Yārkand^{o} ॥ 19
Sābir tilavāñye tāmat yütuy van
yāmat khabạr bōzan ।
tāny^{e} āụ̂ sāhib bā sō^{i}ri sāmān
Yārkand^{o} ॥ 20

14. The sweeper said to the sweeper's wife, "I shall never remember what I have to do. They expect me to provide leather and a cobbler's laces. They are sending me off, my dear, with a leather-cutter and a cobbler's awl." "Yārkand will we conquer for ourselves."

15. And she replied, "Thou shouldst have answered them, O pimp of a sweeper.[1] Thou shouldst have said, 'I know not how to use them.'" "I did, my sweeperess, say that to them, but they heard me not at all." "Yārkand will we conquer for ourselves."

16. The roll-call was cried for the artisans, and a demand was made for workers in iron. Each came bearing his anvil on his head, and leaning on his tongs as if they were a stick. "Yārkand will we conquer for ourselves."

17. The blacksmiths grumbled and complained, "Where are we to look for coals? How can we aright arrange our smithy?" But somehow or other the officials made a makeshift for them, and set them a-forging horseshoes. "Yārkand will we conquer for ourselves."

18. Very pleased did I become, and mighty good it seemed to me that last of all they impressed the barber and the carpenter (of my village), and that I saw them running after the others each with a kerchief of food in his hand.[2] "Yārkand will we conquer for ourselves."

19. Their wives are holding a conference with each other. Say they, "Who is, then, now to support the barber's wife and the carpenter's wife? We shall have to earn our livelihood by hiring ourselves out for spinning thread." "Yārkand will we conquer for ourselves."

20. Ṣābir Oilman[3] only so much say, so long as they shall pay heed unto the news. At length came the Sāhib with all his retinue, saying, "Yārkand will we conquer for ourselves."

[1] This is really a term of affection, much as we sometimes use abusive words in an affectionate sense, or talk of a "poor devil" in the language of pity.

[2] A thoroughly Kāshmīrī sentiment, quite in keeping with the villager's indifference to the troubles of others. The author was evidently on bad terms with the barber and carpenter of his village (Stein).

[3] The name of the poet.

XII. ĀKHUNASẠNZ DALĪL

1. Tạm^{i} süy ås nechiv tsōr tim^{a} nai prütsun bo buḍ^{i} ås tuh^{i} vañyu kyah kār ka^{i}r^{y}u ak^{i} dopus bo kare yimāmat bēy dopus bo parạ bāng bēy dopus bo parạ vāz lokat hi tsorim dopus bo kare tsūr doha ak banyāụ̯ gau pādshạhas tsūri vōt yeli pādshahạ sund garạ rūd vudanye tāñy nerān tōrạ vazīr beye pādshahạsạnz kūr yi vuchuk at^{i} vudañye dop^{u}nak toh^{i} kam chu yimau dop has tsu kus chuk dop^{u}nak bu chus tsūr yimau dop^{u}has ạs^{i} ti che tsūr ka^{i}rik gur^{i} zạ sapud savār ak yi ākhun beye yi pādshāh kūr dop^{u}nas vazīran nēryū toh^{i} nasīyat hasạ karai ak kat yinạ sạ pādshāh kōḍ^{y}i sạ^{i}th kat kuni karak bo hasạ yimau patạ tạ toh^{i} nēr^{y}ū.

2. yim chu pakān pādshāh kōr^{y}i che nạ khabạr yi chu nạ m^{y}e sạ^{i}th ākhun zādạ tas chạ khabạr yi chu vazīr gāsh lug phuleni vat^{y} gur^{y}au p^{y}eṭhạ bun gaye yi pādshāh kūr kul^{y}e ạkis p^{y}eṭh atạ but chulun vuchun at kul e manz lāl yi lāl tulun āyi h^{y}et ạmis ākhun zādas nish tas che khabạr yi chu vazīr vazīr kyĕ ås na yūt gāsh chu pholān tyüt chu yi lāl gah trāvān parzạ nāụ̯ am^{i} pādshāh kōr^{y}e vazīr nạ lāl tuluk sạ^{i}th vạt^{i} shahras akis manz at^{i} vuchuk pār^{y}ehna at^{i} manz b^{y}ēth^{i}.

3. yi chu yivān ạmis pādshahạs nish am^{i} sheharạkis dapān chus bo behe naukar yi chus dapān kya naukrī karak dapān chus bo kare gur^{y}en hạnz kismat yim che yimai kathe karān sakhtsa ak āụ̯ lāl pharōsh ạmis pādshahạs kanạni lāl chis

XII. THE TALE OF THE ĀKHŪN.

1. There was once upon a time an Ākhūn,[1] who had four sons. One day he said to them. "I am now grown old, tell me therefore what professions you intend to follow." Said one, "I'll be a prayer-leader in a mosque." Said another, "I'll call the people to prayer." Said another, "I'll preach sermons." But the fourth and youngest said, "I'll be a thief." So one day he went off to the King's palace to steal something. As he stood outside it there came forth the Vizier and the King's daughter. When they saw him standing there he asked them who they were. "And who art thou?" said they. "I'm a thief," said he. "So are we," said they. Now they had brought out with them two horses, and he straightway mounted on one of them, while the princess got on the other. Then the Vizier said to him, "Go ye two in advance, and, sir, pay thou heed to this one piece of instruction—thou shalt not hold any love-talk with the princess. I will join you later on, but go ye two in advance."

2. So they went on, the princess thinking all the time that it was the Vizier, not the young Ākhūn, who was with her. By and by dawn began to blossom forth, and they dismounted by a stream, and to this went the princess and washed her face and hands. Her eye fell on a ruby lying in the stream. She picked it up and took it to the young Ākhūn, whom all the time she thought to be the Vizier, though it was not him at all. Then, as the dawn blossomed forth, the ruby emitted a brilliant light, and she saw for the first time that it was not the Vizier. So she kept the ruby to herself, and went on with him till they came to a certain city. There they found a small hut in which they made their lodging.

3. The young Ākhūn went to the King of that city, and asked him for employment. "What canst thou do?" asked the King. "I know how to look after horses," answered he. Now, even while they were yet speaking, there came a certain jeweller to sell precious stones to the King. He had two rubies with him. Then

[1] A Musalmān religious teacher.

zạ yi vot^{i} sạyist yi chus dapān pādshahạm ak lāl chu bēb^{a}hā byēk chu khuṭ at manz chu kyum dapān chus pādshāh ti kyatạ pạ^{i}th^{y} å̄y tse bōzạnạ dapān chus yi phīrit pādshahạm tākīt chus manz kyum phuṭạ r^{y}ūn hargā kyum drās nạ adạ yi pādshahạs khush ka^{i}ri ti gats^{y}em karun har gā kyum drās telạ gats^{y}em bakhshāyish diñy.

4. dapān vustād phut^{ạ}ruk yi lāl am^{i} manzạ drāu̯ kyum am^{i} sāthạ tsun has sạyist nāu̯ nạhit lāl shināk pyå̄s nāu̯ gau yi lāl shināk panun garạ doha doha chu kaḍān rātạs bihān chu panạni ga^{i}ri dohas yivān chu lāl pasạnd karạni ạmis pādshahạsund nāyid gatsān chu mast khāsạni ạmis lāl shinākas tat^{i} chu vuchān ạmisunz yi zạnānạ yi å̄s khå̄b sūrat seṭā āu̯ yi nāyid vazīrạs mast khå̄s^{ạ}nas dop^{u}nas ai vazīrạ zạnānạ che amis lāl shinākas yi shuybehe vazīrạsạndi ga^{i}ri ạmis karte kyĕtsa nukhta dop^{u}nas adạ kya yi vazīr gau ạmis pādshahạ sanzi kōḍ^{y}e dop^{u}nas tsạ dap pādshahas m^{y}egatse yis lāl shinākan guḍeñyi lāl pasand kur tạt^{i} hyu byāk lāl āsun dup pādshahạ sạnzi kōḍ^{y}i panạnis mạ^{i}lyis m^{y}e gatse lālas h^{y}u bē bahā lāl āsun āu̯ lāl shināk dop^{u}nas pādshahan disạ lāl ạnit tat lālas hyu āu̯ vōḍạ lāl shināk vōt^{i} paneñye zạnānạ nish byūt tsop^{ạ} ka^{i}rith yi chạs dapān zạnānạ tsi kyā zi chuk phikri gạmut dop^{u}nas phērit ạm^{i} lāl shinākan pādshah chum lāl mangān bēbahā su kạ^{i}ti anạ dop^{u}nas am^{i} zạnānạ gats dap pādshahas ritas kyut dim kharj bo dimai lāl ạnit pādshạhan dyutus kharj ritasumb yi ạnun panun garạ chu bihit khyavān nu chu gatsān pādshahas nu chu gatsān

the young Ākhūn, who now called himself a groom, up and said, " Your Majesty, one of these rubies is beyond price, but the other hath a flaw in it in the shape of a worm." The King asked him how he knew this. Said he in answer, " Sire, of a surety there is a worm inside it. Break it and see. If no worm then come forth from it, do unto me whatsoever your Majesty may please. But if a worm do come forth, I shall deserve a present."

4. Quoth my master :—

They broke the ruby into pieces, and sure enough a worm issued forth from it ; and from that time they gave him the title of " Royal Lapidary " instead of that of " Groom ". So the Lapidary returned home, and the days passed. By night he stayed at home, and each day he attended court to examine rubies. The King's barber came one day to shave him, and there he saw the princess, who passed as the Lapidary's wife. Now she was very fair to look upon, and the barber went off on his rounds to shave the King's Vizier. " Said he, O Vizier, that Lapidary hath a wife, and she would verily adorn the mansion of a Vizier. Thou shouldst find him guilty of some failure in his duty." Quoth the Vizier, " Willingly, and why not ? " and went off to the King's daughter. He told her to tell the King that she wanted another ruby just like the one that the Lapidary had first of all approved as beyond price. So she went to her father and quoth she, " Fain would I have another ruby beyond price, like unto the first." When the Lapidary came that day to the presence the King said to him, " Bring thou me another ruby like unto that one." The Lapidary returned home, and sat down there in silent consternation. Said the woman to him, " Why art thou so anxious ? " Replied he, " The King demandeth from me a ruby beyond price, and where am I to find it ? " Said she, " Go thou and say to the King, ' If thou wilt give me a month's expenses, I will bring thee the ruby.' " Well, the King gave him expenses sufficient for a month, and he brought the money home. There he stayed eating his food, not going to

beye kun rit gau āda divān ches yi su lāl yus tam^{i} kul^{y}e manzạ tu jān gau h^{y}et pādshahas kạr^{ə}nas salām lāl thå̄u̯ nas bōntạ kani.

5. drāu̯ phērit lāl shināk vōt panun garạ rātha kạḍun paneni ga^{i}ri subhas āu̯ nāyid mast khāsạni amis lāl shinākas mast muk^{a}lå̄u̯ nas khāsit tạ drāu̯ nāyid pānas vōt^{i} beye ạmis vazīras nish dopun vazīras kyĕ ʦa kartạ ạmis lāl shinākas ạmis che zạnānạ khōb sūrat sạ shūybihe vazīrạsạndi ga^{i}ri vazīr āu̯ beye ạmis pādshahạ sạnzi kōr^{y}e dop^{u}nas ʦạ mang pādshahas lālan hund truṭ dop am^{i} pādshahạ sanzi koḍ^{y}e panạnis mạ^{i}lis me gaʦi^{y} āsun lālan hund truṭ lāl shināk āu̯ pādshahas nish kạrnas salām pādshah chus dapān lāl hasạ gaʦ^{a}nai āsạn^{i} sethā trạtis sumb āu̯ lāl shināk vōt panun garạ yi chạs dapān zạnānạ lu^{i}t^{i} pạ^{i}ṭh^{i} kyā zi chuk bihith yi chus dapān phērith pādshah chum mangān az lālan hund truṭ su ka^{i}ti anạ bo dop^{u}nas am^{i} zạnānạ k^{y}ĕ chanạ phikir gaʦ pādshahas gaʦe h^{y}un tren ritan kyut kharj dyut^{u}nas pādshahạn kharj āu̯ panun garạ h^{y}et.

6. yi chu khyevān tạ ch^{y}avān yuttāñy yim tre rit gai vu chạs dapān yi zạnānạ ạmis lāl shinākas dapān ches ye tạ^{i}ṭ^{i} m^{y}e tami kulye manzạ lāl tu jāu̯ tami kul^{y}e kul^{y}e gaʦe khasun h^{y}ur pahan ta^{i}ṭ^{i} chiy nāg ta^{i}ṭ^{i} nāgas gaʦe andas kun dob khanun ta^{i}ṭ^{y} dobas manz bih zi kạ^{i}tith tath nāgas p^{y}eṭh yinai guḍeñy she za^{i}n^{y}e srān karạ^{i}ni timan kyĕ kạ^{i}r^{i} zinạ patạ yiyiy tīman shen zanyen hunz ziṭh sạ vasīy tat nāgas srān karạ^{i}ni poshāk trạviy ka^{i}rith

court or anywhere else. When a month had passed the woman gave him the ruby she had picked up out of the stream, and, taking it to the King, he laid it before him with a bow.

5. The Lapidary then left the court and returned home, where he passed the night. Next morning the barber came to shave him. When he had finished he went off to the Vizier. Said he, " Prithee, do somewhat unto that Lapidary. His wife is very beautiful. She would verily adorn the mansion of a Vizier." So the Vizier went again to the King's daughter and told her to ask the King for a ruby necklace. Quoth she to her father, " Fain would I have a ruby necklace." In due course the Lapidary came to the presence and made his bow. Said the King, " Sir, thou must bring unto me a number of rubies sufficient for a necklace." He went home, and the woman whispered to him, " Why art thou sitting here ? " Replied he, " To-day the King demandeth from me a ruby necklace. Whence can I bring one ? " Quoth she to him, " Thou needst not be anxious in the least. Go and take three months' expenses from the King." The King gave him the money and he returned to his house.

6. So there he stayed eating and drinking till the three months were passed. Then the woman said to him, " Thou knowest the stream from whence I picked up that ruby. Go thou up it a little way, and thou wilt come to a spring. Thou must dig a pit close to the source of the spring, and hide thyself therein. At first six females will come to bathe in the spring. Do thou nothing unto them ; but afterwards thou wilt see coming the eldest sister of these six. She also will go down into the spring to bathe.

ba^{i}ṭhis p^{y}eṭh chōn gaŧse gaŧsun ŧsū^{i}r^{i} pạ̄^{i}th^{i} gaŧse ti poshāk tulun.

7. āye she zañye kur timau srān timan kyē vunun na yiman patạ āyi sạtim^{y} za^{i}n^{y} trōv am^{i} poshāk ka^{i}rith bạ^{i}ṭhis p^{y}eṭh pāne vuŧs nāgạs manz āu̯ yi lāl shināk ŧsu^{i}r^{i} pạ̄^{i}th^{y} āu̯ tạ tulun yi ạ^{i}mi sund poshāk gau tạ byūṭh ath dobas manz am^{i} kur srān kạŧs bạ^{i}ṭhis p^{y}eṭh vuchun at^{i} na poshāk diŧsun krēkh dapān che dyau chukạ yinsān chukạ tas khudāyesund chi khasam yim pạ̄^{i}dạ kuruk m^{y}e mạ kar sīras phāsh yi ŧsạ gaŧsiy ti dimai ạmi kurus ālau ạm^{i} dob^{a} manzạ dop^{u}nas dim vādai Khudā yi bo mangai ti gaŧs^{y}em bōzun at^{i} p^{y}éṭh dyut^{u}nas vādai Khudā dyut^{u}nas poshāk poshāk ŧsun am^{i} nạ̄^{i}l^{y} dop^{u}nas kyah chum hukum dop^{u}nas ạm^{i} lāl shinākan ŧse gaŧse h^{y}ün m^{y}e sạ̄^{i}th^{y} pakān chu lāl shināk broh broh yi che pakān patạ patạ.

8. dapān vustād ạmis chu nāv lāl māl pạ^{i}ri vā^{i}t^{i} ạmis lāl shinākạsund gar.

9. dapān vustād yā ạ^{i}mis kathen harān lāl yā chis ạshis harān lāl doho sath sath rāth gaye āda subu āu̯ lāl sath tu^{i}l^{y} lāl shinākan gau h^{y}eth pādshahas kạr^{a}nas salām lāl sath thāu̯ nas bōntạ ka^{i}ni pādshah gau sethā khush.

10. lāl shinākan h^{y}ütus rukhsat vōt panun garạ patai vōtus yi nāyid ạm^{i} khōsus mast mast khāsit drāu̯ vōt yi nāyid vazīras nish ạmis ti khōsun mast dapān chus hā vazīr^{a} ạmis lāl shinākas gamuŧs az pạ̄^{i}dạ b^{y}ēk zạnānạ sa che seṭhā khōbsūrat tạmis guḍe nyechi hạndi khotạ seṭhā khōbsūrat k^{y}ēŧsā kartạ

She will doff her clothes and leave them on the bank. Thou must then go secretly and carry off her garments."

7. The six females came and did their bathing, but to them said he nothing. Afterwards there came the seventh female. She doffed her clothes, and leaving them on the bank descended into the spring. He came secretly and carried off her garments and hid himself again in the pit. When she had finished her bath she went up again on to the bank, and saw that her garments were no longer there. She uttered a loud cry, saying, "Be thou demon or be thou human being, I make to thee an oath by the God who created thee. Put not thou my secret parts to shame, and whate'er thou ask will I give to thee." He then called to her from the pit, "Swear thou to me by God that thou wilt hear and agree to whatsoe'er I shall demand from thee." When she had sworn by God he gave her her garments, and she put them on. Then quoth she, "What is thy command?" and the Lapidary replied, "Thou must come with me." So they went along, the Lapidary in front, and the fairy following behind.

8. Saith my Master :—

Her name was Lālmāl, the Fairy, and they came to the Lapidary's house.

9. And moreover saith my Master :—

I know not which it was, but either at every word she spoke a ruby dropped, or else seven rubies fell each day from her mouth. The night came to an end and dawn appeared. The Lapidary picked up seven rubies and carried them off to the King. Making his bow he laid the seven rubies before him, and mighty pleased became the King.

10. The Lapidary took his leave from the presence and returned home. In due course came the barber and shaved him. When he had finished the barber went off to the Vizier and shaved him also. Said he, "O Vizier, a second wife hath now appeared for that Lapidary. She is very fair to look upon, much more fair even than the first. Prithee do somewhat to him. One of the wives

ạmis lāl shinākas akh che lạ^{i}ki vazīr b^{y}ēk che m^{y}e lāyak dop^{u}nas pyōm hasạ beye vanun pādshah kōḍ^{y}i gau yi vazīr dapān chu ạmis pādshah kōḍ^{y}i tsạ mang mạ^{i}lis m^{y}e gatse āsun rutunạ kuḍ gaye pādshah kūḍ panạnis mạ^{i}lis dapān ches m^{y}e gatse āsun rutun^{a} kuḍ pagā āu̯ lāl shināk dapān chus pādshah ansạ rutun^{a} kuḍ.

11. drāu̯ lāl shināk vōt panun garạ dapān chu yiman zạnānan don pādshah chum mangān rutun^{a} kuḍ su ka^{i}ti anạ bo phērith vutsus lāl māl pạ^{i}ri dop^{u}nas gats pādshahas mang tren ritan k^{y}ut kharj dyut^{u}nas pādshahan āu̯ h^{y}eth panun garạ doha doha chu kaḍān tre r^{y}eth gai āda lekhān che lāl māl pạ^{i}ri kākad dapān che ạ^{i}mis lāl shinākas gats tath nāgas p^{y}eṭh ye^{i}mi manzạ bo añythas tạ^{i}t^{i} manz gatsạ yi kākad trå̄vun tōḍ^{a} khasī atho tạ^{i}t^{i} manz å̄si kuḍ tạ^{i}t^{i} kạ^{i}rzi thaph pān^{a} manz vạ^{i}s^{i} zinạ.

12. gau h^{y}eth yi kākad vōt ath nāgas p^{y}eṭh trå̄vun yi kākad ath nāgas manz h^{y}üthuy yi kākad trå̄vun tyutuy khut å̄dạ athạ a^{i}t^{y} athas manz rutunạ kuḍ ditsun ath thaph ạm^{i} tha^{i}pi sạ^{i}thī āv ạ^{i}mis hots nē^{i}rith hots h^{y}eṭh ti kuḍ h^{y}eth ti āu̯ pānạs vōt panun garạ rāt gaye āda subahanas gau pādshahas karun salām kạ^{i}ḍ^{i}hen thå̄u̯ nas bōnt^{a} ka^{i}ni pādshāh gōs seṭhā khush.

13. h^{y}ütus rukhsat lāl shinākan āu̯ panun garạ āu̯ beye yi nāyid khå̄sun mast ạ^{i}mis lāl shinākas mast khạ^{i}sith drāu̯ vōt ạ^{i}mis vazīras nish beye chus dapān yiy vazīrạ ạ^{i}mis lāl shinākas chuk nạ tsạ vātān kun^{i}kạ^{i}n^{y} ạ^{i}mis kartạ kyētsa gau yi vazīr ạ^{i}mis

is fit for a Vizier, and the other would suit me." Replied the Vizier, "I must, sir, again speak to the King's daughter." So he went and said to her, "Thou shouldst ask of thy father a jewelled bracelet." So the princess went to her father and quoth she to him, "Fain would I have a jewelled bracelet." On the morrow came the Lapidary to the presence, and to him said the King, "Bring me, sir, a jewelled bracelet."

11. The Lapidary went forth and came to his home. Said he to the two women, "The King demandeth of me a jewelled bracelet. Whence am I to bring it?" Then up and said to him Lālmāl, the fairy, "Go thou and ask the King for three months' expenses." The King gave the money to him, and he returned with it to his house. Each day passed day by day, and the three months became completed. Then Lālmāl the Fairy took a paper and wrote upon it. Quoth she to the Lapidary, "Go thou to the spring from which thou hast brought me, and therein cast this paper. Then from the spring a hand will rise, and on it will be a jewelled bracelet. Take hold of it, but descend thou not into the spring."

12. So he went off, taking the paper with him. He flung it into the spring, and even as he did so a hand wearing a jewelled bracelet rose from the water. He grasped hold of the hand, but did so with such force that he pulled the forearm off, and went off home with it and with the bracelet. The night came to an end and at dawn he went to the King. Making his bow he laid the bracelet before him, and mighty pleased became the King.

13. The Lapidary took his leave from the presence and returned home. Again came the barber and shaved him. When he had finished his job he went straight to the Vizier, and again addressed him, "O Vizier, thou dost not in any way get at that Lapidary. Prithee, do thou something to him." The Vizier went to the King's

pādshah kōḍ^{y}i dapān chus tsạ chak pādshah khūḍ tsạ gatsiye āsun akoy kuḍ pādshahas gatse mangun byāk gaye yi pādshah kūḍ dopun panạnis mạ̄^{i}lis m^{y}e gatse āsun byāk kuḍ āu̯ beye lal shināk kạrun salām dapān chus pādshah byāk kuḍ gatse āsun.

14. āu̯ lāl shināk vōṭ panun garạ dapān chu yiman zạnānạn don az chum pādshah mangān byāk rotun^{ạ} kuḍ divān ches lāl māl pạ^{i}ri paneñy vạ̄j dapān ches gats tath nāgas p^{y}eṭh ta^{i}t^{i} nāgas ạ^{i}kith kun chiy pal buḍ ta^{i}t^{i} hāu̯ myēn vạ̄j su pal vu^{i}thī thud tạ^{i}mi tạ^{i}l^{i} chai vath ta^{i}m^{i} va^{i}ti vạz^{i}zạ bun ta^{i}ti chai m^{y}ēn vis sạy diyiy rutunạ kur.

15. drāu̯ yi lāl shināk vōth tath jāye hå̄vun tath palas vạ̄j pal vuth thud vuth ta^{i}mi va^{i}ti bun bun vuchin khå̄tūnạ akh ku^{i}niy zạny a^{i}mi dop^{u}nas ka^{i}ti ōsuk ạ^{i}m^{i} dop^{u}nas lāl māl pạ^{i}riye dopuy rutunạ kur a^{i}mis khå̄tūnī pyau yād ta^{i}misạnzüy mạ̄j å̄s sạ yas rutunạ ka^{i}ris sạ̄^{i}th^{i} huts gayau nē^{i}rith tas che akạy nur tas chu dōd panạnis dilas rāy kạr a^{i}mi khātūnī yāñy m^{y}ēñy mōj vā^{i}t^{i} n^{y}emis manoshas kheye yi å̄s sethā khōbsurat a^{i}mis gau shōk dilas bo kare ạ^{i}mis sạ^{i}th^{i} nēth^{ạ}r voñy yeli māje hund par tav^{ạ} pyau ath jāye gau buñyül ạ^{i}mis dyütun shāp kür^{ạ}nas kanye phul thå̄vun chandạs vå̄tsus mạ̄j uth dop^{u}nas hatai kūḍ^{y}i m^{y}e che yivān māntsạ buy yi chạs nạ h^{y}evān zimạ k^{y}ē a^{i}m^{i} yeli zōr kurnas dop^{u}nas chu manōsh tsạ dim guḍ^{ạ} vādai Khudā bo kya karạs nạ kyē vādai Khudā dyüt^{u}nas a^{i}m^{i} kur chandạ manzạ kañye phul shāp tul^{u}nas manōsh yüthuy å̄s t^{ạ} tüthuy rūd

daughter, and quoth he, "Thou art a King's daughter, shouldst thou have but one bracelet? Yet another shouldst thou ask of the King?" So she departed. Quoth she to her father, "Fain would I have yet another bracelet." Again came the Lapidary to the presence, and to him said the King, "Thou must bring unto me another bracelet."

14. The Lapidary took his leave and came to his own house. Said he to these two women, "To-day doth the King demand of me another jewelled bracelet." Then Lālmāl the Fairy gave him her own ring. Quoth she, "Go thou again unto the spring. Close by one side of it thou wilt find a great rock. Show thou my ring unto that rock, and it will arise and stand upright. Thou wilt find a pathway opening at its foot. Descend thou underground by the path and thou wilt find my crony-girl. She will give to thee a jewelled bracelet."

15. The Lapidary went forth and reached the spot. He showed the ring to the rock and it arose and stood upright. Down the path he went beneath the ground, and, deep down below, he saw a certain lady sitting all alone. Quoth she to him, "Whence comest thou?" Saith he, "Lālmāl the Fairy asketh of thee a jewelled bracelet." Then memory came to the lady. It was her mother whose forearm had been pulled off together with the former jewelled bracelet, and who now had but one arm. For that cause cherished the mother wrath within her heart. So the lady thought to herself, "So soon as my mother cometh she will devour this man." Now he was a mighty personable fellow, and her heart was filled with anxiety on his account, for she had determined to herself to marry him. Just then her mother's footsteps became audible, and the place was shaken by an earthquake. Thereupon the lady uttered a spell over him. She turned him into a pebble, and put it into her pocket. Then came to her her mother, "Aha! my girl," cried she, "I smell the smell of a mortal man." But the lady refused to admit that he had been there. When at last her mother pressed her sore, she said, "There is indeed a man. But first swear thou to me by God that naught wilt thou do unto him." So the mother swore to her by God, and she drew forth the pebble from her pocket, and uttered a spell over it, so that it became a man exactly as he

dop^{u}nas yi chu myōn ha^{i}khi Khudai bo åsan yühoi tsārān yühoi lud^{a}nam mā^{i}ji Khudāyen yi ches dapān mōj zab^{a}r gau bāyen don laḍ kākad a^{i}mi suy a^{i}th^{i} dop^{u}nas mạ̄^{i}jiy lekh tsüy l^{y}ükh a^{i}mi kākad dyütun ạ^{i}mis lāl shinākas a^{i}thi a^{i}mi kur^{a}nas ālau khātūnī dop^{u}nas yi an kākad yūry vuch a^{i}mi khātūni ath l^{y}ükhmut a^{i}misạnzi mā^{i}ji chu voi m^{y}ēn gab^{a}r yi gatse vāt^{a} vunuy mārun a^{i}mis ōs a^{i}mi sāthạ panun dōd pyạmut yād su hats^{y}uk yi kākad tsun^{a}nas tsạ^{i}tith a^{i}mi khåtūnī panun l^{y}ükh^{a}nas kākad ath manz l^{y}ükh^{a}nas chu vai myē̃ bạ̄y tuhund gatse jal^{a}d yün m^{y}e kyā chu yeñyi vål.

16. l^{y}ükhunas kākadas zạbāñy kur^{a}nas na^{i}s^{i}yat dop^{u}nas tut yeli vātak kar^{a} hak salām salām pạ̄^{i}lith dīz^{y}ek kākad tim anạnai khyen tsam ru kare ti ch^{y}ōn khyun gats^{a}nạ badal dyüt^{u}nas sạ̄^{i}th^{i} asl kare dop^{u}nas yi khyēzi ta^{i}ti tihund tsạn^{a}zi bebindạ^{i}r^{i} trå^{i}vith panun khyēzi ta^{i}mi patạ dap^{a}nai tim kash nạ hạna kareñy tat khyuth d^{y}üt^{u}nas shast^{a}ro panje dop^{u}nas tim chi dyav^{a}zāth timan yiye tas^{a}li shast^{a}rvi panje sạ̄^{i}thi.

17. drāu̯ a^{i}ti na^{i}siyat yād h^{y}et vōth thuth karün timan salām dyüt^{u}nak yi kākad a^{i}mis d^{y}ütuk khyen tsam^{a}ru kare a^{i}m^{y}uk tulān chu bus ts^{a}nān bebind^{a}r trạ̄^{i}vith panun chu kaḍān ti chu khyavān a^{i}mi patạ dop^{u}has yimau khash^{a}nạ h^{a}nā kar a^{i}m^{i} kur yi tsü^{i}ri pạ̄^{i}th^{i} shast^{a}ro pañje chuk a^{i}mi sạ̄^{i}th^{i} divān zilla zilla yimau l^{y}ükhas javāb at kākadas l^{y}ükhas asi ch^{y}enạ fursath hazrạ^{i}t^{i} sulaimān chu divān nād hal^{a} bismilla ka^{i}r^{y}u yeñyivōl.

had been before. Quoth she to her mother, "This is he who is unto me as God. For him, and only for him, have I been seeking. It is he, and he alone, O mother, whom God hath sent unto me." Then said her mother, "Good. So let it be. Send thou a letter by his hand unto thy two brethren." Quoth she, "My mother, let it be thou that writest." So the mother wrote a letter, and gave it into the hand of the Lapidary. But the lady called him to her, and asked him to give her the paper. She looked at it, and on it by her mother were written these words, "If ye be indeed my sons, on the instant that he cometh to you, must ye kill this man." The mother had written this because she still bore in her heart the memory of the pain of her lost forearm. But the lady tore the paper into little pieces, and wrote herself another, "If ye be indeed my brethren, quickly must ye come. And for why? Because it is my wedding festival."

16. She wrote for him the paper, and by word of mouth gave she him this instruction, saying, "When thou shalt arrive thither, make thou first a bow, and having louted low, give thou to them this paper. They will offer thee dinner made of leathern pease, but these thou must not eat." As a substitute she gave him real pease to take with him, and said, "These be what thou must eat. Drop thou their leathern pease into the fold of thy breast-cloth and eat thine own pease in their stead. Thereafter they will ask thee to give them a little scratching." For that purpose she gave him a set of iron claws, "For," said she, "they are of a demon race, and these iron claws will give them but a pleasant titillation."

17. Bearing these instructions in his memory he set forth, and reached their abode. He made his bow to them and gave to them the paper. They offered him a dinner of leathern pease. He raised a gobbet of it to his mouth, but let it fall into the fold of his breast-cloth, while at the same time he took out his own pease and kept eating them. Thereafter they asked him to give them a little scratching. So he secretly donned the iron claws and with them scraped and scratched them. Then wrote they an answer to the letter after this manner. "We have no time to come unto thee, for we have been summoned by the holy Solomon. Haste ye, in the name of God, and make ye the wedding festival."

18. vå̄t ạth hå̄u̯ nak yi kākad kākad paḍuk kạruk a^{i}mis sạ^{i}th^{i} yeñy^{i}vōl vũ che yi khå̄tūn dapān a^{i}mis khāv^{a}ndas panạnis yet^{i} rōz kạ kinạ du^{i}n^{i}has manz gatsak bu chạs tsạ tạ^{i}bya ạ^{i}m^{i} dop^{u}nas duny^{i}has manz gatsau dop^{u}nas a^{i}mi khātūnī vuñy yeli nērau myēṅ mōj dạ^{i}p^{i}y khyē tsa mangum chōny gatsạs mangun vat^{a}ranuk muslạ beye khyē mạ^{i}n^{y}g^{a}zạs na vuñy yeli yim sakhr^{y}ai dopuk ạ^{i}mi māje mangun khyē tsa dop^{u}nas dim vat^{a}ranuk mus^{a}lạ tath chu nāu̯ vuts^{a}prang drāu̯ a^{i}ti vạ^{i}ti panun garạ garạ vạ^{i}tith kạrun taiyār roṭhunạ kur gau h^{y}eth pādshahas yi lāl shināk.

19. nạ^{i}ydan bōz lāl shināk vōt gatsān chus nāyid gar^{a} mast kās^{a}ni a^{i}ti vuchān chu triyim khå̄tūnạ drāu̯ a^{i}ti nāyid puth phe^{i}rith vōt vazīras nish dapān chu a^{i}mis vazīras ha vazīrạ a^{i}mis lāl shinākas che az triyim khātūnạ yiman don hạndi khuṭạ khōb-sūrath sạ che lāyiki pādshāh akh che lāyiki vazīr b^{y}ēk che m^{y}e lāyak ạ^{i}mis lāl shinākas kar the khyē tsa dapān chus vazīr az vane bo pādshahas suy pādshāh kạ^{i}ri ạ^{i}mis khyē tsa va^{i}r^{y} dāth su mạ^{i}ri zạnānạ tre n^{y}emau ạ^{i}s^{i} dop vazīran pādshahas pādshahạm ạ^{i}mis lāl shinākas che zạnānạ tre titsạ chenạ pādshāhī manz pādshahạm ta^{i}mis lāl shinākas rath tạ kh^{y}ē tsa nukhtạ su guts galun tim^{a} zanānạ tre kar^{u} huk dākh^{i}li mahalạ khān pādshahan kạr fik^{a}ra dopun mangạ has khyētsa chīz ti chu anān så̄ruy vuñy dapas bo m^{y}ēnis mạ^{i}lisunz khabar gatse aneñy su cha jan^{a} tas kinạ dōzakas.

18. He returned to the lady and her mother, and showed them the reply. They read it and carried out the wedding between him and her. Then said the lady to him who was now her husband, "Here wilt thou stay, or wilt thou return unto the world of men? Behold I am thy humble slave." So he said that he would return to the world of men, and quoth the lady to him, "Now, when we shall set forth, my mother will tell thee to ask of her a gift. And thou must ask for but one thing, a certain skin mat. Ask thou for it alone, and for naught else." So, as they were preparing for their journey her mother said to him, "Ask thou of me some gift," and he said to her "Give me the skin mat that is called the *wutsha prang*, or 'flying-couch'." Well, they went forth from there and reached his home. As soon as they arrived she made ready for him a jewelled bracelet, and the Lapidary took it to the King.

19. The barber heard that the Lapidary had come home, and goes to his house to shave him. There sees he the third lady, and straight returns he to the Vizier. Said he to him, "O Vizier, to-day that Lapidary hath a third lady, more fair to look upon than the other two. She is fit for the King. Another is fit for a Vizier, and yet another would suit me. Prithee, do thou somewhat to this Lapidary." Quoth the Vizier to him, "To-day will I tell the King, and His Majesty himself will lay some trap for him. Then he will die, and the three women will be ours." So the Vizier said to the King, "Your Majesty, that Lapidary hath women three, and women like unto them are not in the whole kingdom. Sire, prithee, seize thou upon some fault of this Lapidary, and destroy him. Then will the three women become inmates of thy harem." The King considered a while and said, "No matter what thou mayst ask of him, that all and sundry doth he bring. Now will I say unto him, "Thou must bring me news of my father, whether he be in heaven or whether he be in hell."

20. dapān vustād āu̯ lāl shināk pādshahas kạrun salām pādshāh chus dapān az tāñy yi mʸe vunmai ti bōzuth tsʸe az gatse mēⁱnis mā̩ⁱlisunz khabạr aneñy su cha janatas manz kinạ dōzakas drāu̯ lāl shināk vōt panun garạ dapān chu aⁱti yiman zạnānạn tren az chum dapān pādshāh mēⁱnis mā̩ⁱlⁱ sunz khabᵊr aneñy bo kya kare ath su che khabạr kā̩ⁱtʸa vạⁱri gamutʸ tas momᵊtis yi vutsạs khå̄tūn yi hoi yi yasạ rothunạ kạⁱrⁱ ā̊s karān sạ ā̊s pạⁱri ba Khudā aⁱmi dopᵘnas khʸē chạ nạ fikᵊr gats hạs kharᵊj beye dapus pādshahas chōnʸ gatse zūn sombᵊrun mā̩ⁱdānas manz zūn gatse sombᵊrun bē shumār.

21. sombᵊrau pādshahạn zūn bēshumār ạⁱtⁱ pʸeṭh khuṭ yi lāl shināk yi muslᵊhan vatạⁱrith ạⁱtⁱ pʸeṭh byōṭh pāne ạⁱmis dopun pādshahas tsạ kya gatsiy anun mā̩ⁱlⁱsund nishānạ yi vothus pādshah dopᵘnas akh gatsiy anun janᵊ tukh mʸeva beye gatsiy anun mʸēⁱnis mā̩ⁱlⁱsandi daskatạ khath dopun yiman diyu yath zinis nār so pā̩ⁱri.

22. dapān vustād yimau yeli ath zinis nār dyuth yivān chu nạ kuni bōzᵊnạ yi lāl shināk lāl shinākan dyuth ath musᵊlas kasᵊm dopᵘnas mʸe gatse vātun panun garᵊ kah lagimnạ dēshun dapān tuvⁱy ạⁱmⁱ lāl shinākan ạch mutsᵊrin tạ vōtᵘmuth garạ panun ạⁱmi khā̊ tūnī kạr kå̄ma habjōshī kạrun mʸeva janᵊ tukh dạn taiyār beye likhun khath ath kạrun ạⁱmis pādshahᵊsạndis mā̩ⁱlⁱsund daskath beye mohur aⁱtⁱ manz likhun pādshahas chōnʸ gatsạ mʸe nish vātun vazīr hʸeth beye nāyid hʸeth tithai pā̩ⁱṭhⁱ yithạ

20. And saith my Master :—

The Lapidary came to the King and made his bow. Quoth the King to him, "Hitherto hast thou hearkened unto whatsoever command I gave to thee. To-day must thou bring unto me news of my father, whether he be in heaven or whether he be in hell." The Lapidary departed and came to his own house. Quoth he to these three women, "To-day the King telleth me to bring news of his father. What am I to do? How know I even how many years have passed since he hath died?" Then up and spake the lady who had made the jewelled bracelet (now she was a fairy who was obedient unto God), "Let nothing prey upon thy mind. Go thou, and ask of him expenses. Then say thou to the King, 'Thou must gather together for me firewood. In the plain let there be gathered together bundles of fuel beyond count.'"

21. The King assembled and piled firewood beyond count, and the Lapidary ascended thereon. He spread upon it the skin mat, and thereon he took his seat. Quoth he to the King, "What token from thy father shall I bring?" and up and said the King, "First must thou bring unto me a fruit from the garden of paradise, and secondly must thou bring unto me a letter signed by my father." Said the Lapidary to the people standing round, "Set ye the firewood alight on all four sides."

22. And moreover saith my Master :—

When they had set the pyre alight, the Lapidary could no longer be seen for fire and smoke. He uttered a charm to the skin mat, saying, "I would arrive at mine own house, but have a care that no one see it." He closed his eyes, and when he opened them he found himself at home. Then that lady did a deed. Of the seven metals[1] she prepared a fruit, a pomegranate of the Garden of Heaven, and moreover she wrote a letter to which she put the signature of the King's father, and sealed it with his seal. And this was what she wrote to the King: "Thou must come unto me

[1] The *haft-jōsh* is an amalgam of iron, antimony, lead, gold, tin, copper, and silver.

pạ^{i}ṭh^{y} lāl shināk m^{y}e nish vōt kakạd kạrun havālạ ạ^{i}mis lāl shinākas beye dyūth^{u}nas athas khyạth yi dạn.

23. ạtāñy gai ŧsōr do yi nār gạmut ŧsetạ path rōd^{ə}mut sūr yi lāl shināk drāu̯ longū^{i}ṭh^{i} kạ^{i}rith sulạ voth ath sūras manz divān chu duleñy naz^{ə}r bāzau kạ^{i}r^{i} naz^{ə}r khābạrdārau niye khab^{ə}r dop^{u}has pādshahạm ạ^{i}mi sūrạ manzạ gaŧsān che sus^{ə} rārai yi ma ā^{i}s^{i} lāl shināk āmut yim che yimai kathạ karān nazạr chak ōkun āu̯ vōḍạ lāl shināk athas kh^{y}ạth h^{y}eth dạn beyes athas kh^{y}ạth h^{y}eth khath kạ^{i}rin pādshahạs salām dạn thāu̯nas bōnt^{ə} ka^{i}ni khath thāu̯nas bōnt^{ə} ka^{i}ni yi khath muŧs^{ə}run pạḍun ath l^{y}ūkhmut bo kyā chus jan^{ə} tas manz chōn^{y} gaŧsạ vātun yūr^{y} vazīr h^{y}eth beye nāyid h^{y}eth jal^{ə}d.

24. pādshāh chu karān fik^{ə}ra m^{y}e dapyau yi lāl shināk ga^{i}li yi āu̯ mạ^{i}lisạnz m^{y}e khabạr h^{y}eth dapān pādshah ạ^{i}mis lāl shinākas bu kh^{y}ạthạ pạ^{i}ṭh^{y} vāte tat jan^{ə}tas manz dop^{u}nas lāl shinākan yūth z^{y}ūn m^{y}e kyuth sōmb^{ə}rå̄vuth tīth^{i} tre gaŧsun somb^{ə}rāva^{i}n^{i} jal^{ə}d vātak jan^{ə} tas manz somb^{ə} rau pādshahan z^{y}ūn bēshumār ạ^{i}t^{i} p^{y}eṭh karanå̄vun vat^{ə}run ạ^{i}t^{i} p^{y}eṭh khuṭh pāne beye vazīr beye nāyid d^{y}ūthuk zinas nār ŧso pạ^{i}r^{i}.

25. dapān vustād dud yi pādshah beye vazīr beye nāyid trin^{ə} vai gạ^{i}l^{i} vōt ạth lāl shinākas nish su vazīr yus vazīr pādshah kūr h^{y}eth å̄s ŧsalān tạ sam^{ə} kukh å̄khun khuṭh suy vōt ạ^{i}mis lāl shinākạsund garạ pane vạ^{i}n^{i} ka^{i}rikh kathe bāṭhạ vonus ạ^{i}m^{i} lāl

with thy Vizier and with thy barber, just in the same manner as the Lapidary hath come unto me." This paper she made over to the Lapidary, and in his hand she laid the pomegranate.

23. By this time four days had passed and the fire became extinct, leaving naught but ashes. The Lapidary went forth wearing only his loin-cloth, and rolled himself in these ashes. The discerners then discerned, and the newsmen brought the news. Cried they, "Your Majesty, there cometh a sound as of rustling from the ashes. Can it be that the Lapidary is returned?" And while they were yet speaking these words and gazing towards the pyre, there came forth from it the Lapidary, in the one hand holding a pomegranate, and in the other the letter. Having made his bow to the King, he laid the pomegranate and the letter before him. The King opened the letter and read it, and this was its contents, "I, of a truth, am in heaven. Thou must come hither speedily, with thy Vizier and with thy barber."

24. The King considered awhile, "I said unto myself that this Lapidary would come to destruction, and, lo, he hath come to me with news from my father." Quoth he to the Lapidary, "How can I convey myself to that abode of bliss?" Replied the Lapidary, "Thou must gather together three times so much firewood as thou didst gather for me, and then speedily wilt thou arrive in heaven." The King gathered together fuel beyond count. Upon it he made them spread a mat, and upon it he ascended and sat, himself with the Vizier and the barber. They set the pyre alight on all four sides.

25. And my Master saith :—

Burnt up was the King, burnt up was the Vizier, and burnt up was the barber. The three became utterly destroyed. And from his home came to the Lapidary's house that first Vizier, the one who had been eloping with the princess when he met the young Ākhūn. Together held they mutual converse, and the Lapidary told him of his journey, and of all the villainy that the Vizier and the barber

shinākan yi panun safar yüs a^i^m^i^ nāyidan tạ vazīran a^i^mis å̊s pēsh on muth dop^u^nas paneñy khå̊tūn ninsạ pānạs yesạ yi lāl māl pạ^i^r^i^ å̊s tas d^y^üthun rukhsath yesạ yi patạ añyēn z^y^ēnith sạ thå̊vun pānas.

26. dapān vustād su vazīr byōth pād^a^shāhī kar^a^ni lāl shinăk byōth vazīrī kar^a^ni.—aslā malaikum vālai kum salām.

had done unto him. Said he to him, "Take, sir, thine own lady to thyself." But as for Lālmāl the Fairy, he gave her leave to return to her home, while she whom last of all he had won for himself, her he kept with him as his wife.

26. And saith my Master :—

The Vizier ascended the vacant throne and ruled right royally, and the Lapidary was appointed by him to the Viziership.

And may the peace be upon you, and on you be peace.

THE TEXT OF THE TALES

AS TRANSCRIBED BY

PAṆḌIT GŌVINDA KAULA

With interlinear translation into English

I

1.	**Shĕhan-shāh**	**Sultān-i-Mahmōd-i-Gaznavī**
	The-king-of-kings	Sulṭān-of-Maḥmūd-of-Ghaznī

ôs^{u}	**karān**	**pāna**	**mulkan**	**pöravī.**
was	making	himself	(of-his-)lands	protection.

2.	**Phakīr**	**lögith**	**ôs^{u}**	**phērān**	**wāna-wān**
	Faqīr	having-taking-the-appearance-of	he-was	wandering	from-shop-to-shop

"myāni-ah^{a}day	**āsi**	**mā**	**kā̃h**	**nôtuwān."**
"(In-)my-time	may-there-be	I-wonder-if	anyone	feeble."

3.	**Jāyĕ-akis**	**ös^{i}**	**karān**	**dwā-yi-khör**
	(In-)place-a-certain	they-were	making	prayer-of-welfare

ad^{a}la-tȧm^{i}-sandi-söty	**āsakh**	**cĕshma**	**sēr.**
justice-his-by	were-of-them	the-eyes	satisfied.

4.	**Jāyĕ-akis**	**wuchun**	**hānzāh**	**akh**	**alīl**
	(In-)place-a-certain	was-seen-by-him	a-certain-fisherman	one	wretched

muhima-sötin	**ôs^{u}**	**gamot^{u}**	**suy**	**zalīl.**
poverty-by	was	gone	he-verily	brought-low.

5.	**Muhima-sötin**	**ôs^{u}**	**trāwān**	**āh**	**ta**	**wōsh,**
	Poverty-by	(he-)was	emitting	sighs	and	groans,

muhima-sötin	**tas**	**na**	**rūd^{u}mot^{u}**	**kā̃h-ti**	**hōsh.**
poverty-by	to-him	not	remained	any-even	sense.

6. **Yōra zālāh ôs^{u} lāyān gāṭa sān**
Whence a-certain-net (he-)was casting skill with

tōra zālas ôsus-na kĕ̄h khasān.
thence to-the-net was-for-him-not anything rising.

7. **Dopus shĕhan "kar mĕ sötin böj^{i}-baṭh**
It-was-said-to-him by-the-king, "make me with sharing

"lāy zālāh, yād-i-Alāh dilas raṭh."
"cast a-single-net, memory-of-God to-the-heart seize."

8. **Lôyun zālāh tōra khot^{u} tas gāḍa-hath**
Was-cast-by-him a-single-net thence arose for-him fish-a-hundred

pātashĕhas bōnṭh-kun āv suy hĕth.
the-king before came he-verily having-taken(-them).

9. **Gāḍa-hatas badal dyut^{u}nas mŏhara-dyār**
For-the-fish-hundred in-exchange was-given-by-him-to-him coin-wealth

lāl nigīn māl mŏktay wūṭha-bār.
rubies jewels property pearls-verily camel-loads.

10. **Rāth barith pātashĕhan dyutus nād**
Night having-passed by-the-king was-given-to-him a-summons

"ts^{a}y chukh myôn^{u} shĕrīkh nāmurād.[1]
"thou-verily art my sharer without-hope.

11. **"Muhim kāsawun^{u} hĕkmat-i-Parwardigār,**
"Poverty expeller (is-)the-skill-of-Providence,

"tāph shĕhul^{u} sarda garam now^{u} bāhār.
"sunshine cold coolness warmth new spring.

[1] *Nāmurād* is the word given by Hātim. A version of the poem current in Śrīnagar has *bā-murād*, with hope. In Kāshmīrī, *nā-murād* means "without hope or expectation".

12.	**“Wanayĕy,**	**‘zan**	**banda**	**mônzur**	**zāsanuy**[1]
	“‘kātsa-hĕkmüts^{ü}	**muhim**	**tagiy**	**kāsunuy.’”**	
	“‘by-how-much-skill	poverty	will-be-possible-for-thee	to-be-expelled-verily.’”	

13.	**Ȧth^{i}-andar**	**chuy**	**wustādāh**	**wanān**	**zār,**
	This-verily-in	is-verily	a-certain-teacher	saying	prayer,

“jumala	**ālam**	**banda**	**Ahmad**	**wumĕdwār.”**
“(on-Him-from-whom-is-)the-entire	world	the-slave	Aḥmad	(is-) hopeful.”

---

[1] The meaning of the line is unknown. Hātim gives it as what he has learnt by tradition. As regard *zāsanuy*, informants in Śrīnagar tell me that it is not a Kāshmīrī word. Hātim says that it is an “old” word which is unintelligible to him. The Śrīnagar version is :—

“Wanay,	**‘yiy**	**zān,**	**banda,**	**mônzur**	**tsĕ**	**āsunuy,’**
“I-would-say-to-thee	‘this	know,	slave,	accepted	by-thee	it-is-to-be,’

which is intelligible.

II.—TŌTA-SÜNZ^{ü} KATH

PARROT-OF THE-STORY

1. Dapān wustād,—
1. (Is) saying the-teacher,—

Shĕhar akh gav, Shĕhar-ĕ-Īrān. Tàt^{i}
Country one went (i.e. is), the-country-of-Īrān. There

ôs^{u} pātashĕhāh; tamis^{ü}y chuh nāv
there-was a-certain-king; to-him-verily is the-name

Bạh^{a}dūr Khān. Tàm^{i} ôs^{u} kor^{u}mot^{u} bāg
Bahādur Khān. By-him was made a-garden

zanānan-kyut^{u}. Tath ös^{ü}-na wath görzānas.
women-for. For-it was-not a-path for-a-stranger.

Tath bāgas-manz gav pöda phakīrāh.
That garden-in went (i.e. became) manifest a-certain-faqīr.

Nazar-bāzav kür^{ü} nazar. Khabar-dārav
By-the-watchers was-made sight. By-the-informers

niyĕ khabar amis-pātashĕhas. Dopukh,
was-brought information to-that-king. It-was-said-by-them,

"phakīrāh tsāv bāgas-manz." Būzun
"a-certain-faqīr entered the-garden-in." Was-heard-by-him

pātashĕhan, hyotun söty wazīr.
by-the-king, was-taken-by-him in-company the-vizier.

Gay tath-bāgas-manz, wuchun ati phakīr.
They-went that-garden-in, was-seen-by-him there the-faqīr.

2. Lachĕ-nôw^{u} chuy har-wati bīnāh.
2. He-who-has-a-hundred-thousand-names (i.e. God) is-verily on-every-path seeing.

Bōz, wŏphādörī ankāh.
Hear, loyalty (is) a-rara-avis.

"Hā Phakīrō,	**yōr**	**kōr**	**tsākhō?**
"Ho Faqīr-O,	here	where	didst-thou-enter-O?

"Katikō	**chukh?**	**Kati-pĕṭha**	**ākhō?"**
"Of-where	art-thou?	Where-from	didst-thou-come-O?"

Phakīr	**dapān,—**
The-faqīr	(is) saying,—

"Kor^{u}	**mĕ**	**sölāh.**	**Tuhond^{u}**	**khĕv**	**mĕ**	**kyāh?"**
"Was-made	by-me	a-stroll.	Your	was-eaten	by-me	what?"

Bōz,	**wŏphādörī**	**ankāh.**
Hear,	loyalty	(is) a-rara-avis.

3. Pātashĕhas	**bōnṭha-kani**	**pōshĕ-thür^{u}.**
To-the-king	front-towards	(was) a-flower-shrub.

Ath^{i}-tal	**mumot^{u}**	**bulbulāh.**	**Yĕli**
It-verily-below	(was) dead	a-certain-nightingale.	When

yimau	**amis-phakīras**	**khashĕm**	**kor^{u},**	**tĕli**	**pĕv**
by-them	to-that-faqīr	wrath	was-made,	then	fell

phakīr	**pathar**	**wasith,**	**mumot^{u}**	**bulbul**
the-faqīr	downwards	having-tumbled,	the-dead	nightingale

gav	**thod^{u}**	**wŏthith.**	**Pātashĕhas**	**hôwun**
became	erect	having-arisen.	To-the-king	was-shown-by-him

yih	**vir^{i}d.**	**Gav**	**nīrith;**	**phīrith**
this	magic-power.	He-went	having-emerged;	having-returned

biyĕ	**āv,**	**bulbul**	**mūd^{u}**	**biyĕ,**	**phakīr**
again	he-came,	the-nightingale	died	again,	the-faqīr

gav	**biyĕ**	**zinda.**	**Hyotun**	**nērun,**	**yim**
became	again	alive.	It-was-begun-by-him	to-go-forth,	they

chis	**karān**	**zāra-pāra.**	**Dapān**
are-to-him	making	entreaties.	Saying

chis,—
they-are-to-him,—

"Hā	**phakīra,**	**khizmath**	**karay,**
"Ho	Faqīr-O,	service	will-I-do-to-thee,

"Dŏda-harȧk^{i}	**khös^{i}**	**hō**	**baray.**
"Milk-cream-of	cups	O	will-I-fill-for-thee.

"Khāsa	**pŏlāv**	**macāma**	**khĕkh-na?"**
"Special	pilaos	(and) *macāmas*	wilt-thou-not-eat?"

Bōz,	**wŏphādörī**	**ankāh.**
Hear,	loyalty	(is) a-rara-avis.

4. Yus	**vir^{i}d**	**phakīras**	**ôs^{u},**	**suy**
What	magic-power	to-the-faqīr	was,	that-verily

bôwun	**amis-pātashĕhas.**	**Ȧm^{i}-pātashĕhan**
was-confided-by-him	to-that-king.	By-that-king

bôw^{u}	**wazīras.**
it-was-confided.	to-the-vizier.

Kor^{u}	**tarbyĕth**	**pātashĕhan**	**wazīras,**
Was-made	instruction	by-the-king	to-the-vizier,

Suti	**mah^{a}ram**	**korun**	**ath-sīras.**
He-also	intimately-acquainted	was-made-by-him	for-this-secret.

Gay	**sölas**	**shikāras**	**yĕg-jāh.**
They-went	for-excursion	for-hunting	together.

Bōz,	**wŏphādörī**	**ankāh.**
Hear,	loyalty	(is) a-rara-avis.

Tōta mumot^{u} wuchukh dar biyābān,
A-parrot dead was-seen-by-them in the-forest,

"Hā wazīrō, āsihē shūbān.
"Ho Vizier-O, it-would-have-been beautiful.

"Zuv amis-manz thāvtan sāthāh."
"(Thy-) soul this-one-in place-please-it for-a-certain-time."

Bōz, wŏphādörī ankāh.
Hear, loyalty (is) a-rara-avis.

Dop^{u} wazīran,
It-was-said by-the-vizier,

"Pātashĕham, yüts^{ü}-kôl^{u} mumot^{u},
"King-my, for-a-long-time (it-is-) dead,

"Phakh chus yiwān, khabar
"Stink is-from-it coming, news (i.e. who knows?)

kar chuh gamot^{u}.
when it-is gone (dead).

"Chusna ṭhaharān; wanta-sa kara kyāh."
"I-am-not waiting (i.e. able to stay here); say-please-sir I-shall-do what."

Bōz, wŏphādörī ankāh.
Hear, loyalty (is) a-rara-avis.

5. Pātashĕh karān zāra-pāra wazīras
The king (is) making entreaties to-the-vizier

ami-bāpath. "Bŏh wuchahan tōta kyuth^{u}
this-for. "I would-see-it the-parrot how

āsihē shūbān." Ȧm^{i} būz^{u}nas-na
it-would-be beautiful." By-this-one was-heard-by-him-for-him-not

wazīran kĕ̆h.
by-the-vizier anything.

Dapān wustād,—
(Is) saying the-teacher,—

Amis ôs^{u} dilas-manz dagāy. Wuñ tsāv
To-him was the-heart-in disloyalty. Now entered

pātashĕh amis-tōtas-manz, panun^{u} moḍ^{u} tshunun-
the-king this-parrot-in, his-own body was-dashed-

trövith. Tōta wọth^{u} thod^{u}, chuh
down-by-him. The-parrot arose erect, it-is

phērān. Wazīran kür^{u} köm^{ü}, tsāv
moving-round. By-the-vizier was-done a-deed, he-entered

ath-pātashĕha-sandis-maḍis-manz. Yiy ôs^{u} amis
that-king-of-body-in. This-verily was to-him

dar dil.
in heart.

Pĕv pĕtarun pātashĕhas pānas,
(That-load-which) fell to-carry-out to-the-king himself,

Bôr^{u} lodun wazīras nādānas.
(That-) load was-laid-by-him to-the-vizier the-fool.

Ôsus dagāy zāgān dādkhāh.
There-was-to-him disloyalty watching a-petitioner.

Bōz, wŏphādörī, ankāh.
Hear, loyalty (is) a-rara-avis.

6. Tōta chuh hawā-yi-asmān, wazīr
The-parrot is (in) the-air-of-heaven, the-vizier

chuh pātashĕha-sandis-maris-manz. Wọth^{u} thod^{u}.
is the-king-of-body-in. He-arose erect,

khoth^{u} guris lashkari-manz gav.
mounted to-the-horse the-army-in went.

Dop^{u}nakh, "mūd^{u} wazīr, guri-pĕṭha
It-was-said-by-him-to-them, "died the vizier, horse-from

wasith-pĕv."
having-tumbled-he-fell."

Khabardārav niyĕ say khabarāh.
By-the-informers was-brought that-very one-piece-of-news.

Bōz, wŏphādörī ankāh.
Hear, loyalty (is) a-rara-avis.

7\. **Ȧm^{i}-wazīran yĕli kür^{u} köm^{ü}, ṭsāv**
By-that-vizier when was-done the-deed, he-entered

pātashĕha-sandis-maris-manz, tuj^{ü}n athas-kĕth
the-king-of-body-in, was-raised-by-him the-hand-in

shĕmshēr, ath-pananis-maris korun rēza.
a-sword, to-that-his-own-body was-made-by-him piece(s).

Ath-lashkari dopun, "nīriv tīrandāz biyĕ
To-that-army it-was-said-by-him, "go-forth archers also

bandūkbāz. Yus māriwa tōta, tamis
gunners. Who will-kill-of-you a-parrot, to-him

baniv bakh^{a}cöyish." Ȧm^{i}-tōtan yĕli
there-will-become a-present." By-that-parrot when

būz^{u}, ta ṭsol^{u}. Gav tas phakīras-
it-was-heard, then he-fled. He-wẹnt that fakīr-

nishĕ, yus tath-bāgas-manz ôs^{u} tami-dŏha.
near, who that-garden-in was (on-) that-day.

Hukum dyutun^{ü}y tīrandāzan,
Order was-given-by-him-verily to-the-archers,

"Kan thȧv^{i}tav myānĕn-nāzan."
"Ear place-ye-please to-my-blandishments."

Tōta	**māranas**	**dyut^{u}nakh**	**photuwāh.**
The-parrot	for-killing	was-given-by-him-to-them	a-certain-decision.

Bōz	**wŏphādörī**	**ankāh.**
Hear,	loyalty	(is) a-rara-avis.

8. **Yus as^{a}l ôs^{u} pātashāh, suh chuh tōtas-manz phakīras-nishin. Suh tōta kaīsi môr^{u}-na. Dŏha-aki drāv yih pātashĕh sölas shikāras. Wôt^{u} jāyĕ-akis. Ati wuch^{ü}n miñĕ-mür^{ü}. Amis^{ü}y kür^{ü}kh lār, Ün^{ü}kh lashkari-manz. Dop^{u}nakh ȧm^{i}-pātashĕhan, "yĕs-kȧn^{i} yih ȶaliv, tas dimav gardan."**

Who real was king, he is the-parrot-in the-fakīr-near. That parrot by-any-one was-killed-not. On-day-one issued this king for-excursion for-hunting. He-arrived at-place-one. There was-seen-by-him a-hind. To-this-one-verily was-made-by-them pursuit, She-was-brought-by-them the-army-in. It-was-said-by-him-to-them by-this-king, "whom-from-near she may-escape, to-him I-will-give the-neck."

9. **Dapān wustād,—**
(Is) saying the-teacher,—

Ami-miñĕ-mari tuj^{ü} wŏṭh, pātashĕha-sandi-kala-pĕṭh^{i} ȶhuñ^{ü}n wŏṭh, ȶüj^{ü}. Löris

By-this-hind was-raised a-leap, the-king-of-head-over was-thrown-by-her a-leap, she-fled. They-ran-for-her

pata. Yus suh tōta ôs^{u}, yüh ôs^{u} phakīras-
after. Who that parrot was, he was the-fakīr-

nishĕ. Phakīr ôs^{u} söhib-ĕ-āgāh. Dopun
near. The-fakīr was a-master-intelligent. It-was-said-by-him

amis-tōtas, yĕs-manz yih pātashĕh ôs^{u},
to-this-parrot, whom-in this king was,

dop^{u}nas, "gatsh, sa, nēr. Az labakh
it-was-said-by-him-to-him, "go, sir, go-forth. To-day wilt-thou-take

panun^{u} moḍ^{u}." Yim chih amis-miñĕ-marĕ-pata
thine-own body." Who are this-hind-after

lārān, nakha rōzān chĕkhna.
running, near remaining she-is-to-them-not.

10. Dāpān wustād,—
(Is) saying the-teacher,—

Ati ôs^{u} mumot^{u} hāputh. Pātashāh tsāv
Here was a-dead bear. The-king entered

amis-hāpatas-manz. Lāryāv. Yus yih
that-bear-in. He-ran. Which this

pātashāha-sond^{u} mor^{u} ôs^{u} yih trôwun
king-of body was this was-abandoned by-him

atiy.
there-verily.

Shod^{u} būzun tōtan. Lāryāv.
News was-heard-by-him by-the-parrot. He-ran.

Kuli-dadari-manz-hau prāryāv.
Tree-hole-in he-waited.

Mor^{u}	**lobun.**	**Kår^{i}tōs**	**marhabāh.**
The-body	was-taken-by-him.	Make-please-ye-for-him	a-wish-of-good-luck.

Bōz,	**wŏphādörī**	**ankāh.**
Hear,	loyalty	(is) a-rara-avis.

11.

Tōta	**pĕv**	**atiy**	**pathar.**	**Yih**	**tsāv**
The-parrot	fell	there-verily	down.	He	entered

pātashāh	**pananis**	**maris-manz.**	**Yus**	**yüh**	**wazīr**
the-king.	his-own	body-in.	Who	this	vizier

ôs^{u},	**suh**	**chuh**	**hāpatas-manz.**	**Pātashāh**	**as^{a}l**
was,	he	is	the-bear-in.	The-king	real

yus	**ôs^{u},**	**suh**	**khot^{u}**	**guris-pĕṭh.**	**Dopun**
who	was,	he	mounted	horse-upon.	It-was-said-by-him

yiman	**lōkan,**	**"möryūn**	**hāputh."**	**Lôy^{u}has**
to-these	people,	"kill-ye-him	the-bear."	Fired-by-them-at-him

bandūkh,	**phuṭ^{o}r^{u}has**	**zang.**	**Onukh**
a-gun,	was-broken-by-them-for-him	the-leg.	He-was-brought-by-them

raṭith	**pātashāhas-nish.**	**Dop^{u}nas**	**pātashāhan,**
having-seized	the-king-near.	It-was-said-by-him-to-him	by-the-king,

"tsĕ	**kür^{u}tham**	**dagāy.**	**Bŏh**	**mārahath-na,**
"by-thee	was-done-by-thee-to-me	disloyalty.	I	should-kill-thee-not,

kyāh	**karahö?**	**Lōkh**	**dapanam,**	**'hāputh**
what	should-I-do?	People	will-say-to-me,	'a-bear

chus	**wazīr.'**	**Tsĕ**	**chuy**	**panun^{u}**
is-to-him	vizier.'	By-thee	is-by-thee	thine-own

mor^{u} gôl^{u}mot^{u}. Wumāh thāwath. Ts̲^{a}h
body destroyed. Now-not I-may-keep-thee. Thou

hāputh wazīr. Bŏh, hasa, mārath.”
a-bear vizier. I, sir, will-kill-thee.”

12. Dapān wustād,—
(Is) saying the-teacher,—

Onukh zyun^{u}. Zôlukh hāputh.
There-was-brought-by-them firewood. He-was-burnt-by-them the-bear.

Hath waīsi gav, kam yā jyāday,
A-hundred (years) in-age, went, less or more,

Āv Bạh^{a}dūr-Khānas pyāday.
Came to-Bahādur-K̲h̲ān the-messenger (of Death).

Kar, Wahab-Khāra, “Ạlāh, Ạlāḥ.”
Make, Wahb-the-blacksmith-O, “Allāh, Allāh.”

Bōz, wŏphādŏrī ankāh.
Hear, loyalty (is) a-rara-avis.

III.—SŌDĀGARA-SŪNZ^{Ū} KATH

MERCHANT-OF STORY

1. **Sōdāgār gav sōdāhas. Gari ös^{ü}s**
A-merchant went for-trade. At-home was-to-him

zanāna. Say gayĕ mushtākh phakīras-
the-wife. She-verily went (i.e. was) enamoured for-mendicant-

akis wārayāhas-kālas. Dŏha-aki āv sōdāgār
one for-a-long-time On-day-one came the-merchant

gara panun^{u} māl hĕth. Pātashĕhas
house his-own goods having-brought. To-the-king

gayĕ khabar "sōdāgar wôt^{u}." Pātashāh
went news "the-merchant arrived." The-king

drāv sölas rāth-kyut^{u}, wôt^{u}
issued-forth for-an-excursion night-by, he-arrived

sōdāgara-sond^{u}. Chuh atiy wŏdañĕ,
(at) the-merchant's (house). He-is there-verily standing,

pahar chuh gamot^{u} röts^{ü}-hond^{u}, yih sōdāgar-
a-watch is gone the-night-of, this merchant's-

bāy wŏ̈tsh^{ü}, wŏḍi-pĕṭh hĕ̈ts^{ü}n bata-tröm^{ü}.
wife arose, crown-of-head-on was-taken-by-her a-cooked-rice-copper-dish.

Pātashāh chuh wuchān tsūri-pöṭhin.
The-king is watching theft-like (i.e. secretly).

Sōdāgar-bāy drāyĕ brūh-brūh, pātashāh
The-merchant's-wife went-forth in-front-in-front, the-king

chuh pakān pata-pata. Wöt^{i} mödānas-
is walking after-after. They-arrived a-plain-

akis-manz.	**Ati**	**ôs^{u}**	**phakīr**	**nāra-han**
one-in.	There	was	the-mendicant	fire-a-small

zölith.	**Kür$^{\ddot{u}}$s**	**ami**	**salām,**	**bata**
having-kindled.	Was-made-to-him	by-her	a-bow,	cooked-rice

thow^{u}nas	**bōnṭha-kani,**	**dop^{u}nas,**	**"khĕh."**
was-placed-by-her-for-him	front-in,	it-was-said-by-her-to-him,	"eat."

Am^{i}	**tul^{u}**	**tshōṭa,**	**lôyun**	**amis-sōdāgar-bāyĕ,**
By-him	was-raised	a-stick,	it-was-struck-by-him	to-that-to-the-merchant's-wife,

dop^{u}nas	**"tsir^{i}**	**kyāzi**	**āyĕkh?"**	**Dop^{u}nas**
it-was-said-by-him-to-her	"late	why	didst-thou-come?"	It-was-said-by-her-to-him

ami	**phīrith,**	**"az**	**ôsum**	**āmot^{u}**	**panun^{u}**
by-her	in-answer,	"to-day	was-to-me	come	my-own

khāwand,	**tạmiy**	**gōm**	**tsēr,**	**khētam**
husband,	by-that-verily	went-for-me	delay,	eat-for-me

wuñ	**bata."**	**Dop^{u}nas**	**ạm^{i}-phakīran,**
now	the-cooked-rice."	It-was-said-by-him-to-her	by-this-mendicant,

"bŏh	**khĕmay-na.**	**Gŏḍañ**	**dim**	**anith**
"I	will-eat-for-thee-not.	First	give-to-me	having-brought

amis-sōdāgāra-sond^{u}	**kala.**	**Ada**	**khĕmay**
this-merchant-of	head.	Then	I-will-eat-for-thee

bata."	**Pātashāh**	**ôs^{u}**	**wuchān,**	**yih-kĕntshāh**
cooked-rice."	The-king	was	watching,	whatever

yimav-dŏyav	**katha**	**karĕ,**	**tih**	**būz^{u}**
by-these-two	words	were-made,	that	was-heard

pātashĕhan	**sôruy.**
by-the-king	all.

2. Dapān wustād,—
(Is) saying the-teacher,—

Drāyĕ sōdāgar-bāy, wöʦ^{ü} panun^{u}
Went-forth the-merchant's-wife, she-arrived her-own

gara, khüʦ^{ü} hyor^{u}. Pātashāh chuh bŏna-
house, she-mounted above. The-king is below-

kani. Ami ʦoṭ^{u} amis-sōdāgaras kala,
in. By-her was-cut for-that-merchant the-head,

wüʦh^{ü} hĕth rumāli-kĕth. Chĕh
she-descended having-taken (it) a-kerchief-in. She-is

pakān brūh-brūh, pātashāh chuh pata-
walking in-front-in-front, the-king is after-

pata. Wöʦ^{ü} amis-phakīras-nish. Tulun
after. She-arrived that-mendicant-near. Was-raised-by-him

ʦhōṭa, lôyun amis-sōdāgar-bāyĕ. Dop^{u}nas,
the-stick, it-was-struck-by-him to-that-the-merchant's wife. It-was-said-by-him-to-her,

"ʦ^{a}h sapüz^{ü}kh-na amis-pananis-khāwanda-
"thou becamest-not (the wife) this-thine-own-husband-

sünz^{ü}, wun sapadakha myön^{ü}?"
of, now will-thou-become mine?"

3. Pātashāh drāv, wôt^{u} panun^{u} gara.
The-king went-forth, arrived his-own house.

Trôwun arām. Gāsh phŏl^{u}, wŏʦh^{ü}
Was-released-by-him repose (i.e. he took repose). Dawn burst-forth, there-arose

krēkh. Dapān chih, "sōdāgar wāʦāv
an-outcry. Saying they-are, "the-merchant arrived

panun^{u} gara, suy môr^{u} tsūrav."
his-own house, he-verily was-killed by-thieves."

Wöts^{ü} otuy sōdāgar-bāy, dapān chĕh
Arrived there-verily the-merchant's-wife, saying she-is

pātashĕhas, "khāwand āyām, suy
to-the-king, "the-husband came-to-me, he-verily

môr^{u}ham tsūrav." Pātashāhas chĕh khabar,
was-killed-by-them-for-me by-thieves." To-the-king is information,

"yih sōdāgar kȧm^{i} môr^{u}?" Tsẖārān
"this merchant by-whom was-killed?" Seeking

chih pay, sōdāgar kȧm^{i} môr^{u},
they-are a-clue, the-merchant by-whom was-killed,

kaĭsi chuna khasān zima.
to-anyone is-not rising responsibility.

4. Dapān wustād,—
(Is) saying the-teacher,—

Koḍukh yih sōdāgar, zôlukh.
Was-brought-forth-by-them this merchant, he-was-burnt-by-them.

Otuy drāv pātashāh biyĕ söriy chuh
There-verily went-forth the-king and-also all is

wuchān. Āyĕ ȧm^{i}-sünz^{ü} kŏlay, yih chĕh
seeing. She-came him-of the-wife, she is

karān gath. Dapān chĕh, "bŏti
doing the-suttee-procedure. Saying she-is, "I-also

zāla pān." Āyĕ, hĕts^{ü}n
will-burn (my) body." She-came, was-begun-by-her

wŏṭh-tshunün^{ü} nāras-manz. Pātashāh gōs,
a-leap-to-be-taken the-fire-in. The-king went-to-her

kür^{u}nas	**thaph.**	**Dapān**	**chus**	**pātashāh,**
was-made-by-him-to-her	hand-grasping.	Saying	is-to-her	the-king,

"yiy,	**ta**	**tih**	**kyāh?**	**Tiy,**	**ta**	**yih**
"this-if,	then	that	what?	That-if,	then	this

kyāh?"	**Dop^{u}nas,**	**"mĕ**	**trāv**	**yĕla.**
what?"	It-was-said-by-her-to-him,	"for-me	let-go	from-restraint.

Bŏh	**zāla**	**pān."**	**Dop^{u}nas,**	**"nāgas-akis-**
I	will-burn	(my) body."	It-was-said-by-her-to-him,	"spring-one-

pĕṭh	**chĕy**	**myōñ^{ü}**	**dŏda-bĕñĕ.**	**Say**	**waniy**
on	is-verily	my	milk-sister.	She-verily	will-tell-to-thee

amyuk^{u}	**mānĕ."**	**Tröv^{ü}n**	**yĕla,**
of-this	the-meaning."	She-was-let-go-by-him	from-restraint,

zôl^{u}	**ami**	**pān**	**pananis-khāwandas-söty,**
was-burnt	by-her	(her) body	her-own-husband-with,

gayĕ	**khalās.**	**Pagāh**	**drāv**	**pātashāh,**
she-went	(to) freedom (from existence).	Tomorrow	went-forth	the-king,

wôt^{u}	**ath-nāgas-pĕṭh.**	**Wuch^{ü}n**	**ati**
he-arrived	that-spring-upon.	Was-seen-by-him	there

zanānāh,	**amis^{ü}y**	**zanāni**	**chuy**	**dapān**
a-certain-woman,	to-that-very	woman	is-verily	saying

pātashāh,	**"tiy,**	**ta**	**yih**	**kyāh?**	**yiy,**
the-king,	"that-if,	then	this	what?	this-if,

ta	**tih**	**kyāh?"**	**Dop^{u}nas**	**ami**	**zanāni,**
then	that	what?"	Was-said-by-her-to-him	by-that	woman,

“ öṭhi-dŏh^{i}	**dapay**	**bŏh**	**amyuk^{u}**	**jĕwāb.”**
“ after-eight-days	I-will-tell-to-thee	I	of-this	the-answer.”

5. **Dapān wustād,—**
(Is) saying the-teacher,—

Öṭh	**dŏh**	**gay,**	**path-kun**	**pātashĕhas**
Eight	days	went,	afterwards	to-the-king

pĕv	**yād.**	**Lāḍyāv**	**pātashāh**	**tath-nāgas-**
fell	memory.	Ran	the-king	that-spring-

pĕṭh.	**Wuch^{ü}n**	**sŏh**	**zanāna,**	**dop^{u}nas,**
upon.	Was-seen-by-him	that	woman,	was-said-by-him-to-her,

“ wanum	**tami-kathi-hond^{u}**	**mānĕ.”**	**Dop^{u}nas,**
“ tell-to-me	that-word-of	meaning.”	Was-said-by-her-to-him,

“ gatsh,	**an**	**tshāwul**	**biyĕ**	**noṭ^{u}.”**	**Onun**
“ go,	bring	a-goat	and-also	a-jar.”	Was-brought-by-him

tshāwul	**ta**	**noṭ^{u}.**	**Dop^{u}nas,**	**“ was**	**yith-**
a-goat	and	a-jar.	Was-said-by-her-to-him,	“ descend	this-

nāgas-manz,	**noṭ^{u}**	**tshun-phirith.”**	**Dop^{u}nas**
spring-in,	the-jar	put-having-reversed (it).”	Was-said-by-her-to-him

biyĕ,	**“ anun**	**tshāwul**	**kana**	**raṭith,**
also,	“ bring-it	the-goat	by-the-ear	having-seized,

thāwus	**naṭis-pĕṭh**	**kala.”**	**Dop^{u}nas,**	**“ lāyus**
place-of-it	the-jar-upon	the-head.”	Was-said-by-her-to-him,	“ strike-to-it

shĕmshēri-hünz^{ü}	**tsünḍ^{ü}.”**
a-sword-of	stroke.”

6. Dapān,—
(Is) saying (the-teacher),—

Löy^{ü}nas	**shĕmshēri-hünz^{ü}**	**tsünḍ^{ü}.**	**Ami-**
Was-struck-by-him-to-it	the-sword-of	blow.	At-that-

sāta	**gatshān**	**pātashāh**	**göb**
moment	(is) becoming	the-king	invisible

hanga-ta-manga.
unexpectedly.

7. Dapān wustād,—
(Is) saying the-teacher,—

Yih	**chuh**	**wātān**	**bāgas-akis-manz.**
He (i.e. the king)	is	arriving	garden-one-in.

Ati	**chuh**	**wuchān**	**palang**	**pörith.**
There	he-is	seeing	a-bed	prepared.

Ath^{i}-pĕṭh	**khot^{u}**	**pātashāh,**	**trôwun**
It-verily-upon	mounted	the-king,	was-released-by-him

arām.	**Ati**	**āsa**	**par^{i}yĕ.**	**Yimav^{ü}y**
repose.	There	were	fairies.	By-them-verily

nĕv	**tulith**	**pātashāh.**	**T̲s̲ônukh**
was-conducted	having-raised (him)	the-king.	He-was-caused-to-enter-by-them

akis-jāyĕ-manz.	**Sapod^{u}**	**bĕdār.**	**Wuchān**
a-place-in.	He-became	awake.	Seeing

chuh	**jĕnatacĕ**	**jāyĕ.**	**Ati**	**lög^{i}mät^{i}**
he-is	heaven-of	place.	There	were-being-carried-on

nagma.	**Pātashāh**	**chuh**	**mushtākh**
dances-of-women.	The-king	is	enamoured

ath^{i}-tamāshĕs-kun.
this-very-spectacle-towards.

8. Dapān,—
(Is) saying (the-teacher),—

Gayĕ	**yima**	**par^{i}yĕ**	**pānas.**	**Amis**
Went	these	fairies	for-themselves (i.e. *away on their own business*).	To-him

dits^{ü}kh	**kunz.**	**Dop^{u}has,**	**" yith**	**kuṭhis**
was-given-by-them	a-key.	It-was-said-by-them-to-him,	" to-this	to-room

thāv	**kuluph.**	**Wŏth,**	**ats̨h**	**andar."**
apply (i.e. open)	the-lock.	Arise,	enter	within."

Ts̲āv	**andar.**	**Ati**	**wuchun**	**gur^{u}**
He-entered	within.	There	was-seen-by-him	a-horse

zīn	**karith.**	**Koḍun**	**nĕbar**	**thaph**
saddle	having-made.	It-was-brought-forth-by-him	outside	hand-grasping

karith.	**Nĕbar**	**yĕli**	**koḍun,**	**chuh**
having-done.	Outside	when	it-was-brought-forth-by-him,	he-is

wŏdañĕ	**thaph**	**karith.**	**Dop^{u}has,**
standing-still	hand-grasping	having-done.	It-was-said-by-them-to-him,

"khas	**yimis-guris."**	**Khot^{u}**	**amis-guris.**
" mount	to-this-to-horse."	He-mounted	to-that-to-horse.

Yih	**chuh**	**wuchān,**	**satav-zamīnav-tȧl^{i}**
He (i.e. the king)	is	seeing,	the-seven-worlds-below

ti	**nawav-asmānav-pĕṭh^{i}**	**ti,**	**yih-kĕnts̨hāh**
both	the-nine-heavens-above	also,	what-ever

Khŏdā-Söban	**pöda**	**kor^{u}mot^{u}**	**tih**	**wuch^{u}**
by-God-the-Master	created	(was) made	that	was-seen

pātashĕhan.	**Tath^{i}-söty**	**gav**	**mushtākh.**
by-the-king.	That-verily-with	he-became	entranced.

Gōs	**pöda**	**Shētān.**	**Dop^{u}nas,**	**"kyāh**
Became-to-him	visible	Satan.	It-was-said-by-him (Satan)-to-him,	"what

chukh	**wuchān?"**	**Dop^{u}nas**	**pātashĕhan,**
art-thou	seeing?"	It-was-said-by-him-to-him	by-the-king,

"yih-kĕntshāh	**Khŏdā-Söban**	**pöda**	**kor^{u},**
"what-ever	by-God-the-Master	created	was-made,

tih	**chus**	**wuchān."**	**Dop^{u}nas**	**Shētānan**
that	I-am	seeing."	It-was-said-by-him-to-him	by-Satan

phīrith,	**"ami-khŏta**	**hāway**	**bŏh.**	**Yih**
in-reply,	"that-than	(more) will-show-to-thee	I.	This

chĕy	**myöñ^{ü}**	**kunz.**	**Yith-kuṭhis**	**thāv**
is-verily	my	key.	To-this-room	apply

kuluph.	**Wŏth,**	**atsh**	**andar."**	**Tsāv**
the-lock.	Arise,	enter	within."	Entered

pātashāh	**andar.**	**Wuchun**	**ati**	**khar**
the-king	within.	Was-seen-by-him	there	an-ass

ganḍith.	**Dop^{u}nas,**	**"kaḍun**	**nĕbar,**	**khas**
bound.	It-was-said-by-him (Satan)-to-him,	"bring-it-forth	outside,	mount

amis^{ü}y.	**Yih-kĕntshāh**	**Khŏdā-Söban**	**pöda**
to-that-very-one.	What-ever	by-God-the-Master	created

kor^{u},	**tami-pĕṭh^{i}-kani**	**wuchakh**	**biyĕ**
was-made,	that-in-addition-to	thou-shalt-see	more

kĕ̃h."	**Khot^{u}**	**pātashāh**	**amis-kharas.**
something."	Mounted	the-king	to-that-ass.

9. **Dapān wustād,—**
(Is) saying the-teacher,—

Barābar	**wātanôwun**	**panun^{u}**	**gara.**
At-once	he-was-caused-to-arrive-by-him (the-ass)	his-own	house.

Khot^{u}	**hyor^{u}.**	**Phīrith**	**woth^{u}.**	**Wuchun**
He-ascended	up.	Returning	he-descended.	Was-seen-by-him

ati	**na**	**khar.**	**Pātashĕhas**	**āv**	**armān**
there	not	the-ass.	To-the-king	came	longing

tami-bāguk^{u}.	**Wŏ̃h**	**kĕtha-pöṭh^{i}**	**wāti ?**
of-that-garden.	Now	how	will-he-arrive (there) ?

Tot^{u},	**dapān,**	**gav**	**ath^{i}-nāgas-pĕṭh.**
From-there,	(they-are-)saying,	he-went	that-very-spring-on.

Dopun	**tamis-zanāni,**	**"mĕ**	**wanta**
It-was-said-by-him	to-that-to-woman,	"to-me	please-tell

yiy,	**ta**	**tih**	**kyāh ?**	**tiy,**	**ta**	**yih**
this-if,	then	that	what ?	that-if,	then	this

kyāh ?"	**Dop^{u}nas**	**ami**	**zanāni,**	**"anun**
what ?"	It-was-said-by-her-to-him	by-that	by-woman,	"bring-him

panun^{u}	**nĕcyuv^{u},**	**biyĕ**	**an**	**noṭ^{u},**	**biyĕ**
thine-own	son,	also	bring	a-jar,	also

an	**shĕmshēr."**	**Dop^{u}nas,**	**"was**	**yith-**
bring	a-sword."	It-was-said-by-her-to-him,	"descend	this-

nāgas-manz,	**wālun**	**panun^{u}**	**nĕcyuv^{u},**
spring-in,	bring-down-him	thine-own	son,

pāwun	**pathar,**	**thāwus**	**naṭis-pĕṭh**
cause-him-to-fall	down,	place-of-him	the-jar-upon

kala."	**Kanas**	**kür^{ü}nas**	**thaph**	**àm^{i}**
the-head."	To-his-ear	was-done-by-him-to-him	hand-grasping	by-that

pātashĕhan,	**tuj^{ü}n**	**shĕmshēr,**	**lāyi**
by-king,	was-raised-by-him	the-sword,	he-will-strike

amis-nĕcivis,	**kür^{ü}s**	**ami-zanāni**	**thaph**
to-that-to-son,	was-made-for-him	by-that-by-woman	hand-grasping

ath-shĕmshēri.	**Dop^{u}nas,**	**" yiy,**	**gav**
to-that-to-sword.	It-was-said-by-her-to-him,	" this-verily,	became (i.e. is)

tih ;	**tiy,**	**gav**	**yih.**	**Ts^{a}h**	**gōkh**
that ;	that-verily,	became (i.e. is)	this.	Thou	becamest

mushtākh	**bāgas ;**	**bĕñĕ**	**myöñ^{ü}**	**gayĕ**
enamoured	for-the-garden ;	the-sister	mine	became

mushtākh	**phakīras."**
enamoured	for-the-mendicant."

IV.—LĀLA-MALIKUN^{U} WON^{U}MOT^{U} GĔWUN

LĀL-MALLIK-OF	SPOKEN	SONG

1. **Dapān-chuh,—**
Saying-he-is,—

Dayĕ,	**zār**	**wån^{i}may,**	**Khŏdāyĕ,**
O-God,	petitions	are-said-by-me-to-Thee,	O-God,

bōztam	**tay,**
please-to-hear-me	. . . ,

Samsār	**böz^{i}gār.**
The-world	(is) a-deceiver.

2.

Hazrat-i-Ādam	**gŏḍa**	**lod^{u}nam**	**tay,**
Saint Adam	first	was-sent-by-Him-for-me	. . . ,

Malakav	**kor^{u}hay**	**tayār.**
By-angels	he-was-made-by-them-verily	complete.

Phor^{u}	**tas**	**Yiblīs,**	**tati**	**kor^{u}nam** [1]	**tay,**
Was-a-plunderer (i.e. ruined)	for-him	Satan,	from-there	he-was-expelled-by-him-for-me	. . . ,

Samsār	**böz^{i}gār.**
The-world	(is) a-deceiver.

3.

Hazrat-i-Nōh	**chuy**	**wŏlād-i-Ādam**	**tay,**
Saint Noah	is-verily	a-descendant-of-Adam	. . . ,

Phīrith	**gös**	**kuphār.**
Having-become-hostile	went-for-him	the-infidels.

[1] Hātim pronounces this word *kur^{u}nam*, but Śrīnagar paṇḍits *kuḍ^{u}nam* or *koḍ^{u}nam*.

Āh	**tȧm^{i}**	**kor^{u}nay,**	**sȧr^{i}**	**gav**	**ālam**
A-sigh	by-him	was-made-by-him-verily,	flooded (in his tears)	went	the-universe

tay,
. . . ,

Samsār	**bŏz^{i}gār.**
The-world	(is) a-deceiver.

4\.

Hazrat-i-Yīsāh	**kĕ̄h**	**chuna**	**kam**	**tay,**
Saint Jesus	anything	is-not	less	. . . ,

Sŏhiba-sond^{u}	**ṭôṭh^{u}**	**yār.**
The-Master-of	beloved	friend.

Tsŏn	**asmānan-pĕṭh**	**tȧm^{i}**	**sabakh**	**dop^{u}nam**
Four	heavens-upon	by-Him	lecture	was-said-by-Him-for-me.

tay,
. . . ,

Samsār	**bŏz^{i}gār.**
The-world	(is) a-deceiver.

5\.

Hazrat-i-Musāy	**trôwuy**	**kadam**	**tay,**
Saint by-Moses	was-put-forth-verily	a-step	. . . ,

Sŏhiba-sond^{u}	**kara**	**dīdār.**
The-Master-of	I-will-do	seeing.

Kōh-i-Tōra-pĕṭha	**tȧm^{i}**	**katha**	**karĕnam**
Mount-of-Sinai-from-on	by-him	words	were-made-by-him-for-me

tay,
. . . ,

Samsār	**bŏz^{i}gār.**
The-world	(is) a-deceiver.

6.	**Hazrat-i-Yibrāhim**	**kĕ̄h**	**chuna**	**kam**	**tay,**
	Saint Abraham	anything	is-not	less	. . . ,

Putalĕn	**korun**	**nakār.**
(Of-) idols	was-made-by-him	prohibition.

Tȧm^{i}	**kor^{u}**	**dīn-i-Mahmad**	**mahkam**	**tay,**
By-him	was-made	the-faith-of-Muḥammad	established	. . . ,

Samsār	**böz^{i}gār.**
The-world	(is) a-deceiver.

7.	**Marith**	**kabari**	**yĕli**	**wālanam**	**tay,**
	Having-died	in-the-grave	when	they-will-cause-me-to-descend	. . . ,

Panin	**böy^{i}**	**kyāh**	**yār.**
My-own	brethren	or	friends.

Tati	**Lāla-Malikas**	**kyāh**	**hāwanam**	**tay,**
There	to-Lāl-Mallik	what	will-they-show-to-me	. . . ,

Samsār	**böz^{i}gār.**
The-world	(is) a-deceiver.

V.—SŎNARA-SÜNZ^{ü} KATH

THE-GOLDSMITH-OF STORY

1. **Dapān wustād,—**
(Is) saying the teacher,—

Shĕharā akh chuh-ôs^{u}mot^{u}. Tȧt^{i} chuh
A-city one has-been. There is

sŏnar. Suy ôs^{u} tsāṭas bahan-hatan-hond^{u}
goldsmith. He-verily was (of-) pupil twelve-hundred-of

zyuṭh^{u}. Yuhuy ôs^{u}-gaḍān wasth
the-superior. He was-making articles

pātashĕha-sanzĕ-kōrĕ-kit^{i}. Tot^{u} ös^{ü}-gatshān
the-king's-daughter-for. There was-going

sŏnara-sünz^{ü} zanāna hĕth. Aki-dŏha
the-goldsmith-of wife carrying (them). On-one-day

dopus ami-pātashāh-kōri, " sōzun^{u} gatshi
it-was-said-to-her by-that-king's-daughter, " is-to-be-sent it-is-proper

panun^{u} khāwand." Dŏha-aki drāv
thine-own husband." On-day-one went-forth

sŏnar, sŏna-sünz^{ü} wöj^{ü} hĕth,
the-goldsmith, gold-of ring having-taken,

pātashāha-sanzĕ-kōrĕ-kits^{ü}. Ami pasand
king's-daughter-for. By-her approval

kür^{ü}sna. Dop^{u}nas, " yith chĕy
was-made-for-it-not. It-was-said-by-her-to-him, " to-this is-verily

waḍ." Āv pot^{u} phīrith. Wôt^{u}
crookedness." He-came (home) back returning. He-arrived

panun^{u} gara. Pĕv bĕmār.
his-own house. He-fell sick.

2. Amis ôsus pātashāha-sanzĕ-kōrĕ-hond^{u}
To-him was-to-him the-king's-daughter-of

ạsh^{ĕ}kh gŏmot^{u}. Pātashāh-kōrĕ ôs^{u}-gŏmot^{u}
love become. To-the-king's-daughter was-become

amis-sŏnara-sond^{u} ạsh^{ĕ}kh. Dŏda-mājĕ-kun
this-goldsmith-of love. The-foster-mother-to

wanān pātashāh-kūr^{ü},—
(is) saying the-king's-daughter,—

"Zargar-nĕcyuvāh pūr^{u}-khumār.
"A-goldsmith-son (is) full-of-languishment.

"Ḍīshith log^{u}m^{ü}y, dŏda-māji, mot^{u}
"Having-seen-him is-attached-to-me-verily, O-foster-mother, mad

hay amār."
O! desire."

Dŏda-möj^{ü} chĕs-wanān phīrith,—
The-foster-mother is-to-her-saying answering,—

"May kar, kūr^{i}yĕy, shur^{i}-bāshĕ.
"Do-not make, O-daughter, child-talk.

"Lagakh ạsh^{ĕ}kañĕ wālawāshi.
"Thou-wilt-be-caught love-of (in-) the-net.

"Ōra-kani ditay, kūr^{i}, kana-ḍōlī.
"In-that-direction give-verily, daughter, ear-closing.

"Ōra mā lagaham wŏbālī."
"(So that) from-there not mayst-thou-find-thyself-not in-blameworthiness."

3. **Sŏnar chuh bĕmār. Amis chuh**
The-goldsmith is sick. To-him is

ạsh^{e}kun^{u} tab. Amis-sŏnara-sünz^{ü}-kŏlay chĕh
love-of fever. That-goldsmith's-wife is

gāṭ^{ü}j^{ü}. Amis tog^{u} bōzun ȧm^{i}-sond^{u}
clever. To-her it-was-possible to-understand him-of

dôd^{u}. Dapān chĕs, "ts^{a}h hĕch lāyȧn^{i}
the-pain. Saying she-is-to-him, "thou learn to-be-thrown

rīnz^{i}, biyĕ gar sŏna-sȧnd^{i} rīnz^{i} z^{a}h."
balls, also make gold-of balls two."

4. **Dapān wustād,—**
(Is) saying the-teacher,—

Gȧr^{i} ȧm^{i} sŏna-sȧnd^{i} rīnz^{i} z^{a}h.
Were-made by-him gold-of balls two.

Drāv athas-kĕth hĕth rīnz^{i}. Lāyān-
He-went-forth the-hand-in taking balls. Throwing-he-

chuh apör^{i} ta yipör^{i} kañiv^{i}
is in-that-direction and in-this-direction stone-of

ta shĕstrȧv^{i}. Wôt^{u} ot^{u} pātashāha-sanzĕ-
and iron-of (balls). He-arrived there the-king's-

dārĕ-tal. Löyin ati sŏna-sȧnd^{i} rīnz^{i}
window-under. Were-thrown-by-him from-there gold-of balls

z^{a}h pātashāha-sanzi-kōri-halamas-manz. Ami
two the-king's-daughter's-lap-cloth-into. By-her

hôwus ōra phīrith thüḍ^{ü}-kani öna,
was-shown-to-him there-from turning-herself backwards (a) mirror,

biyĕ	**trôwun**	**dāri-kȧn^{i}**	**āb,**	**biyĕ**
again	was-cast-by-her	the-window-through	water,	again

trôwun	**pōshĕ-gọnd^{u},**	**biyĕ**	**trôwun**
was-cast-by-her	(a) flower-bunch,	again	was-cast-by-her

kīh,	**biyĕ**	**tuj^{ü}n**	**shĕstrüv^{ü}**	**salay,**
hair,	again	was-lifted-up-by-her	a-made-of-iron	spike,

dyutun	**ath-dārĕ-handis-dāsas**	**khash.**	**Ȧm^{i}**
was-given-by-her	to-that-window's-sill	a-cut.	By-that

sŏnar[1]	**wuch^{i},**	**āv**	**phīrith,**
goldsmith	they-were-seen,	he-came	(home) returning,

wôt^{u}	**panun^{u}**	**gara.**	**Dop^{u}nas**	**panañĕ-zanāni.**
he-arrived	his-own	house.	It-was-told-by-him-to-her	to-his-own-wife.

Dop^{u}nas,	**"kĕ-hŏ**	**koruth?"**	**Ȧm^{i}**
It-was-said-by-her-to-him,	"what-Sir	was-done-by-thee?"	By-him

won^{u}nas	**phīrith,**	**"rīnz^{i}**	**hay**	**löy^{i}mas.**
it-was-said-by-him-to-her	answering,	"the-balls	O	were-thrown-by-me-to-her.

Tim	**hay**	**gös**	**halamas-manz.**	**Tŏra**	**hay**
They	O	went-for-her	the-lap-cloth-into.	Therefrom	O

hôw^{u}nam	**phīrith**	**thüḍ^{ü}-kani**	**ŏna,**	**biyĕ**
was-shown-by-her-to-me	turning-herself	backwards	(a) mirror,	again

hay	**trôw^{u}nam**	**dāri-kȧn^{i}**	**āb,**	**biyĕ**
O	was-cast-by-her-to-me	the-window-through	water,	again

[1] *Sŏnar* is here the case of the agent; the more usual form would be *sŏnaran*.

trôw^{u}nam	**pōshĕ-gọnd^{u},**	**biyĕ**	**trôw^{u}nam**
was-cast-by-her-to-me	(a) flower-bunch,	again	was-cast-by-her-to-me

kīh,	**biyĕ**	**dyutun**	**shĕstravi-salayi-söty**
hair,	again	was-given-by-her	a-made-of-iron-spike-with

dāsas	**khash."**	**Dop^{u}nas**	**ami**	**phīrith,**
to-the-(window) sill	a-cut."	It-was-said-by-her-to-him	by-her	answering,

"thür^{ü}-kani	**hav**	**hôw^{u}nay**	**öna,**	**kus-tāñ**
"backwards	O	was-shown-by-her-to-thee	(a) mirror,	somebody

ôs^{u}mot^{u}-chus	**wŏpar;**	**āb**	**hav**	**trôw^{u}nay,**
was-(there)-for-her	other;	water	O	was-cast-by-her-to-thee

āb-dawa-kañ	**gat͡shi**	**at͡sun^{u};**	**pōshĕ-gọnd^{u}**
water-drain-by-means-of	it-is-proper	to-enter;	flower-bunch

trôw^{u}nay,	**bāgas-manz**	**gat͡shi**	**at͡sun;**
was-cast-by-her-to-thee,	the-garden-in	it-is-proper	to-enter:

salayi-söty	**hôw^{u}nay,**	**anun^{u}**	**gat͡shi**
spike-by	it-was-shown-by-her-to-thee,	to-be-brought	is-proper

phaharawāv,	**tath**	**chiy**	**pŏlādáv^{i}**	**nēza,**
(a) file,	to-it	are-verily	made-of-steel	railings,

tim	**gat͡shan**	**t͡saṭān^{i};**	**kīh**	**trôw^{u}nay,**
they	are-proper	to-be-cut:	hair	was-cast-by-her-to-thee,

"chĕs	**wālān**	**kangañ."**
"I-am	causing-to-descend	a-comb."

5. **Dapān wustād,—**
(Is) saying the-teacher,—

Drāv	**yih**	**sŏnar**	**shāman-bög^{i},**	**ŧsāv**
Went-off	this	goldsmith	at-evening-about,	he entered

ath-bāgas-manz.	**Wuchun**	**ati**	**palang,**
that-garden-in.	Was-seen-by-him	there	a-bed,

khot^{u}	**ath^{i}-palangas-pĕṭh.**	**Shikasta-söty**
he-mounted	that-very-bed-upon.	His-weakness-owing-to

pĕyĕs	**nĕṇd^{a}r.**	**Āyĕs**	**yih**	**pātashāh-kūḍ^{ü}.**
there-fell-to-him	sleep.	She-came-to-him	this	king's-daughter.

"Shānda	**chĕs-karān**	**khŏr,**	**khŏra**
"From-the-pillow	she-is-for-him-making	the-feet,	from-the-foot

chĕs-karān	**shānd."**	**Yih**	**kĕ̃h**	**hushyār**
she-is-for-him-making	the-pillow."	He	at-all	awake

gōs-na.	**Yutāñ**	**gāsh**	**log^{u}**	**phŏlani.**
became-for-her-not.	In-the-meantime	dawn	began	to-flower.

Pātashāh-kūr^{ü}	**ŧsüj^{ü}**	**panun^{u}**	**gara,**	**path-kun**
The-king's-daughter	fled	her-own	house,	afterwards

gav	**hushyār**	**sŏnar.**	**Yiwān-chuh**	**yiti**
became	awake	the-goldsmith.	Coming-he-is	from-here

panun^{u}	**gara.**	**Wanān-chĕs**	**panüñ^{ü}**	**kŏlay,**
his-own	house.	Saying-she-is-to-him	his-own	wife,

"kĕ-hŏ	**koruth?"**	**Yih**	**chus-dapān**	**phīrith,**
"what-Sir	was-done-by-thee?"	He	is-to-her-saying	answering,

"sa	**nay**	**kĕ̃h**	**āyĕm."**	**Dop^{u}nas**	**ami-**
"she	not-even	at-all	came-to-me."	Was-said-by-her-to-him	by-that-

zanāni,	**"talau**	**yūr^{i}-hond^{u}**	**wŏla."**	**Gav.**
woman,	"O	hither	come."	He-went.

Wuchus	**ami-panañi-zanāni**	**cĕndas.**	**Wuchin**
Was-looked-for-him	by-this-his-own-woman	to-the-pocket.	Were-seen-by-her

ati	**rīnz^{i}**	**z^{a}h**	**sŏna-sảnd^{i},**	**timạy**	**yim**
there	the-balls	two	gold-of,	those-very	which

tami-dŏha	**lāyānas**	**halamas-manz.**	**Dop^{u}nas,**
on-that-day	had-been-thrown-by-him-to-her	lap-cloth-in.	It-was-said-by-her-to-him,

"sa	**chĕy**	**āmütš^{ü},**	**tš^{a}h**	**chukhna**	**gŏmot^{u}**
"she	is-to-thee	come,	thou	art-not	become

hushyār.	**Wuñ,**	**yĕli**	**biyĕ**	**gatšhakh**
awake.	Now,	when	again	thou-shalt-go

kālacĕn,	**tĕli**	**dapay**	**bŏh**	**sabakh."**
at-eventide,	then	I-will-say-to-thee	I	a-lesson."

6. Dapān wustād,—
(Is) saying the-teacher,—

Nam	**dah**	**tul^{i}nas**	**athan-hảnd^{i},**	**akis**
Nails	ten	were-raised-by-her-for-him	the-hands-of,	to-one

ôs^{u}nas	**dyut^{u}mot^{u}**	**sọ̆n^{u}**	**khash.**	**Dop^{u}nas,**
was-by-her-to-it	given	a-deep	cut.	It-was-said-by-him-to-her,

"môr^{u}thas."	**Ami**	**dop^{u}nas**	**phīrith,**
"killed (i.e. wounded)-by-thee-am-I."	By-her	it-was-said-by-her-to-him	answering,

"möl^{i}	**māji**	**chĕsna**	**tšhuñ^{u}mütš^{ü}**	**nöyid**
"by-father	by-mother	I-am-not	put	barber's

sabakas.	**Wŏñ**	**yĕli**	**gatšhakh,**	**tĕli**
to-lesson.	Now	when	thou-wilt-go,	then

dimay	**dawāhan."**	**Ami**	**dyut^{u}nas**
I-will-give-to-thee	a-little-medicine."	By-her	was-given-by-her-to-him

martsa-wãgan	**ratshi-hanā,**	**biyĕ**	**nuna**	**ratshi-**
of-red-pepper	a-very-little,	also	of-salt	a-very-

hanā.	**Dop^{u}nas,**	**" biyĕ**	**yĕli**	**tath-palangas-**
little.	It-was-said-by-her-to-him,	" again	when	that-bed-

pĕṭh	**khasakh,**	**tĕli**	**yiyiy,**	**nĕṇd^{a}r.**
on	thou-wilt-mount,	then	will-come-to-thee,	sleep.

Yih	**dawāh**	**ratshi-han**	**gȧnḍ^{i}zĕs,**	**ada**
This	medicine	a-little-amount	(thou) must-bind-it,	then

yiyiy	**nĕṇd^{a}r**	**shĕh^{ü}j^{ü}."**	**Drāv**	**ati**
will-come-to-thee	sleep	cool."	Went-forth	from-there

sŏnar,	**dawāh**	**ratshi-han**	**hĕ̆ts^{ü}n**
the-goldsmith,	the-medicine	a-little-amount	was-taken-by-him

söty,	**wôt^{u}**	**ath-bāgas-manz,**	**khot^{u}**	**ath-**
with,	he-arrived	that-garden-in,	he-mounted	that-

palangas-pĕṭh,	**chuh**	**prārān**	**tsēr**	**tān̄,**
bed-on,	he-is	waiting	long-time	during,

yih	**kuni**	**yiwān-chĕs-na.**	**Hĕts^{ü}nas**
she	at-all	coming-is-to-him-not.	There-began-for-him

yin̄^{ü}	**nĕṇd^{a}r,**	**athas**	**chus**	**dôd^{u},**	**ath**
to-come	sleep,	to-the-hand	is-for-him	pain,	to-it

chuh	**karith**	**thaph.**	**Dopun,**	**" wun̄**
he-is	having-made	holding.	It-was-said-by-him,	" now-indeed

āyĕ-na,	**yith**	**tshunahö**	**bŏh**	**dödis**
she-came-not,	(if) to-this	I-had-applied	I	to-the-pain

dawāh,	**shĕh^{ü}j^{ü}**	**karahö**	**nẹnd^{a}r."**	**Yuthuy**
the-medicine,	(then) cool	I-should-have-made	sleep."	As-verily

ath-dödis	**tshunun**	**dawāh,**	**tyuthuy**
to-that-pain	was-applied-by-him	the-medicine,	so-verily

pyōs	**wölinjĕ**	**vih,**	**chuh**	**lalawān**
there-fell-to-him	to-the-heart	poison,	he-is	caressing (it)

thod^{u}	**wŏthith.**
upright	having-arisen.

7. **Dapān wustād,—**
(Is) saying the-teacher,—

Āyĕ	**yih**	**pātashāha-sünz^{ü}**	**kūr^{ü}.**	**Amis**
Came	this	king's	daughter.	To-him

moṭh^{u}	**sôruy**	**dôd^{u}.**	**Korun**	**amis-söty**
was-forgotten	all	pain.	Was-done-by-him	her-with

yih	**karun^{u}**	**gotsh^{u}.**	**Pĕyĕkh**	**nẹnd^{a}r.**
what	to-be-done	was-proper.	There-fell-to-them	sleep.

Yut^{u}-tāñ	**gāsh**	**log^{u}**	**phŏlani.**	**Kuṭ^{a}wāl**
Here-up-to (by-this-time)	dawn	began	to-flower.	The-chief-of-police

chuh	**wasān**	**apör^{i}-kiñ**	**āgayi.**	**Wuchun**
is	coming-down	on-that-side-from	for-inspection.	Was-seen-by-him

ati	**pātashāha-sünz^{ü}**	**kūr^{ü}**	**biyĕ**	**sŏnar.**
there	the-king's	daughter	and	the-goldsmith.

Rȧṭ^{i}	**ȧm^{i}-kuṭ^{a}wālan,**	**nīn**	**raṭith,**
They-were-arrested	by-that-chief-of-police,	they-were-taken-by-him	having-arrested,

kȧrin	**hawāla**	**tsrālĕn,**	**kȧrikh**
they-were-made-by-him	in-custody	to-the-constables	they-were-made-by-them

köd.	**Ati**	**ôs^{u}**	**pakān**	**wati**
imprisoned.	There	there-was	going	on-the-road

akhāh.	**Amis^{ü}y**	**dopukh**	**yimav-ködyau-**
a-certain-one.	To-him-verily	it-was-said-by-them	by-these-prisoners-

dŏyav,	**" ts^{a}h,**	**hasa,**	**dizi**	**krēkh**
two,	" thou,	Sir,	must-give	an-outcry

sŏnar-aṭa-pēṭha.	**Dåp^{i}zĕkh,**	**'pātashĕhas**
the-goldsmiths'-market-from.	Thou-must-say-to-them,	'for-the-king (the-king's)

khar	**pĕv**	**kŏng-wāri.**	**Khabar**	**chyā**
ass	fell	in-the-saffron-field.	News	is-there? (there-is-not)

loṭ^{u}	**tsaṭanasa**	**kina**	**hoṭ^{u}**	**tsaṭanas.**
tail	will-they-cut-for-him?	or	throat	they-will-cut-for-him.

Pātashĕhas	**khar**	**pĕv**	**kŏng-wārē.**
The-king's	ass	fell	in-the-saffron-field.

Pakān	**dil**	**gōm**	**tåt^{i}**	**tārē.**
Going	the-heart	became-to-me	there	confused.

Vir	**hĕth**	**wātun^{u}**	**gotsh^{u}**	**sōli-gārē.**
Fine-money	having-taken	to-arrive	was-proper	at-dawn-time.

Nata	**tas**	**pātashāh**	**tati**	**mārē.' "**
Other-wise	him	the-king	there	will-kill.' "

Būz^{u}	**ami-sŏnara-sanzi-zanāni.**	**Drāyĕ**
Was-heard	by-that-goldsmith's-wife.	She-went-forth

bāzar,	**hĕtsan**	**tsŏcĕ,**	**lazan**	**kranjĕ,**
(to) the-market,	were-bought-by-her	loaves,	were-placed by-her	to-a-basket,

wŏtamukh^{i},	**drāyĕ**	**nĕbar**	**pātashāh-kūr^{ü},**
upside-down,	issued	forth	the-king's-daughter,

gayĕ	**panun^{u}**	**gara.**	**Kuṭ^{a}wālan**	**dyut^{u}**
she-went	her-own	house.	By-the-chief-of-police	was-given

rapaṭ	**pātashĕhas.**	**Dop^{u}nas,**	**"pātashāh-kūr^{ü}**
report	to-the-king.	It-was-said-by-him-to-him,	"the-king's-daughter (was)

biyĕ	**ôs^{u}**	**sŏnar**	**bāgas-manz.**	**Timaỵ**
and	was	a-goldsmith	the-garden-in.	They-verily

kyā	**kȧrim**	**kȫd."**	**Pātashāh**	**drāv**
of-course	were-made-by-me	(in) prison."	The-king	went-forth

adālüṭs^{ü}-pĕṭh.	**Ȧnikh**	**yim-rātȧk^{i}-kȫd^{i}**	**z^{a}h.**
the-court-of-justice-on.	Were-brought-by-them	these-of-the-night-prisoners	two.

Wuchikh	**yim**	**bȫṭs^{ü}**	**z^{a}h.**	**Sŏnara-sanzi-**
Were-seen-by-them	these	husband-and-wife	two.	By-the-goldsmith's-

kŏlayi	**gȧnḍ^{i}**	**gul^{i}**	**z^{a}h**	**pātashĕhas.**
wife	were-fastened-together	the-fore-arms	two	to-the-king.

Dop^{u}nas,	**"pātashĕham,**	**ȧs^{i}**	**kyāh**
It-was-said-by-her-to-him,	"my-king,	we	of-a-truth

ös^{i}	**gamȧt^{i}**	**sālas.**	**Tōra**	**kyāh**
were	gone	to-a-marriage-feast.	From-there	of-a-truth

āy	**ta**	**wöt^{i}**	**yith-cyönis-shĕharas-manz.**
(we) came	and	arrived	this-thy-city-in.

Gav	**ṭsĕr.**	**Ada**	**ṭsāy**	**cyönis-bāgas-manz.**
It-became	late.	Then	(we) entered	thy-garden-in.

Ati wuch^{u} palang, khȧt^{i} ath-pěṭh,
There was-seen a-bed, (we) mounted it-upon,

kor^{u} arām, ōra āv cyôn^{u} kuṭ^{a}wāl.
was-made repose, from-there came thy chief-of-police.

Amiy kyāh niy raṭith kȧrin
By-him-verily of-a-truth were-taken having-arrested (we) were-made-by-him

kȯd." Wǫth^{u} kuṭ^{a}wāl, dopun
(in) imprisonment." Arose the-chief-of-police, it-was-said-by-him

pātashěhas, "pātashěham, cyōn^{ü} kūr^{ü}
to-the-king, "my-king, thy daughter

karinam kasam Vig^{i}ñāh nāga-pěṭha.
let-her-make-for-me oath the-Vig^{i}ñāh Nāg-from-on.

Dapān, 'yus ati apoz^{u} kasam karihē,
(People are) saying, 'he-who there untrue oath might-have-made,

suh wŏthihē-na tȧt^{i} thod^{u}, suh ôs^{u}
he would-have-arisen-not there upright, he was

tatiy marān.'" Dop^{u} ami-sŏnara-sanzi-
there-verily dying.'" It-was-said by-that-goldsmith's-

zanāni amis-sŏnaras, "tagiyě yih pātashāh-
wife to-that-goldsmith, "is-she-possible-for-thee this king's-

kūr^{ü} bacāwün^{ü}?" Dop^{u}nas, "hāvtam
daughter to-be-caused-to-escape?" It-was-said-by-him-to-her, "show-please-to-me

wath." Dop^{u}nas, "akh, trāv sôruy
a-way." It-was-said-by-her-to-him, "(for) one (thing), put-off all

pŏshākh, khōran lhun khrāv, biyě
(thy) garments, to-the-feet put-on clogs, and

math sūr, lāg gusôn^{u}. Yěli ot^{u}
rub ashes, appear-like a-mendicant-monk. When there

wātanāwan amis-pātashāh-kōrě, cyôn^{u}
they-shall-cause-to-arrive this-king's-daughter, for-thee

gatshi	**gatshun^{u},**	**amis-pātashāh-kōrĕ**	**karün̄^{ü}**
it-is-proper	to-go,	to-this-king's-daughter	to-be-made

gatshi	**thaph**	**dāmānas,**	**dapun^{u}**	**gatshēs,**
is-proper	seizing	to-the-skirt,	to-say	it-is-proper-to-her,

'mĕ	**dita**	**gŏḍa**	**khörāth.'**	**Sa**	**kyāh**
'to-me	give-please	first	alms.'	She	of-course

hāvi	**ada**	**kasam,**	**cyônuy**	**mŏkh**
will-show	then	the-oath,	thine-only	face

raṭith	**dapi,**	**'hā**	**hàz^{i}**	**Vig^{i}ñāh-nāga,**
having-seized	she-will-say,	'O	holy	O-Vig^{i}ñāh-Nāg,

nĕmis-matis	**siwāh**	**kyāh**	**kür^{u}m-na**	**kō͠si**
to-this-mad-one	except	certainly	was-made-to-me-not	by-anyone

dāmānas	**thaph.'"**
to-the-skirt	seizing.'"

Vig^{i}ñāh	**nāgas**	**wütsh^{ü}y**	**srānas.**
To-the-Vig^{i}ñāh	Nāg	she-descended-verily	for-bathing.

"Kuwa	**zāna**	**maṭi**	**māh**	**lod^{u}nam**	**rāh?**
"How	do-I-know,	on-the-shoulder	I-wonder-how	was-loaded-for-me	the-fault?

Màt^{i}	**thaph**	**löy^{ü}nam**	**ḍōli-dāmānas."**
By-the-mad-one	seizing	was-struck	to-the-skirt-of-the-gusset-of-(my) garment."

Kuṭ^{a}wāl-gānas	**gudariv**	**kyāh?**
To-the-chief-of-police-the-pimp	happened	what?

Söriy	**yār**	**gay**	**pānas**	**pānas.**
All	friends	went	voluntarily	voluntarily.

Kuṭ^{a}wāl-gānas	**gudariv**	**kyāh?**
To-the-chief-of-police-the-pimp	happened	what?

10.	**Pātashāh-kūr^{ü}**	**gayĕ**	**gara,**	**kuṭ^{a}wāl**
	The-king's-daughter	went	home,	the-chief-of-police

dyutukh phahi, sŏnara-sandi^{i} bötsü^{ü}
was-given-by-them on-the-empalement-stake, the-goldsmith-of the-husband-and-wife

z^{a}h chih gari-panani. Sŏnar gav
two are in-the-house-their-own. The-goldsmith became

bĕmār. Yihōy kor^{u}nas ạsh^{ĕ}kun^{u} tab.
ill. This-verily was-made-by-him-for-her of-love the-fever.

Yih ös^{ü} sŏnara-sünz^{ü} zanāna gāṭ^{ü}j^{ü}.
This was the-goldsmith-of wife clever.

Goḍun mŏhara-hatas-akis rosh^{u}. Yih
Was-made-by-her (of) mohars-a-hundred-one a-necklace. This

gonḍun pananis-khāwandas. Pāna
was-tied-by-her to-her-own-husband. She-herself

lôgun saniyās. Amis pör^{ü}n
was-made-to-appear-like-by-her an-ascetic. As-for-him she (he)-was-dressed-by-her

gŏpöl^{i}. Wātanöw^{ü}n pātashāha-sond^{u}
(as) a-dancing-girl. She (he)-was-caused-to-arrive-by-her the-king-of

gara. Dopun amis-pātashĕhas, "yih
at-the-house. It-was-said-by-her to-that-king, "this (girl)

chĕm böy^{i}-kākañ, yih chĕy tsĕ
is-to-me elder-brother's-wife, she is-to-thee to-thee

hawāla. Mĕ chuy gatshun^{u} böyis-nish.
a-deposit. To-me is-verily to-be-gone to-the-brother-near.

Suh chum gamot^{u} sōdāhas. Yih
He is-for-me gone for-merchanting. This (girl)

chĕy myöñ^{ü} gŏpöl^{i} hawāla, yotāñ
is-to-thee my dancing-girl a-deposit, until

âs^{i} yimōy. Yih chĕy pākh, yih
we shall-come-to-thee. She is-verily pure, her

thöv^{i}zĕn panañĕ-kōrĕ-söty." Āyĕ phīrith
you-must-keep-her thine-own-daughter-with." She-came returning

panun^{u} gara. Kĕ̄h kālā gav, āv
(to) her-own house. Some a-time went, came

yih sŏnar biyĕ gara panun^{u}.
this goldsmith again (to) home his-own.

11. Dapān wustād,—
(Is) saying the-teacher,—

Lôgun sōdāgār ami zanāni.
He-was-made-to-appear-like-by-her a-merchant by-that woman.

Wöt^{i} ath-pātashĕha-sandis-shĕharas-manz.
They-arrived that-king's-city-in.

Lôgu ami biyĕ saniyās.
He (she)-was-made-to-appear-like by-her again an-ascetic.

Khāwand thôwun ḍēras-pĕṭh sōdāgār
Her-husband was-placed-by-her a-tent-on a-merchant

lögith, pāna gayĕ pātashĕhas.
being-made-to-appear-like, she-herself went to-the-king.

Gonḍ^{u}nas dāwāh, "dim gŏpöl^{i}."
Was-bound-by-her-to-him a-claim, "give-to-me the-dancing-girl."

Diwān chuh achĕn d^{ü}h. Dapān
Giving he-is to-the-eyes smoke. Saying

chĕs, "dim gŏpöl^{i}.
she-is-to-him, "give-to-me the-dancing-girl.

Prārān	**dŏh**	**gav**	**mĕ**	**bālē.**
Waiting	the-day	went	for-me	for(-my)-girl.

Saniyās	**āmot^{u}**	**gŏpālē."**
The-ascetic	(is) come	for-the-dancing-girl."

Yih	**chus**	**dapān**	**pātashāh**	**phīrith,—**
This	is-to-her	saying	the-king	answering,—

"Saniyāsū,	**mōv**	**lāg**	**jĕnḍa,**	**luh-luh.**
"O-ascetic,	do-not	fix	the-flag (of your claim),	luh-luh.

Khôtūnā	**akh**	**dimay**	**danḍa,**	**luh-luh."**
A-certain-lady	a	I-will-give-to-thee	in-exchange,	luh-luh."

Saniyās	**dapān**	**chus**	**phīrith,—**
The-ascetic	saying	is-to-him	answering,—

"Saniyās	**chusay**	**bĕwāsta,**	**luh-luh.**
"An-ascetic	I-am-verily	without-worldly-ties,	luh-luh.

Danḍa	**hĕmay**	**dukhtar-ē-khāsa,**	**luh-luh."**
An-exchange	I-will-take-from-thee	the-daughter-of-thee-thyself,	luh-luh."

12.	**Dapān**	**wustād,—**
	(Is) saying	the-teacher,—

Mŏhara-hatas	**goḍun**	**rosh^{u},**	**gonḍun**
Of-mohars-a-hundred	was-made-by-him	a-necklace,	it-was-tied-by-him

panañĕ	**kōḍĕ.**	**Kür^{ü}n**	**hawāla**	**amis**
to-his-own	daughter.	She-was-made-by-him	to-the-charge	to-this

saniyāsas.
to-ascetic.

Tānana	**tan^{a}nana**	**tanānay.**
Tānana	tananana	tanānay.

Yim	**kār**	**chĕh**	**karān**	**zanānay.**
These	actions	are	doing	women-only.

Niyĕn	**ta**	**kür^{ü}n**	**hawāla**	**pananis-**
Was-taken-by-her	and	was-made-by-her	to-the-charge	to-her-own-

khāwandas.	**Dop^{u}nas,**	**"ts^{a}h**	**zān,**	**ta**
husband.	It-was-said-by-her-to-him,	"thou	know,	and

yih	**zān."**
(thou) this-woman	know."

VI. YŪSŪPH-ZALĪKHĀ KATH.

YŪSUF-ZULAIKHĀ STORY.

1. **Shāh-i-Yūsūph**	**Zalīkhā,**	**yāra,**	**bōzakh-nā?**
King-Yūsuf	Zulaikhā,	Friend,	wilt-thou-not-hear?

2. **Zalīkhā**	**chĕh**	**wanān,—**
Zulaikhā	is	saying,—

"**Sālas**	**yikh-nā?**	**pŏlāv**	**khĕkh-nā?**
"To-the-feast	wilt-thou-not-come?	*pulāo*	wilt-thou-not-eat?
Yitam	**gāh**	**bĕgāh;**	**yāra,**
Come-thou-please-to-me	in-season	out-of-season;	Friend,
bōzakh-nā?			
wilt-thou-not-hear?			

3. **Sath**	**kuṭh^{i}**	**larĕ**	**chim,**	**cyānĕ-**
Seven	rooms	in-the-house	are-to-me,	for-thy-
lŏhlari	**chim.**			
longing	they-are-to-me.			

Bĕhtam	**sāthā;**	**yāra,**	**bōzakh-nā?"**
Sit-please-for-me	a-moment;	Friend,	wilt-thou-not-hear?"

4. **Putal-khānas**	**byon^{u}**	**byon^{u}**	**pānas**
Of-the-idol-house	separately	separately	of-her-own-accord
Kor^{u}nakh	**pardā;**	"**yāra,**	**bōzakh-nā?"**
Was-made-by-her-for-them	a-veil;	"Friend,	wilt-thou-not-hear?"

5.	**"Ati**	**kyā**	**thôwuth,**	**asĕ-kun**
	"Here	what	was-placed-by-thee,	us-before

hôwuth?"
was-shown-by-thee?"

Dopunas,	**"chum**	**Khŏdā;**	**yāra°?"**
It-was-said-by-her-to-him,	"it-is-to-me	a-God;	Friend, etc.?"

6.	**"Khŏdā**	**gav**	**suy,**	**mani-panañē**
	"God	is	He-alone,	from-the-mind-thine-own

kās	**dŏy.**
expel	the-belief-in-two.

Shōlān	**chuh**	**shĕmāh;**	**yāra°?**
Shining	is	the-lamp-flame;	Friend, etc.?

7.	**Khŏdā**	**chuh**	**kunuy,**	**jalwa**	**dith**
	God	is	one-only,	glory	having-given

drāv	**nonuy.**
He-issued	manifest.

Kañĕ-manz	**chyā**	**mŏdā?**	**yāra°?"**
Stone-in	is-there	meaning?	Friend, etc.?"

8.	**Hazrat-i**	**Yūsūph**	**ŧolu.**	**Pata**	**lāḍyēyĕs**
	Saint	Yūsuf	fled.	After	ran-to-him

Zalīkhā.
Zulaikhā.

Yūsūph	**ŧalān,**	**Zalīkhā**	**lārān.**
Yūsuf	fleeing,	Zulaikhā	running.

Dopunas,	**"yī**	**pazyā?**	**yāra°?"**
It-was-said-by-her-to-him,	"this-indeed	is-it-proper?	Friend, etc.?"

9. **Nālas thaph karith, nyūn**
To-the-neck seizing having-done, he-was-taken-by-her

hātshā kārith.
an-accusation having-made.

Gay pēsh-ĕ-pātashāh. Yāra° ?
They-went before-of-the-king. Friend, etc. ?

10. **Azīz-i-Misar ôs^{u} pātashāh. Amis**
Azīz-i-Misar was the-king. To-him

ôs^{u} zid Hazrat-i Yūsūpha-sond^{u}.
was hatred Saint Yūsuf-of.

Yūsūph kŏd-khān, kāh chus-na bōzān.
Yūsuf (in) the-prison, anyone is-to-him-not listening.

Mŏkali az-Khŏdā. Yāra° ?
He-will-be-released from-God. Friend, etc. ?

11. **Yĕli Yūsūph log^{u} kŏd, ati**
When Yūsuf became imprisoned, there

ös^{i} prŏn^{i} kĕh^{i}. Timau dyūṭh^{u}
were old certain-people. By-them was-seen

khāb. Akis korun töbīr. "Tsĕ
a-dream. To-one was-made-by-him interpretation. "Thee

māriy pātashāh." Môr^{u} pātashāhan.
will-kill-certainly the-king." He-was-killed by-the-king.

Biyis korun töbīr. "Ts^{a}h
To-another was-made-by-him interpretation. "Thou

sapadakh pātashāha-sond^{u} pēshkār. Mĕ-ti,
wilt-become the-king-of head-official. Me-also

hasa, pöv^{i}zi yād."
Sir, please-cause-to-fall memory."

Ködyau khāb ḍyūṭh^{u}, töbīr drākh
By-the-prisoners dream was-seen, interpretation issued-for-them

myūṭh^{u}.
sweet.

Mŏkȧliy phardā; yāra° ?
They-were-released-verily on-the-morrow; Friend, etc.?

12\. **Pātashāh Azīz-i-Misar ḍēshān khāb.**
The-king Azīz-i-Misar (is) seeing a-dream.

Azīz-i-Misar khāba-nishĕ abtar,
Azīz-i-Misar the-dream-from terrified,

Gav bĕdār, wǫth^{u} shōra-gāh. Yāra° ?
Became awake, there-arose an-outcry. Friend, etc.?

13\. **Kamyuk^{u} wǫth^{u} shōra-gāh?**
Of-what arose the-outcry?

Malan, bāban, pīran, phakīran,
Of-priests, of-calendars, of-saints, of-mendicants,

Bani-nā hakīmā? Yāra° ?
Will-there-not-be a-single-wise-man? Friend, etc.?

14\. **Kamyuk^{u} hakīm, ath-khābas yus**
Of-what wise-man, to-this-dream he-who

mānĕ	**tsārihĕ,**	**yus**	**àm^{i}-Azīz-i-Misaran**
the-meaning	might-bring-out,	which	by-this-Azīz-i-Misar

khāb	**ôs^{u}**	**ḍyūṭh^{u}mot^{u} ?**	**Dop^{u}nas**
dream	was	seen ?	It-was-said-to-him

gŏlāman,	**" khābuk^{u}**	**töbīr**	**zāni**
by-the-servant,	" of-the-dream	the-interpretation	will-know

Hazrat-i	**Yūsūph.**
Saint	Yūsuf.

Khābuk^{u}	**töbīr**	**Yūsūphas**	**chuh**	**wöphīr.**
Of-dream	interpretation	to-Yūsuf	is	plentiful.

Dādĕn	**chuy**	**dawā.**	**Yāra° ?"**
Of-pains	he-is-verily	the-remedy.	Friend, etc. ?"

15. **Onukh**	**Hazrat-i**	**Yūsūph.**	**Dop^{u}nas**
Was-brought-by-them	Saint	Yūsuf.	It-was-said-by-him-to-him

pātashĕhan,	**"mĕ**	**ḍyūṭh^{u}**	**khāb.**	**Ath^{i}**
by-the-king,	" by-me	was-seen	a-dream.	For-it-verily

wanum	**töbīr."**	**Dop^{u}nas**	**Yūsūphan,**
say-to-me	the-interpretation."	It-was-said-by-him-to-him	by-Yūsuf,

" kyāh	**ḍyūṭhuth ?"**	**Dop^{u}nas**	**pātashĕhan,**
" what	was-seen-by-thee ?"	It-was-said-by-him-to-him	by-the-king,

" akh	**ḍyūṭhum,**	**hŏkh^{i}**	**nāg**	**sath**
" One	was-seen-by-me,	dry	springs	seven

baritĕn	**nāgan**	**satan**	**cĕwān.**	**Biyĕ**
full	springs	seven	(were) drinking.	Again

ḍyūṭhum,	**khām**	**sath**	**hĕl^{i}**	**wuchim**
was-seen-by-me,	unripe	seven	ears-of-corn	were-seen-by-me

pŏkhtan	**satan**	**hĕlĕn**	**ningalān.**	**Biyĕ**
ripe	seven	ears	(were) swallowing.	Again

wuchĕm	**lāgar**	**gōv^{ü}**	**sath**	**yiwān,**
were-seen-by-me	lean	cows	seven	(were) coming,

mastan	**satan**	**gōv^{ü}n**	**ningalān.**	**Amyuk^{u}**
plump	seven	cows	(were) swallowing.	Of-it

wanum	**töbīr."**	**Dop^{u}nas**	**Yūsūphan,**
tell-to-me	the-interpretation."	It-was-said-by-him-to-him	by-Yūsuf,

"drāg	**wŏthi."**
"a-famine	will-arise."

16. Dapān wustād,—
(Is) saying the teacher,—

Yūsūphan	**mŏkalôw^{u}**	**töbīr**	**wanith,**
By-Yūsuf	was-finished	the-interpretation	having-spoken,

pātashĕhas	**gav**	**asar.**	**Lüj^{ü}s**	**bŏchĕ.**
to-the-king	happened	a-result.	There-was-joined-to-him	hunger.

Dop^{u}nakh,	**"diyūm**	**bata."**	**Ami-wakta**
It-was-said-by-him-to-them,	"give-ye-to-me	food."	At-that-time

pātashāh	**khĕwān**	**ôs^{u}na.**	**Ami-asara-söty**
the-king	eating	was-not.	That-result-owing-to

dop^{u}nakh,	**"jĕl**	**anyūm."**	**Dapān,**
it-was-said-by-him-to-them,	"quickly	bring-ye-to-me."	(People are) saying,

gay	**ta**	**onukh**	**bata.**	**Yih**	**khyōn.**
they-went	and	was-brought-by-them	food.	This	was-eaten-by-him.

Dop^{u}nakh,	**"biyĕ**	**anyūm."**	**Añĕhas**
It-was-said-by-him-to-them,	"again	bring-ye-to-me."	Were-brought-by-them-to-him

dēga	**wŏkavith.**	**On^{u}has**	**ta**
cauldrons	having-drawn-forth.	It-was-brought-by-them-to-him	and

khyōn,	**tasalī**	**kẽh**	**ās-na.**	**Dapān,**
it-was-eaten-by-him,	satisfaction	any	came-to-him-not.	(People are) saying,

ath^{i}-bŏchi-sötiy	**gav**	**marith.**	**Dapān,**
that-very-hunger-owing-to-only	he-went	having-died.	(People are) saying,

pagāh	**dit^{ü}**	**wazīrau**	**wurdī,**	**"pagāh**
next-day	was-given	by-the-Viziers	command,	"to-morrow

wasiv	**söriy**	**yīd^{i}kāh.**	**Yĕs**	**host^{u}**
descend-ye	all	(to) the-ʻĪdgāh.	To-whom	the-elephant

nami,	**pöz**	**bĕhi**	**nĕchi,**	**suy**
will-bow,	the-hawk	will-sit	(on) the-thumb-ring,	he-verily

sapadi	**pātashāh."**	**Dapān,**	**wåth^{i}**
shall-become	king."	(People are) saying,	they-descended

yīd^{i}kāh,	**āv**	**host^{u},**	**namyōv**	**Yūsūphas.**
to-the-ʻĪdgāh,	came	the-elephant,	bowed	to-Yūsuf.

Pöz	**āv,**	**byūṭhus**	**nĕchi.**	**Banyōv**
The-hawk	came,	sat-for-him	(on) the-thumb-ring.	Became

Yūsūph	**pātashāh.**
Yūsuf	king.

Jalŏy hôwun, host^u manganôwun,
Glory was-shown-by-him, the-elephant was-sent-for-by-him,

Yūsūph pātashāh; yāra, bōzakh-nā?
Yūsuf king; Friend, wilt-thou-not-hear?

17. **Tŏrīph-ĕ-Yūsūph, par, Wahab-Khāra, khūb.**
The-praise-of-Yūsuf, recite, Wahb-the-blacksmith-O, thoroughly.

Gatsh parān "lāyilā"; yāra, bōzakh-nā?
Go reciting "the-creed"; Friend, wilt-thou-not-hear?

VII.—NAYĔ-HÜNZ$^{\ddot{u}}$ KATH

REED(-FLUTE)-OF TALE

1. **Bani yĕs dôd^{u}, tas chuh**
Will-happen to-whom pain, to-him is

pānas tiy nanān.
to-himself it-verily being-manifest.

Nayĕ-hond^{u} dôd^{u} nay chĕh pānay
The-reed-flute-of pain the-reed-flute is herself

tiy wanān.
that-verily telling.

2. **Nay chĕh dapān, "Bār-söhib**
The-flute is saying, "The-Almighty

chuy kunuy.
is-verily one-only.

Day^{i} ta ꞩakhi-nishĕ pānas chuy
God-only and anger-from of-His-own-will is-verily

byonuy."
distinct."

3. **Nay chĕh dapān, "Bār-söhib munazāth.**
The-flute is saying, "The-Almighty pure.

Pānas$^{\ddot{u}}$y-kun chuy mushtākh dŏh
Himself-only-towards He-is-verily yearning day

ta rāth.
and night.

4. **Hamud gaꞩhiv tas-Khŏdāyĕs-kun parān,**
Praise go-ye that-God-towards reciting,

Pöda korun ṭhôṭh^{u} Mahmad mizmān.
Created was-made-by-Him the-Beloved Muḥammad the-Guest.

5. **Bār-söhiban söty ditin sāmān.**
By-the-Almighty with (him) were-given-by-Him appliances.

Tsōr yār chis söty söty shūbān.
Four friends are-of-him with with glorious.

6. **Nūra tåm^{i}-sandi pöda korun Ādam.**
By-the-glory Him-of created was-made-by-Him Adam.

Ādamas-söty pöda korun yīdam."
Adam-with created was-made-by-Him this (world)."

7. **Nay chĕh dapān, "lodun Ādam bēnawāh.**
The-flute is saying, "was-sent-forth-by-him Adam destitute.

Ös^{ü} mashīyĕth lari-tala drāyĕs Hawāh."
There-was a-wish, the-side-from-under issued-for-him Eve."

8. **Nay chĕh dapān, "kyāh zabar ôs^{u} suy sāth.**
The-flute is saying, "how excellent was that-very moment.

Yĕmi-sātay pöda kür^{ü}n zuryāth."
At-what-time-verily created was-made-by-Him (the world with its) offspring."

9.	**Nay**	**chĕh**	**dapān,**	**"hāl**	**myônuy**
	The-flute	is	saying,	"condition	my-verily

būz^{i}tav.
hear-please-ye.

Död^{i}laday	**chiv,**	**ta**	**sāthā**	**rūz^{i}tav."**
Pained-if	ye-be,	then	a-moment	wait-please-ye."

10.	**Nay**	**chĕh**	**dapān,**	**"path**	**wanan**
	The-flute	is	saying,	"behind	the-woods

ös^{u}s	**pinhān.**
I-was	concealed.

Shākha-bargau	**söty**	**ös^{u}s**	**shūbān."**
Branch-leaves	with	I-was	beautiful."

11.	**Nay**	**chĕh**	**dapān,**	**"thod^{u}**	**mĕ**
	The-flute	is	saying,	"upright	to-me

ôsum	**bāla-pān.**
was-to-me	the-youthful-body.

Sŏna-kananạy	**grāyĕ**	**dūran**	**chĕs**
Of-the-golden-ears-verily	wavings	to-the-ear-pendants	I-am

diwān.
giving.

12.	**Gayĕmạy**	**gum-röyī,**	**ta**	**tamyukuy**
	There-happened-to-me	going-astray,	and	of-it-verily

gōm	**badal.**
there-happened-to-me	exchange,

Pyōm	**mĕ**	**guṭ^{i}lā**	**lön^{i}-tsūr**	**wötith**	**azal.”**
There-fell-to-me	to-me	a-woodcutter	a-fate-thief	having-arrived	doom.”

13.	**Nay**	**chĕh**	**dapān,**	**“ sak^{a}th**	**mĕ**	**gōm**	**suy**	**kusūr.**
	The-flute	is	saying,	“severe	to-me	happened-to-me	that-very	fault.

Nazari-tȧm^{i}-sanzi-söty	**sapodum**	**ṭŏka-sūr.”**
Seeing-his-owing-to	there-became-to-me	crushing-to-powder.”

14.	**Nay**	**chĕh**	**dapān,**	**“ tsakhi-hot^{u}**	**makh**	**chum**	**diwān.**
	The-flute	is	saying,	“rage-struck	an-axe	he-is-to-me	giving.

Phala	**byon^{u}**	**byon^{u}**	**chĕla**	**māzas**	**chum**	**tulān.**
Splinters	separate	separate	pieces	(of my) flesh	he-is-of-me	raising.

15.	**Mad**	**mĕ**	**ôsum,**	**had**	**pānas**	**chĕs**	**karān.”**
	Pride	to-me	was-to-me,	the-limit	(of) myself	I-am	making.”

Bāla-pānas	**wālanay**	**köts^{ü}**	**chum**	**karān.**
(Of my) youthful-body	humiliation	how-much	he-is-to-me	making.

16.	**Gayē**	**judāh,**	**sŏy**	**judöyī**	**chĕy**
	She-went	apart (from the forest),	that-very	separation	she-is-verily

wanān.
telling.

Ös^{u}	**wadān,**	**alvidāh**	**ös^{u}y**	**karān.**
She-was	lamenting,	last-farewell	was-she-verily	making.

17.	**"Tati**	**wölith**	**wati**	**wati**
	"From-there	having-brought-(me) down	on-the-road	on-the-road

tam	**chum**	**diwān.**
weariness	he-is-to-me	giving.

Wālawunuy	**tŏrka-chānas**	**chum**
Immediately-on-bringing-(me) down (from the forest)	to-a-private-carpenter	he-is-me

k^{a}nān."
selling."

18.	**Nay**	**chĕh**	**dapān,**	**"lari**	**phir^{i}**
	The-flute	is	saying,	"on-the-side	turning

phir^{i}	**chum**	**wuchān.**
turning	he-is-me	inspecting.

Dūri	**rūz^{i}**	**rūz^{i}**	**tōri-dab**	**sak^{a}th**
At-a-distance	remaining	remaining	adze-blows	severe

chum	**diwān."**
he-is-to-me	giving."

19.	**Nay**	**chĕh**	**dapān,**	**"litri-söty**	**yĕli**
	The-flute	is	saying,	"a-saw-with	when

göj^{u}nas,
was-caused-to-melt-by-him-I,

Ạth$^{\ddot{u}}$r$^{\ddot{u}}$	**pĕyĕm**	**yĕli**	**carkas**	**khöj$^{\ddot{u}}$nas."**
A-wool-worm	fell-on-me	when	to-the-lathe	was-caused-to-mount-I."

20.

Yĕli	**carkas**	**khüts$^{\ddot{u}}$**	**amis-tŏrka-**
When	to-the-lathe	she-mounted	that-private-

chānas-nishĕ,	**amis**	**pĕwān**	**panȧn^{i}**	**hamnishīn**
carpenter-near,	to-her	(are) falling	her-own	companions

yād.	**Yiman$^{\ddot{u}}$y-kun**	**chĕh**	**wanān**	**kĕntsāh.**
(in) memory.	Them-only-to	she-is	saying	something.

Ta	**kyāh**	**wani ?**
And	what	will-she-say ?

Nay	**chĕh**	**dapān,**	**"hamnishīn**	**myōn^{i}**
The-flute	is	saying,	"companions	my

rūd^{i}	**kati ?**
remained	where ?

Wȧn^{i}	**bŏh**	**dimahakh,**	**tūr^{i}**	**mā**
Messages	I	would-have-given-to-them,	there-verily	I-wonder-if

rūd^{i}	**aḍa-wati ?**
they-remained	on-midway ?

21.

Hamnishīnan	**sīr**	**panunuy**	**bāwahö;**
To-the-companions	secret	my-own-verily	I-would-explain ;

Sīna	**mutsarith**	**dôd^{u}**	**panunuy**	**hāwahö."**
Bosom	having-opened	pain	my-own-verily	I-would-show."

22.

Nay	**chĕh**	**dapān,**	**"kyāh**	**banyōm ?**
The-flute	is	saying,	"what	happened-to-me ?

kūt^{u}	**chĕs**	**riwān ?**
how-much	am-I	lamenting ?

Dādi-panani	**nāla**	**phȧr[i]yād**	**chĕs**	**diwān."**
By-the-pain-my-own	cries	calls-for-help	I-am	giving."

23.	**Nay**	**chĕh**	**dapān,**	**"nāla**	**dimahö**
	The-flute	is	saying,	"cries	I-would-have-given

mārakan;
(in) the-assemblies;

Banana-rost[u]	**nau**	**kāh**	**ti**	**rōzān**
Fated-sorrow-without	not	anyone	even	remaining

marda-zan."
man-(or) woman."

24.	**Dapān wustād,—**
	(Is) saying the-teacher,—

Kyāh	**wanihē**	**yiman**	**hamnishīnan?**
What	would-she-have-said	to-these	companions?

Yiman	**wanihē**	**yīy.**
To-these	she-would-have-said	this-verily.

Narm	**kȧr[i]**	**kȧr[i]**	**bar[a]m**	**pānas**
Smooth	making	making	auger(-hole)s	to-the-body

chum	**karān;**
he-is-to-me	making;

Wāra	**wuch[i]tōm,**	**māz**	**kōtāh**	**chum**
Thoroughly	inspect-please-ye-me,	the-flesh	how-much	is-to-me

harān.
dropping.

25. **Wadanā**	**bŏh,**	**zadĕ**	**pānas**
Shall-I-not-weep	I,	holes	to-(my) body

tör^{i}nam,
are-caused-to-pass-over-by-him-to-me,

Khām-pŏ̃san	**zīṭh^{i}**	**atha**	**kūt^{i}**	**dör^{i}nam.**
For-cheap-pice	long	arms	how-many	are-place-by-him-on-me.

26. **Dapān wustād,—**
(Is) saying the-teacher,—

Wŏñ	**yĕli**	**khām-pŏ̃san**	**āyĕ-k^{a}nana,**	**wŏñ**
Now	when	for-cheap-pice	she-was-sold,	now

chus	**pĕwān**	**panun^{u}**	**nayistān**	**yād.**
is-to-her	falling	her-own	cane-brake	(in) memory.

Ath^{i}	**nayistānas-kun**	**chĕh**	**wanān**
To-this-very	cane-brake-to	she-is	saying

kĕntshāh.	**Kyāh**	**wani?**
something.	What	will-she-say?

Nay	**chĕh**	**dapān,**	**"nayistānuk^{u}**	**chum**
The-flute	is	saying,	"of-the-canebrake	is-to-me

tamāh.
longing.

Garza-panani	**tshā̃jyām**	**arz-ō-samā."**
For-the-purpose-my-own	was-searched-by-me	earth-and-heaven."

27. **Nay**	**chĕh**	**dapān,**	**"nayistān**	**myôn^{u}**
The-flute	is	saying,	"the-canebrake	my

kyāh	**chuh**	**jān;**
how	it-is	good;

Zāni kyāh tath mānĕ būzith
Will-know ? of-that the-meaning having-heard
gör-zān ?"
an-ignorant-person ?"

28. **Nay chĕh dapān, "nayistān myôn^{u}**
The-flute is saying, "the-canebrake my
kyāh zabar;
how excellent;

Zāni kyāh tath mānĕ būzith
Will-know ? of-that the-meaning having-heard
bē-khabar ?"
an-untaught-person ?"

29. **Nay chĕh dapān, "nayistānüc^{ü}**
The-flute is saying, "of-the-canebrake
yĕs chĕh zān;
to-whom is knowledge;

Zāni suy yus āsi wôt^{u}mot^{u}
Will-know he-only who will-be arrived
lā-makān."
at-Him-Who-has-no-abode-(i.e God)."

30. **Nay chĕh dapān, "kyāh chĕh**
The-flute is saying, "what is
wüñ^{ü}müts^{ü} masnavī?
said the-rhymed-poem ?

Zāni suy yĕs āsi pĕmüts^{ü}
Will-know he-alone to-whom will-be fallen
ạsh^{ĕ}ka chīh."
(of) love a-particle."

31.	**Nay**	**chĕh**	**dapān,**	**"mŏdur[u]**	**mas**
	The-flute	is	saying,	"sweet	wine

kötyāh	**cĕwān,**
how-many	(are) drinking,

Sŏdurabalạy	**nay**	**Subhān**	**chuy**
In-Sŏdarabal-only	the-(story-of-the) flute	Subḥān	is

wanān."
saying."

VIII.—PĀTASHĔHA-SŪNZ^{ū} KATH
KING-OF STORY

1\. **Pātashāhā ôs^{u}. Dapān wustād,—**
A-certain-king was. (Is) saying the-teacher,—

Suy pātashāh ôs^{u} nērān prath-dŏha
That-very king was going-out every-day

ath^{i}-zūnaḍabi-pĕṭh. Ath^{i} ôs^{u} pĕṭha-kani
that-very-roof-bungalow-on. Of-it-verily was the-top-on

ôl^{u} jānāwāran-hond^{u}. Yim ös^{i}
the-nest birds-of. They (king and queen) were

prath-dŏha yihünz^{ü} bōlbösh^{ü} bōzān. Yim
every-day of-these the-chirping hearing. They

ös^{i} pātashāha-sȧnd^{i} bötš^{ü} z^{a}h sĕṭhāh
were the-king-of husband-and-wife two very-much

khŏsh gatšhān. Dŏha-aki bōlbösh^{ü} ati
pleased becoming. On-a-day-one the-chirping there

ös^{ü}na kĕh gatšhān. Dop^{u} ami-pātashāh-bāyi
was-not any occurring. It-was-said by-that-queen

pātashĕhas, "az kōna chĕh gatšhān
to-the-king, "to-day why-not is occurring

bōlbösh^{ü}?" Dapān wuchukh ath ölis.
chirping?" Saying it-was-seen-by-them to-that nest.

Ath^{i}-manz bacĕ z^{a}h mumȧt^{i}. Wölikh
It-verily-in young-ones two (were) dead. They-were-brought-down-by-them

bŏn. Sĕṭhāh phyūr^{u} yiman-pātashĕha-sandĕn-
down. Much regret-occurred to-these-king's-two-

dŏn-bāʦan.	**Ȧnikh**	**wazīr**	**gāṭ^{å}l^{i}**	**gāṭ^{å}l^{i}.**
husband-and-wife.	Were-summoned-by-them	viziers	skilful	skilful.

Dop^{u}hakh,	**"nŏman**	**wuch^{i}tav,**	**kyāh**
It-was-said-by-them-to-them,	"to-these	please-look-ye,	what

chuh	**gamot^{u}?"**	**Wuch^{i}hakh.**	**Yiman**
is	happened?"	They-were-seen-by-them.	To-them (was)

rôṭ^{u}mot^{u}	**konḍ^{u}**	**haṭis.**	**Dānāh-wazīran-åk^{i}**
caused-to-stick	a-thorn	to-the-throat.	By-a-wise-vizier-one

dop^{u}nakh,	**"yih**	**chĕh**	**yiman**	**panüñ^{ü}**
it-was-said-by-him-to-them,	"this	is	to-them	their-own

möj^{ü}	**mumüʦ^{ü}.**	**Ȧm^{i}-naran**	**kür^{u}müʦ^{ü}**	**byēkh**
mother	dead.	By-this-male (bird)	(was) made	a-second

wŏrüz^{ü}.	**Ami**	**chunakh**	**dyut^{u}mot^{u}**
second-wife.	By-her	is-by-her-to-them	given

āmpa-kani	**konḍ^{u}.**	**Amiy**	**chih**	**yim**
mouth-to-mouth-feeding-during	a-thorn.	By-this-verily	are	they

mumåt^{i}."	**Pātashāh**	**wanān**	**pātashāh-bāyĕ,**
dead."	The-king	(is) saying	to-the-queen,

"bŏy	**maray,**	**ʦ^{a}h**	**kår^{i}zi-na**	**kuni."**
"I-if	shall-die-if,	thou	must-make-not	at-all (a second marriage)."

Pātashāh-bāy	**wanān**	**pātashāhas,**	**"bŏy**
The-queen	(is) saying	to-the-king,	"I-if

maray,	**ʦ^{a}h**	**kår^{i}zi-na**	**kuni."**	**Kor^{u}**
shall-die-if,	thou	must-make-not	at-all (a second marriage)."	Was-made

yimau	**driy**	**kasam**	**pānawŏn̄.**	**Yih**	**kyāzi**
by-them	a-vow	oath	mutually.	This	why

korukh	**driy**	**kasam?**	**Dopukh,**	**" asĕ**
was-made-by-them	vow	oath ?	It-was-said-by-them,	" to-us

chih	**gabar**	**z^{a}h ;**	**timan**	**kyāh**	**kari**
are	sons	two ;	to-them	perhaps	will-do

wŏramŏj^{ü}	**yā**	**môl^{u}**	**yiy ?"**
a-step-mother	or	(step-)father	this-very-thing ? "

2. Kĕh	**kālāh**	**gav,**	**pātashāh-bāy**
Some	a-certain-space-of-time	went,	the-queen

mŏyĕ.	**Pātashāh**	**kuni**	**karān**	**chuna,**
died.	The-king	at-all (a second marriage)	making	is-not,

ti-kyāzi	**pānawŏn̄**	**ôsukh**	**dŏyau**	**bātsau**
because	mutually	was-by-them	by-the-two	husband-and-wife

driy	**kasam**	**kor^{u}mot^{u}.**	**Wārayāh**	**kālāh**
vow	oath	made.	Very-long	a-certain-space-of-time

gav,	**āy**	**wazīr.**	**Dopukh**	**pātashĕhas,**
went,	they-came	the-viziers.	It-was-said-by-them	to-the-king,

" pātashĕham,	**nēth^{a}r**	**gatshi**	**karun^{u}."**
" my-king,	marriage-arrangement	is-proper	to-be-done."

Wārayāh	**kāl**	**kĕh**	**bōzān**	**chukhna.**
A-very-long	space-of-time	anything	hearing	he-is-to-them-not.

Kor^{u}has	**zōr**	**wazīrau.**	**Korun**
Was-made-by-them-to-him	force	by-the-viziers.	Was-made-by-him

nēth^{a}r.
marriage-arrangement.

3. **Yim**	**pātashāh-zāda**	**z^{a}h**	**ös^{i}.**	**Tim**
These	princes (king's sons)	two	were.	They

ös^{i}	**parān**	**sabakh.**	**Dŏha-aki**	**kür^{ü}**
were	reading	lesson(s).	On-day-one	was-made

yimau-pānawöñ-bāranyau-dŏyau	**maṣlahath,**	**"mājĕ**
by-these-mutually-brothers-two	consultation,	"to-the-mother

gatshav	**salām**	**hĕth."**	**Bür^{ü}kh**	**tröm^{i}**
we-will-go	a-complimentary-gift	taking."	Was-filled-by-them	a-copper-dish

lālau	**nigīnau.**	**Gay**	**hĕth**
with-rubies	with-jewels.	They-went	having-taken (it)

salāmi	**mājĕ.**	**Tröm^{i}**	**rüṭ^{ü}nakh,**
for-a-complimentary-present	to-the-mother.	The-copper-dish	was-accepted-by-her-from-them,

wuchunāh	**kor^{u}nakh.**	**Gay**	**yim**
a-certain-look	was-made-by-her-to-them.	They-went	these

pātashāh-zāda	**z^{a}h**	**sabakas.**	**Yim**	**chih**
princes	two	to-their-lesson.	These	are

dŏhā	**dŏhā**	**yithay-pöṭhin**	**karān.**	**Dŏha-aki**
each-day	each-day	in-this-very-manner	passing.	On-day-one

gav	**amis-pātashāh-bāyĕ**	**khötir**	**yiman-**
there-occurred	to-this-queen	carnal-desire	these-

wŏranĕcivĕn-hond^{u}.	**Yiman**	**dopun,**	**"tŏh^{i}**
stepsons-of.	To-them	it-was-said-by-her,	"ye

thöviv mĕ-söty salāh." Yimau dop^{u}has,
keep-ye me-with consultation." By-them it-was-said-by-them-to-her,

"ts^{a}h chĕkh möj^{ü}, ȧs^{i} chiy gabar.
"thou art mother, we are-to-thee sons.

Ts̱ĕ ta asĕ wāti-na." Gay pānas
For-thee and for-us it-will-not-be-suitable." They-went of-their-own-accord

sabakas. Kālacĕn āv pātashāh pānun^{u}
to-the-lesson. In-the-evening came the-king (to) his-own

mahalakhān. Pātashāh-bāyi trop^{u}nas
private-apartments. By-the-queen was-shut-by-her-to-him

kuṭh^{u}. Dop^{u}nas, "bar kyāzi koruth
the-room. It-was-said-by-him-to-her, "the-door why is-made-by-thee

band?" Yih chĕs dapān pātashāh-bāy,
shut?" She is-to-him saying the-queen,

"bŏh chĕsa cyōñ^{ü} kŏlay, kina cyānĕn-
"I am-I of-thee the-wife, or thy-

nĕcivĕn-hünz^{ü}?" Pātashāh chus dapān,
sons-of?" The-king is-to-her saying,

"tih kyāh gav?" Dop^{u}nas, "tim
"that what happened?" It-was-said-by-her-to-him, "they

ām lĕkan. Gŏḍa dim tihanza
came-to-me for-(using-)indecent-language. First give-to-me their

wölinjĕ z^{a}h, ada mutsaray bar."
hearts two, then I-will-open-to-thee the-door."

4. Dapān,— dyutun hukum wazīran.
(Folk are) saying,— was-given-by-him the-order to-the-viziers.

Tim ös^{i} parān sabakh tsāṭahāl.
They were reading lessons (in) the-school.

Dop^{u}nakh, "mārawātalan karyūkh
It-was-said-by-him-to-them, "to-the-executioners make-ye-them

hawāla. Timay māranakh." Dapān,—
in-custody. They-verily will-kill-them." (Folk are) saying,—

wôt^{u} wazīr yiman-pātashāhzādan-nishin.
arrived the-vizier to-these-princes-near.

Sĕṭhāh gōs yinsāph. Dop^{u}nakh, "wasiv
Very-much occurred-to-him compassion. It-was-said-by-him-to-them, "come-ye-down

bŏn tsāṭahāla." Dop^{u}nakh, "tsaliv yimi
down from-the-school." It-was-said-by-him-to-them, "flee-ye from-this

shĕhara." Tim tsal^{i}, wazīran kür^{ü}
city." They fled, by-the-vizier was-done

köm^{ü}. Dopun mārawātalan, "möryūkh
a-deed. It-was-said-by-him to-the-executioners, "kill-ye-for-them

hūn^{i} z^{a}h." Mörikh hūn^{i} z^{a}h, kaḍikh
dogs two." Were-killed-by-them dogs two, were-extracted-by-them

yiman wölinjĕ z^{a}h, lazakh ṭökis,
of-them the-hearts two, they-were-put-by-them to-a-tray,

gay hĕth pātashāh-bāyĕ. Dop^{u}has,
they-went taking (them) to-the-queen. It-was-said-by-them-to-her,

"anĕy nŏma pātashāhzādan-hanza
"are-brought-to-thee these the-princes-of

wölinjĕ	**z^{a}h.**	**Thāv**	**darwāza**	**ta**	**raṭh."**
hearts	two.	Open	the-door	and	take-hold-of (them)."

Thôw^{u}nakh	**darwāza,**	**racĕn**	**yima**	**wölinjĕ**
Was-open-by-her-for-them	the-door,	were-seized-by-her	these	hearts

z^{a}h.	**Dop^{u}has,**	**" yima**	**chĕy**	**pātashāhzādan-**
two.	It-was-said-by-them-to-her,	" these	are-for-thee	the-princes-

dŏn-hanza."	**Byūṭh^u**	**ȧt^i**	**pātashöhī**
two-of."	(The king) sat	(i.e. remained) there	sovereignty

karani.
for-doing.

5. Yim	**böy^i-bārȧn^i**	**z^{a}h**	**wöt^i**	**biyis-**
These	brothers-brethren	two	arrived	another-

pātashĕhas-akis-nish.	**Dop^{u}nakh**	**pātashĕhan,**
king-one-near.	It-was-said-by-him-to-them	by-the-king,

" tŏh^i	**chiwa**	**shāhzāda**	**mĕ**	**yiwān-bōzana.**
" ye	are	princes	by-me	being-thought.

Tŏh^i	**wȧn^{i}tav**	**tŏh^i**	**kĕtha-pöṭh^i**	**chiwa**
Ye	please-tell	ye	in-what-manner	are

yōr	**lȧg^{i}mȧt^i.**	**Kyāh**	**sabab**	**chuwa ?"**
here	arrived.	What	reason	is-to-you ?"

Timau	**dop^{u}has**	**yih**	**panun^u**	**gudarun.**
By-them	it-was-said-by-them-to-him	this	their-own	happening.

Dop^{u}nakh,	**" bĕhiv**	**mĕ-nish**	**nōkarī."**
It-was-said-by-him-to-them,	" sit-ye	me-near	in-service."

Dapān,— bīṭh^{i} huzūrī-nōkar. Amis ös^{i}
(Folk are) saying,— they-sat (as) personal-servants. To-this were

pātashĕhas prön^{i} gŏlām z^{a}h. Yim z^{a}h
to-the-king old servants two. These two

ti bīṭh^{i}, gay tsōr. Ts̱ŏn-zanĕn kārin
also sat, They-became four. To-the-four-persons were-made-by-him

zima rātsas tsōr pahar. Gŏḍañukuy
in-charge by-night four watches. The-first-verily

pahar chuh lagān amis-pātashāhzādas-
watch is being-allotted to-this-prince-

ziṭhis-hihis. Dapān,— pātashĕha-sandyau-
the-elder. (Folk are) saying,— by-the-king's-

dŏyau-bātsau trôwukh arām.
two-husband-and-wife was-made-by-them rest.

6. Dapān,— gŏlām chuh wŏdañĕ,
(Folk are) saying,— the-servant is standing (by),

nazar chĕs pātashĕha-sandĕn-dŏn-bātsan-kun.
sight is-of-him the-king-of-two-husband-and-wife-towards.

Yimav^{ü}y-syod^{u} log^{u} wasani shĕhmār
Them-verily-in-front began to-descend a-great-snake

tālawa-kani. Gŏlām chuh wuchān. Yĕli
the-ceiling-from. The-servant is watching. When

yih shĕhmār log^{u} wātani amis-pātashāh-
this great-snake began to-arrive to-this-king's-

bāyĕ-handis-badanas-nīzīkh, āv lārān gŏlām,
wife-of-body-near, he-came running the-slave,

löy^{ü}n shĕmshēr amis-shĕhmāras, hani
was-struck-by-him a-sword to-this-great-snake, in-fragment

hani kår^{i}nas ṭuk^{a}ra, ṭhunun
in-fragment were-made-by-him-of-it pieces, was-placed-by-him

palangas-tal, shĕmshēri-handis-tēgas wolun
the-bed-below, the-sword's-to-the-blade was-wrapped-by-him

phamb. Log^{u} amis-pātashāha-bāyĕ-handis-
cotton-wool. He-began to-this-king's-wife's-

badanas wŏtharani. Dopun, "amis
the-body to-wipe. It-was-said-by-him, "to-this-one

āsi shĕhmāra-sond^{u} zahar lāḍyōmot^{u}."[1]
will-be the-great-snake-of poison brought-into-contract-with.

Amiy mōjub ôs^{u} yih wŏtharān. Pātashāh
For-this-very reason was he wiping. The-king

gav bĕdār. Wuchun gŏlām āmot^{u}
became awake. Was-seen-by-him the-servant come

nīzīkh shĕmshēr hĕth nüñ^{ü}. Ȧm^{i}-sond^{u}
near sword having-taken bare. This-one-of

pahar mŏkalyāv, āv dŏyimis-gŏlāma-sond^{u}
the-watch was-finished, there-came the-second-servant-of

pahar. Āv nīzīkh. Dop^{u}nas pātashĕhan,
the-watch. He-came near. It-was-said-by-him-to-him by-the-king,

"ạy gŏlām, yus-akhāh āgas-pĕṭh bē-wŏphöyī
"ho servant, whoever the-master-on infidelity

kari, tas kyāh wāti karun^{u}?" Yih
may-do, to-him what will-be-proper to-be-done?" This

wọ̄thus gŏlām phīrith, "pātashĕham,
arose-for-him slave answering, "my-king,

[1] So Hātim. Gōvind Kaul writes *lāryōmot^{u}*.

tas	**gatshi**	**kala**	**tsaṭun^{u},**	**biyĕ**	**basta**
to-him	is-proper	the-head	to-be-cut-off,	moreover	his-skin

wālün̄^{ü}.	**Pātashĕham,**	**bŏh**	**wanay**	**dalīlā.**
(is) to-be-brought-down.	My-king,	I	will-tell-to-thee	a-certain-story.

Ts̲^{a}h	**thāvtam**	**tath**	**kan."**
Thou	place-please-for-me	for-that	the-ear."

7.	**Dop^{u}nas**	**gŏlāman,—**	**"suh**	**pātashĕhā**
	It-was-said-by-him-to-him	by-the-servant,—	"that	a-certain-king

akh	**ôs^{u}.**	**Suy**	**gav**	**dŏha-aki**	**sölas**
one	was.	He-verily	went	on-day-one	for-excursion

shikāras	**kunuy**	**zon^{u}.**	**Söty**	**ôsus**	**pöz,**
for-hunting	only-one	person.	With	was-to-him	a-falcon,

wôt^{u}	**jāyĕ-akis,**	**lüj^{ü}s**	**trēsh.**	**Banān**
he-arrived	at-a-place-one,	was-felt-to-him	thirst.	Becoming

chĕsna	**kuni.**	**Wuchun**	**jāyĕ-akis**
is-for-him (alleviation of thirst)-not	anywhere.	Was-seen-by-him	in-a-place-one

āba-srĕhā	**hyuh^{u}.**	**Ath^{i}**	**dyutun**	**bȧr^{i}shi-**
water-moisture	a-little.	At-it-verily	was-given-by-him	his-spear-

söty	**dŏba-hanā.**	**Koḍun**	**bagala-manza**
with	a-hole-small.	Was-withdrawn-by-him	his-armpit-from-in

pyāla.	**Lodun**	**ath-pyālas**	**āb.**	**Hyotun**
a-cup.	Was-filled-by-him	to-that-cup	water.	He-began

cyon^{u}.	**Ās**	**pöz,**	**tshun^{u}nas-trövith.**
to-drink.	Come-to-him	the-falcon,	(the-cup) was-dashed-down-by-it-for-him.

Biyĕ	**borun**	**yih**	**āba-pyāla,**	**hyotun**
Again	was-filled-by-him	this	water-cup,	he-began

cyon^{u}.	**Ās**	**biyĕ**	**yih**	**pöz,**
to-drink.	Came-to-him	again	this	falcon,

tshun^{u}nas-trövith.	**Dŏyi-laṭi**	**tshun^{u}nas-trövith.**
(it) was-dashed-down-by-it-for-him.	On-two-occasion(s)	it-was-dashed-down-by-it-for-him.

Pātashĕhas	**khot^{u}**	**zahar.**	**Trĕyimi-laṭi**
To-the-king	arose	poison (i.e. anger).	On-the-third-occasion

borun.	**Dachini**	**atha**	**chuh**	**ath-pyālas**
it-was-filled-by-him.	With-the-right	with-hand	he-is	to-that-cup

thaph-karith;	**khôwur^{u}**	**atha**	**thôwun**
having-held;	the-left	hand	was-placed-by-him

nĕbar.	**Yuthuy**	**hyotun**	**cyon^{u},**	**tyuthuy**
outside.	Even-as	he-began	to-drink,	even-so

āv	**pöz,**	**tshun^{u}nas-trövith.**	**Dits^{ü}s**	**âm^{i}**
came	the-falcon,	it-was-dashed-down-by-it-for-him.	Was-given-to-it	by-him

thaph,	**roṭun**	**latan-tal,**	**hĕtsanas**	**pakha**
seizing,	was-held-by-him	the-feet-below,	were-taken-by-him-of-it	the-wings

z^{a}h,	**kâḍ^{i}nas**	**tān.**	**Yih**	**yĕli**	**môrun,**
two,	were-torn-off-by-him-of-it	the-limbs.	It	when	was-killed-by-him,

pata	**phyūrus**	**ataty.**	**Wŏñ**	**trēsh**
afterwards	regret-was-felt-to-him	in-that-very-place.	Now	(water to allay) thirst

cĕyĕnna.	**Gav**	**wuchani**	**'ath-ābas**
was-drunk-by-him-not.	He-went	to-see	'to-this-water

āsinā kuni āgur?' Pakān chuh
will-there-not-be somewhere source?' Going is

pātashāh, wôt^{u} jāyĕ-akis. Wuchun
the-king, he-arrived at-a-place-one. Was-seen-by-him

ati shĕhmārā shŏngith, amis^{ü}y nērān
there a-certain-great-snake asleep, to-it-verily issuing

ösa-kani lāl. Yih āb ôs^{u} zahar."
the-mouth-from spittle. This water was poison."

Yih chus wanān gŏlām amis pātashĕhas,
This is-to-him saying the-servant to-this to-king,

"hargāh-kiy suh pātashāh sa trēsh
"if that king that (water-to-allay) thirst

cĕyihē, suh marihē. Wüñ^{ü}y saragī
had-drunk, he would-have-died. Now-verily investigation (if)

karihē, suh pātashāh tas-pözas mārihē-na.
he-had-made, that king to-that-falcon would-not-have-killed.

Pātashĕham, say chĕh dalīl. Saragī
My-king, that-verily is the-story. Investigation

gatshi karüñ^{ü}."
is-proper to-be-made."

8. Mŏkalyāv ȧm^{i}-sond^{u} pahar ti. Āv
Was-finished this-one-of the-watch also. Came

trĕyum^{u} pahar. Z^{a}h gay pānas bīṭh^{i}.
the-third watch. The-two became at-their-own-will seated.

Pātashāh chuh bĕdār. Dapan chuh
The-king is awake. Saying he-is

amis-trĕyimis-paharawölis. Dapān chus, "ạy
to-this-third-watchman. Saying he-is-to-him, "ho

gŏlām, yus-akhāh āgas-pĕṭh dagāy
servant, whoever to-the-master-on faithlessness

kari, tas kyāh wāti karun^{u}?"
may-do, to-him what will-be-proper to-be-done?"

Dop^{u}nas phīrith ȧm^{i}-gŏlāman, "suh
It-was-said-by-him-to-him answering by-that-servant, "he

gatshi sangsār karun^{u}. Bāki, pātashĕham,
is-proper stoning-to-death to-be-done. But, my-king,

saragī gatshi karüñ^{ü}. Bŏh wanay
investigation is-proper to-be-made. I will-tell-to-thee

dalīlā. Ṭs^{a}h thāwum, pātashĕham, kan."
a-certain-story. Thou place-for-me, my-king, ear."

9. **Dapān chus, "suh ôs^{u} sōdāgārā**
Saying he-is-to-him, "that was a-certain-merchant

akh. Suy ôs^{u} sĕṭhāh baktāwār. Tamis
one. He-verily was very prosperous. To-him

pĕv muhim. Tamis^{u}y ôs^{u} hūn^{u}. Byākh
fell poverty. To-him-verily was a-dog. Another

sōdāgārā ôs^{u}. Dop^{u}nas, 'yih hūn^{u}
a-certain-merchant was. It-was-said-by-him-to-him, 'this dog

mā k^{a}nahan?' Dop^{u}nas, 'k^{a}nan.'
I-wonder-if wilt-thou-sell-it?' It-was-said-by-him-to-him, 'I-will-sell-it.'

Dop^{u}nas,	**'karus**	**mŏl.'**	**Kor^{u}nas**
It-was-said-by-him-to-him,	'make-of-it	a-price.'	Was-made-by-him-of-it

mŏl	**rŏpayĕ-hath.**	**Dyut^{u}nas**	**mŏl,**
the-price	a-rupee-hundred.	Was-given-by-him-to-him	the-price,

nyūv	**sōdāgāran**	**yih**	**hūn^{u}.**	**Drāv**
was-taken	by-the-merchant	this	dog.	He-went-forth

sōdā	**hĕth,**	**wôt^{u}**	**jāyĕ-akis.**	**Lüj^{ü}s**
merchandize	taking,	he-arrived	at-place-one.	Came-on-for-him

rāth.	**Rāt^{a}li**	**ʦās**	**ʦūr,**	**nyūhas**
night.	By-night	entered-for-him	thieves,	was-taken-by-them-of-him

yih	**māl.**	**Hūn^{u}**	**chuh**	**wuchān,**	**ȧm^{i}**
this	property.	The-dog	is	seeing,	by-him

kor^{u}-na	**kĕ̃h-ti**	**sadāh.**	**Phọl^{u}**	**gwāsh.**
was-made-not	any-at-all	sound-a.	Broke	the-dawn.

Sōdāgār	**gav**	**bĕdār.**	**Wuchun**	**ta**	**māl**
The-merchant	became	awake.	It-was-seen-by-him	verily	property

na	**kuni.**	**Dapān**	**chuh,**	**'yith**	**kyāh**
not	at-all.	Saying	he-is,	'to-this	what

gōm?'	**Āv**	**yih**	**hūn^{u}.**	**Ȧm^{i}**	**kür^{ü}nas**
happened-to-me?'	Came	this	dog.	By-it	was-made-by-him-of-him

pŏshākas	**thaph.**	**Chus**	**lamān.**	**Hūn^{u}**
to-the-coat	seizing.	He-is-to-him	pulling.	The-dog

drāv	**brũh**	**brũh,**	**pata**	**pata**	**chus**
went-forth	in-front	in-front,	behind	behind	is-of-him

sōdāgār.	**Wātanôwun**	**mödānas-akis-manz.**
the-merchant.	He-was-caused-to-arrive-by-him	to-a-plain-to-one-in.

Wuchun ati tsūrau thow^{u}mot^{u} asond^{u}
Was-seen-by-him there by-the-thieves deposited his

māl. Parzanôwun. Onun panun^{u} māl,
property. It-was-recognized-by-him. Was-brought-by-him his-own property,

yih ôsus ta tih, biyĕ ôs^{u} yimau-
what was-of-him both that, also there-was by-these-

tsūrau biyĕn-sōdāgāran-hond^{u} nyūmot^{u}, ti-ti
thieves other-merchants-of taken, that-also

onun, wātanôwun pananis-ḍēras. Gav
was-brought-by-him, it-was-caused-to-arrive-by-him to-his-own-lodging. He-became

sĕṭhāh khŏsh. Dopun, ‘tamis sōdāgāras
very happy. It-was-said-by-him, ‘to-that merchant

tog^{u}-na amis hūnis mŏl karun.
knowledge-how-was-not to-this dog a-price to-make.

Tamis ôs^{u} pĕmot^{u} muhim, tami-mŏkha
To-him was fallen poverty, on-that-account

togus-na.’”
knowledge-how-to-him-was-not.’”

10. Dapān wustād,—
(Is) saying the-teacher,—

“Amis-hūnis korun mŏl rŏpayĕs
“For-that-dog was-made-by-him price (of) rupee

pānts hath. Lich^{u}n ciṭh^{i}. Yihuy
five hundred. Was-written-by-him a-document. This-verily

tshuñ^{u}n amis-hūnis nŏl^{i}. Dop^{u}nas,
was-put-by-him to-that-dog on-the-neck. It-was-said-by-him-to-it,

'ts^{a}h gatsh pananis-khāwandas-nishin yih
'thou go to-thine-own-master-near this

ciṭh^{i} hĕth.' Gav hūn^{u}, wôt^{u} nazdīkh
document having-taken.' Went the-dog, arrived near

amis-sōdāgāras. Sōdāgāran ḍyūṭh^{u}. Parzanôwun
to-that-merchant. By-the-merchant he-was-seen. Was-recognized-by-him

yih hūn^{u}. Dopun pananĕn bātsan.
this dog. It-was-said-by-him to-his-own family-members.

Dop^{u}nakh, 'hūn^{u} āv phīrith. Ȧm^{i}
It-was-said-by-him-to-them, 'the-dog came returning. By-it

kor^{u} kyāh-tān̄ takhsīr. Amiy
was-done some-or-other fault. For-this-very (reason)

tshunukh-kaḍith. Bal^{i}ki chus cālān
it-has-been-driven-out-by-them. Moreover there-is-to-it a-letter-of-dispatch

nöl^{i}.' Sōdāgār gav phikiri. 'Wun̄
on-the-neck.' The-merchant became in-anxiety. 'Now

kyāh kara? Rŏpayĕ-hath gōm khar^{a}c.'
what shall-I-do? The-rupee-hundred went-for-me expended.'

Koḍun bandūkh, lôy^{u}nas, ta
Was-taken-out-by-him a-gun, was-aimed-by-him-at-it and

môrun. Yĕli môrun ta ada
it-was-killed-by-him. When it-was-killed-by-him then afterwards

phyūrus. Gōs nīzīkh. 'Bŏh wuchaha
grief-came-to-him. He-went-to-it near. 'I would-see

amis kyāh kākaz chuh nöl^{i}.' Yihuy
to-it what paper is on-the-neck.' This-verily

koḍ^{u}nas	**nāla**	**ta**	**muʦorun,**	**ta**
was-taken-off-by-him-of-it	from-the-neck	and	it-was-opened-by-him,	and

wuchun	**ath**	**lyukh^{u}mot^{u}**	**rŏpayĕs**	**pānʦ**
was-seen-by-him	on-it	(was) written	(of-)rupee	five

hath.	**Ada**	**phyūrus**	**sĕṭhāh.**	**Pātashĕham,**
hundred.	Then	grief-came-to-him	exceedingly.	My-king,

say	**chĕh**	**dalīl.**	**Saragī**	**gaʦhi**	**karüñ^{ü}.**
that-verily	is	the-story.	Investigation	is-proper	to-be-made.

Hargāh-ay	**suh**	**sōdāgār**	**gŏḍañiy**	**wuchihē**
If	that	merchant	at-the-very-first-even	had-seen

amis-hūnis	**kyāh**	**chuh**	**nöl^{i},**	**suh**	**hūn^{u}**
to-that-dog	what	is	on-the-neck,	that	dog

mā	**mārihē."**	**Gav**	**ȧm^{i}-sond^{u}**	**pahar.**
not	he-would-have-killed."	Went	him-of	the-watch.

11.	**Āv**	**ʦūrimis-zȧn^{i}-sond^{u}**	**pahar.**	**T̲s̲ūrimis-**
	Came	the-fourth-person-of	watch.	The-fourth-

gŏlāma-sünz^{ü}	**dalīl.**	**T̲s̲ūrimis-gŏlāmas**	**wanān**
servant-of	story.	To-the-fourth-servant	(is) saying

pātashāh,	**"ạy**	**gŏlām,**	**yus-akhāh**	**āgas-pĕṭh**
the-king,	"ho	servant,	whoever	the-master-on

bēwŏphöyī	**kari,**	**tas**	**kyāh**	**wāti**	**karun^{u}?"**
infidelity	may-do,	to-him	what	will-be-proper	to-be-done?"

Dop^{u}nas	**gŏlāman,**	**"pātashĕham,**	**tas**
It-was-said-by-him-to-him	by-the-servant,	"my-king,	to-him

gatshi	**sar**	**tsaṭun^{u},**	**shĕhara-manza**	**dūr**
is-proper	the-head	to-be-cut-off,	the-city-from-in	distant

kaḍun^{u}.	**Pātashĕham,**	**bŏh**	**wanay**
(he-is) to-be-expelled.	My-king,	I	will-tell-to-thee

dalīlā,	**ts^{a}h**	**thāwum**	**kan."**	**Dapān**
a-certain-story,	thou	place-for-me	the-ear."	Saying

chus	**gŏlām.**	**"suh**	**ôs^{u}**	**pātashĕhā**
is-to-him	the-servant.	"that	was	a-certain-king

akh.	**Amis**	**ös^{i}**	**nĕciv^{i}**	**z^{a}h.**	**Timan^{ü}y**
one.	To-him	were	sons	two.	To-them-verily

mŏyĕ	**panüñ^{ü}**	**möj^{ü}.**	**Pātashĕhan**	**kür^{ü}**
died	their-own	mother.	By-the-king	was-made

wŏrüz^{ü}	**zanāna.**	**Sa**	**gayē**	**pātashāhzādan**
second-wife	woman.	She	became	to-the-princes

dŏn	**wŏramöj^{ü}.**	**Yim**	**ös^{i}**	**pātashāhzāda**
to-the-two	stepmother.	These	were	princes

z^{a}h	**sabakas.**	**Tōra**	**āy,**	**amis-wŏramājĕ**
the-two	at-a-lesson.	Thence	they-came,	to-this-stepmother

niyĕkh	**salām,**	**lālau**	**nigīnau**
was-taken-by-them	a-complimentary-gift,	(filled) with-rubies	with-jewels

tröm^{i}.	**Thöv^{ü}kh**	**amis**	**bōnṭha-kani.**
a-copper-dish.	It-was-placed-by-them	to-her	in-front.

Yim	**gay**	**biyĕ**	**sabakas.**	**Dŏhā**	**dŏhā**
These	went	again	to-the-lesson.	Each-day	each-day

chih	**kaḍān.**	**Pātashāh-bāyĕ**	**wuz^{ü}**
they-are	(thus) passing.	To-the-queen	was-aroused

panüñ^{ü}	**rāy.**	**Kyāh**	**wuz^{ü}s?**	**'Bŏh**
her-own	intention.	What	was-aroused-in-her?	'I

karahö yiman-pātashāhzādan-söty gŏnāh.'
would-have-done these-princes-with sin.'

Dŏha-aki wonun yiman-pātashāhzādan-dŏn,
On-a-day-one it-was-said-by-her to-these-princes-two,

'mĕ-söty kariv gŏnāh.' Yimav dop^{u}has,
'me-with do-ye sin.' By-them was-said-by-them-to-her,

'ts^{a}h chĕkh sŏn̄^{ü} möj^{ü}; tsĕ ta asĕ
'thou art our mother; for-thee and for-us

wāti-na.' Pātashāhzāda gay sabakas.
it-will-not-be-suitable.' The-princes went to-the-lesson.

Pātashāh āv darbār murkhas karith.
The-king came the-court dismissed having-made.

Wôt^{u} mahalakhān. Pātashāh-bāyi
He-arrived at-the-private-apartments. By-the-queen

trop^{u}nas darwāza. Darwāza chĕs-na
was-shut-by-her-for-him the-door. The-door she-is-for-him-not

thāwān. Dop^{u}nas, 'yih kyāzi?' Wŏtsh^{ü}s
opening. It-was-said-by-him-to-her, 'this why?' She-rose (in-reply)-to-him

pātashāh-bāy. Dop^{u}nas, 'bŏh chĕsa
the-queen. It-was-said-by-her-to-him, 'I am-I

cyŏn̄^{ü} kŏlay, kina cyānĕn-nĕcivĕn-hünz^{ü}?'
of-thee the-wife, or thy-sons-of?'

Dop^{u}nas pātashĕhan, 'tih kyāh
It-was-said-by-him-to-her by-the-king, 'that what

gav?' Dop^{u}nas, 'tim ām
happened?' It-was-said-by-her-to-him, 'they came-to-me

lĕkan.' **Pātashāh** **chus** **dapān,**
for(-using)-indecent-language.' The-king is-to-her saying,

'wuñ **kyāh** **chuh** **salāh ?'** **Pātashāh-bāy**
'now what is (your) advice ?' The-queen

chĕs **dapān,** **'mĕ** **gaʦhi** **tihanza**
is-to-him saying, 'for-me is-necessary their

wölinjĕ **z^{a}h.** **Tima** **khĕma** **bŏh.** **Ada-kyāh**
hearts two. Them I-will-eat I. Then-of-course

thāway **darwāza.'** **Pātashĕhan** **dyut^{u}**
I-will-open-for-thee the-door.' By-the-king was-given

hukum **wazīras.** **Dop^{u}nas,** **'yim**
an-order to-the-vizier. It-was-said-by-him-to-him, 'these

shāhzāda **z^{a}h** **dikh** **mārawātalan** **athi.**
princes two give-them of-the-executioners in-the-hand.

Yiman **kaḍan** **wölinjĕ** **z^{a}h.'** **Gav**
Of-them they-will-extract the-hearts two.' Went

wazīr. **Wôt^{u}** **ʦāṭahāl,** **yĕti** **yim**
the-vizier. He-arrived at-the-school, where these

shāhzāda **z^{a}h** **ös^{i}.** **Yiman-kun** **kür^{ü}n**
princes two were. Them-towards was-made-by-him

nazarāh. **Sĕṭhāh** **gös** **yim** **pātashāhzāda**
a-single-glance. Exceedingly became-to-him these princes

z^{a}h **khŏsh.** **Dilas** **pyōs** **yinsāph.**
two pleasing. To-the-heart fell-of-him compassion.

Dop^{u}nakh, **'ʦaliv** **yimi-shĕhara** **dūr.'**
It-was-said-by-him-to-them, 'flee-ye from-this-city far.'

Tsȧl^{i}."
They-fled."

12. Dapān wustād,—
(Is) saying the-teacher,—

" Mārawātalan dyut^{u} hukum wazīran,
" To-the-executioners was-given an-order by-the-vizier,

'möryūkh hūn^{i} z^{a}h.' Mārawātalau mör^{i}
'kill-ye-them dogs two.' By-the-executioner were-killed

hūn^{i} z^{a}h, kȧḍikh yiman wölinjĕ
dogs two, were-extracted-by-them of-them the-hearts

z^{a}h, lazakh ṭökis-manz, gay hĕth
two, they-were-placed-by-them a-tray-in, they-went taking

pātashāh-bāyĕ. Pātashāh-bāyi thôw^{u} darwāza.
to-the-queen. By-the-queen was-opened the-door.

Pātashāh chuh karān pātashöhī tȧt^{i}.
The-king is doing ruling there.

13. Shāhzāda z^{a}h āy ƭalān biyis
The-princes two came fleeing to-another

pātashĕhas nish. Pātashĕhan rȧṭ^{i} yim
king near. By-the-king were-taken they

gŏlām. Gŏḍanyuk^{u} pahar āv amis-
(as) servants. The-first watch came to-this-

baḍis-hihis-shāhzādas. Shĕmāh chuh dazān.
the-elder-the-prince. A-lamp-flame is burning.

Pātashāha-sȧnd^{i} z^{a}h böƭ^{ü} chih palangas-
The-king two husband-and-wife are the-bed-

pĕṭh arāmas. Yiman^{ü}y syod^{u} wasān
-on in-rest. To-them-verily in-front descending

chuh shĕhmār. Yih gŏlām chuh kaḍān
is a-great-snake. This servant is drawing

shĕmshēr. Amis-shĕhmāras chuh karān
a-sword. To-this-great-snake he-is making

ṭuk^{a}ra. Ami pata chuh shĕmshēri-handis
pieces. This after he-is to-the-sword's

tēgas walān phamb. Amis-pātashāhbāyĕ-handis-
blade wrapping cotton-wool. To-this-queen's-

badanas ôs^{u} wŏtharān yih zahar amis-
body he-was wiping-off this poison that-

shĕhmāra-sond^{u}. Dopun, 'amis mā
great-snake-of. It-was-said-by-him, 'on-her I-wonder-if

āsim shĕhmāra-sond^{u} zahar.' Ôs^{u}
there-will-be-on-my (queen) the-great-snake-of poison.' He-was

wŏtharān ta pātashāh gav bĕdār.
wiping and the-king became awake.

Dop^{u} pātashĕhan, 'yih ām mārani.'
It-was-said by-the-king, 'he came-to-me for-killing.'

Pātashĕham, say chĕh dalīl. Hargāh-kiy
My-king, that-verily is the-story. If

suh pātashāh sara karihē, pananĕn-
that king testing had-made, to-his-own-

nĕcivĕn-pĕṭh mā diyihē hukum mārawātalan,
sons-on not would-he-have-given the-order to-the-executioners,

'tŏh^{i} möryūkh.' Ada gay tim hūn^{i}
'ye kill-ye-them.' Afterwards went those dogs

z^{a}h māra. Pātashĕham, agar bāwar
two to-death. My-king, if believing

karakh-na,	**suh**	**pātashāh**	**ôs^{u}**	**sônuy**
thou-wilt-not-make,	that	king	was	our-verily

môl^{u}.	**Yih**	**pātashāh**	**gōkh**	**ts^{a}h.**	**Yit^{i}-kyāh**
father.	This	king	art	thou.	Here-on-the-one-hand

chĕh	**shĕmshēr,**	**ȧt^{i}-kyāh**	**chuy**	**palangas-tal**
is	the-sword,	there-on-the-other-hand	is-of-thee	the-bed-below

shĕhmār	**gañĕ**	**karith."**
the-great-snake	pieces	having-made."

14.	**Sĕṭhāh**	**gōkh**	**pātashāh**	**khŏsh.**
	Exceedingly	became-with-them	the-king	pleased.

Akh	**bôy^{u}**	**thôwun**	**wazīr,**	**byākh**	**bôy^{u}**
One	brother	was-appointed-by-him	vizier,	the-other	brother

banôwun	**pātashāh.**
was-made-by-him	a-king.

IX.—GRĪST^{I}-BĀYĔ-HÜNZ^{Ü} TA MÃCH-T^{A}L^{A}RĔ-HÜNZ^{Ü} KATH

IX.—GRĪST^{I}-BĀYĔ-HÜNZ^{Ü}	**TA**	**MÃCH-T^{A}L^{A}RĔ-**
FARMER'S-WIFE-OF	AND	HONEY-BEE-

HÜNZ^{Ü}	**KATH**
OF	STORY

1. **Dapān wustād,—**
(Is) saying the-teacher,—

Yih	**grīst^{i}-bāy**	**ös^{ü}**	**ʦüj^{ü}müʦ^{ü}.**	**Kami-**
This	farmer's-wife	had	fled.	For-what-

bāpath ?	**Kārdāran**	**ta**	**mukadaman**	**ôsus**
reason ?	By-the-overseer	and	by-the-village-headman	had-been-to-her

kor^{u}mot^{u}	**zulm.**	**Amiy-bāpath**	**chĕh**	**ʦüj^{ü}müʦ^{ü}.**
done	tyranny.	For-this-very-reason	she-is	fled.

Wöʦ^{ü}	**wanas-akis-manz.**	**Otuy**	**wöʦ^{ü}s**
She-arrived	forest-one-in.	There-verily	arrived-to-her

mãch-t^{a}l^{ü}r^{ü}.	**Amis**	**āyĕ**	**zabān.**	**Dapān**
a-honey-bee.	To-it	came	speech.	Saying

chĕh	**amis-grīst^{i}-bāyĕ,**	**"ʦ^{a}h**	**kyāzi**	**chĕkh**
she-is	to-this-farmer's-wife,	"thou	why	art

ʦüj^{ü}müʦ^{ü} ?"	**Dop^{u}nas**	**grīst^{i}-bāyi,**	**"mĕ**
fled ?"	Was-said-by-her-to-it	by-the-farmer's-wife,	"to-me

chuh	**gŏmot^{u}**	**zulm."**	**Ami**	**dop^{u}nas**
is	happened	tyranny."	By-that	was-said-by-it-to-her

phīrith	**mãch-t^{a}l^{a}ri,**	**"mĕ-ti**	**chuh**	**gŏmot^{u}**
answering	by-the-bee,	"to-me-also	is	happened

zulm.	**Bŏh**	**chĕs**	**wadān,**	**ʦ^{a}h**	**thāvtam**
tyranny.	I	am	lamenting,	thou	please-place-for-me

kan."	**Wanān**	**mā̃ch-t^{a}l^{ü}r^{ü}**	**grīst^{i}-bāyi**	**kun.**
the-ear."	Saying (is)	the-bee	the-farmer's-wife	to.

"Yitay,	**vĕsī,**	**paran**	**pĕmōs,**
"Come-please,	friend,	at-feet	we-will-fall-of-Him,

karōs	**zārapār.**
we-will-make-to-Him	ejaculations.

Buday	**chĕsay**	**mā̃ch-t^{a}l^{ü}r^{ü},**	**wanuk^{u}**
I-verily	am-Thy	honey-bee,	of-the-forest

jānāwār.
a-winged-creature.

2.	**Kŏha-kŏhai**	**vyūr^{u}āh**	**añām,**	**ös^{ü}s**
	From-every-mountain	flower-nectar	was-brought-by-me,	I-became

ayālbār.
possessed-of-a-large-family.

Balāy	**pĕyin**	**hāpath-gānas,**	**wanan**
Calamity	may-fall	to-the-bear-pimp,	to-the-forests

tsöñ^{ü}nam	**lār.**
was-brought-in-by-him-to-me	running-away.

3.	**Pōtĕn**	**tasandĕn**	**öl^{i}-nāsh**	**korun;**
	To-the-young-ones	of-it	nest-destruction	was-made-by-him;

Söhibō,	**āy-nā**	**ār?**
O-God,	did-there-not-there-come-to-thee	pity?

Buday chĕsay mã̄ch-t^{a}l^{ü}r^{ü}, wanuk^{u}
I-verily am-Thy honey-bee, of-the-forest

jānãwār."
a-winged-creature."

4. **Dapān amis grīst^{i}-bāyĕ yih**
(Is) saying to-this farmer's-wife this

mã̄ch-t^{a}l^{ü}r^{ü}, "yih hāl kor^{u}nam
honey-bee, "this condition was-made-by-him-for-me

wana-manza hāpatan. Wuñ tsajyēyĕs,
the-forest-from-in by-the-bear. Now I-fled,

wütsh^{ü}s grīst^{i}-garas, dapyām, 'kara
I-descended to-a-farmer's-house, it-was-said-by-me (long ago), 'I-will-make

rahath.' Wuchta wuñ kyāh karĕm
ease.' See-please now what will-do-to-me

yih gryūst^{u}, thāvta kan. Bŏh kyāh
this the-farmer, place-please the-ear. I what

wanay?
shall-say-to-thee?

Thūñ^{ü}ā mathith kuṭh^{u}āh thôw^{u}nam,
Fresh-butter having-rubbed a-room was-placed-by-him-for-me,

mōtüñ^{ü} chĕm bŏ̄d^{i}-hāl.
of-death it-is-to-me a-prison.

Bāgán^{i}-āyĕs grīst^{i}-garas, say mĕ
It-was-my-fate (in) the-farmer's-house, that-verily to-me

gayĕm gāl.
became-to me shame.

5. **Drāti-sötin** **kȧsh^{i}** **yĕli** **ʦȧṭ^{i}nam,**
A-sickle-with the-honeycombs when were-cut-by-him-of-me,

kötyāh **khȧtis** **mār.**
how-many arose-for-him (guilt of) murders.

Buday **chĕsay** **mā̃ch-t^{a}l^{ü}r^{ü},** **wanuk^{u}**
I-verily am-Thy honey-bee, of-the-forest

jānāwār."
a-winged-creature."

6. **Mŏkalôw^{u}** **ami-mā̃ch-t^{a}l^{a}ri** **wanith**
Was-finished by-this-honey-bee having-spoken

panun^{u} **dôd^{u}.** **Wun̄** **chĕh** **dapān** **amis-**
her-own pain. Now she-is saying to-this-

grīst^{i}-bāyĕ, **"chĕyĕy** **kĕ̃h** **gŏmot^{u},** **ʦ^{a}-ti**
farmer's-wife, "if-there-is-to-thee anything happened, thou-also

wan." **Wanān** **chĕh** **wun̄** **grīst^{i}-bāy.**
speak." Saying is now the-farmer's-wife.

Dapān **chĕs,** **"Bōz,** **mĕ** **kyāh** **zulm**
Saying she-is-to-it, "hear, to-me what tyranny

chuh **gŏmot^{u}."**
is happened."

Azal **chāwun** **chuh** **samsāras,** **chĕh**
Fate to-be-experienced is in-the-world, there-is

tal **wasün̄^{ü}** **jāy.**
below to-be-descended a-place.

Buday **chĕsay** **grīst^{i}-bāy,** **yōr** **nay**
I-verily am-Thy farmer's-wife, here not-verily

rōzani **āy.**
to-abide we-are-come.

7. **Sōta**	**yĕli**	**mŏtasūt^{i}**	**grēstĕn**	**dilāsa**
In-spring	when	the-accountants	to-farmers	soothing

diṇi	**hay**	**āy,**
to-give	O!	came,

Mŏdaryiv-kathau	**yĕḍāh**	**bür^{ü}kh,**	**zālas**
With-sweet-words	a-belly	was-filled-by-them,	in-a-net

walana-āy.
we-were-surrounded.

8. **Har^{a}da-vizi**	**dard**	**müṭh^{ü}kh,**	**lāyĕni**
In-autumn-time	the-affection	was-forgotten-by-them,	for-beating

tim-hay	**āy.**
they-verily	came.

Buday	**chĕsay**	**grīst^{i}-bāy,**	**yōr**	**nay**
I-verily	am-Thy	farmer's-wife,	here	not-verily

rōzani	**āy.**
to-abide	we-came.

9. **Yim**	**phal**	**wåwim**	**mājĕ-zamīni,**
What	fruits	were-sown-by-me	in-mother-earth,

tim-hay	**papith**	**āy,**
they-verily	ripened	came,

Sọmb^{a}rith	**sörith**	**khalas**	**kårim,**
Having-collected	having-piled	on-the-threshing-floor	they-were-made-by-me,

hatabŏd^{i}-khöris	**drāy.**
to-hundreds-of-kharwār-weight	they-emerged.

10.	**Cakla-cakla**	**mukadam**	**ta**	**paṭhwör^{i}**
	In-each-village-circuit	the-village-head-man	and	the-village-accountant

tōlani	**tim-hay**	**āy,**
to-weigh	they-verily	came,

Buday	**chĕsay**	**grīst^{i}-bāy,**	**yōr**	**nay**
I-verily	am-Thy	farmer's-wife,	here	not-verily

rōzani	**āy.**
to-abide	we-came.

11.	**Öz**ī**z**	**ta**	**miskīn**	**kötyāh,**	**vis^{i}yiy,**
	The-poor	and	penniless	how-many,	O-friend,

halam	**dör^{i}-dör^{i}**	**āy,**
the-lap-cloth	holding-out	came,

Halam	**dit^{i}makh**	**mĕ**	**bár^{i}-bárī,**	**suy**
The-skirts	were-given-by-me-to-them	by-me	filling,	that-verily

chuh	**mŏkalan**	**pāy.**
is	for-salvation	a-means.

12.	**Kalama**	**sötin**	**sawāb**	**likhan,**
	A-pen	with	the-reward-of-good-actions	they-will-write,

yith-nay	**lagĕkh**	**grāy.**
so-that-not	will-happen-to-them	shaking.

Buday	**chĕsay**	**grīst^{i}-bāy,**	**yōr**	**nay**
I-verily	am-Thy	farmer's-wife,	here	not-verily

rŏzani	**āy.**
to-abide	we-came.

X.—RĀJĔ BIKARAMĀJĔTÜÑ$^{\bar{u}}$ KATH

(In the original MSS. of this story, the Hindū word for "king" is regularly written *rājĕ*, instead of the more familiar *rāja* or *rāza*. This spelling is followed in the transcription.)

1. **Dapān wustād,—**
(Is) saying the-teacher,—

Mahaniv^{i}	**tsōr**	**ös^{i}**	**pakān**	**wati.**
Men	four	were	going	by-road.

Ākh	**brūha**	**mödān.**	**Ath^{i}**	**mödānas**
There-came-to-them	in-front	a-plain.	(On) this	plain

yĕli	**hyotukh**	**pakun,**	**låg^{i}**	**wanani**
when	they-began	to-go,	they-began	to-say

pānawüñ,	**"talau,**	**wån^{i}tav**	**dalīlā,**	**yih**
mutually,	"ho,	tell-ye	story-a,	this

mödān	**kaḍōn."**	**Pata-kani**	**ākh**	**byākh**
plain	we-will-pass-over-it."	Afterwards	there-came-to-them	other

shĕkhtsā.	**Amis**	**dopukh,**	**"ts^{a}h**	**wanta**
person-a.	To-him	it-was-said-by-them,	"thou	tell-please

dalīlā,	**yih**	**mödān**	**mŏkalāwahun."**	**Åm^{i}**
story-a,	this	plain	we-will-complete-it."	By-him

dop^{u}nakh	**phīrith,**	**"bŏh,**	**hasa,**
it-was-said-by-him-to-them	in-answer,	"I,	sirs,

wanamōwa	**dalīl.**	**Dalīl,**	**hasa,**	**wanamōwa**
will-tell-to-you	a-story.	Story,	sirs,	I-will-tell-to-you

katha	**pānts.**	**Pāntsan-kathan**	**gatshanam**
tales	five.	For-five-tales	they-will-be-proper-to-me

din^{i}	**rŏpayĕs**	**pānts**	**hath."**	**Yimōv**
to-be-given	of-rupee	five	hundred."	By-them

dop^{u}has	**phīrith,**	**"tsōr**	**hath**	**dimōy**
it-was-said-by-them-to-him	in-answer,	"four	hundred	we-will-give-to-thee

tsōr	**zȧn^{i}.**	**Pöntsyum^{u}**	**hath**	**gay**	**panunuy.**
four	persons.	The-fifth	hundred	became	thine-own-only.

Wan-sa	**katha**	**pānts."**	**Dop^{u}nakh.—**
Tell-sir	the-tales	five."	It-was-said-by-him-to-them.—

"Dyār,	**hasa,**	**chih**	**sapharas.**
"Monies,	sirs,	are	for-a-journey.

Yār,	**hasa,**	**chuh**	**na-āsanas.**
A-friend,	sirs,	is	for-non-existence (of wealth).

Āsh^{e}nāv,	**hasa,**	**chuh**	**āsanas.**
A-near-relation,	sirs,	is	for-existence (of wealth).

Gayĕ	**trih**	**katha.**	**Biyĕ**	**z^{a}h**	**katha,**	**hasa,**
Went	three	tales.	The-other	two	stories,	sirs,

chĕwa,—
are-for-you,—

Sa	**zanāna**	**chĕwana**	**panün^{ü},**
That	woman	is-for-you-not	your-own,

yĕsa	**na**	**āsi**	**pānas-söty.**
who	not	will-be	oneself-with.

Biyĕ,	**hasa,—**
Also,	sirs,—

Yus	**rātas**	**bĕdār**	**rōzi,**
He-who	by-night	awake	will-remain,

suy, hasa, zēni Rājĕ-Bikarmājĕtüñ^{ü}
he-only, sirs, will-win King-Vikramâditya's

kūr^{ü}."
daughter."

Wañĕnakh yima katha pānts. Yim
Were-said-by-him-to-them these tales five. They

chis dapān, "wan-sa dalīl." Yih
are-to-him saying, "tell-sir a-story." He

chukh dapān, "mĕ, hasa, wañĕmōwa
is-to-them saying, "by-me, sirs, were-told-by-me-to-you

katha pānts." Milüv^{ü}kh laḍöy^{i}.
tales five." Was-joined-in-by-them fighting.

Yim chis dapān, "rŏpayĕs tsōr hath
They are-to-him saying, "of-rupee four hundred

nīth; dalīl kĕh wüñ^{ü}th-na; mödān
were-taken-by-thee; story any was-told-by-thee-not; the-plain

chuh wuñĕ pakanay." Amis lôyukh
is still not-having-been-walked." To-him it-was-beaten

yimav-tsōrav-zanĕv. Ȧm^{i} dop^{u}nakh,
by-these-four-persons. By-him it-was-said-by-him-to-them,

"pakiv-sa yitikis-pātashĕhas-nish. Yih
walk-ye-sirs of-here-the-king-near. What

suh dapi, tih karav."
he will-say, that we-will-do."

2. Dapān wustād,—
(Is) saying the-teacher,—

Wöt^{i} pātashĕhas-nish. Dyut^{u}
They-arrived the-king-near. Was-given

phȧr^{i}yād tsōrav-zanĕv. Dop^{u}has,
a-complaint by-the-four-persons. It-was-said-by-them-to-him,

"pātashĕham, yim^{i}-shĕkhtsan khĕy
"my-king, by-this-person were-eaten

asĕ rŏpayĕs tsor hath. Dopun,
for-us of-rupee four hundred. It-was-said-by-him,

'wanamōwa katha pānts.'" Pātashĕhan
'I-will-tell-you tales five.'" By-the-king

dop^{u} amis-shĕkhtsas, "wan-sa kyāh
it-was-said to-this-person, "tell-sir what

won^{u}thakh?" Yih wọthus
was-told-by-thee-to-them?" He arose-to-him

phīrith, "pātashĕham, bŏh wanay katha
in-answer, "my-king, I will-tell-to-thee tales

pānts. Rŏpayĕs gatshanam din^{i}
five. Of-rupee they-are-proper-to-me to-be-given

pānts hath. Ada wanay bŏh katha
five hundred. Then I-will-tell-to-thee I the-tales

pānts." Pātashĕhan kȧḍ^{i} rŏpayĕs
five." By-the-king were-produced of-rupee

pānts hath, ditin amis-shĕkhtsas. Yim
five hundred, they-were-given-by-him to-this-person. These

kȧrin band, pāna kür^{ü}n köm^{ü}āh
were-made-by-him tied-up, by-himself was-done-by-him deed-a

ȧm^{i}-pātashĕhan.	**Pātashöhī-hond^{u}**	**pŏshākh**
by-that-king.	Royalty-of	garment

trôwun,	**gadöyiyĕ-hond^{u}**	**pŏshākh**	**pūrun.**
was-put-off-by-him,	beggary-of	garment	was-put-on-by-him.

Biyĕ	**gȧnḍin**	**lāl**	**sath**	**matshi,**
Also	were-tied-by-him	rubies	seven	on-the-arm,

drāv	**yima**	**katha**	**pānts**	**sara**	**karani.**
he-went-forth	these	tales	five	testing	to-make.

3. Dapān wustād,—
(Is) saying the-teacher,—

Gŏḍañiy	**drāv**	**bĕñĕ-handis-shĕharas-kun.**
At-the-very-first	he-went-forth	his-sister's-city-towards.

Gur^{u}	**chus**	**khasun^{u}.**	**Wôt^{u}**	**yĕli**
A-horse	is-for-him	to-be-mounted.	He-arrived	when

nīzīkh	**ath-bĕñĕ-handis-shĕharas**	**lüz^{ü}n**
near	to-that-sister's-city	was-sent-by-him

shĕch^{i}	**amis-bĕñĕ,**	**"mĕ**	**kyāh**	**chuh**
a-message	to-that-sister,	"to-me	verily	is

pĕmot^{u}	**muhim.**	**Bŏh**	**kyāh**	**yimahö**
fallen	poverty.	I	of-course	should-come

tūr^{i}."	**Ami**	**lüz^{ü}nas**	**bĕñi**	**pot^{u}**
there-even."	By-that	was-sent-by-her-to-him	by-the-sister	back-again

phīrith	**shĕch^{i},**	**"mĕ**	**kyāh**	**rŏzan**
in-answer	a-message,	"to-me	of-course	will-remain

pāma	**wör^{i}vis-manz."**	**Pot^{u}**	**phīrith**
reproaches	my-father-in-law's-house-in."	Back-again	in-answer

lüz^{ü}nas	**biyĕ**	**shĕch^{i},**	**“ mĕ**	**yĕli**	**na**
was-sent-by-him-to-her	again	message,	“ to-me	when	not

bani	**tōr**	**yun^{u},**	**tō-ti**	**gatshĕm**	**ladun^{u}**
will-be-possible	there	to-come,	nevertheless	it-is-proper-to-me	to-be-sent

naphtsas	**kĕntshāh.**	**Ladaham-ay,**	**tath**
for-the-belly	something.	Thou-wilt-send-to-me-if,	to-that

gatshi	**ganḍ**	**karun^{u},**	**pĕṭha**	**gatshĕs**
it-is-proper	a-knot	is-to-be-made,	upon (it)	it-is-proper-for-it

mŏhar	**karüñ^{ü}**	**panüñ^{ü}.”**	**Ami**	**kür^{ü}**
the-seal	to-be-made	thine-own.”	By-that	was-done

bĕñi	**köm^{ü}āh.**	**Lodun**	**panañĕ-kĕnzĕ**
by-the-sister	deed-a.	Was-sent-by-her	(in) her-own-dish-cup

bata-hanā,	**yā**	**tshyoṭ^{u}**	**yā**	**shōtsh.**
a-little-boiled-rice,	(not caring whether it was) either	impure (leavings)	or	purity.

Pĕṭha	**kür^{ü}nas**	**panüñ^{ü}**	**mŏhar,**	**korun**
Upon (it)	was-made-by-her-for-it	her-own	seal,	was-made by-her

rawāna	**amis-böyis.**	**Tȧm^{i}**	**yĕli**	**wuch^{ü}**
dispatching	to-that-brother.	By-him	when	was-seen

bĕñĕ-hünz^{ü}	**mŏhar,**	**roṭun,**	**ȧtiy**
the-sister-of	the-seal,	was-taken-by-him,	in-that-very-place

thôwun-dabövith.
was-buried-by-him.

4.	**Drāv**	**yāra-sanzi-wati.**	**Yĕli**	**wôt^{u}**
	He-went-forth	on-a-friend's-the-road.	When	he-arrived

nīzīkh	**sūzun**	**amis**	**mahanyuv^{u},**	**"yār,**
near	was-sent-by-him	to-him	a-man (saying),	"(thy) friend,

hasa,	**ôy.**	**Pātashöhī**	**chĕsna.**	**Suh,**
sir,	is-come-to-thee.	Royalty	is-to-him-not.	He,

hasa,	**chuy**	**muhimzad."**	**Yāran**	**yĕli**
sir,	is-verily	struck-by-adversity."	By-the-friend	when

būz^{u},	**drāv,**	**wôt^{u}**	**amis-yāras-nish.**
it-was-heard,	he-went-forth,	he-arrived	that-friend-near.

Dapān	**chus,**	**"hā**	**yāra,**	**kati**	**gōham**
Saying	he-is-to-him,	"O	friend-O,	whence	didst-thou-become-for-me

yōr	**pöda?"**	**Pakān**	**chih**	**dŏnaway.**
here	manifest?"	Going	they-are	both.

Amis	**ôs^{u}**	**miskīnī-hond^{u}**	**pŏshākh**	**nöl^{i}.**
To-that-one	was	poverty-of	garment	on-the-neck.

Dapān	**chus,**	**"yāra,**	**yih**	**khal^{a}t-ĕ-shöhī**
Saying	he-is-to-him,	"friend,	this	robe-of-royalty

dita	**mĕ.**	**Yih**	**myôn^{u}**	**pŏshākh**
please-give	to-me.	This	my	garment

tshunta	**ts^{a}h."**	**Yih**	**ās-na-bōzana,**	**"yih**
please-put-on	thou."	This	was-not-considered-by-him,	"this

chuh	**amis**	**miskīnī-hond^{u}**	**pŏshākh";**
is	to-that-one	beggary-of	garment";

yih	**ās-bōzana**	**khal^{a}t-ĕ-shöhī;**	**kami-mŏkha?**
this	was-considered	a-robe-of-royalty;	on-what-account?

Mahabata-söty.	**Gav.**	**Wöt^{i}**	**yāra-sond^{u}**
Affection-through.	He-went.	They-arrived	the-friend-of

gara.	**Yāran**	**kür^{u}nas**	**ziyāphath**
house.	By-the-friend	was-made-by-him-for-him	a-feast

löyik-ĕ-pātashāh.	**Sapañĕs**	**ot^{u}-tāñ**	**z^{a}h**
worthy-of-a-king.	There-happened-to-him	there-up-to	two

katha	**sara.**
statements	in-investigation.

5.	**Drāv**	**wuñ**	**zanāni-handis-shĕharas-kun.**
	He-went-forth	now	(his) wife's-city-towards.

Wôt^{u}	**ath-shĕharas**	**and-kun.**	**Ati**
He-arrived	of-that-city	the-outskirt-towards.	There

ös^{ü}	**buḍ^{ü}**	**zanānā.**	**Byūṭh^{u}**	**àm^{i}-sandi-gari.**
was	an-old	woman-a-certain.	He-stayed	in-her-house.

Dopun	**amis-bujĕ-zanāni,**	**"ditam**	**drôt^{u}.**
It-was-said-by-him	to-that-old-woman,	"please-give-to-me	a-sickle.

Bŏh	**ana**	**yimis-guris-kyut^{u}**	**gāsa."**	**Drāv**
I	will-bring	this-horse-for	grass."	He-went-forth

gāsa	**anani.**	**Wuchun**	**ati**	**gāsa-mödānā,**
grass	to-bring.	Was-seen-by-him	there	grass-plain-a-certain,

ath^{i}	**chuh**	**lōnān.**	**Yih**	**ös^{ü}**	**rakh**
to-it-verily	he-is	reaping.	This	was	the-private-field

pātashĕha-sünz^{ü}.	**Ös^{i}**	**lārān**	**ṭahàl^{i}.**
the-king-of.	Were	running-up	the-grooms.

Nyūkh	**raṭith**	**pananis-mējĕras-nish.**
He-was-taken-by-them	having-seized	their-own-master-of-the-horse-near.

Korukh	**köd.**	**Rāth**	**āyĕ.**	**Amis**
He-was-made-by-them	imprisoned.	Night	came.	To-him

chĕh	**gatshān**	**pöda**	**zanānā**	**akh,**
is	becoming	manifest	woman-a	one,

amis-mējĕras	**ziyāphathā**	**hĕth.**	**Yih**
to-that-master-of-the-horse	dish-of-food-a	having-brought.	He

chuh	**bihith**	**cārpāyi-pĕṭh.**	**Ziyāphath**
is	seated	a-bedstead-on.	The-dish-of-food

thüv^{ü}nas	**bōnṭha-kani.**	**Ath^{i}**	**wȧth^{i}**
was-placed-by-her-for-him	front-in.	To-it-verily	they-descended

khĕni	**dŏnaway.**	**Hanā**	**h^{a}rēyĕkh.**	**Yih**
to-eat	both.	A-little	remained-over-for-them.	This

dyutukh	**amis-ködis.**	**Kor^{u}has**	**ālav,**
was-given-by-them	to-this-prisoner.	Was-made-by-them-to-him	a-call,

"hatō	**ködyau,**	**yih**	**khyuh**	**sōn^{ü}**
"ho	prisoner-O,	this	eat	our

tshĕṭh-han."	**Köd^{i}**	**roṭ^{u},**	**khyōn.**	**Ȧtiy**
waste-food-a-little."	By-the-prisoner	it-was-taken,	it-was-eaten-by-him.	There-verily

chuh	**pananĕ**	**jāyĕ**	**bihith.**	**Yimav-dŏyav**
he-is	in-his-own	in-place	seated.	By-these-two

kür^{ü}	**tamaskhurī;**	**ath-palangas**	**phüṭ^{ü}**
was-made	jesting;	to-that-bedstead	was-broken

tür^{u}.	**Korukh**	**ālav**	**amis-ködis,**	**"ts^{a}h**
the-tenon.	Was-made-by-them	a-call	to-that-prisoner,	"thou

wuchta,	**yith-palangas**	**phüṭ^{ü}**	**tür^{ü},**	**tsĕ**
please-see,	to-this-bedstead	is-broken	the-tenon,	to-thee

mā	**tagiy."**	**Ȧm^{i}**	**dop^{u}nakh,**	**"ān,**
I-wonder-if	it-will-within-thy-power."	By-him	it-was-said-to-them,	"yes,

tagĕm-nā ?	**Hamsāyĕ**	**chim**	**chān."**
will-it-not-be-within-my-power ?	Neighbours	are-to-me	carpenters."

Dop^{u}has,	**"wŏla."**	**Wôt^{u}**	**ot^{u}.**	**Ami-**
It-was-said-by-them-to-him,	"come."	He-arrived	there.	By-that-

zanāni	**parzanôw^{u}**	**panun^{u}**	**khāwand.**
woman	he-was-recognized (as)	her-own	husband.

Ȧm^{i}	**ös^{ü}-parzanöv^{ü}müts^{ü}**	**brōṇth,**	**yĕli**	**yih**
By-him	she-had-been-recognized	before,	when	this

bata-han	**dits^{ü}has.**	**Yih**	**zanāna**	**chĕh**
food-a-little	was-given-by-them-to-him.	This	woman	is

dapān	**amis-mējĕras,**	**"wun**	**kyāh**	**karav ?**
saying	to-this-master-of-the-horse,	"now	what	shall-we-do ?

Yih	**chuh**	**myôn^{u}**	**khāwand.**	**Yih**	**gatshi**
This	is	my	husband.	He	is-proper

mārun^{u}	**rātas-rāth."**	**Hukum**	**dyutun**
to-be-killed	this-very-night."	An-order	was-given-by-him

mārawātalan.	**Dop^{u}nakh,**	**"niyūn**	**yih**
to-the-executioners.	It-was-said-by-him-to-them,	"take-him	this

köd^{i},	**gaʦhi**	**mārun^{u};**	**wölinj^{ü}**	**gaʦhĕs**
prisoner,	he-is-proper	to-be-killed;	the-heart	is-proper-of-him

yūr^{i}	**anün̄^{ü}."**	**Nyūkh**	**yih**	**köd^{i}**
here-even	to-be-brought."	Was-taken-by-them	this	prisoner

shĕharas-nĕbar.	**Ȧm^{i}**	**dyut^{u}nakh**	**sawāl,**
the-city-outside.	By-him	was-given-by-him-to-them	a-petition,

"mĕ	**tröv^{i}tav**	**yĕla,**	**bŏh**	**chalahö**	**atha**
"me	please-to-let-me-loose	from-restraint,	I	would-wash	the-hands

buth^{u},	**Khŏdāyĕs-kun**	**karahö**	**zārapār."**
face,	God-towards	I-would-make	ejaculations."

Trôwukh	**yĕla.**	**Wuch^{ü}n**	**āba-hanā,**
He-was-let-loose-by-them	from-restraint.	Was-seen-by-him	water-a-little,

cholun	**atiy**	**atha**	**buth^{u}.**	**Khŏdā-Söbas-**
was-washed-by-him	there-indeed	the-hands	face.	God-the-Lord-

kun	**korun**	**zārapār.**	**Atha**	**pyōs**
towards	was-made-by-him	ejaculation.	The-hand	fell-of-him

yiman-lālan-satan-pĕṭh,	**yim**	**tati**	**ösis**
these-rubies-seven-on,	which	there	were-of-him

gȧnḍ^{i}mȧt^{i}	**maʦhi.**	**Yiman**	**dopun**	**mārawātalan-**
tied	on-the-arm.	To-these	it-was-said-by-him	to-executioners-

ʦŏn,	**"hata-sa,**	**mĕ**	**trövyuv**	**yĕla.**	**Nŏm**
four,	"O-sirs,	me	let-ye-me	from-restraint.	These

chiwa	**lāl**	**sath.**	**T̲s̲ōr**	**chiwa**	**tŏhĕ**
are-for-you	rubies	seven.	Four	are-for-you	for-you

tsŏn zanĕn. Trih chiwa myön^{i} tŏhĕ-
four persons. Three are-for-you mine you-

nish."
with."

6. Ot^{u}-tāñ karĕn tsōr katha sara.
There-up-to were-made-by-him four statements tested.

Pöntsim^{ü} kath gayĕs mashith. Āv,
The-fifth statement went-for-him forgotten. He-came,

wôt^{u} panun^{u} gara. Biyĕ wanān chuh
he-arrived his-own house. Again saying he-is

timan pāntsan zanĕn, "waniv-sa kyāh
to-those five persons, "say-ye-sirs what

wañĕwa tŏhĕ pānts katha." Yih
were-said-by-you by-you five statements." He

wọthus pot^{u} phīrith,
arose-to-him back-again in-answer,

"Pātashĕham, katsa katha karĕth sara?"
"My-king, how-many statements were-made-by-thee tested?"

Dop^{u}nakh pātashĕhan, "tsōr katha."
It-was-said-by-him-to-them by-the-king, "four statements."

Yimav dop^{u}has, "kusa kusa?"
By-them it-was-said-by-them-to-him, "which which?"

Dop^{u}nakh pātashĕhan,
It-was-said-by-him-to-them by-the-king,

"Āsh^{e}nāv chih pàz^{i}-pöṭh^{i} āsanas.
"Relations are really-truly for-existence (of wealth).

Yār	**chuh**	**na-āsanas.**	**Ti-ti**	**pozuy.**
A-friend	is	for-non-existence (of wealth).	That-also (is)	true-verily.

Zanāna	**sa**	**chĕna**	**panüñ^{ü},**	**yĕsa**	**na**
Woman	that	is-not	one's-own,	who	not

pānas-söty	**chĕh.**	**Ti-ti**	**pozuy.**
oneself-with	is.	That-also	true-verily.

Dyār	**chih**	**bakār**	**sapharas.**	**Ti-ti**
Monies	are	useful	for-a-journey.	That-also

pozuy.
true-verily.

Yima	**tsör**	**katha**	**karĕmav**
These	four	statements	were-made-by-me-for-you

sara.	**Wuñ**	**wanyūm**	**pöntsim^{ü}**	**kath."**
tested.	Now	tell-ye-me	the-fifth	statement."

Dop^{u}nas	**ȧm^{i}**	**shĕkhtsan**	**pot^{u}**	**phīrith,**
It-was-said-by-him-to-him	by-this	by-person	back-again	in-answer,

" rŏpayĕ	**hath**	**gatshĕm**	**dyun^{u}."**	**Dyut^{u}nas**
" rupees	hundred	are-proper-to-me	to-be-given."	Was-given-by-him-to-him

pātashĕhan.	**Dop^{u}nas,—**
by-the-king.	It-was-said-by-him-to-him,—

" Yus	**rātas**	**bedār**	**rōzi,**
" He-who	by-night	awake	will-remain,

suy	**zēni**	**Rājĕ-Bikarmājĕtüñ^{ü}**	**kūr^{ü}."**
he-only	will-win	King-Vikramâditya's	daughter."

7.	**Pātashĕhan**	**kür^{ü}**	**köm^{ü}.**	**Lôgun**
	By-the-king	was-done	a-deed.	Was-imitated-by-him

phakīr. **Gav,** **wôt^{u}** **Rājĕ-Bikarmājĕtun^{u}**
a-faqīr. He-went, he-arrived King-Vikramâditya's

gara. **Nazarbāzav** **kür^{ü}** **nazar,**
house. By-the-watchers was-done watching,

khabardārav **niyĕ** **khabar** **amis-rājĕs.**
by-the-newsmen was-brought news to-this-king.

Dop^{u}has, **"rājĕ-söba,** **phakīrā** **akh**
It-was-said-by-them-to-him, " King-Sir, faqīr-a one

gamot^{u} **pöda.** **Yihuy** **dapān,** **'bŏh**
(is) become manifest. He-verily (is) saying, 'I

zēnan **rājĕ-sünz^{ü}** **kūr^{ü}.'"** **Rājĕ** **wanān**
will-win-her the-king's daughter.'" The-king saying

chukh **pot^{u}** **phīrith,** **"az-tān̄** **kötyāh**
is-to-them back-again in-answer, " today-up-to how-many (are)

gamàt^{i} **rājĕzāda** **ati** **māra!** **Wun̄** **gav**
gone princes here to-death! Now is-gone

yih **phakīr** **hawāla-y-Khŏdā,** **ada** **yā**
this faqīr (in) the-care-of-God, then either

lasi **yā** **mari.** **Gatshiv,** **khölyūn**
he-will-survive or he-will-die. Go-ye, cause-ye-him-to-mount

kuṭhis-manz." **Yĕti** **yih** **rājĕ-sünz^{ü}** **kūr^{ü}**
the-room-in." Where this king's daughter

ös^{ü}, **palang** **trôw^{u}has** **shīrith.** **Khoth^{u}**
was, a-bed was-put-by-them-for-him having-made-ready. Ascended

yih **phakīr** **palangas-pĕṭh.** **Amis-khôtūni**
this faqīr the-bed-on. To-this-lady

dits^{ü}n	**zīr^{ü}.**	**Karĕn**	**amis-söty**	**katha.**
was-given-by-him	a-push.	Were-made-by-him	her-with	speeches.

Katha	**karith**	**kür^{ü}n**	**köm^{ü}.**	**Ath-pŏshākas**
Speeches	having-made	was-done-by-him	a-deed.	(Of) that-garment

kür^{ü}n	**shĕkal**	**yinsān-hish^{ü}.**	**Pāna**
was-made-by-him	a-form	a-human-being-like.	He-himself

drāv	**dūr-pahān,**	**byūṭh^{u}**	**nazari.**	**Shĕmāh**
went-forth	distance-a-little,	he-sat	in-watch.	A-lamp-flame

chuh	**dazān.**	**Amis-khôtūni-handi-shikama-manza**
is	burning.	This-lady's-belly-from-in

drāv	**ạj^{a}dāh.**	**Tsāv**	**ath-pŏshākas-manz,**
issued	a-python.	It-entered	that-garment-in,

yĕth	**yih**	**ȧm^{i}-phakīran**	**yinsān-hyuh^{u}**
which	this	by-this-faqīr	a-human-being-like

kor^{u}mot^{u}	**ôs^{u}.**	**Yih**	**chuh**	**d^{a}nān,**	**tsāp^{i}**
made	was.	This	he-is	shaking,	bites

hĕwān.	**Ati**	**yĕli**	**na**	**yinsān**	**ôs^{u},**
(he is) taking.	Here	when	not	human-being	it-was,

biyĕ	**tsāv**	**yih**	**ạj^{a}dāh**	**khôtūni-shikamas-**
again	entered	this	python	(of)-the-lady's-belly-

manz.	**Ȧm^{i}-phakīran**	**kür^{ü}**	**saragī.**	**Balāy**
in.	By-this-faqīr	was-done	testing.	The-evil-spirit

chĕh	**amis-khôtūni-handis-shikamas-manz.**	**Nĕbar**
is	this-lady's-belly-in.	External

kĕh	**chĕna.**	**Āv**	**phakīr,**	**wôt^{u}**	**biyĕ**
any	is-not.	Came	the-faqīr,	he-arrived	again

ath-palangas-nishĕ.	**Khôtūni**	**dits^{ün}**	**zīr^{ü},**
that-bed-near.	To-the-lady	was-given-by-him	a-push,

katha	**karĕn**	**amis-söty.**	**Ath-pŏshākas**
speeches	were-made-by-him	her-with.	To-that-garment

korun	**biyĕ**	**yinsān-hyuh^{u},**	**gav**	**biyĕ**
it-was-made-by-him	again	a-human-being-like,	went	again

phakīr,	**byūṭh^{u}**	**dūri-pahān.**	**Shĕmāh**	**chuh**
the-faqīr,	he-sat	at-a-distance-a-little.	A-lamp-flame	is

dazön^{i}.	**Athas-kĕth**	**küḍ^{ün}**	**shĕmshēr.**
burning-verily.	The-hand-in	was-drawn-forth-by-him	a-sword.

Amis-khôtūni-handi-shikama-manza	**log^{u}**	**nērani**
This-lady's-the-belly-from-in	began	to-issue

yih	**ạj^{a}dāh.**	**Log^{u}**	**ath-pŏshākas-manz**	**atsani.**
this	python.	It-began	this-garment-in	to-enter.

Tuj^{ün}	**shĕmshēr,**	**chuh**	**amis-ạj^{a}dāhas**
Was-raised-by-him	the-sword,	he-is	to-this-boa-constrictor

katarān,	**môrun,**	**karĕnas**	**gañĕ,**
cutting-to-pieces,	it-is-killed-by-him,	were-made-by-him-of-it	lumps,

tshunun	**ath-palangas-tal.**	**Khot^{u}**	**pāna**
it-was-put-by-him	that-bed-under.	He-mounted	himself

palangas-pĕṭh,	**shĕmshēr**	**dits^{ün}**	**shānd,**
the-bed-upon,	the-sword	was-put-by-him	(under) the-pillow,

ta	**shọng^{u}.**
and	he-went-to-sleep.

8\. **Rāth gayĕ ādā, subuh log^{u} yini.**
The-night went (to) completion, morning began to-come.

Ȧm^{i}-Rājĕ-Bikarmājĕtan dop^{u} mārawātalan,
By-this-King-Vikramâditya it-was-said to-the-executioners,

" gatshiv. Yih phakīr āsi mumot^{u}.
" go-ye. This faqīr will-be dead.

Yŏhay wālyūn. Az-tāñ kötyāh
Him-verily bring-ye-down-him. Today-up-to how-many

rājĕzāda gamȧt^{i} māra, ta yi-ti
princes (are) gone to-death, and this-one-also

āsi mumot^{u}." Khȧt^{i} ath-kuṭhis-manz.
will-be dead." They-ascended this-room-in.

Wuchukh phakīr wāra-kāra zinday.
Was-seen-by-them the-faqīr safe-sound living-verily.

Nazarabāzav kür^{ü} nazar, khabardārav
By-the-watchers was-done watching, by-the-newsmen

niyĕ khabar rājĕs. Dop^{u}has,
was-brought news to-the-king. It-was-said-by-them-to-him,

" Rājĕ-sa, phakīr chuh zinday." Rājĕ-söb
" King-Sir, the-faqīr is living-verily." The-king-Sir

khot^{u} pāna kuṭhis-manz. Karān chuh
ascended himself the-room-in. Doing he-is

mŏbārakh amis-phakīras. Dapān chus,
congratulation to-this-faqīr. Saying he-is-to-him,

" phakīra, ts^{a}h wanta kĕtha-pöṭh^{i} bacyōkh."
" faqīr-O, thou tell-please in-what-manner thou-escapedst."

Dapān chus phakīr, " bĕdār rōzana-söty.
Saying is-to-him the-faqīr, " awake remaining-by.

Rājĕ-sa,	**kar**	**nazar**	**palangas-tal."**	**Rājĕn**
King-Sir,	do	looking	the-bed-under."	By-the-king

kür^{ü}	**nazar.**	**Wuchun**	**palangas-tal**
was-done	looking.	Was-seen-by-him	the-bed-under

balāyā	**akh.**	**Tröv^{ü}müʦ^{ü}**	**phakīran**	**mörith.**
evil-spirit-a	one.	(It-was) put	by-the-faqīr	having-killed.

Dapān	**chuh**	**phakīr**	**amis-rājĕs,**	**"zabān**
Saying	is	the-faqīr	to-this-king,	"promise

kyāh	**chĕy**	**kür^{ü}müʦ^{ü} ?"**	**Rājĕ**	**chus**
what	is-by-thee	made ?"	The-king	is-to-him

dapān,	**"poz^{u}**	**chuh,**	**Khŏdāy**	**chuh**
saying,	"true	is,	God-verily	is

kunuy."	**Phakīr**	**chus**	**dapān,**	**"yih,**
one-only."	The-faqīr	is-to-him	saying,	"this,

hasa,	**chĕy**	**ȧt^{i}**	**panün^{ü}**	**kūr^{ü}.**	**Mĕ**
Sir,	is-to-thee	here-verily	thine-own	daughter.	To-me

di-sa	**panun^{u}**	**nishāna."**	**Diʦ^{ü}nas**	**wöj^{ü}**
give-Sir	thine-own	token."	Was-given-by-him-to-him	a-ring

amis-phakīras.	**Phakīra-sünz^{ü}**	**wöj^{ü}**	**rüṭ^{ü}**
to-this-faqīr.	The-faqīr's	ring	was-taken

ȧm^{i}-rājĕn.
by-this-king.

9. **Drāv**	**phakīr,**	**wôt^{u}**	**panun^{u}**	**shĕhar.**
Went-forth	the-faqīr,	he-arrived	his-own	city.

Phakīriyĕ-hond^{u}	**jāma**	**ʦhunun-kaḍith.**
Faqīrhood-of	coat	was-doffed-by-him.

Pātashöhī-hond^{u} pŏshākh pūrun. Dyutun
Royalty-of robe was-put-on-by-him. Was-given-by-him

hukum lashkari, "nīriv-sa mĕ söty."
order to-the-army, "go-ye-forth-sirs me with."

10. Dapān wustād,—
(Is) saying the-teacher,—

Gŏḍañiy gav ath-bĕñĕ-handis-shĕharas. Yih
At-the-very-first he-went to-that-sister's-city. This

pātashāh-ti ôs^{u} bāj tārān amis^{ü}y-pātashĕhas.
king-also was tribute paying to-this-very-king.

Ün^{ü}n bĕñĕ panün^{ü}, thüv^{ü}nas bōnṭha-kani
Was-brought-by-him the-sister his-own, was-placed-by-him-to-her in-front

sa tami-dŏhüc^{ü} ziyāphath, yĕth tami-
that of-that-day present-of-food, to-which by-that-

bĕñi mŏhar ös^{ü}s pĕṭha kür^{ü}müts^{ü}.
sister seal was-for-it on made.

Dapān chus, "yih chyā mŏhar cyön^{ü}?"
Saying he-is-to-her, "this is seal thine?"

Dop^{u}nas phīrith, "myön^{ü}y chĕh." Dapān
It-was-said-by-her-to-him in-answer, "mine-verily it-is." Saying

chus yih pātashāh, "bŏy kyāh gōs
is-to-her this king, "I-verily of-a-surety am

tami-dŏhuk^{u} miskīn. Pàz^{i}-pöṭh^{i} chuh āsh^{e}nāv
of-that-day the-beggar. Truly is a-relation

āsanas."
for-existence (of wealth)."

11. **Hĕts^{ü}n amis-pātashĕhas-ti lashkar,**
Was-taken-by-him of-that-king-also the-army,

dyutun kadam yāra-sond^{u} kun. Wôt^{u}
was-put-by-him footstep the-friend-of direction. He-arrived

yāras-nish. Yāran kür^{ü} ziyāphath
the-friend-near. By-the-friend was-made a-feast

yiman-dŏn pātashöhiyĕn-kits^{ü}. Rāth küḍ^{ü}kh
these-two kingdoms-for. Night was-passed-by-them

ȧt^{i}, sub^{a}han drāy.
there, at-dawn they-went-forth.

12. **Dyutun kadam ath-hihara-sandis-shĕharas-kun.**
Was-put-by-him footstep that-the-father-in-law's-the-city-towards.

Anān chuh nād dith amis-pātashĕhas.
Bringing he-is call having-given to-this-king.

Dapān chus, "anukh-sa ṭahȧl^{i}. Timav
Saying he-is-to-him, "bring-them-Sir the-grooms. By-them

chuh cyāñĕ-rakhi-manza tsūr roṭ^{u}mot^{u}. Suh
is thy-private-field-from-in a-thief seized. He

kati chukh thôw^{u}mot^{u}?" Ȧnikh ṭahȧl^{i},
where is-by-them put?" Were-brought-by-them the-grooms,

dop^{u}hakh, "yus tŏhĕ tsūr roṭ^{u}wa
it-was-said-by-them-to-them, "what by-you thief was-seized-by-you

rakhi-manza, suh kati chuwa
the-private-field-from-in, he where is-by-you

thôw^{u}mot^{u} ?"	**Yimav**	**won^{u},**	**"pātashĕham,**
put ?"	By-them	it-was-said,	"my-king,

asĕ	**chuh**	**kor^{u}mot^{u}**	**hawāla**	**pananis-**
by-us	he-is	made	in-custody	to-our-own-

apsaras-mējĕras."	**Onukh**	**mējĕr.**	**Dop^{u}has,**
officer-the-master-of-the-horse."	Was-brought-by-them	the-master-of-the-horse.	Was-said-by-them-to-him,

"nŏmav	**ṭahalyav**	**koruy**	**hawāla**	**tsūr,**
"by-these	grooms	was-made-to-thee	in-custody	a-thief,

suh	**kati**	**thôwuth ?"**	**Yih**	**chukh**	**dapān,**
he	where	was-put-by-thee ?"	He	is-to-them	saying,

"mĕ	**ḍyūṭh^{u}-na."**	**Ṭahȧl^{i}**	**chis**	**karān**
"by-me	he-was-seen-not."	The-grooms	are-to-him	making

gawöy^{i},	**"pātashĕham,**	**asĕ**	**kor^{u}**	**tāhkhīth**
witnessing,	"my-king,	by-us	was-made	certainly

amis	**hawāla."**	**Dop^{u}nakh**	**ȧm^{i}-pātashĕhan,**
to-him	in-custody."	Was-said-by-him-to-them	by-this-king,

yus	**tami-dŏha**	**phakīr**	**lögith**	**ôs^{u},**
he-who	on-that-day	faqīr	having-made-himself-to-resemble	was,

suy	**chukh**	**dapān,**	**"anyūkh**	**mārawātal**
he-verily	is-to-them	saying,	"bring-ye-them	the-executioners

tsōr.	**Tim**	**wanan**	**pānay."**	**Ȧnikh**	**tim.**
four.	They	will-say	themselves-verily."	Were-brought-by-them	they.

Dapān	**chukh**	**yih**	**pātashāh,**	**"tŏhĕ-nish**
Saying	is-to-them	this	king,	"you-near

chuh	**amānath**	**tas-phakīra-sond^{u},**	**suh**
is	a-deposit-in-trust	of-that-faqīr,	that

diyiv	**yūr^{i}."**	**Yimav-mārawātalau**	**kür^{ü}**
give-ye	here-verily."	By-these-executioners	was-done

köm^{ü}.	**Kạḍikh**	**yim**	**lāl**	**sath,**	**thövikh**
a-deed.	Were-produced-by-them	these	rubies	seven,	were-put-by-them

pātashĕhas	**bōnṭha-kani.**	**Satav-manza**
to-the-king	in-front.	The-seven-from-in

tulin	**tsōr,**	**kạr^{i}nakh**	**hawāla.**	**Dop^{u}nakh,**
were-lifted-by-him	four,	were-made-by-him-to-them	in-charge.	It was-said-by-him-to-them,

"yim	**kạm^{i}**	**ös^{i}wa**	**dit^{i}mạt^{i}?"**	**Dop^{u}has,**
"these	by-whom	were-to-you	given?"	Was-said-by-them-to-him,

"phakīran-ạk^{i}."	**"Tạm^{i}**	**kami**	**bāpath?"**
"by-faqīr-one."	"By-him	on-what	account?"

"Suh	**ôs^{u}**	**dyut^{u}mot^{u}**	**yim^{i}-mējĕran**
"He	was	given	by-this-master-of-the-horse

mārana-bāpath."	**Dapān**	**chuh**	**pātashāh**
killing-for."	Saying	is	the-king

amis-mējĕras-kun,	**"mĕ**	**chukhnā**	**parzanāwān?**
this-master-of-the-horse-to,	"me	art-thou-not	recognizing?

Bŏy	**kyāh**	**gōs**	**suh**	**phakīr**	**yus**
I-verily	certainly	am	that	faqīr	who

köd	**ôs^{u}than**	**kor^{u}mot^{u}.**	**Gŏḍañ**	**āyĕ**
imprisoned	was-by-thee-he	made.	At-first	came

sa	**khôtūna**	**ziyāphath**	**hĕth.**	**Khĕyĕv**
that	lady	a-dish-of-food	taking.	Was-eaten

yĕkh-jāh.	**H^{a}ryōv**	**tshyoṭ^{u}.**	**Kor^{u}wa**	**mĕ**
in-one-place.	Remained-over	waste-food.	Was-made-by-you	to-me

ālav;	**dop^{u}wam,**	**wŏla**	**ködyau,**	**yih**
a-call;	it-was-said-by-you-to-me,	'come	prisoner-O,	this

khyō	**sôn^{u}**	**tshyoṭ^{u}.'**	**Tami-pata**	**ās**	**bŏh.**
eat	our	waste-food.'	That-after	came	I.

Roṭ^{u}	**mĕ**	**ta**	**khyauv.**	**Tami-pata**
Was-taken	by-me	and	was-eaten.	That-after

kür^{ü}wa	**murdamāzör^{i}.**	**Phüṭ^{ü}wa**	**palangas**
was-made-by-you	laughing-joking.	Was-broken-for-you	of-the-bedstead

tür^{ü}.	**Kor^{u}wa**	**mĕ**	**ālav,**	**'ts^{a}h**	**mā**
the-tenon.	Was-made-by-you	to-me	a-call,	'thou	I-wonder-if

zānakh	**yith-palangas**	**wāṭh**	**karith?'**
thou-wilt-know	to-this-bedstead	joining	having-made?'

Mĕ	**dopum^{a}wa,**	**'ān̄,**	**zāna-nā?**	**Hamsāyĕ**
By-me	it-was-said-by-me-to-you,	'yes,	shall-I-not-know?	A-neighbour

chum	**chān.'**	**Palangas**	**dyutum^{a}wa**
is-to-me	a-carpenter.'	To-the-bedstead	was-given-by-me-for-you

wāṭh	**karith.**	**Ami-panan̄i-zanāni**	**parzanôwus.**
joining	having-made.	By-this-my-own-wife	I-was-recognized.

Dop^{u}nay	**tsĕ,**	**'yüh**	**chuh**	**myôn^{u}**
It-was-said-by-her-to-thee	to-thee,	'this	is	my

khāwand.	**Yih**	**chuh**	**āmot^{u}**	**phakīr**
husband.	He	is	come	a-faqīr

lögith.	**Yih**	**gaʦhi**	**rātas-rāth**	**mārun^{u}.'**
having-made-himself-to-resemble.	He	is-proper	this-very-night	to-be-killed.'

Kor^{u}thas	**hawāla**	**nŏman-mārawātalan.**
Was-made-by-thee-I	in-charge	to-these-executioners.

Yiman	**āv**	**ār**	**myôn^{u}.**	**Yimav**	**trôw^{u}has**
To-them	came	pity	of-me.	By-them	was-let-by-them-I

yĕla.	**Yiman**	**ditim**	**lāl**	**sath.**	**T̲sōr**
from-restraint.	To-them	were-given-by-me	rubies	seven.	Four

ditim	**ʦŏn-zanĕn,**	**trih**	**thöv^{i}màt^{i}**	**amānath.**
were-given-by-me	to-four-persons,	three	placed	as-deposit.

Yit^{i}-kyāh	**chim**	**tim**	**lāl**	**trih,**	**ʦōr**
Here-in-fact	are-to-me	those	rubies	three,	four

chim	**dit^{i}màt^{i}**	**nŏman-ʦŏn-zanĕn.**	**Yit^{i}-kyāh**
are-by-me	given	to-these-four-persons.	Here-in-fact

chiy	**tim**	**ti."**	**Khôl^{u}nas**	**zima**
are-verily	those	also."	Was-caused-to-mount-by-him-on-him	the-responsibility

takhsīr.
(for) the-crime.

13. Dapān wustād,—
(Is) saying the-teacher,—

Dyutun	**hukum**	**panañi-lashkari.**	**Koḍun**
Was-given-by-him	the-order	to-his-own-army.	Was-dragged-out-by-him

yih	**mējĕr**	**ti,**	**yih**	**panüñ^{ü}**	**zanāna**
this	master-of-the-horse	both,	this	his-own	wife

ti. Khananôwun khŏḍ, ŧhananövin
and. Was-caused-to-be-dug-by-him a-pit, were-caused-to-be-cast

dŏnaway ath-khŏḍas, karanöv^{ü}n kañĕ-küñ^{ü}.
both (into) that-pit, was-caused-to-be-done-by-him lapidation.

Atiy chuh likhān söhib-i-kitāb,—
Here-verily is writing a-master-of-books,—

"Shrākh, sar^{a}ph, mạkh^{a}r-i-zan,
"A-knife, a-serpent, coquetry-of-a-woman,

bē-wŏphā."
treacherous."

14. Drāv ati phīrith yih pātashāh.
Went-forth from-there returning this king.

Wôt^{u} ot^{u} Rājĕ-Bikarmājĕtun^{u} gara.
He-arrived there King-Vikramāditya's house.

Diwān chih rājĕs khabar, "pātashāh
Giving they-are to-the-king news, "a-king

chuh āmot^{u} pananĕn-bāŧan." Rājĕ chukh
is come for-his-own-people-of-the-house (i.e. wife)." The-king is-to-them

dapān, "sa chĕh phakīra-sünz^{ü}.
saying, "she is a-faqīr-of.

Pātashāha-sünz^{ü} chĕna." Pātashāh chus
A-king-of she-is-not." The-king is-to-him

dapān, "bŏy gōs suh phakīr. Mĕ-nishĕ
saying, "I-verily am that faqīr. Me-near

chuh cyôn^{u} nishāna, ŧĕ-nishĕ chuh
is thy token, thee-near is

myôn^{u} nishāna." Dapān chus rājĕ,
my token." Saying is-to-him the-king,

"tami-dŏhüc^{ü} phakīrī kyāh gayĕ? azic^{ü}
"of-that-day faqīrhood why was? of-today

pātashŏhī kyāh gayĕ?" Dapān chus
royalty why became?" Saying is-to-him

pātashāh, "mĕ āsa hĕtsamatsa katha
the-king, "by-me were taken statements

pānts mŏl^{i}. Timay ôsus sara karān.
five at-a-price. Them-verily I-was tested making.

Tamiy ôsum lôg^{u}mot^{u} phakīr." Rājĕn
Therefore was-by-me taken-the-semblance-of a-faqīr." By-the-king

kür^{ü} köm^{ü}. Dit^{i}nas söty panàn^{i}
was-done a-deed. Were-given-by-him-to-him in-company his-own

böts^{ü}. Drāv, wôt^{u} pananis-shĕharas-
people-of-the-house (i.e. wife). He-went-forth, he-arrived his-own-city-

manz. Chuh karān rājy. Wa-salām,
in. He-is doing ruling. And-the-peace,

wa-yikrām.
and-respect.

XI.—PHŌRSAṬ SÖHIBUN^{u} SHĀR YĔLI YĀRKAND ZĒNANI GAV

XI.—PHŌRSAṬ	**SÖHIBUN^{u}**	**SHĀR**	**YĔLI**
XI.—FORSYTH	SĀHIB-OF	POEM	WHEN

YĀRKAND	**ZĒNANI**	**GAV**
YĀRKAND	TO-CONQUER	HE-WENT

Yiy	**mĕ**	**ḍyūṭh^{u}may,**	**tī**	**gatshta**
What-verily	by-me	was-seen-by-me-verily,	that-verily	please-go-thou

bōzān.
hearing.

Yārkand	**anōn**	**zēnān.**	**1**
Yārkand	we-shall-bring-it	conquering.	1

Gŏḍañ	**dop^{u}**	**Māl^{i}kāñi,**	**"kus**	**kari**
First	was-said	by-the-Queen,	"who	will-do

yuhay	**kār ?**
this-very	work ?

Phōrsaṭ	**chuh**	**zōrāwār.**
Forsyth	is	powerful.

Rājĕ,	**bĕh**	**Yārkand,**	**bāj**	**gatsh**
O-king,	sit-thou	(in) Yārkand,	tribute	go

tārān.
taking.

Yārkand	**anōn**	**zēnān."**	**2**
Yārkand	we-shall-bring-it	conquering."	2

Landana-pĕṭha	**Yārkand**	**yimav**	**kor^{u}**
London-from	(up to) Yārkand	by-whom	was-done

tay.
authority.

Mashhūr,	**hā,**	**tsŏpôr^{u}**	**gay.**
Celebrated,	Ha,	on-all-sides	they-became.

Gŏḍañ	**Sŏnamargi**	**chāwān**	**pōshĕ-mödān.**
First	at-Sonamarg	(they-were) enjoying	(the-odours-of) the-flower-meadows.

Yārkand	**anōn**	**zēnān.**	**3**
Yārkand	we-shall-bring-it	conquering.	3

Hukm-i-Māhrāj	**Bŏṭanis**	**brōh**	**drāv,**
The-order-of-the-Mahārāja	to-Tibet	in-advance	issued,

"Baltī,	**tum**	**āgē**	**jāv.**
"O-Baltīs,	you	ahead	go-ye.

Pīchē	**jāwō**	**Kashmīr**	**nālē**	**cālān."[1]**
Afterwards	go-ye	to-Kashmīr	with	a-certificate-of-dispatch."

Yārkand	**anōn**	**zēnān.**	**4**
Yārkand	we-shall-bring-it	conquering.	4

Rasad	**say**	**tsŏpôr^{u}**	**kür^{ü}hay**	**taraphan.**
Assembling	that-very	on-all-sides	was-made-by-them-for-you	in-(all) directions.

Gŏḍa	**log^{u}**	**Marāz-i-Pargan.**
At-first	was-reached	Marāz-of-the-Pargana.

Tim	**wadān**	**ösī,**	**"kot^{u}**	**lāg^{i}**	**gör-zān?"**
They	lamenting	were,	"where	(are we) arrived	ignorant-ones?"

Yārkand	**anōn**	**zēnān.**	**5**
Yārkand	we-shall-bring-it	conquering.	5

Timan	**Bŏṭa-garan**	**Köshir^{i}**	**thöv^{i}k^{i},**
In-those	Tibetan-houses	Kāshmīrīs (were)	stationed,

[1] This speech of the Mahārāja of Kashmīr is meant to be in Hindī.

Bŏṭa-böy^{i}	**brũh**	**nyöv^{i}k^{i}.**
The-Tibetan-brothers	in-advance (were)	dispatched.

Gur^{i}	**bīṭh^{i}**	**ḍākas,**	**zŏmba**	**chih**
Horses	were-stationed	for-the-post,	yaks	are

gāsa	**sārān.**
grass	conveying-and-piling.

Yārkand	**anōn**	**zēnān.**	**6**
Yārkand	we-shall-bring-it	conquering.	6

Barāyĕ	**kŏmbakas**	**zanānan**	**chih**
In-the-way-of	for-reinforcement	women	they-are

sọmb^{a}rān,
collecting,

Zyun^{u}	**ta**	**gāsa**	**wartāwān.**
Firewood	and	grass	distributing.

Ajĕ	**āsa**	**pyāwal,**	**kẽh**	**āsa**	**dujān.**
Half (i.e. some)	were	fresh-from-childbed,	some	were	pregnant.

Yārkand	**anōn**	**zēnān.**	**7**
Yārkand	we-shall-bring-it	conquering.	7

Gur^{i}	**manganöv^{i}hay**	**kŏkar-gāman,**
Horses	were-demanded-by-them	(in)-fowl-villages,

"Chuh"	**karun^{u}**	**yim**	**na**	**zānan.**
"Tchk" (is)	to-be-made (by-those)	who	not	know (how to make the sound).

"Hár^{i} hár^{i}"	**karān**	**ös^{i}**	**timan**
"Hár^{i} hár^{i}"	making	they-were	them

pakanāwān.
causing-to-go.

Yārkand	**anōn**	**zēnān.**	**8**
Yārkand	we-shall-bring-it	conquering.	8

Kala	**kȧnⁱ**	**dŏmbijᵘ**	**chĕs,**	**laṭi**
Head	in-the-direction	crupper	is-to-it,	tail

kȧnⁱ	**lākam,**
in-the-direction	bridle,

Gāsa-raz	**kaññĕkh**	**mahkam.**
A-grass-rope (was)	the-rear-binding-rope[1]	strong.

Gāsa-gȧnḍⁱ	**ta**	**zacĕ-zīn**	**pūrith**	**sôruy**
Grass-packsaddles[2]	and	rag-saddles	having-saddled	entire

sāmān.
appliance.

Yārkand	**anōn**	**zēnān.**	**9**
Yārkand	we-shall-bring-it	conquering.	9

Rasad	**kȧrⁱthan**	**ȧnⁱhay**	**nān-gār,**
Proportionate-division	having-made	were-brought-by-them	menial-cultivators,

Maṭi	**chikh**	**panȧnⁱ-panȧnⁱ**	**kār.**
On-the-shoulder	are-to-them	each-his-own	works.

Gĕjĕ	**karĕkh**	**krālan**	**gŏḍañ**	**lĕjĕ**
Bundles-of-grass	were-made-by-them	for-the-potters	at-first	cooking-pots

sārān.
conveying-and-piling.

[1] *Kaññĕkh* is the term used for the two ropes attached at the back of a Kāshmīrī saddle, to secure blankets, etc. (Stein).

[2] *ganḍⁱ* is the term used for the Turkestan packsaddle, which consists of two straw-filled pommels joined in front (Stein).

Yārkand	**anōn**	**zēnān.**	**10**
Yārkand	we-shall-bring-it	conquering.	10

Krāji	**dop^{u}**	**khāwandas,**	**" nādāna**
By-the-potter's-wife	it-was-said	to-the-husband,	" foolish

krālau,
potter-O,

Kathō-kit^{i}	**kōndi**	**wālav ?**
What-for (pots)	into-the-potter's-oven	shall-we-bring-down ?

Kōm^{ü},	**hav,**	**chĕh**	**pakawüñ^{ü},**	**öm^{i}**
The-business,	O,	is	one-that-marches,	uncooked (things)

gatshu	**trāwān."**
go	leaving-behind."

Yārkand	**anōn**	**zēnān.**	**11**
Yārkand	we-shall-bring-it	conquering.	11

Gūr^{i}	**dop^{u}**	**gūr^{i}-bāyĕ,**	**" dŏnaway**
By-the-cowherd	it-was-said	to-the-cowherd's-wife,	" both

nērav,
let-us-go-forth,

Gōv^{ü}-kits^{ü}	**jāy**	**shērav.**
Cow-for	a-place	we-will-arrange.

Wŏḍi	**pĕṭh**	**hĕh**	**gāsa-lôw^{u},**	**gōv^{ü}**
The-head	on	carry	a-grass-handful,	the-cows

gatshan	**lārān."**
will go	running."

Yārkand	**anōn**	**zēnān.**	**12**
Yārkand	we-shall-bring-it	conquering.	12

Khŏni	**kĕth**	**dŏda-noṭ^{u}**	**wārĕ**	**hĕth**
The-haunch	on	a-milk-pail	earthen-pots	taking

bāri	**drāv.**
in-a-load	he-went-forth.

Lōkan	**chuh**	**sapharun^{u}**	**tāv.**
To-the-people	is	of-the-journey	exhaustion.

Tāhkhīth	**dŏda-gūr^{u}**	**Jĕnatuk^{u}**	**bāgwān.**
Of-a-certainty	the-milk-herd	of-Paradise	(is) the-garden-watcher.

Yārkand	**anōn**	**zēnān.**	**13**
Yārkand	we-shall-bring-it	conquering.	13

Wātāl^{i}	**dop^{u}**	**wāt^{a}jĕ,**	**"bŏ-nay**	**sara**
By-the-Mihtar	it-was-said	to-the-Mihtar's-wife,	"I-not	shall-remember

zāh.
ever.

Chim	**mangān**	**dālomuy**	**ta**	**kāh.**
They-are-from-me	asking	leather-only	and	cobbler's-lace.

Tsŏratsh	**ta**	**ör^{ü}**	**hĕth,**	**mĕ-ti,**
Leather-cutter	and	awl	having-taken,	me-also,

hay,	**pakanāwān."**
O,	(they are) causing-to-go."

Yārkand	**anōn**	**zēnān.**	**14**
Yārkand	we-shall-bring-it	conquering.	14

"Phīrith	**dåp^{i}zihĕkh,**	**wātal-gānau,**
"In-answer	you-should-have-said-to them,	Mihtar-pimp-O,

Dȧp^{i}zihĕkh, ‘ȧs^{i} nau zānav.’”
You-should-have-said-to-them, ‘we not know (how-to-use-them.’”)

“Dapyāmakh, wāt^{a}j^{i}, kĕ̄h nay
“It-was-said (long ago) by-me-to-them, O-Mihtar's-wife, any-thing not

chim bōzān.”
they-are-to-me listening.”

Yārkand anōn zēnān. **15**
Yārkand we-shall-bring-it conquering. 15

Shumār būz^{ü}, hay, töyiphdāran.
Counting was-heard, O, of-the-artisans.

Mang lüj^{ü} ahan-gārān.
A-request was-made for-iron-workers.

Wŏḍi pĕṭh yīran hĕth shranz
The-head on the-anvil having-taken the-tongs

ḍakhanāwān.
leaning-upon.

Yārkand anōn zēnān. **16**
Yārkand we-shall-bring-it conquering. 16

Khārav dit^{i} bārav, “yĕngar kati
By-the-blacksmiths were-given grumblings, “charcoals from-where

tshārav ?
shall-we-search-for ?

Wān kati jān shērav ?”
A-shop (i.e. smithy) where good shall-we-arrange ?”

Hāl kyāh kor^{u}hakh, nāl
Arrangement somehow-or-other was-made-by-them-for-them, horse-shoes

garanāwān.
getting-made.

Yārkand anōn zēnān. **17**
Yārkand we-shall-bring-it conquering. 17

Khŏsh kyāh gōsay, amôb^{u} gav jān.
Pleased certainly I-became-verily, very it-became good.

Pata nyūkh nöyid ta chān.
Afterwards was-taken-by-them barber and carpenter.

Bata-düj^{ü} athi hĕth pata chikh lārān.
Food-kerchief in-the-hand taking (others) after are-to-them running.

Yārkand anōn zĕnān. **18**
Yārkand we-shall-bring-it conquering. 18

Mạslahath karān tima āsa pānawöñ.
Consultation making they (fem.) were amongst-themselves.

"Kusuy kari nāyĕz^{ü} ta chöñ^{ü}?
"Who will-do (i.e. support) the-barber's-wife and the-carpenter's-wife?

Katawañ karith, hay, karav guzarān."
The-wages-of-spinning having-done, O, we-shall-make a-livelihood."

Yārkand anōn zēnān. **19**
Yārkand we-shall-bring-it conquering. 19

Söbir Tilawāñi, tāmath yutuy wan,
O-Ṣābir Oilseller, so-long this-much say,

Yāmath khabar bōzan.
As-long-as the-news they-will-hear.

Tāñ āv Söhib bā-sôruy-sāmān.
At-length came the-Sāhib with-all-pomp.

Yārkand anōn zēnān. **20**
Yārkand we-will-bring-it conquering. 20

XII.—ÔKHUNA-SÜNZ^{ü} DALĪL.

XII.—RELIGIOUS-TEACHER-OF THE-STORY.

1.	**Ôkhunā**	**akh**	**ôs^{u}·**	**Tamis^{ü}y**	**ös^{i}**
1.	Religious-teacher-a-certain	one	was.	To-him-verily	were

nĕciv^{i}	**tsōr.**	**Timan^{ü}y**	**pryutshun,**	**"bŏh**
sons	four.	To-them-verily	it-was-asked-by-him,	"I

buḍyōs,	**tŏh^{i}**	**waniv**	**kyāh**	**kariv."**
am-grown-old,	ye	say-ye	what	ye-will-do."

Ȧk^{i}	**dopus,**	**"bŏh**	**kara**	**yimāmath."**
By-one	it-was-said-to-him,	"I	will-do	leading-prayers-in-a-mosque."

Biy^{i}	**dopus,**	**"bŏh**	**para**	**bā̃g."**
By-the-second	it-was-said-to-him,	"I	will-recite	the-call-to-prayers."

Biy^{i}	**dopus,**	**"bŏh**	**para**	**wāz."**
By-another	it-was-said-to-him,	"I	will-recite	sermons."

Lŏk^{a}ṭ^{i}-hih^{i}	**tsūrim^{i}**	**dopus,**	**"bŏh**	**kara**
By-the-youngest	by-the-fourth	it-was-said-to-him,	"I	will-do

tsūr^{ü}."	**Dŏhā**	**akh**	**banyāv,**	**gav**
thieving."	Day-a-certain	one	happened,	he-went

pātashĕhas	**tsūri.**	**Wôt^{u}**	**yĕli**	**pātashĕha-sond^{u}**
to-the-king	for-thieving.	He-arrived	when	the-king's

gara,	**rūd^{u}**	**wŏdañĕ,**	**tā̃n**	**nērān**	**tōra**
house,	(while) he-remained	standing,	in-the-meantime	(was)-coming-forth	from-there

wazīr biyĕ pātashĕha-sünz^{ü} kūr^{ü}. Yih
the-vizier and-also the-king's daughter. He

wuchukh ati wŏdañĕ. Dop^{u}nakh, "tŏh^{i}
was-seen-by-them there standing. It-was-said-by-him-to-them, "you

kam chiwa?" Yimau dop^{u}has, "ȶ^{a}h
who are?" By-them it-was-said-by-them-to-him, "thou

kus chukh?" Dop^{u}nakh, "bŏh chus
who art?" It-was-said-by-him-to-them, "I am

ȶūr." Yimau dop^{u}has, "ȧs^{i}-ti chih
a-thief." By-them it-was-said-by-them-to-him, "we-also are

ȶūr." Kȧḍikh gur^{i} z^{a}h. Sapod^{u}
thieves." Were-brought-out-by-them horses two. He-became

sawār akh yih ôkhun, biyĕ yih
mounted one this religious-teacher, and-the-other this

pātashāh-kūr^{ü}. Dōp^{u}nas wazīran, "nīriv
king's-daughter. It-was-said-by-him-to-him by-the-vizier, "go-forth

tŏh^{i}. Nasīyĕth, hasa, karay akh
ye. Instruction, Sir, I-will-make-to-thee one

kath, yina-sa pātashāh-kōrĕ söty kath
word, that-not-Sir the-king's-daughter with conversation

kuni karakh. Bŏh, hasa, yimawa
in-any-respect thou-wilt-make. I, Sir, will-come-to-you

pata, ta tŏh^{i} nīriv."
after, and ye go-ye-forth."

2. Yim chih pakān. Pātashāh-kōrĕ
2. They are going-along. To-the-king's-daughter

chĕna khabar, "yih chuna mĕ söty
is-not belief, "this is-not me with

ôkhun-zāda." Tas chĕh khabar, "yih
the-teacher's-son." To-her is belief, "this

chuh wazīr." Gwāsh log^{u} phŏlani.
is the-vizier." Dawn began to-break.

Wȧth^{i} guryau pĕṭha bŏn. Gayĕ yih
They-descended the-horses from down. She-went this

pātashāh-kūr^{ü} kŏli akis pĕṭh, atha
king's-daughter to-a-stream one on, hands

buth^{u} cholun. Wuchun ath-kŏli-manz
face was-washed-by-her. Was-seen-by-her that-stream-in

lāl. Yih lāl tulun, āyĕ hĕth amis
a-ruby. This ruby was-taken-up-by-her, she-came taking (it) that

ôkhun-zādas nish. Tas chĕh khabar,
teacher's-son near. To-her is belief,

"yih chuh wazīr." Wazīr kĕ̃h ôs^{u}na.
"this is the-vizier." The-vizier anyone he-was-not.

Yūt^{u} gwāsh chuh phŏlān, tyūt^{u} chuh
As-soon-as dawn is breaking, so-soon is

yih lāl gāh trāwān. Parzanôw^{u} ami
this ruby light giving-forth. He-was-recognized by-that

pātashāh-kōri wazīr na. Lāl tulukh
king's-daughter the-vizier not. The-ruby was-carried-by-them

söty, wöt^{i} shĕharas akis manz. Ati
with (them), they-arrived to-city to-one in. There

wuch^{u}kh pāri-hanā. Ath^{i} manz bīṭh^{i}.
was-seen-by-them a-small-hut. It-verily in they-sat.

3. Yih chuh yiwān amis atikis
3. He is coming to-that of-that-place

pātashĕhas nish ami shĕharakis. Dapān
king near of-that city. Saying

chus, "bŏh bĕha nōkar." Yih chus
he-is-to-him, "I will-sit (as) servant." He is-to-him

dapān, "kyāh nōkarī karakh?" Dapān
saying, "what service wilt-thou-do?" Saying

chus, "bŏh kara gurĕn-hünz^{u}
he-is-to-him, "I will-do horses-of

khazmath." Yim chih yimay katha
service." They are these-verily words

karān. Shĕkhtsāh akh āv lāl-pharōsh
making. Person-a-certain one came ruby-seller

amis pātashĕhas k^{a}nani. Lāl chis
to-this king to-sell. Rubies are-to-him

z^{a}h. Yih wŏth^{u} söyīsth. Yih chus
two. This arose groom. He is-to-him

dapān, "pātashĕham, akh lāl bēbahā,
saying, "my-king, one ruby (is) priceless,

bēkh chuh khŏṭ^{u}. Ath manz chuh
the-other is flawed. To-it in is

kyom^{u}." Dapān chus pātashāh, "tih
a-worm." Saying is-to-him the-king, "that

kĕtha-pöṭh^{i} ôy tsĕ bōzana?" Dapān
in-what-manner came-to-thee to-thee (forming passive) into-knowledge?" Saying

chus yih phīrith, "pātashĕham,
he-is-to-him he in-reply, "my-king,

tāhkhīth chus manz kyom^{u}. Phuṭ^{a}ryūn.
certainly there-is-to-it inside a-worm. Break-ye-it.

Hargāh kyom^{u} drās-na, ada yih
If a-worm issued-from-it-not, then what

pātashĕhas khŏsh kari, tih gatshĕm
to-the-king pleased will-make, that it-is-proper-to-me

karun^{u}. Hargāh kyom^{u} drās, tĕli
to-be-done. If a-worm issued-from-it, then

gatshĕm bakh^{a}cöyish dinü^{ü}."
is-proper-to-me a-present to-be-given."

4. Dapān wustād,—
4. (Is) saying the-teacher,—

Phuṭ^{o}rukh yih lāl. Ami manza drāv
Was-broken-by-them this ruby. From-it from-in issued

kyom^{u}. Ami sāta tshun^{u}has "söyīsth"-nāv
a-worm. At-that time was-cast-by-them-to-him "groom"-name

nahīth, "lāl-shĕnākh" pyōs nāv.
having-cancelled, "lapidary" fell-to-him name.

Gav yih lāl-shĕnākh panun^{u} gara.
Went this lapidary his-own house.

Dŏhā	**dŏhā**	**chuh**	**kaḍān.**	**Rātas**
Day-a	day-a	he-is	passing.	By-night

bĕhān	**chuh**	**panani**	**gari,**	**dŏhas**
sitting-down	he-is	in-his-own	house,	by-day

yiwān	**chuh**	**lāl**	**pasand**	**karani.**	**Amis**
coming	he-is	rubies	approved	for-making.	This

pātashĕha-sond^{u}	**nöyid**	**gatshān**	**chuh**	**mast**
king-of	barber	going	is	hair

kāsani	**amis**	**lāl-shĕnākas.**	**Tati**	**chuh**
for-shaving	to-this	lapidary.	There	he-is

wuchān	**ȧm^{i}-sünz^{ü}**	**yih**	**zanāna.**	**Yih**	**ös^{ü}**
seeing	him-of	this	woman.	She	was

khōbsūrath	**sĕṭhāh.**	**Āv**	**yih**	**nöyid,**
beautiful	very.	Came	this	barber,

wazīrās	**masṭ**	**kôs^{u}nas.**	**Dop^{u}nas,**
of-the-vizier	the-hair	was-shaved-by-him-of-him.	It-was-said-by-him-to-him,

"ay	**wazīra,**	**zanānā**	**chĕh**	**amis**
"O	vizier,	woman-a	is	to-this

lāl-shĕnākas.	**Yih**	**shūbihĕh**	**wazīra-sandi**
lapidary.	She	would-have-been-becoming	of-the-vizier

gari.	**Amis**	**karta**	**kĕntshāh**	**nŏktāh."**
in-the-house.	To-him	please-make	some	fault-a."

Dop^{u}nas,	**"ada-kyāh."**	**Yih**	**wazīr**	**gav**
It-was-said-by-him-to-him,	"certainly."	This	vizier	went

amis	**pātashĕha-sanzĕ**	**kōrĕ,**	**dop^{u}nas,**	**"ts^{a}h**
to-that	king-of	daughter,	it-was-said-by-him-to-her,	"thou

daph pātashĕhas, ‘mĕ gatshi yus
say to-the-king, ‘to-me is-necessary what

lāl-shĕnākan gŏḍañiy lāl pasand kor^{u},
by-the-lapidary at-the-very-first ruby approved was-made,

tath^{i} hyuh^{u} byākh lāl āsun^{u}.’”
that-verily like another ruby to-be.’”

Dop^{u} pātashĕha-sanzi kōri pananis
Was-said by-the-king’s daughter to-her-own

mölis, “mĕ gatshi lālas-hyuh^{u} bĕbahā
father, “to-me is-necessary the-ruby-like a-priceless

lāl āsun^{u}.” Āv lāl-shĕnākh. Dop^{u}nas
ruby to-be.” Came the-lapidary. It-was-said-by-him-to-him

pātashĕhan, “dis lāl anith, tath
by-the-king, “give-to-her a-ruby having-brought, to-that

lālas hyuh^{u}.” Āv ōra lāl-shĕnākh, wôt^{u}
ruby like.” Came thence the-lapidary, he-arrived

panañĕ zanāni nish. Byūṭh^{u} tshŏpa
to-his-own woman near. He-sat silence

karith. Yih chĕs dapān zanāna, “ts^{a}h
making. This is-to-him saying woman, “thou

kyāzi chukh phikiri gŏmot^{u}?” Dop^{u}nas
why art in-anxiety become?” It-was-said-by-him-to-her

phīrith ȧm^{i} lāl-shĕnākan, “pātashāh
in-answer by-this lapidary, “the-king

chum lāl mangān bēbahā. Suh kati
is-from-me a-ruby demanding priceless. That from-where

ana?"	**Dop^{u}nas**	**ami**	**zanāni,**	**"gatsh,**
shall-I-bring?"	It-was-said-by-her-to-him	by-that	woman,	"go,

daph	**pātashĕhas,**	**'rĕtas**	**kyut^{u}**	**dim**
say	to-the-king,	'for-a-month	for	give-to-me

khar^{a}j,	**bŏh**	**dimay**	**lāl**	**anith.'"**
expenses,	I	will-give-to-thee	a-ruby	having-brought.'"

Pātashĕhan	**dyutus**	**khar^{a}j**	**rĕtas**	**sumb^{u}.**
By-the-king	was-given-to-him	expenses	for-a-month	adequate.

Yih	**onun**	**panun^{u}**	**gara.**	**Chuh**	**bihith**
This	was-brought-by-him	his-own	house.	He-is	seated

khĕwān.	**Nu**	**chuh**	**gatshān**	**pātashĕhas,**
eating.	Not-at-all	he-is	going	to-the-king,

nu	**chuh**	**gatshān**	**biyĕ-kun.**	**Rĕth**
not-at-all	he-is	going	other-where.	The-month

gav	**ādā.**	**Diwān**	**chĕs**	**yih**	**suh**
went	completion.	Giving	is-to-him	she	that

lāl,	**yus**	**tami**	**kŏli**	**manza**	**tujyān.**
ruby,	which	from-that	stream	from-in	was-taken-up-by-her.

Gav	**hĕth**	**pātashĕhas,**	**kür^{ü}nas**	**salām,**
He-went	taking (it)	to-the-king,	was-made-by-him-to-him	a-bow,

lāl	**thôw^{u}nas**	**bōṇtha-kani.**
the-ruby	was-placed-by-him-of-him	in-front.

5. Drāv	**phīrith**	**lāl-shĕnākh,**	**wôt^{u}**
5. Went-forth	back-again	the-lapidary,	he-arrived

panun^{u}	**gara.**	**Rāthāh**	**küḍ^{ü}n**	**panani**
his-own	house.	Night-a	was-passed-by-him	in-his-own

gari. **Sub^{a}has** **āv** **nöyid** **mast** **kāsani**
house. In-the-morning came the-barber hair to-shave

amis **lāl-shĕnākas.** **Mast** **mŏkalôw^{u}nas**
of-that lapidary. Hair was-completed-by-him-for-him

kösith, **ta** **drāv** **nöyid** **pānas.**
having-shaved, and went-forth the-barber of-his-own-accord.

Wôt^{u} **biyĕ** **amis** **wazīras-nish.** **Dopun**
He-arrived again to-that vizier-near. It-was-said-by-him

wazīras, **"kĕntshāh** **karta** **amis**
to-the-vizier, "something please-to-do to-that

lāl-shĕnākas. **Amis** **chĕh** **zanāna** **khōbsūrath**
lapidary. To-him is the-woman beautiful

sĕṭhāh. **Söh** **shūbihĕh** **wazīra-sandi**
very. She would-have-been-becoming of-the-vizier

gari." **Wazīr** **āv** **biyĕ** **amis**
in-the-house." The-vizier came again to-that

pātashĕha-sanzĕ **kōrĕ.** **Dop^{u}nas,** **"ts^{a}h**
king's daughter. It-was-said-by-him-to-her, "thou

mang **pātashĕhas** **lālan-hond^{u}** **troṭ^{u}."**
demand to-the-king rubies-of necklace."

Dop^{u} **ami** **pātashĕha-sanzi** **kōri**
It-was-said by-that king's daughter

pananis **mölis,** **"mĕ** **gatshiy** **āsun^{u}**
to-her-own father, "to-me is-necessary-from-thee to-be

lālan-hond^{u} **troṭ^{u}."** **Lāl-shĕnākh** **āv**
rubies-of a-necklace." The-lapidary came

pātashĕhas	**nish.**	**Kür^{u}nas**	**salām.**	**Pātashĕh**
to-the-king	near.	Was-made-by-him	a-bow.	The-king

chus	**dapān,**	**"lāl,**	**hasa,**	**gatshanay**
is-to-him	saying,	"rubies,	sir,	are-required-from-thee

āsàn^{i}	**sĕṭhāh**	**traṭis**	**sumb^{i}."**	**Āv**
to-be	many	for-a-necklace	adequate."	Came

lāl-shĕnākh,	**wôt^{u}**	**panun^{u}**	**gara.**	**Yih**
the-lapidary,	he-arrived	his-own	house.	She

chĕs	**dapān**	**zanāna**	**lŏt^{i}-pöṭh^{i},**	**"kyāzi**
is-to-him	saying	woman	gently,	"why

chukh	**bihith?"**	**Yuh**	**chus**	**dapān**
art-thou	seated?"	He	is-to-her	saying

phīrith,	**"pātashĕh**	**chum**	**mangān**	**az**
in-reply,	"the-king	is-from-me	demanding	today

lālan-hond^{u}	**troṭ^{u}.**	**Suh**	**kati**	**ana**
rubies-of	a-necklace.	That	whence	will-I-bring

bŏh?"	**Dop^{u}nas**	**ami**	**zanāni,**	**"kĕh**
I?"	It-was-said-by-her-to-him	by-that	woman,	"any

chĕna	**phikir^{ü}.**	**Gatsh,**	**pātashĕhas**	**gatshi**
is-not	anxiety.	Go,	of (i.e. from)-the-king	it-is-necessary

hyon^{u}	**trĕn**	**rĕtan-kyut^{u}**	**khar^{a}j."**
to-take	for-three	months-for	expenses."

Dyut^{u}nas	**pātashĕhan**	**khar^{a}j,**	**ta**	**āv**
Was-given-by-him-to-him	by-the-king	expenses,	and	he-came

panun^{u}	**gara**	**hĕth.**
his-own	house	taking (the money).

6. Yih	**chuh**	**khĕwān**	**ta**	**cĕwān.**
6. He	is	eating	and	drinking.

Yot^{u}-tāñ	**yim**	**trih**	**rĕth**	**gay,**	**wuñ**
As-soon-as	these	three	months	went,	now

chĕs	**dapān**	**yih**	**zanāna**	**amis**
she-is-to-him	saying	this	woman	to-that

lāl-shĕnākas.	**Dapān**	**chĕs,**	**"yĕtảt^{i}**	**mĕ**
lapidary.	Saying	she-is-to-him,	"where	by-me

tami	**kŏli**	**manza**	**lāl**	**tujyāv,**	**tamiy**
from-that	stream	from-in	the-ruby	was-taken-up,	along-that-very

kŏli	**kŏli**	**gatshi**	**khasun^{u}**	**hyor^{u}-pahān.**
along-stream	along-stream	it-is-necessary	to-ascend	up-stream-a-little.

Tati	**chĕy**	**nāg.**	**Tath^{i}**	**nāgas**	**gatshi**
There	is-verily	a-spring.	To-that-verily	spring	is-necessary

andas-kun	**dŏb**	**khanun^{u}.**	**Tath^{i}**
the-end-at	a-pit	to-be-dug.	To-that-very

dŏbas-manz	**bĕh^{i}zi**	**khaṭith.**	**Tath**
pit-in	you-must-sit	having-concealed-yourself.	To-that

nāgas-pĕṭh	**yinay**	**gŏdañiy**	**shĕh**	**zañĕ**
spring-on	will-come-before-thee	at-the-very-first	six	females

srān	**karani.**	**Timan**	**kẽh**	**kar^{i}zi-na.**
bathing	to-do.	To-them	anything	you-must-do-not.

Pata	**yiyiy**	**timan**	**shĕn**	**zañĕn**
Afterwards	will-come-before-thee	of-those	six	females

zĕṭh^{ü}. Sa wasiy tath nāgas srān
the-eldest-sister. She will-descend-before-thee to-that spring bathing

karani. Pŏshākh trāviy kaḍith baṭhis
to-do. Garment she-will-leave-before-thee having-taken-off to-the-bank

pĕṭh. Cyôn^{u} gatshi gatshun^{u}
on. For-thee it-is-necessary to-be-gone

tsüri-pöṭh^{i}, gatshi tih pŏshākh tulun^{u}."
thieving-like (i.e. secretly), is-necessary that garment to-be-taken-up."

7. Āyĕ shĕh zañĕ. Kor^{u} timau
7. Came six females. Was-done by-them

srān. Timan kĕ̄h wonun-na. Yiman
bathing. To-them anything was-said-by-him-not. To-them

pata āyĕ satim^{ü} züñ^{ü}, trôw^{u} ami
after came a-seventh female, was-left by-her

pŏshākh kaḍith baṭhis-pĕṭh, pāna
the-garment having-taken-off the-bank-on, she-herself

wütsh^{ü} nāgas-manz. Yih lāl-shĕnākh ăv
descended the-spring-in. This lapidary came

tsüri-pöṭh^{i}. Āv ta tulun yih
secretly. He-came and was-taken-up-by-him this

ȧm^{i}-sond^{u} pŏshākh, gav ta byūṭh^{u}
her-of the-garment, he-went and sat

ath dŏbas-manz. Ami kor^{u} srān.
to-that pit-in. By-her was-done bathing.

Khüts^{ü} baṭhis pĕṭh. Wuchun ati
She-ascended to-the-bank on. Was-seen-by-her there

na	**pŏshākh.**	**Dits^{u}n**	**krēkh.**	**Dapān**
not	the-garment.	Was-given-by-her	a-cry.	Saying

chĕh,	**"dĕv**	**chukha?**	**yinsān**	**chukha?**
she-is,	"demon	art-thou?	human-being	art-thou?

tas	**Khŏdāyĕ-sond^{u}**	**chuy**	**kasam**	**yĕm^{i}**
of-that	God-of	is-to-thee	an-oath	by-whom

pöda	**korukh.**	**Mĕ**	**ma**	**kar**
created	thou-was-made.	For-me	do-not	make

sīras	**phāsh.**	**Yih**	**tsĕ**	**gatshiy,**	**tih**
of-my-secret	disgracing.	What	to-thee	is-necessary-to-thee,	that

dimay."	**Ȧm^{i}**	**korus**	**ālav**	**ami**
I-will-give-to-thee."	By-him	was-made-to-her	a-call	from-that

dŏba-manza.	**Dop^{u}nas,**	**"dim**	**wāda-y-Khŏdā,**
pit-from-in.	It-was-said-by-him-to-her,	"give-to-me	the-promise-of-God,

yih	**bŏh**	**mangay,**	**tih**	**gatshĕm**	**bōzun^{u}."**
what	I	shall-demand-of-thee,	that	will-be-certainly-for-me	to-be-heard."

Ath^{i}	**pĕṭh**	**dyut^{u}nas**	**wāda-y-Khŏdā.**
That-verily	upon	was-given-by-her-to-him	the-promise-of-God.

Dyut^{u}nas	**pŏshākh.**	**Pŏshākh**	**tshon^{u}**
Was-given-by-him-to-her	the-garment.	The-garment	was-put-on

ami	**nöl^{i}.**	**Dop^{u}nas,**	**"kyāh**	**chum**
by-her	on-the-neck.	It-was-said-by-her-to-him,	"what	is-to-me

hukum?"	**Dop^{u}nas**	**ȧm^{i}**	**lāl-shĕnākan,**
the-order?"	It-was-said-by-him-to-her	by-that	lapidary,

"tsĕ	**gatshiy**	**yun^{u}**	**mĕ-söty."**	
"for-thee	it-is-necessary	to-come	me-with."	
Pakān	**chuh**	**lāl-shĕnākh**	**brũh**	**brũh,**
Going-along	is	the-lapidary	in-front	in-front,

yih	**chĕh**	**pakān**	**parī**	**pata**	**pata.**
this	is	walking	fairy	after	after.

8. **Dapān wustād,—**
(Is) saying the-teacher,—

Amis	**chuh**	**nāv**	**Lālmāl**	**Parī.**
To-her	is	name	Lālmāl	Fairy.

Wöt^{i}	**amis**	**lāl-shĕnāka-sond^{u}**	**gara.**
They-arrived	to-that	lapidary's	house.

9. **Dapān wustād,—**
(Is) saying the-teacher,—

Yā	**amis**	**kathan**	**chih**	**harān**	**lāl,**
Either	for-her	of-the-words	are	dropping	rubies,
yā	**chis**	**ös^{ü}üs**[1]	**harān**	**lāl**	**dŏha**
or	they-are-to-her	of-the-mouth	dropping	rubies	each-day
sath	**sath.**	**Rāth**	**gayĕ**	**ādā.**	**Subuh**
seven	seven.	Night	went	to-completion.	Morning

āv.	**Lāl**	**sath**	**tul^{i}**	**lāl-shĕnākan.**
came.	Rubies	seven	were-taken-up	by-the-lapidary.
Gav	**hĕth**	**pātashĕhas.**	**Kür^{ü}nas**	**salām.**
He-went	taking (them)	to-the-king.	Was-made-by-him-to-him	a-bow.

Lāl	**sath**	**thàv^{i}nas**	**bōnṭha-kani.**
Rubies	seven	were-placed-by-him-of-him	in-front.
Pātashāh	**gav**	**sĕṭhāh**	**khŏsh.**
The-king	became	very-much	pleased.

[1] So Gōvind Kaul. Stein's transcript has *ashis*, "for a tear."

10. **Lāl-shĕnākan**	**hyotus**	**rukhsath.**
By-the-lapidary	was-taken-from-him	leave-to-depart.

Wôt^{u}	**panun^{u}**	**gara.**	**Patay**	**wôtus**
He-arrived	his-own	house.	Afterwards-verily	arrived-to-him

yih	**nöyid.**	**Ȧm^{i}**	**kôsus**	**mast.**	**Mast**
this	barber.	By-him	was-shaved-for-him	the-hair.	Hair

kösith	**drāv,**	**wôt^{u}**	**yih**	**nöyid**	**wazīras-**
having-shaved	he-went-forth,	arrived	this	barber	the-vizier-

nish.	**Amis**	**ti**	**kôsun**	**mast.**	**Dapān**
near.	For-him	also	was-shaved-for-him	the-hair.	Saying

chus,	**"hā**	**Wazīra,**	**amis**	**lāl-shĕnākas**
he-is-to-him,	"O	Vizier,	to-that	lapidary

gamüts^{ü}	**az**	**pöda**	**byākh**	**zanānā.**	**Sa**
(is) become	today	manifest	another	a-certain-woman.	She

chĕh	**sĕṭhāh**	**khōbsūrath.**	**Tamis**
is	very	beautiful.	Of-that

gŏḍañicĕ-handi	**khŏta**	**sĕṭhāh**	**khōbsūrath.**
first-one	than	more	beautiful.

Kĕntshāh	**karta**	**amis**	**lāl-shĕnākas.**	**Akh**
Something	please-to-do	to-that	lapidary.	One

chĕh	**löyik-i-wazīr,**	**bēkh**	**chĕh**	**mĕ**
is	worthy-of-the-vizier,	the-other	is	for-me

öyikh."	**Dop^{u}nas,**	**"pyōm,**	**hasa,**	**biyĕ**
worthy."	It-was-said-by-him-to-him,	"it-is-fallen-to-me,	sir,	again

wanun	**pātashĕh-kōrĕ."**	**Gav**	**yih**	**wazīr.**
to-speak	to-the-king's-daughter."	Went	this	vizier.

Dapān	**chuh**	**amis**	**pātashĕh-korĕ,**	**"ts^{a}h**
Saying	he-is	to-that	king's-daughter,	"thou

mang	**mölis,**	**'mĕ**	**gatshi**	**āsun**
demand	to (-your)-father,	'to-me	is-necessary	to-be

raṭ^{a}na-kor^{u}.'"	**Gayĕ**	**pātashĕh-kūr^{ü}**	**pananis**
a-jewel-bracelet.'"	Went	the-king's-daughter	to-her-own

mölis.	**Dapān**	**chĕs,**	**"mĕ**	**gatshi**
father.	Saying	she-is-to-him,	"to-me	is-necessary

āsun	**raṭ^{a}na-kor^{u}."**	**Pagāh**	**āv**	**lāl-shĕnākh.**
to-be	a-jewel-bracelet."	Next-day	came	the-lapidary.

Dapān	**chus**	**pātashĕh,**	**"an,**	**sa,**	**raṭ^{a}na-kor^{u}."**
Saying	is-to-him	the-king,	"bring,	sir,	a-jewel-bracelet."

11.	**Drāv**	**lāl-shĕnākh,**	**wôt^{u}**	**panun^{u}**
	Went-forth	the-lapidary,	he-arrived	his-own

gara.	**Dapān**	**chuh**	**yiman**	**zanānan**	**dŏn,**
house.	Saying	he-is	to-these	women	two,

"pātashĕh	**chum**	**mangān**	**raṭ^{a}na-kor^{u}.**
"the-king	is-from-me	demanding	a-jewel-bracelet.

Suh	**kati**	**ana**	**bŏh?"**	**Phīrith**	**wŏtsh^{ü}s**
That	from-where	shall-I-bring	I?"	In-answer	arose-to-him

Lālmāl	**Parī.**	**Dop^{u}nas,**	**"gatsh,**	**pātashĕhas**
Lālmāl	Fairy.	It-was-said-by-her-to-him,	"go,	of (i.e. from)-the-king

mang	**trĕn**	**rĕtan-kyut^{u}**	**khar^{a}j."**	**Dyut^{u}nas**
demand	for-three	months-for	expenses."	Was-given-by-him-to-him

pātashĕhan.	**Āv**	**hĕth**	**panun^{u}**	**gara.**
by-the-king.	He-came	taking (them)	his-own	house.

Dŏhā	**dŏhā**	**chuh**	**kaḍān.**	**Trih**	**rĕth**
Day-a	day-a	he-is	passing.	Three	months

gay	**ādā.**	**Likhān**	**chĕh**	**Lālmāl**	**Parī**
went	to-completion.	Writing	is	Lālmāl	Fairy

kākad.	**Dapān**	**chĕh**	**amis**	**lāl-shĕnākas,**
a-paper.	Saying	she-is	to-that	lapidary,

"gatsh	**tath**	**nāgas**	**pĕṭh,**	**yĕmi-manza**
"go	to-that	spring	on,	which-from-in

bŏh	**üñ^{u}thas.**	**Tath^{i}-manz**	**gatshi**	**yih**
I	was-brought-by-thee-I.	It-verily-in	is-necessary	this

kākad	**trāwun^{u}.**	**Tōra**	**khasiy**	**atha.**
paper	to-be-thrown.	Therefrom	will-arise-to-thee	a-hand.

Tath^{i}-manz	**āsiy**	**kor^{u}.**	**Tath^{i}**	**kȧr^{i}zi**
It-verily-on	will-be-for-thee	a-bracelet.	To-that-verily	you-must-do

thaph.	**Pāna**	**manz**	**wȧs^{i}zi-na."**
seizing.	You-yourself	within	you-must-not-descend."

12.

Gav	**hĕth**	**yih**	**kākad.**	**Wôt^{u}**
He-went	taking	this	paper.	He-arrived

ath	**nāgas-pĕṭh.**	**Trôwun**	**yih**	**kākad**
to-that	spring-on.	Was-thrown-by-him	this	paper

ath	**nāgas-manz.**	**Yuthuy**	**yih**	**kākad**
to-that	spring-in.	As-verily	this	paper

trôwun,	**tyuthuy**	**khot^{u}**	**ōra**	**atha.**
was-thrown-by-him,	so-verily	there-rose	from-there	a-hand.

Ath^{i}	**athas-manz**	**raṭ^{a}na-kor^{u}.**	**Dits^{ü}n**
To-that-very	hand-on	a-jewel-bracelet.	Was-given-by-him

ath	**thaph.**	**Ami**	**thapi**	**sötiy**	**āv**
to-it	seizing.	By-that	grasp	by-means-of-only	came

amis	**hoʦ^u**	**nīrith.**	**Hoʦ^u**	**hĕth**	**ti,**
of-it	the-forearm	coming-forth.	The-forearm	taking	both,

kor^u	**hĕth**	**ti,**	**āv**	**pānas,**	**wôt^u**
the-bracelet	taking	and,	he-came (home)	for-himself (i.e. without opposition),	he-arrived

panun^u	**gara.**	**Rāth**	**gayĕ**	**ādā.**
his-own	house.	The-night	went	to-completion.

Sub^{a}hanas	**gav**	**pātashĕhas.**	**Kür^{ü}n**
At-dawn	he-went	to-the-king.	Was-made-by-him

salām.	**Kȧr^i-han**	**thüv^{ü}nas**	**bōnṭha-kani.**
a-bow.	The-bracelet	was-put-by-him-of-him	in-front.

Pātashĕh	**gōs**	**sĕṭhāh**	**khŏsh.**
The-king	became-to-him	very-much	pleased.

13. Hyotus	**rukhsath**	**lāl-shĕnākan,**	**āv**
Was-taken-from-him	leave-to-depart	by-the-lapidary,	he-came

panun^u	**gara.**	**Āv**	**biyĕ**	**yih**	**nöyid,**
his-own	house.	Came	again	this	barber,

kôsun	**mast**	**amis**	**lāl-shĕnākas.**	**Mast**
was-shaved-by-him	the-hair	for-this	lapidary.	Hair

kösith	**drāv,**	**wôt^u**	**amis**	**wazīras-nish.**
having-shaved	he-went-forth,	he-arrived	to-that	vizier-near.

Biyĕ	**chus**	**dapān,**	**"Wazīra,**	**amis**
Again	he-is-to-him	saying,	"Vizier-O,	to-that

lāl-shĕnākas chukhna ʦ^{a}h wātān
lapidary thou-art-not thou getting-at

kuni-kani. Amis karta kĕnʦhāh." Gav
in-any-way. To-him please-to-do something." Went

yih wazīr amis pātashĕh-kōrĕ. Dapān
this vizier to-that king's-daughter. Saying

chus, "ʦ^{a}h chĕkh pātashĕh-kūr^{ü}. T̲sĕ
he-is-to-her, "thou art the-king's-daughter. To-thee

gaʦhiyĕ āsun^{u} okuy kor^{u}? Pātashĕhas
is-proper-for-thee to-be one-only bracelet? To-the-king

gaʦhi mangun^{u} byākh." Gayĕ yih
is-necessary to-be-demanded another." Went this

pātashĕh-kūr^{ü}. Dopun pananis mölis,
king's-daughter. It-was-said-by-her to-her-own father,

"mĕ gaʦhi āsun^{u} byākh kor^{u}." Āv
"for-me is-necessary to-be another bracelet." Came

biyĕ lāl-shĕnākh. Kür^{ü}n salām. Dapān
again the-lapidary. Was-made-by-him a-bow. Saying

chus pātashĕh, "byākh kor^{u} gaʦhiy
is-to-him the-king, "another bracelet is-necessary-for-thee

āsun^{u}."
to-be."

14. Āv lāl-shĕnākh, wôt^{u} panun^{u}
Came the-lapidary, he-arrived his-own

gara. Dapān chuh yiman zanānan dŏn,
house. Saying he-is to-these women two,

"Az chum pātashĕh mangān byākh
"today is-from-me the-king demanding another

rạt^{a}na-kor^{u}." **Diwān** **chĕs** **Lālmāl** **Parī**
jewel-bracelet." Giving is-to-him Lālmāl Fairy

panüñ^{ü} **wöj^{ü}.** **Dapān** **chĕs,** **"gatsh**
her-own ring. Saying she-is-to-him, "go

tath **nāgas-pĕṭh.** **Tath^{i}** **nāgas** **akith-kun**
to-that spring-on. To-that-very spring on-one-side

chuy **pal** **boḍ^{u}.** **Tath^{i}** **hāv** **myöñ^{ü}**
is-verily a-rock great. To-it-verily show my

wöj^{ü}. **Suh** **pal** **wŏthiy** **thod^{u}.** **Tami**
ring. That rock will-rise-for-thee erect. From-it

tȧl^{i} **chĕy** **wath.** **Tamiy** **wati** **wȧs^{i}zi**
below is-for-thee a-path. By-that-very path you-must-descend

bŏn. **Tati** **chĕy** **myöñ^{ü}** **vĕs.** **Say**
beneath. There is-verily my crony. She-verily

diyiy **rạt^{a}na-kor^{u}."**
will-give-to-thee a-jewel-bracelet."

15. **Drāv** **yih** **lāl-shĕnākh.** **Wôt^{u}**
Went-forth this lapidary. He-arrived

tath **jāyĕ.** **Hôwun** **tath** **palas** **wöj^{ü}.**
to-that place. Was-shown-by-him to-that rock the-ring.

Pal **wọth^{u}** **thod^{u}.** **Woth^{u}** **tamiy** **wati**
The-rock arose erect. He-descended by-that-very path

bŏn. **Bŏn** **wuch^{ü}n** **khôtūnā** **akh,**
beneath. Beneath was-seen-by-him a-certain-lady one,

kuñ^{ü}y **züñ^{ü}.** **Ami** **dop^{u}nas,** **"kati**
a-single woman. By-her it-was-said-by-her-to-him, "whence

ôsukh?" Åm^{i} dop^{u}nas, "Lālmāl Par^{i}yi
wast-thou?" By-him it-was-said-by-him-to-her, "By-Lālmāl Fairy

dopuy raṭ^{a}na-kor^{u}." Amis khôtūni
is-asked-from-thee a-jewel-bracelet." To-this lady

pyauv yād. Tåm^{i}-sünz^{ü} möj^{ü} ös^{ü} sa,
fell remembrance. Her mother was she,

yĕs raṭ^{a}na-karis-söty hoṭs^{u} gayāv
of-whom the-jewel-bracelet-with the-forearm went

nīrith. Tas chĕh ük^{u}y nür^{ü}. Tas
going-away. Of-her is one-only arm. Of-her

chuh dôd^{u} pananis dilas. Rāy kür^{ü}
is pain to-her-own heart. Consideration was-made

ami khôtūni, "yāñ myöñ^{ü} möj^{ü}
by-that lady, "as-soon-as my mother

wāti, nĕmis manōshĕs khĕyi." Yih
will-arrive, (to-)this man she-will-eat." He

ôs^{u} sĕṭhāh khōbsūrath. Amis gav
was very beautiful. To-her became

shĕkh dilas, "bŏh kara amis-söty
anxiety to-the-heart, "I will-make this-one-with

nēth^{a}r." Wuñ yĕli māje̮-hond^{u} partawa
marriage." Now when the-mother-of sound-of-approach

pyauv, ath jayĕ gav buñul^{u}. Amis
fell, to-that place there-became an-earthquake. To-him

dyutun shāph. Kor^{u}nas kañi-phol^{u},
was-given-by-her a-charm-word Was-made-by-her-of-him a-pebble,

thôwun	**cĕndas.**	**Wöts^{ü}s**	**möj^{ü}**	**ot^{u}.**
it-was-put-by-her	in-the-pocket.	Arrived-to-her	the-mother	there.

Dop^{u}nas,	**"hatay,**	**kōriy,**	**mĕ**	**chĕh**
It-was-said-by-her-to-her,	"hullo,	O-daughter,	to-me	is

yiwān	**mō̃tsa-bŏy."**	**Yih**	**chĕsna**	**hĕwān-zima**
coming	man-stink."	She	is-to-her-not	admitting

kē̃h.	**Ami**	**yĕli**	**zōr**	**kor^{u}nas,**
anything.	By-her	when	force	was-made-by-her-to-her,

dop^{u}nas,	**"chuh**	**manōsh.**	**T̲s^{a}h**	**dim**
it-was-said-by-her-to-her,	"there-is	a-man.	Thou	give-to-me

gŏḍa	**wāda-y-Khŏdā**	**'bŏh**	**kyāh**	**karas-na**
at-first	a-promise-of-God	'I	verily	will-do-to-him-not

kē̃h.'"	**Wāda-y-Khŏdā**	**dyut^{u}nas.**	**Ami**
anything.'"	Promise-of-God	was-given-by-her-to-her.	By-her

koḍ^{u}	**cĕnda-manza**	**kañi-phol^{u},**	**shāph**
was-brought-forth	the-pocket-from-in	the-pebble,	the-charm

tul^{u}nas,	**manōsh**	**yuthuy**	**ôs^{u},**	**ta**
was-raised-by-her-from-him,	a-man	as (-before)-exactly	he-was,	and

tyuthuy	**rūd^{u}.**	**Dop^{u}nas,**	**"yih**	**chuh**
so-exactly	he-remained.	It-was-said-by-her-to-her,	"this	is

myôn^{u}	**hakh-i-Khŏdāy.**	**Bŏh**	**ös^{ü}san**
my	duty-of-God (i.e. husband as sacred to me as God).	I	was-him

yihuy	**tshāḍān.**	**Yihuy**	**lod^{u}nam,**
this-very-one	seeking.	He-verily	was-sent-by-Him-to-me

mājiy,	**Khŏdāyĕn."**	**Yih**	**chĕs**	**dapān**
O-mother,	by-God."	This	is-to-her	saying

möj^{ü},	**"zabar**	**gav.**	**Bāyĕn**	**dŏn**	**lad**
the-mother,	"excellent	it-is.	To-brothers	two	send

kākad	**amis^{ü}y**	**athi."**	**Dop^{u}nas,**
a-paper	of-this-very-one	by-the-hand."	It-was-said-by-her-to-her,

"mājiy,	**likh**	**ts^{a}y."**	**Lyukh^{u}**	**ami,**
"O-mother,	write	thou-verily,"	Was-written	by-her,

kākad	**dyutun**	**amis**	**lāl-shĕnākas**
the-paper	was-given-by-her	to-that	lapidary

athi.	**Ami**	**kor^{u}nas**	**ālav**	**khôtūni.**
in-the-hand.	By-that	was-made-by-her-to-him	a-call-of-summons	by-the-lady.

Dop^{u}nas,	**"yih**	**an**	**kākad**	**yūr^{i}."**
It-was-said-by-her-to-him,	"this	bring	paper	even-hither."

Wuch^{u}	**ami**	**khôtūni.**	**Ath**	**lyukh^{u}mot^{u}**
It-was-inspected	by-that	lady.	(In)-to-it	(was) written

ȧm^{i}-sanzi	**māji,**	**"chiway**	**myön^{i}**	**gabar,**
by-her	mother,	"ye-are-if	my	sons,

yih	**gatshi**	**wātawunuy**	**mārun^{u}."**
this-person	is-necessary	immediately-on-arrival	to-be-killed."

Amis	**ôs^{u}**	**ami**	**sāta**	**panun^{u}**	**dôd^{u}**
To-her	was	at-that	time	her-own	pain

pĕmot^{u}	**yād**	**suh**	**hatsyuk^{u}.**	**Yih**
fallen	(in) memory	(viz.) that (pain)	of-the-forearm.	This

kākad	**tshun^{u}nas-tsaṭith**	**ami**	**khôtūni.**
paper	was-torn-to-pieces-by-her-for-him	by-that	lady.

Panun^{u}	**lyukh^{u}nas**	**kākad.**	**Ath**	**manz**
Her-own	was-written-by-her-for-him	a-paper.	To-that	in

lyukh^{u}nas,	**"chiway**	**myön^{i}**	**böy^{i},**	**tuhond^{u}**
was-written-by-her-on-it,	"ye-are-if	my	brothers,	of-you

gaʦhi	**jĕl^{a}d**	**yun^{u},**	**mĕ**	**kyāh**	**chuh**
is-necessary	quickly	the-coming,	for-me	verily	is

yĕñĕwôl^{u}."
a-marriage-festival."

16.	**Lyukh^{u}nas**	**kākadas,**	**zaböñ^{ü}**
	Was-written-by-her-on-it	to-(on)-the-paper,	by-word-of-mouth

kür^{ü}nas	**nás^{i}yĕth.**	**Dop^{u}nas,**	**"tot^{u}**	**yĕli**
was-made-by-her-to-him	instruction.	It-was-said-by-her-to-him,	"there	when

wātakh,	**karahakh**	**salām.**	**Salām**	**pölith**
thou-wilt-arrive,	thou-wilt-make-to-them	a-bow.	The-bow	having-fulfilled

dizikh	**kākad.**	**Tim**	**ananay**	**khĕn**
thou-must-give-to-them	the-paper.	They	will-bring-to-thee	food

ʦamruw^{u}	**kara.**	**Tih**	**cyôn^{u}**	**khyon^{u}**
leathern	pease.	That	thy	eating

gaʦhi-na."	**Badal**	**dyut^{u}nas**	**söty**	**as^{a}l**
is-not-proper."	Instead	were-given-by-her-to-him	with (him)	real

kara.	**Dop^{u}nas,**	**"yih**	**khĕzi**	**tati.**
pease.	It-was-said-by-her-to-him	"this	you-must-eat	there.

Tihond^{u}	**tshân^{i}zi**	**bĕbi-andar^{ü}y**	**trövith,**
Their (pease)	you-must-let-fall	your-breast-pocket-within	having-let-go,

panun^{u}	**khĕzi.**	**Tami**	**pata**	**dapanay**
your-own	you-must-eat.	From-that	after	they-will-say-to-thee

tim,	**'kashĕna-hanā**	**karüñ^{u}.'"**	**Tath-kyut^{u}**
they,	'scratching-a-little	is-to-be-done.'"	That-for

dyut^{u}nas	**shĕstruw^{u}**	**panja.**	**Dop^{u}nas,**	**"tim**
was-given-by-her-to-him	an-of-iron	claw.	It-was-said-by-her-to-him,	"they

chih	**dĕwa-zāth.**	**Timan**	**yiyi**	**tasalī**
are (of)	demon-race.	To-them	will-come	a-pleasant-feeling

shĕstravi	**panja-sötiy."**
from-the-of-iron	claw-by-means-of-only."

17.	**Drāv**	**ati**	**nàs^{i}yĕth**	**yād**	**hĕth.**
	He-went-forth	from-there	the-instruction	(in) memory	taking.

Wôt^{u}	**tot^{u},**	**kür^{ü}n**	**timan**	**salām.**
He-arrived	there,	was-made-by-him	to-them	a-bow.

Dyut^{u}nakh	**yih**	**kākad.**	**Amis**	**dyutukh**
Was-given-by-him-to-them	this	paper.	To-him	was-given-by-them

khĕn	**tsamruw^{u}**	**kara.**	**Amyuk^{u}**	**tulān**
food	leathern	pease.	Of-it	raising

chuh	**bus^{u},**	**tshanān**	**chuh**	**bĕbi-andar**
he-is	a-hand-mouthful,	letting-it-fall	he-is	his-breast-pocket-within

trövith.	**Panun^{u}**	**chuh**	**kaḍān**	**ti**	**chuh**
having-let-go.	His-own	he-is	taking-forth	and	is

khĕwān.	**Ami**	**pata**	**dop^{u}has**	**yimau,**
eating.	From-that	after	it-was-said-by-them-to-him	by-them,

"kashĕna-hanā	**kar."**	**Ȧm^{i}**	**koḍ^{u}**	**yih**
"scratching-a-little	do."	By-him	was-brought-forth	this

ťsūri-pöṭh^{i}	**shĕstruw^{u}**	**panja,**	**chukh**
secretly	of-iron	claw,	he-is-to-them

ami-söty	**diwān**	**z^{a}lā-z^{a}lā.**	**Yimaŭ**	**lyukhus**
from-this-by-means-of	giving	a-scraping-a-scraping.	By-them	was-written-to-it

jĕwāb	**ath**	**kākadas.**	**Lyukh^{u}has,**	**"asĕ**
an-answer	to-that	paper.	It-was-written-by-them-on-it,	"to-us

chĕna	**phursath.**	**Hazrat-i-Sulaymān**	**chuh**
is-not	leisure.	His-Highness-Solomon	is

diwān	**nād.**	**Hala!**	**bismillā,**	**kariv**
giving	summons.	Be-quick!	in-the-name-of-God,	make-ye

yĕñĕwôl^{u}."
the-marriage-festival."

18.	**Wôt^{u}**	**ot^{u},**	**hôw^{u}nakh**	**yih**	**kākad.**
	He-arrived	there,	was-shown-by-him-to-them	this	paper.

Kākad	**porukh,**	**korukh**	**amis-söty**
The-paper	was-read-by-them,	was-made-by-them	him-with

yĕñĕwôl^{u}.	**Wuñ**	**chĕh**	**yih**	**khôtūnā**
a-marriage-festival.	Now	is	this	lady

dapān	**amis**	**khāwandas**	**pananis,**	**"yit^{i}**
saying	to-that	husband	her-own,	"here

rōzakha,	**kina**	**dun^{i}yāhas**	**manz**	**gatshakh?**
wilt-thou-remain,	or	to-the-world	in	wilt-thou-go?

Bŏh	**chēs**	**tsĕ**	**töb^{i}yāh."**	**Ȧm^{i}**	**dop^{u}nas,**
I	am	to-thee	an-humble-servant."	By-him	it-was-said-by-him-to-her,

"dun^{i}yāhas-manz	**gatshav."**	**Dop^{u}nas**	**ami**
"the-world-in	we-shall-go."	It-was-said-by-her-to-him	by-that

khôtūni,	**"wuñ**	**yĕli**	**nērav**	**myōñ^{ü}**
lady,	"now	when	we-shall-go-forth	my

möj^{ü}	**dapiy,**	**'kĕntshāh**	**mangum.'**	**Cyôn^{u}**
mother	will-say-to-thee,	'something	ask-for-from-me.'	Of-thee

gatshēs	**mangun^{u}**	**watharanuk^{u}**	**musla.**
is-proper-from-her	to-be-demanded	of-a-spreading-out (i.e. for a mat)	the-skin.

Biyĕ	**kĕh**	**mȧng^{i}zēs-na."**	**Wuñ**	**yĕli**
Other	anything	you-must-demand-from-her-not."	Now	when

yim	**sakharyēy,**	**dopukh**	**ami**	**māji,**
they	made-ready-to-set-out,	it-was-said-to-them	by-that	mother,

"mangun^{u}	**kĕntshāh."**	**Dop^{u}nas,**	**"dim**
"is-to-be-demanded	something."	It-was-said-by-him-to-her,	"give-to-me

watharanuk^{u}	**musla.**	**Tath**	**chuh**	**nāv**
of-spreading-out (i.e. for a mat)	the-skin.	To-it	is	the-name

'wutsha-prang.'"	**Drāv**	**ati,**	**wöt^{i}**	**panun^{u}**
'the-flying-couch.'"	He-went-forth	from-there,	they-arrived	their-own

gara.	**Gara**	**wötith**	**korun**	**tayār**
house.	The-house	having-arrived	was-made-by-her	ready

ṛat^{a}na-kor^{u}.	**Gav**	**hĕth**	**pātashĕhas**	**yih**
a-jewel-bracelet.	Went	taking (it)	to-the-king	this

lāl-shĕnākh.
lapidary.

19.	**Nöyidan**	**būz^{u},**	**"lāl-shĕnākh**	**wôt^{u}."**
	By-the-barber	it-was-heard,	"the-lapidary (has)	arrived."

Gatshān	**chus**	**nöyid**	**gara**	**mast**
going	is-for-him	the-barber	(to) the-house	hair

kāsani.	**Ȧt^{i}**	**wuchān**	**chuh**	**trĕyim^{u}**
to-shave.	Here-verily	seeing	he-is	the-third

khôtūna.	**Drāv**	**ati**	**nöyid**	**pot^{u}**
lady.	Went-forth	from-there	the-barber	back-again

phīrith.	**Wôt^{u}**	**wazīras-nish.**	**Dapān**	**chuh**
returning.	He-arrived	the-vizier-near.	Saying	he-is

amis	**wazīras,**	**"ha**	**wazīra,**	**amis**
to-that	vizier,	"O	Vizier-O,	to-that

lāl-shĕnākas	**chĕh**	**az**	**trĕyim^{u}**	**khôtūna,**
lapidary	is	to-day	a-third	lady,

yiman	**dŏn-handi-khŏta**	**khōbsūrath.**	**Sa**
these	two-than	beautiful.	She

chĕh	**löyik-i-pātashāh,**	**akh**	**chĕh**
is	worthy-of-the-king,	one	is

löyik-i-wazīr,	**byākh**	**chĕh**	**mĕ**	**löyikh.**
worthy-of-the-vizier,	another	is	of-me	worthy.

Amis	**lāl-shĕnākas**	**karta**	**kĕntshāh."**
To-that	lapidary	please-do	something."

Dapān	**chus**	**wazīr,**	**"az**	**wana**	**bŏh**
Saying	is-to-him	the-vizier,	"to-day	I-will-speak	I

pātashĕhas.	**Suy**	**pātashāh**	**kari**	**amis**
to-the-king.	That-very	king	will-do	to-him

kĕntshāh	**wöridāth.**	**Suh**	**mari,**	**zanāna**
some	occurrence (i.e. device).	He	will-die,	the-women

trĕh	**nimav**	**às^{i}."**	**Dop^{u}**	**wazīran**
three	we-shall-take	we."	It-was-said	by-the-vizier

pātashĕhas,	**"pātashĕham,**	**amis**	**lāl-shĕnākas**
to-the-king,	"my-king,	to-that	lapidary

chĕh	**zanāna**	**trĕh,**	**titsha**	**chĕna**
are	women	three,	such (women)	are-not

pātashöhī-manz.	**Pātashĕham,**	**tamis**
the-kingdom-in.	My-king,	to-that

lāl-shĕnākas	**raṭhta**	**kĕntshāh**	**nŏkhta.**
lapidary	please-seize	some	point (i.e. fault).

Suh	**gotsh^{u}**	**galun^{u}.**	**Tima**	**zanāna**	**trĕh**
He	was-proper	to-be-destroyed.	Those	women	three

karuhukh	**dökhil-i-mahala-khāna."**	**Pātashĕhan**
make-thou-them	entered-of-the-private-apartments-of-the-palace."	By-the-king

kür^{ü}	**phikirāh.**	**Dopun,**	**"mangahas**
was-made	a-thinking.	It-was-said-by-him,	"(If) thou-wilt-

kĕntshāh	**cīz,**	**tih**	**chuh**	**anāṇ**	**sôruy.**
any	thing,	that	he-is	bringing	all-even.

Wuñ	**dapas**	**bŏh,**	**'myönis**	**möl^{i}-sünz^{ü}**
Now	I-will-say-to-him	I,	'my	father-of

khabar	**gatshi**	**anüñ^{ü},**	**suh**	**chwā**
news	is-proper	to-be-brought,	he	is-he-?

jĕnatas	**kina**	**dōzakas.' "**
in-heaven	or	in-hell.' "

20. Dapān wustād,—
(Is) saying the-teacher,—

Āv	**lāl-shĕnakh,**	**pātashĕhas,**	**kür^{ü}n**
Came	the-lapidary,	to-the-king,	was-made-by-him

salām.	**Pātashāh**	**chus**	**dapān,**	**"az-tāñ**
a-bow.	The-king	is-to-him	saying,	"today-up-to

yih	**mĕ**	**won^{u}may,**	**tih**	**būzuth**	**tsĕ.**
what	by-me	was-said-by-me-to-thee,	that	was-heard-by-thee	by-thee.

Az	**gatshi**	**myönis**	**möl^{i}-sünz^{ü}**	**khabar**
Today	is-proper	my	father-of	news

anüñ^{ü},	**suh**	**chwā**	**jĕnatas-manz**	**kina**
to-be-brought,	he	is-he-?	heaven-in	or

dōzakas."	**Drāv**	**lāl-shĕnākh,**	**wôt^{u}**	**panun^{u}**
hell-(in)."	Went-forth	the-lapidary,	he-arrived	his-own

gara.	**Dapān**	**chuh**	**ȧt^{i}**	**yiman**	**zanānan**
house.	Saying	he-is	there	to-these	women

trĕn,	**"az**	**chum**	**dapān**	**pātashāh,**
three.	"today	is-to-me	saying	the-king

'myönis möl^{i}-sünz^{ü} khabar anüñ^{ü}.' Bŏh
'my father-of news (is) to-be-brought.' I

kyāh kara? Ath sŏh chyā khabar,
what shall-do? Of-that that is-there-? news,

kötyāh warihy gamàt^{i} tas mumatis?"
how-many years (are) gone to-him dead?"

Yih wŏtsh^{ü}s khôtūna. Yihai yih,
This arose (-in-reply)-to-him lady. She-verily (was) she,

yĕsa ratˌ^{a}na-kàr^{i} ös^{ü} karān. Sa ös^{ü}
who jewel-bracelets was making. She was

parī bā-Khŏdā. Ami dop^{u}nas, "kĕntshāh
a-fairy (who-obeyed-) God. By-her it-was-said-by-her-to-him, "any

chĕna phikir^{ü}. Gatsh, hĕs khar^{a}j,
is-not anxiety. Go, take-from-him expenses,

biyĕ dapus pātashĕhas, 'cyôn^{u} gatshi
also say-to-him to-the-king, 'of-thee is-proper

zyun^{u} sọmb^{a}run^{u}; mödānas-manz zyun^{u}
firewood to-be-collected; the-plain-in firewood

gatshi sọmb^{a}run^{u} bĕ-shumār."
is-proper to-be-collected countless.'"

21. **Sọmb^{a}rôw^{u} pātashĕhan zyun^{u}**
Was-collected by-the-king firewood

bĕ-shumār. Ath-pĕṭh khot^{u} yih lāl-shĕnākh
countless. It-on mounted this lapidary

yih musla-han watharith. Ath^{i}-pĕṭh
this the-piece-of-skin spreading-out It-verily-on

byūṭh^{u} pāna. Amis dopun pātashĕhas,
sat he-himself. To-him was-said-by-him to-the-king,

"tsĕ kyāh gatshiy anun^{u} möl^{i}-sond^{u}
"to-thee what is-proper-to-thee to-be-brought father-of

nishāna?" Yih wọthus pātashĕh,
token?" This arose (in-reply)-to-him king,

dop^{u}nas "akh gatshiy anun^{u}
it-was-said-by-him-to-him "one is-proper-for-thee to-be-brought

jĕnatuk^{u} mĕwa, biyĕ gatshiy anun^{u}
of-heaven a-fruit, second is-proper-for-thee to-be-brought

myönis möl^{i}-sandi daskhata khath."
my father of with-signature a-letter."

Dopun yiman, "diyiv yith zinis nār
It-was-said-by-him to-them, "give-ye to-this firewood fire

tsöpör^{i}."
on-the-four-sides."

22. Dapān wustād,—
(Is) saying the-teacher,—

Yimau yĕli ath zinis nār dyut^{u},
By-them when to-this firewood fire was-given,

yiwān chuna kuni bōzana yih
coming (passive) is-not at-all in-possibility-of-seeing (passive) this

lāl-shĕnakh. Lāl-shĕnākan dyut^{u} ath
lapidary. By-the-lapidary was-given to-that

muslas	**kas^{a}m.**	**Dop^{u}nas,**	**“mě**	**gatshi**
leather	a-charm.	It-was-said-by-him-to-it.	“for-me	it-is-proper

wātun^{u}	**panun^{u}**	**gara.**	**Kā̃h**	**gatshěm-na**
to-arrive	my-own	house.	Anyone	is-proper-for-me-not

ḍēshun^{u}.”	**Ṭuvyēyě**	**ȧm^{i}**	**lāl-shěnākan**
to-be-seen.”	Were-closed	by-that	lapidary

achě.	**Mutsarěn,**	**ta**	**wôt^{u}mot^{u}**	**gara**
the-eyes.	They-were-opened-by-him	and	(he-was) arrived	house

panun^{u}.	**Ami**	**khôtūni**	**kür^{ü}**	**köm^{ü}.**
his-own.	By-that	lady	was-done	an-act.

Hab-jūshī	**korun**	**měwa**	**jěnatuk^{u}**	**dön^{ü}**
Of-the-seven-metals	was-made-by-her	a-fruit	of-heaven	a-pomegranate

tayār,	**biyě**	**lyukhun**	**khath,**	**ath**
prepared,	also	was-written-by-her	a-letter,	to-it

korun	**amis**	**pātashěha-sandis**	**möl^{i}-sond^{u}**
was-made-by-her	that	king's	father-of

daskhath,	**biyě**	**mŏhar.**	**Ath^{i}-manz**
signature,	also	seal.	It-verily-in

lyukhun	**pātashěhas,**	**“cyôn^{u}**	**gatshi**
was-written-by-her	to-the-king,	“of-thee	it-is-proper

mě-nish	**wātun^{u},**	**wazīr**	**hěth,**	**biyě**
me-near	to-arrive,	vizier	having-taken,	also

nöyid	**hěth,**	**tithay**	**pöṭh^{i},**	**yěthay**
the-barber	having-taken,	in-that-very-kind-of	manner,	in-what-very-kind-of

pöṭh^{i}	**lāl-shĕnākh**	**mĕ-nish**	**wôt^{u}."**	**Kākad**
manner	the-lapidary	me-near	arrived."	The-paper

korun	**hawāla**	**amis**	**lāl-shĕnākas,**	**biyĕ**
was-made-by-her	in-charge	to-that	lapidary,	also

dyut^{u}nas	**athas-kĕth**	**yih**	**dön^{ü}.**
was-given-by-her-to-him	the-hand-in	this	pomegranate.

23.

Ŏtāñy	**gay**	**tsōr**	**dŏh.**	**Yih**	**nār**
There-verily	went	four	days.	This	fire

gŏmot^{u}	**tshĕta,**	**path**	**rūd^{u}mot^{u}**	**sūr.**
(was) become	extinguished,	behind	(was) remained	ash.

Yih	**lāl-shĕnākh**	**drāv**	**langūṭ^{i}**	**karith.**
This	lapidary	came-forth	langōṭī	having-made (i.e. having-put-on).

Suli	**wŏṭh^{u},**	**ath**	**sūras-manz**	**diwān**
At-dawn	he-arose,	that	ash-in	giving

chuh	**ḍulàn^{i}.**	**Nazarbāzav**	**kür^{ü}**	**nazar,**
he-is	rollings.	By-the-inspectors	was-made	inspection,

khabardārav	**niyĕ**	**khabar.**	**Dop^{u}has,**
by-the-informers	was-brought	information.	It-was-said-by-them-to-him,

"pātashĕham,	**ami**	**sūra-manza**	**gatshān**	**chĕh**
"my-king,	that	ash-from-in	going	is

susarāray.	**Yih**	**mā**	**āsi**	**lāl-shĕnākh**
a-rustling.	This,	I-wonder-if	will-be	the-lapidary

āmot^{u} ?"	**Yim**	**chih**	**yimay**	**katha**	**karān,**
come ?"	They	are	these-very	words	making,

nazar	**chĕkh**	**ō-kun,**	**āv**	**wōḍa**

lāl-shĕnākh, athas-kĕth hĕth dön^{ü},
the-lapidary, the-hand-in taking the-pomegranate,

biyis athas-kĕth hĕth khath. Kür^{ü}n
the-other hand-in taking the-letter. Was-made by-him

pātashĕhas salām, dön^{ü} thôw^{u}nas
to-the-king a-bow, the-pomegranate was-placed-by-him-of-him

bōnṭha-kani, khath thôw^{u}nas bōnṭha-kani.
in-front, the-letter was-placed-by-him-of-him in-front.

Yih khath mutsorun, porun. Ath
This letter was-opened-by-him, it-was-read-by-him. (In-) it

lyukh^{u}mot^{u}, "bŏh, kyā, chus jĕnatas-manz.
(was) written, "I, of-a-surety, am heaven-in.

Cyôn^{u} gatshi wātun^{u} yūr^{i}, wazīr
Of-thee is-proper to-arrive here-even, the-vizier

hĕth, biyĕ nöyid hĕth, jĕl^{a}d."
taking, also the-barber taking, quickly."

24. Pātashāh chuh karān phikirāh,
The-king is making a-thinking,

"mĕ dapyāv, 'yih lāl-shĕnākh gali.'
"by-me it-was-long-ago-said, 'this lapidary will-be-destroyed.'

Yih āv möl^{i}-sünz^{ü} mĕ khabar hĕth."
He came the-father-of to-me news taking."

Dapān pātashāh amis lāl-shĕnākas,
(Is) saying the-king to-that lapidary,

"bŏh kĕtha-pöṭh^{i} wāta tath jĕnatas-manz?"
"I how shall-arrive to-that heaven-in?"

Dop^{u}nas lāl-shĕnākan, "yuth^{u} zyun^{u}
It-was-said-by-him-to-him by-the-lapidary, "as firewood

mĕ-kyut^{u} sọ̆mb^{a}rôwuth, tithiy trĕh
me-for was-collected-by-thee, so-even three (times)

gatshan sọ̆mb^{a}rāwạn^{i}; jĕl^{a}d wātakh
are-proper to-be-collected; quickly thou-wilt-arrive

jĕnatas-manz." Sọ̆mb^{a}rôw^{u} pātashĕhan zyun^{u}
heaven-in." Was-collected by-the-king firewood

bĕ-shumār. Ath^{i}-pĕṭh karanôwun watharun^{u},
countless. It-verily-on was-caused-to-be-made a-mat,

ath^{i}-pĕṭh khot^{u} pāna biyĕ wazīr biyĕ
it-verily-on he-mounted himself also the-vizier also

nöyid. Dyutukh zinis nār tsöpör^{i}.
the-barber. Was-given-by-them to-the-firewood fire on-the-four-sides.

25. Dapān wustād,—
(Is) saying the-teacher,—

Dod^{u} yih pātashāh, biyĕ wazīr,
Was-burnt-up this king, also the-vizier,

biyĕ nöyid, trĕnaway gạl^{i}. Wôt^{u} ot^{u}
also the-barber, the-three were-destroyed. Arrived there

lāl-shĕnākas-nish suh wazīr, yus wazīr
the-lapidary-near that vizier, which vizier

pātashĕh-kūr^{ü} hĕth ôs^{u} tsalān, ta
the-king's-daughter taking was fleeing, and

samokhukh ôkhun-koṭ^{u}, suy wôt^{u}
was-met-by-them the-religious-teacher's-son he-verily arrived

amis	**lāl-shĕnāka-sond^{u}**	**gara.**	**Pānawöñ**
to-that	lapidary's	house.	Mutually

karĕkh	**katha-bātha.**	**Wonus**	**ȧm^{i}**
were-made-by-them	conversations.	It-was-said-to-him	by that

lāl-shĕnākan	**yih**	**panun^{u}**	**saphar,**
lapidary	this	his-own	travelling (i.e. experiences of his journey),

yus	**ȧm^{i}**	**nöyidan**	**ta**	**wazīran**	**amis**
which	by-that	barber	and	by-the-vizier	to-him

ôs^{u}	**pēsh**	**on^{u}mot^{u}.**	**Dop^{u}nas,**	**"panüñ^{ü}**
was	in-front	brought.	It-was-said-by-him-to-him,	"thine-own

khôtūna	**nin-sa**	**pānas."**	**Yĕsa**	**yih**
lady	take-her-sir	for thyself."	Who	this

Lālmāl	**Parī**	**ös^{ü},**	**tas**	**dyutun**	**rukhsath.**
Lālmāl	Fairy	was,	to-her	was-given-by-him	leave-to-depart.

Yĕsa	**yih**	**pata**	**üñ^{ü}n**	**zīnith,**	**sa**
Who	this	afterwards	was-brought-by-him	having-conquered,	she

th̆ôwun	**pānas.**
was-kept-by-him	for-him-self.

26. **Dapān wustād,—**
(Is) saying the-teacher,—

Suh	**wazīr**	**byūṭh^{u}**	**pātashöhī**	**karani.**
That	vizier	sat	sovereignty	to-do.

Lāl-shĕnākh	**byūṭh^{u}**	**wazīrī**	**karani.**
The-lapidary	sat	viziership	to-do.

Aslāmalaikum,	**wālaikum**	**salām.**
The-peace-be-upon-you,	and-upon-you	be-peace.

VOCABULARY OF ALL THE WORDS IN GŌVINDA KAULA'S TEXT

[*Roman numerals refer to the number of the story, and Arabic numerals to the section. To save space, when several Arabic numerals come together, tens are generally not repeated. Thus, xii, 21, 6, means xii, 21, 26. The order of words is based on the alphabetical order of the consonants, without any regard to the vowels. The latter come into consideration only in cases in which the same consonant or consonants are followed or separated by different vowels. Thus, the different words containing the consonants* kn *will be found in the succession* kan, kăn[i], kani, kina, kōna, kun, kuni, *and* kun[u]. *All words beginning with vowels are arranged together at the commencement of the Vocabulary, their mutual order being determined by their consonants. The letter ñ follows n, and ts follows t. For purposes of alphabetical order v and w are counted as the same letter. In other respects the alphabetical order is that of the English alphabet.*]

a, ĕ, interrog. suff.; *gatshiyĕ,* is it proper? xii, 13; *sapadakha,* wilt thou become? iii, 2; *tagiyĕ,* will it be possible for thee? v, 8, 9; *tsaṭanasa,* will they cut off for him? v, 7.

ā, interrog. suff.; *chwā,* is he? xii, 21.

ā, suff. of indef. art., see *āh.*

ĕ, i, y, iẓāfat; *dukhtar-ĕ-khāsa,* (your) own daughter, v, 11; *khal[a]t-ĕ-shōhī,* robe of royalty, x, 4 (bis); *lŏyik-ĕ-pātashāh,* worthy of a king, x, 4; *pēsh-ĕ-pātashāh,* before the king, vi, 9; *söhib-ĕ-āgāh,* master intelligent, ii, 9; *shĕhar-ĕ-Yīrān,* the country of Persia, ii, 1; *tōrīph-ĕ-Yūsūph,* praise of Yūsuf, vi, 17; *Azīz-i-Misar,* N.P., vi, 10, 2 (bis), 4; *dōkhil-i-mahalakhāna,* brought into the harem, xii, 19; *dīn-i-Mahmad,* the faith of Muḥammad, iv, 6; *hakh-i-Khŏdāy,* duty due to God, xii, 15; *hukm-i-Māhrāj,* order of the Mahārāja, xi, 4; *hĕkmat-i-Parwardigār,* the power of Providence, i, 11; *kōh-i-Tōra,* Mount Sinai, iv, 5; *lŏyik-i,* worthy of, xii, 10, 19 (bis); *maḳhᵃr-i-zan*, coquetry of a woman, x, 13; *söhib-i-kitāb*, a master of books, x, 13; *wŏlād-i-Ādam*, a descendant of Adam, iv, 3; *yād-i-Alāh*, memory of God, i, 7; *dwā-yi-khör*, a prayer for welfare, i, 3; *hawā-yi-asmān*, the air of heaven, ii, 6; *hawāla-y-Khŏdā*, in the care of God, x, 7; *wāda-y-Khŏdā*, an oath by God, xii, 7 (bis), 15 (bis); irregular use, *hazrat-i-Ādam*, and so on, iv, 2, etc.; *hazrat-i-Sulaymān*, his highness Solomon, xii, 17; *hazrat-i-Yūsūph*, etc., his highness Yūsuf, etc., vi, 8, etc.; *Shāh-i-Yūsūph*, id., vi, 1; *Sultān-i-Mahmōd-i-Gaznavī*, Sulṭān Maḥmūd of Ghaznī, i, 1; *Marāz-i-Pargan*, the Pargana of Marâz, xi, 5.

ī, interj.; *vĕsī*, O female friend, ix, 1; cf. *ⁱyih*.

ō 1, and; *arz ō samā*, earth and heaven, vii, 26.

ō 2, in *ō-kun*, in that direction, xii, 23.

āb, m. water, v, 4; v, 4 (bis); vii, 7 (bis); *-dawa-kañ*, (enter) through the water-drain, v, 4; *āba-hanā*, f. a little water, x, 5; *-pyāla*, water-cup, vii, 7; *-srĕhā*, water-moisture, viii, 7; *ābas*, to the water, viii, 7.

abtar, terrified, vi, 12.

achⁱ, f. an eye; pl. nom. *ṭuvyēyĕ achĕ*, the eyes were closed, xii, 22; dat. *achĕn, diwān chuh achĕn dᵘh*, he is putting smoke in her eyes, i.e. he is abusing her, v, 11.

aḍ, in *aḍa-wati*, midway, vii, 20.

ada, then, iii, 1; v, 6, 9 (bis); viii, 3, 10; x, 2, 7; xii, 3; afterwards, viii, 10, 13; introducing apodosis of a conditional sentence, v, 8; *-kyāh*, then of course, of course, certainly, viii, 11; xii, 4.

ādā, m. completion; — *gatshun*, (of a period of time) to be completed, to come to an end, to elapse, pass, x, 8; xii, 4, 9, 11, 2.

oḍᵘ, half; f. pl. *ajĕ*, half, i.e. some, xi, 7.

adal, m. justice; *adᵃla söty*, by means of justice, i, 3.

adālath, f. a court of justice; *adālütsᵘ-pĕṭh*, (went) to the court of justice, v, 9.

Ādam, m. N.P., Adam, iv, 2, 3; vii, 6, 7; sg. dat. *ādamas-söty*, together with A., vii, 6.

āga, m. a master ; sg. dat. *āgas-pĕṭh*, (infidelity) to a master, viii, 6, 8, 11.

āgē (Hindī), ahead, in front, xi, 4.

āgāh, *söhib-ĕ-āgāh*, an intelligent master, ii, 9.

agar, if, viii, 13.

āgur, m. source (of a stream), viii, 7.

āgay, f. information ; *āgayi*, for inspection, v, 7.

āh 1, *ā*, suff. of indefinite art. ; *dŏhā dŏhā*, each day, every day, viii, 3 ; *dalīlā*, a story, viii, 6, 8, 11 ; x, 1 (bis) ; *hakīmā*, a single wise man, vi, 13 ; *hātshā*, an accusation, vi, 9 ; *kĕ̃h kālā* (v, 10), or *kĕ̃h kālāh* (viii, 2), some short time (elapsed) ; *mödānā*, a plain, x, 5 ; *pardā*, a veil, vi, 4 ; *pātashāhā*, a certain king, viii, 1 ; *sōdāgārā*, a merchant, viii, 9 ; *shĕhmārā*, a python, viii, 7 ; *shĕharā*, a city, v, 1 ; *shĕkhtsā*, a person, x, 1 ; *āba-srĕhā*, a water moisture, a trickle of water, viii, 7 ; *sāthā*, (sit, wait) a moment, vi, 3 ; vii, 9 ; *thūñ^{u}ā*, a (piece of) fresh butter, ix, 4 ; *z^{a}lā z^{a}lā*, a scratch a scratch, a continuous scratching, xii, 17 ; *zanānā*, a woman, x, 5 ; xii, 4, 10 ; *ziyāphathā*, a dish of food, x, 5 ; *akhāh*, a certain person, v, 7 ; *yus akhāh*, whoever, viii, 6, 8, 11 ; *ankāh*, a rara avis, ii, 2, etc., see *ankā* ; *hānzāh*, a boatman, i, 4 ; *köm^{u}āh*, a deed, x, 2, 3 ; *kuṭh^{u}āh*, a room, ix, 4 ; *kötyāh*, how many a ! ix, 5, 11 ; xii, 29 ; *marhabāh*, a wish of good luck, ii, 10 ; *nĕcyuvāh*, a son, v, 2 ; *nazarāh*, a glance, viii, 11 ; *phakīrāh*, a faqīr, ii, 1 (bis) ; *photawāh*, a decree, ii, 7 ; *pātashĕhāh*, a king, ii, 1 ; *phikirāh*, a thought, xii, 19, 24 ; *rāthāh*, a night, xii, 5 ; *sadāh*, a sound, viii, 9 ; *sölāh*, an excursion, ii, 2 ; *sāthāh*, for a short time, ii, 4 ; *töb^{i}yāh*, an humble servant (fem.), xii, 18 ; *wuchunāh*, a look, viii, 3 ; *wārayāh kālāh*, a long time (elapsed), viii, 2 ; *wārayāh kāl*, for a long time, viii, 2 ; *wustādāh*, a teacher, i, 13 ; *vyūr^{u}āh*, a little nectar, ix, 2 ; *yĕḍāh*, a belly, ix, 7 ; *zālāh*, a net, i, 6, 7, 8 ; *zanānāh*, a woman, iii, 4.

Followed by *akh*, *ôkhūnā akh*, a certain religious teacher, xii, i ; *balāyā akh*, an evil thing, x, 8 ; *dŏhā akh*, one day, xii, 1 ; *hānzāh akh*, a certain fisherman, i, 4 ; *dānāh wazīran ȧk^i*, by a certain wise vizier, viii, 1 ; *khôtūnā akh*, a certain lady, v, 11 ; xii, 15 ; *phakīrā akh*, a certain faqīr, x, 7 ;

pātashĕhā akh, a certain king, viii, 7, 11; *sōdāgārā akh*, a certain merchant, viii, 9; *shĕharā akh*, a certain city, v, 1; *shĕkhtsāh akh*, a certain person, xii, 3; *zanānā akh*, a certain woman, x, 5.

āh 2, m. a sigh, iv, 3; pl. nom. *āh*, i, 5.

ahᵃd, m. lifetime, time; abl. sg. with emph. *y*, *ahᵃday*, i, 2.

Ahmad, m. N.P., Aḥmad.

ahan-gār, m. a blacksmith; pl. dat. *ahan-gārān*, m.c. for *-gāran*, xi, 16.

ạjᵃdāh, m. a python, a boa-constrictor, x, 11 (ter); sg. dat. *ạjᵃdāhas* (in sense of acc.), x, 7.

okᵘ, one, a, a certain; with emph. *y*, masc. *okuy*, one only, xii, 13; fem. *ükᵘy*, one only, xii, 15; ag.sg.masc. subst. *ȧkⁱ*, by one (sc. son); adj. *phakīran ȧkⁱ*, by a certain faqīr, x, 12; *dānāh wazīran ȧkⁱ*, by a certain wise Vizier, viii, 1; sg. abl. masc. *aki dŏha*, on a certain day, one day, v, 1; *dŏha aki*, id. ii, 8; iii, 1; v, 1; viii, 1, 3 (bis), 7, 11; sing. dat. masc. subst. *akis*, v, 6; vi, 11; adj. *bāgas akis manz*, in a certain garden, iii, 7; *mŏhara hatas akis roshᵘ*, a necklace of one hundred mohars, v, 10; *mödānas akis manz*, in a certain plain, iii, 1; viii, 9; *nāgas akis pĕṭh*, on a certain spring, iii, 4; *phakīras akis*, for a certain faqīr, iii, 1; *pātashĕhas akis nish*, (arrived) near a certain king, viii, 5; *shĕharas akis manz*, (arrived) at a certain city, xii, 2; *wanas akis manz*, in a certain forest, ix, 1; fem. *akis jāyĕ manz*, into a certain place, iii, 7; *jāyĕ akis*, in (at) a certain place, ii, 8; viii, 7 (ter), 9; *jāyĕ akis . . . jāyĕ akis*, in one place . . . in another place, i, 3, 4; *kŏli akis pĕṭh*, (went) to the bank of a certain stream, xii, 2.

akh, one, a, a certain one, a certain. In these tales, when used as an indefinite article, it follows the noun with which it is in agreement, as in *ôkhunā akh*, a certain religious teacher, xii, 1; *balāyā akh*, an evil thing, x, 8; *dŏhā akh*, one day, xii, 1; *hānzāh akh*, a certain fisherman, i, 4; *khôtūnā akh*, a certain lady, v, 11; xii, 15; *phakīrā akh*, a certain faqīr, x, 7; *pātashĕhā akh*, a certain king, viii, 7, 11; *sōgādārā akh*, a certain merchant, viii, 9; *shĕhar akh*, a certain city, ii, 1; *shĕharā akh*, a certain city, v, 1; *shĕkhtsāh akh*, a certain person, xii, 3; *zanānā akh*, a certain woman, x, 5. It will be observed that, except in one instance (ii, 1), the suffix *ā* or *āh* of the indefinite article is always added to the noun.

When used as a definite numeral the word precedes the noun in the one instance occurring in these tales, viz. *akh kath*, one word, xii, 1. So also when opposed to "other" in the following: *akh . . . bēkh* (or *byākh*), the one . . . the other, viii, 14; xii, 3, 10, 19; *akh . . . biyĕ*, in the first place . . . in the second place, v, 9; vi, 15; xii, 1, 21.

With suffix of the indefinite article, *akhāh*, a certain person, v, 1; *yus akhāh*, whoever, viii, 6, 8, 11.

ākh, *ākhō*, see *yun*ᵘ.

ôkhun, m. a religious teacher, a doctor of divinity, xii, 1; with suff. of indef. art., *ôkhunā akh*, a certain religious teacher, xii, 1; *ôkhun-koṭ*ᵘ, the son of a r.t., xii, 25; *-zāda*, id., xii, 2; sg. dat. *-zādas nish*, (came) to the r.t.'s son, xii, 2.

akith, on one side; *nāgas akith kun*, on one side of the spring, xii, 14.

*ôl*ᵘ, m. a bird's nest, viii, 1; sg. dat. *ölis*, viii, 1.

A̱lāh, m. God, i, 7; ii, 12.

alīl, wretched, miserable, poverty-stricken, i, 4.

ālam, m. the world, the universe, i, 13; iv, 3.

*öl*ⁱ*-nāsh*, m. destruction of house and home, ix, 3.

ālav, m. a call, a cry; *—karun*, to call out (to a person), x, 5 (bis), 12 (bis); xii, 7, 15.

alvidāh (= *al-widā'*), m. — *karun*, to make a last farewell, vii, 16.

ām, etc., see *yun*ᵘ.

*ôm*ᵘ, raw, uncooked; masc. pl. nom., *öm*ⁱ, xi, 11.

*amôb*ᵘ, very, excessively, xi, 18.

amānath, m., a deposit in trust, x, 12; *—thāwun*, to place as a deposit, to put in deposit, x, 12.

āmpa, f. pl., the feeding of one bird by another, beak to beak; *-kani*, by means of this method of feeding, viii, 1.

amār, m. desire, longing, v, 2.

*āmot*ᵘ, *āmüts*ᵘ, see *yun*ᵘ.

öna, *aina*, m. a mirror, v, 4 (ter).

unᵘ, sign of gen., generally used with persons, but used with *ạshᵉkh* (*ạshᵉkunᵘ*), love, v, 2, 3, 10.

and, m., end, extremity; *andas-kun*, at the end, at the extremity, xii, 6; *wôtᵘ shĕharas and-kun*, he arrived at the outskirts of the city.

andar, adv. within, iii, 8 (ter); postpos. governing dat., within, in, i, 13; xii, 17; *andarᵘy*, id., xii, 16.

ankā (= *'anqā*), m. a phœnix, a rara avis, something very rare; with suff. of indef. art. *ankāh*, ii, 2 (bis), 3, 4 (ter), 5, 6, 7, 10, 12.

anun, to bring, to fetch, ii, 8, 11, 12; iii, 1, 5, 9; v, 4, 8, 9; vi, 15, 16; viii, 4, 9; ix, 2; x, 5, 10, 12; xi, 10; xii, 4, 5, 10, 11, 15, 16, 19, 20, 21; to bring, to call, summon, viii, 1; *anun nād dith*, having called to bring, to summon, send for, x, 12; *pēsh anun*, to bring before (a person); to cause (him) to experience, to subject (him) to, xii, 25; *anun zīnith* (xii, 25) or *anun zēnān* (xi, 1, 2, etc.), to conquer and carry off, to conquer and appropriate to oneself; *anith dyunᵘ*, to bring and give, to bring to a person, xii, 4 (bis).

inf. of purpose, *anani*, x, v; fut. pass. part. with *gatshun* 1, *anun*, v, 4; *anunᵘ*, xii, 21 (ter); fem. *anüñü*, x, 5; xii, 19, 20 (bis); conj. part. *anith*, iii, 1: xii, 4 (bis).

pres. part., forming pres. *anān chuh*, x, 12; *chuh anān*, xii, 19.

1 past part. forming past, *onᵘ*, fem. *üñᵘ*; m. sg. with suff. 3 sg. ag. *onun*, iii, 5; viii, 9 (bis) 12, 4; with suff. 3 pl. ag. *onukh*, ii, 11, 12; vi, 15, 16; x, 12; with ditto and suff. 3 sg. dat. *onᵘhas*, vi, 16; m. pl. with suff. 3 pl. ag. *ȧnikh*, v, 9; viii, 1; x, 12 (bis); *ȧnⁱhay* (poet.), xi, 10; f. sg. with suff. 2 sg. ag. and 2 sg. nom. *üñᵘthas*, xii, 11; with suff. 3 sg. ag. *üñᵘn*, x, 10; xii, 25; with suff. 3 pl. ag. *üñᵘkh*, ii, 8; f. pl. with suff. 2 sg. dat. *añĕy*, viii, 4; with suff. 3 pl. ag. and 3 sg. dat. *añĕhas*, vi, 16; perf. part. *onᵘmotᵘ*; m. pl. *ȧnⁱmȧtⁱ*, v, 8 (for plup.); m. sg. forming plup. m. sg. 3 *ósᵘ onᵘmotᵘ*, xii, 25; 2 past part. *añāv*, forming 2 past, with suff. 1 sg. ag. *añām*, ix, 2.

fut. sg. 1 *ana*, x, 5; interrog. *ana*, xii, 4, 5, 11; pl. 1, with suff. 3 sg. acc. *anōn*, xi, 1, etc.; pl. 3, with suff. 2 sg. dat. *ananay*, xii, 16.

impve. sg. 2, *an*, iii, 5, 9 (bis); xii, 10, 15; with suff. 3 sg. acc. *anun*, iii, 5, 9; with suff. 3 pl. acc. *anukh*, x, 12; 2 pl. with suff. 1 sg. dat. *anyūm*, vi, 16 (bis); with suff. 3 pl. acc. *anyūkh*, x, 12.

āñ, yes, x, 5, 12.

apör[i], in that direction, v, 4; *-kin*[i], from on that side, v, 7. Cf. *yipör*[i].

apsar, m. an officer; sg. dat. *apsaras*, x, 12.

apoz[u], untrue, v, 9.

ār, m. pity; *āy-nā ār*, did not pity come to thee? ix, 3; *yiman āv ār myôn*[u], pity for me came to them, x, 12.

ōr, there; *ōra*, from there, thence, v, 2, 4; xii, 4, 12; from there, equivalent to "from some unnamed place", v, 9; from there, thereupon, then (opposed to *yōra*), v, 8; *ōra-kani*, in that direction, v, 2. Cf. *wōḍa*.

ör[ü], f. a shoemaker's awl, xi, 14.

arām, m. repose; — *karun*, to repose, v, 9; — *trāwun*, to repose, go to bed, lie down (on a bed), take rest, iii, 3, 7; viii, 5; sg. dat. *arāmas*, at rest, sleeping, viii, 13.

armān, m. longing; — *āv*, longing came, iii, 9.

arz-ō-samā f. (= *arẓ o samā*) earth and heaven, vii, 26.

ās, see *yun*[u].

ös, m. the mouth; *ösa-kani* (issuing) from the mouth, viii, 7; *chis ös*[u]*s harān* (rubies) are dropping from her mouth, xii, 9.

ạshkh, m. lo ve, v, 2 (bis); *ạsh*[ĕ]*ka chīh*, a particle of love, vii, 30; sg. gen. *ạsh*[ĕ]*kun*[u] (not *ạsh*[ĕ]*kuk*[u]), v, 3, 10; do. f. dat. *ạsh*[ĕ]*kañĕ*, v, 2.

āsh[ĕ]*nāv*, m. a near relation, x, 1, 6, 10.

as[a]*l*, real, ii, 8, 11; xii, 16.

aslāmalaikum (= *as-salām 'alaikum*), the peace be upon you, xii, 26.

asmān, m. heaven, ii, 6; pl. dat. *asmānan pĕṭh*, on the heavens, iv, 4; pl. abl. *asmānav pĕṭh*[i], above the heavens, iii, 8.

āsun, conj. 2, to be, to exist (as a verb subst.), i, 3; ix, 2; ii, 1, 4, 7, 8, 9, 10; iii, 7; v, 1, 9, 10; vi, 10, 11; vii, 7, 8, 10;

viii, 1 (bis), 3, 5, 7 (bis), 9, 11 (ter), 13 (bis); x, 1, 5 (bis), 7 (bis); xi, 7 (bis); xii, 1, 2, 4, 11, 15 (ter), 20, 25; to become, i, 3; ix, 2; xii, 15. Often used with dat. of possession, *phakīras ôsᵘ*, the faqīr had, ii, 4; *amis ôsᵘ*, he had, ii, 5; vi, 10; x, 4; *ôsᵘ amis*, he had, ii, 5; *ösᵘs*, he had (a wife), iii, 1; *ôsum*, I had, vii, 11, 15; *ôsus*, he had, viii, 7, 9; *ābas āsinā*, has not the water? viii, 7; *tamis ôsᵘ*, he had, viii, 9; *amis ösⁱ*, he had (sons), viii, 11; *tamisᵘy ösⁱ*, he had (sons), xii, 1.

inf. *āsunᵘ*, xii, 4; sg. dat. *āsanas*, for existence (of wealth), i.e. when wealth exists, x, 1 (bis), 6, 10; fut. pass. part. m. sg. *āsun*, xii, 10 (bis); *āsunᵘ*, xii, 4 (bis), 5, 13 (ter); with emph. *y*, *āsunuy*, i, 12 (v.l.); pl. *āsànⁱ*, xii, 5.

past sg. masc. *ôsᵘ*, was, ii, 4, 5 (bis), 7, 8, 9, 10, 11; v, 1, 9 (*pātashāh-kūrᵘ biyĕ ôsᵘ sŏnar bagas-manz*, the princess and also the goldsmith were in the garden); vi, 10 (bis); vii, 8; viii, 1 (bis), 7 (bis), 9 (bis), 11, 13; x, 4, 7; xii, 1, 15 (bis); *ôsᵘ-na*, he was not, xii, 2; *ôsum*, I had, vii, 11, 15; *ôsus*, he had, viii, 7, 9; *kati ôsukh*, whence wast thou? where have you come from? xii, 15.

Forming impf. *ôsᵘ gaḍān*, he used to make, v, 1; *ôsᵘ karān*, he was making, i, 1; *ôsᵘ lāyān*, he was casting (a net), i, 6; *ôsᵘ marān*, he was dying, v, 9; *ôsᵘ nērān*, he used to go out, viii, 1; *ôsᵘ phērān*, he was wandering, i, 2; *ôsᵘ pakān*, he was going along, v, 7; *ôsᵘ tārān*, he was paying (tribute), x, 10; *ôsᵘ trāwān*, he was emitting, i, 5; *ôsᵘ tsalān*, he was absconding, xii, 25; *ôsᵘ wuchān*, he was watching, iii, 1; *ôsᵘ wŏtharān*, he was wiping, viii, 6, 13; *khĕwān ôsᵘ-na*, he used not to eat, vi, 16; *ôsus karān*, I was making, x, 14; *ôsus-na khasān*, was not rising for him, i, 6; *ôsus zāgān*, (disloyalty) was waking in him, ii, 5.

Forming plup. *ôsᵘ onᵘmotᵘ*, had been brought, xii, 25: *ôsᵘ dyūṭhᵘmotᵘ*, had been seen, vi, 14; *ôsᵘ dyutᵘmotᵘ*, had been given, x, 12; *ôsᵘ gamotᵘ*, he had become, i, 4; *ôsᵘ gŏmotᵘ*, had befallen, v, 2; *ôsᵘ korᵘmotᵘ*, had been made, ii, 1 (bis): *korᵘmotᵘ ôsᵘ*, had been made, x, 7; *ôsᵘ nyūmotᵘ*, had been taken, viii, 9; *ôsᵘ pĕmotᵘ*, had fallen, viii, 9; xii,

15 ; *ôsukh kor*^{u}*mot*^{u}, had been made by them, viii, 2 ; *ôsum āmot*^{u}, (to-day) he came to me, iii, 1 ; *phakīr ôsum lôg*^{u}*mot*^{u}, I dressed as a faqīr, x, 14 ; *ôs*^{u}*nas dyut*^{u}*mot*^{u} *khash*, she gave a cut (to one of) his (nails), v, 6 ; *ôsus gŏmot*^{u}, (love) befel him, v, 2 ; *ôsus kor*^{u}*mot*^{u}, had been done to her, ix, 1 ; *ôs*^{u}*than kor*^{u}*mot*^{u}, he was made by thee, x, 12.

Forming plup. with conj. part. *ôs*^{u} *zölith*, he had kindled, iii, 1 ; *ôs*^{u} *lögith*, he had dressed himself as (a faqīr), x, 12.

m. pl. *ös*^{i}, they were, etc., vi, 11 ; viii, 3, 5, 11 (ter) ; xii, 1 ; forming impf. *ös*^{i} *bōzān*, they were listening to, viii, 1 ; *ös*^{i} *gatshān*, they were becoming, they used to be, viii, 1 ; *ös*^{i} *karān*, they were making, i, 3 ; *karān ös*^{i}, they were making, xi, 8 ; *ös*^{i} *lārān*, they were running, x, v ; *ös*^{i} *pakān*, they were walking, x, 1 ; *ös*^{i} *parān*, they were reading, viii, 3, 4 ; *wadān ösī* (m.c.), they were lamenting, xi, 5.

Forming plup. *ös*^{i} *gamàt*^{i}, v, 9 ; *ösis gàṇḍ*^{i}*màt*^{i}, they had been tied (on) his (arm), x, 5 ; *ös*^{i}*wa dit*^{i}*màt*^{i}, they had been given to you, x, 12.

f. sg. *ös*^{ü}, she was, etc., v, 10 ; vii, 7 ; x, 5 (bis), 7 ; xii, 4, 15, 20, 25 ; *ös*^{ü}*na*, it (f.) was not, ii, 1 ; *ös*^{ü}*s*, I was, vii, 10 ; I became, ix, 2 ; *ös*^{ü}*s*, he had (a wife), iii. 1.

Forming impf. *ös*^{ü} *gatshān*, she used to go, v, 1 ; *ös*^{ü} *karān*, she used to make, xii, 20 ; *ös*^{ü} *wadān*, she was lamenting, vii, 16 ; *ös*^{ü}*na gatshān*, (chirping f.) was not occurring, viii, 1 ; *ös*^{ü}*s shūbān*, I (f.) was beautiful, vii, 10 ; *ös*^{ü}*san tshāḍān*, I was seeking for him, xii, 15 ; *ös*^{ü}*y karān*, she verily was making, vii, 16.

Forming plup. *ös*^{ü} *parzanöv*^{ü}*müts*^{ü}, she had been recognized, x, 5 ; *ös*^{ü} *tsüj*^{ü}*müts*^{ü}, she had absconded, ix, 1 ; *ös*^{ü}*s kür*^{ü}*müts*^{ü}, (a seal, f.) had been made on it, x, 10.

f. pl. *āsa*, they (f.) were, iii, 7 ; xi, 7 (bis) ; *āsakh*, the (eyes f.) of them were (satisfied), i, 3.

Forming impf. *karān āsa*, they (f.) were making, xi, 19.

Forming plup. *āsa hĕtsamatsa*, they (f.) were taken, x, 14.

fut. sg. 3, *āsi*, he (etc.) will be, x, 1 ; *āsinā*, will there not be ? i, 2 ; *ābas āsinā*, has not the water ? viii, 7 ; *āsim* (for *āsĕm*), there will be (on) my (queen), viii, 13; *āsiy*, there will be for thee, xii, 11.

Forming fut. perf. *mā āsi āmot*ᵘ, I wonder can he have come, xii, 23; *āsi lāryōmot*ᵘ, is probably polluted, viii, 6; *āsi mumot*ᵘ, he is probably dead, x, 8 (bis).

Forming fut. subjunctive, *āsi pĕmüts*ᵘ̈, (on whom a particle of love) will have fallen; vii, 30; *āsi wôt*ᵘ*mot*ᵘ, (he who) will have arrived, vii, 29.

past cond. forming durative past cond. sg. 3, *āsihē shūbān*, it would be excellent, ii, 4, 5.

perf. m. sg. 3, *chuh ôs*ᵘ*mot*ᵘ, has been, i.e. was, v, 1; *ôs*ᵘ*mot*ᵘ *chus*, (someone) was (near) her, v, 4.

asar, m. a result, vi, 16; *asara-söty*, owing to the result, vi, 16.

*ȧt*ⁱ, here, there (near), viii, 4; x, 11; xii, 20; here verily, x, 8; xii, 19; *yit*ⁱ*-kyāh* . . . *ȧt*ⁱ*-kyāh*, here, on the one hand . . . there on the other hand, viii, 13; *ȧtiy*, in that very place, x, 3, 5.

ati, here, there (near), ii, 1, 8, 10; iii, 1, 4, 7, (ter), 8 (bis), 9; v, 5, 7 (bis), 9 (bis); vi, 5, 11; viii, 1, 7, 9; x, 5 (bis), 7 (bis); xii, 1, 2, 7; from there, v, 4, 6; x, 14; xii, 17, 18, 19; *atiy*, there verily, ii, 10, 11; iii, 1, x, 5; in regard to this, x, 13; sg. gen. *atyuk*ᵘ, of there; m. sg. dat. *atikis pātashĕhas nish*, (came) to the king of that place.

*ot*ᵘ, there, v, 4, 9; x, 5, 14; xii, 15, 18, 25; *ot*ᵘ *tāñ*, up to there, by that time, x, 4, 6; *otuy*, there verily, iii, 4; ix, 1.

[*ath*], this, that (near, or within sight).

subst. an. m. sg. ag. *ȧm*ⁱ, ii, 5; iii, 1; v, 4 (bis), 8; viii, 7, 9 (bis), 10; x, 1 (bis), 5 (ter); xii, 7, 10, 15, 17, 18; *ȧmiy*, by him verily, v, 9; an. m. sg. dat. *amis*, ii, 4 (of a dead parrot), 5 (bis); iii, 8; v, 2, 3, 7, 10 (dat. comm.); vi, 10; viii, 6, 10 (*amis kyāh chuh nöl*ⁱ), what is on his neck ?), 11; x, 1, 1 (*amis lôyukh*, they beat him, *bhāvē prayōga*), 4 (ter), 5, 12; xii, 4, 5, 10 (*amis kôsun mast*, he shaved him), 12 (meaning of genitive), 13, 15 (bis), 18, 19, 21, 25; *amis*ᵘ̈*y* to this one verily, ii, 8; v, 7; viii, 7 (*amis*ᵘ̈*y ösa-kani*, from its (an.) mouth); xii, 15 (*amis*ᵘ̈*y athi*, by the hand of this very one); sg. m. gen. *ȧm*ⁱ*-sond*ᵘ, v, 3; viii, 6, 8, 10; *ȧm*ⁱ-

sünz^{u}, iii, 4 (bis) ; *asond*^{u}, viii, 9 ; f. sg. ag. *ami*, iii, 1 (bis), 2, 4 ; v, 1, 4 (bis), 6 (bis), 11 ; viii, 1 ; xii, 7 (ter), 15 (quater), 20 ; f. sg. dat. *amis*, v, 3, 7 ; vii, 20 ; viii, 11 ; ix, 1 ; x, 7 ; xii, 8, 9 (*amis kathan*, on her words), 15 (bis) ; f. sg. gen. *àm*^{i}*-sond*^{u}, xii, 7 ; *àm*^{i}*-sandi*, x, 5 ; *àm*^{i}*-sanzi*, xii, 15.

subst. inan. sg. abl. *ami*, ii, 5 ; iii, 8 ; viii, 13 ; xii, 4, 17 (bis) ; *amiy* (for this very reason, etc.), viii, 1, 10 ; ix, 1 ; viii, 6 ; sg. gen. *amyuk*^{u}, iii, 4 ; vi, 15 ; xii, 17 ; sg. dat. *ath*, v, 6, 9 ; viii, 10 ; xii, 3, 12, 15 (bis), 20 (*ath khabar*, news about that), 21, 22, 23 ; *ath*^{i} (emph. ^{i}), i, 13 ; ii, 3 ; iii, 7 ; vi, 15 ; viii, 1 (bis), 7 ; x, 5 (sense of acc.) ; xii, 2, 7, 21, 22, 24 (bis).

adj. an. sg. m. ag. *àm*^{i}, ii, 4, 7 (bis), 8 ; iii, 1, 9 ; v, 4, 7 ; vi, 14 ; viii, 1, 8 ; x, 2, 6, 7 (bis), 8 (bis), 12 ; xii, 4, 7, 22, 25 (bis). dat. *amis*, ii, 1, 3, 4, 5, 9, 10 ; iii, 1, 2 (ter), 8 (bis), 9 ; v, 2 (agreeing with gen.), 3 (do.), 8, 9 (bis), 10, 12 ; vii, 20 ; viii, 5 (bis), 6, 7, 8, 9, 10 (quater), 13 (ter) ; x, 1, 2 (bis), 3, 4, 5, (quater) 7, 7 (for acc.), 8 (ter), 11, 12 ; xii, 2, 3 (bis), 4 (ter), 4 (with gen.), 5 (bis), 5 (with gen.), 6, 8, 10 (bis), 11, 12, 13 (ter), 15, 18, 19 (quater), 22, 22 (with gen.), 24, 25 ; (with emph. *y*), *amis*^{ü}*y*, iii, 8 ; x, 10 ; f. ag. *ami*, ii, 9 ; iii, 4, 9 (bis) ; v, 1, 5 (bis), 7, 9, 11 ; viii, 1 ; ix, 1, 6 ; x, 3 (bis), 5, 12 ; xii, 2, 4, 5, (bis), 15 (quater), 18 (bis), 22 ; sg. dat. *amis*, ii, 9 ; iii, 1, 2 ; v, 9 (for acc.) ; viii, 3, 6, 6 (with gen.), 11, 13 ; ix, 1, 4, 6 ; x, 3, 5, 7 (quater), 7 (with gen.), 10, 13, 15 ; (with emph. *y*), *amis*^{ü}*y*, iii, 4.

adj. inan. sg. abl. *ami*, iii, 6 ; vi, 16 (bis) ; xii, 3 (with gen.), 4, 7, 12, 15, 23 ; sg. dat. *ath*, ii, 4, 5, 7 (bis) ; iii, 4, 9 ; v, 4, 5, 6 (ter), 11 ; vi, 14 ; viii, 1, 7 (ter) ; x, 3, 5 (bis), 7 (sexies), 8, 10, 12, 13 ; xii, 2, 7, 12 (bis), 15, 17, 22 (bis), 23 ; (with emph. ^{i}) *ath*^{i}, iii, 7, 9 ; v, 5 ; vi, 16 ; vii, 26 ; viii, 9 ; xii, 12.

aṭh, m. a market ; sg. abl. *aṭa-pĕṭha*, v, 7.

atha, m. a hand, forearm, viii, 7 (bis) ; x, 5 ; xii, 11, 12 ; pl. nom. vii, 25 (*zīṭh*^{i} *atha dārån*^{i}, to stretch out the arms) ; x, 5 (bis), xii, 2 ; sg. abl. *athi*, viii, 11 (*athi dyun*^{u}, to make over to so and so), xi, 18; xii, 15 (bis); pl. gen. *athan-handi*, v, 6; sg. dat. *athas*, v, 6; *athas-kĕth*, in the hand, ii, 7; v, 4; x, 7; xii, 22 (— *dyut*^{u}, put into the hand), 23; *athas-manz*, (a bracelet) on the hand, xii, 12.

öṭh, eight, iii, 5; *öṭhi dŏh*^{i}, after eight days, iii, 4.

ath^{ü}*r*^{ü}, f. a wool-worm; a wood-worm, vii, 19.

ŏtāñy, there verily, xii, 33.

ataty, in that very place, viii, 7.

atsun, to enter (*manz*, into).

impve. sg. 2, *atsh*, iii, 8 (bis); inf. and fut. part. pass. *atsun*, v, 4 (bis) (with *gatshun* 1); *log*^{u} *atsani*, began to enter, x, 7; n. ag. *atsawunuy*, even as I enter, v, 8; fut. sg. 1, *atsayō*, I will enter, O! v, 7.

past m. sg. 2, *tsākhō*, didst thou enter, O! ii, 2; 3 *tsāv*, ii, 1, 5 (bis), 7, 10, 11; iii, 8 (bis); v, 5; x, 7 (bis); pl. 3, *tsāy*, v, 9; *tsās*, they entered for him, viii, 9.

āv, see *yun*^{u}.

ay 1, if; *yiy*, if this, iii, 4 (bis), 9; *tiy*, if that, iii, 4 (bis), 9; *dŏd*^{i}*lad-ay*, if (ye are) pained, vii, 9; *hargāh-ay*, if (he had done), viii, 10; *hargāh ki-y*, if (he had done), viii, 7, 13; *ladaham-ay*, if thou wilt send to me, x, 3; *chiway*, if ye are, xii, 15.

ay 2, O! *kūriyay* (addressed by a nurse to a princess), O daughter! v, 2; *ay wazīra* (addressed by an inferior), O vizier! xii, 4.

ạy, O! *ạy gŏlām*, O slave! (addressed by a superior), viii, 6, 8, 11.

āy, *āyĕ*, see *yun*^{u}.

^{i}*yiy*, in *vis*^{i}*yiy*, O friend (*vĕs*, fem.), ix, 11. Cf. *ī* and (in v, 2) *kūr*^{i}*yĕy*.

ôy, see *yun*^{u}.

āyĕkh, see *yun*^{u}.

ayālbār, possessed of a large family, ix, 2.

āyām, *āyĕm*, *āy-nā*, *āyĕs*, see *yun*^{u}.

az 1, to-day, ii, 9; iii, 1; viii, 1; xii, 5, 10, 14, 19 (bis), 20 (bis); *az tāñ*, up to to-day, till now, x, 7, 8; xii, 20. sg. gen. f. *azic*^{ü}, x, 14.

az 2, from; *az Khŏdā*, from God, vi, 10.

azal, m. fate, doom, vii, 12; ix, 6.

özīz, poor; m. pl. nom. *özīz*, ix, 11.

Azīz-i-Misar, N.P., vi, 10, 12 (bis); sg. ag. *-misaran*, vi, 14.

bā; *parī bā-Khŏdā*, a fairy who obeys God, xii, 20; *āv bā-sôruy-sāmān*, he came with all (his) paraphernalia, xi, 20.

bĕ, *bē*, prefix of privation; *bē-bahā*, priceless, xii, 3, 4 (bis); *bĕ-shumār*, countless, xii, 20, 1, 4; *bē-khabar*, untaught, ignorant, vii, 28; *bē-wŏphā*, treacherous, x, 13; *bē-wŏphöyī*, treachery, infidelity, viii, 6, 11; *bē-wāsta*, without worldly ties, v, 11.

bāba, m. a holy man, a Calandar; *bāban* (among) Calandars, vi, 13.

bĕb, f. the breast-pocket; sg. dat. *bĕbi andar* (xii, 17) or *bĕbi-andar^{ü}y* (xii, 16), in the breast pocket.

bacĕ, m. the young of any animal; pl. nom. *bacĕ*, viii, 1.

bŏchĕ, f. hunger; — *lüj^{ü}s*, he became hungry, vi, 16; *bŏchi-sötiy*, merely owing to hunger, vi, 16.

bacun; 2 past, *bacyōkh*, thou escapedst, x, 8.

bacāwun, to save; inf. fem. *tagiyĕ bacāwüñ^{ü}*, do you know how to save her? v, 9.

b$\tilde{\bar{o}}$d^{i}, m. a prisoner; *b$\tilde{\bar{o}}$d^{i}-hāl*, f. a prison, ix, 4.

bŏḍ^{u}; *hata-bŏd^{i}*, hundreds, ix, 9.

boḍ^{u}, great, xii, 14; *baḍis-hihis*, to the elder (prince), viii, 13.

buḍ^{u}, old; *buḍ^{u} zanāna*, an old woman, x, 5; *bujĕ zanāni*, to the old woman, x, 5.

badal, m. exchange, vii, 12; prep. governing dat. in exchange (for), i, 9; adv. instead, xii, 16.

badan, m. the body; sg. dat. *badanas*, viii, 6 (bis), 13.

buḍun, to be old; 2 p. m. sg. 1 *buḍyōs*, I am grown old, xii, 1.

bĕdār, awake, iii, 7; viii, 8; — *gatshun*, to wake (from sleep), vi, 12; viii, 6, 9, 13; — *rōzun*, to keep awake, x, 1, 6, 8.

bāg, m. a garden, ii, 1; sg. gen. *armān bāguk^{u}*, longing for the garden, iii, 9; dat. *mushtākh bāgas*, enamoured of the garden, iii, 9; *bāgas-manz*, in, or into, the garden, ii, 1 (ter), 7 (bis); v, 4, 5, 6, 9 (bis).

b$\tilde{a}$g, m. the Musalmān call to prayer; — *parun*, to cry the call to prayer, xii, 1.

bög^{i}, in *shāman-bög^{i}*, at about evening, v, 5.

bĕgāh; *gāh bĕgāh*, in and out of season, vi, 2.

bagal, m.; *bagala-manza*, from under his armpit, viii, 7.

bāgȧnⁱ ; *bāgȧnⁱ āyĕs*, it was my fate, ix, 4.

bög^arun ; fut. pass. part. f. pl. *bög^arañĕ*, (loaves) must be divided, v, 8 ; 1 p. f. pl. *bög^arĕn*, she divided (the loaves), v, 8 ; 2 p. f. sg. *bög^arēm-ay*, I divided it (f.), O ! v, 7.

bāgwān, m. a garden-watcher, a gardener, xi, 13.

bŏh, I, ii, 5, 11 (bis) ; iii, 1, 4 (bis), 8 ; v, 5, 6 ; vii, 20, 5 ; viii, 3, 6, 8, 10, 11 (quater) ; ix, 1, 4 ; x, 1, 2 (bis), 3, 5 (bis), 7, 12 ; xii, 1, 4, 11, 19, 23 ; *bŏ-nay*, I (shall) not, xi, 14 (poet.) ; *bŏ ti*, I also, iii, 4 ; *bŏy*, if I, viii, 1 (bis) ; I verily, x, 10, 2, 4 ; *buday*, I verily (poet.), ix, 1, 3, 5, 6, 8, 10, 12.

asĕ, us, to us, etc., viii, 1, 3, 11 ; x, 2, 12 (bis) ; xii, 17 ; *asĕ-kun hôwuth*, thou showedst before us, vi, 5 ; *ȧsⁱ*, we, v, 9, 10 ; viii, 3 ; xi, 15 ; xii, 19 ; *ȧsⁱ-ti*, we also, xii, 1.

mĕ, me, to me, etc., iii, 4, 9 ; v, 8, 9, 10, 11 ; vii, 11, 2, 3 ; viii, 11 ; ix, 1, 4, 6 ; x, 3 (bis), 4, 5 (bis), 8, 12 (bis), 5 ; xii, 4 (bis), 5 (bis), 7, 10 (bis), 13, 22, 24 (bis) ; by me, ii, 2 (bis) ; vi, 15 ; viii, 5 ; ix, 11 ; x, 1, 12 (ter), 14 ; xi, 1 ; xii, 6, 20, 4 ; *mĕ-kyutᵘ*, xii, 24 ; *mĕ löyikh*, fit for me, xii, 10 (bis) ; *mĕ nish*, near me, viii, 5 ; xii, 22 (bis) ; *mĕ nishĕ*, near me, in my possession, x, 14 ; *mĕ ôsum*, I had, vii, 15 ; *mĕ sötin*, (share) with me, i, 7 ; *mĕ söty*, together with me, viii, 3, 11 ; x, 9 ; xii, 2, 7 ; *mĕ-ti*, to me also, ix, 1 ; me also, vi, 11 ; xi, 14.

bah, card., twelve ; *ťsāṭas bahan-hatan-hondᵘ zyuṭhᵘ*, the master of twelve hundred pupils, v, 1.

Baḥ^adūr Khān, m. N.P., Bahādur K͟hān, ii, 1 ; sg. dat. — *khānas*, ii, 12.

bĕhun, to sit down, vi, 3, 16 (bis) ; x, 7 ; xii, 4 (bis), 6, 7, 21 ; to sit down in a place, take up a position, xi, 2 ; to be stationed, posted (at a particular place), xi, 6 ; to remain, stay (in a certain place), take up one's abode, viii, 4 ; x, 5 ; xii, 2, 4 ; to sit down at a work, set to work, xii, 26 (bis) ; to be employed (in a certain business), viii, 5 (ter) ; to sit down (after finishing a work), to rest, viii, 8 ; *byūṭhᵘ nazari*, he sat watching ; *nōkar bĕhun*, to sit down as a servant, take service, xii, 3.

conj. part. in sense of past part. *bihith*, seated, x, 5 (bis) ; xii, 4, 5 ; fut. sg. 1, *bĕha*, xii, 3 ; 3, *bĕhi*, vi, 16 ; impve. sg. 2

bĕh, xi, 2 ; pl. 2, *bĕhiv*, viii, 5 ; pol. impve. sg. 2, *bĕhtam*, sit please for me, sit to please me, vi, 3 ; fut. impve. *bĕh*[i]*zi*, you must sit, xii, 6 ; pres. masc. sg. 3, *bĕhān chuh*, xii, 4 ; past masc. sg. 3, *byūṭh*[u], viii, 4 ; x, 5, 7 (bis) ; xii, 4, 7, 21, 6 (bis) ; *byūṭhus*, sat (on) his (thumb-ring), vi, 16 ; m. pl. 3, *bīṭh*[i], viii, 5 (bis), 8 ; xi, 6 ; xii, 2.

bahār, m. the season of spring, i, 11.

bāj, m. tribute ; — *tārun*, to collect tribute, x, 10 ; xi, 2.

bôj[u], m. in *bŏj*[i]*-baṭh*, sharing, partnership, i, 7.

bāki, conj. but.

bēkh, see *byākh*.

bakh[a]*cöyish*, f. a present, a gift, ii, 7 ; xii, 3.

bakār, useful, x, 6.

Bikarmājĕth, m. N.P., Vikramāditya ; sg. ag. *bikarmājĕtan*, x, 8 ; gen. m. — *jĕtun*[u], x, 7, 14 ; f. — *jĕtüñ*[u], x, 1, 6.

baktāwār, prosperous, viii, 9.

bāl, m. a child ; *bāla-pān*, a youthful body, the graceful body of a child, vii, 11 ; sg. dat. *-pānas*, vii, 15.

bāl, f. a girl ; sg. dat. *bālē*, m.c. for *bāli*, v, 11.

bōl, m. speech ; *bōl-bōsh*[ü], the chirping of birds, viii, 1 (ter).

bulbul, m. a nightingale, ii, 3 (bis) ; with suff. of indef. art. *bulbulāh*, ii, 3.

bal[i]*ki*, conj. moreover.

Baltī, m. a Baltī, an inhabitant of Baltistān ; voc. pl. *baltī*, xi, 4 (Hindōstānī).

balāy, f. a calamity, evil (ix, 2), an evil genius, evil spirit, devil, fiend (x, 7, 8) ; with suff. of indef. art. *balāyā akh*, an evil spirit, x, 8 ; *balāy pĕyin*, may calamity fall on him, ix, 2.

bĕmār, adj. sick, ill, v, 1, 3 ; — *gatshun*, to become sick, v, 10 ; — *pyon*[u], to fall ill, v, 1.

bŏn, adv. down, below, xii, 15 ; — *wasun*, to descend, viii, 4 ; xii, 2, 14, 15 ; *bŏna-kani*, below, down below, iii, 2.

band, adj. shut, tied up ; *bar band karun*, to shut the door, viii, 3 ; *kărin band*, he tied up (rupees), x, 2.

banda, m. a slave, i, 13 ; voc. *banda*, i, 13.

bandūk-bāz, m. a gunner ; pl. nom. *bandūk-bāz*, ii, 7.

bandūkh, m. a gun, viii, 10; —*lāyun*, to fire a gun, ii, 11; cf. viii, 10.

bīnāh, m. one who sees, ii, 2.

banun, to become, vi, 16; to be, vi, 13; to happen, ii, 7; vii, 22; viii, 7; xii, 1; to become, turn out, viii, 7; to be possible, x, 3; *banun*, inf., is used to mean "fate", especially "evil fate", hence *banana-rost*ᵘ, free from fated sorrow, vii, 23.

fut. sg. 3, *bani*, vi, 13; vii, 1; x, 3; with *v* added (I say to you, "there will happen"), *baniv*, ii, 7; pres. sg. f. 3 with suff. 3rd pers. sg. dat. *banān chĕs-na*, viii, 7; II past, *banyōv*, vi, 16; with suff. 1 pers. sg. dat. *banyōm*, vii, 22; III past, *banyāv*, xii, 1.

bōnṭh; *bōnṭha-kani*, in front (governing dat.), ii, 3; iii, 1; viii, 11; x, 5, 10, 2; xii, 4, 9, 12, 23 (bis); *pātashĕhas bōnṭh-kun*, (laid) before the king, i, 8; cf. *brōnṭh*.

bēnawāh, adj. destitute, vii, 7.

banāwun, to make; I past with suff. 3 pers. sg. ag. *banôwun*, viii, 14.

bĕñĕ, f. a sister, iii, 9; x, 3, 10; sg. ag. *bĕñi*, x, 3 (bis), 10; gen. *bĕñĕ-hond*ᵘ, x, 3 (ter), 10; *dŏda-bĕñĕ*, a milk-sister, a foster sister, iii, 4.

*buñul*ᵘ, m. an earthquake, xii, 15 (*gav*, took place).

bāpath, postpos. for; *mārana bāpath*, he was made over for killing, i.e. to be killed, x, 12; *ami bāpath*, for this reason, on this account, ii, 5; *amiy bāpath*, for this very reason, ix, 1; *kami bāpath*, for what reason? why? ix, 1; with what purpose? x, 12.

bar, m. a door; —*band karun*, to lock the door, viii, 3; —*mutsarun*, to open the door, viii, 3.

bār (1); *Bār Khŏdāyō*, O Great God! v, 7; *Bār-Sōhib*, the Almighty, vii, 2, 3, 5.

bār (2); m. a load; *wūnṭa-bār* (pl. nom.), camel loads, i, 9.

*bôr*ᵘ, m. a load, ii, 5; sg. abl. *hĕth bāri*, taking in a load, xi, 13.

barābar, adv. at once, iii, 9.

barg, m. a leaf; pl. abl. *bargau-sōty*, owing to leaves, vii, 10.

brōh, adv. (an order) in advance, beforehand, xi, 4.

brūh, adv. in advance, in front, beforehand, xi, 6; *brūh brūh*, (walking) in front, iii, 1, 2; viii, 9; xii, 7; cf. *pata pata*, s.v. *pata*; *ākh brũh*, there came to them in front, there appeared before them, x, 1.

barᵃm, m. an auger, a drill (poet. for *barma*); *barᵃm pānas chum karān*, he is making auger(-holes) in my body, vii, 24.

bārànⁱ, m. pl. a pair of uterine brothers, viii, 5; ag. *bāranyau*, viii, 3.

barun, to fill, ii, 3; viii, 3, 7 (bis); ix, 7, 11; *rāth barũñᵘ*, to pass the night, i, 10.

freq. part. *bàrⁱ bàrī* (for *bàrⁱ bàrⁱ*, m.c.), ix, 11; conj. part. *barith*, i, 10; fut. sg. 1, with suff. 2nd pers. sg. dat. *baray*, ii, 3; past masc. sg. with suff. 3 sg. ag. *borun*, viii, 7 (bis); fem. sg. with suff. 3 pl. ag. *bürᵘkh*, viii, 3; ix, 7.

brōnṭh, adv. of time, before, previously, x, 5; cf. *bōnṭh*.

barish, f. a spear; sg. abl. *barishi söty*, (dug) with his spear, viii, 7.

borutᵘ, adj. full; pl. dat. (for acc.) *barítĕn*, vi, 15.

bārav, m. pl. grumbling; — *dinⁱ*, to grumble, xi, 17.

barāyĕ, prep. for the sake of; on account of; for the purpose of; by way of; — *kŏmbakas*, by way of reinforcement, in order to give help, xi, 7.

busᵘ, m. a gobbet or mouthful of food put into the mouth at one time, xii, 17.

bāshĕ, f. babbling of a child; *shurⁱ-bāshĕ*, infantile talk, v, 2.

bĕ-shumār, adj. countless, xii, 20, 1, 4.

bismillā, interj., *bi'smi'llāh*, in the name of God! xii, 17.

basta, f. the skin; — *wālũñᵘ*, to flay, viii, 6.

bata, m. cooked rice, iii, 1 (ter); food generally, vi, 16 (bis); *-düjᵘ*, f. a cloth holding a quantity of boiled rice, xi, 18; *-han*, a little boiled rice, x, 5; *-hanā*, usually f., but m. in x, 3; *-trômᵘ*, a copper dish holding cooked rice, iii, 1.

baṭh, m. *böjⁱ-baṭh*, sharing; — *karun*, to divide into shares amongst partners, to take one's own share and give out the other shares, i, 7.

bāth, f. word, speech, language; *katha-bātha*, nom. pl. conversations, xii, 25 (we should expect *-bāta*).

bīṭhⁱ, see *bĕhun*.

bŏṭa, m. a Tibetan, esp. an inhabitant of Baltistān; *-böy*[i], m. pl. Tibetan brothers, xi, 6; *-garan*, in Tibetan houses, xi, 6.

boṭh[u], m. the bank of a river; *baṭhis-pĕṭh*, on the bank, xii, 7; (ascended) on to the bank, xii, 6, 7.

buth[u], m. the face, x, 5 (bis); xii, 2.

bŏṭun[u], Tibet, esp. Baltistān or Little Tibet, or Ladakh; sg. dat. *bŏṭanis*, xi, 4.

böts[ü], m. the members of a family, the people of a house, viii, 10; a husband and wife, v, 9, 10; viii, 1 (bis), 2, 5, 6, 13; a wife (politely), x, 14 (bis); *sŏnara-sȧnd*[i] *böts*[u] *z*[a]*h*, the goldsmith and his wife, v, 10; *pātashĕha-sȧnd*[i] (*z*[a]*h*) *böts*[ü], the king and queen, viii, 1 (bis), 5, 6, 13; pl. nom. *böts*[ü], v, 9, 10; viii, 1, 13; x, 14; pl. dat. *bātsan*, viii, 1, 6, 13; x, 14; ag. *bātsau*, viii, 2, 5.

bāwun, to make manifest, explain a secret, confide a secret, ii, 4 (bis); vii, 21; past m. sg. *bôw*[u], ii, 4; with suff. 3 sg. ag. *bôwun*, ii, 4; past cond. sg. 1, *bāwahö*, vii, 21.

bē-wŏphā, adj. treacherous, x, 13.

bē-wŏphöyī, f. infidelity, viii, 6, 11.

bāwar, m. belief, faith; — *karun*, to believe, viii, 13.

bē-wāsta, adj. without worldly ties, v, 11.

bāy, f. a lady, a mistress; used as a suffix to indicate the wife of a man of a certain trade or profession; thus, *gūr*[i]*-bāy*, a cow-herd's wife, xi, 12; *grīst*[i]*-bāy*, a farmer's wife, ix, 1, 4, 6, 8, 10, 12; *pātashāh-bāy*, a king's wife, a queen, viii, 1, 2, 3, 4, 6, 11, 12, 13; *sōdāgar-bāy*, a merchant's wife, iii, 1, 2, 3. sing. nom. iii, 1 (bis), 2, 3; viii, 1, 2, 3, 11 (bis); ix, 1, 6 (bis), 8, 10, 2; dat. *bāyĕ*, iii, 1, 2; viii, 1, 3, 4, 11, 2; ix, 1, 4, 6; xi, 12; gen. *bāyĕ-hond*[u], viii, 6, 13; ag. *bāyi*, viii, 1, 3, 11, 2; ix, 1; *grīst*[i]*-bāyi*(for *-bāyĕ*)*-kun*, (saying) to the farmer's wife, ix, 1.

biyĕ (properly abl. of *byākh*, q.v.), adv. again, once more, iii, 3 (ter); v, 4, 5, 6, 10, 1; vi, 15, 6; viii, 7 (bis), 11; x, 3, 6, 7 (quater); xii, 5 (bis), 10, 3 (ter); again, also, ii, 7; iii, 5, 9 (bis); v, 3, 4 (bis), 6, 8; x, 1, 2; xii, 20, 2 (quater), 3, 4 (bis), 5 (bis); *biyĕ kĕh*, something more (iii, 8), anything else (xii, 18); *biyĕ kun*, anywhere else, xii, 4.

conj. again, moreover, viii, 6; and, v, 7, 9 (bis); and also, iii, 4, 5; *akh . . . biyĕ*, in the first place . . . in the second place, both . . . and, v, 9; vi, 15; xii, 21; *ta . . . biyĕ*, both . . . and, viii, 9.

bŏy, f. a smell, scent, stink, xii, 15.

*bôy^u^*, m. a brother, viii, 14 (bis); sing. dat. *bŏyis*, v, 10; x, 3; pl. nom. *bŏy^i^*, iv, 7; xi, 6; xii, 15; dat. *bāyĕn*, xii, 15; *bŏy^i^-bārán^i^*, uterine brothers, viii, 5; *bŏy^i^-kākañ*, an elder brother's wife, v, 10.

biyābān, m. a forest, ii, 4.

byākh, *byēkh*, or *bēkh*, pron. adj. another, the other, one more, hence often, "a second," in the sense of "one more"; sing. nom. *byākh*, viii, 9, 14; x, 1; xii, 4, 10 (fem.), 3 (ter), 4, 9 (fem.); *byēkh*, viii, 1 (fem.); *bēkh*, xii, 3, 10 (fem.); sg. dat. *biyis*, viii, 5, 13; vi, 11; xii, 23; m. sg. ag. *biy^i^*, xii, 1 (bis); fem. pl. nom. *biyĕ*, x, 1; m. pl. dat. *biyĕn*, viii, 9. The sing. abl. of this word *biyĕ* or *biyi* is used as an adv. meaning "again", "once more", "also", and as a conjunction meaning "moreover", "and". See s.v. *biyĕ*.

*byon^u^*, adj. separate, apart. *byon^u^ byon^u^*, adv. separately, each apart, vi, 4; vii, 14; *byunuy*, He alone is apart from all things, or discrete (of God), vii, 2.

bōzun, to hear, ii, 1, 2 (bis), 3, 4 (ter), 5, 6, 7 (bis), 10 (bis), 2; iii, 1; iv, 1; v, 7; vi, 1, etc.; vii, 9, 27, 8; ix, 6; x, 4; xi, 20; xii, 7, 19; to listen to, ii, 5; vi, 10; viii, 1, 2; xi, 1, 15; to obey, heed, xii, 20; *shumār būz^ü^*, the counting was heard, i.e. the roll-call was read out, xi, 16.

In the pass. this verb usually means "to be visible" (xii, 22), or "to be considered (as such and such)", "to seem" (viii, 5; x, 4 (bis)), or "to be known or recognized (as such and such)", xii, 3.

inf. *bōzun*, abl. (forming pass.) *bōzana*, viii, 5; x, 4 (bis); xii, 3, 22; fut. pass. part. *gatshĕm bōzun^u^*, you must hear me. xii, 7; conj. part. *būzith*, vii, 27, 8; impve. sg. 2, *bōz*, ii, 2 (bis), 3, 4 (ter), 5, 6, 7, 10, 2; ix, 6; pol. sg. 2, with suff. 1st pers. sg. acc. *bōztam*, please to hear me; pl. 2, *būz^i^tav*, please hear ye, vii, 9; fut. sg. 2 neg. interrog. *bōzakh-nā*, wilt thou not hear? vi, 1 ff.; plur. 3, *bōzan*, xi, 20; pres. part. *bōzān*, hearing, *gatsh bōzān*, go attentively, xi, 1; pres. m. sg. 3 neg. with suff. 3 sg. acc. *chus-na bōzān*, he is not listening to him, vi, 10; with suff. 3 pers. pl. acc. *bōzān chukh-na*, he is not listening to them, viii, 2; m. pl. 3 with suff. 1 pers. sg. acc. *chim bōzān*, they are listening to me, xi, 5; imperf. m. pl. 3, *ösᶦ bōzān*, viii, 1; past m. sg. *būzᵘ*, ii, 7; iii, 1; v, 7; x, 4; xii, 19; with suff. 2nd pers. sg. ag. *būzuth*, xii, 20; with suff. 3rd pers. sg. ag. *būzun*, ii, 1, 10; also with suff. 3 pers. sg. acc. and neg. *būzᵘnas-na*, he did not listen to him, ii, 5; f. sg. *būzᵘ̈*, xi, 16.

bözᶦgār, m. a deceiver, cheat, iv, 1, etc.

bāzar, m. a market, a bazaar, v, 7.

chīh, f. a particle, a very small amount of anything, vii, 30.

chuh 1, the cry used in urging on a horse, xi, 8. Cf. *hárᶦ hárᶦ*.

chuh 2, verb substantive and auxiliary verb.

(*a*) Verb subst. 1 sg. masc. *chus*, I am, xii, 1, 23; fem. *chĕs*, xii, 18; 2 sg. masc. *chukh*, thou art, i, 10; ii, 2; xii, 1; fem. *chĕkh*, viii, 3, 11; xii, 13; sg. 3 masc. *chuh*, he is, ii, 6, 8, 11; iii, 1, 2, 7, 8; v, 1, 8; vi, 7, 14; vii, 27; viii, 6, 8, 10, 1; x, 1, 4, 5, 6, 7, 8, 10, 2; xi, 2; xii, 2, 3, 15; fem. *chĕh*, she is, v, 3; vii, 29; viii, 7, 10, 3; x, 6, 7, 10, 4; xi, 11; xii, 10, 9; 1 pl. masc. *chih*, we are, xii, 1; 2 pl. m. *chiv*, (if) ye be, vii, 9 (poet.); *chiwa*, ye are, xii, 1; 3 pl. m. *chih*, they are, v, 8, 10, 3; x, 1, 6; xii, 16.

neg. 3 sg. masc. *chuna*, he is not, iii, 3; iv, 4, 6; xii, 2; fem. *chĕna*, x, 6, 7, 14; xii, 2 (*kōrĕ chĕna khabar*, there is no news for the daughter, i.e. she does not know), 5, 20; 3 pl. fem. *chĕna*, xii, 19.

interrog. *chĕsa*, am I (fem.)? viii, 3, 11; *chukha*, art thou (masc.)? xii, 7; *chwā*, is he? xii, 19, 20; *chyā*, is she? v, 7; vi, 7; x, 10; xii, 20.

emph. *chusay*, I (masc.) am verily, v, 11; 3 sg. masc. *chuy*, is verily, ii, 2: iv, 3; vi, 14; vii, 2, 3; x, 4; xii, 14; fem. *chĕy*, iii, 4, 8; v, 1, 10; xii, 6, 14; 3 pl. masc. *chiy*, v, 4; x, 12; fem. *chĕy*, viii, 4. Possibly, in some of these cases, the final *y* is not the emphatic particle, but is the suffix of the 2nd pers. sg. dat., used as a sort of *dativus commodi.* Note that *chĕy,* xii, 6, is apparently masc. although fem. in form. The true subject is *kŏl* in the preceding sentence. Cf. *chĕyĕy,* ix, 6.

Conditional. 2 pl. masc. *chiway,* if ye are, xii, 15.

Used in possessive phrases (*tamis,* etc.). *chuh nāv,* (his) name is (so and so), ii, 1; xii, 8, 18; *amis chuh tab,* he has fever, v, 3; *lūkan chuh tār,* the people have exhaustion (i.e. are exhausted), xi, 13; *tas chuh dôdᵘ,* she has pain, xii, 15; *mĕ-nishĕ chuh nishāna,* I have a token, x, 14; *tsĕ nishĕ chuh nishāna,* x, 14; *pātashĕhas chĕh khabar,* the king has news, iii, 3; so *tas chĕh khabar,* xii, 2, she has news, she believes; similarly *chĕh* in xii, 4, 5 (he has a wife), 15 (*tas chĕh ükᵘy nürᵘ,* she has only one arm), 19; *amis chĕh zanāna trĕh,* he has three wives, xii, 19; *asĕ chih gabar zᵃh,* we have two sons, viii, 1; neg. *asĕ chĕna phursath,* we have no leisure, xii, 17.

With pronominal suffixes. 1st pers. sg. masc. *chum,* v, 8 (my (husband) is (sick)); vi, 5 (*chum khŏdā,* it is my god); vii, 26 (*chum tamāh,* I have longing); x, 12 (I have); xii, 7, *kyāh chum hukum,* (what order (have you) for me); fem. *chĕm,* v, 10 (*chĕm böyⁱ-kākañ,* she is my sister-in-law); ix, 4 (*mōtüñᵘ chĕm bŏdⁱ-hāl,* it is to me a prison-house of death); 3 pl. masc., vi, 3 (*sath kuṭhⁱ lari chim,* there are seven rooms in my house); vi, 3 (*cyāñĕ lŏhlari chim,* they are (to fulfil) my longing for you); x, 5 (*hamsāyĕ chim,* I have neighbours).

2nd pers. sing., 1 fem. *chĕsay,* I (fem.) am thy, ix, 3, 5, etc.; 3 sg. masc. *chuy,* is of thee, viii, 13; *Khŏdāyĕ-sondᵘ chuy kasam,* the oath of God is to thee, I adjure thee by God, xii, 7; fem. *chĕy,* she is of thee, v, 10; x, 8 (you have her); xii, 14 (there is a road (*wath,* fem.) for thee); conditional, *chĕyĕy,* if there be to thee, ix, 6. *N.B.*—This last is masculine although feminine in form. Cf. *chĕy* in xii, 6. 1 pl. masc. *chiy* (*ȧsⁱ chiy gabar,* we are in the position of sons to thee).

3rd pers. sing., 3 masc. *chus,* is to him, he has something masculine, ii, 11; v, 6 (*athas chus dôdᵘ,* his hand is sore);

viii, 9 (*pata chus*, he is behind him); viii, 10 (*chus cālān nōl*ⁱ, he has a letter of dispatch on his neck); xii, 3 (*chus manz*, there is in it); fem. *chĕs*, viii, 6 (*nazar chĕs bātsan-kun*, he looks towards the husband and wife); xi, 9 (*kala-kån*ⁱ *dŏmbij*ᵘ *chĕs*, the crupper is close to its head); neg. *pātashōhī chĕsna*, he has no royal state, x, 4; 3 pl. masc. *lāl chis z*ᵃ*h*, he has two rubies, xii, 3.

2nd pers. plur., 3 sg. m. *kyāh sabab chuwa*, what reason have you? viii, 5; fem. neg. *chĕwana panüñ*ᵘ, she is not your own, x, 1; 3 plur. masc. *tsōr chiwa tŏhĕ*, *trih chiwa myōn*ⁱ *tŏhĕnish*, four are for you, and three are mine in your charge, x, 5; fem. *chĕwa*, they (fem.) are for you, x, 1.

3rd pers. pl., 3 sg. fem. *chhĕkh*, *nazar chĕkh ō-kun*, their look is (directed) thither, xii, 23; 3 pl. masc. *chikh kār*, they have works, xi, 10.

(*b*) Auxiliary. (1) With present participle. sg. 1 masc. *chus wuchān*, I see, iii, 8; fem. *chĕs diwān*, I give, vii, 22; *chĕs karān*, I make, vii, 15; *chĕs riwān*, I lament, vii, 22; *chĕs wadān*, I lament, ix, 1; *chĕs wālān*, I cause to descend, v, 4.

sg. 2 masc. *chukh wuchān*, thou seest, iii, 8.

sg. 3 masc. *anān chuh*, he brings, x, 12; *chuh anān*, xii, 19; *bĕhān chuh*, he sits down, xii, 4; *chuh cĕwān*, he drinks, xii, 6; *dapān chuh*, he says, iv, 1; viii, 8, 9; x, 8, 12; xii, 10, 1, 4, 9, 20; *diwān chuh*, he gives, v, 11; xii, 23; *chuh diwān*, xii, 17; *chuh dazān*, is burning, viii, 13; x, 7; *gatshān chuh*, he goes, xii, 4; *chuh gatshān*, xii, 4; *chuh kaḍān*, he abstracts, he passes time, viii, 13; xii, 4, 11, 17; *chuh khĕwān*, he eats, xii, 6, 17; *chuh karān*, he does, makes, viii, 12, 13; x, 8, 14; xii, 24; *chuh katarān*, he cuts, x, 7; *chuh lagān*, he is being attached, viii, 5; *chuh lēkhān*, he writes, x, 13; *chuh lalawān*, he caresses, v, 6; *chuh lōnān*, he reaps, x, 5; *chuh lāyān*, he throws, v, 4; *chuh nanān*, it is manifest, vii, 1; *gwāsh chuh phŏlān*, dawn is breaking, xii, 2; *chuh phērān*, it moves about, ii, 5; *chuh pakān*, he goes forward, iii, 1; *pakān chuh*, viii, 7; xii, 7; *chuh prārān*, he is waiting, v, 6; *chuh shōlān*, is flaming, vi, 6;

chuh tulān, he is raising, xii, 17; *chuh gāh trāwān,* is emitting light, xii, 2; *chuh tshunān,* he is letting fall, xii, 17; *chuh wuchhān,* he sees, iii, 1, 4, 7, 8; viii, 6, 9; xii, 4; *wuchān chuh,* iii, 7; xii, 19; *chuh walān,* he wraps, viii, 13; *wanān chuh,* he says, x, 6; *chuh wasān,* he is coming down, v, 7; *wasān chuh,* viii, 13; *chuh wātān,* he arrives, iii, 7; *chuh yiwān,* he comes, xii, 3; *yiwān chuh,* v, 5; xii, 4.

sg. 3 fem. *chĕh dapān,* she says, vii, 2, 3, 7, 8; ix, 6; x, 5; xii, 18; *dapān chĕh,* iii, 3, 4; ix, 1; xii, 7, 11; *chĕh gatshān,* she goes, becomes, x, 5; *gatshān chĕh,* xii, 23; *chĕh karān,* she does, iii, 4; *likhān chĕh,* she writes, xii, 11; *chĕh pakān,* she goes forward, iii, 2; xii, 7; *chĕh wanān,* she says, vi, 2; vii, 1, 20, 6; *wanān chĕh,* ix, 6; *chĕh yiwān,* she comes, xii, 15.

pl. 2 masc. *chiwa yiwān bōzana,* you appear to be, viii, 5.

pl. 3 masc. *dapān chih,* they say, iii, 3 (people say); *diwān chih,* they give, x, 14; *chih harān,* (rubies) are dropping, xii, 9; *chih kaḍān,* they pass the time, viii, 11; *chih karān,* they do, make, viii, 3; xii, 3, 23; *chih lārān,* they run, ii, 9; *chih pakān,* they go forward, xii, 2; *pakān chih,* x, 4; *chih sọ̄mb^arān,* they collect, xi, 7; *chih sārān,* they collect, xi, 6; *chih tshārān,* they seek, iii, 3.

pl. 3 fem. *chĕh karān,* they do, v, 12; *chĕh gatshān,* they occur, viii, 1.

neg. sg. 1 masc. *chusna ṭhah^arān,* I am not standing, ii, 4; 2 masc. *chukhna wātān,* thou art not reaching, xii, 13; 3 masc. *chuna karān,* he does not make, viii, 2; *yiwān chuna bōzana,* he cannot be seen, xii, 22.

neg. interrog. *chukhnā parzanāwān,* dost thou not recognize, x, 12.

emph. sg. 3 masc. *chuy dapān,* he verily says, iii, 4; *chuy wanān,* he verily says, i, 13; vii, 31; fem. *chĕy wanān,* she verily says, vii, 16.

With pronominal suffixes. 1st person; sg. 3 masc. *chum dapān,* he says to me, xii, 20; *chum diwān,* he gives to me, vii, 14, 7, 8; *chum harān,* my (flesh) is dropping, vii, 24; *chum k^anān,* he sells me, vii, 17; *chum karān,* he makes for me, vii, 15, 24; *chum mangān,* he is asking from me, xii, 4, 5, 11, 4; *māzas chum tulān,* he is raising (bits of) my flesh, vii, 14; *chum wuchān,* he is inspecting me, vii, 18.

pl. 3 masc. *chim bōzān,* they listen to me, xi, 15; *chim mangān,* they are asking from me, xi, 14.

3rd person sing.; sg. 3 masc. *chus dapān,* he says to him or her, v, 5, 11; viii, 3, 11 (bis); x, 8 (bis), 14; xii, 3, 13, 20; *dapān chus,* iii, 4; v, 11; viii, 9; x, 8, 10 (bis), 14; xii, 3, 5, 10 (bis), 13 (bis), 19; *chus lamān,* he pulls him, viii, 9; *chus pĕwān,* falls to her, vii, 26; *chus wanān,* he says to him, viii, 7; *chus yiwān,* (stink) is coming from it, ii, 4.

3rd pers. plur.; pl. 3 masc. *pata chikh lārān,* they are running after them, xi, 18.

neg. *bōzān chukhna,* he is not listening to them, viii, 2; fem. neg. *rōzān chĕkhna,* she is not remaining for them, ii, 9.

(2) With emph. pres. part. *chuh dazōn*^{i}, he is verily burning, x, 7.

(3) With perfect participle. sg. 1 fem. neg. *chĕsna tshuñ*^{ü}*müts*^{ü}, I have not been set (to learn), v, 6; sg. 2 masc. *chukh gŏmot*^{u}, thou hast gone, xii, 4; neg. *chukhna gŏmot*^{u}, thou didst not become, v, 5; fem. *chĕkh tsüj*^{ü}*müts*^{ü}, thou hast fled, ix, 1.

sing. 3 masc. *chuh āmot*^{u}, he has come, x, 12, 4; *chuh ôs*^{u}*mot*^{u}, he has been, v, 1; *chuh gamot*^{u}, has gone, etc., ii, 4; iii, 1; viii, 1; *chuh gŏmot*^{u}, ix, 1, 6; *chuh kor*^{u}*mot*^{u}, he has been made, x, 12; *chuh pĕmot*^{u}, it has befallen, x, 3; *chuh roṭ*^{u}*mot*^{u}, he has been arrested, x, 12; fem. *chĕh mumüts*^{ü}, she is dead, viii, 1; *chĕh tsüj*^{ü}*müts*^{ü}, she has fled, ix, 1; *chĕh wüñ*^{ü}*müts*^{ü}, it (fem.) has been said, vii, 30.

plur. 2 masc. *chiwa làg*^{i}*màt*^{i}, ye have arrived, viii, 5.

plur. 3 masc. *chih mumàt*^{i}, they are dead, viii, 1.

With pronominal suffixes. 1st person; sg. 3 masc. *chum gamot*^{u}, he has gone for me (*dativus commodi*), v, 10; pl. 3 masc. *chim dit*^{i}*màt*^{i}, I have given them, x, 12.

2nd person sg.; sg. 3 masc. *chuy gôl*^{u}*mot*^{u}, thou hast destroyed, ii, 11; fem. *chĕy āmüts*^{ü}, she has come to thee, v, 5; *chĕy kür*^{ü}*müts*^{ü}, thou hast made it (fem.), x, 8.

3rd pers. sg. ag. and pl. dat.; sg. 3 masc. *chunakh dyut^{u}mot^u*, she has given to them, viii, 1.

3rd pers. sg. dat.; sg. 3 masc. *kus-tāñ ôs^{u}mot^u chus wŏpar*, somebody else was with her, v, 4.

2nd pers. pl.; sg. 3 masc. *chuwa thôw^{u}mot^u*, you have deposited, x, 12.

3rd pers. pl.; sg. 3 masc. *chukh thôw^{u}mot^u*, they have deposited, x, 12.

(4) With future passive participle; sg. 3 masc. *chuh chāwun*, (one's fated lot) must be experienced, ix, 6; fem. *chĕh wasüñ^ü*, it is to be descended (a place, fem.), ix, 6; emph. *chuy gatshun*, (I) must certainly go, v, 10; with suff. 3rd pers. sg. dat. *chus khasun*, he must mount, x, 3; with suff. 2nd pers. plur. *dapun chuwa*, (whatever) is to be said by you, v, 8.

(5) With conjunctive participle; sg. 2 masc. *chukh bihith*, thou art seated, xii, 5; sg. 3 masc. *chuh bihith*, he is seated, x, 5; xii, 4; *chuh karith thaph*, he is holding (it), v, 6; viii, 7.

(6) With negative conjunctive participle; *chuh pakanay*, it is not yet walked over, x, 1.

chĕl, f. a piece, fragment; pl. nom. *chĕla*, vii, 14.

chalun, to wash; past sg. m. with suff. 3rd pers. sg. ag. *cholun*, x, 5; xii, 2; past cond. sg. 1 *chalahö*, x, 5.

chān, m. a carpenter, x, 12; xi, 18; sg. dat. *chānas*, vii, 17, 20; pl. nom. *chān*, x, 5.

chöñ^ü, f. a carpenter's wife, xi, 19.

chāwun, to experience (ix, 6); to enjoy (xi, 3); fut. pass. part. sg. m. *chāwun*, ix, 6; pres. part. *chāwān*, xi, 3.

cakla, m. a group of villages, a village circle, ix, 10.

cālān, m. a letter of dispatch, an invoice, viii, 10; xi, 4.

cĕnda, m. a pocket; sg. dat. *cĕndas*, v, 5; xii, 15; abl. *cĕnda*, xii, 15.

carkh, m. a lathe; sg. dat. *carkas khālun*, to put on to a lathe, vii, 19; *carkas khasun*, to be put on to a lathe, vii, 20.

cārpāy, f. a bedstead; sg. dat. *cārpāyi*, x, 5.

cĕshma, m. an eye; pl. nom. *cĕshma*, i, 3.

ciṭh^i, f. a document, viii, 10 (bis).

cyon^u, to drink; inf. *hyotun cyon^u*, he began to drink, viii, 7 (ter);

pres. part. *cĕwān*, vi, 15; vii, 31; pres. m. sg. 3, *chuh cĕwān*, xii, 6; past. sg. f. neg. with suff. 3 pers. sg. ag. *trēsh cĕyĕnna*, he did not drink water, viii, 7; past cond. sg. 3, *trēsh cĕyihē*, (if) he had drunk water, viii, 7.

cyônᵘ, poss. pron. thy; sg. m. nom. *cyônᵘ*, v, 9; x, 14; xii, 16, 8; *cyônᵘ gatshi*, thou shouldst, v, 9; xii, 6, 20, 2, 3; emph. *cyônuy*, thine verily, v, 9; dat. *cyönis*, v, 9 (bis); pl. m. dat. *cyānĕn*, viii, 3, 11.

fem. sg. nom. *cyöñᵘ*, v, 9; viii, 3, 11; x, 10; dat. *cyāñĕ*, vi, 3; x, 12.

cīz, m. a thing, xii, 19.

dab, m. a fall from a height; *tōri-dab*, the fall, or blow, of an adze, vii, 18.

ḍab, f. (in *zūna-ḍab*), a covered wooden balcony on the roof of a house; sg. dat. *ḍabi*, viii, 1.

dŏb, m. a hole, or pit, in the ground, xii, 6; sg. dat. *dŏbas*, xii, 6, 7; sg. abl. *dŏba*, xii, 7; *dŏba-hanā*, a small hole in the ground, viii, 7 (*N.B.* masc.).

dabāwun, to press, squeeze; *daböwith thāwun*, to press into (the ground), to conceal (in the ground), x, 3.

dachyunᵘ, adj. right (not left); m. sg. abl. *dachini atha*, with the right hand, viii, 7.

dŏd, m. milk; *dŏda-bĕñĕ*, f. a milk-sister, a foster sister, iii, 4; *dŏda-gūrᵘ*, m. a milk cowherd, a milkman, xi, 13; *dŏda-har*, m. cream of milk, ii, 3; *dŏda-möjᵘ*, f. a foster mother, v, 2 (ter); *dŏda-noṭᵘ*, a milk-pail, xi, 3.

dodᵘ, see *dazun*.

dôdᵘ, m. pain, agony, anguish (mental or physical), v, 3, 6, 7; vii, 1 (bis), 21; ix, 6; xii, 15; sg. dat. *dödis*, v, 6 (bis); abl. *dādi*, vii, 22; pl. dat. *dādĕn*, vi, 14; *tas chuh dôdᵘ pananis dilas*, she has pain in her heart, xii, 15.

dādkhāh, m. a petitioner; *ôsus dagāy zāgān dādkhāh*, disloyalty (to the king) was watching in him as a petitioner, ii, 5.

dödⁱlad, adj. pained, afflicted; with *ay*, if, suffixed, *dödⁱlad-ay*, vii, 9.

dīdār, adj. seeing; *söhiba-sondᵘ kara dīdār*, I will do seeing of the master, I will see the master, iv, 5.

dēg, f. a large metal pot, a cauldron; pl. nom. *dēga*, vi, 16.

dagāy, f. disloyalty (cf. *dādkhāh*), ii, 5 (bis), 11 ; *āgas-pěṭh dagāy karūñᵘ*, to show faithlessness to one's master, viii, 8.

dᵘh, m. smoke ; *diwān chuh achěn dᵘh*, he puts smoke in (her) eyes, he abuses her, v, 11.

dah, card., ten, v, 6.

dŏh, a day ; *dŏh gav*, the day passed, v, 11 ; *dŏh ta rāth*, night and day (adverbially), vii, 3 ; with suff. of indef. art. *dŏhā akh banyāv*, a certain day came, xii, 1 ; *dŏhā dŏhā kaḍun*, to pass each day, viii, 3, 11 ; xii, 4, 11 ; sg. dat. *dŏhas*, by day (cf. *rātas*, by night), xii, 4 ; abl. *tami dŏha*, on that day, ii, 7 ; v, 5 ; x, 12 ; *dŏha*, by day, on each day, xii, 9 ; *aki dŏha* (v, 1) or *dŏha aki* (ii, 8 ; iii, 1 ; v, 1 ; viii, 1, 3 (bis), 7, 11), on a certain day ; *prath dŏha*, every day (adv.), viii, 1 (bis) ; gen. *dŏhukᵘ*, x, 10 ; fem. *dŏhücᵘ*, x, 10, 14 ; pl. nom. *dŏh gay*, days elapsed, iii, 5 ; xii, 23. Note the adverbial form, *öṭhi dŏhᶦ*, after eight days, iii, 4.

düjᵘ, f. a square piece of cloth, a napkin, a kerchief ; *bata-düjᵘ*, a kerchief containing food, xi, 18.

dujān, adj. pregnant, xi, 7 (f. pl.).

ḍākh, m. the post (for letters) ; sg. dat. *ḍākas*, xi, 6.

dökhil, adj. entered ; *karuhukh dökhil-i-mahala-khāna*, bring them into your harem, xii, 19.

ḍakhanāwun, to lean upon (a stick or the like) ; pres. part. *ḍakhanāwān*, xi, 16.

dukhtar, f. a daughter ; *dukhtar-ĕ-khāsa*, (your) own daughter, v, 11.

dil, m. the heart, mind, soul, v, 7 ; *dar dil*, in the heart, ii, 5 ; sg. dat. *dilas*, i, 7 ; ii, 5 ; xii, 15 ; *dilas pyōs yinsāph*, his heart was filled with pity, viii, 11 ; *dôdᵘ dilas*, pain in the heart, xii, 5.

ḍölᶦ, the gusset of a garment ; in *ḍōli-dāmānas*, v, 9, to the skirt of the gusset of the garment, i.e. to the skirt of the garment. The sg. abl. *ḍāli* has been altered to *ḍōli* m.c. See *dāmān*.

ḍölī, f. in *kana-ḍölī*, closing of the ear, refusal to hear, v, 2.

dalīl, f. a story, tale, narrative, viii, 7, 10, 1, 3 ; x, 1 (quater) ; with suff. of indef. art. *dalīlā*, viii, 6, 8, 11 ; x, 1 (bis).

*dālom*ᵘ, m. leather; with emph. *y dālomuy*, nothing but leather, xi, 14.

*ḍulun*ᵘ, m. the act of rolling; pl. nom. *ḍulànⁱ diwān chuh*, he is rolling himself, xii, 23.

dilāsa, m. soothing, consolation; — *dyun*ᵘ, to soothe, ix, 7.

*dŏmbij*ᵘ, f. a crupper, xi, 9.

dāmān, the skirt of a garment; sg. dat. *dāmānas thaph karüñ*ᵘ, to seize the skirt of a person in entreaty, begging, in making improper advances, or the like, v, 9 (bis); *ḍōli-dāmānas-thaph lāyüñ*ᵘ, id., v, 9 (see *ḍōl*ⁱ), with the double meaning.

dānāh, adj. wise; *dānāh wazīran*, by a wise vizier, viii, 1.

dīn, m. faith, religion; *dīn-i-Mahmad*, the religion of Muḥammad, iv, 6.

*dōn*ᵘ, m. a pomegranate, xii, 22 (bis), 23 (bis).

danḍ, m. punishment, fine; sg. abl. *danḍa dyun*ᵘ, to give in compensation (for harm, etc., done), v, 11; *danḍa hyon*ᵘ, to take in compensation, v, 11.

*d*ᵃ*nun*, to shake out (clothes), to shake (clothes); pres. 3 m. sg. *chuh d*ᵃ*nān*, x, 7.

dŏnaway, card. both. x. 4, 5, 13; xi, 12.

duniyā, m. the world; sg. dat. *dunⁱyāhas*, xii, 18 (bis).

dapun, to say (the person addressed is usually put in the dat., sometimes with *kun* added, as in *dapān chuh amis mĕjĕras kun*, he says to this master of the horse, x, 12); to send word asking for something, xii, 15.

inf. *dapun gatshis*, you must say to her, v. 9; fut. pass. part. *dapun chuwa*, (whatever) is to be said by you, (whatever) you have to say, v, 8; pres. part. *dapān wuchukh*, as they said (this), they looked, viii, 1.

impve. sg. 2, *daph*, xii, 4; say to him, *dapus*, xii, 20; fut. *dàpⁱzĕm*, you must say to me, v, 8; *dàpⁱzĕm-na*, you must not say to me, v, 8; *dàpⁱzĕkh*, you must say to them, v, 7; past, *dàpⁱzihĕkh*, you should have said to them, xi, 15 (bis).

fut. sg. 1, *dapay*, I will say to thee, iii, 4; v, 5; *dapas*, I will say to him, xii, 19; 3. *dapi*, he will say, x, 1; she will say, v, 9; *dapiy*, she will say to thee, xii, 18; pl. 3, *dapanam*, they will say to me, ii, 11; *dapanay*, they will say to thee, xii, 16.

pres. (often used as historical pres.), *dapān* (pres. part. alone used without auxiliary), say, (he or she) says, ii, 1, 2, 5, 9, 10, 12; iii, 2, 4, 5, 6, 7, 8, 9; v, 1, etc.: vii, 3, etc.; viii, 1, 10; ix, 4; x, 7; xii, 4, 24; they say, i.e. people say, iii, 9; v, 9; vi, 16 (ter); viii, 4; sg. m. 3, *dapān chuh*, he says, iv, 1; viii, 8, 9; x, 8, 12; xii, 10, 11, 14, 19, 20; *chuy dapān*, he says verily, iii, 4; *dapān chum*, he says to me, xii, 20; he says to him or her, *chus dapān*, v, 5, 11; viii, 3, 11 (bis); x, 8 (bis), 14; xii, 3, 13, 20; *dapān chus*, iii, 4; v, 11; viii, 9; x, 4, 8, 10 (bis), 14; xii, 3, 5, 10 (bis), 3 (bis), 9; he says to them, *chukh dapān*, x, 1, 12 (ter), 4; f. she says, *chĕh dapān*, vii, 2, 7, 8; ix, 6; x, 5; *dapān chĕh*, iii, 3, 4; ix, 1; xii, 7, 11; she says to him or her, *chĕs dapān*, viii, 3, 11; xii, 4, 15; *dapān chĕs*, v, 3, 11; ix, 6; xii, 10, 4; pl. m. 3, *dapān chih*, they say, i.e. people say, iii, 3; they say to him, *chis dapān*, x, 1 (bis); *dapān chis*, ii, 3.

past sg. 3 m. *dop*[u], said, ii, 4; v, 9; viii, 1, 13; x, 2, 8; xi, 2, 11, 2, 4; xii, 4, 5, 9.

dopum, I said; I said to you, *dopum*[a]*wa*, x, 12.

dopun, he or she said, ii, 7, 9, 11; iii, 9; v, 6, 8, 9, 10; viii, 3, 4, 6, 9, 10, 3; x, 2, 5 (bis); xii, 5, 13, 9, 21 (bis); asked from thee, *dopuy*, xii, 15; said to him, *dopus*, i, 7; v, 1; xii, 1; he said for me, *dop*[u]*nam*, iv, 4; she said to thee, *dop*[u]*nay*, x, 12; he or she said to him or her, *dop*[u]*nas*, ii, 9, 11; iii, 1 (quater), 2, 4 (ter), 5 (quinquies), 8 (quater), 9 (ter); v, 1, 4 (ter), 5 (bis), 6 (ter), 8, 9 (quater), 12; vi, 5, 8, 14, 5 (quater); viii, 3 (bis), 6, 7, 8, 9 (ter), 10, 1 (sexies); ix, 1 (bis); x, 6 (bis), 10; xii, 1, 4 (sexies), 5 (bis), 7 (ter), 10, 1, 5 (septies), 6 (ter), 8 (ter), 20, 1, 2, 4, 5; he or she said to them, *dop*[u]*nakh*, ii, 6, 8; v, 8 (bis); vi, 16 (ter); viii, 1, 4 (ter), 5 (bis), 10, 1; x, 1 (ter), 5 (bis), 6 (bis), 12 (quater).

dop[u]*wa*, you said; you said to me, *dop*[u]*wam*, x, 12.

dopukh, they said, ii, 1; v, 7; viii, 1, 2; x, 1; xii, 18;

they said to me, *dop^{u}ham*, v, 8; they said to him, *dop^{u}has*, iii, 8 (bis); v, 8; viii, 3, 4 (bis), 5, 11; x, 1, 2, 5, 6, 7, 8, 12 (bis); xii, 1 (bis), 17, 23; they said to them, *dop^{u}hakh*, viii, 1; x, 12.

3 past, 3 sg. m. *dapyāv*, said long ago, xii, 24; I said long ago, *dapyām*, ix, 4; I said long ago to them, *dapyāmakh*, xi, 15.

dar, prep. in; *dar biyābān*, in the forest, ii, 4; *dar dil*, in the heart, ii, 5.

ḍēra, m. a lodging, a temporary residence, viii, 9; a tent, v, 11; sg. dat. *ḍēras*, viii, 9; *ḍēras-pĕṭh*, in a tent, v, 11.

dör^ü, f. a window; sg. gen. *dārĕ-handis dāsas*, to the sill of the window, v, 4; abl. *dāri-kán^i*, (thrown) through the window, v, 4 (bis); dat. *dārĕ-tal*, under the window, v, 4.

dūr 1, an ear-pendant; pl. dat. *dūran*, vii, 11.

dūr 2, distant; *dūr kaḍun*, to expel, banish, viii, 11; *shĕhara dūr*, far from the city, viii, 11; abl. *dūri rōzun*, to remain at a distance, vii, 18; note, *drāv dūr-pahān*, he went a short way off, x, 7; but *byūṭh^u dūri-pahān*, he sat at a little distance, x, 7.

darbār, m. a court (a king's), viii, 11.

dard, m. affection, ix, 8.

drāg, m. a famine, vi, 15.

dārun, to place, etc.; freq. part. *halam dör^i dör^i*, holding out the lapcloth, i.e. begging for alms, ix, 11; past masc. pl. 3, *zīṭh^i atha dör^{i}nam*, long arms are stretched over me, vii, 25.

drôt^u, m. a sickle, x, 5; sg. abl. *drāti-sötin*, by means of a sickle, ix, 5.

drāv, etc., see *nērun*.

darwāza, m. a doorway; — *thāwun*, to open a door, viii, 4 (bis), 11 (bis), 2; — *trop^{u}nas*, she shut the door against him, viii, 11.

drāy, etc., see *nērun*.

driy, f. a vow; *driy kasam karun*, to make a vow, viii, 1 (bis), 2.

dās, m. a window-sill; sg. dat. *dāsas*, v, 4 (bis).

ḍēshun, to see; fut. pass. part. *kāh gatshĕm-na ḍēshun^u*, no one may see me, xii, 22; conj. part. *ḍīshith*, having seen, v, 2;

pres. part. (for pres. tense), *ḍēshān*, (is) seeing, vi, 12; past m. sg. 3, *ḍyūṭh^u*, was seen, vi, 11 (bis), 5; viii, 10; *ḍyūṭh^u-na*, was not seen, x, 12; *ḍyūṭhum*, I saw, vi, 15 (bis); *ḍyūṭh^um-ay*, I verily saw, xi, 1; *ḍyūṭhuth*, thou sawest, vi, 15; plup. m. sg. 3, *ôs^u ḍyūṭh^umot^u*, (a dream) had been seen.

daskhath, m. a signature; — *karun*, to make a signature, sign, xii, 21; abl. *ath korun möl^i-sandi daskhata*, she signed it with the father's signature, xii, 22.

dwā, m. a prayer; *dwā-yi-khör*, a prayer for welfare, i, 3.

dawā (vi, 14), *dawāh* (v, 6 (quater)), m. a medicine, a remedy; *dawā-han*, f. a little medicine, v, 6.

dĕv, a demon, xii, 7; sg. abl. *dĕva-zāth*, the demon-race, the tribe of demons, xii, 16.

dav, m. a channel, drain; abl. *āb-dawa-kañ*, (enter) through the water drain, v, 4.

dawāh, see *dawā*.

dāwāh, m. a claim; — *ganḍun*, to make a claim, v, 11.

Day, m. God; *day^i*, God only, vii, 2; voc. *dāyĕ*, O God! iv, 1.

dŏy, the belief in two, dualism, as opposed to monotheism, vi, 6.

dŏyum^u, ord., second; m. sg. dat. *dŏyimis gulāma-sond^u*, of the second servant, viii, 6.

dyun^u, to give; to make over a person to another's charge, viii, 11.

anith dyun^u, to bring and give, xii, 4; *dab dyun^u*, to give blows, vii, 18; *dyutun bär^ishi-söty dŏba-hanā*, he made a small hole in the ground with his spear, viii, 7; *achĕn d^uh diwān chuh*, he is giving smoke in the eyes, he abuses, v, 11; *ḍulän^i din^i*, to roll oneself about, xii, 23; *dilāsa dyun^u*, to comfort, ix, 7; *danḍa dyun^u*, to give in compensation, v, 11; *tas gardan diñ^ü*, to behead him, ii, 8; *grāyĕ chĕs diwān*, I am causing to wave, vii, 11; *hukum dyun^u*, to give an order, x, 5, 9, 13; *halam bär^i bär^i dyun^u*, to fill the lap-skirt (of a beggar), to give alms, ix, 11: *jalwa dyun^u*, (of God) to give forth glory, to become manifest, vi, 7; *kadam dyun^u*, to set forth (*kun* = to), x, 11, 2; *khash dyun^u*, to cut, v, 4, 6; *krēkh diñ^ü*, to make an outcry, v, 7; xii, 7; *karith dyun^u*, to do completely, x, 12; *muslas dyut^u kas^am*, he pronounced a charm over the skin, xii, 22; *makh dyun^u*, to hit with an axe, vii, 14 ; *anun nād dith*, to send for (a person), summon, x, 12 ; xii, 17 ; *nāla dimahö*, I would give cries, vii, 23 ; *nār dyun*ᵘ, to set alight (to), to set on fire (dat. of obj.), xii, 21, 2, 4 ; *phahi dyun*ᵘ, to impale, v, 10 ; *pharyād dyun*ᵘ, to lay a complaint, x, 2 ; *phash dyun*ᵘ, to rub, v, 4 ; *rukhsath dyun*ᵘ, to give leave to depart, xii, 25 ; *rapaṭ dyun*ᵘ, to make a report, v, 9 ; *shĕmshēr dits*ᵘ*n shānd*, he put the sword under the pillow, x, 7 ; *amis shāph dyun*ᵘ, to pronounce a charm over him, xii, 15 ; *sawāl dyun*ᵘ, to present a petition, x, 5 ; *tam chum diwān*, he is causing me to be weary, vii, 17 ; *thaph diñ*ᵘ̈, to seize (dat. of obj.), viii, 7 ; xii, 12 ; *wāday Khŏdā dyun*ᵘ, to swear by God, xii, 7 ; *wurdī diñ*ᵘ̈, to give an order, vi, 16 ; *wŏtamukh*ⁱ *dyun*ᵘ, to put on upside down, v, 9 ; *zīr*ᵘ *diñ*ᵘ̈, to give a push, x, 7 (bis).

inf. *dyun*ᵘ ; sg. obl. *dini*, in order to give, ix, 7 ; fut. pass. part. m. sg. *rŏpayĕ hath gatshĕm dyun*ᵘ, you must give me 100 rupees, x, 6 ; so, m. pl. *gatshanam din*ⁱ, you must give them to me, x, 1 ; f. sg. *gatshĕm bakh*ᵃ*cöyish diñ*ᵘ̈, you must give me a present, xii, 3 ; conj. part. *dith*, vi, 7 ; x, 12.

impve. sg. 2, *dih* ; *di-sa*, give, sir, x, 8 ; *dim*, give to me, iii, 1 ; v, 11 (bis) ; viii, 3 ; xii, 4, 7, 15, 8 ; *dis*, give to her, xii, 4 ; *dikh*, give to them, viii, 11 ; pl. 2, *diyiv*, give ye, x, 12 ; xii, 21 ; give ye to me, *diyūm*, vi, 16 ; pol. impve. sg. 2, *dita*, please give thou, v, 9 ; x, 4 ; with emph. *y*, *ditay*, v, 2 ; please give to me, *ditam*, x, 5 ; fut. *dizikh*, thou must give to them, xii, 16.

fut. sg. 1, *dima* ; I shall give to thee, *dimay*, v, 6, 11 ; xii, 4, 7 ; with irreg. suff. 2nd person pl. *dimav*, (I say to you) I shall give, ii, 8 ; 3, *diyi* ; she will give to thee, *diyiy*, xii, 14 ; pl. 1, *dimaw* ; we shall give to thee, *dimōy*, x, 1.

pres. m. sg. 3, *chuh diwān*, he gives, v, 11 ; xii, 17 (bis), 22 ; he gives to me, *chum diwān*, vii, 14, 7, 8 ; pl. 3, *diwān chih*, they give, x, 14 ; f. sg. 1, *chĕs diwān*, I give, vii, 11, 22 ; 3, *chĕh diwān* ; she gives to him, *diwān chĕs*, xii, 4, 14.

past m. sg. *dyut*ᵘ, he was given, v, 9 ; viii, 11, 2 ; x, 2 ; xii, 22 (bis) ; I gave for you, *dyutum*ᵃ*wa*, x, 12 ; gave to him, *dyutus*, i, 10 ; xii, 4 ; he or she gave, *dyutun*, v, 4 (bis) ;

viii, 4, 7 ; x, 5, 9, 11, 2, 3 ; xii, 15 (bis), 25 ; with emph. *y*, *dyutun*^{ü}*y*, ii, 7 ; he or she gave to him or her, *dyut*^{u}*nas*, i, 9 ; v, 6 ; viii, 9 ; x, 6 ; xii, 5, 7 (bis), 11, 5, 6 (bis), 22 ; he or she gave to them, *dyut*^{u}*nakh*, ii, 7 ; x, 5 ; xii, 17 ; *dyutukh*, they gave, v, 10 ; x, 5 ; xii, 17, 24 ; pl. *dit*^{i}, they were given, xi, 17 ; I gave, *ditim*, x, 12 (bis) ; I gave to them, *dit*^{i}*makh*, ix, 11 ; he or she gave, *ditin*, vii, 5 ; x, 2 ; he gave to him, *dit*^{i}*nas*, x, 14.

f. sg. *dits*^{ü}, she was given, vi, 16 ; given to him, *dits*^{ü}*s*, viii, 7 ; he gave, *dits*^{ü}*n*, x, 7 (ter) ; xii, 7, 12 ; he or she gave to him or her, *dits*^{ü}*nas*, v, 9 ; x, 8 ; they gave, *dits*^{ü}*kh*, iii, 8 ; they gave to him, *dits*^{u}*has*, x, 5.

perf. m. sg. *chunakh dyut*^{u}*mot*^{u}, she has given to them, viii, 1 ; pl. *chim dit*^{i}*măt*^{i}, I have given, x, 12.

plup. m. sg. *ôs*^{u} *dyut*^{u}*mot*^{u}, had been given, x, 12 ; she had given to him, *ôs*^{u}*nas dyut*^{u}*mot*^{u}, v, 6 ; pl. they had been given to you, *ös*^{i}*wa dit*^{i}*măt*^{i}, x, 12.

past cond. sg. 1, *dimahö*, vii, 23 ; I would have given to them, *dimahakh*, vii, 20 ; 3, *mā diyihē*, he would not have given, viii, 13.

dyār, m. pl. coined money, wealth, x, 1, 6 ; *mŏhara-dyār*, coin-wealth, money in cash, i, 9.

dōzakh, m. hell ; sg. dat. *dōzakhas* (for *dōzakhas-manz*), in hell, xii, 19, 20.

dazun, to burn ; pres. m. sg. 3, *chuh dazān*, (a lamp) is burning, viii, 13 ; x, 7 ; with emph. ^{i}, *chuh dazōn*^{i}, is verily burning, x, 7 ; past sg. m. 3, *dod*^{u}, he was burnt up, xii, 25.

gŏb, adj. invisible ; — *gatshun*, to become invisible, iii, 6.

gobur, m. dial. for *gọbur*, a son ; pl. nom. *gabar*, viii, 1, 3 ; xii, 15.

gāḍ, f. a fish ; *gāḍa-hath*, a hundred fish, i, 8, 9.

gĕ̤ḍ^{ü}, a bunch or handful of grass or the like ; pl. nom. *gĕjĕ* ; *gĕjĕ karañĕ*, to make bundles of grass, hence, met. to crowd together, xi, 10.

gŏḍ, m. a beginning ; abl. *gŏḍa*, first, at first, iv, 2 ; v, 9 ; viii, 3 ; xi, 5 ; xii, 15.

gaḍun, i.q. *garun*, q.v.

gŏḍañ, adv. first, at first, iii, 1 ; x, 12 ; xi, 2, 3, 10 ; emph. *gŏḍañiy*, at the very first, viii, 10 ; x, 3, 10 ; xii, 4, 6.

gŏḍañuk^u, adj. first, the first, viii, 13 ; with emph. *y*, *gŏḍañukuy*, the very first, viii, 5 ; f. gen. *gŏḍañicĕ-handi khŏta*, (more beautiful) than the first, xii, 10.

gudarun, conj. 3, to happen, occur ; inf. *gudarun*, a happening, occurrence, viii, 5 ; 2 past m. sg. 3, *gudariv*, for *gudaryōv*, v, 9.

gadöyi, f. begging, mendicity, the condition of a beggar ; sg. gen. *gadöyiyĕ-hond^u*, x, 2.

gāh, m. brightness, brilliancy, lustre ; — *trāwun*, to emit light, x, 2.

gāh, m. a place, a time, a turn ; *gāh bĕgāh*, in and out of season, vi, 2 ; *shōra-gāh*, a time or opportunity for outcry, a proclamation, vi, 13.

gĕjĕ, see *gĕḍ^ü*.

göj^ünas, see *gālun*.

gāl, f. a feeling of shame caused by another's action, mortification, humiliation, ix, 4.

gul^u, m. the forearm ; *gul^i ganḍàn^i*, to stand in a reverent attitude, with the arms folded in front, v, 9.

gŏlām, m. a servant, a slave, viii, 6 (quinquies), 7, 11, 3 (bis) ; sg. dat. *gŏlāmas*, viii, 11 ; ag. *gŏlāman*, vi, 14 ; viii, 7, 8, 11 ; voc. *ay gŏlām*, viii, 6, 8, 11 ; pl. nom. *gŏlām*, viii, 5, 13.

galun, to be destroyed ; fut. pass. part. *suh gotsh^u galun^u*, he must be destroyed, xii, 10 ; fut. sg. 3, *gali*, xii, 24 ; past. m. pl. 3, *gàl^i*, xii, 25.

gālun, to destroy ; to cause to waste away ; past f. sg. *göj^ünas*, he caused me (fem.) to waste away, he pared me down, vii, 19 ; perf. m. sg. *chuy gôl^umot^u*, thou hast destroyed, ii, 11.

gām, m. a village ; pl. dat. *gāman*, xi, 8.

gumröyī, f. going astray ; *gayĕm gumröyī*, I went astray (lit. going astray happened to me), vii, 12.

gamot^u, *gŏmot^u*, *gōmot^u*, see *gatshun*.

gān, m. the keeper of a brothel, a prostitute's bully ; used as a term of contempt after another noun, as in *hāpath-gān*, a wretch of a bear (ix, 2); *kuṭ^a^wāl-gān*, the wretch of a police-captain (v, 9); *wātal-gān*, a wretch of a sweeper (xi, 15). sg. dat. *gānas*, v, 9 (bis); ix, 2; voc. *gānau*, xi, 15 (used by a wife to her husband).

ganḍ, m. a knot; *tath ganḍ karun*, to tie it up (in a parcel), x, 3.

*gŏnḍ^u^*, m. a posy, bunch; *pōshĕ-gŏnḍ^u^*, a posy of flowers, v, 4 (ter).

*gonḍ^u^*, m. the Turkestan pack-saddle, consisting of two straw-filled pommels joined in front; pl. nom. *gànḍ^i^*, xi, 9.

ganḍun, to tie, to bind, iii, 8 (an ass was tied up), v, 6; the thing to which the object is tied is put in the dat. (v, 10, 2; x, 2, 5). *gul^i^ ganḍàn^i^*, to stand in a reverent attitude with the arms folded, v, 9; *dāwāh ganḍun*, to present a claim in court, v, 11. Conj. part. (in sense of past part. pass.) *ganḍith*, iii, 8; impve. fut. *gànḍ^i^zĕs*, you must tie it, v, 6; past m. sg. *gonḍun*, he or she tied, v, 10, 2; *dāwāh gonḍ^u^nas*, she made a claim to him, v, 11; m. pl. *gànḍ^i^*, were bound, v, 9; *gànḍin*, he tied them, x, 2; plup. m. pl. *ösis gànḍ^i^màt^i^*, he had tied them on it, x, 5.

gŏnāh, m. sin; — *karun*, to sin, viii, 11 (bis).

*gūñ^u^*, a piece or gobbet of flesh or the like; pl. nom. *gañĕ karith*, having cut up, viii, 13; *chuh katarān gañĕ*, he cuts it into lumps, x, 7.

*gŏpöl^i^*, f. a female dancer, a singing girl, v, 10 (bis), 11 (bis).

gār, see *āhan-gār* and *nān-gār*.

gara, m. a house; — *gatshun*, to go to a house, to go home, v, 9, 10; xii, 4 (bis), 19; — *tsalun*, to run away home, v, 5; — *wātun*, to arrive at a house, to reach home, iii, 2, 3 (bis); v, 1, 4; x, 4, 6, 7, 14; xii, 1, 5 (ter), 8, 10, 1, 2, 4, 8 (bis), 20, 2 (bis), 5; — *wātanāwun*, to cause to arrive at a house, to bring (a person) home, iii, 9; v, 10; — *yun^u^*, to go home, iii, 1; v, 5, 10 (bis); xii, 11, 3; sg. dat. *garas*, ix, 4 (bis); abl. *gari*, at home, iii, 1; v, 10; xii, 5 (bis); *gari bĕhun*, to sit down in a house, to stay at home, x, 5; xii, 4 (bis); pl. dat. *garan* (for *garan-manz*), xi, 6.

gārē, see *gūr^ū^*.

gör, in *gör-zān*, adj. an ignorant person, hence, an unknown person, a stranger, vii, 27; xi, 5; sg. dat. *gör-zānas*, ii, 1.

gur^u, m. a horse, iii, 8 ; x, 3 ; sg. dat. *guris-kyut*^{u}, (grass) for the horse, x, 5 ; *guris khasun*, to mount a horse, ii, 11 ; iii, 8 (bis) ; *guris wŏthun*, to mount a horse, ii, 6 ; abl. *guri-pĕṭha wasith pyon*^{u}, to fall from one's horse, ii, 6 ; pl. nom. *gur*^{i}, horses, xi, 6, 8 ; xii, 1 ; gen. *gurĕn-hünz*^{ü} *khazmath*, service of horses, groom's work, xii, 3 ; abl. *wȧth*^{i} *guryau-pĕṭha bŏn*, they dismounted, xii, 2.

gūr^u, m. a cowherd ; *dŏda-gūr*^{u}, a milk-seller, xi, 13 ; sg. ag. *gūr*^{i}, xi, 12 ; *gūr*^{i}*-bāy*, f. a cowherd's wife, xi, 12.

gür^ü, f. a space of twenty minutes ; any particular moment of time ; abl. *sōli-gārē* (m.c. for *suli-gari*), at dawn time, v, 7.

gardan, f. the neck ; *tas gardan diñ*^{ü}, to behead him, ii, 8.

garm, adj. warm ; used as subst., warmth, i, 11.

garun or *gaḍun*, conj. 1, to make, form, fashion, forge, work metals ; impve. sg. 2, *gar*, v, 3 ; imperf. m. sg. 3, *ôs*^{u} *gaḍān*, he used to make, v, 1 ; past m. sg. *goḍun*, he or she made, v, 10, 2 ; pl. *gȧr*^{i}, were made, v, 4.

garanāwun, conj. 1, to get made, to make (with help), prepare ; pres. part. *garanāwān*, xi, 17.

grāy, f. shaking ; — *lagüñ*^{ü}, shaking to be experienced, to be unsteady, impermanent, ix, 12 ; pl. nom. *grāyĕ diñĕ*, to cause to wave, vii, 11.

gryūst^u, m. a farmer, ix, 4 ; sg. ag. *grīst*^{i}*-bāy*, a farmer's wife, ix, 1 (quater), 4, 6 (ter), 8, 10, 2 ; *grīst*^{i}*-gara*, a farmer's house, ix, 4 (bis) ; pl. dat. *grīstĕn*, ix, 7.

gar^a*z*, m. design, view, purpose ; abl. *garza panani*, for my own purpose, vii, 26.

görzān, see *gör*.

gāsa, grass, hay, x, 5 (bis) ; xi, 6, 7 ; *gāsa-gonḍ*^{u}, a pack-saddle made of grass, xi, 9 ; *gāsa-lôw*^{u}, a handful of grass, as much as is grasped by the hand near the root when cutting it, xi, 12 ; *gāsa-mödān*, a grassy mead, a grass-field, x, 5 ; *gāsa-raz*, a hay or straw rope, xi, 9.

gāsh or (viii, 9 ; xii, 2 (bis)) *gwāsh*, brightness, dawn ; — *phŏlun*, dawn to break, iii, 3 ; v, 5, 7 ; viii, 9 ; xii, 2.

gusôñ^u, m. a mendicant monk, v, 9.

gāṭa, m. skill, cleverness ; sg. abl. *gāṭa-sān*, with skill, i, 6.

gath, f. in *gath karüñ*ᵘ, (of a widow) to do the *satī* ceremony, to become *satī*, iii, 4.

*gāṭ*ᵘ*j*ᵘ, see *gāṭul*ᵘ.

*gāṭul*ᵘ, adj. skilful, clever; m. pl. nom. *gāṭ*ᵃ*l*ⁱ *gāṭ*ᵃ*l*ⁱ, several skilful (viziers), viii, 1; f. sg. nom. *gāṭ*ᵘ*j*ᵘ, v, 3, 10.

*guṭyul*ᵘ, a man who wields a *guṭil*, or axe for splitting logs into planks, a woodcutter; with suff. of indef. art. *guṭ*ⁱ*lā*, a certain woodcutter, vii, 12.

gatshun 1, conj. 2, to be right, proper, advisable; to be necessary, requisite. Constructed with the future passive participle, either actively or passively. It appears in these stories either in the future (sg. 3 *gatshi*, pl. 3 *gatshan*) or in the past tense (m. sg. 3 *gotsh*ᵘ). In the future it has the sense of the present. The forms are all easily recognizable in the examples given below.

A. Actively. *kāh gatshĕm-na ḍēshun*ᵘ, no one may see me, xii, 22.

B. Passively. Here the personal subject is either not expressed, or else is put in the dative or in the genitive.

(*a*) Personal subject not expressed, *anun*ᵘ *gatshi phaharawāv*, a file is necessary to be brought, i.e. you must bring a file, v, 4; so, *khabar* (f.) *gatshi anüñ*ᵘ, you must bring news, xii, 19, 20; *gatshi atsun*ᵘ, you must enter, v, 4; *g. hyon*ᵘ *khar*ᵃ*j*, you must take expenses, xii, 5; *dŏb g. khanun*ᵘ, you must dig a pit, iii, 6; *g. khasun*ᵘ, you must go up, xii, 6; *karun*ᵘ *g. ganḍ*, you must tie up, x, 3; *nēth*ᵃ*r g. karun*ᵘ, you must arrange a marriage, viii, 2; *suh g. sangsār karüñ*ᵘ, lapidation is to be done (to) him, he is to be stoned, viii, 8; *sargī g. karüñ*ᵘ, you must investigate, viii, 7, 8, 10; *g. karüñ*ᵘ *thaph*, you must seize, v, 9; *g. mangun*ᵘ *byākh*, you must ask for another, xii, 13; *yih g. mārun*ᵘ, you must kill him, x, 5 (bis), 12, 5; *sōzun*ᵘ *g. sŏnur*, you must send the goldsmith, v, 1; *g. pŏshākh tulun*ᵘ, you must take up the garment, xii, 6; *g. kākad trāwun*ᵘ, you must throw the paper, xii, 11; *tas g. kala* (*sar*) *tsaṭun*ᵘ, you must cut off his head, viii, 6, 11.

With pron. suff. *gatshĕm bakh*ᵃ*cöish* (f.) *diñ*ᵘ, you must give me a present, xii, 3; *gatshĕm bōzun*ᵘ, you must hear me, xii, 7; *rŏpayĕ-hath gatshĕm dyun*ᵘ, you must give me a hundred rupees (sing.), x, 6; *tih gatshĕm karun*ᵘ, you must do that to me, xii, 3; *kĕntshāh gatshĕm ladun*ᵘ, you must send me something, x, 3; *wŏlinj*ᵘ *gatshĕs anüñ*ᵘ, his heart must be brought (here), x, 5; *dapun*ᵘ *gatshĕs*, you must say to her, v, 9; *gatshĕs mŏhar karüñ*ᵘ, you must seal it, x, 3; *tsĕ kyāh gatshiy anun*ᵘ, what must (I) bring to thee? xii, 21; *kor*ᵘ *gatshiy āsun*ᵘ, I want a bracelet from thee, xii, 13.

tsŏcĕ (f. pl.) *gatshan bög*ᵃ*rañĕ*, loaves are to be distributed, you must distribute loaves, v, 8; *tithiy trĕh gatshan sǫmb*ᵃ*rāwån*ⁱ, you must collect three times as many, xii, 24; *tim gatshan tsaṭån*ⁱ, they must be cut, v, 4.

With pron. suff. *gatshanam din*ⁱ *rŏpayĕs pānts hath*, you must give me five hundred rupees, x, 1, 2; *lāl gatshanay āsån*ⁱ, rubies are required to be from thee, I want rubies from thee, xii, 5.

*suh gotsh*ᵘ *galun*ᵘ, he was proper to be destroyed, you should have destroyed him, xii, 19; *yih karun*ᵘ *gotsh*ᵘ, (that) which was proper to be done, v, 7; *wātun*ᵘ *gotsh*ᵘ, it was proper to arrive, I should have arrived, v, 7.

(*b*) Personal subject expressed in dative. *mĕ gatshi āsun*ᵘ (*kor*ᵘ), to me (a bracelet) is proper to be, i.e. I want (a bracelet), xii, 4 (bis), 10 (bis), 13; *mĕ gatshiy āsun*ᵘ *troṭ*ᵘ, I want a necklace from thee, xii, 5; *mĕ gatshi wātun*, I must arrive, xii, 22; *yih tsĕ gatshiy*, (that) which thou wantest, xii, 7; *gatshiy anun*ᵘ *mĕwa* (*khath*), thou must bring a fruit (a letter), xii, 21; *tsĕ gatshiyĕ āsun*ᵘ *okuy kor*ᵘ, oughtest thou to have only one bracelet? xii, 13; *tsĕ gatshiy yun*ᵘ, thou must come, xii, 7. Note *mĕ gatshi tihanza wŏlinjĕ*, I want their hearts, where the grammatical subject is plural, while the verb is singular, viii, 11.

(*c*) Personal subject expressed in genitive. *cyôn*ᵘ *gatshi gatshun*, thou must go, v, 9; xii, 6; *tih cyôn*ᵘ *khyon*ᵘ *gatshi-na*, thou must not eat that, xii, 16; *cyôn*ᵘ *gatshĕs mangun*ᵘ *musla*, thou must ask her for the skin, xii, 18; *cyôn*ᵘ *gatshi zyun*ᵘ *sǫmb*ᵃ*run*ᵘ, thou must collect firewood, xii, 20 ; *cyôn*^{u} *gatshi wātun*^{u}, thou must arrive, xii, 22, 3 ; *tuhond*^{u} *gatshi yun*^{u}, you must come, xii, 15.

gatshun 2, conj. 3, to go, i, 4 ; ii, 1, 3, 4, 6, 7, 9, et passim (the place or person to which one goes is usually in the dative, e.g. x, 10 ; xii, 4, 10, 2 ; cf. however, *gayĕ kŏli akis pĕṭh*, she went to the bank of a stream, xii, 2) ; to go, disappear, die, ii, 4 ; to go, elapse (of a period of time), iii, 1, 5 ; v, 10, 1 ; viii, 2 (bis), 10 ; xii, 6, 20, 3 ; to become, iii, 4, 9 ; viii, 11 ; ix, 4 ; xi, 3, 18 ; to happen, occur, ii, 12 ; v, 8 ; vi, 16 ; vii, 12 (bis), 3 ; viii, 1 (ter), 3 (bis) ; ix, 1, 6 (bis) ; xii, 15, 23 (*kyāh gōm*, what happened to me ? viii, 9 ; *kyāh gav*, what is the matter ? viii, 11 ; *kyāh gayĕ*, what was (fem.) it ? x, 14 ; *gayĕ trih katha*, three stories happened, i.e. there, you have had your three stories, x, 1).

The past tense " became " is often used in the sense of " am ", " is ", etc. Thus, ii, 1 ; iii, 9 ; v, 7 ; vi, 6 (*khŏdā gav suy*, God is He alone, i.e. God is one, there is no duality about Him) ; viii, 13 ; x, 1, 10 (*kyāh gōs*, of course I am, I am no other than), 2 (id.), 4 ; xii, 15 (*zab*^{a}*r gav*, it is all right).

Often in idiomatic phrases (mostly nominal compounds), as *ādā gatshun*, to be completed, come to an end (of night, a month, etc.), x, 8 ; xii, 4, 9, 11, 2 ; *ạsh*^{ĕ}*kh g.*, love to befall a person, v, 2 (bis) ; *bĕdār g.*, to become awake, awake, wake up, vi, 12 ; viii, 6, 9, 13 ; *g. bĕmār*, to fall sick, v, 10 ; *gay pānas bīṭh*^{i}, they sat down at liberty from their turn of duty, viii, 8 ; *gŏb g.*, to disappear, iii, 6 ; *g. panun*^{u} *gara*, to go home, xii, 4 ; *hushyār g.*, to become awake, to wake up, v, 5 (bis) ; *khalās g.*, to go free, to be released from this mortal coil, to die, iii, 4 ; *rŏpayĕ hath gōm khar*^{a}*c*, expenditure of the hundred rupees happened to me, I have spent the hundred rupees, viii, 10 ; *khŏsh g.*, to become pleased, happy, viii, 1, 9, 14 ; xi, 18 ; xii, 9, 12 ; *gōs yiṁn z*^{a}*h khŏsh*, these two were pleasing to him, he felt affection for them, viii, 11 ; *māra gatshun*, to suffer a violent death, viii, 13 ; x, 7, 8 ; *mushtākh g.*, to become entranced, enamoured, iii, 8, 9 ; *g. pŏda*, to become manifest, appear, become visible, turn up, ii, 1 ; iii, 8 ; x,

4, 5, 7; xii, 10; *phikiri g.*, to go into anxiety, to become anxious, viii, 10; xii, 4; *amis gav shĕkh*, she felt hesitation, xii, 15; *sàr*[i] *gatshun*, to be drowned, iv, 3; *g. thod*[u] *wŏthith*, to stand up, ii, 3; *tsĕr gav*, it has become late, it is too late, v, 9; *nār gŏmot*[u] *tshĕta*, the fire had become extinguished, xii, 23; *gōs yinsāph*, he felt pity, viii, 4; *mĕ-ti chuh gŏmot*[u] *zulm*, I also have experienced tyranny, ix, 1.

With a present participle, *gatshun* indicates continuous action, as in *gatshta bōzān*, keep hearing, listen attentively to the whole, xi, 1; *gatshiv parān*, recite ye continually, vii, 4; similarly vi, 17; *gatsh tārān*, take tribute, and go on doing so perpetually, xi, 2; *gatshu trāwān*, go on leaving behind (at every stage), xi, 11.

With a conjunctive participle it forms frequent compounds, most of them the so-called "Intensives". Thus, *hĕth gatshun*, to take away (Hindī *lē jānā*), v, 1; viii, 3 (bis), 4, 10, 2; xii, 4, 9, 12, 8; *marith gatshun* (Hindī *mar jānā*), to die, vi, 16; *kath mashith gayĕs*, he forgot the statement, x, 6; *nīrith gatshun*, to go forth, ii, 3; xii, 15; *phīrith gatshun*, to become hostile, iv, 3.

fut. pass. part. *mĕ chuy gatshun*[u], it is verily to be gone by me, i.e. I must really go, v, 10; *cyôn*[u] *gatshi gatshun*[u], thou must go, v, 9; xii, 6; pres. part. *gatshān*, see pres. and imperf.; past part. *gamot*[u] or *gŏmot*[u], see perf. and plup.

impve. sg. 2 *gatsh*, ii, 9; iii, 5; vi, 17; viii, 10; xi, 2; xii, 4, 5, 11 (bis), 4, 20; poetical, *gatshu*, xi, 11; pl. 2 *gatshiv*, vii, 4; x, 7, 8; pol. sg. 2 *gatshta*, xi, 1.

fut. sg. 2 *gatshakh*, v, 5, 6; xii, 18; 3 *gatshi*, v, 8; pl. 1, *gatshav*, viii, 3; xii, 18; 3 *gatshan*, xi, 12.

pres. m. sg. 3 *gatshān*, iii, 6; *chuh gatshān*, xii, 4; *gatshān chuh*, xii, 4; with pron. suff. 3 pers. sg. dat. *gatshān chus*, he goes (to shave) him, xii, 19; f. sg. 3 *chĕh gatshān*, x, 5; viii, 1; *gatshān chĕh*, xii, 23; imperf. f. sg. 3 *ös*[ü] *gatshān*, v, 1; neg. *ös*[ü]*na gatshān*, viii, 1; m. pl. 3 (two subjects, one masc., the other fem.), *ös*[i] *gatshān*, viii. 1.

I past m. sg. 1 *gōs*, x, 10, 2, 4; emphatic, *gōsay*, I verily became (pleased), xi, 18; m. sg. 3 *gav*, viii, 10, 1 (bis), 3;

x, 4, 7 (ter), 10; xi, 1, 18; xii, 1, 4 (quater), 7, 9 (bis), 10, 2 (bis), 3, 5 (ter), 8; with suff. 1st pers. sg. dat. *gōm*, he went to me, etc., iii, 1; v, 7; vii, 12, 3; viii, 9, 10; with suff. 3rd pers. sg. dat. *gōs*, he went to him or her, etc., iii, 4, 8; viii, 4, 10, 1; xii, 12; neg. *gōs-na*, went not for her, v, 5; with suff. 3rd pers. pl. dat. *gōkh*, he became (pleased) with them, viii, 14; m. pl. 3 *gay*, ii, 1, 4; iii, 5; v, 9; vi, 9 (he and she), 16; viii, 3 (ter), 4, 5, 8, 11 (bis), 2, 3; x, 1; xi, 3; xii, 6, 11, 23; with suff. 3rd pers. sg. dat. *gös*, they went for him or her, etc., iv, 3; v, 4.

f. sg. 3 *gayĕ*, iii, 1 (bis), 4, 9; v, 9, 10, 1; x, 8, 14 (bis); xii, 2, 9, 10, 2, 3; with suff. of 1st pers. sg. dat. *gayĕm*, ix, 4; emph. *gayĕmay*, it (fem.) verily happened to me, vii, 12; with suff. of 3rd pers. sg. dat. *kath gayĕs mashith* (see above), x, 6; f. pl. 3 *gayĕ*, iii, 8; x, 1.

II past, went a long time ago, m. sg. 3 *gayāv*, xii, 15; f. sg. 3 *gayē* (for *gayēyĕ*), vii, 16; viii, 11.

perf. m. sg. 2 *chukh gŏmotu*, xii, 4; neg. *chukh-na gŏmotu*, v, 5; 3 *gamotu*, x, 7; *gŏmotu*, xii, 23; *chuh gamotu*, ii, 4; iii, 1; v, 10; viii, 1; *chuh gŏmotu*, ix, 1 (bis), 6; with suff. 2nd pers. sg. dat. *chĕyĕy* (not *chuyĕy*) *gŏmotu*, (cf. *chĕy nāg*, xii, 6), ix, 6; pl. 3 *gamȧti*, x, 7, 8; xii, 20; f. sg. 3 *gamütsü*, xii, 10.

plup. m. sg. 3 *ôsu gamotu*, i, 4; v, 2; with suff. 3rd pers. sg. dat. *ôsus gŏmotu*, (love) had befallen him, v, 2; pl. 1 *ösi gamȧti*, v, 9.

gāv, f. a cow; sg. dat. *gōvü*, xi, 12; pl. nom. *gōvü*, vi, 15; xi, 12 (bis); pl. dat. (in sense of acc.) *gōvün*, vi, 15.

gĕwun, m. a song, iv (title).

gwāsh, see *gāsh*.

gawöyi, f. evidence, testimony; *chis karān gawöyi*, they give evidence to him, x, 12.

Gaznavī, of or belonging to the town of Ghaznī, i, 1.

guzarān, m. a livelihood; — *karun*, to make a livelihood, xi, 19.

ha, O! (inferior addressing superior); *ha*, *Wazīr-a*, O Vizier, xii, 19. Cf. the next.

hā, O!, ha!; as exclamation, xi, 3; governing voc., with *-a*;

hā phakīr-a, O Faqīr, ii, 3; *hā Vigiñāh nāg-a*, O Vigiñāh Nāg, v, 9; *hā yār-a*, O friend, x, 4; *hā Wazīr-a* (address by an inferior), O Vizier, xii, 10; with *-ō*; *hā phakīr-ō*, O Faqīr, ii, 2; *hā wazīr-ō*, O Vizier (address by a superior), ii, 4.

hau, pleonastic suff. (poet.), ii, 10.

hŏ, pleonastic suff. added to *kyāh*, *kĕhŏ*, what? (addressed by wife to her husband), v, 4, 5.

hab-jushī, composed of the seven metals (*haft-jōsh*), i.e. iron, antimony, lead, gold, tin, copper, and silver, xii, 22.

hĕchun, to learn; impve. sg. 2 *hĕch lāyȧn*ⁱ *rīnz*ⁱ, learn to throw balls, v, 3.

had, a limit; *had pānas karun*, to make a limit for oneself, to consider oneself perfect, vii, 15.

hihur, a father-in-law; sg. gen. *hihara-sandis shĕharas-kun*, towards the father-in-law's city, x, 12.

hakh, m. right, duty; *hakh-i Khŏdāy*, duty of God, i.e. (a husband), sacred to me as God, xii, 15.

*hǫkh*ᵘ, dry (of a river); pl. nom. *hŏkh*ⁱ, vi, 15.

hakīm, m. a wise man, a sage, vi, 14; with suff. of indef. art. *hakīmā*, a single wise man, vi, 14.

hukum, *hukm*, m. an order, command; *kyāh chum hukum*, what order have you for me, xii, 7; *hukm-i-Māhrāj*, the order of the Mahārāja, xi, 4; *hukum dyun*ᵘ, to give an order, ii, 7; viii, 4, 11, 2, 3; x, 5, 9, 13.

hĕkmath, f. cleverness, skill, contrivance; *hĕkmat-i-Parwardigār*, the power of Providence, i, 11; sg. abl. *hĕkmüts*ᵘ, i, 12.

hāl, m. condition, state, vii, 9; ix, 4; *hāl kyāh kor*ᵘ*hakh*, an arrangement of affairs was somehow or other made by them, xi, 17.

hāl, f. a house; *bŏ̄d*ⁱ*-hāl*, a prison, ix, 4.

hala, interj. expressing urgency, look sharp! be quick, xii, 17.

halam, m. a skirt, a lap-cloth, apron, ix, 11; *halam dārun*, to hold out the lap-cloth for alms, to beg, ix, 11; sg. dat. *halamas*, v, 4 (bis), 5.

hamud, m. praise; *h. parun*, to recite praises, vii, 4.

hamnishīn, m. a companion, a familiar friend; pl. nom., id., vii, 20 (bis); dat. *hamnishīnan*, vii, 21, 4.

hamsāyĕ, m. a neighbour, x, 12 ; pl. nom., id., x, 5.

han, dim. suff. f. *bata-han*, a little cooked rice, a little food, x, 5 ; *dawā-han*, a little medicine, v, 6 ; *kår^i-han*, a small bracelet, xii, 12 ; *musla-han*, a piece of skin, xii, 21 ; *nāra-han*, a small fire, iii, 1 ; *ratshi-han*, a very little (of something), v, 6 (bis) ; *tshĕṭh-han*, a little waste food, x, 5.

hanā, a small quantity, x, 5 ; dim. suff. (f. unless otherwise stated) *āba-hanā*, a little water, x, 5 ; *bata-hanā*, a little cooked rice, x, 3 (masc.) ; *dŏba-hanā*, a small hole or pit, viii, 7 (masc.); *kashĕna-hanā*, a little scratching, a small amount of scratching, xii, 16, 17 ; *pāri-hanā*, a small hut, xii, 2 ; *ratshi-hanā*, a very little (of something), v, 6.

hani-hani, in small pieces, in fragments, viii, 6.

hūn^u, m. a dog, viii, 9 (sexies), 10 (quater) ; sg. dat. *hūnis*, viii, 9, 10 (ter) ; pl. nom. *hūn^i*, viii, 4 (bis), 12 (bis).

hond^u, postpos. of gen.

A. Added to fem. sg. nouns ; m. sg. nom. *gadöyīyĕ-hond^u*, of beggary, x, 2 ; *kōrĕ-hond^u*, of the daughter, v, 2, 9 ; *kathi-hond^u*, of a word, iii, 5 ; *mājĕ-hond^u*, of a mother, xii, 15 ; *miskīnī-hond^u*, of beggary, x, 4 (bis) ; *nayĕ-hond^u*, of a reed flute, vii, 1 ; *phakīriyĕ-hond^u*, of faqīrhood, x, 9 ; *pātashōhī-hond^u*, of royalty, x, 2, 9 ; *röts^ü-hondu*, of night, iii, 1 ; dat. *bĕñĕ-handis*, of the sister, x, 3 (bis), 10 ; *bāyĕ-handis*, of the wife, viii, 6, 13 ; *dārĕ-handis*, of the window, v, 4 ; *khôtūni-handis*, of the lady, x, 7 ; *shĕmshĕri-handis*, of the sword, viii, 13 ; *zanāni-handis*, of the wife, x, 5 ; abl. *gŏḍañicĕ-handi-khŏta*, than the first, xii, 10 ; *khótūni-handi*, of the lady, x, 7 (bis) ; fem. sg. nom. *bĕñĕ-hünz^u*, of the sister, x, 3 ; *nayĕ-hünz^u*, of the reed flute, vii, 1 ; *shĕmshĕri-hünz^ü*, of a sword, iii, 5, 6.

B. Added to plural nouns ; m. sg. nom. *sōdāgāran-hond^u*, of merchants, viii, 9 ; *wŏranĕcivĕn-hond^u*, of step-sons, viii, 3 ; *hatan-hond^u*, of hundreds, v, 1 ; *jānāwāran-hond^u*, of birds, viii, 1 ; *lālan-hond^u*, of rubies, xii, 5 (ter) ; abl. *dŏn-handi-khŏta*, than two, xii, 9 ; pl. nom. *athan-hånd^i*, of hands, v, 6 ; f. sg. nom. *gurĕn-hünz^ü*, of horses, xii, 3 ; *nĕcivĕn-hünz^u*, of sons, viii, 3, 11 ; *yihünz^u*, of these, viii, 1 ; pl. nom. *dŏn-*

hanza, of two, viii, 4; *pātashāhzādan-hanza*, of princes, viii, 4; *tihanza*, their, viii, 3.

C. Added to an adverb; *yuri-hond*ᵘ, hither, v, 5.

hanga ta manga, adv. unexpectedly, iii, 6.

*hönz*ü, m. a boatman; with suff. of indef. art. *hānzāh*, i, 4.

hāputh, m. a bear, ii, 10, 1 (ter), 2; *hāpath-gān*, a bear pimp, a bear referred to abusively, ix, 2; sg. dat. *hāpatas*, ii, 10, 1; ag. *hāpatan*, ix, 4.

har 1, every; *har wati*, on every path (fem.), ii, 2.

har 2, m. cream; sg. gen. *dŏda-hȧrȧk*ⁱ, (cups) of milk-cream, ii, 3.

*hȧr*ⁱ *hȧr*ⁱ, the cry used in driving a cow, xi, 8. Cf. *chuh* 1.

harud, m. autumn; *har*ᵃ*da-vizi*, in autumn time, ix, 8.

hargāh, if; *hargāh drās-na*, if it do not issue from it, xii, 3 (bis); *hargāh-ay wuchihē*, if he had seen, viii, 10; *hargāh kiy cĕyihē*, if he had drunk, viii, 7; *hargāh kiy karihē*, if he had done, viii, 13.

*h*ᵃ*run*, to remain over and above; 2 past m. sg. 3, *h*ᵃ*ryōv*, x, 12; f. sg. 3, with suff. 3 pers. pl. dat. *h*ᵃ*ryēyĕkh*, x, 5.

harun, to drop; pres. sg. 3 *māz chum harān*, my flesh is dropping, vii, 24; pl. 3 *lāl chih harān*, rubies are dropping (from her mouth), xii, 9 (bis).

hasa, interj. sir! ii, 11; v, 7; vi, 11; x, 4 (bis), 8; xii, 1 (bis), 5, 10; sirs! x, 1 (passim).

hōsh, m. sense, i, 5.

hushyār, awake; —*gatshun*, to awake (intrans.), v, 5 (ter).

*host*ᵘ, m. an elephant, vi, 16 (ter).

hata, interj.; *hata-sa*, O sirs! x, 5; *hatay*, hullo! (a mother speaking to her daughter), xii, 15.

hatō, interj.; *hatō ködyau*, ho prisoner! x, 5.

*hot*ᵘ, smitten; *tsakhi-hot*ᵘ, smitten by rage, full of rage, vii, 14.

*hoṭ*ᵘ, m. the throat; — *tsaṭun*, to cut the throat, v, 7; sg. dat. *haṭis*, viii, 1.

hath, a hundred; *gāḍa-hath*, a hundred fish, i, 8; *hath waīsi*, a hundred (years) in age, ii, 12; *rŏpayĕ-hath*, a hundred rupees, viii, 9, 10 (with verb in sg.); x, 6 (ditto); *rŏpayĕs pānts hath*, five hundred rupees, viii, 10 (bis); x, 1, etc.; sg. dat. *gāḍa-hatas*, for the hundred fish, i, 9; *mŏhara-hatas* (*akis*) *rosh^u*, a necklace of one hundred mohars, v, 10, 12; pl. dat. *tsāṭas* (sic) *bāhan hatan-hond^u*, of twelve hundred pupils, v, 1; *hata-bọ̆d^u*, hundreds, ix, 9; *hatabŏd^i-khôr^u*, weighing hundreds of kharwārs, ix, 7.

hots^u, m. the forearm, xii, 12 (bis), 15; sg. gen. *hatsyuk^u*, xii, 15.

hātsh, f. an accusation; with suff. of indef. art. *hātshā*, vi, 9.

hav, interj. O (addressed by a woman to her husband), v, 4; xi, 11. Cf. *hay*.

hawā, m. air, atmosphere; *hawā-yi-asmān*, the air of heaven, ii, 6.

hawāh, f. Eve, vii, 7.

hawāla, m. deposit, consignment, charge, v, 10; *hawāla-y-Khŏdā*, in the care of God, x, 7; *hawāla karun*, to put in so and so's (dat.) charge, to make over (to) as a deposit, v, 7, 12 (bis); viii, 4; x, 12 (quinquies); xii, 22.

hāwun, to show, make manifest; *kasam hāwun*, to make oath, swear, v, 9; impve. sg. 2 *hāv*, xii, 14; pol. with suff. 1st pers. sg. dat. *hāvtam*, please show to me, v, 9; fut. sg. 1, with suff. 2nd pers. sg. dat. *hāway*, I will show to thee, iii, 8; 3, *hāvi* v, 9; pl. 3, with suff. 1st pers. sg. dat. *hāwanam*, they will show to me, iv, 7; 1 past m. sg. with suff. 2nd pers. sg. ag. *hôwuth*, thou showedst, vi, 5; with suff. 3rd pers. sg. ag. *hôwun*, vi, 16; xii, 15; ditto, with suff. 1st pers. sg. dat. *hôw^unam*, she showed to me, v, 4; ditto, with suff. 2nd pers. sg. dat. *hôw^unay*, she showed to thee, v, 4; ditto, with suff. 3rd pers. pl. dat. *hôw^unakh*, he showed to them, xii, 18; with suff. 3rd pers. sg. dat. *hôwus*, showed to him, v, 4; past cond. sg. 1 *hāwahö*, vii, 21.

hay, interj. O! (addressed by a man to his wife), v, 4 (passim); xi, 14, 6, 9; (addressed by woman to woman), v, 2; ix, 7, 9.

hāy, interj., as exclamation, O! v, 7.

hyuh^u, adj. like; m. sg. nom. *lālas hyuh^u*, like a ruby, xii, 4 (bis); *tath^i hyuh^u*, exactly like that, xii, 4; *yinsān hyuh^u*, like a human being, x, 7 (bis); dat. *baḍis hihis*, to the elder (prince), viii, 13; *ziṭhis hihis*, to the elder (prince), viii, 5; ag. *lŏk^{ā}ṭ^i hih^i*, by the youngest, xii, 1; f. sg. nom. *yinsān hish^ü*, like a man, x, 7.

hyol^u, an ear (of corn, etc.); pl. nom. *hĕl*^{i}, vi, 15; pl. dat. *hĕlĕn*, vi, 15.

hyon^u, to take, ii, 1; iii, 1, 2; v, 1, 4, 6, 7 (bis); viii, 7; x, 5, 11; xi, 12, 3, 4, 6, 8; xii, 5, 12, 20, 22, 23; to begin, *hyotun cyon*^{u}, he began to drink, viii, 7 (ter); *hyotun nērun*, he began to go forth, ii, 3; *hyotukh pakun*, they began to go, x, 1; *hĕts*^{ü}*n wŏṭh tshunüñ*^{ü}, she began to leap, iii, 4; *hĕts*^{ü}*nas yiñ*^{ü} *nẹnd*^{a}*r*, sleep began to come to him, v, 6. The conj. part. *hĕth*, having taken, may often be translated "with", as in *vir hĕth*, with the fine, v, 7; *drāv sōdā hĕth*, he went off with merchandize, viii, 9; *wazīr hĕth*, taking the Vizier, i.e. taking the Vizier along with you, xii, 23; *pātashāh-kūr*^{ü} *hĕth tsalān*, running away with the princess, xii, 25.

danḍa hyon^u, to take in compensation, v, 11; *khabar hĕñ*^{ü}, to bring news, xii, 24; *mŏl*^{i} *hyon*^{u}, to buy, x, 14; *rukhsath hyon*^{u}, to take leave, depart, xii, 10, 3; *tsāp*^{i} *hĕn*^{i}, to take bites, to bite, x, 7; *yād hyon*^{u}, to keep in memory, xii, 17; *zima hyon*^{u}, to take responsibility (for), to admit, xii, 15.

hĕth gatshun (Hindī *lē jānā*), to take away, v, 1; viii, 3 (bis), 4, 10, 2; xii, 4, 9, 12, 8; *hĕth yun*^{u} (Hindī *lē ānā*), to bring, i, 8; iii, 1; viii, 6; x, 12; xii, 2, 5, 11.

fut. pass. part. m. sg. *hyon*^{u}, xii, 5; conj. part. *hĕth*, i, 8; iii, 1, 2; v, 1 (bis), 4, 7 (bis); viii, 3 (bis), 4, 6, 9, 10, 2; x, 5, 12; xi, 13, 4, 6, 8; xii, 2, 4, 5, 9, 11, 2 (bis), 7, 8, 22, 3 (bis), 4, 5; impve. sg. 2, *hĕh*, xi, 12; with suff. 3rd pers. abl. *hĕs*, take from him, xii, 20; fut. sg. 1, with suff. 2nd pers. sg. abl. *hĕmay*, I will take from thee, v, 11; pres. m. sg. 3, *chuh hĕwān*, x, 7; f. sg. 3, with suff. 3rd pers. sg. dat. and neg. *chĕsna hĕwān zima*, she does not admit to her, xii, 15; past m. sg. 3, with suff. 3rd pers. sg. ag. *hyotun*, ii, 1, 3; viii, 7 (ter); with suff. 3rd pers. sg. abl. *hyotus*, took from him, xii, 10, 13; with suff. 3rd pers. pl. ag. *hyotukh*, x, 1; f. sg. with suff. 3rd pers. sg. ag. *hĕts*^{ü}*n*, iii, 1, 4; v, 6; x, 11; ditto, with suff. 3rd pers. sg. dat. *hĕts*^{ü}*nas*, v, 6; pl. with suff. 3rd pers. pl. ag. *hĕtsan*, v, 7; ditto, with suff. 3rd pers. sg. gen. *hĕtsanas*, viii, 7; perf. part. f. pl. *hĕtsamatsa*, x, 14.

*hyor*ᵘ, adj. upwards; — *khasun*, to go upstairs, iii, 2, 9; *-pahān khasun*, to go a short way up stream, xii, 6.

hāzⁱ, as a title of respect, holy, v, 9.

huzūrī nōkar m. a personal servant, viii, 5.

hazrath, a title of respect, saint; *hazrat-i-Ādam*, Saint Adam, iv, 2; *hazrat-i-Nōh*, Saint Noah, iv, 3; *hazrat-i-Yīsāh*, Saint Jesus, iv, 4; *hazrat-i-Musāy*, Saint Moses, iv, 5; *hazrat-i-Yibrāhim*, Saint Abraham, iv, 6; *hazrat-i-Yūsūph*, Saint Joseph, vi, 8, 10, 14, etc.; *hazrat-i-Sulaymān*, Saint Solomon, xii, 17.

judāh, apart; *gayĕ judāh*, she went apart, she became separated, vii, 16.

judöyī, fem. separation, vii, 16.

jāh, a place, in *gay yĕg-jāh*, they went together, ii, 4; *khĕyĕv yĕkh-jāh*, (you) ate together, x, 12. Cf. *jāy*.

jĕl, i.q. *jĕlᵃd*, quickly, vi, 16.

jĕlᵃd or *jĕl* (q.v.), adv. quickly, xii, 15, 23, 4.

jalwa, m. glory; — *dyun*ᵘ, to give forth glory; — *dith*, giving forth glory, in all His glory (of God), vi, 7; with emph. *y*, *jalŏy hôwun*, he manifested glory, vi, 16.

jalŏy, see *jalwa*.

jāma, m. a coat, x, 9.

jumala, m. entirety; *jumala ālam*, (He who is the source of) the whole world, God, i, 13.

jān, adj. good, vii, 27; xi, 17, 8.

jĕṇḍa, m. a flag; — *lāgun*, to set up a flag, to insist on a claim, v, 11.

jĕnath, m. heaven; sg. dat. *jĕnatas* (for *jĕnatas-manz*), xii, 19; *jĕnatas-manz*, in heaven, xii, 20, 3, 4; sg. gen. m. *jĕnatuk*ᵘ, of heaven, xi, 13; xii, 21, 2; fem. pl. *jĕnatacĕ jāyĕ*, places of heaven, iii, 7.

jānāwār, m. a winged creature, a bird, ix, 1, 3, 5; pl. gen. *jānāwāran-hond*ᵘ, viii, 1.

jāv, for Hindī *jāō*, go ye, xi, 4.

jāwō, for Hindī *jāō*, go ye, xi, 4.

jĕwāb, m. an answer, reply, iii, 4; xii, 17.

jāy, f. a place (cf. *jāh*), ix, 6; xi, 12; sg. dat. *panañĕ jāyĕ*, (seated) in his own place, x, 5: *ath jāyĕ gav buñul*ᵘ, there occurred an earthquake in that place, xii, 15; *wôt^u tath jāyĕ*, he arrived at that place, xiii, 15; *wôt^u jāyĕ akis*, he arrived at a certain place, ii, 8; viii, 7 (ter), 9; *tsônukh akis jāyĕ-manz*, they led him into a certain place, iii, 7; *jāyĕ akis . . . jāyĕ akis*, in one place . . . in another place, i, 3, 4; pl. nom. *jāyĕ*, iii, 7.

jyāday, more; *kam yā jyāday*, (a hundred) less or more, ii, 12.

kĕ, see *kyāh*, 1.

kabar, f. a grave, a tomb; sg. dat. *kabari wālun*, to cause to descend into a grave, to inter, iv, 7.

köd, m. prison; — *karun*, to imprison, v, 7, 9 (bis); x, 5, 12; — *lagun*, to become imprisoned, v, 8; vi, 11; *köd-khān* (not *-khāna*), a prison, v, 8; pl. dat. *-khānan*, v, 7, 8.

kūḍ^ü, see *kūr^u*.

köd^i, m. a prisoner, a person imprisoned, v, 8; sg. dat. *ködis*, x, 5 (bis); ag. *köd^i*, x, 5; voc. *ködyau*, x, 12; *hatō ködyau*, x, 5; pl. nom. (and acc.) *köd^i*, v, 8, 9; ag. *ködyau*, v, 7, vi, 11.

kadam, m. a step; — *dyun^u*, to set forth, x, 11, 12; — *trāwun*, to step forward, iv, 5.

kaḍun, or (iv, 2; viii, 3) *karun*, to extract, pull out, viii, 4, 11, 2; to drag forth (e.g. a person from his house), x, 13; to bring forth, bring out, lead forth, iii, 4, 8 (ter); xii, 1; to take out (of a receptacle), viii, 7, 10; xii, 17 (bis); to bring forth, produce, exhibit, x, 2, 12; xii, 15; to tear out or off, dislocate, viii, 7; to take off (from something to which the object is attached), viii, 10; to expel, banish, iv, 2; viii, 11; to take off clothes, v, 9 (bis); xii, 6, 7; to draw (a sword), viii, 13; x, 7; to pass a (period of time), viii, 3, 11; x, 11; xii, 4, 5, 11; to while away the time (on a journey), x, 1; *kaḍith tshunun*, to drive out, viii, 10; to take off, doff (clothes), x, 9.

fut. pass. part. sg. m. *gatshi kaḍun*, he should be expelled, viii, 11; conj. part. *kaḍith*, viii, 10; x, 9; xii, 6, 7. Impve. sg. 2 with suff. 3rd pers. sg. acc. *kaḍun*, iii, 8; fut. pl. 1, with suff. 3rd pers. sg. acc. *kaḍōn*, x, 1; pl. 3 *kaḍan*, viii, 11; pres. masc. sg. 3 *chuh kaḍān*, viii, 13; xii, 4, 11, 17; pl. 3 *chih karān*, viii, 3 ; *chih kaḍān*, viii, 11 ; past sg. m. *koḍ*[u], xii, 15, 7 ; with suff. 3 pers. sg. ag. *koḍun*, iii, 8 ; v, 9 ; viii, 7, 10, 3 ; with ditto and suff. 1 pers. sg. dat. *kor*[u]*nam*, iv, 2 ; with ditto and suff. 3rd pers. sg. dat. *koḍ*[u]*nas*, viii, 10 ; with suff. 3rd pers. pl. ag. *koḍukh*, iii, 4 ; pl. *kåḍ*[i], x, 2 ; with suff. 3rd pers. sg. ag. and 3rd pers. sg. gen. *kåḍ*[i]*nas*, viii, 7 ; with suff. 3rd pers. pl. ag. *kåḍikh*, viii, 4, 12 ; x, 12 ; xii, 1 ; f. sg. with suff. 3rd pers. sg. ag. *küḍ*[ü]*n*, x, 7 ; xii, 5 ; with suff. 3rd pers. pl. ag. *küḍ*[u]*kh*, x, 11.

kāh, f. the leather lace used by shoemakers for sewing together the parts of leather shoes or the like, used where English cobblers use thread, xi, 14.

kĕ̃h, anything, something ; m. sg. nom. *kā̊h*, anyone, i, 2 ; vi, 10 ; xii, 22 ; *kā̊h-ti*, even anyone, vii, 23 ; *kaīsi*, to anyone, iii, 3 ; by anyone, ii, 8 ; *kŏ̈si*, by anyone, v, 9 ; *kĕ̃h*, anything, i, 6 ; ii, 5 ; iv, 4, 6 ; v, 8 ; viii, 2 ; ix, 6 ; xi, 15 ; xii, 6, 7, 15 (bis) ; *biyĕ kĕ̃h*, something more, iii, 8 ; anything else, xii, 8 ; *na kĕ̃h*, not at all, ii, 5 ; v, 5 (bis) ; xii, 2.

As adj. *kā̊h köd*[i], any prisoner, v, 8 ; *kā̊h-ti hōsh*, any sense at all, i, 5 ; *kĕ̃h*[i] *prön*[i], some old (prisoners), vi, 11 ; *kĕ̃h*, any (inanimate thing), vi, 16 ; viii, 1 ; x, 1, 7 ; xii, 5 ; some women, xi, 7 ; *kĕ̃h kālā(h)*, some little time, v, 10 ; viii, 2 ; *kĕ̃h-ti*, any (sound) at all, viii, 9.

kĕ-hŏ, see *kyāh* 1.

kīh, m. loose hair (from the head), combings, v, 4 (ter).

kŏh, *kōh*, m. a mountain ; *kōh-i-tōra*, Mount Sinai, iv, 5 ; *kŏha-kŏhai*, on every mountain, ix, 2.

khāb, m. a dream, sg. dat. *khābas*, vi, 14 ; abl. *khāba*, vi, 12 ; gen. *khābuk*[u] *töbīr*, the interpretation of a dream, vi, 14 ; *khāb ḍēshun*, to see a dream, have a dream-vision, vi, 11 (bis), 2, 4, 5.

khūb, adv. well, thoroughly, vi, 10.

khabar, f. information ; news, tidings, xi, 20 ; notice, care, heed, xii, 2 (ter) ; *bē-khabar*, an untaught person, vii, 28 ; —*anüñ*[u], to bring news, xii, 19, 20 (bis) ; *(tas) chĕh khabar*, there is information (to him), (he) knows (all about it), iii, 3 ; there is heed (to him), (he) believes, (he) is under the impression (that), xii,

2 (ter); *chyā khabar*, is there news? hence, (I) don't know, how am (I) to know? how can (I) know? v, 7; xii, 20; *khabar diñ^u*, to give news, x, 14; *tas khabar gayĕ*, news went to him, information was given to him, iii, 1; *khabar hĕth yun^u*, to bring news, xii, 24; *khabar kar*, news when? i.e. who knows when (such and such a thing happened)? ii, 4; — *niñ^u*, to bring news or information, ii, 16; x, 7, 8; xii, 23; *khabarāh*, a piece of news, ii, 6.

khabardār, m. an informer, spy, scout, newsman; pl. ag. *khabardārav*, ii, 1, 6; x, 7, 8; xii, 23.

khōbsūrath, adj. beautiful, xii, 4, 5, 10 (bis), 5, 9.

khŏḍ, a pit; x, 13; sg. dat. *khŏḍas*, x, 13.

Khŏdā, m. God, vi, 5, 6, 7; x, 7; *Khŏdāy*, verily God, God alone, x, 8; *az Khŏdā*, from God, vi, 10; *bā-Khŏdā*, one who believes in God, a true believer, xii, 20; *wāda-y-Khŏdā*, a promise of God, an oath by God, xii, 7, 15 (bis); *hakh-i-Khŏdāy*, the duty of God alone, i.e. a husband as sacred to the wife as God, xii, 15; sg. dat. *Khŏdāyĕs*, vii, 4; x, 5; ag. *Khŏdāyĕn*, xii, 15; gen. *Khŏdāyĕ-sond^u-chuy kasam*, (I) adjure thee by God, xii, 7; voc. *Khŏdāyĕ*, O God! iv, 1; *bar Khŏdāyō*, O Great God! v, 7; *Khŏdā-Söb*, God the Master, God, sg. dat.*-söbas*, x, 5; ag. *-söban*, iii, 8 (ter).

khöj^unas, see *khālun*.

khal, m. a threshing floor; sg. dat. *khalas karun*, to put (crops) on the threshing floor, ix, 9.

khālun, caus. of *khasun*, to cause to mount, to take (upstairs), x, 7; to fix (on to a lathe), vii, 19; *zima khālun*, to cause responsibility to mount, to prove responsible, x, 12; impve. pl. 2, with suff. 3rd pers. sg. acc. *khölyūn*, cause ye him to mount, x, 7; past. masc. with suff. 3rd pers. sg. ag. and 3rd pers. sg. dat. *khôl^unas*, x, 12; fem. with suff. 3rd pers. sg. ag. and 1st pers. sg. nom. *khöj^unas*, vii, 19.

khalās, adj. free; — *gatshun*, to die, iii, 4.

khalath, m. a robe of honour; *khal^at-ĕ-shōhī*, a royal robe of honour, a magnificent robe of honour, x, 4 (bis).

khām, adj. raw, unripe, green, vi, 15; of small value, cheap; *khām pōsa*, the pice formerly current in Kashmīr, of small value compared to the British pice worth about a farthing, now becoming current; vii, 25, 6.

khumār, m. intoxication; languor of love, languishment; *pūr*ᵘ-*khumār*, full of languishment, one who intoxicates another with love, v, 2.

khān, a certain title, used as part of a proper name in *Baḥ*ᵃ*dūr Khān* = Bahādur Khān, ii, 1; sg. dat. — *khānas*, ii, 12.

khāna, m. a house, sg. dat. *khānas*, vi, 4; *köd-khāna*, a prison, sg. nom (m.c.) *köd-khān*, vi, 10; pl. dat. *köd-khānan*, v, 7, 8; *mahala-khāna*, a palace, xii, 19.

khĕn, m. food, xii, 16, 17.

khŏn, f. the haunch; sg. dat. *khŏni-kĕth*, (carrying) on the haunch, xi, 13.

khanun, to dig; fut. pass. part. m. sg. *gatshi dŏb khanun*ᵘ, you must dig a pit, xii, 6.

khananāwun, to cause to be dug; past m. sg. with suff. 3rd pers. sg. ag. *khananôwun*, x, 13.

khar, m. an ass; iii, 8, 9; v, 7 (bis); sg. dat. *khot*ᵘ *kharas*, he mounted the ass, iii, 8.

khār, m. a blacksmith; sg. voc. *khāra*, ii, 12; vi, 17; pl. ag. *khārav*, xi, 17; *Wahab Khār*, or Wahb the Blacksmith, is the name of the author of stories ii and vi.

khŏr (v, 5) or *khōr* (v, 9), m. the foot; sg. dat. *khōran*, v, 9; *shānda karun khŏr*, to go from the pillow to the foot of the bed, v, 5; *khŏra karun shānd*, to go from the foot of the bed to the pillow, v, 5.

khör, m. welfare; *duā-yi-khör*, a prayer for welfare, a blessing, i, 3.

*khôr*ᵘ, a thing which weighs a *khār* or *kharwār*, i.e. an ass's load; sg. dat. *hatabŏd*ⁱ*-khŏris drāy*, they turned out (i.e. amounted) to hundreds of *kharwārs*, ix, 9.

*khar*ᵃ*c* (viii, 10) or *khar*ᵃ*j* (xii, 4, etc.), m. expenditure; expenses, money to be spent for any purpose; xii, 4 (bis), 5 (bis), 11, 20; *khar*ᵃ*c gōm*, expenditure has occurred by me, I have spent, viii, 10.

khörāth, m. alms, v, 9.

khrāv, m. the clog, patten, or wooden soles worn by Kāshmīrīs in winter; nom. (acc.) plur. *khrāv*, v, 9.

khāsa, adj. peculiar, special; personal, own; choice, select, excellent, ii, 3; *dukhtar-ĕ-khāsa*, thine own daughter, v, 11.

*khôs*ᵘ, m. a kind of metal cup; pl. nom. *khös*ⁱ, ii, 3.

khash, m. a cut; — *dyun*ᵘ, to cut, v, 4 (bis), 6.

khŏsh, adj. pleased, happy; — *gatshun*, to become happy, to become pleased, viii, 1, 9; xii, 9; — *gōsay*, I became pleased about thee, xi, 18; *gōs* —, he became pleased with him, xii, 12; *gōkh*, —, he became pleased with them, viii, 14; *gös* —, they became pleasing to him, i.e. he loved them, viii, 11; *yih pātashĕhas* — *kari*, that which will make the king pleased, whatever will please the king, xii, 3.

khashĕm, m. anger, wrath; *yimau amis phakīras* — *kor*ᵘ, by them to that faqīr wrath was made, i.e. they were made angry with the faqīr, ii, 3.

khasun (1 p.p. *khot*ᵘ or *khoth*ᵘ), to rise, arise; to rise, come up (out of water), i, 6, 8; xii, 11, 2; to rise, go up, go upstairs, iii, 2, 9; x, 8 (bis); xii, 7; to get up on to (e.g. on to a bed, or a funeral pyre, governing dat., with or without *pĕṭh*), iii, 7; v, 5, 6, (bis) 9; x, 7 (bis); xii, 21, 4; to mount (a horse, etc., *guris* or *guris-pĕṭh*), ii, 6, 11; iii, 8 (quater); to ride (a horse), (*gur*ᵘ *chus khasun*ᵘ, he has a horse on which to ride), x, 3; *carkas khüts*ᵘ̈, she mounted on to the lathe, she was fixed on the lathe (for being turned), vii, 20; *kŏli kŏli khasun*, to go up stream, xii, 6; *kaīsi chuna khasān zima*, the responsibility rises on no one, no one can be made responsible, or, as we should say, the responsibility falls on no one, iii, 3; *kötyāh khâtis mār*, how many murders have risen for him, i.e. of how many murders is he guilty! ix, 5; *pātashĕhas khot*ᵘ *zahar*, poison arose to the king, i.e. he became enraged, viii, 7.

Fut. pass. part. sg. m. *khasun*ᵘ, x, 3; xii, 5 (*gatshi khasun*ᵘ, you must go up); impve. sg. 2 *khas*, iii, 8 (bis); fut. sg. 2 *khasakh*, v, 6; 3 with suff. 2nd pers. sg. dat. *khasiy*, xii, 11 (there will arise before you); pres. m. sg. 3 neg. *chuna khasān*, iii, 3; imperf. sg. m. 3 with suff. 3rd pers. sg. dat. neg. *ôsus-na khasān*, i, 6; 1 past sg. m. 3 *khot*ᵘ, i, 8; ii, 11; iii, 7, 8 (bis), 9; v, 5, 6; viii, 7; x, 7, 8; xii, 12, 21, 4; *khoth*ᵘ, ii, 6; x, 7; pl. 1 *khâtⁱ*, v, 9 (we, i.e. one m. and one f.);

3 *khăt*[i], x, 8; with suff. 3rd pers. sg. dat. *khătis*, ix, 5; f. sg. 3 *khüts*[u], iii, 2; vii, 20; xii, 7.

khŏta, postpos. than; *dŏn-handi khŏta*, (more beautiful) than the two, xii, 19; *gŏḍañicĕ-handi khŏta*, (more beautiful) than the first (girl), xii, 10. In *ami khŏta hāway bŏh*, iii, 8, I will show thee more than that, the word "more" is not expressed.

khọ̆ṭ[u], adj. false, base, counterfeit; (of a jewel) flawed, xii, 3.

khath, m. a letter, a document, xii, 22, 3 (ter); *mŏl*[i]*-sandi daskhata khath*, a letter signed by (my) father, xii, 21.

khaṭun, to conceal; conj. part. *khaṭith*, having concealed (sc. yourself), secretly, xii, 6.

khôtūna, f. a noble woman, a lady, x, 12; xii, 18, 9 (bis), 20, 5; with suff. of indef. art. *khôtūnā akh*, a certain lady, v, 11; xii, 15; sg. dat. *khôtūni*, x, 7 (bis); xii, 15; ag. *khôtūni*, xii, 15 (quater), 8, 22; gen. *khôtūni-handis shikamas-manz* (x, 7) or *khôtūni-shikamas-manz* (x, 7), in the lady's belly; *khôtūni-handi shikama-manza*, from in the lady's belly, x, 7 (bis).

khötir, m. carnal desire, viii, 3.

khāwand, m. a master, a lord, viii, 10 (of a dog); a woman's husband, iii, 1, 2, 3, 4; v, 1, 8, 10, 1, 2; x, 5 (bis), 12; xi, 11; xii, 18; sg. dat. *khāwandas*, iii, 4; v, 8, 10, 2; xi, 11; xii, 18; *khāwandas nishin*, (go) to (your) master, viii, 10; sg. gen. fem. *khāwanda-sünz*[u], iii, 2.

khôwur[u], adj. left (not right); — *atha*, the left hand, viii, 7.

khyon[u], to eat; to consume unlawfully, misappropriate, x, 2.

inf. obl. *wăth*[i] *khĕni*, they got down (in order) to eat, x, 5; fut. pass. part. m. sg. *tih cyôn*[u] *khyon*[u] *gatshi-na*, you must not eat that, xii, 16; pres. part. *chuh bihith khĕwān*, he is seated eating, xii, 4; impve. sg. 2, *khĕh*, iii, 1; (dial.) *khyuh*, x, 5; (dial.) *khyō*, x, 12; pol. sg. 2, with suff. 1st pers. sg. dat. *khĕtam*, eat for my sake, iii, 1; fut. sg. 2, *khĕzi*, xii, 16 (bis).

fut. sg. 1 *khĕma*, viii, 11; with suff. 2nd pers. sg. dat. *khĕmay*, I will eat for thy sake, iii, 1; do. with neg. *khĕmay-na*, I will not eat for thy sake, iii, 1; 2, with neg. interrog. *khĕkh-nā*, wilt thou not eat? ii, 3; vi, 2; 3, *khĕyi*, xii, 15.

pres. m. sg. 3 *chuh khĕwān*, xii, 6, 17 ; imperf. m. sg. 3, with neg. *khĕwān ôsᵘ-na*, he used not to eat, vi, 16.

1 past m. sg. *khyauv*, x, 12 ; *khĕv*, ii, 2 ; with suff. 3rd pers. sg. ag. *khyōn*, vi, 16 (bis) ; x, 5 ; pl. (dial. for *khyēy*) *khĕy*, x, 2 ; f. sg. with suff. 2nd pers. pl. ag. (dial. for *khĕyĕwa*) *khĕyĕv*, x, 12.

khazmath (xii, 3) or *khizmath* (ii, 3), f. service ; *gurĕn-hünzᵘ khazmath karakh*, I will do service of horses for them, i.e. I will do groom's work, xii, 3.

kākad, m. paper, a piece of paper, xii, 11, 2, 5 (quinquies), 6, 7, 8 (bis), 22 ; — *likhun*, to write a paper, xii, 11 ; sg. dat. *kākadas*, xii, 16, 7 ; cf. *kākaz*.

kākañ, f. the wife of the eldest son in a Hindū family ; *böyⁱ-kākañ*, an elder brother's wife, v, 10.

kŏkur, m. a fowl ; *kŏkar-gām*, a fowl village, a village the speciality of which is rearing fowls, xi, 8.

kākaz, m. paper, viii, 10. Cf. *kākad*.

kāl, time ; with suff. indef. art. *kĕh kālā gav* (v, 10) or *kĕh kālāh gav* (viii, 2), some short time passed ; *wārayāh kālāh gav*, a very long time passed, viii, 2 ; *wārayāh kāl*, for a very long time, viii, 2 ; sg. dat. *wārayāhas kālas*, for (during) a long time, iii, 1.

kala, the head, iii, 1, 5, 9 ; *kala tsaṭun*, to behead, iii, 2 ; viii, 6 ; abl. *kala-kànⁱ*, in the direction of the head, at the head end (of an animal), xi, 9 ; *kala-pĕṭhⁱ tshunüñᵘ wŏṭh*, to leap over (so and so's) head, ii, 9.

kŏl, f. a small river, a stream ; sg. dat. *kŏli-manz*, in the stream, xii, 2 ; *gayĕ kŏli akis pĕṭh*, she went to the bank of a stream, xii, 2 ; abl. *kŏli kŏli khasun*, to go up along the stream, to go up stream, xii, 4 ; *kŏli-manza*, from in the stream, xii, 4.

kôlᵘ, adj. of or belonging to time ; *yütsᵘ-kôlᵘ*, of or belonging to a long time ago, ii, 4.

kulᵘ, m. a tree ; abl. *kuli-dadari-manz*, in the tree-hole, in the hole in the tree, ii, 10.

kālacĕn, adv. in the evening, at eventide, v, 5 ; viii, 3.

kalam, m. a pen ; *kalama sötin likhun*, to write with a pen, ix, 12.

kuluph, m. a lock. — *thāwun*, to open a lock, to unlock a door, iii, 8 (bis).

kŏlay, f. a wife, iii, 4; v, 3, 5; viii, 3, 11; sg. ag. *kŏlayi*, v, 9.

kam 1, adj. less, deficient, iv, 4, 6; *kamyā jyāday*, less or more, more or less, ii, 12.

kam 2, *kȧmⁱ*, *kami*, see *kyāh* 1.

kömᵘ, f. a thing done, a deed; a business; *kömᵘ chĕh pakawüñᵘ*, the business is one that marches, i.e. it involves marching, xi, 11; in the stories, *kürᵘ kömᵘ*, he, she, or they, did a deed, is equivalent to the English, "what do you think he, she, or they did," "what did he do but," ii, 5, 7; viii, 4; x, 7 (bis), 12, 4; xii, 22; so, with suff. of indef. art. *kürᵘn* (x, 2) or *kürᵘ* (x, 3) *kömᵘāh*.

kŏmbakh, m. help, aid, assistance, the reinforcement (of an army); sg. dat. *barāyĕ kŏmbakas*, in order to help, by way of help, as a reinforcement, xi, 7.

kamyukᵘ, see *kyāh* 1

kan, m. the ear; — *thawun* (ii, 7) or — *thāwun* (viii, 6, 8, 11; ix, 1, 4), to apply the ear, to lend the ear, to listen attentively; sg. dat. *kanas kürᵘnas thaph*, he seized him by the ear, iii, 9; abl. *kana-ḍōlī diñᵘ* (poet.), to give ear-closing, to refuse to listen, v, 2; *kana raṭith*, holding (a goat) by the ear, iii, 5; pl. dat. with emph. *y*, *kananạy*, vii, 11.

kȧnⁱ, postpos. signifying—

(*a*) direction, as in *kala-kȧnⁱ*, in the direction of the head, at the head end (of an animal), xi, 9; *laṭi-kȧnⁱ*, at the tail end, xi, 9.

(*b*) route, as in *dāri-kȧnⁱ*, (cast) out through the window, v, 4 (bis).

(*c*) direction from, as in *yĕs-kȧnⁱ*, from whom (it will escape), ii, 8.

Cf. *kani*, *kun*, *kāñ*, and *kiñ*.

kani, postpos. signifying—

(*a*) locality, as in *bŏna-kani*, (he is standing) below, downstairs, iii, 2; *bōnṭha-kani*, in front, before (governing dat.), ii, 3; iii, 1; viii, 11; x, 5, 10, 2; xii, 4, 9, 12, 23 (bis); *athⁱ-pĕṭha-kani*, on the top of it verily, viii, 1.

(*b*) direction towards, as in *ōra-kani*, in that direction, v, 2.

(*c*) direction from, as in *tālawa-kani*, (down) from the ceiling, viii, 6; *ösa-kani*, issuing from the mouth, viii, 7.

(*d*) other miscellaneous relations as in *thürü-kani* (v, 4) or *thüḍü-kani* (v, 4 bis), (turning) backwards (from there); *pata-kani*, afterwards, x, 1; *kuni-kani*, in any way, xii, 13; *āmpa-kani*, by means of beak-to-beak feeding, viii, 1; *tami-pĕṭhi-kani*, in addition to that, iii, 8.

Cf. *kàni*, *kun*, *kāñ*, and *kiñ*.

kina, conj. or. Used to indicate an alternative in an interrogative sentence, v, 7; viii, 3, 11; xii, 18, 9, 23.

kōna, adv. why not? viii, 1 (why is there no chirping?).

kun, postpos. governing dat., meaning—

(*a*) towards, viii, 6, 11; x, 3, 5, 12; similarly *ō-kun*, in that direction, xii, 23; *mustākh kun*, enamoured of, yearning for, iii, 7; vii, 3; *biyĕ-kun*, (he does not go) anywhere else, xii, 4.

(*b*) to (after verbs of saying, addressing, etc.), v, 2; vii, 4, 20, 6; ix, 1; x, 5 (bis); x, 12.

(*c*) in, at, *bōnṭh-kun*, i, 8, (came) before (the king); *wôtu shĕharas and-kun*, he arrived at the outskirts of the city, x, 5; *andas-kun*, at the end, xii, 6.

(*d*) other meanings, *nāgas akith kun*, on one side of the spring, xii, 14; *asĕ-kun hôwuth*, thou showedst before us, vi, 5; *path-kun*, afterwards, iii, 5; v, 5; at the back (of a place), in the rear, v, 8.

(with gen.) *yāra-sondu kun*, (he set out) in the direction of his friend's abode, x, 11.

Cf. *kàni*, *kani*, *kāñ*, and *kiñ*.

kuni, adv. at all, in any respect, v, 6; viii, 1 (bis), 2, 9; xii, 1, 22; anywhere, viii, 7; somewhere, viii, 7; *kuni-kani*, in any way, xii, 13.

kunu, num. adj., only one; with emph. *y*, One only (of God), vi, 7; vii, 2; x, 8; *kunuy zonu*, only one person, all alone, viii, 7; fem. *küñüy züñü*, xii, 15.

kōnda, f. a potter's kiln; sg. abl. *kōndi wālun*, to put (unbaked pots) into a kiln for baking, xi, 11.

*koṇḍ*ᵘ, m. a thorn, viii, 1 (bis).
kangañ, f. a comb ; *chĕs wālān kangañ*, I am combing (my hair), v, 4.
kŏng-wörü, f. a saffron-garden or -field ; sg. dat. (for loc.), *kŏng-wāri*, or (m.c.) *kŏng-wārī*, v, 7.
kᵃnun, to sell ; inf. abl. *āv kᵃnani*, he came (in order) to sell, xii, 3 ; *āyĕ kᵃnana* (pass.), she was sold, vii, 26 ; fut. sg. 1 with suff. 3rd pers. sg. acc. *kᵃnan*, I will sell it, viii, 9 ; 2, with same suff. *mā kᵃnahan*, I wonder if thou wilt sell it, viii, 9 ; pres. sg. 3, with suff. 1st pers. sg. acc. *chum kᵃnān*, he is selling me, vii, 17.
kĕntsāh (vii, 20) or (usually) *kĕntshāh*, indef. pron. something, vii, 20, 6 ; x, 3 ; xii, 18 (bis) ; — *karun*, to do something, esp. to do something malicious, xii, 5, 10, 3, 9 ; *yih-kĕntshāh*, whatever, iii, 1, 8 (ter) ; v, 8.

As adj. some, xii, 4, 19 (bis) ; any, xii, 19.
kĕnzü, f. a kind of cup with a foot to it ; Musalmān women eat their rice out of it. Sg. dat. *kĕnzĕ*, x, 3.
kunz, f. a key, iii, 8 (bis).
kāñ, postpos. by means of ; *āb-dawa-kāñ*, (enter) by means of (i.e. through) the water-drain, v, 4.

Cf. *kànⁱ*, *kani*, *kiñ*, and *kun*.
kiñ (for *kinⁱ*), postpos. in *apörⁱ-kiñ*, from that direction, v, 7.

Cf. *kànⁱ*, *kani*, *kun*, and *kāñ*.
küñü, f. a stone ; sg. dat. *kañĕ-manz*, in a stone, iv, 7 ; *kañĕ-küñü*, punishment of death by stoning, lapidation, x, 13 ; abl. *kañi-pholᵘ*, a pebble, xii, 15 (bis).
kaññĕkh, ? gender, the apparatus consisting of two ropes attached at the back of a Kāshmīrī saddle, to secure blankets, etc., xi, 9.
kañuwᵘ, adj. made of stone ; m. pl. nom. *kañivⁱ*, v, 4.
kuphār, m. pl. infidels, non-Muslims (for *kuffār*, Ar. pl. of *kāfir*), iv, 3.
kar, adv. when ? ii, 4.
kār, m. an action, a deed, a work, xi, 2 ; pl. nom. *kār*, v, 12 ; xi, 10.
kara, m. a pea, pease, xii, 16 (ter), 7.
kāra, in *wāra-kāra*, safe and sound, x, 8.

kōr, adv. where ? ii, 2.

*kor*ᵘ, m. a bracelet, xii, 11, 2, 3 (ter); *ṛatᵃna-kor*ᵘ, a bracelet of jewels, xii, 10, 1, 2, 4 (bis), 5, 8; *kårⁱ-han*, f. a little bracelet, xii, 12; sg. dat. *ṛatᵃna-karis-söty*, xii, 15; pl. nom. *ṛatᵃna-kårⁱ*, xii, 20.

*kūr*ᵘ̈, or (v, 5, 12) *kūḍ*ᵘ̈, f. a daughter, v, 7 (bis), 9; x, 1, 6, 7 (bis), 8; xii, 1; *pātashāh-kūr*ᵘ̈, (v, 2, 5, 8 (bis), 9 (ter), 10; xii, 1, 2) or *pātashāh-kūḍ*ᵘ̈ (v, 5); or *pātashĕh-kūr*ᵘ̈ (xii, 10, 3 (bis), 25), a king's daughter, a princess; sg. dat. *kōḍĕ*, v, 12; *kōrĕ*, xii, 4, 5; *pātashāh-kōrĕ*, v, 2, 9 (ter); xii, 2, 10, 13; *pātashĕh-kōrĕ*, xii, 10; *kōrĕ-kyut*ᵘ, for the daughter, v, 1 (bis); *kōrĕ-söty*, with the daughter, v, 10; *pātashāh-kōrĕ-söty*, with the princess, xii, 1; gen. *kōrĕ-hond*ᵘ, v, 2; *pātashāh-kōrĕ-hond*ᵘ, v, 9; ag. *kōri*, xii, 4, 5; *pātashāh-kōri*, v, 1; xii, 2; abl. *kōri-halamas manz*, in the lap-cloth of the daughter, v, 4; voc. *kūrⁱ*, v, 2; *kūrⁱyĕy*, v, 2; *kōriy*, xii, 15 (all addressed by an elder woman to a younger woman).

kārdār, m. the Hindū overseer of a village, a government official whose duty it is to collect the Mahārāja's share of the grain; sg. ag. *kārdāran*, ix, 1.

*kröj*ᵘ̈, f. a potter's wife; cf. *krāl*; sg. ag. *krāji*, xi, 11.

krēkh, f. an outcry; — *diñ*ᵘ̈, to raise an outcry, to cry out, v, 7; xii, 7; — *wöthüñ*ᵘ̈, an outcry to arise, iii, 3.

krāl, m. a potter; cf. *kröj*ᵘ̈; sg. ag. *krālan*, xi, 10; voc. *krālau* (addressed by a woman to her husband), xi, 11.

karun 1; to do, ii, 4, 11 (bis); iii, 8; v, 4, 5, 7 (bis), 12; viii, 1, 3, 4, 6 (bis), 8 (bis), 10 (bis), 1 (quater), 2; ix, 4; x, 3, 5, 8 (bis); xi, 2, 19 (bis); xii, 1 (quater), 3 (bis), 6, 15, 7, 20, 6 (bis); to make, i, 1, 3, 7; ii, 1 (bis), 2, 3 (bis), 4 (bis), 5, 10, 2; iii, 1, 4, 8; iv, 2, 3, 6; v, 2, 5 (bis), 6, 9, 10; vi, 9, 11 (bis); vii, 4, 6 (bis), 8, 15 (bis), 6, 24 (ter); viii, 1 (bis), 2 (ter), 3 (bis), 5, 7, 9 (bis), 11 (bis), 3 (quater); ix, 3, 4 (bis); x, 1, 3, 4, 5, 7 (bis), 8, 12 (bis); xi, 5, 8 (bis), 10 (bis), 7, 9 (bis); xii, 1, 4, 7, 15 (bis), 7, 8 (bis), 9 (bis), 20 (bis), 2 (bis), 3, 4, 5; to make something out of something else, to turn one thing into another, *pŏshākus kür*ᵘ̈*n shĕkal yinsān hish*ᵘ̈, he made the shape of a man out of his clothes, he folded them up to look like a man, x, 7 (bis); *kȧñ^i-phol^u kor^unas*, she (uttered a charm and) turned him into a pebble, xii, 15; to make another marriage, to take a second wife, (*wŏrüz^ü zanāna*, or some such words, being understood), viii, 1 (bis), 2; *khalas karun*, to put (crops) on the threshing floor, ix, 9; *karith dyun^u* (= Hindī *kar dēnā*), to complete, finish, x, 12.

Nominal compounds are very commonly made with this verb. The following examples by no means pretend to form a complete list: *ālav karun*, to call out (to a person, dat.), x, 5 (bis), 12 (bis); xii, 7; *arām karun*, to repose, rest, sleep, v, 9; *band k.*, to tie up, x, 2; *dīdār k.*, to do seeing, to see (gen. of obj.), iv, 5; *driy kasam k.*, to swear, to take an oath, viii, 1; *gañĕ karañĕ*, to make into pieces, to cut flesh into gobbets, x, 7; *gath karüñ^ü*, (of a widow) to perform the *satī* ceremony, to become suttee, iii, 4; *gawöy^i karüñ^ü*, to give evidence, x, 12; *hawāla karun*, to make over (to so and so, dat.) for safe custody, to put into so and so's charge, v, 7, 12 (bis); viii, 4; x, 12 (quinquies); *köd karun*, to imprison, v, 7, 9 (bis); x, 5, 12; *khŏsh karun*, to please, gratify (dat. of person), xii, 3; *khizmath* (ii, 3) or *khazmath* (xii, 3) *karun*, to do service, to act as a servant; *köm^u karüñ^ü*, to do a deed (for the special meaning of this compound, see *köm^ü*), ii, 5, 7; viii, 4; x, 2, 7 (bis), 12, 4; xii, 22; *kĕntshāh karun*, to do something, esp. to do something malicious, xii, 5, 10, 3, 9 (bis); *kashĕna-hanā karüñ^ü*, to do a little scratching, to scratch a person (at his request), xii, 16; *kasam karun*, to make oath, to swear, v, 9; viii, 1; *katha karañĕ*, to utter words, to speak, say, iii, 1; iv, 5; xii, 23; to converse, x, 7 (ter); xii, 3; *langūṭ^i karüñ^ü*, to put on a loin-cloth; *lār karüñ^ü*, to run after, pursue (dat. of obj.), ii, 8; *mŏhar karüñ^ü*, to seal (dat. of obj.), x, 3 (bis), 10; *mŏl karun*, to fix a price, agree to a price, viii, 9 (bis), 10; *putalĕn korun nakār*, he prohibited idols, iv, 6; *nȧs^iyĕth karüñ^ü*, to give instructions, xii, 16; *nēth^ar karun*, to make preparations for a marriage, to marry (*amis söty*, him), viii, 2; xii, 15; *nazar karüñ^ü*, to look, x, 7, 8 (bis); xii, 23; *pöda karun*, to create, iii, 8 (bis); xii, 7; *pardā karun*, to veil, cover with a veil (dat. of obj.), vi, 4; *pasand karun*, to approve (acc. of obj.), v, 1; xii, 4 (bis); *rājy karun*, to do ruling, to rule, x, 14; *rawāna karun*, to dispatch, x, 3; *maris karun rēza*, he cut the corpse to pieces, ii, 7; *salām karüñ*ᵘ, to make a salaam, to bow, xii, 4, 5, 9, 12, 3, 6, 7; *sara karun*, to inquire into, test, prove the truth about, investigate concerning, viii, 1, 3; x, 2, 6 (ter), 14; *saragī karüñ*ᵘ, id., viii, 7 (bis), 8, 10; x, 7; *srān karun*, to bathe, xii, 6 (bis), 7 (bis); *thaph karüñ*ᵘ, to seize, lay hold of, grasp (dat. of obj.), iii, 8, 9 (bis); v, 6, 9 (bis); vi, 9; viii, 7, 9; xii, 11; *ṭukara karänⁱ*, to make pieces, to cut to pieces (dat. of obj.), viii, 6; *tay karun*, to do authority, to exercise sway, xi, 3; *tayār karun*, to make ready, to make and have ready, to make, xii, 22; *tshŏpa karith*, silently, in silence, xii, 4; *wuchunāh karun*, to do a seeing, to take a glance at (dat. of obj.), viii, 3; *wŏrüzᵘ zanāna karüñ*ᵘ, to take a second wife, (of a man) to make a second marriage, viii, 11; *zulm karun*, to exercise tyranny, ix, 1; *gurᵘ zīn karith*, a horse ready saddled, iii, 8; *zōr karun*, to make force, to show force, to insist, xii, 15; *zāra-pār karun*, to make lamentations, to lament, ix, 1; to utter pious ejaculations, x, 5 (bis); to make earnest entreaties, ii, 3, 5; *ziyāphath karüñ*ᵘ, to make a feast, x, 11.

inf. *tamis togᵘ-na karun*, he did not know how to make, viii, 9; sg. abl. forming inf. of purpose, *karani*, viii, 4; x, 2; xii, 4, 6 (bis), 26; fut. pass. part. sg. m. sg. *karunᵘ*, it is to be made, it must be made, xi, 8; *gatshi karunᵘ*, viii, 2, 8; x, 3; xii, 3; *gotshᵘ karunᵘ*, v, 7; *wāti karunᵘ*, viii, 6, 8, 11; f. sg. *karüñ*ᵘ, it is to be done, please do, xii, 16; *gatshi karüñ*ᵘ, v, 9; viii, 7, 8, 10; x, 3; conj. part. *karith*, iii, 8 (bis); vi, 9 (bis); viii, 11, 3; x, 7, 12; xi, 19; xii, 4, 23; *zānakh karith*, thou wilt know how to make, x, 12; in adjectival sense, *zīn karith*, (a horse) ready saddled, iii, 8; *chuh karith thaph*, he holds, v, 6; viii, 7; irreg. conj. part. *kärⁱthan*, xi, 10; freq. part. *kärⁱ kärⁱ*, vii, 24.

impve. sg. 2 *kar*, i, 7; ii, 12; v, 2; x, 8; xii, 17; neg. *ma kar*, xii, 7; with suff. 3rd pers. sg. gen. *karus*, viii, 9;

with suff. 3rd pers. pl. acc. (irreg.) *karuhukh*, make thou them, xii, 19; 3, with suff. 1st pers. sg. dat. *karinam*, let her make for me, v, 9; pl. 2 *kariv*, viii, 11; xii, 17; with suff. 3rd pers. pl. acc. *karyūkh*, make ye them, viii, 4; pol. impve. sg. 2 *karta*, xii, 4, 5, 10, 3, 9; pl. 2 with suff. 3rd pers. sg. dat. *kårⁱtōs*, please make ye for him, ii, 10; impve. fut. *kårⁱzi*, xii, 11; neg. *kårⁱzi-na*, viii, 1 (bis); xii, 6.

fut. sg. 1 *kara*, ii, 4; iv, 5; viii, 10; ix, 4; xii, 1 (bis), 3, 15, 20; with suff. 2nd pers. sg. dat. *karay*, ii, 3; xii, 1; with suff. 3rd pers. sg. dat. and neg. *karas-na*, xii, 15; 2 *karakh*, xii, 1, 3; neg. *karakh-na*, viii, 13; with suff. 3rd pers. pl. dat. *karahakh*, thou wilt make to them, xii, 16; 3, *kari*, viii, 1; xi, 2, 19; xii, 3, 19; with suff. 1st pers. sg. dat. *karĕm*, ix, 4; pl. 1 *karav*, x, 1, 5; xi, 19; with suff. 3rd pers. sg. dat. *karōs*, ix, 1; 2 *kariv*, xii, 1; pres. subj. sg. 3 *kari*, viii, 6, 8, 11.

pres. m. sg. 3 *karān*, he (is) making, ii, 5; *chuh karān*, viii, 12, 3; x, 14; xii, 24; *karān chuh*, x, 8; neg. *chuna karān*, viii, 2; with suff. 1st pers. sg. gen. or dat. *chum karān*, vii, 15 (dat.), 24 (gen.); pl. 3 *chih karān*, viii, 3; xii, 3, 23; with suff. 3rd pers. sg. dat. *chis karān*, ii, 3; x, 12; f. sg. 1, *chĕs karān*, vii, 15; 3 *chĕh karān*, iii, 4; with suff. 3rd pers. sg. dat. *chĕs karān*, v, 5 (bis); pl. 3 *chĕh karān*, v, 12.

imperf. m. sg. 1, *ôsus karān*, x, 14; sg. 3 *ôsᵘ karān*, i, 1; pl. 3 *ösⁱ karān*, i, 3; *karān ösⁱ*, xi, 8; f. sg. 3 *ösᵘ karān*, xii, 20; emph. *ösᵘy karān*, vii, 16; pl. 3 *āsa karān*, xi, 19.

past m. sg. *korᵘ*, ii, 2, 3, 4; iii, 8 (bis); iv, 6; v, 9; viii, 1, 9, 10, 2; xi, 3; xii, 4, 7 (bis).

With suff. 2nd pers. sg. dat. *koruy*, x, 12; ag. *koruth*, v, 4, 5; viii, 3; with do. and suff. 1st pers. sg. nom. *korᵘthas*, x, 12; with do. and suff. 1st pers. sg. dat. *korᵘtham*, ii, 11.

With suff. 3rd pers. sg. dat. *korus*, xii, 7; ag. *korun*, ii, 4, 7; iv, 6; v, 7; vi, 11 (bis); vii, 4, 6 (bis); viii, 2, 10; ix, 3; x, 3, 5, 7; xii, 18, 22 (ter); emph. *korᵘnay*, iv, 3; and with suff. 1st pers. sg. dat. *korᵘnam*, ix, 4; and with suff. 3rd pers.

sg. dat. *kor*ᵘ*nas*, v, 10 ; viii, 9 ; xii, 15 (ter) ; and with suff. 3rd pers. pl. dat. *kor*ᵘ*nakh*, vi, 4 ; viii, 3.

With suff. 2nd pers. pl. ag. *kor*ᵘ*wa*, x, 12 (bis).

With suff. 3rd pers. pl. ag. *korukh*, viii, 1 ; x, 5 (bis) ; xii, 7, 18 ; and with suff. 2nd pers. sg. dat. *kor*ᵘ*hay*, iv, 2 ; and with suff. 3rd pers. sg. dat. *kor*ᵘ*has*, viii, 2 ; x, 5 ; and with suff. 3rd pers. pl. dat. *kor*ᵘ*hakh*, xi, 17.

pl. with suff. 1st pers. sg. ag. *kårim*, v, 9 ; ix, 9 ; with suff. 2nd pers. sg. ag. *kårith*, v, 7 ; with suff. 3rd pers. sg. ag. *kårin*, v, 7, 9 ; viii, 5 ; x, 2 ; and suff. 3rd pers. sg. gen. *kår*ⁱ*nas*, viii, 6 ; and suff. 3rd pers. pl. dat. *kår*ⁱ*nakh*, x, 12.

f. sg. *kür*ᵘ̈, ii, 1, 5, 7 ; viii, 3, 4, 11 ; x, 3, 5, 7 (ter), 8 (bis), 11, 2, 4 ; xii, 15, 9, 22, 3 ; with suff. 1st pers. sg. dat. and neg. *kür*ᵘ̈*m-na*, v, 9 ; with suff. 3rd pers. sg. dat. *kür*ᵘ̈*s*, iii, 1, 9 ; and neg. *kür*ᵘ̈*sna*, v, 1 ; ag. *kür*ᵘ̈*n*, v, 12 (bis) ; vii, 8 ; viii, 11 ; x, 2, 7 (bis) ; xii, 12, 3, 7, 20, 3 ; and suff. 3rd pers. sg. dat. *kür*ᵘ̈*nas*, iii, 4, 9 ; viii, 9 ; x, 3, 4 ; xii, 4, 5, 9, 16 ; with suff. 2nd pers. pl. ag. *kür*ᵘ̈*wa*, x, 12 ; with suff. 3rd pers. pl. ag. *kür*ᵘ̈*kh*, ii, 8 ; and suff. 3rd pers. sg. dat. *kür*ᵘ̈*hay*, xi, 5.

pl. *karĕ*, iii, 1 ; with suff. 1st pers. sg. ag. and 2nd pers. pl. dat. (irreg.) *karĕmav*, x, 6 ; suff. 2nd pers. sg. ag. *karĕth*, x, 6 ; with suff. 3rd pers. sg. ag. *karĕn*, x, 6, 7 (bis) ; and suff. 1st pers. sg. dat. *karĕnam*, iv, 5 ; and with suff. 3rd pers. sg. gen. *karĕnas*, x, 7 ; with suff. 3rd pers. pl. ag. *karĕkh*, xi, 10 ; xii, 25.

perf. m. sg. *chuh kor*ᵘ*mot*ᵘ, x, 12 ; f. sg. with suff. 3rd pers. sg. dat. for ag. *chĕy kür*ᵘ̈*müts*ᵘ̈, x, 8.

plup. m. sg. *kor*ᵘ*mot*ᵘ, iii, 8 ; *ôs*ᵘ *kor*ᵘ*mot*ᵘ, ii, 1 ; *kor*ᵘ*mot*ᵘ *ôs*ᵘ, x, 7 ; with suff. 2nd pers. sg. ag. and 3rd pers. sg. acc. for nom. *ôs*ᵘ*than kor*ᵘ*mot*ᵘ, thou hadst made him, x, 12 ; with suff. 3rd pers. sg. dat. *ôsus kor*ᵘ*mot*ᵘ, ix, 1 ; with suff. 3rd pers., pl. ag. *ôsukh kor*ᵘ*mot*ᵘ, viii, 2 ; f. sg. *kür*ᵘ̈*müts*ᵘ̈, viii, 1 ; with suff. 3rd pers. sg. dat. *ös*ᵘ̈*s kür*ᵘ̈*muts*ᵘ̈, x, 10.

cond. past sg. 1, *karahö*, ii, 11 ; v, 6 ; viii, 11 ; x, 5 ; 3, *karihē*, v, 9 ; viii, 7, 13.

karun 2, see *kaḍun*.

krünḍᵘ, f. a basket, v, 9; *kranjĕ ladun*, to put into a basket, v, 7.

karanāwun, to cause to be made; past m. sg. with suff. 3rd pers. sg. ag. *karanôwun*, he caused (a mat) to be made (i.e. spread), xii, 24; f. sg. with same suff. as *karanövᵘn*, x, 13.

kaīsi, *kō̃si*, see *kĕ̃h*.

kus, *kusa*, *kusuy*, see *kyāh* 1.

koshᵘ, a honeycomb; pl. nom. *kȧshⁱ*, ix, 5.

Kashmīr (Hindī, not Kāshmīrī), Kashmīr, xi, 4. The Kāshmīrī word is *Kashīrᵘ*. Cf. *kôshyurᵘ*.

kashun, to scratch; inf. abl. *kashĕna-hanā kariiñᵘ*, to do a little scratching, to scratch (somebody) a little, xii, 16, 7.

kôshyurᵘ, m. (f. *köshirᵘ*), an inhabitant of Kashīrᵘ, or Kashmīr; pl. nom. *köshirⁱ*, xi, 6.

kasam or (xii, 2, *kasᵃm*), m. an oath; a charm, an incantation; *Khŏdāyĕ-sondᵘ chuy kasam*, there is an oath to thee of God, I adjure thee by God, xii, 7; — *karun*, to take an oath, to swear, v, 9 (bis); *driy kasam karun*, to take an oath, to swear, viii, 1 (bis), 2; — *hāwun*, to take an oath, swear by, v, 9; *muslas dyutᵘ kasᵃm*, he uttered a charm over the skin (cf. *shāph*), xii, 22.

kāsun, to expel, i, 12; vi, 6; to shave (hair); *mast kāsun*, to shave (so and so, dat.), xii, 4 (bis), 5 (bis), 10 (ter), 3 (bis), 9.

inf. obl. (inf. of purpose) *kāsani*, xii, 4, 5, 19; fut. pass. part. with emph. *y*, *muhim tagiy kāsunuy*, poverty will be able to be expelled for thee, thou wilt know how to expel poverty, i, 12; conj. part. *kösith*, xii, 10, 3; *mast mŏkalôwᵘnas kösith*, he finished shaving him, xii, 5.

impve. sg. 2, *kās*, vi, 6; past m. sg. with suff. 3rd pers. sg. ag. (*amis*) *kôsun mast*, he shaved him, xii, 10, 3; with ditto, and suff. 3rd pers. sg. dat. *mast kôsᵘnas*, he shaved him, xii, 4; with suff. 3rd pers. sg. dat. *kôsus mast*, shaved him, xii, 10.

kusūr, m. a fault; *gōm suy kusūr*, that very fault happened to me, i.e. that was my bad luck (for some fault of mine), vii, 13.

kāsawunᵘ, one who expels, i, 11.

kati, adv. where? (*kätⁱ* of the grammars), vii, 20; x, 12 (ter); xi, 17;

from where ? whence ? (*kati* of the grammars), x, 4 ; xi, 17 ; xii, 4, 5, 11, 5 ; *kati-pĕṭha*, from where ? whence ? ii, 2.

*kot*ᵘ, adv. where ? xi, 5.

*koṭ*ᵘ, a son, esp. a clever son ; *ôkhun-koṭ*ᵘ, the son of a doctor of divinity, xii, 25.

*kūt*ᵘ, pron. adj. how much ? pl. how many ? m. sg. nom. *kūt*ᵘ, vii, 22 ; *kōtāh*, vii, 24 ; pl. nom. *kūt*ⁱ, vii, 25 ; *kaityāh*, ix, 5, 11 ; *kötyāh*, vii, 31 ; x, 7, 8 ; xii, 20 ; f. sg. nom. *köts*ᵘ, vii, 15 ; ag. *kātsa*, i, 12 ; pl. nom. *katsa*, x, 6.

kitāb, f. a book ; *sōhib-i-kitāb*, a master of books, a celebrated writer, x, 13.

kath, f. (this word is the equivalent of the Hindī *bāt*), a word, an uttered word, ix, 7 ; xii, 9 ; a word, a statement, iv, 5 ; x, 4, 6 (many times), 14 ; a matter, circumstance, affair, iii, 5 ; xii, 1 ; a story, tale, narrative, v (title) ; vii, 1 ; viii, 1 ; x, 1 (many times), 2 (many times) ; *katha-bātha*, pl. conversations, xii, 25 ; *katha-karañĕ*, to converse, iii, 1 ; x, 7 (ter) ; xii, 3 ; to say (such and such) words, xii, 23 ; *kōri söty kath karūñ*ᵘ, to hold speech with the girl, i.e. to make improper overtures to her, xii, 1. In x, 1 ff., the point of the story consists in a misunderstanding of the word *kath*, one person of the company means "a statement", the others mean "a tale".

sg. nom. *kath*, v, 1 ; vii, 1 ; viii, 1 ; x, 6 (bis) ; xii, 1 (bis) ; gen. *kathi-hond*ᵘ, iii, 5 ; pl. nom. *katha*, iii, 1 ; iv, 5 ; x, 1 (many times) ; 2 (many times), 4, 6 (many times), 7 (ter), 14 ; xii, 3, 23, 5 ; dat. *kathan*, x, 1 ; xii, 9 ; abl. *kathan*, ix, 7.

kathō, see *kyāh* 1

kĕth, postpos. governing dat. in, on ; *athas kĕth*, in the hand, ii, 7 ; v, 4 ; x, 7 ; xii, 22, 3 (bis) ; *khŏni-kĕth*, on the haunch, xi, 13 ; *rumāli kĕth*, in a kerchief, iii, 2.

kĕtha, adv. ; *kĕtha-pöṭh*ⁱ, how ? in what manner ? iii, 9 ; v, 8 ; viii, 5 ; x, 8 ; xii, 3, 24.

kōtāh, see *kūt*ᵘ.

*kuṭh*ᵘ, m. a room, viii, 3 ; with suff. of indef. art. *kuṭh*ᵘ*āh*, ix, 4 ; sg dat. *kuṭhis*, iii, 8 (bis) ; x, 7, 8 (bis) ; pl. nom. *kuṭh*ⁱ, vi, 3.

katikō, adj. of or belonging to where ? ii, 2 (poet.). Cf. *kati*.

katarun, to cut to pieces ; pres. m. sg. 3, *chuh katarān*, x, 7.

kuṭ^a^wāl, m. a chief of police, a *kōṭwāl*, v, 7, 9 (bis), 10 ; sg. ag. *kuṭ^a^wālan*, v, 7, 8, 9 ; *kuṭ^a^wāl-gānas* (sg. dat.), to the wretch of a police captain, v, 9 (see *gān*).

katawañ, f. the wages of spinning ; — *karüñ^ü^*, to earn money by spinning, xi, 19.

kaityāh, *kötyāh*, see *kūt^u^*.

katsa, *kātsa*, see *kūt^u^*.

*kits^ü^*, see *kyut^u^*.

*köts^ü^*, see *kūt^u^*.

kuwa, adv. how ? v, 9.

kiy, in *hargāh-kiy*, if, viii, 7, 13. See *hargāh*.

kyā, see *kyāh*, 1 and 4.

kyāh 1 or *kyā* 1, interrog. pron. who ? what ?

As subst. an. m. sg. nom. *kus*, who ? xi, 2 ; xii, 1 ; *kusuy*, who verily ? xi, 19 ; ag. *kàm^i^*, by whom ? iii, 3 (bis) ; x, 12 ; pl. nom. *kam*, who ? xii, 1.

subst. inan. *kyā*, what ? vi, 5 ; *kyāh*, what ? ii, 2, 4, 11 ; iii, 4 (quater), 8, 9 (bis) ; iv, 7 ; v, 9 (bis) ; vi, 15 ; vii, 20, 2, 4, 6, 30 ; viii, 1, 3, 6, 8, 9, 10 (ter), 1 (quater) ; ix, 4 (bis) ; x, 2, 5, 6, 8 ; xii, 1, 7, 20.

kĕ-hŏ, what, sir (colloquial, addressed by a woman to her husband), v, 4, 5 ; dat. *kath* ; poet. colloquial, *kathō-kit^i^* (pots) for what ? xi, 11 ; abl. *kami-bāpath*, for what ? why ? on what account ? ix, 1 ; x, 12 ; *kami-mŏkha*, on what account ? x, 4 ; gen. *kamyuk^u^*, of what ? vi, 13, 4.

kyāh sabab chuwa, what is your reason ? viii, 5 ; *kyāh gatshiy anun^u^ nishāna*, what is to be brought to thee as a token ? xii, 21.

adj. f. inan. nom. *kusa kusa*, which (of several) ? x, 6 (bis).

*mĕ kyāh zulm chuh gŏmot^u^*, (hear) what tyranny has happened to me, ix, 6.

an. masc. *kus-tāñ wŏpar*, some one else, v, 4 ; inan. *kyāh-tāñ takhsīr*, some fault of other, viii, 10.

kyāh 2, adv. why ? x, 14 (bis) ; how ? vii, 8, 27, 8.

kyāh 3, an expletive implying interrogation, vii, 27, 8.

kyāh 4 or *kyā* 2 (v, 9 ; xii, 23), an expletive common in the colloquial language, impossible to translate, but approximately equivalent to the English "why !", "of course," "certainly," "verily," "you see," or something of the sort, v, 8, 9 (many times) ; viii, 1 ; ix, 10 ; x, 3 (ter), 12 ; xi, 18 ; xii, 15 (bis), 23 ; *yit*^{i} *kyāh*, "here, in fact," or "here, you see," x, 12 (bis) ; *yit*^{i} *kyāh* . . . *ȧt*^{i} *kyāh*, here on the one hand you see . . . there on the other hand you see, viii, 13 ; *ada-kyāh*, then of course, of course, certainly, viii, 11 ; xii, 4.

kyāh 5, conj., or, iv, 7.

kyom^{u}, m. a worm, xii, 3 (ter), 4.

kyut^{u}, postpos. for. This, like the postpositions of the genitive, is adjectival, and agrees with the governing noun. Thus : m. sg. nom. *bāg zananan-kyut*^{u}, a garden for the women, ii, 1 ; *guris-kyut*^{u} *gāsa*, grass for the horse, x, 5 ; *rĕtas-kyut*^{u} *kharj*, expenditure for a month, xii, 4 ; *trĕn rĕtan-kyut*^{u} *kharj*, expenditure for three months, xii, 5, 11 ; *tath-kyut*^{u} *shĕstruw*^{u} *panja*, an iron claw for that, xii, 16 ; *zyun*^{u} *mĕ-kyut*^{u}, firewood for me, xii, 24. With a special adverbial meaning indicating time, *rāth-kyut*^{u}, by night, iii, 1.

m. pl. nom. *wasth pātashĕha-sanzĕ kōrĕ-kit*^{i}, articles for the king's daughter, v, 1 ; *kathō-kit*^{i}, (pots) for what ? xi, 11.

f. sg. nom. *wōj*^{ü} *pātashāha-sanzĕ kōrĕ-kits*^{ü}, a ring for the king's daughter, v, 1 ; *ziyāphath pātishōhiyĕn-kits*^{ü}, a feast for the kingdoms, x, 11 ; *gōv*^{ü} *kits*^{ü} *jāy*, a place for the cow, xi, 12.

kyuth^{u}, adv. how ? ii, 5.

kyāzi, adv. why ? iii, 1 ; v, 8 ; viii, 1, 3, 11 ; ix, 1 ; xii, 4, 5 ; *ti-kyāzi*, because, viii, 2.

lā, in *Lā-makān*, without a dwelling-place, an epithet of the Deity, vii, 29.

labun, to take ; fut. sg. 2, *labakh*, ii, 9 ; past m. sg. with suff. 3rd pers. sg. ag. *lobun*, ii, 10.

lach, m. a hundred thousand, a *lākh* ; *lachĕ-nôw*^{u}, m. He Who has a hundred thousand names, an epithet of the Deity, ii, 2.

lich^{ü}*n*, see *likhun*.

ladun, to send, iv, 2 ; vii, 7 ; x, 3 (many times) ; xii, 15 ; to put or place (into or on a receptacle, such as a basket or tray), v, 7 ; viii, 4, 12 ; to fill (a cup with water, *pyālas āb ladun*), viii, 7 ; to place or impose (a burden), ii, 5 ; *maṭi rāh ladun*, to impose a crime on the shoulder, to charge (a person, gen. or dat.) with a crime, v, 9.

fut. pass. part. m. sg. *gatshĕm ladun*^{u} *kĕntshāh*, you must send me something, xii, 15 ; impve. sg. 2, *lad*, xii, 15 ; fut. sg. 2, with suff. 1st pers. sg. dat. and conditional suff. *ladaham-ay*, if thou wilt send to me, x, 3 ; past m. sg. with suff. 3rd pers. sg. ag. *lodun*, ii, 5 ; vii, 7 ; viii, 7 ; x, 3 ; ditto and with suff. 1st pers. sg. dat. *lod*^{u}*nam*, iv, 2 ; v, 9 ; xii, 15 ; f. sg. with suff. 3rd pers. sg. ag. *lüz*^{ü}*n*, x, 3 ; ditto and with suff. 3rd pers. sg. dat. *lüz*^{ü}*nas*, x, 3 (bis) ; pl. with 3rd pers. sg. ag. *lazan*, v, 7 ; with suff. 3rd pers. pl. ag. *lazakh*, viii, 4, 12.

lāḍun 1 and 2, see *lārun* 1 and 2.

laḍöy^{i}, f. fighting ; *milüv*^{ü}*kh laḍöy*^{i}, fighting was joined by them, i.e. they began to quarrel, x, 1.

lagun, to be joined (to), connected (with) ; to be felt, experienced, (*amār lagun*, desire to be felt, v, 2 ; *bŏchĕ lagüñ*^{ü}, hunger to be felt, vi, 16 ; *trĕsh lagüñ*^{ü}, thirst to be felt, viii, 7 ; in all these cases the person is put in the dat.) ; to come into existence (*mang lüj*^{ü}, a demand was made, xi, 16) ; to occur, happen, become (*rāth lagüñ*^{ü}, night to come on, viii, 9) ; to become liable to, to incur (*köd lagun*, to incur imprisonment, to be imprisoned, v, 8 ; vi, 11) ; to be experienced (*grāy lagüñ*^{ü}, shaking to be experienced, to be unsteady, to be impermanent, ix, 12, dat. of pers. experiencing) ; to be attached (to), find oneself in a certain condition (*lagun wŏbāli*, to find oneself in blameworthiness, to incur guilt, viii, 5) ; to be caught (*wālawāshi lagun*, to be caught in a net, v, 2) ; to arrive at (a place), viii, 5 ; xi, 5 ; (conversely), (of a place), to be reached, to be arrived at, xi, 5 ; (of a work) to be allotted (to so and so), viii, 5 ; to begin.

In the meaning " to begin ", this verb is used with the oblique infinitive in *-ni* of another verb to form inceptive compounds. Thus, *atsani lagun*, to begin to enter, x, 7 ;

nērani l., to begin to issue, x, 7 ; *phŏlani l.*, (of the dawn) to begin to break, v, 5, 7 ; xii, 2 ; *wanani l.*, to begin to say, x, 1 ; *wasani l.*, to begin to descend, viii, 6 ; *wŏtharani l.*, to begin to wipe, viii, 6 ; *wātani l.*, to begin to arrive, viii, 6 ; *yini l.*, to begin to come, x, 8. In all these cases, the verb *lagun* is in the past tense.

fut. sg. 2, *lagakh*, v, 2 ; with prohibitive neg. repeated as a suff. *mā lagah-a-m*, mayst thou not find thyself, v, 2 ; 3, *lagi*, with suff. 3rd pers. pl. dat. *lagĕkh*, ix, 12 ; pres. m. sg. 3, *chuh lagān*, viii, 5.

past m. sg. *log*ᵘ, v, 5, 7 ; vi, 11 ; viii, 6 (ter), 7 (bis), 8 ; xi, 5 ; xii, 2 ; with suff. 1st pers. sg. dat. and emph. *y*, *log*ᵘ*m*ᵘ*y*, v, 2 ; pl. *lȧg*ⁱ, x, 1 ; xi, 5 ; f. sg. *lüj*ᵘ, xi, 16 ; with suff. 3rd pers. sg. dat. *lüj*ᵘ*s*, vi, 16 ; viii, 7, 9 ; perf. m. pl. 2, *chiwa lȧg*ⁱ*mȧt*ⁱ, viii, 5.

cond. past sg. 1, *lagahö*, v, 8.

lāgun, to apply ; to fix (*jĕnḍa lāgun*), to fix a flag, set up a flag, insist on a claim, v, 11) ; to assume the character of (so and so), make oneself look like (so and so), dress oneself up as (so and so), disguise oneself as (so and so), i, 2 ; v, 9, 10, 1 (ter) ; x, 7, 12 (bis), 4 ; to cause to come into existence, to be carried on (*lög*ⁱ*mȧt*ⁱ *nagma*, dances were being carried on, iii, 7).

conj. part. *lögith*, i, 2 ; v, 11 ; x, 12 (bis) ; impve. sg. 2, *lāg*, v, 9, 11 ; past m. sg. with suff. 3rd pers. sg. ag. *lôgun*, v, 10, 1 (bis) ; x, 7 ; perf. m. pl. (auxiliary omitted), *lög*ⁱ*mȧt*ⁱ, iii, 7 ; plup. m. sg. with suff. 1st pers. sg. ag. *ôsum lôg*ᵘ*mot*ᵘ, x, 14.

lāgar, adj. lean, thin ; f. pl. nom. *lāgar*, vi, 15.

luh-luh, a meaningless refrain added in songs, v, 11 (four times).

*lŏhlür*ᵘ, f. longing, eager desire ; sg. abl. *lŏhlari*, vi, 3.

*lĕj*ᵘ, f. a cooking pot ; pl. nom. *lĕjĕ*, xi, 10.

*lüj*ᵘ, *lüj*ᵘ*s*, see *lagun*.

lĕkh, f. indecent language, immoral proposals made to a woman ; pl. dat. *lĕkan*, viii, 3, 11.

lōkh, m. pl. people ; pl. nom. ii, 11 ; dat. *lōkan*, ii, 11 ; xi, 13. According to the Kaśmīraśabdâmrta (II, i, 66), in standard Kāshmīrī this word is *lūkh*, and retains the long *ū* throughout all its cases.

likhun, to write; impve. sg. 2, *likh*, xii, 15; fut. pl. 3, *likhan*, ix, 12; pres. m. sg. 3, *chuh likhān*, x, 13; f. sg. 3, *likhān chĕh*, xii, 11; part. m. sg. *lyukh*^{u}, xii, 15; with suff. 3rd pers. sg. ag. *lyukhun*, xii, 22 (bis); ditto and with suff. 3rd pers. sg. dat. *lyukh*^{u}*nas*, xii, 15 (bis), 6; with suff. 3rd pers. sg. dat. *lyukhus*, xii, 17; with suff. 3rd pers. pl. ag. and 3rd pers. sg. dat. *lyukh*^{u}*has*, xii, 17; f. sg. with suff. 3rd pers. sg. ag. *lich*^{ü}*n*, viii, 10; perf. (auxiliary omitted) m. sg. *lyukh*^{u}*mot*^{u}, viii, 10; xii, 15, 23.

lākam, m. a bridle, xi, 9.

lŏkuṭ^u, adj. small; *lŏkuṭ*^{u} *hyuh*^{u}, the younger of one or more brothers, sg. ag. *lŏk*$^{\dot{a}}$*ṭ*^{i} *hih*^{i}, xii, 1.

lāl 1, m. a ruby, xii, 2 (quater), 3, 4 (many times), 6; sg. dat. *tath lālas hyuh*^{u}, like that ruby, xii, 4 (bis); pl. nom *lāl*, i, 9; x, 2; 5, 12 (ter); xii, 3, 5, 9; dat. *lālan-pĕṭh*, on the rubies, x, 5; gen. *lālan-hond*^{u}, xii, 5 (ter); abl. *lālau*, viii, 3, 11; *lāl-pharōsh*, m. a ruby-seller, a jeweller, xii, 3; *lāl-shĕnākh*, m. a ruby-tester, a lapidary, xii, 4, 5, etc.; sg. dat. *lāl-shĕnākas*, xii, 4 (bis), 5, 6, 10, 1, 3, 5, 9 (several times), 22, 4, 5, gen. *lāl-shĕnāka-sond*^{u}, xii, 8, 25; ag. *-shĕnākan*, xii, 4 (bis), 7, 9, 10, 3, 22 (ter), 4, 5.

lāl 2, f. spittle, saliva, viii, 7.

Lālmāl, N.P. f. xii, 8, 11 (bis), 4, 5 (indeclinable in composition), 25.

Lāla-Malikh, N.P. m.; sg. gen. *Lāla-Malikun*^{u}, iv, title; dat. *Lāla-Malikas*, iv, 7.

lalawun, to caress; to caress, in order to relieve pain, to soothe, fondle, stroke, v, 6; pres. m. sg. 3, *chuh lalawān*, v, 6.

lamun, to pull, drag; pres. m. sg. 3, with suff. 3rd pers. sg. dat. *chus lamān*, he is pulling him, viii, 9.

lôn^u, m. fate; *lôn*^{i}*-tsūr*, a fate-thief, a destroyer of good luck, vii, 12.

Landan, m. London; sg. abl. *Landana-pĕṭha*, xi, 3.

langūṭ^i, f. a loin-cloth; — *karith*, wearing only a loin-cloth, xii, 23.

lōnun, to reap; pres. sg. 3, *chuh lōnān*, x, 5.

lar, f. the side (of the body); sg. abl. *lari*, vii, 18; *lari-tala*, from under the side (of Eve's birth from Adam), vii, 7.

lār, f. running, pursuit; running away, fleeing; — *karüñ*ᵘ, to pursue, ii, 8; *lār tsānüñ*ᵘ, to pursue, ix, 2.

*lür*ᵘ, f. a house; dat. *larĕ*, vi, 3.

lārun 1 or (iii, 5; vi, 8) *lāḍun* 1, to run; *pata lārun*, to run after, to pursue (ii, 9; vi, 8; xi, 18).

pres. part. *lārān*, vi, 8; viii, 6; xi, 12; pres. m. pl. 3, *chih lārān*, ii, 9; with suff. 3rd pers. pl. dat. *chikh lārān*, xi, 18; imperf. m. pl. 3, *ös*ⁱ *lārān*, x, 5; 1 past m. pl. with suff. 3rd pers. sg. dat. *lōris*, ii, 9; III past m. sg. *lāryāv*, ii, 10; *lāḍyāv*, iii, 5; f. sg. with suff. 3rd pers. sg. dat. *lāḍyēyĕs*, vi, 8.

lārun 2 or *lāḍun* 2, to be brought into contact with, to touch (of oil or other liquid dirtying a person); perf. *lāryōmot*ᵘ (Gōvind Kaul) or *lāḍyōmot*ᵘ (Hātim), viii, 6 (*amis zahar l.*, the poison has touched her).

lashkar, f. an army, x, 11; sg. dat. *lashkari*, ii, 7; x, 9, 13; *lashkari-manz*, in the army, ii, 6, 8.

lasun, to survive (a danger); fut. sg. 3, *lasi*, x, 7.

*lọ̆t*ᵘ, adj. light, gentle; *lŏt*ⁱ*-pöṭh*ⁱ, gently, xii, 5.

*loṭ*ᵘ, the tail of an animal, v, 7; abl. *laṭi-kån*ⁱ, in the direction of the tail, towards the tail (and not towards the head), xi, 9.

lath, f. a foot; pl. dat. *roṭun latan tal*, he held it under his feet, i.e. he stood upon it, viii, 7.

laṭh, f. an occasion, time, turn; sg. dat. *dŏyi laṭi*, on two occasions, twice, viii, 7; *trĕyimi laṭi*, on the third occasion, viii, 7.

*lit*ᵘ*r*ᵘ, f. a saw; abl. *litri-söty*, with (by means of) a saw, vii, 19.

*lôw*ᵘ, m. in *gāsa-lôw*ᵘ, a bundle of grass, xi, 12.

*lyukh*ᵘ, etc., see *likhun*.

löyikh, adj. fit, worthy; *mĕ löyikh*, worthy of me, xii, 10, 9; *löyik-ĕ-pātashāh*, worthy of a king, x, 4; *löyik-i-wazīr*, worthy of a vizier, xii, 10, 19; *löyik-i-pātashāh*, worthy of a king, xii, 19.

lāyilā, the Musalmān creed, a corruption of the Arabic *lā ilāha illa-llāhu*, there is no god, but *the* God, vi, 17.

lāyun, to strike, hit, beat, iii, 1 (dat. of obj.), 2 (dat. of obj.), 9 (dat. of obj.); ix, 8; x, 1 (*amis lôyukh*, they beat him, *bhāvē prayōga*); (*shĕmshēri-hünz*ᵘ *tsünḍ*ᵘ *lāyüñ*ᵘ, to strike a blow with a sword, iii, 5, 6; *thaph dāmānas lāyüñ*ᵘ, to strike a grasp to a skirt, to seize the skirt, v, 9; *bandūkh lāyun,* to aim and fire a gun, ii, 11; viii, 10); to cast, to throw, i, 6, 7, 8; v, 3, 4 (ter), 5.

inf. dat. (inf. of purpose) *lāyěni,* ix, 8; fut. pass. part. m. pl. *hěch lāyanⁱ rīnzⁱ,* learn to throw balls, v, 3; impve. 2, *lāy,* i, 7; with suff. 3rd pers. sg. dat. *lāyus,* iii, 5; fut. sg. 3, *lāyi,* iii, 9; pres. m. sg. 3, *lāyān chuh,* v, 4; imperf. m. sg. 3, *ôsᵘ lāyān,* i, 6.

I past m. sg. with suff. 3rd pers. sg. ag. *lôyun,* i, 8; iii, 1, 2; ditto and suff. 3rd pers. sg. dat. *lôyᵘnas,* viii, 10; with suff. 3rd pers. pl. ag. *lôyukh,* x, 1; ditto and suff. 3rd pers. sg. dat. *lôyᵘhas,* ii, 11; pl. with suff. 1st pers. sg. ag. and suff. 3rd pers. sg. dat. *löyⁱmas,* v, 4; with suff. 3rd pers. sg. ag. *löyin,* v, 4; f. sg. with suff. 3rd pers. sg. ag. *löyᵘn,* viii, 6, ditto and suff. 1st pers. sg. dat. *löyᵘnam,* v, 9; ditto and suff. 3rd pers. sg. dat. *löyᵘnas,* iii, 6.

III past m. sg. with suff. 3rd pers. sg. ag. and 3rd pers. sg. dat. *lāyānas,* he had thrown a long time ago to her, v, 5.

lüzᵘ, see *ladun.*

ma or (poet. v, 2) *may,* prohibitive adv., used with impve. *ma kar,* do not make, xii, 7. Cf. *mā* 1.

mā 1, or (poet. v, 11) *mōv,* prohibitive adv. With 2 sg. fut., in v, 2 it is repeated, under the form of *m,* as a suffix to the verb, *mā lagaham* (*lagakh+a+m,* in which the *a* is a junction vowel), mayst thou not find thyself. It is also used as a negative in the apodosis of a conditional sentence, as in *hargāh-ay wuchihē . . . mā mārihē,* if he had seen . . . he would not have killed, viii, 10 (but cf. *mārihē-na,* viii, 7); *hargāh-kiy sara karihē . . . mā diyihē hukum,* if he had investigated, . . . he would not have given the order, viii, 13. Cf. *ma* and *na.*

mā 2, or (poet. v, 9) *māh,* adv. indicating a question asked with hesitation, equivalent to "I wonder if", "can it be possible that?" i, 2; v, 8, 9; vii, 20; viii, 9, 13; x, 5, 12; xii, 23.

mě, see *bŏh.*

mŏbārakh, adj. blessed; — *karun,* to congratulate, x, 8.

măch-tᵃlᵘrᵘ, f. a honey-bee, ix, 1 (ter), 3, 4, 5; sg. ag. *măch-tᵃlᵃri,* ix, 1, 6.

macīma, m. N. of a certain dainty, a kind of rice pudding, cooked with *ghī* and spices, and coloured, ii, 3.

mad, m. pride, vii, 15.

mŏdā, f. (Ar. *mudda'ā*), meaning, object, vi, 7.

modu, see *mor*[u].

mūd[u], see *marun*.

mödān, m. an open field, plain, x, 1 (quater); with suff. of indef. art. *gāsa-mödānā*, a certain grass plain, x, 5; sg. dat. *mödānas*, iii, 1; viii, 9; x, 1; xii, 20; pl. nom. (acc.) *pōshĕ-mödān*, the flower-meadows, xi, 3.

mŏdur[u], adj. sweet, vii, 31 (wine); pl. abl. *mŏdaryiv kathau*, with sweet words, ix, 7.

māh, see *mā* 2.

mahabath, m. affection, love; sg. abl. *mahabata-söty*, through affection, x, 4.

mahkam, adj. made firm, firm, stable, strong, xi, 9 (of a rope); strong, established, which cannot be abrogated, iv, 6 (of a religion).

mahala-khān, or (xii, 19) *-khāna*, m. the private apartments of a palace, the harem, viii, 3, 11; *dökhil-i-mahalakhāna*, (of a woman) brought into the harem, xii, 19.

muhim, m. poverty, i, 11, 2; viii, 9 (bis); x, 3; sg. abl. *muhima-sötin*, through (i.e. owing to) poverty, i, 4, 5 (bis); *muhim-zad*, poverty stricken, x, 4.

Mahmad, m. N.P. Muḥammad, iv, 6; vii, 4.

Mahmōd, m. N.P. Maḥmūd; — *-i-Gaznavī*, Maḥmūd of G͟haznī, i, 1.

mahanyuv[u], m. a man, x, 4; pl. nom. *mahaniv*[i], x, 1.

mŏhar, f. a seal, x, 3, 10; xii, 22; N. of a certain coin, a gold mohur; *mŏhar karūñ*[u], to seal, x, 3 (bis), 10; *mŏhara-dyār*, wealth of mohurs, much money, i, 9; *mŏhar-hatas rosh*[u], a necklace worth a hundred mohurs, v, 10, 12.

māhrāj, m. (a Hindī word), the Mahārāja of Kashmīr, xi, 4.

mah[a]*ram*, adj. familiar (with), intimately acquainted (with), ii, 4 (with a secret, dat.).

möj[u], f. a mother, viii, 1, 3, 11 (bis); xii, 15 (quater), 8; sg. dat. *mājĕ*, viii, 3 (bis); gen. *mājĕ-hond*[u], xii, 15; ag. *māji*, v, 6; xii, 15, 8; voc. *mājiy*, xii, 15 (bis); *mājĕ-zamīn*, mother-earth, ix, 9; *wŏra-mŏj^u*, a stepmother, viii, 1.

mōjub, m. a reason; *amiy mōjub*, for this reason, viii, 6.

mējĕr, m. a major (corr. of the English word), a superior officer, e.g. a master-of-the-horse, x, 12, 13; sg. dat. *mējĕras*, x, 5 (ter), 12 (bis); ag. *mējĕran*, x, 12.

mukadam, m. a certain revenue official, the village headman, ix, 10; sg. ag. *mukadaman*, ix, 1.

makh, m. an axe; *makh dyun^u*, to apply, or wield, an axe (dat. of obj.), vii, 14.

mŏkh, m. the face; *mŏkh raṭun*, to seize the face, gaze on the face, v, 9; abl. *mŏkha*, on account of; *tami mŏkha*, on that account, viii, 9; *kami mŏkha*, on what account, x, 4.

mạkh^ara, m. coquetry; *mạkh^ar-i-zan*, a woman's coquetry, woman's wiles, x, 13.

mŏkalun, to be completed, finished, viii, 6, 8; to be released, to escape, v, 8; vi, 10, 1; *mŏkalan pāy*, a device for escape, a way of salvation, ix, 11.

inf. obl. abl. *mŏkalan* (poet. for *mŏkalana*), ix, 11; fut. sg. 3, *mŏkali*, v, 8; vi, 10; 1 past m. pl. with emph. *y*, *mŏkåliy*, vi, 11; 3 past m. sg. *mŏkalyāv*, viii, 6, 8.

mŏkalāwun, to finish, to complete, vi, 16; ix, 6; x, 1; xii, 5; to release, set free, v, 8.

wanith mŏkalāwun, to finish speaking, vi, 16; ix, 6; *kösith m.*, to finish shaving, xii, 5.

fut. pass. part. f. sg. *tagiyĕ mŏkalāwüñ^ü*, do you know how to get her released? v, 8; fut. pl. 1, with suff. 3rd pers. sg. acc. *mŏkalāwahun*, we shall complete it, x, 1; 1 past m. sg. *mŏkalôw^u*, vi, 16; ix, 6; with suff. 3rd pers. sg. ag. and 3rd pers. sg. dat. *mŏkalôw^unas*, he finished (shaving) him, xii, 5.

makān, m. a dwelling-place, see *lā*.

mŏkta, m. a pearl; pl. nom. with emph. *y*, *mŏktay*, pearls verily, i, 9. This word is elsewhere usually spelt *mŏkhta*.

māl, m. goods, property, i, 9; iii, 1; viii, 9 (quater).

mala, m. a Musalmān priest, a Mullah; pl. dat. *malan*, vi, 13

mŏl, m. the price (of anything), viii, 9; — *karun*, to fix the price, viii, 9 (bis).

môlᵘ, m. a father, viii, 13; *wōra-möjᵘ yā môlᵘ*, a stepmother or (step)father, viii, 1; sg. dat. *mölis*, xii, 4, 5, 10 (bis), 3; gen. *mölⁱ-sondᵘ*, xii, 19, 20 (bis), 1 (bis), 2, 4; ag. *mölⁱ*, v, 6.

Malikh, N.P. See *Lāla-Malikh*.

malakh, m. an angel; pl. ag. *malakav* (for *malakau*), iv, 2.

mulkh, m. a country, district; pl. dat. *mulkan*, i, 1.

màlⁱköñᵘ, f. a queen, esp. Queen Victoria of England; sg. ag. *màlⁱkāñi*, xi, 2.

milawun, to join, unite (transitive); 1 past f. sg. with suff. 3rd pers. pl. ag. *milüvᵘkh laḍöyⁱ*, fighting was joined by them, they began to fight among themselves, x, 1.

mumotᵘ, see *marun*.

man, f. the mind; sg. abl. *mani*, vi, 6. This word is usually m., but here it is certainly feminine, with a fem. adj. (*panañĕ*, for *panañi*, m.c.) in agreement with it.

mānĕ, m. meaning, purport, iii, 4, 5; vii, 27, 8; *khābas mānĕ tsārun*, to tell the meaning of a dream, vi, 14.

mang, f. a request; — *ladüñᵘ*, to make a request, make a demand, xi, 16.

manga, see *hanga ta manga*.

mangun, to ask for, demand; fut. pass. part. m. sg. *mangunᵘ*, it is to be demanded, you must demand, xii, 18; with *gatshi*, xii, 13, 8; impve. sg. 2, *mang*, xii, 5, 10, 1; with suff. 1st pers. sg. dat. *mangum*, ask from me, xii, 18; fut. with suff. 3rd pers. sg. dat. and neg. *màngⁱzĕs-na*, you must not ask from her, xii, 18; indic. fut. sg. 1, with suff. 2nd pers. sg. dat. *mangay*, I shall ask from thee, xii, 7; 2, with suff. 3rd pers. sg. dat. *mangahas*, thou wilt demand from him, xii, 19; pres. m. sg. 3, with suff. 1st pers. sg. dat. *chum mangān*, he is asking from me, xii, 4, 5, 11, 4; pl. 3, with same suff. *chim mangān*, they are asking from me, xi, 14.

manganāwun, to send for, summon (by another); past m. sg. with suff. 3rd pers. sg. ag. *manganôwun*, vi, 16; pl. with suff. 3rd pers. pl. ag. and with emphatic suffix *ay*, *gurⁱ manganövⁱhay*, they actually sent for horses, xi, 8.

manōsh, m. a man, a human being, xii, 15 (bis); sg. dat. (for acc.) *manōshĕs*, xii, 15.

manz, adv. inside, xii, 11 (descend inside).

postpos. governing dat. in; on (in special cases only); into.

in, *ath-manz*, in it, xii, 3, 15; *ath^i-m.*, in it verily, viii, 1; xii, 2, 22; *bāgas-m.*, in the garden, ii, 1, 7; *chus manz*, he is inside it, xii, 3; *dŏbas-m.*, in the pit, xii, 6, 7; *dadari-m.*, in the hollow, ii, 10; *dilas-m.*, in the heart, ii, 5; *hāpatas-m.*, in the bear, ii, 11; *janatas-m.*, in heaven, xii, 20, 3; *kŏli-m.*, in the stream, xii, 2; *kañĕ-m.*, in a stone, vi, 7; *maris-m.*, in the body, ii, 6; *pātashŏhī-m.*, in the kingdom, xii, 19; *sūras-m.*, in the ashes, xii, 23; *tōtas-m.*, in the parrot, ii, 8; *wŏr^ivis-m.*, in the father-in-law's house, x, 3; *yĕs-m.*, in whom, ii, 9.

on, *athas-m.*, (a bracelet) on the hand (arm), xii, 12; *mödānas-m.*, on the plain, xii, 20; *ṭŏkis-m.*, (jewels) on a tray, viii, 12; *tath^i-m.*, (a bracelet) on even it (sc. a hand), xii, 11.

into, (on to), *amis-m.*, (put) into this (bear), ii, 4; *bāgas-m.*, (went, entered, arrived) into the garden, ii, 1 (bis); iii, 7; v, 4, 5, 6, 9 (bis); *dun^iyāhas-m.*, (go) into the world, xii, 18 (bis); *halamas-m.*, (throw, etc.) into the lap-skirt, v, 4 (bis), 5; *hāpatas-m.*, (entered) into the bear, ii, 10; *janatas-m.*, (arrive, etc.) into heaven, xii, 24 (bis); *jāyĕ-m.*, (enter) into a place, iii, 7; *kuṭhis-m.*, (ascend) into the room, x, 7, 8 (bis); *laskari-m.*, (go, etc.) into the army, ii, 6, 9; *mödānas-m.*, (arrived) on to a plain, iii, 1; viii, 9; *maḍ(r)is-m.*, (enter) into a body, ii, 5, 6, 7, 11; *nāgas-m.*, (descend, throw) into a spring, iii, 5, 9; xii, 7, 12; *nāras-m.*, (leap) into the fire, iii, 4; *pŏshākas-m.*, (entered) into the garment, x, 7 (bis); *shĕharas-m.*, (entered, arrived) into the city, v, 9, 11; x, 14; xii, 2; *shikamas-m.*, (entered) into the belly, x, 7 (bis); *tath^i-m.*, (throw) into it verily, xii, 11; *tōtas-m.*, (entered) into the parrot, ii, 5; *wanas-m.*, (arrived) into a forest, ix, 1.

manza, postpos. governing abl. from in; *ami-manza*, from in it, xii, 4; *bagala-m.*, from in (i.e. from under) the armpit, viii, 7; *cĕnda-m.*, from in (i.e. out of) the pocket, xii, 15; *dŏba-m.*, from in the pit, xii, 7; *kŏli-m.*, from in the stream, xii, 4, 6;

rakhi-m., (seized) from in (i.e. seized in and brought from) the field, x, 12 (bis); *shĕhara-m.*, from in (i.e. from) the city, viii, 11; *shikama-m.*, from in the belly, x, 7 (bis); *sūra-m.*, from in the ashes, xii, 23; *satav-m.*, from in (i.e. from among) the seven, x, 12; *wana-m.*, from in the forest, ix, 4; *yĕmi-m.*, from in which, xii, 11.

mônzūr, approved, accepted, i, 12.

munazāth (= *munazzat*), pure (of God), vii, 1.

miñĕ-mürü, f. a hind, ii, 8; dat. *-marĕ*, ii, 9; ag. *-mari*, ii, 9.

mār, m. killing, slaughter; *māra gatshun*, to die a violent death, x, 7, 8, 13.

moru, or (ii, 5, 9) *moḍu*, m. the body of man or beast, ii, 5, 9, 10 (bis), 1; sg. dat. *maris*, ii, 7; *maris-manz*, ii, 6, 7, 11; *maḍis-manz*, ii, 5.

mürü, f. see *miñĕ-mürü*.

mard, m. a man; *marda-zan*, man or woman, vii, 23.

murdamāzörī, f. laughing and joking, amorous sport, x, 12. The word is a corruption of the Persian *mardum āzārī*. In that language *mardum āzār*, a tormenter of men, is colloquially used to mean "a lovely woman". Hence *mardum āzārī* would mean lit. "the conduct of a man with a lovely woman", i.e. "amorous sport."

marhabā, interj. welcome! hail! God bless you!; with suff. of indef. art. *kăritōs marhabāh*, make ye a God bless you for him, wish him good luck, ii, 10.

māraka (= *ma'raka*), m. an assembly; pl. dat. *mārakan*, (in) the assemblies, vii, 23.

murkhas (= *murakhkhas*), dismissed, allowed to depart; — *karun*, to dismiss (a court), viii, 11.

marun, irreg. to die; conj. part. *marith*, having died, i.e. after death, iv, 7; *marith gatshun* (= Hindī *mar jāna*), to die, vi, 16.

fut. sg. 1, *bŏy mara-y*, if I shall die, viii, 1 (bis); 3, *mari*, x, 7; xii, 19; imperf. *ôsu marān*, he was dying, he used to die, i.e. (in former times, if he did so) he always died, v, 9.

past sg. m. 3, *mūdu*, ii, 3, 6; sg. f. 3, *mŏyĕ*, viii, 2, 11.

perf. part. m. sg. *mumotu*, dead, ii, 3 (bis), 4 (bis), 10; dat. *kötyāh warihy gamăti mumatis*, how many years have passed for him dead, i.e. how many years it is since he died, xii, 20; pl. *mumāt*^{i}, viii, 1; perf. m. pl. 3, *chih mumāt*^{i}, they have died, viii, 1; fut. perf. *āsi mumot*^{u}, he is probably dead, x, 8 (bis).

cond. past sg. 3, *marihē*, viii, 7.

mārun, to kill; to strike, wound (v, 6).

inf. dat. *māranas*, for killing, (a decision) to kill, ii, 7; abl. *mārana-bāpath*, (given) for killing, x, 12; *ām mārani*, he came to kill me, viii, 13; fut. pass. part. *gatshi mārun*^{u}, he must be killed, x, 5 (bis), 12, 5; conj. part. *mörith trāwun* (= Hindī *mār ḍālnā*), to kill, slay, x, 8.

impve. pl. 2, with suff. 3rd pers. sg. acc. *möryūn*, ii, 16; with suff. 3rd pers. pl. acc. or dat. *möryūkh*, viii, 4, 12, 3; indic. fut. sg. 1, with suff. 2nd pers. sg. acc. *mārath*, ii, 11; 3, *mārē* (m.c. for *māri*), v, 7; with emph. *y*, *māriy*, vi, 11; with suff. 2nd pers. pl. gen. *yus māriwa*, he who among you will kill, ii, 7; pl. 3, with suff. 3rd pers. pl. acc. *māranakh*, viii, 4.

past m. sg. *môr*^{u}, iii, 3 (ter); vi, 11; neg. *môr*^{u}*-na*, ii, 8; with suff. 2nd pers. sg. ag. and 1st pers. sg. nom. *môr*^{u}*thas*, thou didst wound me, v, 6; with suff. 3rd pers. sg. ag. *môrun*, viii, 7, 10 (bis); x, 7; with suff. 3rd pers. pl. ag. and 1st pers. sg. dat. *môr*^{u}*ham*, they killed him for me (dat. ethicus), iii, 3; pl. *mör*^{i}, viii, 12; with suff. 3rd pers. pl. sg. *mörikh*, viii, 4.

cond. past 1, with suff. 2nd pers. sg. ag. and neg. *mārahath-na*; 3, neg. *mā mārihē*, he would not have killed, viii, 10; *mārihē-na*, he would not have killed, viii, 7; both being in apodosis of a cond. sentence.

martsa-wāgun, m. red pepper; *martsa-wāgan ratshi-hanā*, a little red pepper, a small amount of red pepper, v, 6.

māra-wātul, m. an executioner; pl. nom. (for acc.) *mārawāta*^{i}, x, 12; dat. *mārawātalan*, viii, 4 (bis), 11, 2, 3; x, 5 (bis), 12; ag. *mārawātalau*, viii, 12; x, 12; Cf. *wātul*.

Marāz, m. N. of the south-east end of the Valley of Kashmīr; *Marāz-i-pargan*, the Pargana, or fiscal division, of Marāz. xi, 5.

mas, m. wine, vii, 31.

Musā, Moses ; sg. ag. *musāy*, iv, 5.
mashhūr, celebrated, renowned, xi, 3.
mashun, to be forgotten ; (with subj. in dat.) to forget ; conj. part. *kath gayĕs mashith*, he forgot the statement, x, 6 ; past part. m. sg. *amis moṭhᵘ*, he forgot, v, 7 ; f. sg. 1 with suff. 3rd pers. pl. dat. *müṭhᵘkh*, (love, fem.) was forgotten to them, they forgot (love), ix, 8.
mushtākh, enamoured (of), entranced (with), usually governing dat., iii, 1, 9 (bis) ; *m.* · *athⁱ tamāshĕs-kun*, enamoured of that spectacle, iii, 7 ; *m. tathⁱ-söty*, entranced with that also, iii, 8 ; *pānasᵘy-kun mushtākh*, (God has) yearnings only for Himself ; i.e. He alone is free from imperfections, and if He has yearnings, they can only be for Himself, as all things consist in Him, vii, 3 ; *mushtākh gatshun*, to become entranced, etc., iii, 1, 7, 8.
mashīyĕth, f. a wish, vii, 7.
miskīn, m. a beggar, one who is poverty-stricken, x, 10 ; pl. nom. *miskīn*, ix, 11.
miskīnī, f. poverty, beggary ; sg. gen. *-hondᵘ*, x, 4 (bis).
musla, m. a piece of skin, xii, 18 (bis) ; dim. *musla-han*, f. a piece of skin, xii, 21 ; sg. dat. *muslas*, xii, 22.
maslahath, f. consultation ; — *karüñᵘ*, to consult together, viii, 3 ; xi, 19.
masnavī, f. a rhymed poem, vii, 30.
Misar, see Azīz-i-Misar.
mast, m. hair ; *mast kāsun* (personal obj. in dat.), to shave, xii, 4 (bis), 5 (bis), 10 (ter), 3 (bis), 9.
masᵃth, adj. plump, well-favoured (of cattle). This adjective is here inflected to agree with a fem. noun in dat. pl., *mastan*, vi, 15.
motᵘ, adj. mad, v, 2 ; subst. m. a mad man ; sg. dat. *nĕmis matis siwāh*, except this madman, v, 9 ; ag. *mätⁱ*, v, 9.
moṭᵘ, the space between the shoulders, the upper part of the back, sg. abl. *maṭi*, v, 9 ; xi, 10.
mōth, m. death ; Death personified, hence sg. gen. f. *mōtüñᵘ*, (a prison-house) of Death, ix, 4.
mathun, to rub ; conj. part. *mathith*, having rubbed (butter on

something), ix, 4 ; impve. sg. 2, *math*, rub (ashes on the body), v, 9.

mŏtasūtⁱ (for *mutaṣaddī*), m. an accountant ; pl. nom. *mŏtasūtⁱ*, ix, 7.

matsh, f. the arm ; sg. abl. *matshi*, x, 5.

mōtsh, m. a contemptuous term used by demons or the like for a man ; sg. abl. *mōtsha-bŏy*, f. the smell of a man, xii, 15.

mutsarun, to open ; — a door (viii, 3) ; — a letter (viii, 10 ; xii, 23) ; — the eyes (xii, 22) ; *sīna* —, to open the bosom, to declare one's inmost thoughts and sorrows (vii, 21).

conj. part. *mutsarith*, vii, 21 ; fut. sg. 1, with suff. 2nd pers. sg. dat. *mutsaray*, viii, 3 ; past sg. m. with suff. 3rd pers. sg. ag. *mutsorun*, viii, 10 ; xii, 23 ; f. pl. with same suff. *mutsarĕn*, xii, 22.

mĕwa, m. a fruit, xii, 21, 2.

mōv, poet. for *mā* 1 (v, 11), q.v.

may, poet. for *ma* (v, 2), q.v.

mŏyĕ, see *marun*.

myônᵘ, possess. pron. my, i, 10 ; vii, 27, 8 ; x, 4, 5, 12 (bis), 4 ; xii, 15 ; with emph. *y*, *myônuy*, vii, 9 ; m. sg. dat. *myönis*, xii, 19, 20 (bis), 1 ; abl. *myāni*, i, 2 ; pl. nom. *myönⁱ*, vii, 20 ; x, 5 ; xii, 15 (bis) ; dat. *myānĕn*, ii, 7 ; f. sg. nom. *myöñᵘ*, iii, 2, 4, 8, 9 ; v, 10 ; xii, 14 (bis), 5, 8 ; with emph. *y*, *myöñᵘy*, x, 10.

myūṭhᵘ, adj. sweet, pleasant, vi, 11 (of the interpretation of a dream).

māz, m. flesh, vii, 24 ; sg. dat. *māzas*, vii, 14.

mizmān, m. a guest, vii, 4.

na, adv. neg. not. It is not used with the simple or with the polite impve. (see *ma*, *mā* 1), but is used as a prohibitive with the fut. imperative. In a direct statement it is usually suffixed to the verb, as in *môrᵘ-na*, did not kill, and if the verb has pronominal suffixes it follows them, as in *mārahath-na*, I should not have killed thee. Before it the suffix *kh* does not become *h*, as in *chukh-na*, not *chuhana*, thou art not. It is used in this way, suffixed to a verb in i, 6 ; ii, 1, 4, 8, 9, 11 ; iii, 1, 2, 3 ; iv, 4, 6 ; v, 6 (ter), 9 (bis) ; vi, 10, 6 (bis) ; viii,

1, 2, 3, 7 (ter), 9 (bis), 11 (bis), 3; x, 1 (ter), 4 (bis), 6, 7, 12, 4; xii, 2 (bis), 3, 7, 15 (bis), 6, 7, 22. With the fut. impve., we have *dáp'zĕm-na*, you must not say to me, v, 8; *kár'zi-na*, you must not make, viii, 1; xii, 6; *wás'zi-na*, you must not descend, xii, 11; *máng'zĕs-na*, you must not demand from her, xii, 18.

It is also occasionally employed in other parts of the sentence, as in *na rūdᵘmotᵘ*, there was not remaining, i, 5; *wuchun ati na khar*, he did not see the ass there, iii, 9; *wuchun ta māl na kuni*, he saw that there was no property, viii, 9; *wuchun ati na pŏshākh*, she saw that her clothes were not there, xii, 7. This is most common in subordinate clauses, as in *yĕli na bani*, when it is not possible, x, 3; *yĕsa na pānas-söty chĕh*, (the woman) who is not with you, x, 6; *yĕli na yinsān ôsᵘ*, when it was not a man, x, 7; *yim na zānan*, they who do not know, xi, 8.

It is sometimes used as a privative prefix, as in *na-āsanas*, for non-existence, x, 1, 6.

With emph. *y*, it becomes *nay* 1, as in *sa nay kĕ̄h āyĕm*, she did not come at all to me, v, 5; *yŏr nay rōzani āy*, we did not come here to stay, ix, 6, 8, 10, 2; *yith nay lāgĕkh grāy*, so that they may not be at all shaken, ix, 12; *bŏ-nay sara zāh*, I shall never remember, xi, 14; *kĕ̄h nay chim bōzān*, they do not listen to me at all, xi, 15. This word should not be confused with *nay* 2, q.v.

nā, negative interrogative suffix in *āsi-nā*, will there not be? viii, 7; *āyĕ-nā*, did there not come? ix, 3; *bani-nā*, will there not be? vi, 13; *bōzakh-nā*, wilt thou not hear? vi, 1, etc.; *khĕkh-nā*, wilt thou not eat? ii, 3; vi, 2; *chukh-nā parzanāwān*, dost thou not recognize? x, 12; *tagĕm-nā*, will it not be within my power? i.e. of course it will be, x, 5; *wada-nā*, shall I not weep? vii, 25; *yikh-nā*, wilt thou not come? vi, 2; *zāna-nā*, shall I not know? x, 12.

nau, i.q. *na* (poet.); *nau kāh-ti*, no one at all, vii, 23; *nau zānav*, we do not know, xi, 15.

nu, adv. neg. in *nu chuh gatshān pātashĕhas*, *nu chuh gatshān biyĕ-kun*, he goes neither to the king not does he go anywhere else, xii, 4.

nĕbar, adv. outside, iii, 8 (ter); viii, 7; x, 7; postpos. *shăharas nĕbar*, (he was taken) outside the city, x, 5.

nĕchi, see *nĕṭh*ᵘ.

*nĕcyuv*ᵘ, m. a son, iii, 9 (bis); with suff. of indef. art. *zargar-nĕcyuvāh*, a goldsmith's son, v, 2; sg. dat. (for acc.) *nĕcivis*, iii, 9; pl. nom. *nĕciv'*, viii, 11; xii, 1; dat. *nĕcivĕn-pĕṭh*, on the sons, viii, 13; gen. *nĕcivĕn-hünz*ᵘ, viii, 3, 11.

nād, m. a call, a summons; *nād dyun*ᵘ, to summon, i, 10; x, 12; xii, 17.

nādān, m. a fool; sg. dat. *nādānas*, ii, 5; voc. *nādāna*, xi, 11.

nāg, a spring (of water) (usually looked upon as sacred, where it issues from a mountain side), xii, 6; sg. dat. *nāgas*, v, 9; xii, 6; *nāgas-manz*, (descended, etc.) into the spring, iii, 5, 9; xii, 7, 12; *nāgas-pĕṭh*, (went, etc.) up to, or on to the bank of, a stream (a common idiom), iii, 4 (bis), 5, 9; xii, 6 (bis), 11, 2, 4; *nāgas akith kun*, on one side of the spring, xii, 14.

sg. abl. *kasam nāga-pĕṭha*, an oath from by the stream, an oath made on the bank of the spring, calling the spring to witness, v, 9; voc. *nāga*, v, 9; pl. nom. *nāg*, vi, 15; dat. (for acc.) *nāgan*, vi, 15.

nagma, m. a melody, song; in Kāshmīrī, a dance of women; pl. nom., id., iii, 7.

nigīn, m. a jewel; pl. nom. id., i, 9; ag. *nigīnau*, (a tray filled) with jewels, viii, 3, 11.

Nōh, m. Noah, iv, 3.

nahīth tshunun, to cancel, make void, xii, 4.

nakha, adv. near, ii, 9.

nŏkhta (xii, 19) or *nŏkta* (xii, 4), m. a point; hence a particular on which one can condemn a person; *tamis raṭh-ta kĕntshāh nŏkhta*, seize some point (in) him, bring a charge of some fault against him, get up something against him, catch him tripping, xii, 19; so *kar-ta kĕntshāh nŏktāh* (with suff. of indef. art.), xii, 4.

nakār, m. prohibition; — *karun*, to prohibit (dat. of obj. prohibited), iv, 6.

nōkar, m. a servant; *nōkar bĕhun*, to sit down as a servant, to take service, xii, 3; pl. nom. *huzūrī-nokar běhan*[i], to sit down as personal servants, to be employed as such, viii, 5.

nōkarī, f. service; *kyāh nōkarī karakh*, what service wilt thou do? what employment dost thou want? xii, 3; *běhiv mě-nish nōkarī*, be employed (in) my service, take service with me, viii, 5.

nŏkta, see *nŏkhta*.

nāl 1, m. a horse-shoe; pl. nom. *nāl*, xi, 17.

nāl 2, m. the neck; sg. dat. *nālas*, vi, 9; abl. *nāla*, v, 9; viii, 10. Cf. *nöl*[i].

nāla, f. pl. cries, lamentation; nom. (acc.) *nāla diñě*, to utter cries, to lament, vii, 22, 3.

nālē, postpos. (Hindī), with, xi, 4.

nöl[i], adv. on the neck (cf. *nāl* 2), viii, 10 (ter); — *tshunun*, to put round the neck, viii, 10; *amis ôs*[u] *pŏshākh nöl*[i], he had garments on his neck, i.e. he was wearing garments, x, 4; *pŏshākh tshon*[u] *ami nöl*[i], she put the garment on her neck, i.e. she dressed herself, xii, 7.

nam, a nail (of the finger or toe); pl. nom. *nam*, v, 6.

namun, to bow; fut. sg. 3, *nami*, vi, 16; 2 past m. sg. 3, *namyōv*, vi, 16.

němis, see *nŏth*.

nāmurād, adj. unsuccessful; in Kāshmīrī, without hope, without expectation, i, 10.

non[u], adj. naked; bare (of a sword), viii, 6; manifest, hence, glorious, vi, 7; with emph. *y*, *nonuy*, vi, 7; f. sg. nom. *nüñ*[ü], viii, 6.

nun, m. salt; sg. abl. *nuna-ratshi-hanā*, a little salt, v, 6. (Elsewhere the word is written *nūn*.)

nĕnd[a]*r*, f. sleep; — *karüñ*[ü], to sleep, v, 6; — *pĕñ*[ü], sleep to fall, v, 5, 7; — *yiñ*[ü], sleep to come, v, 6 (ter); *yiyiy nĕnd*[a]*r shĕh*[ü]*j*[ü], sleep will come to thee cold, i.e. thou wilt cease to be sleepy; but it also means "cool sleep will come to thee", and is misunderstood by the hearer in this sense, v, 6 (bis).

ningalun, to swallow; pres. part. *ningalān*, vi, 15 (bis).

nān-gār, m. a menial cultivator, xi, 10.

nanun, to become manifest; pres. m. sg. 3, *chuh nanān*, vii, 1.

naphts, m. the belly ; sg. dat. *naphtsas*, x, 3.
nar, m. a male ; (of a bird) a cock, viii, 1 ; sg. abl. *naran*, viii, 1.
nār, m. fire ; *zinis nār dyun*ᵘ, to set fire to the firewood, xii, 21, 2, 4 ; *nār gŏmot*ᵘ *tshēṭa*, the fire (had) become extinguished, xii, 23 ; sg. dat. *nāras-manz*, (leap) into the fire, iii, 4 ; abl. *nāra-han zölith*, having kindled a little fire, iii, 1.
nūr, m. light, brilliancy, glory ; sg. abl. *nūra*, vii, 6.
*nür*ᵘ, f. the arm (from shoulder to wrist), xii, 15.
narm, adj. smooth, vii, 24.
nērun, irreg. to go forth, come forth, issue, emerge ; to issue, turn out, happen (as the result of something), vi, 11 ; to be issued (of an order), xi, 4 ; *hatabŏd*ⁱ*-khöris drāy*, they turned out (i.e. amounted to) hundreds of *kharwārs*, ix, 9 ; *nīrith gatshun*, to issue forth and be gone (Hindī *nikal jānā*), ii, 3 ; xii, 15 ; *nīrith yun*ᵘ, to come forth (Hindī *nikal ānā*), xii, 12.

inf. *hyotun nērun*, he began to go forth, ii, 3 ; *log*ᵘ *nērani*, began to issue, x, 7 ; conj. part. *nīrith*, ii, 3 ; xii, 12, 5 ; pres. part. *nērān*, viii, 7 ; impve. sg. 2, *nēr*, ii, 9 ; pl. 1, *nērav*, xi, 12 ; 2, *nīriv*, ii, 7 ; xii, 1 (bis) ; *nīriv-sa*, go ye forth, sirs, x, 9 ; indic. fut. pl. 1, *nērav*, xii, 18 ; imperf. *nērān*, xii, 1 ; m. sg. 3, *ôs*ᵘ *nērān*, viii, 1.

1 past m. sg. 3, *drāv*, ii, 8 ; iii, 1, 3, 4 (bis) ; v, 1, 4, 5, 6, 9 ; vi, 7, 11 ; viii, 9 (bis) ; x, 2, 3, 4 (bis), 5 (bis), 7 (bis), 9, 14 (bis) ; xi, 4, 13 ; xii, 4, 5 (bis), 10, 1, 3, 5, 7, 8, 9, 20, 3 ; with suff. 3rd pers. sg. dat. *drās*, issued from it, xii, 3 ; *drās-na*, did not issue from it, (if it does not) issue from it, xii, 3 ; pl. 3, *drāy*, ix, 9 ; x, 11 ; f. sg. 3, *drāyĕ*, iii, 1, 2 ; v, 7 (bis) (*drāyĕ bāzar*, she went forth to the bazaar), 9 ; with suff. 3rd pers. sg. dat. *drāyĕs*, she issued from his (side), vii, 7.
*nērawun*ᵘ, n. ag. one who goes forth ; as adv. as I go forth, v, 8.
nāsh, m. destruction, see *öl*ⁱ*-nāsh*, ix, 3.
nish, near, the equivalent of the Hindī *pās*, and governing the dative ; *mĕ-nish*, near me, by me, viii, 5 ; forming datives of possession, *tsĕ-nish*, in thy possession, x, 14 ; *tŏhĕ-nish*, in your possession, x, 5, 12. After a verb of motion, and governing a noun signifying a person, it means " to ". Thus :

ôkhun-zādas nish, (brought it) to the teacher's son, xii, 2; *böyis-nish,* (go) to the brother, v, 10; *lāl-shĕnākas-n.*, (came) to the lapidary, xii, 25; *mĕ-n.*, (came) to me, xii, 22; *mĕjĕras-n.*, (brought him) to the master of the horse, x, 5; *phakīras-n.*, (came) to the mendicant, iii, 2; *pātashāhas-n.*, (brought him) to the king, ii, 11; *pātashĕhas-n.*, (came, etc.) to the king, viii, 5, 13; x, 1, 2, 3, 5; *wazīras-n.*, (came) to the Vizier, xii, 5, 10, 3; *yiman-n.*, (she came) to these (persons), v, 8; *yāras-n.*, (came) to the friend, x, 4, 11; *zanāni-n.*, (came) to the woman, xii, 4. Cf. *nishĕ* 1 and *nishin.*

nishĕ 1, i.q. *nish,* q.v.; *phakīras-nishĕ,* (he was) near (i.e. with) the mendicant, ii, 9; *tŏrka-chānas-nishĕ,* near (i.e. in the house of) the cabinet maker, vii, 20; *mĕ-nishĕ,* in my possession, x, 14; governing dat. of person and following a verb of motion, *mĕ-nishĕ,* (came) to me, xii, 22; *phakīras-nishĕ,* came to the mendicant, ii, 7; *wazīras-nishĕ,* (he came) to the vizier, xii, 19; governing inan. noun, *palangas-nishĕ,* he came near the bed, x, 7; Cf. *nish* and *nishin.*

nishĕ 2, postpos. governing abl. (= Hindī *pās-sē*), from near, from; *khāba-nishĕ abtar,* terrified from (i.e. at) the dream, vi, 12; *ʦakhi-nishĕ byonuy,* distinct from (i.e. absolutely without) anger, vii, 2.

nishāna, m. a token (given as a sign of recognition), x, 8, 14 (bis); xii, 21.

nishin, postpos. governing dat, i.q. *nish* and *nishĕ* 1; *phakīras-nishin,* (he was) near (i.e. with) the mendicant, ii, 8; *khāwandas-nishin,* (go) to (your) master, viii, 10; *pātashāh-zādan-nishin,* (came) to the princes, viii, 4. Cf. *nish* and *nishĕ* 1.

nas'yĕth (xii, 16, 7) or *nasīyĕth,* f. admonition, advice (xii, 1), instruction; — *karüñ^{ü}*, to advise, give instruction, xii, 16; *nasīyĕth karay akh kath,* I will give thee one piece of instruction (xii, 1).

nata, conj. (if) not then, (if so and so does) not (happen) then, otherwise, v, 7.

noṭ^{u}, m. a jar, a pitcher, iii, 5 (ter), 9; *dŏda-noṭ^{u}*, a milk-jar, xi, 13; sg. dat. *naṭis-pĕṭh,* on the jar, iii, 5, 9.

nĕth see ***nŏth.***

nẹ̆thᵘ, f. a thumb-ring; sg. abl. *nĕchi*, vi, 16.

nŏth or ***nĕth***, pronoun defective, said to be used mainly by villagers, as the equivalent of *yih* 1, this. It has no nominative, and *nĕth* is the inan. sg. dat. In declension it runs parallel to *ath*, q.v.

As a substantive we have m. pl. dat. (for acc.) *nŏman*, (look at) these, viii, 1.

As adjective we have m. sg. dat. *nĕmis matis siwāh*, excepting this madman, v, 9; *nĕmis manōshĕs*, to this man, xii, 15; m. pl. nom. *nŏm lāl*, these rubies, x, 5; f. pl. nom. *nŏma wŏlinjĕ*, these hearts, viii, 4; dat. *nŏman mārawātalan*, to these executioners, x, 12; *nŏman zanĕn*, to these persons, x, 12; ag. *nŏmav ṭahalyav*, by these grooms, x, 12.

nēthᵃr, m. a marriage-arrangement; — *karun*, to make a marriage, to marry (so and so, *amis söty*, xii, 15), viii, 2 (bis); xii, 15.

nôtuwān, adj. feeble, i, 2.

nav, card. nine; pl. abl. *nawav asmānav-pĕṭhⁱ*, above the nine heavens, iii, 8.

nāv, m. a name, ii, 1; xii, 4 (bis); *amis chuh nāv*, her name is, xii, 8; *tath chuh nāv*, its name is, xii, 18.

nowᵘ, adj. new, i, 11.

nôwᵘ, see *Lachĕ-nôwᵘ*, s.v. *lach*.

nay 1, see *na*.

nay 2, f. a reed-flute, vii, passim; gen. m. *nayĕ-hondᵘ*, vii, 1; f. *nayĕ-hüñzᵘ*, vii, 1.

nöyid, m. a barber, xi, 18; xii, 4 (bis), 5 (bis), 10 (bis), 3, 9 (bis), 22, 3, 4, 5; *nöyid-sabakh*, a barber-lesson, instruction in barber's work, v, 6; sg. ag. *nöyidan*, xii, 19, 25. Cf. *nāyĕzᵘ*.

nyunᵘ, irreg. to take, v, 12; vi, 9; viii, 9 (ter), 11; x, 1, 5 (bis); xi, 18; xii, 19, 25; to bring (news), ii, 1, 6; x, 7, 8; xii, 23; *raṭith nyunᵘ*, to arrest, capture (a prisoner), v, 7, 9; x, 5; *tulith nyunᵘ*, to lift up and take away, to raise (a person from a bed) and lead (him) away, iii, 7.

impve. sg. 2, with suff. 3rd pers. sg. acc. *nin*, xii, 25; pl. 2, with same suff., *niyūn*, x, 5; indic. fut. pl. 1 *nimav*, xii, 19.

1 past m. sg. *nyūv*, viii, 9; *nĕv*, iii, 7; with suff. 3rd

pers. sg. ag. *nyūn*, vi, 9; with suff. 3rd pers. pl. ag. *nyūkh*, x, 5 (bis); xi, 18; with ditto, and also suff. 3rd pers. sg. gen. *nyūhas*, viii, 9; pl. *niy*, v, 9; with suff. 2nd pers. sg. ag. *nīth*, x, 1; with suff. 3rd pers. sg. ag. *nīn*, v, 7.

f. sg. *niyĕ*, ii, 1, 6; x, 7, 8; xii, 23; with suff. 3rd pers. sg. ag. *niyĕn*, v, 12; with suff. 3rd pers. pl. ag. *niyĕkh*, viii, 11.

plup. m. sg. *ôs*ᵘ *nyūmot*ᵘ, viii, 9.

nayistān, m. a place where canes or reeds grow, a cane-brake, vii, 26, 7, 8; dat. *nayistānas-kun*, (saying) to the cane-brake, vii, 26; gen. m. *nayistānuk*ᵘ, vii, 26; f. *nayistānüc*ᵘ̈, vii, 29.

nyāwun, to cause to be taken, to cause to be taken away, to have dispatched; 1 p.p. *nyôw*ᵘ. In xi, 6, this is given a pleonastic suffix *ku*, forming *nyôw*ᵘ*-k*ᵘ, of which the m. pl. nom. is *nyöv*ⁱ*-k*ⁱ.

*nāyëz*ᵘ̈, f. a barber's wife, xi, 19. Cf. *nöyid*.

nāz, m. blandishment, coaxing; pl. dat. *nāzan*, ii, 7 (applied by a man to soldiers).

nēza, m. a spear; iron railings or the like round a garden, etc. (v, 4); pl. nom. *nēza*, v, 4.

nazdīkh, postpos. near; *sōdāgāras-n.*, (he arrived) near (i.e. came to) the merchant, viii, 10.

nīzīkh, adv. near, viii, 6 (bis); x, 4; *gōs n.*, he went near it, viii, 10; postpos. governing dat., near, *badanas-n.*, (came) near the body, viii, 6; *shĕharas-n.*, (he came) near the city, x, 3.

nazar, f. look, regard, glance; observation, inspection, watching; — *chĕs bātsan-kun*, his sight is (i.e. eyes are) directed towards the married pair, viii, 6; — *chĕkh ō-kun*, their eyes were directed thither, xii, 23; *nazarāh*, a single glance; *nazarāh karüñ*ᵘ, to take one look at a person, viii, 11; *nazar karüñ*ᵘ̈, to look at, observe, inspect, watch, ii, 1; x, 7, 8 (ter); xii, 23; dat. *byūṭh*ᵘ *nazari*, he sat for looking, he sat in watch, x, 7; *nazari tàm*ⁱ*-sanzi söty*, owing to his looking at (me), vii, 13.

nazarbāz, m. a watcher, a watchman, a detective; pl. ag. *nazarbāzav*, ii, 1; x, 7, 8; xii, 23.

pīchē (Hindī), adv. afterwards, xi, 4.

pöda, adj. born, created; manifest, manifested; — *karun*, to create, iii, 8 (ter); vii, 4, 6 (bis), 8; xii, 7; — *gatshun*, to become manifest, to become visible, to come into sight, ii, 1; iii, 8; x, 4, 5, 7; xii, 10.

pagāh, adv. to-morrow, iii, 4; vi, 16; on the following day, next day, vi, 16; xii, 10.

phahi in *phahi dyun*^{u}, to impale, v, 10.

phaharawāv, m. a file, a rasp, v, 4.

phakh, m. an evil smell, a stink, ii, 4.

phakīr, m. a religious mendicant, a faqīr, i, 2; ii, 1, 2, 3 (bis), 9; iii, 1; x, 7 (many times), 8 (many times), 9, 12 (bis), 4 (bis); — *lāgun*, to dress oneself as a faqīr, pretend to be a faqīr, x, 12; with suff. of indef. art. *phakīrāh*, ii, 1 (bis); *phakīrā akh*, x, 7; sg. dat. *phakīras*, ii, 3, 4, 7, 8, 9; iii, 1, 2, 9; x, 8 (bis); ag. *phakīran*, iii, 1; x, 7, 8, 12; gen. *phakīra-sond*^{u}, x, 12; f. — *sünz*^{u}, x, 8, 14; voc. *phakīra*, ii, 3; x, 8; *phakīrō*, ii, 2; pl. dat. *phakīran* (for gen.), vi, 13; ag. *phakīrav*, v, 8.

phakīrī, f. the condition or state of a religious mendicant, faqīr-hood, x, 14; sg. gen. *phakīriyĕ-hond*^{u}, x, 9.

phikir^{ü}, f. thought, consideration, reflection; concern, solicitude, anxiety; *kĕh chĕna phikir*^{ü} (xii, 5) or *kĕtshāh chĕna phikir*^{ü} (xii, 20), there is no anxiety, there is no reason to be anxious; with suff. of indef. art. *phikirāh karüñ*^{ü}, to do a thinking, to consider, reflect, xii, 19, 24; *phikiri gatshun*, to go into anxiety, to become anxious, viii, 10; xii, 4.

phal 1, m. a fruit; pl. nom. *phal*, ix, 9.

phal 2, f. a small piece, a splinter; pl. nom. (for acc.) *phala*, vii, 14.

phol^{u}, m. a grain, hence any small round object, such as a pearl, etc.; *kañi-phol*^{u}, a pebble, xii, 15 (bis).

phŏlun, to flower; to break (of the dawn), iii, 3; v, 5, 7; viii, 9; xii, 2 (bis); inf. obl. *phŏlani logun*, to begin to break, v, 5, 7; xii, 2; pres. m. sg. 3, *chuh phŏlān*, xii, 2; past m. sg. 3, *phọ̆l*^{u}, iii, 3; viii, 9.

phamb, m. cotton-wool, viii, 6, 13.

pahān, a dim. suff. *drāv dūr-pahān*, he went forth a little distance, x, 7; *byūṭh*^{u} *dūri-pahān*, he sat down at a little distance, x, 7; *khasun hyor*^{u}*-pahān*, to go a little distance up-stream, xii, 6.

pahar, m. a division of time consisting of three hours, an eighth part of a day, a watch, viii, 5 (bis), 6 (bis), 8 (bis), 10, 1, 3; *röts^ü-hond^u pahar*, a watch of the night, iii, 1; sg. abl. *patimi pahara*, at the last watch (of the night), v, 8; pl. nom. *pahar*, viii, 5.

phardā, adv. to-morrow, on the morrow, vi, 11.

pharun, to cause loss, to be a plunderer or robber; past m. sg. 3, *phor^u tas Yiblīs*, Satan caused loss to him, plundered him, ruined him, iv, 2.

phērun, to go round, wander about, i, 2; ii, 8; to return, go back; to feel regret, be grieved, viii, 1, 7, 10 (bis), (all with dat. of subject); *thüḍ^ü-kani phērun*, to turn oneself backwards, to turn the back (on a person), v, 4.

conj. part. *phīrith*, having returned; with or without *pot^u*, very common in the meaning "back again", as in *phīrith yun^u*, to come back, return, ii, 3; v, 10; viii, 10; esp. to return home, go home, v, 1, 4; so *phīrith nērun* (x, 14) or *phīrith pot^u nērun* (xii, 19), to go forth back again; *phīrith wasun*, to come down again (after going upstairs), iii, 9; with verbs of saying, it means "in answer"; thus, *phīrith dapun*, to say in answer, to reply, iii, 1, 8; v, 4, 5, 6, 8, 11 (bis); viii, 8; ix, 1; x, 1 (bis), 6, 10; xi, 15; xii, 3, 4, 5 (bis); so *phīrith wanun*, to reply, v, 2, 4; *wanun pot^u phīrith*, id., x, 7; *phīrith ladun*, to send (a message) in reply, x, 3 (bis); with *wŏthun*, to arise, we have *wọ̆thus phīrith*, he up and replied to him, viii, 6; x, 2; *wọ̆thus pot^u phīrith*, id., x, 6; *wŏtsh^üs phīrith*, she up and answered him, xii, 11. With *gatshun*, we have *phīrith gatshun*, to go having turned away, i.e. to become hostile, iv, 3.

pres. m. sg. 3, *chuh phērān*, ii, 5; imperf. m. sg. 3, *ôs^u phērān*, i, 2.

past m. sg. 3, *phyūr^u*, viii, 1; with suff. 3rd pers. sg. dat. *phyūrus*, viii, 7, 10 (bis).

phirun, to turn something round; freq. part. *phir^i phir^i*, turning (me) round and round, vii, 18; conj. part. *phirith tshunun*, to turn upside down, iii, 5.

pharōsh, m. a seller; *lāl-pharōsh*, a ruby-seller, a jeweller, xii, 3.

Phōrsaṭ, m. N.P., Sir Douglas Forsyth, xi, 2.
phursath, f. leisure, freedom from duties, xii, 17.
paharawôl^{u}, m. a man who keeps a watch, a watchman, sentry; sg. dat. *-wōlis*, viii, 8.
phår^{i}*yād*, m. a lamentation, cry for help or redress, complaint; — *dyun*^{u}, to lay a complaint, cry for redress, vii, 22; x, 2.
phāsh, m. abusive language reflecting on a woman's chastity; *mĕ ma kar sīras phāsh*, do not accuse my secret (parts) of unchastity, do not disgrace me by letting me remain naked, xii, 7.
phaṭun, to be broken; past f. sg. 3, *phüṭ*^{ü}, iii, 5; with suff. 2nd pers. pl. dat. *phüṭ*^{ü}*wa*, x, 12.
phuṭ^{a}*run*, to break (trans.); impve. pl. 2 with suff. 3rd pers. sg. acc. *phuṭ*^{a}*ryūn*, xii, 3; past m. sg. with suff. 3rd pers. pl. ag. *phuṭ*^{o}*rukh*, xii, 4; ditto and 3rd pers. sg. dat. *phuṭ*^{o}*r*^{u}*has*, ii, 11.
photuwāh, m. a decree, order, ii, 7. This word has here the suff. of the indef. art. added.
phyūr^{u}, etc., see *phērun*.
pakh, f. a wing; pl. nom. *pakha*, viii, 7.
pākh, adj. pure, spotless, undefiled, virginal (of a woman), v, 10.
pŏkhta, adj. ripe; as subst. pl. dat. (for acc.) *pŏkhtan*, vi, 15.
pakun, to walk, to go, to go along; inf. *hyotukh pakun*, they began to go, x, 1; neg. conj. part. *mödān chuh wuñĕ pakanay*, the plain is still not having been walked, i.e. we have not yet passed over it, x, 1; pres. part. *pakān*, going, i.e. as I go, v, 7; impve. pl. 2, *pakiv-sa*, go ye, sirs, x, 1; pres. m. sg. 3, *chuh pakān*, iii, 11; *pakān chuh*, viii, 7; xii, 7; pl. 3, *chih pakān*, xii, 2; *pakān chih*, x, 4; f. sg. 3, *chĕh pakān*, iii, 2; xii, 7; imperf. m. sg. 3, *ôs*^{u} *pakān*, v, 7; pl. 3, *ös*^{i} *pakān*, x, 1.
pakanāwun, to cause to go, to set on the march (xi, 14); to drive an animal (xi, 8); pres. (aux. omitted) m. pl. 3, *pakanāwān*, xi, 4; imperf. m. pl. 3, *ös*^{i} *pakanāwān*, xi, 8.
pakawun^{u}, n. ag., f. sg. nom. *pakawüñ*^{ü}, one who marches, xi, 11.
pal, m. a rock, xii, 14 (bis), 15; sg. dat. *palas*, xii, 15.
pŏlāduw^{u}, adj. made of steel; m. pl. nom. *pŏlādåv*^{i}, v, 4.

pālun, to protect; *salām pāluñu*, to make a bow, to salute reverently (xii, 16); conj. part. *pölith*, xii, 16.

palang, m. a bedstead, cot, bed, iii, 7; v, 5, 9; x, 7; sg. dat. *palangas*, v, 5, 6 (ter); viii, 13 (bis); x, 5, 7 (quater), 8 (bis), 12 (bis); *palangas türu*, the tenon of the bedstead, x, 5, 12.

pŏlāv, m. a dish made of rice boiled in soup, with flesh, spices, etc., vi, 2; pl. nom. *pŏlāv*, ii, 3.

pām, f. a reproach; pl. nom. *mĕ rōzan pāma*, reproaches will remain (upon) me, i.e. I shall get a bad name, x, 3.

pān, m. the body, the human body, iii, 4 (ter); *bāla-pān*, a youthful body, a youthful condition, vii, 11, 5; sg. dat. *pānas*, vii, 24, 5.

pāna, reflex. pron. self; myself, vii, 15; thyself, xii, 11, 25; himself, i, 1; ii, 5; vi, 4; vii, 1, 2, 3; x, 2, 7 (bis), 8; xii, 5, 12, 21, 4; herself, v, 9, 10, 1; vii, 1; xii, 7; oneself (indef.), x, 1, 6,; themselves, iii, 8; viii, 3, 8; x, 12. This word is equivalent to the Hindī *āp*.

sg. nom. *pāna*, i, 1; v, 10, 1; x, 7 (bis), 8; xii, 7, 11, 21, 4; with emph. *y*, sg. nom. *pānay*, vii, 1; pl. nom. *pānay*, x, 12.

dat. (sg. unless otherwise stated), ii, 5; iii, 8 (pl.); v, 9; vi, 4; vii, 1, 2, 15; viii, 3 (pl.), 8 (pl.); x, 1, 6; xii, 5, 12, 25 (bis); with emph. *y*, *pānasuy*, vii, 3; *had pānas chĕs karān*, I am making a limit for myself, i.e. I consider myself perfect, vii, 15.

ag. sg. *pāna*, x, 2.

gen. *panunu*, q.v., s.v.

The dat. *pānas* is often used adverbially, to signify "voluntarily", "of one's own free will", "of one's own accord", vi, 4; vii, 2. Especially, with verbs of motion, it signifies "to go of one's own accord", hence, simply, "to go off", "start off", as in *pānas gatshun*, to go away on one's own business, to go away, to go home, iii, 8; v, 9; viii, 3; *pānas nērun*, to go forth on one's own business, xii, 5; *pānas yunu*, to set out home, xii, 12; so *gay pānas bīṭhi*, they sat down free from duty, they rested after finishing their turn of duty, viii, 8; *gay pānas pānas*, they went away each on his own business, or each to his own home, v, 9.

pinhān, adj. secret, hidden, concealed.

panja, a claw, xii, 16, 7; sg. abl. *panja-sötiy*, only by using the claw, xii, 16.

*panun*ᵘ, poss. adj. reflex. (usually considered as the genitive of *pāna*) own, the equivalent of the Hindī *apnā*. My own, iii, 1; iv, 7; vii, 21 (bis), 2, 6; x, 12; xii, 22; thine own, ii, 9, 11; iii, 2, 9 (bis); v, 1, 10; vi, 6; viii, 10; x, 1, 3, 8 (bis); xii, 16, 25; his own, ii, 5, 7, 11; iii, 1, 3 (bis), 9; v, 1, 4 (bis), 5 (ter), 10, 2; viii, 3, 9 (bis), 10, 3; x, 5, 6, 9, 10, 3 (bis), 4 (ter); xii, 4 (quater), 5 (quater), 10, 1 (bis), 2, 3, 4, 7, 20, 2, 5; her own, iii, 2, 4; v, 5, 8, 9 (bis), 10 (bis), 2; vii, 20, 6; viii, 11; ix, 6; x, 3 (bis), 5; xii, 4, 5, 10, 3, 4, 5 (ter), 8; one's own (indef.), x, 6; our own, x, 12; your own, x, 1; their own, v, 10; viii, 1, 5, 11; x, 5; xii, 18; *panun*ᵘ *panun*ᵘ, each his own, xi, 10.

m. sg. nom. *panun*ᵘ, ii, 5, 9, 11; iii, 1 (bis), 2, 3 (bis), 9 (ter); v, 1 (bis), 4, 5 (bis), 9, 10; vii, 21, 6; viii, 3, 5, 9; ix, 6; x, 5, 6, 8, 9; xii, 4 (bis), 5 (ter), 10, 1 (bis), 2, 3, 4, 5 (bis), 6, 7, 8 (bis), 20, 2 (bis), 5; with emph. *y*, *panunuy*, x, 1; dat. *pananis*, ii, 7; iii, 2, 4; v, 8, 10, 2; viii, 9, 10; x, 5, 12, 4; xii, 4, 5, 10, 3, 5, 8; abl. *panani*, v, 10; vii, 21, 2, 6; xii, 4, 5; pl. nom. *panàn*ⁱ, vii, 20; x, 14; *panàn*ⁱ *panàn*ⁱ, xi, 10; *panin* (m.c. for *panàn*ⁱ), iv, 7; dat. *pananĕn*, viii, 10, 3, 4.

f. sg. nom. *panüñ*ᵘ, v, 5; viii, 1, 11 (bis); x, 1, 3 (bis), 6, 8, 10, 3; xii, 14, 25; dat. *panañĕ*, v, 4, 10, 2; x, 5; xii, 4; ag. *panañi*, v, 5; x, 12; abl. *panañi*, x, 3, 13; *panañē* (m.c. for *panañi*), vi, 6.

pānts, card. five; *katha pānts* (f. pl. nom.) five statements, x, 1 (several times), 14; *pānts katha*, x, 6; *rŏpayĕs pānts hath*, five hundred rupees, viii, 10 (bis); x, 1, 2 (bis); pl. dat. *pāntsan kathan*, for five statements, x, 1; *pāntsan zanĕn*, to the five men, x, 6.

*pöntsyum*ᵘ, ord. fifth, x, 1; f. sg. nom. *pöntsim*ᵘ, x, 6 (bis).

pānawöñ or *pānawüñ*, adv. mutually; *pānawöñ*, viii, 1, 2; xi, 19;

xii, 25 ; *pānawüñ*, x, 1. This word is equivalent to the Hindī *āpas-mẽ*.

papun, to ripen ; conj. part. *papith yun*ᵘ, to become ripe, ix, 9.

par, m. a foot ; pl. dat. *paran*, (we fall) at (his) feet, ix, 1.

pāra, see *zāra-pāra*, s.v. *zār*.

parī, f. a fairy, xii, 7, 8, 11 (bis), 4, 20, 5 ; sg. ag. *par*ⁱ*yi*, xii, 15 ; pl. nom. *par*ⁱ*yĕ*, iii, 7, 8.

pīr, m. a saint, a spiritual guide or father, the head of a religious order ; pl. dat. (for gen.) *pīran*, vi, 13 ; ag. *pīrav*, v, 8.

*pör*ᵘ, f. a hut ; dim. f. sg. nom. *pāri-hanā*, a hovel, a small hut, xii, 2.

*pūr*ᵘ, adj. full, in *pūr*ᵘ*-khumār*, full of languishment, v, 2.

parda, m. a veil ; with suff. of indef. art. *pardā kor*ᵘ*nakh*, she put a veil over them, she hid them under a veil, vi, 4.

pargan, m. a certain fiscal division, a parish, a " pargana ", xi, 5.

*prôn*ᵘ, adj. old, of former times ; m. pl. nom. *prön*ⁱ, vi, 11 ; viii, 5.

parun, to read, xii, 18, 23 ; to read, study, viii, 3, 4 ; to recite (a holy name, or a charm, etc.), vi, 17 (bis) ; vii, 4 ; xii, 1 (bis).

pres. part. *parān gatshun*, to go reciting, i.e. to recite continually, vi, 17 ; vii, 4 ; impve. sg. 2, *par*, vi, 17 ; indic. fut. sg. 1, *para*, xii, 1 (bis) ; imperf. m. pl. 3, *ös*ⁱ *parān*, viii, 3, 4 ; past m. sg. with suff. 3rd pers. sg. ag. *porun*, xii, 23 ; with suff. 3rd pers. pl. ag. *porukh*, xii, 18.

pārun, to prepare, make ready (a bed) ; conj. part. (in sense of past part.) *palang pörith*, a bed prepared, iii, 7.

pörun, to put (a garment) on, x, 2, 9 ; to clothe (a person), v, 10 ; past m. sg. with suff. 3rd pers. sg. *pūrun*, x, 2, 9 ; f. sg. with same suff. *pör*ᵘ*n*, v, 10 ; *pūrith*, having put on (a saddle to a horse), xi, 9.

prang, m. a bed, a couch ; *wutsha-prang*, a flying couch, = the magic carpet of our fairy tales, xii, 18.

prārun, to wait for (a person), v, 6, 11 ; to watch (for an opportunity), ii, 10 ; pres. part. *prārān*, v, 11 ; pres. m. sg. 3, *chuh prārān*, v, 6 ; 2 past m. sg. 3, *prāryāv*, ii, 10.

prath, a distributive preposition, as in *prath-dŏha*, on each day, every day, viii, 1 (bis).

pritshun, to ask ; 1 past m. sg. 3, with suff. 3rd pers. sg. ag. *timanᵘy pryutshun*, he asked them, xii, 1.

partawa, m. the sound of a footstep, a footfall, xii, 15 (*pyauv*, fell).

pöravī, f. following ; hence (in Kāshmīrī) protection ; — *karüñᵘ*, to protect, i, 1.

Parwardigār, m. the Cherisher, the Provider, Providence, an epithet of the Deity, i, 11.

parzanāwun, to recognize ; pres. m. sg. 2 neg. interrog. *chukh-nā parzanāwān*, dost thou not recognize ? x, 12 ; past m. sg. *parzanôwᵘ*, x, 5 ; xii, 2 ; with suff. 1 sg. nom. *parzanôwus*, I was recognized, x, 12 ; with suff. 3rd pers. sg. ag. *parzanôwun*, viii, 9, 10; plup. f. sg. 3, *ösᵘ parzanövᵘmütsᵘ*, x, 5.

pö̃sa, m. N. of a small copper coin, a pice ; *khām pö̃sa*, see *khām*. pl. dat. *pösan*, vii, 25, 26.

pēsh, adv. and prep., in front, before ; *gay pēsh-ĕ-pātashāh*, they went before the king, they were taken into the king's presence, vi, 9 ; *amis pēsh anun*, to bring before him, to cause him to experience (trouble), xii, 25.

pōsh, m. a flower ; *pōshĕ-gọndᵘ*, a bunch of flowers, a nosegay, v, 4 (ter) ; *pōshĕ-mödān*, a flower-meadow, a field of flowers, xi, 3 ; *pōshĕ-thürᵘ*, a flower-shrub, ii, 3.

pŏshākh, m. a robe, a garment, v, 9 (bis) ; x, 2 (bis), 4 (ter), 9 ; xii, 6 (bis), 7 (several times) ; — *trāwun*, to put off a garment, disrobe oneself ; sg. dat. *ath pŏshākas kürᵘn shĕkal yinsān-hyuhᵘ* or *ath pŏshākas korun yinsān-hyuhᵘ*, he made the garment into the shape of a man, x, 7 ; *pŏshākas-manz*, (entered) into the garment, x, 7 ; *àmᶦ kürᵘnas pŏshākas thaph*, he (the dog) caught hold of his coat, viii, 9.

pēshkār, m. a certain high official ; in vi, 11, a chief clerk.

pasand, adj. approved ; — *karun*, to approve of, v, 1 ; xii, 4 (bis).

pata, adv. after, afterwards, viii, 7 ; xi, 18 ; xii, 6, 25 ; with emph. *y*, *patay*, xii, 10 ; *pata-kani*, afterwards, x, 1 ; with verbs of motion, *pata pata*, (to go along) after, to follow, iii, 1, 2 ; viii, 9 ; xii, 7. Cf. *brũh brũh*, s.v. *brũh*.

postpos. This governs the dative in the case of animate objects, and the ablative in the case of inanimate objects. It also governs pron. suffixes in the dative. Thus :—

A. Animate dative. *miñĕ-marĕ pata lārān,* running after the hind, ii, 9; *yiman pata,* after these (women came another), xii, 7.

B. Inanimate ablative. *ami pata,* after this, viii, 13; xii, 17; *tami pata,* after that, x, 12; xii, 16.

C. Governing suffixes. *lōris pata,* they ran after her, ii, 9; *pata lāḍyēyĕs,* she ran after him, vi, 8; *yimawa pata,* I will come after you, I will follow you, xii, 1; *pata chikh lārān,* they are running after them, xi, 18.

pot[u], backwards, back again; — *yun[u],* to come back, return, v, 1; — *phērun,* id., xii, 19; — *phīrith,* common as adv., back again, in return, in reverse, esp. common with verbs of saying, to say back again, to say in reply, x, 3, 6 (bis), 7.

pūt[u], the young of any animal or insect, esp. a dear child; pl. dat. *pōtĕn,* ix, 3 (young ones of a bee).

path, adv. behind; *path rōzun,* to remain behind, remain over and above, xii, 23; *path-kun,* afterwards, iii, 5; v, 5; in the rear, v, 8.

prep. governing dat. *path wanan,* at the back of the forests, deep in the forest, vii, 10.

pĕṭh, postpos. governing dat., on, upon, in various shades of meaning. Thus:—

on, upon, *asmānan pĕṭh,* on the heavens, iv, 4; *palangas-pĕṭh,* (lying) on the bed, viii, 13; *wŏḍi-pĕṭh,* (carry) on the crown of the head, iii, 1; xi, 12, 6.

on to, upon, *lālan-pĕṭh,* (the hand fell) upon the rubies, x, 5; *naṭis-pĕṭh,* (put) upon the jar, iii, 5; *cārpāyi-pĕṭh,* (sat down) upon the bed, x, 5, so *ath-pĕṭh,* (sat) on it, xii, 21; *ath[i]-pĕṭh,* on it verily, xii, 21; *zūnaḍabi-pĕṭh,* (going forth) on to the roof-bungalow, viii, 1.

on to (with verbs of mounting, etc.), *guris-pĕṭh,* (mounted) the horse, ii, 11; *ath[i] pĕṭh,* (got up) on to it (a bed), iii, 7; so *palangas pĕṭh,* (got up) on to the bed, v, 5, 6 (bis), 9 (*ath*); x, 7 (bis); *baṭhis-pĕṭh,* (ascended) on to the bank of the river, xii, 7; *ath[i]-pĕṭh,* (ascended) on to it (a pyre), xii, 24.

down on to, *baṭhis-pĕṭh,* (put) down on the bank, xii, 6, 7.

With certain words it is used in the sense of "to" after

a verb of motion. Thus *adālütsü-pĕṭh*, (went) to the court of justice, v, 9; *kŏli-akis-pĕṭh*, (went) to (the bank of) a stream, xii, 2; *nāgas-pĕṭh*, (arrived, etc.) at the spring, (went) to (the bank of) the spring, iii, 4, 5, 9 (bis); xii, 6, 11, 2, 4.

on, close by, *nāgas-pĕṭh chĕh*, she is (i.e. lives) close by a spring, iii, 4.

It means "in" in *khāwand thôuun ḍēras-pĕṭh*, she put her husband in a tent, v, 11.

It means "on", i.e. "with regard to", "towards", in *āgas-pĕṭh* (infidelity) to a master, viii, 6, 8, 11; *nĕcivĕn-pĕṭh*, (an order) concerning or against (his) sons, viii, 13.

Forming adv. *ath^i-pĕṭh*, thereupon, xii, 7.

pĕṭha, postpos. governing abl. from on, as in *guri-pĕṭha*, (fell) from on (his) horse, fell off his horse, ii, 6; *guryau-pĕṭha*, (dismounted) from (their) horses, xii, 2; *Kōh-i-Tōra-pĕṭha*, (commandments given) from on Mt. Sinai, iv, 5.

from (generally), as in *kati-pĕṭha*, where from? whence? ii, 2; *Landana-pĕṭha*, from London, xi, 3; *sŏnar-aṭa-pĕṭha*, (a cry raised) from (i.e. in) the goldsmiths' market, v, 7.

In special cases it means simply "on", like *pĕṭh*, as in *pĕṭha kür^unas mŏhar*, on it she put a seal, x, 3, in which *pĕṭha* governs the dat. pron. suff. *as*. Similarly x, 3 (again), and x, 10.

Another special meaning occurs in *karin kasam nāga pĕṭha*, let her make an oath from on (the bank of) (i.e. by) the spring, v, 9.

pĕṭha-kani, on the top of (it = *ath^i*), viii, 1.

pĕṭh^i, postpos. governing abl., on, above, in various shades of meaning. Thus:—

nawav asmānav pĕṭh^i, above the nine heavens, iii, 8.

kala-pĕṭh^i, (leaped) over (his) head, ii. 9.

tami-pĕṭh^i-kani, in addition to that, iii, 8.

pöṭh^i or *pöṭhin*, adv. used with other words to indicate manner. It may be added either to adjectives or to adverbs, and in the latter case is pleonastic. It converts adjectives into adverbs of manner, and when the adjective is declinable it is put, before *pöṭh^i*, into the case of the agent. Thus:—

Added to an adjective, *lŏṭ*-*pöṭh*[i] (*lŏṭ*[u]), gently, xii, 5; *pàz*[i]-*pöṭh*[i] (*poz*[u]), really, truly, x, 6, 10.

Added to an adverb, *kĕtha-pöṭh*[i], how? in what manner? iii, 9; v, 8; viii, 5; x, 8; xii, 3, 24; *tithay-pöṭh*[i], in that very manner, exactly so, xii, 23; *yĕthay-pöṭh*[i], in what very manner, exactly as, xii, 22; *yithay-pöṭhin*, in this very manner, exactly thus, viii, 3.

We occasionally find this word added to the agent case of a substantive. Thus, from *tsūr*[u], theft, we have *tsūri-pöṭh*[i], theft-like, i.e. secretly, xii, 6, 7, 17; so *tsūri-pöṭhin*, iii, 1.

pathar, adv. on the flat ground; hence, down, in phrases such as *pathar wasun*, to fall to the ground, ii, 3; *pathar pyon*[u], id., ii, 11; *pāwun pathar*, to throw down on the ground, iii, 9.

paṭhwör[i], m. a village accountant, ix, 10.

putol[u], an idol; pl. dat. *putalĕn*, iv, 6; *putal-khāna*, an idol house, a temple or room in which idols are worshipped, sg. dat. *-khānas*, vi, 4.

pĕtarun, to be responsible for the carrying out of any work; *pyon*[u] *pĕtarun*, a load of responsibility to fall on a person, ii, 5.

pātashāh (पातशाह) or *pātashĕh* (पातशह्) a king. This word is given with either of these spellings almost at random in the stories as written in the *nāgarī* character. I have followed them in this.

sg. nom. *pātashāh*, ii, 8, 10, 1 (bis); iii, 1 (ter), 2 (bis), 3, 4 (several times), 5, 6, 7 (ter), 8; v, 7, 9, 11; vi, 9, 10, 1, 2, 6 (quater); viii, 1 (bis), 2, 3 (bis), 6, 7 (ter), 8, 11 (ter), 2, 3 (quater), 4 (bis); x, 4, 10 (bis), 2 (bis), 4 (quater); xii, 3, 4, 9, 19 (bis), 20 (bis), 4 (bis), 5; *-bāy*, a king's wife, a queen, viii, 1 (bis), 2, 3 (quater), 4, 6 (bis), 11 (quater), 2 (bis), 3 (bis); *-kūḍ*[u] (= *-kūr*[u], bel.), v, 5; *-kūr*[u], a king's daughter, a princess, v, 2 (bis), 5, 8 (bis), 9 (several times), 10; xii, 1 (bis), 2 (ter). With suff. of indef. art. *pātashāhā*, viii, 1.

pātashĕh, ii, 5, 8, 9; xii, 5, 10, 1, 2, 3, 4; *pātashĕh-kūr*[u], a princess, xii, 10 (ter), 3 (ter), 5, 21, 5. With suff. of indef. art. *pātashĕhā akh*, viii, 7, 11; *pātashĕhāh*, ii, 1.

sg. dat. *pātashāhas*, iii, 3; viii, 1.

pātashěhas, i, 8; ii, 1, 3 (bis), 4, 5, 11; iii, 1, 3, 5, 9; v, 7 (bis), 9 (ter), 10, 1; vi, 16; viii, 1, 2, 5 (bis), 7 (bis), 13; x, 1, 2, 10, 1, 2 (bis); xii, 1, 3 (ter), 4 (quater), 5 (ter), 9, 11, 2, 3, 8, 9 (bis), 20 (bis), 1, 2, 3.

sg. ag. *pātashāhan*, ii, 11; vi, 11; viii, 5.

pātashěhan, i, 10; ii, 1, 4 (bis), 8; iii, 1, 8 (bis), 9; vi, 15 (bis); viii, 6, 11 (ter), 3 (bis); x, 2 (ter), 6 (bis), 7, 12; xii, 4 (bis), 5, 11, 9, 21, 4.

sg. gen. *pātashāha-sond*^{u}, ii, 10; v, 10; vi, 11; *sȧnd*^{i} (m. pl.), viii, 1, 13; *-sünz*^{u}, v, 7 (bis); viii, 1; x, 14; *-sanzě*, v, 2, 4; *-sanzi*, v, 4; xii, 4.

pātashěha-sond^{u}, xii, 1, 4; *-sandis*, ii, 5, 6, 7; v, 11; xii, 22; *-sandi*, ii, 9; *-sanděn*, viii, 1, 6; *-sandyau*, viii, 5; *-sünz*^{u}, x, 5; xii, 1; *-sanzě*, v, 1 (bis); xii, 4, 5; *-sanzi*, xii, 5.

pātashöhī, f. royalty, sovereignty, the state or condition of a king, x, 2, 4, 9; a kingdom, x, 11; xii, 19; — *karüñ*^{u}, to rule, exercise sovereignty, viii, 12; x, 4; xii, 26; sg. loc. *patashöhī-manz*, xii, 19; gen. *-hond*^{u} *pŏshākh*, a royal robe, x, 2, 9; pl. dat. *pātashöhiyěn-kyut*^{u}, x, 11.

pātashěham, interj. my king! your Majesty! ii, 4; v, 9 (bis); viii, 2, 6 (bis), 7, 8 (bis), 10 (bis), 3; x, 2 (bis), 6, 12 (bis); xii, 3 (bis), 19 (bis), 23.

pātashāhzāda, m. a king's son, a prince; sg. dat. *-zādas*, viii, 5; pl. nom. *-zāda*, viii, 3 (bis), 11 (ter); dat. *-zādan*, viii, 4 (bis), 11 (bis); gen. *-zādan-hond*^{u}, viii, 4.

patyum^{u}, adj. last, final; m. sg. abl. *patimi pahara*, at the last watch (of the night), v, 8.

pāwun, to cause to fall; impve. sg. 2, with suff. 3rd pers. sg. acc. *pāwun pathar*, cause him to fall down, iii, 9; fut. impve. *mě pöv*^{i}*zi yād*, cause memory of me to fall, i.e. make (so and so) remember me, vi, 11.

pay, m. a clue (for discovering a thief, etc.), iii, 3.

pāy, m. a means; *mŏkalan pāy*, a means of salvation, ix, 11.

pyāday, m. a messenger; the messenger of death, x, 12.

pyāla, m. a cup, viii, 7; *āba-pyāla*, a water-cup, viii, 7; sg. dat. *lodun pyālas āb*, he filled the cup with water, viii, 7; *pyālas chuh thaph karith*, he holds the cup, viii, 7.

pyon^u^, to fall, vii, 19 ; x, 5 ; to fall, throw oneself down (before a person, in humility), ix, 1 ; to fall (into a place), to trespass (into a garden or the like), v, 7 (bis) ; to fall (of sound, on a person's ears), xii, 15 ; to fall to a person's lot, to happen to him, to be felt by him, vii, 30 (love) ; viii, 9 (bis) (poverty), 11 (pity) ; ix, 2 (calamity) ; x, 3 (adversity) ; to fall (of sleep), v, 5, 7 ; to fall (in a person's way), to be encountered, vii, 12.

wasith pyon^u^, to fall down (= Hindī *gir paṛnā*), ii, 3, 6 ; *pyon*^u^ *pathar*, to fall to the ground, to fall down, ii, 11 ; *bĕmār pyon*^u^, to fall sick, v, 1 ; *pyon*^u^ *pĕtarun*, a load of responsibility to fall (on a person, dat.), ii, 5 ; *pyōm wanun*, it is fallen to me to speak, I shall have to speak, xii, 10 ; *pyōs nāv*, a name fell to him, he was named (so and so), xii, 4 ; *yād pyon*^u^, memory to fall to so and so, so and so to remember, iii, 5 ; vii, 20 ; xii, 15 ; *amis dôd*^u^ *ôs*^u^ *pĕmot*^u^ *yād*, she remembered the pain, xii, 15 ; *chus pĕwān nayistān yād*, she remembers the cane-brake, vii, 26.

impve. sg. 3, *pĕyin*, ix, 2 ; indic. fut. pl. 1, with suff. 3rd pres. sg. dat. *pĕmōs*, ix, 1 ; pres. m. sg. 3, with suff. 3rd pers. sg. dat. *chus pĕwān*, vii, 26 ; m. pl. 3, *pĕwān*, vii, 20.

past m. sg. 3, *pyauv*, xii, 15 (bis) ; *pĕv*, ii, 3, 5, 6, 11 ; iii, 5 ; v, 1, 7 (bis) ; viii, 9 ; with suff. 1st pers. sg. dat. *pyōm*, vii, 12 ; xii, 10 ; with suff. 3rd pers. sg. dat. *pyōs*, v, 6 ; viii, 11 ; x, 5 ; xii, 4 ; f. sg. 3, with suff. 1st pers. sg. dat. *pĕyĕm*, vii, 19 ; with suff. 3rd pers. sg. dat. *pĕyĕs*, v, 5 ; with suff. 3rd pers. pl. dat. *pĕyĕkh*, v, 7.

perf. m. sg. 3, *chuh pĕmot*^u^, x, 3 ; plup. m. sg. 3, *ôs*^u^ *pĕmot*^u^, viii, 9 ; xii, 15 ; fut. subj. f. sg. 3, *āsi pĕmüts*^u^, vii, 30.

pyāwal, adj. (of a woman), fresh from childbirth ; f. pl. *pyāwal*, xi, 7.

pöz, m. a hawk, falcon, vi, 16 (bis) ; viii, 7 (quater) ; sg. dat. (for acc.) *pözas*, viii, 7.

poz^u^, adj. true, x, 8 ; with emph. *y*, as adv. *pozuy*, x, 6 (ter) ; m. sg. ag. *pàz*^i^-*pöṭh*^i^, really, truly, x, 6, 10 ; see *pöṭh*^i^.

pazun, to be proper = *gatshun* 1, and used in the same way, the future being used in the sense of the present.

fut. sg. 3, interrog. *yī pazyā*, is this proper ? is this right ? vi, 8.

racĕn, see *raṭun*.

rūdⁱ, *rūdᵘ*, *rūdᵘmotᵘ*, see *rōzun*.

rāh, m. a fault ; *maṭi rāh ladun*, to impose a fault on (so and so's) shoulder, to charge a person with a crime, v, 9.

rahath (? gender) (= pers. *rāḥat*), rest, repose, ease, tranquillity. *kara rahath*, I will make ease, I shall be at ease, ix, 4.

rājĕ, m. a king (esp. a Hindū king) (the usual form of this word is *rāza*, but in these stories it only occurs in Nos. x and xi, and, there, under the form *rājĕ*), x, 7, 8, 14 (ter) ; sg. dat. *rājĕs*, x, 7, 8 (bis), 14 ; ag. *rājĕn*, x, 8 (bis), 14 ; gen. *rājĕ-sünzᵘ*, the king's (daughter), x, 7 (bis) ; voc. *rājĕ*, xi, 2 (addressed by Queen Victoria to Sir Douglas Forsyth).

In composition we have voc. *rājĕ-sa*, Your Majesty ! x, 8 (bis) ; *rājĕ-sōb* (nom. sg.), His Majesty, x, 8 ; voc. *rājĕ-sōba*, Your Majesty ! x, 7 ; *rājĕ-bikarmājĕth*, King Vikramāditya, ag. *-bikarmājĕtan*, x, 8 ; gen. f. *-bikarmājĕtüñᵘ*, x, 6.

rājy, m. ruling (as a king) ; — *karun*, to rule, x, 14.

rājĕzāda, a prince ; pl. nom. *rājĕzāda*, xi, 7.

rakh, f. a plain kept for the pasturage of the king's cattle, x, 5 ; sg. dat. *rakhi*, x, 12 (bis).

rukhsath, m. permission to depart, leave of absence, *congé* ; — *dyunᵘ*, to give a person leave to depart, to dismiss, xii, 25 ; — *hyonᵘ*, to take leave to depart, to take leave, xii, 10, 3.

rumāl, f. a handkerchief, kerchief, towel ; sg. dat. *rumāli-kĕth*, in a kerchief, iii, 2.

rīnzⁱ, see *ryūnzᵘ*.

rapaṭ, m. a report (the English word) ; — *dyunᵘ*, to make a report, v, 9.

rŏpay, m. a rupee ; *rŏpayĕ-hath*, a hundred rupees, viii, 9, 10 ; x, 6 ; *rŏpayĕs tsōr hath*, four hundred rupees, x, 1, 2 ; *rŏpayĕs pānts hath*, five hundred rupees, viii, 10 (bis) ; x, 1, 2 (bis).

rasad, f. assembling of provisions, etc., xi, 5 ; share, portion, quota, proportionate division, xi, 10 ; — *karüñᵘ*, to collect supplies, xi, 5 ; — *kårⁱthan ånⁱhay nān-gār*, menial cultivators were brought in (from the villages), (each village) providing its proportionate quota, xi, 10.

rosh^u, m. a necklace, v, 10, 12.

rost^u (f. *rütsh^ü*), an adjectival suffix signifying "without"; *banana-rost^u*, without what is fated, (no one) escapes from what is fated, vii, 23.

rāth 1, m. night; sg. dat. *rātas*, by night, x, 1, 6; xii, 4; *rātas-rāth*, on this very night, x, 5, 12; sg. gen. m. pl. *rātåk^i*, of last night, v, 9.

rāth 2, f. night; — *āyĕ*, night came, x, 5; — *barüñ^ü*, to pass the night, i, 10; — *lagüñ^ü*, night to come on, viii, 9; — *kaḍüñ^ü*, to pass the night, x, 11; xii, 5; — *gayĕ ādā*, the night went to completion, the night came to an end, x, 8; xii, 9, 12; with suff. of indef. art. *rāthāh*, xii, 5; sg. gen. *röts^ü-hond^u*, iii, 1.

rāth 3, adv. *dŏh ta rāth*, day and night, i.e. always, continually, vii, 3; *rāth-kyut^u*, by night. Cf. *rātsas*.

rĕth, m. a month, sg. dat. *rĕtas*, pl. nom. *rĕth*, dat. *rĕtan*, as in the following: *rĕtas-kyut^u khar^{a}j* or *rĕtas khar^{a}j*, a month's expenditure, salary for a month, xii, 4; *trĕn rĕtan-kyut^u khar^{a}j*, salary for three months, xii, 5, 11; *rĕth gav ādā*, a month went to completion, a month came to an end, xii, 4; *trih rĕth gay ādā*, three months came to an end, xii, 11; *trih rĕth gay*, three months passed, xii, 6.

rāt^{a}li, adv. by night, viii, 9.

raṭ^{a}n, m. a jewel; *raṭ^{a}na-kor^u*, a bracelet of jewels, xii, 10, 12, 14 (bis), 15 (bis), 18, 20.

raṭun, to take hold of, grasp, seize, iii, 5; to seize, capture, ii, 11; to arrest (a prisoner), v, 7 (bis), 9; x, 5, 12 (bis); to take hold of, take, accept, viii, 3, 4 (bis); x, 3, 5, 8, 12; *gŏlām raṭun*, to engage as a servant, viii, 13; *latan tal raṭun*, to hold under the feet, viii, 7; *mŏkh raṭun*, to seize (so and so's) face, to look intently at, v, 9; *kĕtshāh nŏkhta raṭun*, to find some fault with (dat.), to get up some charge against, xii, 19; *yād raṭun*, to seize the memory, to keep on the memory, i, 7.

conj. part. *raṭith*, ii, 11; iii, 5; v, 7, 9 (bis); x, 5; impve. sg. 2, *raṭh*, i, 7; viii, 4; pol. sg. 2, *raṭhta*, xii, 19; past sg. m. *roṭ^u*, x, 5, 12; with suff. 3rd pers. sg. ag. *roṭun*, viii, 7; x, 3;

with suff. 2nd pers. pl. ag. *roṭ^u^wa*, x, 12 ; pl. *råṭ^i^*, v, 7 ; viii, 13 ; f. sg. *rüṭ^u^*, x, 8 ; with suff. 3rd pers. sg. ag. and 3rd pers. pl. abl. *rüt^u^nakh*, viii, 3 ; pl. with suff. 3rd pers. sg. ag. *racĕn*, viii, 4 ; perf. m. sg. 3, *chuh roṭ^u^mot^u^*, x, 12.

rāṭun, to cause to be grasped, to cause to stick ; perf. part. m. sg. *rôṭ^u^mot^u^*, viii, 1 (of a thorn).

ratsh, f., a very small amount of (anything) ; *ratshi-han*, v, 6 (bis), or *ratshi-hanā*, v, 6 (bis), id.

rātsas, adv. by night, viii, 5. Cf. *rāth*, 3.

rawāna, adj. dispatched, sent ; — *karun*, to dispatch, x, 3.

riwun, to lament ; pres. f. sg. 1, *chĕs riwān*, vii, 22.

rāy, f. belief, judgment, opinion ; thought, meditation, deliberation ; an intention, viii, 11 ; — *karüñ^u^*, to consider, think, xii, 15.

*ryūnz^u^*, a ball (such as children play with) ; pl. nom. *rīnz^i^*, v, 3 (bis), 4 (several times), 5.

raz, f. a rope ; *gāsa-raz*, a grass rope, xi, 9.

rēza, m. a piece, a fragment ; — *karun*, to cut to fragments.

rōzun, to remain, continue, i, 5 ; ii, 9 ; vii, 18, 20 (bis), 3 ; x, 1, 6, 8 ; xii, 1, 15, 8 ; to wait a while, to wait, vii, 9 ; to abide, continue in one place, ix, 6, 8, 10, 2 ; *path rōzun*, to remain behind, to remain over and above, to be all that is left, xii, 23 ; *pāma rōzan*, reproaches will remain, i.e. (I) shall get a bad name, x, 3.

inf. abl. *bĕdār rōzana-söty*, by means of remaining awake, x, 8 ; forming inf. of purpose, *rōzani āy*, came in order to stay, x, 6, 8, 10, 2 ; freq. part. *rūz^i^ rūz^i^*, remaining continually, vii, 18 ; pres. part. *rōzān*, vii, 23 ; perf. part. *rūd^u^mot^u^*, i, 5 ; xii, 23 ; impve. pol. pl. 2, *rūz^i^tav*, vii, 9 ; indic. fut. sg. 2 interrog. *rōzakha*, xii, 18 ; 3, *rōzi*, x, 1, 6 ; pl. 3, *rōzan*, x, 3 ; pres. f. sg. 3, with suff. 3rd pers. pl. dat. *nakha rōzān chĕkh-na*, she does not remain near them, ii, 9 ; past m. sg. 3, *rūd^u^*, xii, 1, 15 ; pl. 3, *rūd^i^*, vii, 20 (bis).

sa 1, see *tih*.

sa 2, a vocative suff., equivalent to our " sir " or " sirs ". Attached to :—

(*a*) A noun, *rājĕ-sa*, Your Majesty ! x, 8 (bis).

(*b*) Verbs, *an-sa*, bring, sir, xii, 10 ; *anukh-sa*, bring them, sir, x, 12 ; *di-sa*, give, sir, x, 8 ; *gatsh-sa*, go, sir, ii, 9 ; *nin-sa*, take her, sir, xii, 25 ; *nīriv-sa*, go forth, sirs, x, 9 ; *pakiv-sa*, walk, sirs, x, 1 ; *wan-sa*, tell, sir, x, 1 (bis), 2 ; *wanta-sa*, please tell, sir, ii, 4 ; *waniv-sa*, say, sirs, x, 6.

(*c*) A conjunction, *yina-sa*, that not, sir, xii, 1.

(*d*) An interjection, *hata-sa*, O, sirs, x, 5.

söb (= *ṣāḥib*), an honorific suffix ; *rājĕ-söb*, His Majesty, x, 8 ; sg. voc. *rājĕ-söba*, Your Majesty ! x, 7 ; *Khŏdā-Söb*, God ; sg. dat. *Khŏdā-Söbas*, x, v ; ag. *Khŏdā-Söban*, iii, 8 (bis).

sabab, m. a reason, cause, viii, 5.

subuh, m. morning, dawn, x, 8 ; xii, 9 ; *sub*^a^*han*, adv. in the morning, at dawn, x, 11 ; *sub*^a^*hanas*, id., xii, 12 ; *sub*^a^*has*, id., xii, 5.

Subhān, m. N.P., Subḥān, N. of the author of the 7th story in this collection, — The Tale of the Reed-flute.

sabakh, m. a lecture, lesson, reading ; *sabakh dapun*, to teach a lesson, iv, 4 ; v, 5 ; — *parun*, to read a lesson, to study, viii, 3, 4 ; sg. dat. *sabakas*, viii, 3 (bis), 11 ; *sabakas āsun*, to be at a lesson, to be at school, viii, 11 ; *chĕs-na tshuñ*^ü^*-müts*^ü^ *nöyid sabakas*, I (fem.) was not taught a barber's lesson, I did not learn barber's work, v, 6.

Söbir Tilawôñ^u^, m. N.P., Ṣābir, the oilseller, N. of the author of the 11th story in this collection, — How Forsyth Sāhib went to conquer Yārkand.

sadāh, m. a sound, viii, 9.

sōdā, m. goods, wares, merchandise, viii, 9 ; marketing, bargaining, acting as a merchant, iii, 1 ; v, 10 ; sg. dat. *sōdāhas*, iii, 1 ; v, 10.

sōdāgar [iii, 3 (bis), 4] or *sōdāgār* [iii, 1 (ter), 3 ; v, 11 (bis) ; viii, 9 (bis), 10 (bis)], m. a merchant ; with suff. of indef. art. *sōdāgārā*, viii, 9 ; *sōdāgārā akh*, viii, 9 ; sg. dat. *sōdāgaras*, iii, 2 ; *sōdāgāras*, viii, 9, 10 ; ag. *sōdāgāran*, viii, 9, 10 ; gen. *sōdāgara-sond*^u^, iii, 1 ; *sōdāgāra-sond*^u^, iii, 1 ; pl. gen. *sōdāgāran-hond*^u^, viii, 9.

sōdāgar-bāy, f. a merchant's wife, iii, 1 (bis), 2, 3 ; sg. dat. *-bāyĕ*, iii, 1, 2.

Sŏdurabal, m. N. of a place in Kashmīr ; with emph. *y*, *Sŏdurabalạy*, only in Sŏdurabal, vii, 31.

sŏh, suh, see *tih.*

shĕch[i], f. a message ; — *ladüñ*[ü], to send a message, x, 3 (ter).

söhib, m. a possessor, owner, lord, great man ; a European gentleman, xi, 20 (referring to Sir Douglas Forsyth) ; a title of courtesy added to the name of a European gentleman, *Phōrsaṭ söhibun*[u] (of Mr. Forsyth), xi, title ; God, iv, 4, 5 ; ix, 3 ; *söhib-ĕ āgāh,* an intelligent master, i.e. a master of recondite learning, a profound magician, ii, 9 ; *söhib-i-kitāb,* a master of books, a famous author, x, 13 ; sg. gen. *Söhiba-sond*[u], of God, iv, 4, 5 ; *Phōrsaṭ söhibun*[u] (treated as part of a proper name), xi, title ; sg. voc. *Söhibō,* O God ! ix, 3.

Bār-Söhib, the Almighty, vii, 2, 3 ; ag. — *Söhiban,* vii, 5.

shūbun, to shine ; to be beautiful, ii, 4, 5 ; vii, 10 ; to be beautiful, to be glorious, vii, 5 ; to be becoming, to suit, be worthy, be proper, xii, 4, 5.

pres. m. pl. 3, with suff. 3rd pers. sg. gen. *chis shūbān,* vii, 5 ; imperf. f. sg. 1, *ös*[ü]*s shūbān,* vii, 10 ; durative past conditional, *āsihē shūbān,* it would have been (i.e. it must have been, it probably was) beautiful, ii, 4 ; (I would see) how beautiful it was, ii, 5 ; past cond. sg. 3, *shūbihĕh,* xii, 4, 5.

shod[u], m. news, intelligence, ii, 10.

shāh, shĕh 1, m. a king ; *shĕhan-shāh,* a king of kings, an emperor, i, 1 ; *shāh-i-yūsūph,* King Joseph, vi, 1 ; sg. ag. *shĕhan,* i, 7.

shĕh 2, card. six. *shĕh zañĕ,* six females, xii, 6, 7 ; pl. dat. *shĕn köd-khānan,* for six prisons, v, 7 ; *shĕn zañĕn,* for (of) six females, xii, 6.

shöhī, f. royalty ; *khal*[a]*t-ĕ-shöhī,* a robe of honour of royalty, a royal robe, x, 4 (ter).

shĕhul[u] 1, m. coolness, cold, i, 11.

shĕhul[u] 2, adj. cool ; (of sleep) cold, the reverse of deep, v, 6 ; f. sg. nom. *yiyiy nẹ̆nd*[a]*r shĕh*[ü]*j*[ü], sleep will come to thee cold, i.e. you will lose the desire to sleep, but it also means cool (refreshing) sleep will come to you, and is misunderstood by the hearer in this sense, v, 6 (bis).

shĕhmār, m. a great snake, a huge poisonous python, viii, 6 (bis) ; 13 (bis) ; with suff. of indef. art. *shĕhmārā,* viii, 7 ; sg. dat. *shĕhmāras,* viii, 6, 13 ; gen. *shĕhmāra-sond*[u], viii, 6, 13 (bis).

shĕhar, m. a city, x, 9; a country, ii, 1; *shĕhar-ĕ-Yirān*, the land of Persia, ii, 1; with suff. of indef. art. *shĕharā*, v, 1.

sg. dat. *shĕharas*, (went) to the city, x, 10; *nīzīkh shĕharas*, (arrived) near the city, x, 3; *shĕharas and-kun*, (arrived) at the outskirts of the city, x, 5; *shĕharas-kun*, (went, etc.) towards the city, set out for the city, x, 3, 5, 12; *shĕharas-manz*, in the city, v, 11; x, 14; into the city, v, 9; *shĕharas akis-manz*, (arrived) at a certain city, xii, 2; *shĕharas nĕbar*, (he was taken) outside the city, x, 5.

gen. *shĕharakis*, (to the king) of the city, xii, 3.

abl. *shĕhara dūr*, far from the city, viii, 11; *shĕhara-manza*, from in the city, viii, 11; *tsaliv yimi shĕhara*, flee ye from this city, xiii, 11.

shāhzāda, a prince; sg. dat. *-zādas*, viii, 13; pl. nom. *-zāda*, viii, 5, 11 (bis), 3.

shākh, f. a branch; *shākha-bargau-söty*, (beautiful) with the leaves of (my) branches, vii, 10.

shĕkh, m. anxiety; — *gatshun*, anxiety to occur, anxiety to be felt, v, 8; xii, 15.

shĕkh^{a}ts, m. a person, an individual; with suff. of indef. art. *shĕkhtsā*, x, 1; *shĕkhtsāh akh*, xii, 3; sg. dat. *shĕkhtsas*, x, 2 (bis); ag. *shĕkhtsan*, x, 2, 6.

shĕkal, f. a form, shape; *pŏshākas kür^{ū}n shĕkal yinsān-hish^{ü}*, he folded his clothes into the shape of a man, x, 7.

shikam, m. the belly; sg. dat. *shikamas-manz*, (entered) into (her) belly, x, 7 (bis); abl. *shikama-manza*, (issued) forth from (her) belly, x, 7 (bis).

shikār, m. hunting, sport, the chase; sg. dat. *shikāras*, ii, 4, 8; viii, 7.

shikast, m. weakness, sickness; sg. abl. *shikasta-söty*, owing to (his) weak condition, v, 5.

shōlun, to shine, flame (of a lamp); pres. sg. m. sg. 3, *shōlān chuh*, vi, 6.

shām, m. evening; *shāman-bög^{i}*, at about evening, at eventide, v, 5.

shĕmāh, m. the flame of a lamp, vi, 6; viii, 13; x, 7 (bis).

shumār, f. counting, enumeration; *shumār būz^{u}*, the counting was heard, i.e. the roll-call was heard, the roll was called, xi, 16. Cf. *bĕ-shumār.*

shĕmshēr, f. a sword, viii, 6, 13 ; x, 7 ; — *kaḍüñ*ᵘ, to draw a sword, viii, 13 ; x, 7 ; — *lāyüñ*ᵘ, to give a blow with a sword, viii, 6 ; — *tulüñ*ᵘ, to raise a sword (in order to strike), ii, 7 ; iii, 9 (ter) ; x, 7 ; sg. dat. *kür*ᵘ*s thaph shĕmshēri*, she seized the sword, iii, 9 ; gen. *shĕmshēri-hond*ᵘ *tēg*, the blade of a sword, viii, 6, 13 ; *shĕmshēri-hünz*ᵘ *tsünḍ*ᵘ, a blow of a sword, a sword-cut, iii, 5, 6.

shānd, m. a bed-pillow ; *shānd dyun*ᵘ, to put (anything) under one's pillow, x, 7 ; *khōra chĕs karān shānd*, she goes from the foot of the bed to the pillow, v, 5 ; sg. abl. *shānda*, v, 5.

shŏngun, to go to sleep ; past m. sg. 3, *shọng*ᵘ, x, 7. The conj. part. *shŏngith*, having gone to sleep, is used as an adjective, meaning " asleep ", viii, 7.

shĕnākh, m. one who recognizes, in *lāl-shĕnākh*, one who recognizes rubies, a lapidary. See *lāl-shĕnākh*, s.v. *lāl* 1.

shāph, m. a charm, spell, incantation ; *amis shāph dyutun*, she pronounced a spell over him, xii, 15 ; *shāph tul*ᵘ*nas*, she took the spell off him, xii, 15. Cf. *kas*ᵃ*m.*

shār, m. a poem, xi, title.

shōr, m. in *shōra-gāh*, an outcry, vi, 12, 3.

*shur*ᵘ, m. an infant, a child ; *shur*ⁱ*-bāshĕ*, child-talk, infantine babbling, v, 2.

shrākh, f. a knife, x, 13.

shĕrīkh, m. a sharer, partner, i, 10.

shērun, to put in order, to arrange ; conj. part. *shīrith trāwun*, to make ready (for a person), x, 7 ; fut. pl. 1, *shērav*, xi, 12, 7.

shranz, ? m. a blacksmith's tongs, xi, 16.

*shĕstruw*ᵘ, adj. made of iron, xii, 16, 7 ; m. sg. abl. *shĕstravi*, xii, 16 ; pl. nom. *shĕstrāv*ⁱ, v, 4 ; fem. sg. nom. *shĕstrüv*ᵘ, v, 4 ; abl. *shĕstravi*, v, 4.

Shētān, m. Satan, iii, 8 ; sg. ag. *Shētānan*, iii, 8.

shōtsh, m. purity, the condition of not being defiled, hence (x, 3) pure (i.e. undefiled) food.

sakharun, to prepare to set out, make ready to depart.
II past, m. pl. 3, *sakharyēy*, xii, 18.

sak^{a}th, adj. hard, severe, vii, 13, 18.

sāl, a feast, vi, 2; a wedding feast, v, 9; sg. dat. *sālas*, v, 9; vi, 2.

söl, m. a stroll, ramble, walk, taking the air, excursion, with suff. of indef. of art. *sölāh*, ii, 2; sg. dat. *sölas*, ii, 4, 8; iii, 1; viii, 7.

sul^u, dawn; *suli*, at dawn, xii, 23; *sōli-gārē* (m.c. for *suli-gari*), at dawn time, v, 7.

salāh, m. advice, viii, 11; *thāviv mĕ-söty salāh*, make ye a consultation with me, i.e. have an understanding with me, have an intrigue with me, viii, 3.

salām, f. peace (in Arabic formulas), x, 14; xii, 26; a bow, salutation; a complimentary present, viii, 3 (bis), 11; — *karüñ^u*, to make a bow, to salute, iii, 1; xii, 4, 5, 9, 12, 3, 6, 7, 20, 3; — *pālüñ^u*, id., xii, 16; sg. dat. *salāmi*, viii, 3.

sultān, m. a Sultan; *Sultān-i-Mahmōd-i-Gaznavī*, Sultān Maḥmūd of G͟haznī, i, 1.

salay, f. a spike, v, 4; sg. abl. *salayi-söty*, with, or by means of, a spike, v, 4 (bis).

Sulaymān, m. N.P. Solomon, xii, 17.

samā, m. heaven; *arz o samā*, earth and heaven, vii, 26.

sumb^u, adj.; adequate (for), sufficient (for); *rĕtas sumb^u*, (money) sufficient for a month, xii, 4; m. pl. nom. *lāl traṭis sumb^i*, rubies enough for a necklace, sufficient to make a necklace, xii, 5.

sǫmb^{a}run, to collect, bring together, amass; fut. pass. part. m. sg. *cyôn^u gatshi sǫmb^{a}run^u*, you must collect, xii, 21; conj. part. *sǫ̆mb^{a}rith*, ix, 9; pres. m. pl. 3, *chih sǫmb^{a}rān*, xi, 7.

sǫ̆mb^{a}rāwun, i.q. *sǫmb^{a}run*; fut. pass. part. m. pl. *gatshan sǫ̆mb^{a}rāwān^i*, they must be collected, xii, 24; past m. sg. *sǫ̆mbarôw^u*, xii, 21, 4; with suff. 2nd pers. sg. ag. *sǫ̆mb^{a}rôwuth*, xii, 24.

samakhun, to meet a person, have an interview with, to encounter; past m. sg. with suff. 3rd pers. pl. ag. *samokhukh*, xii, 25.

sāmān, m. requisites, materials, appliances, vii, 5; xi, 9; pomp and circumstance, xi, 20; *sôruy sāmān*, the entire appliance, xi, 9; *bā-sôruy-sāmān*, with all pomp, xi, 20; pl. nom. *sāmān*, vii, 5.

samsār, the world, iv, 1, etc.; sg. dat. *samsāras*, for *samsāras-manz*, in the world, ix, 6.

sān, postpos. with; *gāṭa-sān*, with skill, skilfully, i, 6.

sīna, m. the bosom, vii, 21.

sŏn, m. gold; sg. gen. *sŏna-sond^{u}*, made of gold; m. pl. nom. *sŏna-sȧnd^{i}*, v, 3, 4 (bis), 5; f. sg. *sŏna-sünz^{ü}*, v, 1; *sŏna-kan*, an ear adorned with golden ears; pl. dat. with emph. *y*, *sŏna-kananạy*, vii, 11.

sọ̆n^{u}, adj. deep; — *khash*, a deep cut, v, 6.

sôn^{u}, possess. pron. our, x, 12; with emph. *y*, *sônuy*, viii, 13; f. sg. nom. *söñ^{ü}*, viii, 11; x, 5.

sond^{u}, postpos. of gen. Added

A. to masc. sg. animate nouns. *gŏlāma-sond^{u}*, of the servant, viii, 6; *khŏdāyĕ-sond^{u}*, of God, xii, 7; *lāl-shĕnāka-sond^{u}*, of the lapidary, xii, 8, 25; *möl^{i}-sond^{u}*, of the father, xii, 21, 2; *phakīra-sond^{u}*, of the faqīr, x, 12; *pātashāha-sond^{u}*, of the king, ii, 10; v, 10; vi, 11; *pātashĕha-sond^{u}*, of the king, xii, 1, 4; *sōdāgara-sond^{u}*, of the merchant, iii, 1; *sōdāgāra-sond^{u}*, id., iii, 1; *Söhiba-sond^{u}*, of the Master (i.e. of God), iv, 4, 5; *shĕhmāra-sond^{u}*, of the python, viii, 6, 13; *sŏnara-sond^{u}*, of the goldsmith, v, 2; *yāra-sond^{u}*, of the friend, x, 4, 11; *Yūsūpha-sond^{u}*, of Joseph, vi, 10; *zȧn^{i}-sond^{u}*, of the person, viii, 11.

hihara-sandis, of the father-in-law, x, 12; *pātashĕha-sandis*, of the king, ii, 5, 6, 7; v, 11; xii, 22.

möli-sandi, of the father, xii, 21; *patashĕha-sandi*, of the king, ii, 9; *wazīra-sandi*, of the vizier, xii, 4, 5.

pātashāha-sȧnd^{i}, of the king, viii, 1, 13; *sŏnara-sȧnd^{i}*, of the goldsmith, v, 10.

pātashĕha-sandĕn, of the king, viii, 1, 6.

pātashĕha-sandyau, of the king, viii, 5.

gŏlāma-sünz^{ü}, of the servant, viii, 11; *khāwanda-sünz^{ü}*, of the husband, iii, 2; *möl^{i}-sünz^{u}*, of the father, xii, 19, 20 (ter); *phakīra-sünz^{ü}*, of the faqīr, x, 8, 14; *pātashāha-sünz^{ü}*, of the king, v, 7 (bis); viii, 1; x, 14; *pātashĕha-sünz^{ü}*, of the king, x, 5; xii, 1; *rājĕ-sünz^{ü}*, of the king, x, 7 (bis); *sŏnara-sünz^{u}*, of the goldsmith, v, 1, 3, 10.

pātashāha-sanzĕ, of the king, v, 2, 4 ; *pātashĕha-sanzĕ*, of the king, v, 1 (bis) ; xii, 4, 5.

pātashāha-sanzi, of the king, v, 4 ; xii, 4 ; *pātashĕha-sanzi*, of the king, xii, 5 ; *sŏnara-sanzi*, of the goldsmith, v, 7, 9 (bis) ; *yāra-sanzi*, of the friend, x, 4.

B. Used with masc. sg. inan. noun, to indicate the material of which a thing is made. *sŏna-sȧndⁱ*, made of gold, v, 3, 4 (bis), 5 ; *sŏna-sūñzᵘ*, id., v, 1.

C. With sg. an. pron. m. or f. *ȧmⁱ-sondᵘ*, of him, v, 3 ; viii, 6, 8, 10 ; of her, xii, 7.

ȧmⁱ-sandi, of her, x, 5 ; *tȧmⁱ-sandi*, of him, i, 3 ; vii, 6.

ȧmⁱ-sünzᵘ, of him, iii, 4 ; xii, 4 ; *ȧmⁱ-sanzi*, of her, xii, 15 ; *tȧmⁱ-sünzᵘ*, of her, xii, 15 ; *nazari tȧmⁱ-sanzi-sŏty*, owing to his seeing (me), vii, 13.

sangsār, m. lapidation, stoning (the punishment), viii, 8.

Sŏnamarg, f. N. of a *marg* or mountain plateau in the Sind valley of Kashmīr, celebrated for its flowery meads. It is a favourite camping ground for European visitors ; sg. dat. *Sŏnamargi*, at Sŏnamarg, xi, 3.

sŏnar, m. a goldsmith, v, 1 (bis), 3, 5 (bis), 6, 7, 9, 10 (bis) ; sg. dat. *sŏnaras*, v, 9 ; gen. *sŏnara-sondᵘ*, v, 2 ; *-sȧndⁱ* (m. pl. nom.), v, 10 ; *-sünzᵘ* (f. sg. nom.), v, 1, 3, 10 ; *-sanzi* (f. sg. ag.), v, 7, 9 (bis).

sg. ag. irreg. *sŏnar* (for *sŏnaran*), v, 4.

sŏnar-aṭh, the goldsmiths' market, the goldsmiths' quarter (of a town), v, 7.

This word is more usually *sonur* or *sonᵃr*.

saniyās, m. a kind of Hindū ascetic, a *Saṁnyāsin*, v, 10, 11 (quater) ; sg. dat. *saniyāsas*, v, 12 ; voc. (poet.) *saniyāsū*, v, 11.

sapadun, *sapanun*, to become.

fut. sg. 2, *sapadakh*, vi, 11 ; interrog. *sapadakha*, iii, 2 ; 3, *sapadi*, vi, 16 ; past m. sg. 3, *sapodᵘ*, iii, 7 ; *sapodᵘ sawār*, he became mounted, he mounted (a horse), xii, 1 ; with suff. 1st pers. sg. dat. *sapodum*, there became to me (crushing), I became (crushed), vii, 13 ; f. sg. 2 with neg. suff. *sapüzᵘkh-na*, thou didst not become, iii, 2 ; pl. with suff. 3rd pers. sg. dat.

sapañĕs zᵃh katha sara, two statements became tested for him, i.e. he had two statements tested, x, 4.

saphar, m. travelling, a journey, xii, 25; sg. dat. *sapharas*, x, 1, 6 (bis); gen. (poet. for *sapharukᵘ*) *sapharunᵘ*, xi, 3.

sapañĕs, see *sapadun*.

sar, m. the head; *sar tsaṭun*, to behead, viii, 11.

sara 1, m. investigation, testing, x, 4; *sara karun*, to test, viii, 13; x, 2, 6 (ter), 14. In this phrase, the grammatical object is the thing tested, as in *karĕn tsōr katha* (f. pl.) *sara*, he tested four statements (x, 6). Similarly *sapañĕs zᵃh katha sara*, two statements became tested for him, i.e. he had two statements tested (x, 4). Cf. *saragī*.

sara 2, see *sarun*.

sȧrⁱ, an old word, now used in compounds such as *sȧrⁱ gatshun*, to be flooded, to be covered with a flood of water, iv, 3.

sēr, adj. satisfied, contented, i, 3.

sīr, m. a secret, a mystery, ii, 4; *sīr bāwun*, to explain a secret, vii, 21; *mĕ ma kar sīras phāsh*, do not accuse my secret (parts) of unchastity, i.e. do not disgrace me by letting me remain naked, xii, 7.

sôrᵘ, adj. all. This word is always used with emph. *y*; m. sg. nom. *sôruy*, iii, 1; v, 7, 9; xi, 9; xii, 19; *bā sôruy sāmān*, with all pomp, xi, 20; pl. nom. *sōriy*, iii, 4; v, 9; vi, 16.

sūr, m. ashes, xii, 23; *sūr mathun*, to rub ashes over one's body (like a Hindū ascetic), v, 9; *ṭŏka-sūr*, ashes of crushing, i.e. crushing into a powder like ashes, crushing to powder, vii, 13.

sg. dat. *sūras-manz*, in the ashes, xii, 23; abl. *sūra-manza*, from amid the ashes, xii, 23.

sarda, m. coolness, i, 11.

saragī, f. investigation, testing, viii, 7 (bis), 8, 10; x, 7. Cf. *sara* 1.

srĕh, m. moisture; with suff. of indef. art. *ūba-srĕhā*, a water-moisture, a slight trickle of moisture, viii, 7.

srān, m. bathing; — *karun*, to bathe (oneself), xii, 6 (bis), 7 (bis); sg. dat. *srānas*, v, 9.

sarun, to remember; fut. sg. 1, *sara*, xi, 14.

sārun, to carry goods from one place to another, and there to collect them, to pile up; conj. part. *sörith*, ix, 9; pres. part. *sārān*, xi, 10; pres. m. pl. 3, *chih sārān*, xi, 6.

sar^{a}*ph*, m. a serpent, x, 13.

susurāray, f. a rustling sound, xii, 23.

suti, see *tih*.

sath, card. seven; (preceding noun) *sath kuṭh*^{i}, seven rooms, vi, 3; *sath hĕl*^{i}, seven ears of corn, vi, 15; (following noun) *nāg sath*, seven springs, vi, 15; *göv*^{ü} *sath*, seven cows, vi, 15 (fem.); *lāl sath*, seven rubies, x, 2, 5, 12 (bis); *dŏha lāl sath sath*, seven rubies each day, xii, 9.

pl. dat. *satan köd-khānan*, to seven prisons, v, 8; *satan hĕlĕn* (for acc.), seven ears of corn, vi, 15; *satan göv*^{ü}*n* (for acc.) seven cows (fem.), vi, 15; *nāgan satan* (for acc.), seven springs, vi, 15; *lālan satan pĕṭh*, on the seven rubies, x, 5; abl. *satav-manza*, from among the seven, x, 12; *satav zamīnav tal*^{i}, below the seven worlds, iii, 8.

sāth, m. a particular instant of time, a moment, vii, 8; with suff. of indef. art. *sāthāh*, during a moment of time, for a short time, ii, 4; *sāthā*, id., vi, 3; vii, 9.

sg. abl. *ami sāta*, at that time, iii, 6; xii, 4, 15; with emph. *y*, *yĕmi sātay*, at what time verily, vii, 8.

sōth, m. the season of spring; *sōta*, in the spring time, ix, 7.

sĕṭhāh, adj. very much; *sĕṭhāh yinsāph*, great pity, viii, 4. adv. very, very much, exceedingly. With adj. preceding the word qualified, as in viii, 1, 9 (bis); or following it as in *khōbsūrath sĕṭhāh*, very beautiful, xii, 4, 5; but *sĕṭhāh khōbsūrath*, xii, 10, 5; *khŏta sĕṭhāh khōbsūrath*, much more beautiful than, xii, 10. With a verb, *sĕṭhāh gav khŏsh*, became much pleased, viii, 11; xii, 9; so *sĕṭhāh gōkh khŏsh*, viii, 14, but *gōs sĕṭhāh khōsh*, xii, 12; *sĕṭhāh phyūr*^{u}, they regretted extremely, viii, 1; *phyūrus sĕṭhāh*, he regretted extremely, viii, 10.

sötin, postpos. i.q. *söty*, q.v. governing dat.; *mĕ-sötin*, (share) with me, i, 7.

Governing abl., with, by means of; *drāti-sötin*, (cut) with a sickle, ix, 5; *kalama-sötin*, (write) with a pen, ix, 12; with, by means of, owing to; *muhima-sötin*, owing to poverty, i, 4 (bis).

söty, adv. with, together with ; *söty dyun*^{u}, to give with (a person), to give as a companion, vii, 5 ; x, 14 ; xii, 16 ; *söty hyon*^{u}, to take (a person) with (one), to take as a companion, ii, 1 ; v, 6 ; *söty tulun*, to carry along (with one), xii, 2 ; *söty-söty*, continually in (one's) company, vii, 5.

postpos. governing dat. and abl.

A. Governing dat. with, together with, in various shades of meaning ; thus,

amis-söty, in company with her, v, 7 ; *khāwandas-söty*, (burnt) together with her (dead) husband, iii, 4 ; *kōrĕ-söty*, (keep her) in (your) daughter's society, v, 10 ; *mĕ-söty*, in company with me, in my company, xii, 2 ; (come) with me, xii, 7 ; (go) with me, x, 9. We have it governing a pronominal suffix in the dat. in *söty ôsus*, (a falcon) was with him, viii, 7.

With, in the sense of consultation with, etc., *mĕ-söty* (intrigue) with me, viii, 3 ; (sin ye) with me, viii, 11 ; *pātashāhzādan-söty*, (sin) with the princes, viii, 11.

Together with, simultaneously with ; *ādamas-söty*, (created) simultaneously with Adam, vii, 6.

Together with, along with ; *karis-söty*, (the arm was pulled off) together with the bracelet, xii, 15.

(a marriage) with (so and so) in *amis-söty*, xii, 15, 8.

(conversation) with (so and so), *amis-söty*, x, 7 (bis) ; *kōrĕ-söty*, xii, 1.

Special meanings are *pānas-söty*, with oneself, under one's own control, x, 1, 6 ; *tath-söty mushtākh*, enamoured of that, iii, 8.

B. Governing abl., with, by means of ; *ami-söty*, (scratches) with it, xii, 17 ; *bār*^{i}*shi-söty*, (dug) with (his) spear, viii, 7 ; *litri-söty*, (cut) with a saw, vii, 19 ; *bĕdār rōzana-söty* (escaped) by keeping awake, x, 8 ; *salayi-söty*, (scratched) with a spike, v, 4 (bis) ; with emph. *y, panja-sötiy*, (a pleasant feeling arose) merely owing to (the application of) the (iron) claw, xii, 16 ; *thapi-sötiy*, merely by means of the grasp, xii, 12.

With, by means of, owing to ; *ad*^{a}*la söty*, (contented) owing to his justice, i, 3 ; *asara-söty*, owing to the result, vi, 16; *bargau-söty*, owing to the leaves, vii, 10; *mahabata-söty*, owing to affection, x, 4; *nazari-söty*, owing to (his) seeing (me), vii, 13; *shikasta-söty*, (fell asleep) owing to weakness, v, 5; with emph. *y*, *bŏchi sötiy*, owing only to hunger, vi, 16.

satyum^u, ord. seventh; m. sg. dat. *satimis*, v, 7; f. sg. nom. *satim*^{u}, xii, 7.

sawāb, m. meed, reward (of good works, of faith, etc.), ix, 12.

siwāh, postpos. with the exception of, except, save; *nĕmis matis siwāh*, with the exception of this madman, v, 9.

sawāl, m. asking, questioning; solicitation; a petition, application; — *dyun*^{u}, to present or make a petition, x, 5.

sawār, adj. mounted, riding (on); *sawār sapadun*, to mount, ride, xii, 1.

say, *sŏy*, *suy*, see *tih*.

syod^u, adj. straight; as adv. *yimau syod*^{u}, straight in front of them, viii, 6, 13.

söyīsth, m. a horse-attendant, a groom, syce, xii, 3, 4.

sōzun, to send; fut. pass. part. m. sg. nom. *sōzun*^{u} *gatshi panun*^{u} *khāwand*, you must send your husband, v, 1; past m. sg. with suff. 3rd pers. sg. ag. *sūzun*, x, 4.

ta 1, conj. and, i, 5; iii, 5; v, 4, 9, 12; *et passim*; *ta — biyĕ*, both . . . and, viii, 9.

ta 2, conj. introducing the apodosis of a conditional sentence, as in *yi-y, ta tih kyāh ? ti-y, ta yih kyāh ?* if this, then (*ta*) what (is) that ? if that, then (*ta*) what (is) this ? iii, 4 (bis), 9; so vii, 9; after *yĕli*, when, *yĕli būz*^{u}, *ta tsol*^{u}, when he heard, then he fled, ii, 7; *yĕli môrun, ta ada phyūrus*, when he had killed (the dog), then afterwards he grieved, viii, 10.

ta 3, illative conjunction, hardly translatable, equivalent to the Hindī *tō*. In the following passage translated " verily ", but this is merely written for want of a better word, viii, 9.

ti, conj. also, viii, 5, 8; x, 10, 1, 2; xii, 10. Often used as an enclitic, as in *ås*^{i}*-ti*, we also, xii, 1; *mĕ-ti*, me also, vi, 11; ix, 1; xi, 14; *su-ti*, he also, ii, 4; *ti-ti*, that also, viii, 9; x, 6 (ter); *ts*^{a}*-ti*, thou also, ix, 6; *yi-ti*, this one also, x, 8.

and, xii, 17.

even; *kăh-ti*, any even, i, 5; anyone even, vii, 23; *kĕh-ti*, any at all, viii, 9.

ti . . . *ti*, both . . . and, iii, 8; x, 13; xii, 12; *tō-ti*, nevertheless, x, 3.

tī, see *tih*.

tō, in *tō-ti*, nevertheless, x, 3.

tab, m. fever, v, 3, 10.

töb[i], c.g. an humble servant, a subject; with suff. of indef. art. *töb*'*yăh*, f. (of a woman), xii, 18.

töbīr, m. interpretation (of a dream), vi, 11, 4 (bis), 5 (bis), 6; — *karun*, to interpret, vi, 11, 16.

tēg, m. the blade (of a sword); sg. dat. *tēgas*, viii, 6, 13.

tagun, to be known how to be done, to be possible, used as a quasi-impersonal passive, to make potential compounds. It is generally used to indicate mental possibility, while *hĕkun* (which does not occur in these tales) indicates physical possibility. Its use with the infinitive or future passive participle will be clear from the following:—

fut. sg. 3, *tagi*, it will be possible; with suff. 1st pers. sg. dat. and interrog. neg. *tagĕm-nā*, will it not be possible for me? i.e. of course I can, of course I know how, x, 5; with suff. 2nd pers. sg. dat. *muhim tagiy kăsunuy*, poverty would have been known how to be verily expelled for thee, thou wouldst have been able to expel poverty, i, 15; *ṭsĕ mā tagiy*, I wonder if (*mā*) it will be possible for thee, I wonder if you know how (to make it right), x, 5; with the same suffix and the interrogative suffix *tagiyĕ mŏkalāwüñ*[u], will she be possible for thee to be released? do you know how to release her? v, 8; *tagiyĕ yih pātashāh-kūr*[u] *bacāwüñ*[u], can you save this princess? v, 9.

past m. sg. *amis tog*[u] *bōzun dôd*[u], to her the pain was possible to be understood, she could understand the pain, v, 3; with suff. 3rd pers. sg. dat. and neg. *togus-na* (or *tamis tog*[u]*-na*) *mŏl karun*, to fix a price was not known how to him, i.e. he did not know how to fix a price, he could not fix a fair price, viii, 9 (bis).

cond. past sg. 3, with suff. 1st pers. sg. dat. *tih yĕli tagihēm*, if that had been known how to me, i.e. if I had known how, v, 8.

tih, pron. he, she, it, that.

ANIMATE. SUBST. MASC. sg. nom. *suh*, ii, 8, 11 (bis); v, 9 (bis), 10; viii, 7, 8; x, 1, 4, 12 (quater); xii, 5, 19 (ter), 20. Used idiomatically in introducing the hero of a story, as *suh pātashĕhā akh ôs*^{u}, that king one was, equivalent to "once upon a time there was a king", viii, 7; so viii, 9, 11; *su-ti*, he also, ii, 4; *suy*, he verily, i, 4, 8; iii, 3 (bis); v, 1; vi, 16; viii, 7, 9; x, 12; xii, 25; he only, he alone, vi, 6; vii, 29, 30; x, 1, 6.

dat. *tas*, to him, i, 5, 8; ii, 8; iv, 2; v, 7; vii, 1; viii, 6 (bis), 8, 11 (bis); *tamis*, ii, 7; viii, 9 (bis); *tamis*^{ü}*y*, to him verily, ii, 1; viii, 9; xii, 1.

ag. *tàm*^{i}, by him, ii, 1; iv, 3, 4, 5, 6; x, 3, 12.

gen. (*tàm*^{i}*-sond*^{u}), his; *tàm*^{i}*-sandi*, i, 3; vii, 6; *-sanzi*, vii, 13.

pl. nom. *tim*, they, v, 4 (bis), 8; viii, 3 (bis), 4 (bis), 11; x, 12 (bis); xi, 5; xii, 16 (ter); *timạy*, they verily, v, 9; viii, 4; *tim-hay*, they verily, ix, 8, 9, 10.

dat. *timan*, to them, them, viii, 1; xi, 8; xii, 16, 7; *timan*^{ü}*y*, to them verily, them verily, viii, 11; xii, 1.

ag. *timau*, by them, vi, 11; *timav*, x, 12.

gen. *tihond*^{u}, their, xii, 16; *tihanza*, viii, 3, 11.

FEM. sg. nom. *sa*, she, v, 5 (bis), 9; viii, 11; x, 14; xii, 6, 10, 5, 9, 20, 5; *sŏh*, xii, 5; *say*, she verily, iii, 1, 4; xii, 14.

dat. *tas*, to her, xii, 2 (bis), 15 (bis), 25.

gen. (*tasond*^{u}), her, *tasandĕn*, ix, 3; (*tàm*^{i}*-sond*^{u}), *tàm*^{i}*-sünz*^{ü}, xii, 15.

pl. nom. *tima*, they, them (acc.) (fem.), viii, 11; xi, 9; *timay*, them verily (fem.), x, 14.

dat. *timan*, to them (fem.), xii, 6 (bis), 7.

ag. *timau*, by them (fem.), xii, 7.

ADJ. MASC. sg. nom. *suh*, that, ii, 8, 9 (bis); viii, 7 (bis), 10 (bis), 3 (bis); x, 12 (bis), 4; xii, 25, 6; *suy*, that very, xii, 19.

dat. *tas*, to that, that, ii, 7 ; vii, 4 ; viii, 7 ; x, 12 ; xii, 7, 20 ; *tamis*, to that, viii, 9 ; xii, 19.

pl. nom. *tim*, those, viii, 13.

dat. *timan*, to those, x, 6.

FEM. sg. nom. *sa*, that, x, 1, 6, 12 ; *sŏh*, iii, 5.

dat. *tamis*, to that, iii, 9 ; xii, 10.

ag. *tami*, by that, x, 10.

pl. nom. *tima*, those, xii, 19.

INANIMATE. SUBST. (m. or f.). sg. nom. *tih*, that, iii, 4 (bis), 9 ; viii, 3, 9, 11 ; x, 1 ; xii, 3 (bis), 7, 16, 9. As a correlative to a preceding relative, iii, 1, 8 (bis) ; v, 8 (bis) ; xii, 7, 20 ; *ti-kyāzi*, because, viii, 2 ; *ti-ti*, that also, viii, 9 ; x, 6 (ter) ; *tiy*, that verily, vii, 1 (bis) ; iii, 9 ; *tī*, that verily, xi, 1 ; *tiy*, (for *tih* + *ay*), if that, iii, 4 (bis), 9.

dat. *tath*, for that, for it, ii, 1 ; v, 4 ; vii, 27, 8 ; viii, 6 ; x, 3 ; xii, 16, 8 ; *tath*[i], to that verily, iii, 8 ; xii, 4, 11 (ter), 4.

ag. *tàmiy*, by that verily, iii, 1.

abl. *tami pata*, after that, x, 12 ; xii, 16 ; *tami-pĕṭh*[i] *kani*, in addition to that, iii, 8 ; *tami-tàl*[i], below it, xii, 14 ; *tamiy*, therefore, x, 14.

gen. *tamyukuy*, of it verily, vii, 12.

ADJ. As an adjective the masculine and feminine forms are commonly used in the sg. nom., even when agreeing with inanimate nouns. In one case the inanimate form of the pronoun is used, viz. *tih pŏshākh*, that garment, xii, 6. Other examples are :—

MASC. sg. nom. *suh*, that, xii, 4 (ruby) (bis), 11 (bracelet), 4 (rock), 5 (pain) ; *suy*, that very, ii, 4 (magic power, correlative) ; vii, 8 (time), 13 (fault) ; ix, 11 (action).

dat. *tath*, to that, etc., ii, 1 (bis), 7 ; iii, 5 ; v, 6 ; xii, 4, 6 (bis), 11, 4, 5, 24 ; *tath*[i], to that very, xii, 6 (bis), 14.

abl. *tami*, from that, etc., ii, 7 ; v, 5 ; viii, 9 ; x, 12 ; agreeing with inan. gen. masc. iii, 9 ; x, 10 (bis), 4.

pl. nom. *tim*, those, x, 12 (bis) ; *timay*, those very, v, 5.

dat. *timan*, to those, xi, 6.

FEM. sg. nom. *sa*, that, viii, 7 (thirst) ; x, 10 (dish of food) ; *sŏh*, xii, 20 (news) ; *say*, that very, ii, 6 (news) ; viii, 7 (story), 10 (id.), 3 (id.); ix, 4 (prison); xi, 5 (assembling); *sŏy*, vii, 16 (separation).

dat. *tath jāyĕ*, at that place, xii, 15.

abl. *tami kŏli manza*, from in that stream, xii, 4, 6; *tamiy kŏli kŏli*, along that very stream, xii, 6; *tamiy wati*, by that very road, xii, 14, 5.

gen. *tami kathi-hond*ᵘ, of that story, iii, 5.

tŏhĕ, *tŏh*ⁱ, see *tsᵃh*.

thaḍ or *thar*, f. the back; sg. obl. *thüḍ*ᵘ̈ or *thür*ᵘ̈ 1 (for *thür*ᵘ̈ 2, see s.v.); sg. abl. *thüḍ*ᵘ*-kani* (v, 4, bis), *thür*ᵘ*-kani* (v, 4), (turning herself) backwards (from there).

*thod*ᵘ, adj. erect, upright, standing up, ii, 3; vii, 11; — *wŏthun*, to stand up, ii, 5, 6; v, 6, 9; xii, 14, 5.

ṭhaharun, to stay in expectation, to await, wait; pres. f. sg. 1, neg. *chus-na ṭhaharān*, I am not waiting, i.e. I am not going to stay here, I cannot stop here (on account of the evil smell), ii, 4.

tāhkhīth (for *taḥqīq*), adv. of a certainty, certainly, assuredly, x, 12; xi, 13; xii, 3.

*ṭahol*ᵘ, m. a groom, x, 5, 12 (quater).

*tihond*ᵘ, *tihanza*, see *tih*.

*tuhond*ᵘ, possessive pron. your, ii, 2; xii, 15. Cf. *tsᵃh*.

*thüñ*ᵘ̈, f. fresh butter. With suff. of indef. art. *thüñ*ᵘ*ā*, ix, 4.

thaph, f. a grasp with the hand; sg. abl. *thapi-söṭiy*, merely by means of the grasp, xii, 12.

— *diñ*ᵘ̈, to seize, take hold of, *thaph dits*ᵘ̈*s*, he seized it, viii, 7; *dits*ᵘ̈*n ath thaph*, he seized it, he grasped it, xii, 12; — *karüñ*ᵘ̈, to take hold of; *kür*ᵘ̈*nas thaph*, he took hold of her, iii, 4; *kür*ᵘ̈*s thaph shĕmshēri*, he took hold of the sword, iii, 9; *kanas kür*ᵘ̈*nas thaph*, he took hold of him by the ear, iii, 9; *karüñ*ᵘ̈ *gatshi thaph dāmānas*, you must seize hold of (her) skirt, v, 9; *kür*ᵘ̈*s-na kūsi dāmānas thaph*, no one has seized hold of (my) skirt, v, 9; *ȧm*ⁱ *kür*ᵘ̈*nas pŏshākas thaph*, he caught hold of him by his garment, viii, 9; *tath*ⁱ *kār*ⁱ*zi thaph*, you must take hold of it, xii, 11; *thaph karith*, having (previously) grasped, i.e. holding, iii, 8 (bis) (of holding the bridle of, or leading, a horse); *athas chuh thaph karith*, he is holding (his) hand, v, 6; *nālas thaph karith*, holding him by the neck, vi, 9; *chuh thaph karith pyālas*, he is holding the cup, viii, 7; — *lāyüñ^u^*, i.q. — *karüñ^u^*, v, 9 (poet.).

*thür^ü^* 1, see *thaḍ*.

*thür^ü^* 2, f. a shrub; *pōshĕ-thür^u^*, a flower-shrub, ii, 3.

*ṭhôṭh^u^*, adj. beloved, dear, vii, 4; i.q. *ṭôṭh^u^*, q.v.

*thöv^i^k^i^*, see *thawun*.

thawun or *thāwun* (this verb is the equivalent of the Hindī *rakhnā*), to place, put, deposit, ii, 4; iii, 1, 5, 9; v, 11; vi, 5; viii, 7, 9, 11; ix, 4; x, 5, 10, 2 (quater); xii, 4, 9, 12, 5, 23; to keep, ii, 11; v, 10; xii, 25; to station (a person in a certain place), xi, 6; to appoint (a person to a post), *akh bôy^u^ thôwun wazīr*, he appointed one brother Vizier, viii, 14.

amanāth thāwun, to place as a deposit, to give in trust, x, 12; *thôwun dabövith*, to press (into the ground), to hide in the ground, to bury, x, 3; *thāwun darwāza*, to open a door, viii, 4 (bis), 11 (bis), 2; *thāwun kuluph*, to unlock, iii, 8 (bis); *thăwun kan*, to apply the ear, to give ear, attend, pay attention (to), listen (to), ii, 7; viii, 6, 8, 11; ix, 1, 4; *thāviv mĕ-söty salāh*, keep an understanding with me, have an intrigue with me, viii, 3.

perf. part. m. sg. nom. *thow^u^mot^u^*, viii, 9.

impve. sg. 2, *thāv*, iii, 8 (bis); viii, 4; with suff. 1st pers. sg. dat. *thāwum*, viii, 8, 11; with suff. 3rd pers. sg. gen. *thāwus*, iii, 5, 9; pl. 2, *thöviv*, viii, 3; pol. sg. 2, *thāvta*, ix, 4; with suff. 1st pers. sg. dat. *thāvtam*, viii, 6; ix, 1; with suff. 3rd pers. sg. acc. *thāvtan*, ii, 4; pl. 2, *thàv^i^tav*, ii, 7; fut. with suff. 3rd pers. sg. acc. *thöv^i^zĕn*, v, 10.

fut. and pres. subj. sg. 1, with suff. 2nd pers. sg. acc. *wumāh thāwath*, I may not now keep thee, ii, 11; with suff. 2nd pers. sg. dat. *thāway darwāza*, I will open for thee the door, viii, 11.

pres. f. sg. 3, with suff. 3rd pers. sg. dat. and neg. *chĕs-na thāwān*, viii, 11.

past masc. sg. *thôw^u^*, viii, 12; with suff. 2nd pers. sg. ag. *thôwuth*, vi, 5; x, 12; with suff. 3rd pers. sg. ag. *thôwun*, v, 11; viii, 7, 14; x, 3; xii, 15; with same, and also with suff. 1st pers. sg. dat. *thôw^u^nam*, ix, 4; with same, and also with suff. 3rd pers. sg. dat. *thôwᵘnas*, iii, 1 ; xii, 4, 23 (bis) ; with same, and also with suff. 3rd pers. pl. dat. *thôwᵘnakh*, viii, 4, 9.

pl. with suff. 3rd pers. sg. ag. and also with suff. 3rd pers. sg. dat. *thåvⁱnas*, xii, 9; with suff. 3rd pers. pl. ag. *thövikh*, x, 12.

fem. with suff. 3rd pers. sg. ag., *thövüⁿn*, xii, 25 ; with same, and also with suff. 3rd pers.

sg. dat. *thüvüⁿnas*, x, 5, 10 ; xii, 12 ; with suff. 3rd pers. pl. ag. *thövükh*, viii, 11.

perf. m. sg. with suff. 2nd pers. pl. ag. *chuwa thôwᵘmotᵘ*, x, 12 ; with suff. 3rd pers. pl. ag. *chukh thôwᵘmotᵘ*, x, 12 ; pl. (without auxiliary) *thövⁱmåtⁱ*, x, 12.

Altogether irregular is the peculiar form *thövⁱ-kⁱ* (xi, 6). This is the m. pl. of the past *thôwᵘ*, with a pleonastic suffix *-kᵘ* added. So that we get *thôwᵘ-kᵘ*, m. pl. nom. *thövⁱ-kⁱ*.

tujü, *tujyāv*, etc., see *tulun*.

ṭôkᵘ, m. a tray ; sg. dat. *ṭökis*, viii, 4 ; *ṭökis-manz*, viii, 12.

ṭŏkh, m. crushing ; sg. abl. *ṭŏka-sūr*, ashes of crushing, crushing into powder like ashes, crushing to powder, vii, 13.

takhsīr, m. a crime, a fault, viii, 10 ; x, 12.

ṭukᵃra, m. a piece, fragment ; pl. nom. *ṭukᵃra karåⁿⁱ*, to break or cut into pieces, viii, 6 : *shĕhmāras chuh karān ṭukᵃra*, he cuts the python to pieces, viii, 13.

ti-kyāzi, see *tih*.

tal, adv. below ; *tal wasun*, to descend, ix, 6 ; postpos. governing dat., below ; *athⁱ-tal*, below it verily, ii, 3 ; *dārĕ-tal*, under the window, v, 4 ; *latan-tal*, under the feet, viii, 7 ; *palangas-tal*, under the bed, viii, 6, 13 ; x, 7, 8.

tala, postpos. governing abl. ; *lari-tala*, issued from under the side, vii, 7.

tålⁱ, postpos. governing abl. ; *satav zaminav tålⁱ*, below the seven worlds, iii, 8 ; *tami tålⁱ*, below it, xii, 14.

talau, interj. O ! Ho ! v, 5 (addressed by a woman to her husband) ; x, 1 (addressed by men to men).

tĕli, adv. then, ii, 3 ; v, 5, 6 (bis) ; xii, 3.

tōlun, to weigh (something) ; inf. sg. obl. *tōlani āy*, they came to weigh, ix, 10.

tulun, to raise, take up, lift up, iii, 1, 2, 7 ; v, 4 ; x, 12 ; xii, 2, 4, 6 (bis), 7, 9, 17 ; *māzas chum tulān*, he is raising bits of my flesh, i.e. cutting bits out of me, vii, 14 ; *nam tulân^{i}*, to cut (another's) nails, to manicure, v, 6 ; *shĕmshēr tulüñ^{u}*, to raise, i.e. to draw, a sword, ii, 7 ; iii, 9 ; x, 7 ; *shāph tulun*, to raise (i.e. undo) a charm, xii, 15 ; *tulun söty*, to carry along with one, xii, 2 ; *wŏṭh tulüñ^{u}*, to leap, ii, 9.

fut. pass. part. m. sg. *gatshi pŏshākh tulun^{u}*, you must take up the garment, xii, 6 ; conj. part. *tulith*, iii, 7 ; pres. m. sg. 3, *tulān chuh*, xii, 17 ; with suff. 1st pers. sg. gen. *chum tulān*, vii, 14 ; 1 past m. sg. *tul^{u}*, iii, 1 ; with suff. 3rd pers. sg. ag. *tulun*, iii, 2 ; xii, 2, 7 ; with ditto, and with suff. 3rd pers. sg. gen. *tul^{u}nas*, xii, 15 ; with suff. 3rd pers. pl. ag. *tulukh*, xii, 2 ; pl. *tul^{i}*, xii, 9 ; with suff. 3rd pers. sg. ag. *tulin*, x, 12 ; with ditto, and with suff. 3rd pers. sg. gen. *tul^{i}nas*, v, 6 ; f. sg. *tuj^{ü}*, ii, 9 ; with suff. 3rd pers. sg. ag. *tuj^{ü}n*, ii, 7 ; iii, 9 ; v, 4 ; x, 7 ; 3 past m. sg. *tujyāv*, xii, 6 ; with suff. 3rd pers. sg. ag. *tujyān*, xii, 4.

t^{a}l^{ü}r^{ü}, f. a bee ; *măch-t^{a}l^{ü}r^{ü}*, a honey-bee, ix, 1, 3, 4, 5 ; sg. ag. *-t^{a}l^{a}ri*, ix, 1, 6.

tālav, m. the ceiling of a room ; sg. abl. *tālawa-kani*, down from the ceiling, viii, 6.

tilawôñ^{u}, m. an oil-seller, an oilman ; sg. voc. *tilawāñi*, xi, 20.

tam, m. weariness (from walking, travelling, etc.) ; — *dyun^{u}*, to cause such weariness, vii, 17.

tâm^{i}, *tami*, *tim*, *tima*, *timau*, see *tih*.

tum, you (Hindōstānī), xi, 4.

tamāh, m. longing, longing desire, vii, 26.

timan, see *tih*.

tamis, see *tih*.

tamāshĕ, m. an entertainment, exhibition, sight, show, spectacle ; sg. dat. *mushtākh tamāshĕs-kun*, enamoured of the spectacle, iii, 7.

tamaskhurī, f. jesting, joking.

tāmath, adv. so long (of time) ; *tāmath . . . yāmath*, so long . . . as, xi, 20.

timav, *tamiy*, *tâmiy*, *timay*, *timay*, see *tih*.

tān, m. a limb of the body; pl. nom. *tān*, viii, 7.

tānana, tan^{a}nana, tanānay, meaningless words, introduced into a verse, like our "fol-de-riddle-i-do", v, 12.

tāñ, adv. and postpos. as far as, up to, as in *ot^{u}-tāñ*, up to there, i.e. by that time, x, 4, 6; *az-tāñ*, up to to-day, until to-day, x, 7, 8; xii, 20; *tsēr-tāñ*, up to lateness, i.e. during a long time, v, 6; *yot^{u}-tāñ*, up to where, i.e. as soon as, xii, 6; *yut^{u}-tāñ*, up to here, i.e. by this time, in the meantime, v, 7.

Used as a suffix implying indefiniteness added to an interrogative pronoun, as in *kus-tāñ wŏpar*, someone else, v, 4; *kyāh-tāñ takhsīr* some fault or other, viii, 10.

By itself, *tāñ* is used in the sense of *yut^{u}-tāñ*, abl., xi, 20; xii, 1.

tāph, m. sunshine, i, 11.

tārē, see *tör^{ü}*.

tōr 1, m. Mount Sinai; sg. abl. *tōra-pĕṭha*, from on Mount Sinai, iv, 5.

tōr 2, adv. there, x, 3.

tōra, adv. therefrom, thence, i, 6, 8; v, 4, 9; viii, 11; xii, 1, 11.

tūr^{i}, adv. there verily, even there, vii, 20; x, 3.

tör^{ü}, f. delay; sg. abl. *tārē* (m.c. for *tāri*), with delay, hence, as adv. confusedly, v, 7.

tūr^{i}, see *tōr* 2.

tūr^{ü}, f. an adze; sg. abl. *tōri-dab*, the blow of an adze, vii, 18.

tür^{ü}, f. a tenon (in carpentry), x, 5, 12.

tarbyĕth, f. instruction, tuition, ii, 4, where the word is treated as m. It is usually f.

trĕh or *trih*, card. three; *trih*, x, 1, 12 (as subst.); *trih katha*, three statements, x, 1; *lāl trih*, three rubies, x, 12; *trih rĕth*, three months, xii, 6, 11; *zanāna trĕh*, three women, xii, 19 (ter); *tithiy trĕh*, three times as much, xii, 24; pl. dat. *trĕn rĕtan-kyut^{u} khar^{a}j*, expenses for three months, xii, 5, 11; *yiman zanānan trĕn*, to these three women, x, 20.

tŏrka-chān, m. a carpenter, turner, cabinet maker, who is not a village servant, but who works independently on his own account; sg. dat. *-chānas*, vii, 17, 20.

tröm[i], f. a copper dish, or tray, viii, 3 (bis), 11.

tröm[ü], f. i.q. *tröm*[i], iii, 1.

tārun, to cause to pass over; *bāj tārun*, to take tribute (from a subordinate king, etc.), x, 10; xi, 2; *zadĕ pānas tārañĕ*, to cause holes to pass over a person's body, to bore holes in it, vii, 25; pres. part. *tārān*, xi, 2; imperf. m. sg. 3, *ôs*[u] *tārān*, xi, 2; past m. pl. with suff. 3rd pers. sg. ag. and 1st pers. sg. gen. *tör*[i]*nam*, vii, 25.

tīrandāz, m. an archer, a bowman; pl. nom. *tīrandāz*, ii, 7; dat *tīrandāzan*, ii, 7.

trĕnaway, card. all three, the three, xii, 25.

taraph, m. a direction; pl. dat. as adv. *taraphan*, in all directions, xi, 5.

törīph, m. praise: *törīph-ĕ-Yūsūph*, praise of Joseph, vi, 17.

trapun, to shut (a room, viii, 3), (a door, viii, 11); past m. sg. with suff. 3rd pers. sg. ag. and 3rd pers. sg. dat. *trop*[u]*nas*, she shut (the door,—room) against him, viii, 3, 11.

trēsh, f. thirst; — *cĕñ*[ü], to drink thirst, i.e. to drink water to allay thirst, to drink water, viii, 7 (bis); — *lagüñ*[ü], thirst to be felt, to become thirsty, viii, 7.

troṭ[u], m. a necklace, xii, 5 (ter); sg. dat. *lāl traṭis sumb*[i], rubies sufficient for a necklace.

trāwun, to let go, let loose; to abandon, leave behind, ii, 10; xi, 11; to emit, give forth, i, 5 (sighs); xi, 11 (light); to cast, throw, v, 4 (many times); xii, 11, 2; to put off, doff (garments), v, 9; x, 2.

trāwun ārām, to take repose, iii, 3, 7; viii, 5; *trāwun kadam*, to put forth a step, to step forward, iv, 5; *trāwun yĕla*, to let go free, to release, iii, 4 (bis); x, 5 (ter), 12.

tshanun trövith, to let drop, throw down, xii, 16, 7; *tshunun trövith*, to throw or dash down and cast away, ii, 5; viii, 7 (bis)

trāwun kaḍith, to take off, doff (clothes), xii, 6; *trāwun mörith*, to kill (= Hindī *mār ḍālnā*), x, 8; *palang trāwun shīrith*, to make ready a bed, x, 7.

fut. pass. part. *gatshi kākad trāwun*[u], you must throw the paper, xii, 11; conj. part. *trövith*, ii, 5; viii, 7 (bis); xii,

16, 7; pres. part. *trāwān*, xi, 11; perf. part. sg. f. *tröv*ᵘ*-müts*ᵘ, x, 8.

impve. sg. 2, *trāv*, iii, 4; v, 9; pl. 2, *trövyuv* (for *tröviv*), x, 5; pol. pl. 2, *tröv*ⁱ*tav*, x, 5; fut. sg. 3, with suff. 2nd pers. sg. dat. *trāviy*, xii, 6; pres. m. sg. 3, *chuh trāwān*, xii, 2; imperf. m. sg. 3, *ôs*ᵘ *trāwān*, i, 5.

past m. sg. *trôw*ᵘ, xii, 7; with emph. *y*, *trôwuy*, iv, 5; with suff. 3rd pers. sg. ag. *trôwun*, ii, 10; iii, 3, 7; v, 4 (ter); x, 2; xii, 12; with ditto, and suff. 1st pers. sg. dat. *trôw*ᵘ*nam*, v, 4 (ter); with ditto, and suff. 2nd pers. sg. dat. *trôw*ᵘ*nay*, v, 4 (ter); with suff. 3rd pers. pl. ag. *trôwukh*, viii, 5; x, 5; with ditto, and suff. 3rd pers. sg. dat. *trôw*ᵘ*has*, x, 7, 12.

past f. sg. with suff. 3rd pers. sg. ag. *tröv*ᵘ*n*, iii, 4.

*trĕyum*ᵘ, ord. third, viii, 8; m. sg. dat. *trĕyimis*, viii, 8.

f. sg. nom. *trĕyim*ᵘ, xii, 19 (bis); abl. *trĕyimi laṭi*, on the third occasion, viii, 7.

tas, *tasond*ᵘ, see *tih*.

tasalī, m. satisfaction; — *ās-na*, satisfaction did not come to him, he did not become satisfied, vi, 16.

*tàt*ⁱ, adv. there, in that place, ii, 1; v, 1, 7, 9; viii, 12.

tati, adv. from there, thence, iv, 2; vii, 17; there, in that place (for *tàt*ⁱ), iv, 7; v, 7; x, 5; xii, 4, 6, 14, 6; with emph. *y*, *tatiy*, there verily, v, 9.

tōta, m. a parrot, ii, 4, 5 (bis), 6, 7 (bis), 8, 9, 11; sg. dat. *totas*, ii, 9; *tōtas-manz*, ii, 5, 8; ag. *tōtan*, ii, 7, 10.

*tot*ᵘ, adv. there, in that place, v, 1; xii, 7, 16; from there, thence, iii, 9.

tath, *tath*ⁱ, see *tih*.

*ṭôṭh*ᵘ, adj. beloved, iv, 4; i.q. *ṭhôṭh*ᵘ, q.v.

tithay, adv.; *tithay pöṭh*ⁱ, in that very manner, xii, 22. Cf. *tyuth*ᵘ.

tāv, m. fever caused by starvation; hence, exhaustion generally as in *sapharun*ᵘ *tāv*, exhaustion of the journey, exhaustion from long travel, xi, 13.

ṭuwun, to close (the eyes); 2 past f. pl. *ṭuvyēyĕ achĕ*, he closed his eyes, xii, 22.

tay 1, a pleonastic word put at the end of a line of verse, iv, 1 ff.

tay 2, m. authority; — *karun*, to rule, xi, 3.

tiy, that verily ; if that ; see *tih*.

töyiphdār, m. an artizan ; pl. dat. *-dāran*, xi, 16 (for genitive).

tayār, adj. ready, complete ; — *karun*, to make ready, to complete, prepare, iv, 2 ; xii, 18, 22.

tyūt^u, adv. so soon ; *yūt^u* . . . *tyūt^u*, as soon as . . . so soon, xii, 2.

tyuth^u, adj. such, of that kind ; m. pl. nom. with emph. *y*, *tithiy trĕh*, three times so many, xii, 24 ; f. pl. nom. *titsha*, such (women), xii, 19.

tyuth^u (with emph. *y*, *tyuthuy*) is often used adverbially to mean "so", "exactly so", v, 6 ; viii, 7 ; xii, 12, 5. Cf. *tithay*. In viii, 7, it means "at that very time".

tyuth^u is correlative of *yuth^u*, and *tyuthuy* of *yuthuy*.

tsĕ, see *ts^{a}h*.

tsŏcĕ, see *tsö̆ṭ^ŭ*.

ts^{a}h, thou, ii, 11 ; iii, 2 (fem.), 9 ; v, 3, 5, 7, 12 ; vi, 11 ; viii, 1 (bis), 3 (fem.), 6, 8, 10, 1 (fem. bis), 3 ; ix, 1 (bis) ; x, 1, 4, 5, 8, 12 ; xii, 1, 4 (bis), 5, 10, 3 (bis), 5 ; *ts^a-ti*, thou also, ix, 6 ; *ts^{a}y*, thou verily, i, 10 ; xii, 15.

sg. acc.-dat. *tsĕ*, v, 10 ; vi, 11 ; viii, 3, 11 ; x, 5, 12 ; xii, 3, 7 (bis), 13, 8, 21 ; *tsĕ-nishĕ*, in thy possession, x, 14.

ag. *tsĕ*, i, 12 (v.l.) ; ii, 11 (bis) ; xii, 20.

gen. For this, the possessive pronoun *cyôn^u* is used, q.v.

pl. nom. *tŏh^i*, viii, 3, 5 (ter), 13 ; xii, 1 (quater).

acc.-dat. *tŏhĕ-nish*, in your possession, x, 5, 12.

ag. *tŏhĕ*, x, 12.

gen. For this, the possessive pronoun *tuhond^u* is used, q.v.

tshāḍun or *tshāḍun*, to seek for, search for ; imperf. f. sg. 1, with suff. 3rd pers. sg. acc. *ös^{ū}san tshāḍān*, I (fem.) was seeking for him, xii, 15 : 3 past m. sg. with suff. 1st pers. sg. ag. *tshājyām*, I searched (earth and heaven), vii, 26. Cf. *tshārun*.

tshājyām, see *tshāḍun*.

tshanun or *tshunun* (*tshanun* is used only in villages), to cast, throw ; to put, place, viii, 6 ; x, 7 ; to put on (clothes), v, 9 (bis) ; x, 4 ; to apply (an ointment, medicine, etc.), v, 6 (bis) ; — *nöl^i*, to put on the neck, tie on to the neck, viii, 10 ; to put on (clothes), xii, 7 ; — *sabakas*, to put to a lesson, to teach, v, 6; *wŏth tshunüñ^ü*, to throw a leap, to leap, ii, 9; iii, 4; — *kaḍith*, to drive out, expel, viii, 10; to doff clothes, x, 9; — *nahīth*, to cancel, xii, 4; — *phirith*, to put upside down, iii, 5; — *trövith*, to let drop, throw down, xii, 16, 7; to dash down and cast away, ii, 5; viii, 7 (bis); — *tsaṭith*, to tear to pieces, xii, 15.

fut. pass. part. f. sg. *tshunüñ^ü*, iii, 4; perf. part. f. sg. neg. *chĕsna tshuñ^ümüts^ü sabakas*, I have not been taught, v, 6.

impve. sg. 2, *tshun*, iii, 5; v, 9; pol. sg. 2, *tshun-ta*, x, 4; fut. *tshån^izi*, xii, 16.

pres. m. sg. 3, *tshanān chuh*, xii, 17.

past m. sg. *tshon^u*, xii, 7; with suff. 3rd pers. sg. ag. *tshunun*, ii, 5; v, 6, 9 (bis); viii, 6; x, 7, 9; with ditto, and with suff. 3rd pers. sg. dat. *tshun^unas*, viii, 7 (bis); xii, 15; with suff. 3rd pers. pl. ag. *tshunukh*, viii, 10; with ditto, and with suff. 3rd pers. sg. dat. *tshun^uhas*, xii, 4; f. sg. with suff. 3rd pers. sg. ag. *tshuñ^ün*, ii, 9; viii, 10.

past cond. sg. 1, *tshunahö*, v, 6.

tshananāwun (village form for *tshunanāwun*), to cause to be cast; past pl. m. with suff. 3rd pers. sg. ag. *tshananövin*, x, 13.

tshŏpa, in *tshŏpa karith*, having made silence, in silence, xii, 4.

tshārun, a dialectic form of *tshāḍun*, q.v., to search for, seek; pres. m. pl. 3, *tshārān chih*, iii, 3; fut. pl. 1, *tshārav*, xi, 17.

tshĕta, adj. extinct; *nār gŏmot^u tshĕta*, the fire had become extinct, xii, 23.

tshōṭa, m. a stout stick, a club, iii, 1, 2.

tshāwul, a he-goat, iii, 5 (ter).

tshyoṭ^u, m. remains or leavings of food, orts, refuse, offal; hence, food which, as such, is considered to be defiled, x, 3, 12 (bis); fem. *tshĕṭ^ü-han*, a little waste food, x, 5.

tsüj^ü, etc., see *tsalun*.

tsakh, fem. rage; sg. abl. *tsakhi-hot^u*, m. full of rage, vii, 14; *tsakhi-nishĕ*, from anger, vii, 2.

tsalun, to flee, run away, ii, 7, 9; v, 5; vi, 8 (bis); viii, 4 (bis), 11 (bis), 3; ix, 1 (ter), 4; xii, 25; to escape by flight, ii, 8.

pres. part. *tsalān*, vi, 8; viii, 13; impve. pl. 2, *tsaliv*, viii, 4, 11; pres. subj. sg. 3, with irreg. suff. 2nd pers. pl. dat.

tsaliv, (I say) to you he may escape, ii, 8; imperf. m. sg. 3, *ôs^u tsalān*, xii, 25.

1 past, m. sg. 3, *tsol^u*, ii, 7; vi, 8; pl. 3, *tsȧl^i*, viii, 4, 11; f. sg. 3, *tsüj^ü*, ii, 9; v, 5.

2 past, f. sg. 1, *tsajyēyĕs*, I (fem.) fled, ix, 4.

perf. f. sg. 3, *chĕh tsüj^ümüts^ü*, ix, 1; 2, *chĕkh tsüj^ümüts^ü*, ix, 1; pluperf. f. sg. 3, *ös^u tsüj^ümüts^ü*, ix, 1.

tsamruw^u, adj. made of leather, leathern, xii, 16, 7.

tsŏn, see *tsōr*.

tsünḍ^ü, f. a blow, a stroke; —*lāyüñ^ü*, to strike a blow (with a sword), iii, 5, 6.

tsānun, to cause to enter; to bring in; past m. sg. with suff. 3rd pers. pl. ag. *tsônukh*, iii, 7; f. with suff. 3rd pers. sg. ag. and 1st pers. sg. *tsöñ^ünam lār*, he caused pursuit to enter for me, i.e. he caused me to run away, ix, 2. Causal of *atsun*, q.v.

tsop^u, m. a bite; pl. nom. *tsȧp^i hĕn^i*, to take bites, to bite repeatedly, x, 7.

tsŏpôr^u, adv. on all four directions, on all sides, ii, 3, 5; *tsŏpör^i*, id., xii, 21, 4.

tsēr, m. delay; — *gatshun*, delay to occur (to a person), to be delayed, to be late, iii, 1; v, 9; *tsēr-tāñ*, up to lateness, during a long time, v, 6.

tsīr^i, adv. late, iii, 1.

tsōr, card. four, x, 12 (ter); *gay tsōr*, they became four, viii, 5; following qualified noun, *mahaniv^i tsōr*, four men, x, 5; *mārawātal tsōr*, four executioners, x, 12; *nĕciv^i tsōr*, four sons, xii, 1.

Preceding qualified noun, *tsōr dŏh*, four days, xii, 23; *tsōr hath*, four hundred, x, 1 (bis); *tsōr katha* (f.), four statements, x, 6 (ter); *tsōr pahar*, four watches, viii, 5; *tsōr yār*, four friends, vii, 5; *tsōr zȧn^i*, four persons, x, 1 (bis).

pl. dat. *mārawātalan tsŏn*, to four executioners, x, 5; *tsŏn asmānan-pĕṭh*, on the four heavens, iv, 4; *tsŏn zanĕn*, to the four persons, viii, 5; x, 5 (bis), 12.

ag. *tsōrav zanĕv*, by four persons, x, 1, 2.

tsūr, m. a thief, x, 12 (ter); xii, 1; *lŏn^i-tsūr*, a fate-thief, a destroyer of good luck, vii, 12.

pl. nom. *tsūr*, viii, 9; xii, 1; ag. *tsūrav*, iii, 3 (bis); *tsūrau*, viii, 9 (bis).

tsūrü, f. theft; — *karüñu*, to do thieving, to be a professional thief, xii, 1; sg. dat. *gav tsūri* (for *tsūrĕ*), he went to steal, xii, 1; ag. *tsūri-pöṭhi*, like theft, secretly, xii, 6, 7, 17; *tsūri-pöṭhin*, id., iii, 1.

tsrôlu, m. a police spy, a detective. In v, the word is used in the sense of a police constable. pl. dat. *tsrālĕn*, v, 7.

tsārun, to pick out, select; past cond. sg. 3, *mānĕ tsārihĕ* (for *tsārihē*), he who might pick out (i.e. explain) the meaning, vi, 14.

tsōratsh, (?) f., a leather-cutter (the tool), xi, 14.

tsūryumu, ord. fourth; m. sg. dat. *tsūrimis*, viii, 11 (ter); ag. *tsūrimi*, xii, 1.

tsŏṭü, f. a loaf; pl. nom. *tsŏcĕ*, v, 7 (bis), 8 (bis).

tsāṭh, m. a pupil; sg. dat. *tsāṭas bāhan hatan-hondu*, (a leader) of twelve hundred pupils, v, 1.

tsāṭahāl, m. a school, viii, 4, 11; abl. *-hāla*, viii, 4.

tsaṭun, to cut, to tear. *tsaṭith tshanun*, to tear (a paper) to pieces, xii, 15; *sar* (or *kala*) *tsaṭun*, to behead, iii, 2; viii, 6, 11.

fut. pass. part. m. sg. *tas gatshi kala* (or *sar*) *tsaṭunu*, his head should be cut off, viii, 6, 11; pl. *tim gatshan tsaṭàni*, they must be cut, v, 4; conj. part. *tsaṭith*, xii, 15; fut. pl. 3, with suff. 3rd pers. sg. dat. *tsaṭanas*, they will cut for him, v, 7; do. interrog. *tsaṭanasa*, v, 7; past m. sg. *tsoṭu*, iii, 2; pl. with suff. 3rd pers. sg. ag. and 1st pers. sg. gen. *tsàṭinam*, ix, 5.

wa, conj. used in the corrupt Arabic phrase, *wa-salām*, *wa-yikrām*, and the peace, and the respect, a polite ending to a story, equivalent to "may peace and respect be upon the hearers", x, 14.

wŏbāl, f. a guilty condition, blameworthiness; sg. dat. *wŏbālī* (m.c. for *wŏbāli*), v, 2.

wuchun, to see; to look at, inspect, v, 5; vii, 18, 24; viii, 1, 3; to watch, iii, 1; viii, 6, 9.

inf. nom. with suff. of indef. art. *wuchunāh korunakh*, she made a look at them, i.e. she looked at them, viii, 3; abl. forming inf. of purpose, *wuchani*, in order to see, viii, 7.

impve. pol. sg. 2, *wuchta*, ix, 4; x, 5; pl. 2, *wuchitav*, viii, 1; with suff. 1st pers. sg. acc. *wuch*[i]*tōm,* please inspect me, vii, 24; indic. fut. sg. 2, *wuchakh,* iii, 8.

pres. m. sg. 1, *chus wuchān,* iii, 8; 2, *kyāh chukh wuchān,* what dost thou see? iii, 8; 3, *chuh wuchān,* iii, 1, 4, 7, 8; viii, 6, 9; xii, 4; *wuchān chuh,* iii, 7; xii, 19; with suff. 1st pers. sg. acc. *chum wuchān,* vii, 18; imperf. m. sg. 3, *ôs*[u] *wuchān,* iii, 1.

past m. sg. *wuch*[u], iii, 8; v, 9; xii, 15; with suff. 3rd pers. sg. gen. *wuchus chĕndas,* (she) looked into his pocket, v, 5; with suff. 3rd pers. sg. ag. *wuchun,* i, 4; ii, 1; iii, 8 (bis), 9; v, 5, 7 (with two singular grammatical subjects—one fem., the other, the nearer, masc.); viii, 6, 7 (bis), 9 (bis), 10; x, 5, 8; xii, 2, 7; with suff. 3rd pers. pl. ag. *wuchukh,* ii, 4; x, 8; xii, 1; *ath ölis wuchukh,* they looked at that nest, viii, 1; pl. *wuch*[i], v, 4; with suff. 1st pers. sg. ag. *wuchim,* vi, 15; with suff. 3rd pers. sg. ag. *wuchin,* v, 5; with suff. 3rd pers. pl. ag. *wuchikh,* v, 9; with ditto, and also suff. 3rd pers. pl. nom. *wuch*[i]*hakh,* they were seen by them, viii, 1.

f. sg. *wuch*[ü], x, 3; with suff. 3rd pers. sg. ag. *wuch*[ü]*n,* ii, 8; iii, 4, 5; x, 5; xii, 15; with suff. 3rd pers. pl. ag. *wuch*[u]*kh,* xii, 2; pl. with suff. 1st pers. sg. ag. *wuchĕm,* vi, 15.

past cond. sg. 1, *wuchaha* (for *-hö,* similarly the next), I would see, i.e. I should like to see, viii, 10; with suff. 3rd pers. sg. acc. *wuchahan,* I should like to see it, ii, 5; 3, *wuchihē,* viii, 10.

waḍ, f. crookedness, v, 1.

wāda, m. (*wa'da*), a vow. With *izāfat, wāda-y-Khŏda,* a vow by God; *wāday-Khŏdā dyun*[u], to swear by God, to make a vow in God's name, xii, 7 (bis), 15 (bis).

wŏḍ, f. the crown of the head; sg. dat. *wŏḍi-pĕṭh,* on the crown of the head, iii, 1; xi, 12, 6.

wōḍa, adv. from there, xii, 23. Cf. *ōra,* s.v. *ōr.*

wadun, to lament, to weep; fut. 1, neg. interrog. *wadanā,* shall I not weep? vii, 25; pres. f. sg. 1, *chĕs wadān,* ix, 1; imperf. f. sg. 3, *ös*[ü] *wadān,* vii, 16; m. pl. 3, *wadān ös*[i], xi, 5.

wŏdañĕ, erect, standing up, iii, 1, 8; viii, 6; — *rōzun,* to remain standing, to stand, xii, 1; *yih uuchukh ati wŏdañĕ*, they saw him standing there, xii, 1.

wāday, see *wāda*.

Vigiñāh, m. N. of a certain forest goddess; *Vigiñāh Nāg*, a spring sacred to her, v, 9 (ter).

Wahab, m. a Musalmān proper name, Wahb. *Wahab-Khār*, Wahb the Blacksmith, N. of the author of stories ii and vi; voc. *Wahab-Khāra*, ii, 12; vi, 17.

vih, m. poison; *pyōs wŏlinjĕ vih*, poison fell into his heart, i.e. he became in an agony of pain, v, 6.

wŏ̃h, adv. now, iii, 9; i.q. *wŏñ*, q.v.

wöjᵘ, f. a finger-ring, v, 1; x, 8 (bis); xii, 14 (bis), 15.

wakth, m. time; sg. abl. *ami wakta*, at that time, vi, 16.

wŏkawun, to draw forth, bring out; conj. part. *anun wŏkavith*, to draw out (e.g. from a store-room) and bring, vi, 16.

wŏla, see *yunᵘ*.

wŏlād, m. offspring, issue, progeny; *wŏlād-i-Ādam*, a descendant of Adam, iv, 3.

walaikum (borrowed from Arabic), and on you, xii, 26. Cf. *wa*.

walun, to wrap round anything; *tēgas walun phamb*, to wrap cotton wool round the blade (of a sword), viii, 6, 13; *zālas walun*, to wrap round in a net, to entangle in a net, ix, 7. Inf. abl. forming pass. *walana yunᵘ*, ix, 7; pres. m. sg. 3, *chuh walān*, viii, 13; past m. sg. with suff. 3rd pers. sg. ag. *wolun*, viii, 6.

wālun (causal of *wasun*), to cause to descend, to bring down, iii, 9; vii, 17 (bis); x, 8; xi, 11; *bŏn wālun*, id., viii, 1; *basta wālüñᵘ*, to bring the skin down, to flay a person alive, viii, 6; *kabari wālun*, to cause to descend into a tomb, to bury (a dead man), iv, 7; *kangañ wālüñᵘ*, to cause a comb to descend, to comb the hair, v, 4.

fut. pass. part. f. sg. *wālüñᵘ*, viii, 6; conj. part. *wölith*, vii, 17; n. ag. m. sg. nom. with emph. *y*, *wālawunuy*, immediately on bringing down, vii, 17; impve. sg. 2, with suff. 3rd pers. sg. acc. *wālun*, iii, 9; pl. 2, with same suff. *wālyūn*; indic. fut. pl. 1, *wālav*, xi, 11; 3, with suff. 1st pers. sg. acc. *wālanam*, iv, 7; pres. f. sg. 1, *chĕs wālān*, v, 4; past m. pl. with suff. 3rd pers. pl. ag. *wölikh*, viii, 1.

*wölinj*ᵘ, f. the heart, x, 5; sg. dat. *wölinjĕ*, v, 6; pl. nom. *wölinjĕ*, viii, 3, 4 (ter), 11 (bis), 2.

wālanay, f. bringing down; humiliation, humbling (a proud person), vii, 15.

*wālawösh*ⁱ, f. a kind of net made of hair (*wāl*), for catching birds or animals; sg. dat. (in sense of loc.) *-wāshi* (poet. for *wāshĕ*), v, 2.

wumēdwār, adj. hopeful, i, 13.

wumāh, a negative adv. signify "now not", as in *wumāh thāwath*, now I may not keep thee, how can I keep thee now, ii, 11.

wan, m. a forest, a wood; sg. dat. *wanas akis-manz*, (she arrived) in a certain forest, ix, 1; abl. *wana-manza*, from in the forest, ix, 4; gen. *wanuk*ᵘ, ix, 1, 3, 5; pl. dat. *wanan*, ix, 2; *path wanan*, at the back of the woods, vii, 10.

wān, m. a shop, i, 2 (bis); a shop, in the sense of a working place, e.g. a blacksmith's shop, xi, 17; abl. *wāna-wān*, from shop to shop, i, 2.

*won*ᵘ, m. a thing said (properly past part. of *wanun*); *wånⁱ dinⁱ*, to give sayings, to send messages, xi, 20.

wanun, to say, speak, till; *wanun phīrith*, to say in reply, to answer, v, 4; *wanun pot*ᵘ *phīrith*, id., x, 7.

inf. *pyōm wanun*, it fell to me to speak, I shall have to speak, xii, 10; abl. *lågⁱ wanani*, they began to say, x, 1; conj. part. *wanith*, vi, 16; *mŏkalôw*ᵘ *ami wanith*, she finished telling, ix, 6; perf. part. *won*ᵘ*mot*ᵘ, a thing said, iv, title; f. *wüñ*ᵘ*müts*ᵘ, vii, 30.

impve. sg. 2, *wan*, ix, 6; xi, 20; *wan-sa*, tell, sir, x, 1 (bis), 2; with suff. 1st pers. sg. dat. *wanum*, tell (say) to me, iii, 5; vi, 15 (bis); pl. 2, *waniv, kyāh kariv*, say ye what ye will do, xii, 1; *waniv-sa*, say ye, sirs, x, 6; with suff. 1st pers. sg. dat. *wanyūm*, tell ye me, x, 6; pol. sg. 2, *wanta*, iii, 9; x, 1, 8; *wanta-sa*, say please, sir, ii, 4; pl. 2, *wån*ⁱ*tav*, viii, 5; x, 1.

fut. sg. 1, *wana*, xii, 19; with suff. 2nd pers. sg. dat. *wanay*, I shall (would) say to (tell) thee, i, 12 (v.l.); viii, 6, 8, 11; ix, 4; x, 2 (bis); with suff. 2nd pers. pl. dat. *wanamōwa*, (a village form), x, 1 (bis), 2; 3, *wani*, vii, 20, 6;

with suff. 2nd pers. sg. dat. *waniy,* iii, 4; pl. 3, *wanan,* x, 12.

pres. m. sg. 3, (without auxiliary) *wanān,* v, 2 (to, *kun*); viii, 1 (bis), 11; ix, 1; *wanān chuh,* x, 6; with emph. *y, chuy wanān,* i, 13; vii, 3; with suff. 3rd pers. sg. dat. *chus wanān,* viii, 7; with suff. 3rd pers. pl. dat. *wanān chukh,* x, 7; f. sg. 3, *chĕh wanān,* vi, 2; vii, 1, 20, 6; *wanān chĕh,* ix, 6; with emph. *y, chĕy wanān,* vii, 16; with suff. 3rd pers. sg. dat. *chĕs wanān,* v, 2; *wanān chĕs,* v, 5.

past m. sg. *won*^{u}, x, 12; with suff. 1st pers. sg. ag. and 2nd pers. sg. dat. *won*^{u}*may,* I said to thee, xii, 20; with suff. 2nd pers. sg. ag. and 3rd pers. pl. dat. *won*^{u}*thakh,* thou saidst to them, x, 2; with suff. 3rd pers. sg. dat. *wonus,* said to him, xii, 25; with suff. 3rd pers. sg. ag. *wonun,* he said, viii, 11; neg. *wonun-na,* xii, 7; with suff. 3rd pers. sg. ag. and 3rd pers. sg. dat. *won*^{u}*nas,* v, 4; pl. with suff. 1st pers. sg. ag. and 3rd pers. sg. dat. *wån*^{i}*may,* iv, 1.

f. sg. with suff. 2nd pers. sg. ag. *wüñ*^{ü}*th,* x, 1; pl. with suff. 1st pers. sg. ag. and 2nd pers. pl. dat. *wañĕmōwa* (a village form), x, 1; with suff. 3rd pers. sg. ag. and 3rd pers. pl. dat. *wañĕnakh,* x, 1; with suff. 2nd pers. pl. ag. *wañĕwa,* x, 6.

past cond. sg. 3, *wanihē,* vii, 24 (bis).

wŏñ, adv. now, v, 6; vii, 26 (bis); viii, 7. Cf. *wŏh.*

wuñ, even now, now indeed, now, immediately, ii, 5; iii, 1, 2; v, 5, 6, 8; viii, 10, 1; ix, 4 (bis), 6 (bis), x, 5 (bis), 6, 7; xii, 6, 15, 8 (ter), 9; *wuñĕ,* now and on, still, still more, x, 1; *wuñ*^{ü}*y,* i.q. *wuñ,* viii, 7.

wŏphā, see *bē-wŏphā.*

wŏphādörī, f. loyalty, fidelity, faithfulness, ii, 2 (bis), 3, 4 (ter), 5, 6, 7, 10, 2.

wŏphöyī, see *bē-wŏphöyī.*

wöphīr, adj. (m.c. for *wöphir*), abundant, plentiful; *töbīr Yūsūphas chuh wöphīr,* there is abundant interpretation to Joseph, i.e. he is full of interpretation, vi, 14.

wŏpar, adj. other; *kus-tāñ wŏpar,* someone else, v, 4.

wāra 1, adj. well, safe, in good condition; *wāra-kāra,* safe and sound, x, 8.

wāra 2, adv. well, thoroughly, properly, vii, 24.

vir, ? gend., a fine (in money); *vir hěth*, bringing the money (to pay a fine), v, 7.

*wör*ᵘ 1, f. a kind of small earthen pot; pl. nom. *wārě*, xi, 13.

*wör*ᵘ 2, f. a garden, a field plot in which flowers (e.g. saffron) are cultivated; sg. abl. *wāri* and (m.c.) *wārē*, in the (saffron-) field, v, 7.

*vir*ⁱ*d*, m. skilled practice; hence, magic skill, magic power, ii, 3, 4.

wöridāth, ? gend. an occurrence, incident; *kari amis kěntshāh wöridāth*, he will do some occurrence to him, i.e. he will devise something against him, xii, 19.

warihy, m. a year; pl. nom. *warihy*, xii, 20.

*wŏra-mŏj*ᵘ, f. a step-mother, viii, 1, 11; sg. dat. *-mājě*, viii, 11.

*wŏra-něcyuv*ᵘ, a step-son; pl. gen. *-něcivěn-hond*ᵘ, viii, 3.

wartāwun, to deal out (to), distribute, apportion, dispense; pres. m. pl. 3, (*chih*) *wartāwān*, xi, 7.

wārayāh, adj. very much, excessive; *wārayāh kāl* (viii, 2) or — *kālāh* (viii, 2), or — *kālas* (iii, 1), for (during) a very long time.

*wöryuv*ᵘ, m. the house of a man's father-in-law, the house of a wife's father; sg. dat. *wörivis-manz*, x, 3.

*wŏrüz*ᵘ, f. the second wife of a widower, — *karüñ*ᵘ, (of a widower) to take a second wife, viii, 1, 11. (The word also means a woman who has married a second time, after the death of her first husband.)

věs, f. a female friend, a female crony, xii, 14; sg. voc. *věsī*, ix, 1; *vis*ⁱ*yiy*, ix, 11.

waīs, f. the age (of a person); sg. dat. *hath waīsi gav*, he went in age a hundred (years), i.e. he lived for a hundred years, ii, 12.

wōsh, m. a sigh, a groan; pl. nom. *ôs*ᵘ *trāwān āh ta wōsh*, he was emitting sighs and groans, i, 5. This word is more usually written *wŏsh*. It is here probably altered to *wōsh* for the sake of rhyme.

wasun, to descend, go down, come down, iii, 2, 5, 9 (bis); v, 9; vi, 16 (bis); viii, 6, 13; ix, 4, 6; x, 5; xii, 6, 7, 11; to come down (in the sense of coming along), to descend (upon a place), v, 7; *wasun bŏn*, to descend, get down, viii, 4; xii, 14, 5; *tal wasun*, to go down below, ix, 6; *wàth[i] guryau pĕṭha bŏn*, they dismounted from the horses, xii, 2; *wasith pyon[u]*, to fall down, tumble down, ii, 3, 6 (= Hindī *gir paṛnā*).

inf. sg. obl. *log[u] wasani*, he began to descend, viii, 6; fut. pass. part. f. sg. *chĕh tal wasüñ[ü] jāy*, there is a place to be descended below, i.e. there is a place to which one must (in the end) descend (sc. the grave), i.e. we must all die, ix, 6; conj. part. *wasith*, ii, 3, 6.

impve. pres. sg. 2, *was*, iii, 5, 9; pl. 2, *wasiv*, vi, 16; viii, 4; fut. *wàs[i]zi*, xii, 14; with neg. *wàs[i]zi-na*, xii, 11; indic. fut. sg. 3, with suff. 2nd pers. sg. dat. *wasiy*, she will descend in thy presence, xii, 6.

pres. m. sg. 3, *chuh wasān*, v, 7; *wasān chuh*, viii, 13.

past m. sg. 3, *woth[u]*, iii, 9; xii, 15; pl. 3, *wàth[i]*, vi, 16; x, 5 (m. and f. subject); xii, 3 (m. and f. subject); f. sg. 1, *wütsh[ü]s*, ix, 4; 3, *wütsh[ü]*, iii, 2; xii, 7; with emph. *y*, *wütsh[ü]y*, v, 9.

wustād, m. a preceptor, tutor, teacher; esp. the teacher from whom the reciter learnt the stories in this book. Very common in the phrase *dapān wustād*, "the teacher says," as in ii, 1, 5, 9, 10, 2, *et passim*; *wustādāh*, a certain teacher, i, 13.

wasth, m. an article, a thing; pl. nom. (for acc.) *wasth*, v, 1.

vis[i]yiy, see *vĕs*.

wath, f. a way, a road, a path, v, 9; xii, 14; *tath ös[ü]-na wath*, there was no path into it, i.e. no one was allowed to enter it, ii, 1; sg. abl. *wati*, (going) by or along a road, v, 7; x, 1; xii, 14, 5; *drāv yāra-sanzi wati*, he went forth by the road of his friend, i.e. he took the road to his friend's house, x, 4; *aḍa-wati*, on half the road, half-way, mid-way, vii, 20; *har-wati*, on every path, ii, 2; *wati wati*, along the road, vii, 17.

wāṭh, m. joining, uniting, junction, repairing something broken; *wāṭh karun*, to repair, join broken pieces, x, 12 (bis).

wŏṭh, f. a leap, jump; — *tulüñ[ü]*, to leap, ii, 9 (bis); — *ṭshunüñ[ü]*, id. iii, 4.

woth[u], see *wasun*.

wọ̆th[u], see *wŏthun*.

wŭṭh, m. a camel ; abl. *wŭṭha-bār*, m. pl. camel-loads, i, 9.

wŏthun, to arise, rise, ii, 3 ; iii, 1, 8 (bis) ; v, 6, 9 ; vi, 12, 3 ; xii, 3, 23 ; to arise (of some immaterial thing), to come into existence, to happen, iii, 3 (an outcry) ; vi, 15 (a famine) ; (with dat. of person), to rise in reply to a person, to up and answer, viii, 11 ; xii, 20 ; *phīrith wŏthun*, having replied to rise, to rise and answer, to up and answer, viii, 6 ; x, 2, 6 ; xii, 11 ; *wŏthun thod*ᵘ, to rise erect, to stand up, ii, 5, 6 ; v, 6, 9 ; xii, 14, 5.

conj. part. *wŏthith*, ii, 3 ; v, 6 ; impve. sg. 2, *wŏth*, iii, 8 (bis) ; indic. fut. sg. 3, *wŏthi*, vi, 15 ; with suff. 2nd pers. sg. dat. *wŏthiy thod*ᵘ, (the rock) will stand up before thee, xii, 14.

past m. sg. 3, *wọthᵘ*, ii, 5, 6 ; v, 9 ; vi, 12, 3 ; xii, 3, 15, 23 ; with suff. 3rd pers. sg. dat. *wọthus*, he up and answered him, viii, 6 ; x, 2, 6 ; xii, 21.

f. sg. 3, *wŏtshᵘ̈*, iii, 1, 3 ; with suff. 3rd pers. sg. dat. *wŏtshᵘ̈s*, she up and answered him, viii, 11 ; xii, 11, 20.

cond. past sg. 3, neg. *wŏthihĕ-na thod*ᵘ, he would not have stood up, i.e. he would not have been able to stand up, v, 9.

watharun, to spread out ; inf. sg. gen. *watharunuk*ᵘ *musla*, a skin of spreading out, a leather mat, xii, 18 (bis) ; conj. part. *watharith*, xii, 21.

*watharun*ᵘ, m. a mat, a carpet, xii, 24.

wŏtharun, to wipe clean ; inf. obl. *log*ᵘ *wŏtharani*, he began to wipe clean, viii, 6 ; imperf. m. sg. 3, *ôs*ᵘ *wŏtharān*, viii, 6, 13 (bis).

wātᵘ̈jᵘ̈, see *wātul*.

wātul, m. a sweeper, a mihtar ; sg. ag. *wātalⁱ*, xi, 14 ; voc. (addressed by his wife) *wātal-gānau*, O pimp of a mihtar, xi, 15 ; f. *wātᵘ̈jᵘ̈*, a mihtar's wife, sg. dat. *wātᵃjĕ*, xi, 14 ; voc. *wātᵃjⁱ*, xi, 15. Cf. *māra-wātul*.

wŏtamukhⁱ, adv. upside down, v, 9.

wātun, to arrive, come to, come up to, reach, ii, 8 ; iii, 1 (ter), 2 (bis), 3 (ter), 4, 7, 9 ; v, 1, 4 (bis), 6, 7, 8, 9, 11 ; vii, 12, 29 ; viii, 4, 5, 6, 7 (bis), 9, 10, 1 (bis) ; ix, 1 (bis) ; x, 2, 3, 4 (ter), 5 (bis), 6, 7 (bis), 9, 11, 4 (bis) ; xii, 1, 2, 4, 5 (ter), 8, 10 (ter), 1, 2 (bis), 3, 4, 5 (ter), 6, 7, 8 (ter), 9 (bis), 20, 2 (quater), 3, 4 (bis), 5 (bis) ; to arrive at (a person, dat.), get at (him), circumvent (him), xii, 13; to be suitable, to be proper, to be convenable (in this sense, the fut. is used in the sense of the present, like *gatshi*, see *gatshun* 1); *tsĕ ta asĕ wāti-na*, is not proper for thee and for us, viii, 3, 11; *kyāh wāti karun*ᵘ, what should be done? viii, 6, 8, 11.

In the sense of "arriving" if the object is a person, it is usually put in the dative governed by *nish*, as in *wôt*ᵘ *lālshĕnākas-nish*, he came to the lapidary, xii, 25; so *mĕ-nish*, to me, xii, 22 (bis); *wazīras-nish*, to the vizier, xii, 5, 10, 3, 9; *yāras-nish*, to (his) friend, x, 4, 11; *zanāni-nish*, to the woman, xii, 4. Or it may be indicated by a pronominal suffix, as in *wôtus*, he came to him, xii, 10; *wötsᵘ̈s*, she came to her, ix, 1; xii, 15.

If the object is not a person it may remain simply in the nom. form of the acc. as in *wôt*ᵘ *panun*ᵘ *shĕhar*, he arrived at his own city, x, 9; *wôt*ᵘ *gara*, he reached the house, iii, 3; v, 1, 4; x, 4, 6, 14; xii, 1, 5, etc.; or it may be put in the dative, as in *wôt*ᵘ *tath jāyĕ*, he arrived at that place, xii, 15; or a postposition may be used, as in *wôt*ᵘ *shĕharas-kun*, he arrived at the city, x, 5; or (with *manz*) *chuh wātān bāgas-manz*, he arrives in a garden, iii, 7; so *janatas-manz*, in heaven, xii, 24 (bis); *shĕharas-manz*, in the city, x, 14; xii, 2; *wanas-manz*, in a forest, ix, 1; or (with *pĕṭh*) *wôt*ᵘ *nāgas pĕṭh*, he arrived at the spring, iii, 4; xii, 12. It will be observed that the word *shĕhar*, a city, may be used either by itself or with *kun* or with *manz*.

inf. obl. *log*ᵘ *wātani*, he began to arrive, viii, 6; fut. past part. m. sg. nom. *gotsh*ᵘ *wātun*ᵘ, v, 7; *gatshi wātun*ᵘ, xii, 22 (bis); perf. part. m. sg. nom. *wôt*ᵘ*mot*ᵘ, xii, 22; conj. part. *wötith*, vii, 12; xii, 18.

fut. sg. 1, *wāta*, xii, 24; 2, *wātakh*, xii, 16, 24; 3, *wāti*, iii, 9; viii, 6, 8, 11; xii, 15; neg. *wāti-na*, viii, 3, 11; pres. m. sg. 2 neg. *chukh-na wātān*, xii, 13; 3, *chuh wātān*, iii, 7.

past m. sg. 3, *wôt*ᵘ, ii, 8; iii, 1 (bis), 3, 4; v, 1, 4 (bis), 6; viii, 4, 7 (bis), 9, 10, 1 (bis); x, 3, 4 (bis), 5 (bis), 6, 7 (bis), 9, 11, 4 (bis); xii, 1, 4, 5 (ter), 10 (bis), 1, 2 (bis), 3, 4, 5, 7, 8, 9 (bis), 20, 2, 3, 5 (bis); with suff. 3rd pers. sg. dat. *wôtus*, xii, 10; pl. *wöt*^{i}, iii, 1 (m. and f. subject); v, 9 (ditto), 11; viii, 5; x, 2, 4; xii, 2 (m. and f. subject), 8 (ditto), 18 (ditto).

f. sg. 3, *wöts*^{ü}, iii, 2 (bis), 3; v, 8; ix, 1; with suff. 3rd pers. sg. dat. *wöts*^{ü}*s*, ix, 1; xii, 15.

fut. perf. m. sg. 3, *āsi wôt*^{u}*mot*^{u}, vii, 29.

3 past m. sg. 3, *wātsāv*, iii, 3.

wātanāwun, to cause to arrive; fut. pl. 3, *wātanāwan*, v, 9; past m. sg. with suff. 3rd pers. sg. ag. *wātanôwun*, iii, 9; viii, 9 (bis); f. sg. with same suff. *wātanöw*^{ü}*n*, v, 10.

wātawun^{u}, n. ag. of *wātun*, one who arrives, with emph. *y*, as adv. *wātawunuy*, immediately on arriving, xii, 15.

wöts^{ü}, see *wātun*.

wŏtsh^{u}, see *wŏthun*.

wütsh^{ü}, see *wasun*.

wutsha-prang, m. a flying couch, equivalent to the flying carpet of English fairy-tales, xii, 18.

wöts^{ü}*s*, *wātsāv*, see *wātun*.

wawun, to sow; past m. pl. with suff. 1st pers. sg. ag. *wåwim*, ix, 9.

vyūr^{u}, m. flower-nectar; with suff. of indef. art. *vyūr*^{u}*āh*, a little nectar, a drop of nectar, ix, 2.

wāz, m. a sermon (Musalmān); pl. nom. (for acc.) *wāz*, xii, 1.

viz, f. a time, a season; abl. *harda-vizi*, in the autumn season, ix, 8.

wuzun, to awake, be awakened, aroused; past f. sg. 3, *wuz*^{ü}, viii, 11; with suff. 3rd pers. sg. dat. *wuz*^{ü}*s*, viii, 11. In both cases of an evil desire.

wazīr, m. a prime-minister, a vizier, ii, 1, 6 (bis), 11 (ter); viii, 4, 11, 4; xii, 1, 2 (quater), 4, 5, 10 (bis), 3, 9 (bis), 22, 3, 4, 5 (ter), 6; sg. dat. *wazīras*, ii, 4 (bis), 5 (bis); viii, 11; xii, 4, 5, 5 (*nish*), 10 (*nish*), 3 (*nish*), 9, 9 (*nish*); ag. *wazīran*, ii, 4, 5 (bis), 7; viii, 1, 4, 12; xii, 1, 19, 25; gen. *wazīra-sandi gari*, in the vizier's house, xii, 4, 5; voc. *ay wazīra* (addressed by a subordinate), xii, 4; *wazīra* (ditto), xii, 13; *ha wazīra* (ditto), xii, 19; *hā wazīra* (ditto), xii, 10; *hā wazīrō* (addressed by a superior), ii, 4; pl. nom. *wazīr*, viii, 1, 2; dat. *wazīran*, viii, 4; ag. *wazīrau*, vi, 16; viii, 2.

wazīrī, f. the post or office of a vizier, viziership, xii, 26.

y (*izāfat*), see *ĕ*, *i*, *y*.

yā, conjunct. or, ii, 12; viii, 1; *yā* . . . *yā*, either . . . or, x, 3, 7; xii, 9.

yi 1 (*izāfat*), see *ĕ*, *i*, *y*.

yi 2, *yī*, see *yih* 1.

Yiblīs, m. Iblīs, Satan, the Devil, iv, 2.

Yibrāhim, Abraham (the Patriarch), iv, 6.

yād, m. memory, remembrance; *yād-i-Alāh*, memory of God, i, 7; *nás*[i]*yĕth yād hĕth*, keeping the advice in mind, xii, 17; *yād pāwun*, to cause memory to fall, to cause to be remembered, (dat. of obj. remembered), vi, 11; *yād pyon*[u], memory to fall, remembrance to come (to so and so), iii, 5; vii, 20; xii, 15; *amis dôd*[u] *ôs*[u] *pĕmot*[u] *yād*, to her the pain has fallen (as) memory, i.e. she bore in mind the pain, xii, 15; *chus pĕwān nayistān yād*, the canebrake falls to her as a memory, she remembers the canebrake, vii, 26.

yĕḍ, f. the belly; with suff. of indef. art. *yĕḍāh*, ix, 7.

yīdam, m. (corruption of the Sanskrit *idam*), this (world), vii, 6.

yīd[i]*kāh*, m. an *'Īdgāh*, the common outside a town where Musulmāns celebrate the 'Īd services (put by an anachronism in Joseph's time), vi, 16 (bis).

yĕg-jāh, see *yĕkh-jāh*.

yih 1, pron. demonstr. this; (referring to a person or thing near by, or just referred to), he, she, it. See *nŏth* or *nĕth*.

ANIMATE. SUBST. MASC. sg. nom. *yih*, this (referring to a male), xii, 2 (bis), 15; he, ii, 9, 11; iii, 7, 8; v, 5; viii, 6, 13; x, 1, 2, 5 (bis), 6, 12 (bis); xii, 1, 3 (quater), 6, 15, 24, and others; *yuh* (for *yih*[u]), he, xii, 5; *yüh*, this, ii, 9; x, 12; with emph. *y*, *yihuy*, he verily, x, 7; xii, 15; *yŏhay*, him verily (nom. form of acc.), x, 8; *yuhuy*, x, 1; *yi-ti*, this one also, x, 8.

pl. nom. *yim*, they (masc.), ii, 3; viii, 1, 3, 13; x, 1 (bis); xii, 2, 3, 23; they (one masc. and one fem.), xii, 18.

dat. *yiman*, to them (masc.), vii, 24; viii, 1, 3, 11; x, 12 (bis); xii, 21; to them (masc. and fem.), v, 8; in sense of gen., of them, viii, 1, 4, 11, 12 ; with emph. *y*, *yiman*$^{\ddot{u}}$*y*, to them verily, vii, 20 ; viii, 13.

ag.-abl. *yimau*, by them, ii, 3 ; viii, 1, 3, 5 ; xii, 1 (bis), 17 (bis), 22 ; *yimav*, v, 8 ; viii, 11 ; x, 6, 12 ; *yimōv*, x, 1 ; with emph. *y*, *yimav*$^{\ddot{u}}$*y syod*^{u}, in front of them verily, viii, 6 (m. and f.).

gen. (f. nom.) *yihünz*$^{\ddot{u}}$, of these (birds, masc.), viii, 1.

FEM. sg. nom. *yih*, this (referring to a female), v, 10 (ter), 12 ; x, 8 ; xii, 25 ; she, ii, 8 ; iii, 4 ; v, 6, 10 (ter) ; viii, 3 ; xii, 4 (ter), 15, 20 ; with emph. *y*, *yihay*, she verily, xii, 20.

pl. dat. *yiman pata*, after them, xii, 7.

ag. with emph. *y*, *yimav*$^{\ddot{u}}$*y*, by them verily, iii, 7.

ADJ. MASC. sg. nom. *yih*, this, ii, 8, 9 ; iii, 3, 4 ; v, 5, 10, 1 ; viii, 6 (bis), 7, 9 (ter), 10, 3 (bis) ; ix, 4 (bis) ; x, 5, 7 (bis), 8, 10 (bis), 3, 4 ; xii, 1, 3, 4 (ter), 7, 10 (ter), 3 (bis), 5 (bis), 8, 21 (ter), 2, 4, 5, and others ; *yüh*, in *yus yüh wazīr ôs*^{u}, he who was this vizier, ii, 11.

dat. *yimis*, to this, iii, 8 ; x, 5.

ag. *yim*^{i}, by this, x, 2, 12.

pl. nom. *yim*, these, v, 9 ; viii, 1 (m. and f.), 3 (bis), 5 (bis), 11 (quater).

dat. *yiman*, to these, ii, 11 ; vii, 24 ; viii, 1, 3, 4, 11 (bis) ; x, 5.

ag. *yimau*, by these, v, 7 ; viii, 3, 9 ; *yimav*, iii, 1 ; x, 1, 5 ; x, 12 (bis).

FEM. sg. nom. *yih*, this, iii, 1 ; v, 7, 8, 9, 10 ; viii, 1 ; ix, 1, 4 ; x, 7 ; xii, 1, 2, 4 (bis), 5, 6, 7, 13, 5, 8, 20, 5, and perhaps others.

pl. nom. *yima*, these, iii, 8.

dat. *yiman*, to these, xii, 11, 4, 9, 20.

INANIMATE. SUBST. MASC. sg. nom. *yih*, this, iii, 4 (bis), 8, 9 (bis) ; vi, 16 ; viii, 7, 11 ; x, 4, 5 (bis), 7, 12 ; xii, 4 (bis), 16, 23, and others ; it, viii, 7 ; with emph. *y*, *yī*, this indeed, vi, 8 ; *yihuy*, this verily, viii, 10 (bis) ; *yiy*, this very thing, viii, 1 ; this verily, ii, 5 ; *yīy*, this verily, vii, 24 ; iii, 9 ; with conj. *ay*, if, *yiy*, if this, iii, 4 (bis), 9.

dat. *yith*, to this, v, 1, 6 ; viii, 9 ; xii, 21.

pl. nom. *yim*, these (referring to masc. inan. things), x, 2, 12; *yima* (referring to fem. inan. things), viii, 4.

Adj. sg. nom. *yih*, this, ii, 3, 10 (bis); v, 6; viii, 1, 5, 7 (bis), 9, 10, 3; x, 1, 4 (bis), 5; xii, 7, 11, 2, 5 (bis), 7 (bis), 8, 22, 3 (bis), 5, and others; with emph. *y*, *yihōy*, verily this, v, 10; *yuhay*, this very, xi, 2.

dat. *yith*, to this, iii, 5, 8 (bis), 9; v, 9; x, 5, 12.

abl. *yimi*, from this, viii, 4, 11.

pl. nom. *yim*, these (masc. things), v, 12; x, 12; xii, 6; *yima*, these (fem. things), v, 8; viii, 4: x, 1, 2, 6; with emph. *y*, *yimay* (fem.), these very, xii, 3, 23.

dat. *yiman*, to these, x, 5.

It will be observed that when emph. *y* is added to *yih*, the word takes several varying forms. As occurring in these tales they are as follows: *yihuy* (an. m. and inan.), *yihay* (an. f.), *yihōy* (inan.), *yuhuy* (an. m.), *yŏhay* (an. m.), *yuhay* (inan.), *yiy* (inan.), *yīy* (inan.), *yī* (inan.).

yih 2, pron. rel. who, which, what. In construction, the antecedent clause as a rule contains a demonstrative or other pronoun as correlative, but in the following cases there is no correlative pronoun:—

(*a*) Relative clause preceding antecedent clause, ii, 9; xi, 3, 8.

(*b*) Antecedent clause preceding relative clause, v, 7.

When there is a correlative pronoun it is most usually some form of the demonstrative pronoun *tih*, q.v., as in—

(*a*) Relative clause preceding antecedent clause, ii, 4, 7, 8 (bis), 11; iii, 1, 8 (ter); v, 8, 9; vi, 16; vii, 1, 29; viii, 6, 8, 9, 11; ix, 9; x, 1 (bis), 6, 12 (bis); xi, 1; xii, 3, 7 (bis), 20, 2.

(*b*) Antecedent clause preceding relative clause, ii, 7; v, 5; vii, 8, 29, 30; x, 1, 6, 10, 2; xii, 4, 7, 11, 5, 25.

Or the correlative pronoun may be some form of *yih* 1, as in (in every case the antecedent clause preceding), x, 5; xii, 20, 5.

Or it may be some form of the pronoun *ath*, as in (antecedent clause in each case preceding), ii, 9; vi, 14; x, 7.

In vi, 14, the antecedent is the genitive of the interrogative pronoun *kyāh*, i.e. *kamyuk*ᵘ, of what?

Sometimes the correlative pronoun is used twice, once immediately after the relative, and again in the antecedent clause, which in this case follows the relative clause. The repeated correlative is not necessarily the same as the one after the relative pronoun. Thus, *yus suh tōta ôs*ᵘ, *yüh ôs*ᵘ *phakīras nishĕ*, who he (i.e. he who) was the parrot, he was with the faqīr, ii, 9; so *yus yüh wazīr ôs*ᵘ, *suh chuh hāpatas-manz*, he who was the vizier, he is (now) in the bear, ii, 11; *yus yih pātashāha-sond*ᵘ *mor*ᵘ *ôs*ᵘ, *yih trôwun*, that which was the body of the king, that he abandoned, ii, 10; *yĕsa yih Lālmāl Parī ös*ᵘ, *tas dyutun rukhsath*, she who was the Fairy Lālmāl, to her he gave leave to depart, xii, 25; *yĕsa yih pata üñ*ᵘ*n zīnith, sa thöv*ᵘ*n pānas*, she whom he had won and afterwards brought home, her he kept for himself, xii, 25.

Like the demonstrative pronouns, the relative pronoun has animate and inanimate forms, and either of these may be substantival or adjectival. But in some cases in which we should look upon the relative as a substantive it is treated as an adjective. This is specially the case when the antecedent correlative is an adjective. In such a case the relative, even if not in direct agreement with a noun, also takes the adjectival form. Thus, *suh lāl, yus tujyān*, xii, 4, that ruby which she had taken up. Here we have the inanimate adjectival form *yus*, because the antecedent correlative, *suh*, is an adjective. The inanimate substantival form would be *yih*. Similarly, *yih panun*ᵘ *saphar, yus nöyidan ôs*ᵘ *pēsh on*ᵘ*mot*ᵘ, this (*yih*) his suffering, which he experienced at the hands of the barber, xii, 25.

The following forms of this pronoun occur in these tales:—

ANIMATE. SUBST. MASC. sg. nom. *yus*, ii, 7 (bis), 8, 11; v, 9; vi, 14; vii, 29; x, 1, 6, 12 (bis); *yus-akhāh*, whoever, viii, 6, 8, 11.

dat. *yĕs*, ii, 8, 9; vi, 16; vii, 1, 29, 30.

ag. *yĕm*ⁱ, xii, 7.

pl. nom. *yim*, ii, 9; xi, 8.

ag. *yimav*, xi, 3.
FEM. sg. nom. *yĕsa*, x, 6 ; xii, 20, 5.
dat. *yĕs*, xii, 15.
ADJ. MASC. sg. nom. *yus*, ii, 9, 11 ; x, 12 ; xii, 25.
FEM. sg. nom. *yĕsa*, x, 1 ; xii, 25.
INANIMATE. SUBST. sg. nom. *yih*, v, 7 ; viii, 9 ; x, 1 ; xii, 6, 7 (bis), 20 ; with emph. *y*, *yiy*, what verily, xi, 1 ; *yih-kĕntshāh*, whatever, iii, 1, 8 (ter) ; v, 8.
dat. *yĕth*, x, 7, 10.
abl. *yĕmi*, xii, 11.
pl. nom. (masc.) *yim*, v, 5 ; x, 5.
ADJ. sg. nom. *yus*, ii, 4, 10 ; vi, 14 ; xii, 4, 25.
abl. *yĕmi sātay*, at what time verily, vii, 8.
pl. nom. (masc.) *yim*, ix, 9.

yuh, *yüh*, see *yih* 1.

*yihünz*ᵘ, see *yih* 1.

yihay, *yihōy*, *yihuy*, *yŏhay*, *yuhay*, *yuhuy*, see *yih* 1.

yikh, see *yun*ᵘ.

yĕkh-jāh, adv. in one place, (of two persons) together, x, 12 ; *yĕg-jāh*, id., ii, 4.

yikrām, in *wa-salām wa-yikrām*, interj. (may) both the peace and respect (be on you) (corrupt Arabic), x, 14.

yĕl, m. pulling (with the arms), restraint ; abl. *yĕla trāwun*, to release from restraint, to let a person go, iii, 4 (bis) ; x, 5 (ter), 12.

yĕli, relative adv. when, at what time, ii, 3, 7 (bis) ; iii, 8 ; iv, 7 ; v, 5, 6 (bis), 9 ; vi, 11 ; vii, 19 (ter), 26 ; viii, 6, 7, 10 ; ix, 5, 7 ; x, 1, 3 (ter), 4 (bis), 5, 7 ; xi, 1 ; xii, 1, 15 (bis), 6, 8, 22. In v, 8, " when " is used in the sense of " if ".

*yĕm*ⁱ, *yĕmi*, see *yih* 2.

yim 1, *yima*, *yimau*, *yim*ⁱ, *yimi*, see *yih* 1.

yim 2, see *yih* 2.

yimahö, see *yun*ᵘ.

yimāmath, ? gender, the office of a leader of prayers in a mosque, *bŏh kara yimāmath*, I shall act as prayer-leader in a mosque, I shall adopt the profession of such a leader, xii, 1.

yiman, *yiman*ᵘ*y*, *yimis*, see *yih* 1.

yāmath, adv. as long as, *tāmath . . . yāmath*, so long . . . as, xi, 20.

yimav 1, *yimōv*, *yimav^{ü}y*, see *yih* 1.

yimav 2, see *yih* 2.

yimawa, see *yun^{u}*.

yimay, see *yih* 1.

yimōy, see *yun^{u}*.

yina, conj. that not. *karay akh kath, yina-sa kath karakh*, I say to thee one word, viz. that, sir, you will not make conversation, i.e. I tell you one thing,—do not converse, xii, 1.

yini, see *yun^{u}*.

yun^{u}, to come, i, 8; ii, 2, 3, 12; iii, 1 (bis), 3, 4 (bis); v, 5 (quinquies), 6 (bis,) 7, 9 (bis), 10, 1; vi, 2 (bis), 15, 6 (bis); viii, 2, 3 (bis), 6 (bis), 7 (ter), 8, 9, 11 (ter), 3 (ter); ix, 1, 3, 6, 7, 8 (bis), 12; x, 1, 3 (bis), 4, 5, 6, 7, 12 (quinquies), 4; xi, 20; xii, 1, 3 (bis), 4 (quater), 5 (ter), 6 (bis), 7 (quinquies), 10, 2, 3 (bis), 4, 5 (bis), 6, 20, 3 (bis), 4.

āv armān, longing came (to the king), i.e. he felt longing, iii, 9; *bāgȧn^{i} yun^{u}*, to come by (one's) share, to obtain on 's share allotted by fate, to receive one's fated portion, ix, 4; *brūha yun^{u}*, to come in front, to be seen in front of a person, to come into sight, x, 1; *bŏy yiñ^{ü}*, a smell to come, a smell to be perceived, xii, 15; *gara panun^{u} yun^{u}*, to come to one's own house, to go home, v, 10 (bis); xii, 5, 13; *lārān yun^{u}*, to come running, viii, 6; *nĕnd^{a}r yiñ^{ü}*, sleep to come, v, 6 (bis); *āv tsūrimis zȧn^{i}-sond^{u} pahar*, the watch of the fourth man came, i.e. it was now the time for him to go on watch, viii, 11; *phakh chus yiwān*, a stink comes from it, i.e. it stinks, ii, 4; *rāth āyĕ*, night came, x, 5; *subuh log^{u} yini*, morning began to come, x, 8; so *subuh āv*, morning came, xii, 9; *tasalī ās-na*, satisfaction did not come to him, i.e. he was not satisfied, vi, 16; *āyĕ zabān*, speech came, i.e. she became able to speak, ix, 1.

With conj. parts. we have *hĕth yun^{u}*, having taken to come, i.e. to bring, to take with one (Hindī *lē ānā*), iii, 1; viii, 6; xii, 2, 5, 11, 2; *nīrith yun^{u}*, to come forth, xii, 12; *phīrith yun^{u}*, to come back, to return, v, 1, 4, 10 (bis).

With the abl. of the infinitive of another verb *yun*^{u} forms a passive, as in *k*^{a}*nana yun*^{u}, to be sold, vii, 26 ; *walana yun*^{u}, to become wrapped up, ix, 7. The passive of *bōzun*, to hear, *bōzana yun*^{u}, means (1) (potentially) to be visible, xii, 22 ; or (2) to be considered as such and such, to appear to be such and such, viii, 5; x, 4 (bis); or (3) to be known, recognized, as such and such, xii, 3.

inf. *mě na bani yun*^{u}, to come will not be possible for me, i.e. I shall not be able to come, x, 3 ; *tsě gatshi yun*^{u}, thou must come, xii, 7 ; *tuhond*^{u} *gatshi yun*^{u}, you must come, xii, 15 ; abl. *subuh log*^{u} *yini*, morning began to come, x, 8 ; fut. pass. part. f. *hĕts*^{ū}*nas yiñ*^{ü} *nĕnd*^{a}*r*, sleep began to come to him, v, 6 ; perf. part. m. sg. *āmot*^{u}, come (H. *āyā huā*), viii, 6.

impve. sg. 2 (irreg.) *wŏla*, v, 5 ; x, 5, 12 ; pol. sg. 2, *yita*, with emph. *y*, *yitay*, ix, 1 ; with suff. 1st pers. sg. dat. *yitam*, please come to me, vi, 2.

fut. sg. 1, *yima*, with suff. 2nd pers. pl. dat. *yimawa*, I will come to you, xii, 1 ; 2, with neg. interrog. *yikh-nā*, wilt thou not come ? vi, 2 ; 3, *yiyi*, xii, 16 ; with suff. 2nd pers. sg. dat. *yiyiy*, will come to thee, v, 6 (bis) ; xii, 6 ; pl. 1, *yimav*, with suff. 2nd pers. sg. dat. *yimōy*, we shall come to thee, v, 10 ; 3, *yin*, with suff. 2nd pers. sg. dat. *yinay*, they will come before thee, xii, 6.

pres. m. sg. 3, *chuh yiwān*, xii, 3 ; *yiwān chuh*, v, 5 ; xii, 4 ; neg. *yiwān chuna*, xii, 22 ; with suff. 3rd pers. sg. abl. *chus yiwān*, is coming from it, ii, 4 ; pl. 2, *chiwa yiwān*, viii, 5 ; f. sg. 3, *chĕh yiwān*, xii, 15 ; with suff. 3rd pers. sg. dat. and neg. *chĕs-na yiwān*, v, 6 ; imperf. f. pl. 3 (auxiliary omitted) *yiwān*, vi, 15.

1 past m. sg. 1, *ās*, x, 12 ; 2 (with vocative suff. *ō*) *ākhō*, ii, 2 ; 3, *āv*, i, 8 ; ii, 3, 12 ; iii, 1, 9 ; v, 1, 4, 9, 10 ; vi, 16 (bis) ; viii, 3, 6 (ter), 7, 8, 9, 10, 1 (bis), 3 ; x, 6, 7, 12, 20 ; xii, 3, 4 (ter), 5 (quinquies), 7 (bis), 9, 10, 11, 2 (bis), 3 (ter), 4, 20, 3, 4 ; with suff. 1st pers. sg. dat. *ām*, viii, 13 ; with suff. 2nd pers. sg. dat. *ôy*, x, 4 ; xii, 3 ; irreg. with neg. interrog. *āy-nā*, did there not come to thee ? ix, 3 ; with suff. 3rd pers.

sg. dat. *ās*, viii, 7 (bis); x, 4; with neg. *ās-na*, vi, 16; x, 4; with suff. 3rd pers. pl. dat. *ākh*, x, 1 (bis).

pl. 1, *āy*, v, 9 (m. and f.); x, 6, 7, 8, 12; 3, *āy*, viii, 2, 11, 3; ix, 7, 8; with suff. 1st pers. sg. dat. *ām*, viii, 3, 11.

fem. sg. 1, *āyĕs*, ix, 4; 2, *āyĕkh*, iii, 1; 3, *āyĕ*, iii, 4 (bis); v, 5, 7, 10; vii, 26; ix, 1; x, 5, 12; xii, 2, 7; with neg. *āyĕ-na*, v, 6; with neg. interrog, ix, 3; with suff. 1st pers. sg. dat. *āyĕm*, v, 5; pl. 3, *āyĕ*, xii, 7.

3 past m. sg. 3, *āyāv*, with suff. 1st pers. sg. dat. *āyām*, iii, 3.

perf. m. sg. 3, *āmot*^{u} (without auxiliary), v, 11; *chuh āmot*^{u}, x, 12, 4; f. sg. 3, with suff. 2nd pers. sg. dat. *chĕy āmüts*^{ü}, v, 5; plup. m. sg. 3, with suff. 1st pers. sg. dat. *ôsum āmot*^{u}, iii, 1; fut. perf. m. sg. 3, *mā āsi āmot*^{u}, I wonder if he has come, xii, 23.

cond. past sg. 1, *yimahö*, x, 3.

yĕngur, charcoal, pl. nom. *yĕngar*, xi, 17.

yinsān, m. a human being, a man, x, 7; xii, 7; *-hyuh*^{u}, like a human being, x, 7 (bis); fem. *-hish*^{ü}, x, 7.

yinsāph, m. compassion, — *gōs* (viii, 4) or *dilas yinsāph pyōs* (viii, 11), he felt compassion.

yinay, see *yun*^{u}.

yāñ, adv. as soon as, xii, 15.

yiñ^u, see *yun*^{u}.

yĕñĕwôl^u, m. the bridegroom's party in a marriage festival; hence, a marriage festival (from the bride's point of view), xii, 15; — *karun*, to hold a marriage festival, xii, 17, 18.

yipör^i, adv. in this direction, v, 4. Cf. *apör*^{i}.

yār, m. a friend, iv, 4; x, 1, 4, 6; sg. dat. *yāras*, x, 4, 11; ag. *yāran*, x, 4 (bis), 11; gen. *yāra-sond*^{u}, x, 4, 11; *yāra-sanzi wati*, on the friend's road, on the road to (his) friend, x, 4; voc. *yāra*, O friend, vi, 1, etc.; x, 4 (bis); pl. nom. *yār*, iv, 7; v, 9; vii, 5.

yōr, adv. here, in this place, ii, 2; viii, 5; ix, 6, 8, 10, 2; x, 4.

yōra 1, adv. hence, from this place, v, 8.

yōra 2, rel. adv. whence, from what place (with *tōra* as correlative), i, 6.

yūr^i, adv. emph. form of *yōr*, even here, hither; *diyiv yūr^i*, give ye (them) even here, produce them, x, 12; *wōlinj^u gatshēs yūr^i anūñ^u*, bring his heart here (hither), x, 5; *an kākad yūr^i*, bring the paper here (hither), xii, 15; *cyôn^u gatshi wātun^u yūr^i*, you must come here (hither), xii, 23; sg. gen. *yūr^i-hond^u wŏla*, come here! v, 5.

Yārkand, m. the town of Yarkand, in Central Asia, xi, 1, etc.

yīran, f. an anvil, xi, 16.

Yīrān, m. Iran, Persia, ii, 1.

yĕs, yĕsa, yus, see *yih* 2.

Yīsāh, m. Jesus, iv, 4.

Yūsūph, m. Yūsuf, Joseph, vi, 1, etc.; sg. dat. *yūsūphas*, vi, 14, 16; ag. *yūsūphan*, vi, 15 (bis); gen. *yūsūpha-sond^u*, vi, 10.

yĕti, adv. where, in the place which, viii, 11; x, 7.

yit^i, adv. here, xii, 18; *yit^i-kyāh . . . ȧt^i-kyāh*, here you see on the one hand . . . there you see on the other hand, viii, 13; *yit^i-kyāh . . . yit^i-kyāh*, here you see . . . and here you see, x, 12.

yiti, adv. from here, hence, v, 5, 8; here, v, 8; sg. gen. *yityuk^u*, m. sg. dat. *yitikis pātashĕhas-nishĕ*, to the king of this place, x, 1.

yi-ti, see *yih* 1.

yot^u, adv. where; *yot^u-tāñ*, up to which place, i.e. until, as soon as, xii, 6. Cf. *yotāñ*.

yut^u 1, adj. this much, with emph. *y*, *yutuy*, xi, 20. This word is usually spelt *yūt^u*.

yut^u 2, adv. *yut^u-tāñ*, up to here, i.e. in the meantime, v, 7. Cf. *yutāñ*.

yūt^u, adv. *yūt^u . . . tyūt^u*, as soon as . . . so soon, xii, 2.

yĕth, see *yih* 2.

yith, see *yih* 1.

yith-nay, conj. so that not, in order that not, ix, 12.

yĕtha, adv. how, in the manner which; with emph. *y*, *yĕthay pōṭh^i*, in what very manner, exactly as, xii, 2.

yitha, adv. thus, in this manner; with emph. *y*, *yithay pōṭhin*, in this very manner, viii, 3.

yuth^u, adj. and adv. as, of what kind, xii, 24 (correlative *tyuth^u*);

with emph. *y*, *yuthuy*, as verily, even as, exactly as (correl. *tyuthuy*), v, 6 ; xii, 12, 5 ; even as, at the very time that, viii, 7 (correl. *tyuthuy*).

yitam, see *yun*^{u}.

yotāñ, adv. until, (contraction of *yot*^{u}*-tāñ*, see *yoṭ*^{u}), v, 10.

yutāñ, adv. in the meantime, (contraction of *yut*^{u}*-tāñ*, see *yut*^{u}), v, 5.

yitay, see *yun*^{u}.

yĕtȧt^i, adv. where, in the place where, xii, 6.

yutuy, see *yut*^{u} 1.

yüts^ü, adj. much, very, *yüts*^{ü}*-kôl*^{u}, for a long time, ii, 4.

yiwān, see *yun*^{u}.

yiy 1, *yīy*, see *yih* 1.

yiy 2, see *yih* 2.

yiyi, *yiyiy*, see *yun*^{u}.

zabān, f. tongue, speech, language ; — *karüñ*^{ü}, to say a thing ; hence, to promise, x, 8 ; — *āyĕ*, speech came (to it), it became able to speak (of a bee), ix, 1 ; sg. abl. *zaböñ*^{ü}, by word of mouth, xii, 16.

zab^a*r*, adj. superior, excellent, vii, 8, 28 ; — *gav*, it became excellent, as an interj. all right ! xii, 15.

zacĕ, see *züṭ*^{ü}.

zāda, m. at end of compound, a son ; *ôkhun-zāda*, the son of a religious teacher, xii, 2 ; sg. dat. *ôkhun-zādas*, xii, 2 ; *pātashāh-zāda*, a king's son, a prince, sg. dat. *-zādas*, viii, 5 ; pl. nom. *-zāda*, viii, 3 (bis), 11 (ter) ; dat. *-zādan*, viii, 4 (bis) 11 (bis) ; gen. *-zādan-hond*^{u}, viii, 4 ; *shāh-zāda*, a prince ; sg. dat. *-zādas*, viii, 13 ; pl. nom. *-zāda*, viii, 5, 11 (bis), 3.

zod^u, m. a hole ; f. *züd*^{u} (pl. nom. *zadĕ*), a small hole, vii, 25.

zid, m. hatred : *amis ôs*^{u} *zid Yūsūpha-sond*^{u}, he hated Joseph, vi, 10.

zāgun, to watch for, to be wide awake and on the alert ; imperf. m. sg. 3, with suff. 3rd pers. sg. dat. *ôsus dagāy zāgān dādkhāh*, disloyalty, (like) a petitioner, was watching in him, ii, 5.

z^a*h*, card. two, viii, 8, 11 ; following noun qualified, *bacĕ z*^{a}*h*, two young ones, viii, 1 ; *böy*^{i}*-bārȧn*^{i} *z*^{a}*h*, two brothers, viii, 5 ; *böts*^{u} *z*^{a}*h*, the two members of a family, husband and wife, v, 9, 10 ; viii, 1 ; *gabar z*^{a}*h*, two sons, viii, 1 ; *gul*^{i} *z*^{a}*h*, the two fore-arms, v, 9 ; *gŏlām* z^a*h*, two servants, viii, 5 ; *gur*[i] z^a*h*, two horses, xii, 1 ; *hūn*[i] z^a*h*, two dogs, viii, 4, 12 (bis), 3 ; *kŏd*[i] z^a*h*, two prisoners, v, 9 ; *lāl chis* z^a*h*, he has two rubies, xii, 3 ; *nĕciv*[i] z^a*h*, two sons, viii, 11 ; *pātashāh-zāda* z^a*h*, two princes, viii, 3 (bis), 11 ; *rīnz*[i] z^a*h*, two balls, v, 3, 4 (bis), 5 ; *shāh-zāda* z^a*h*, two princes, viii, 11 ; *wŏlinjĕ* z^a*h*, two hearts, viii, 3, 4 (ter), 11, 2 ; *yim* z^a*h*, these two, viii, 5.

Preceding noun qualified, z^a*h kŏd*[i], two prisoners, v, 8 ; z^a*h katha*, two statements, x, 1, 4.

sg. abl. *dŏyi laṭi*, on two occasions, viii, 7.

pl. dat. *dŏn*, viii, 11 ; following noun qualified, *bāyĕn dŏn*, to the two brothers, xii, 15 ; *pātashāh-zādan dŏn*, to the two princes, viii, 11 ; *yiman dŏn pātashŏhiyĕn kits*[ü], for the kingdoms of these two, x, 11 ; *zanānan dŏn*, to two women, xii, 11, 4 ; preceding qualified noun, *dŏn bātsan*, to the husband and wife (see *bŏts*[ü] z^a*h*, ab.), viii, 1, 6.

pl. gen. *pātashāh-zādan dŏn-hanza*, of the two princes, viii, 4 ; *yiman dŏn-handi-khŏta*, than these two, xii, 19.

pl. ag. *bāranyau dŏyau*, by the two brothers, viii, 3 ; *kŏdyau dŏyav*, by the two prisoners, v, 7 ; *yimav dŏyav*, by these two, iii, 1 ; x, 5 ; *dŏyau bātsau*, by the husband and wife, viii, 2, 5.

zāh, adv. ever, at any time ; *na zāh*, never, xi, 14.

zahar, m. poison, viii, 6, 7, 13 (bis) ; *pātashĕhas khot*[u] *zahar*, poison rose to the king, i.e. he became enraged, viii, 7.

z^a*l*, m. scratching (with the nails) ; with suff. of indef. art. z^a*lā*-z^a*lā*, a continuous scratching, xii, 17.

zāl, m. a net ; with suff. of indef. art. *zālāh lāyun*, to cast a net (to catch fishes), i, 6, 7, 8 ; sg. dat. *zālas*, i, 6 ; *zālas walana yun*[u], to be caught in a net, ix, 7.

Zalīkhā, f. N.P. Zulaikhā (the wife of Potiphar, in the story of Joseph), vi, 1, etc.

zalīl, adj. brought low, humbled, i, 4.

zulm, m. tyranny ; — *karun*, to do tyranny, ix, 1 ; *mĕ chuh zulm gŏmot*[u], tyranny has been done to me, ix, 1 (bis), 6.

zālun, to set on fire, to kindle, to burn ; conj. part. *zŏlith*, iii, 1 ; fut. sg. 1, *zāla*, iii, 4 (bis) ; past m. sg. *zôl*[u], iii, 4 ; with suff. 3rd pers. pl. ag. *zôlukh*, ii, 12 ; iii, 4.

zima, m. responsibility; *zima karun*, to make a responsibility; *tsŏn zanĕn kărin zima tsōr pahar*, four watches were made a responsibility to the four men, i.e. each was put in charge of a watch, viii, 5; *zima hyon*ᵘ, to take responsibility, i.e. to confess, admit, *yih chĕs-na hĕwān zima kĕ̃h*, she does not admit anything, xii, 15; *zima khālun*, to cause a responsibility, to mount; *khôl*ᵘ*nas zima takhsīr*, he caused the responsibility (for) the crime to mount on him, i.e. he proved him guilty, x, 12; *zima khasun* responsibility to mount; *kaīsi chuna khasān zima*, on no one does the responsibility mount, i.e. no one could be proved guilty, iii, 3.

zŏmba, m. a Yak; pl. nom. *zŏmba*, xi, 6.

zamīn, f. earth, land, ix, 9; the world, land, as opposed to the sky, iii, 8; sg. dat. *mājĕ-zamīni*, in mother earth, ix, 9; pl. abl. *satav zamīnav tăl*ⁱ, below the seven worlds, iii, 8.

zan, f. a woman; *marda-zan*, man or woman, vii, 23; *mạkh*ᵃ*r-i-zan*, the coquetry of a woman, x, 13.

zān, f. knowledge, understanding, vii, 29; *gŏr-zān*, adj. ignorant, vii, 27; xi, 5.

zīn, m. a saddle; *gur*ᵘ *zīn karith*, a horse ready saddled, iii, 8; pl. nom. *zacĕ-zīn*, rag-saddles, saddles made of rags, xi, 9.

*zon*ᵘ, m. a man, a male person; *kunuy zon*ᵘ, only one person; *gav kunuy zon*ᵘ, he went alone; sg. gen. *zăn*ⁱ*-sond*ᵘ, viii, 11; pl. nom. *zăn*ⁱ, x, 1; dat. *zanĕn*, viii, 5; x, 5, 6, 12 (bis); ag. *zanĕv*, x, 1, 2. Cf. *züñ*ᵘ.

zūn, f. moonlight; *zūna-ḍab*, f. a kind of roof-bungalow, or small erection on the roof of a house, in which people sit to enjoy the moonlight; sg. dat. *-ḍabi*, *-pĕṭh*, on the roof-bungalow, viii, 1.

zinda, adj. living, alive, ii, 3; with emph. *y*, *zinday*, x, 8 (bis).

zang, f. the leg, ii, 11.

zanāna, f. a woman; ii, 1; iii, 4 (ter), 5, 9 (ter); v, 5 (bis), 11, 2; viii, 11; x, 1, 5 (several times), 6; xi, 7; xii, 4 (several times), 5 (ter), 6, 10, 1, 4, 9 (ter), 20; a wife, iii, 1; v, 1, 4, 7, 9, 10; x, 5, 12, 3.

sg. nom. iii, 1, 5; v, 1, 10; viii, 11; x, 1, 5, 6, 13; xii, 4 (bis), 5 (bis), 6; with suff. of indef. art. *zanānā*, x, 5; xii,

4, 10; *zanānāh,* iii, 4; *zanānā akh,* x, 5; sg. dat. *zanāni,* iii, 4, 9; v, 4; x, 5; xii, 4; ag. *zanāni,* iii, 4, 9 (bis); v, 5 (bis), 7, 9, 11; x, 5, 12; xii, 4, 5; gen. *zanāni-handis,* x, 5; pl. nom. *zanāna,* xii, 19 (ter); with emph. *y, zanānay,* only women, v, 12; dat. *zanānan,* ii, 1; xi, 7; xii, 11, 4, 20.

zānun, to know; to know how, x, 12; xi, 8, 15; impve. sg. 2, *zān,* i, 12; *tsᵃh zān ta yih zān,* (a woman addressing a man and a woman) do thou (the man) know, and do this woman (i.e. thou, this woman) know, v, 9; fut. (often in sense of pres.) *kuwa zāna,* how do I know, v, 9; with neg. interrog. *zāna-nā,* do I not know? i.e. of course I know, x, 12; 2, *zānakh karith,* thou wilt know how to make, x, 12; 3, *zāni,* vi, 14; vii, 27, 8, 9, 30; pl. 1, *ásⁱ na zānav,* we do not know how (sc. to work), xi, 15; 3, *yim na zānan,* who do not know how (sc. to make a certain sound), xi, 8.

zēnun, to conquer (xi, title); to win (x, 1, 6, 7); *zēnān anun,* to conquer (a country), xi, 1, 2, etc.; *zīnith anun,* to capture (a person), xii, 25; inf. obl. (inf. of purpose) *zēnani,* xi, title; conj. part. *zīnith,* xii, 25; pres. part. *zēnān,* xi, 1, 2, etc.; fut. sg. 3, *zēni,* x, 1, 6; pl. 3, *zēnan,* x, 7.

zinis, see *zyunᵘ*.

zūñᵘ, f. a female person, a woman, xii, 7, 15; pl. nom. *zañĕ,* xii, 6, 7; dat. *zañĕn zēṭhᵘ,* the eldest of the females, xii, 6. Cf. *zonᵘ,* of which this is the fem.

zār, a prayer, supplication (made in misery or sorrow), i, 13; pl. nom. *zār,* iv, 1; *zāra-pār,* m. ejaculatory prayers, ix, 1; x, 5 (bis); *zāra-pāra,* m. entreaty, coaxing request, ii, 3, 5.

zōr, m. force; — *karun,* to use (moral) force, to insist, viii, 2; xii, 15.

zīrᵘ, f. a push, shove, nudge; — *diñᵘ,* to push, etc., x, 7 (bis).

zargar, m. a goldsmith; *zargar-nĕcyuvāh,* a young goldsmith, v, 2.

zāra-pār, zāra-pāra, see *zār*.

zōrāwār, adj. powerful, mighty, xi, 2.

zuryāth (for *zurrīyat*), f. progeny, offspring; hence, the offspring of God, the whole world, vii, 8.

zāsanuy, a word used by Hātim in i, 12, but the meaning of which is unknown to him; he gives it as part of the traditional text, a variant reading is *tsĕ āsunuy*.

züṭü, f. a rag; sg. dat. *zacĕ-zīn*, rag-saddles, saddles made of rags, xi, 9.

zāth, f. a race, tribe, caste; *dĕwa-zāth*, of demon race, xii, 16.

zĕṭhü, see *zyuṭhᵘ*.

zīṭhⁱ, see *zyūṭhᵘ*.

zuv, m. the soul, ii, 4.

zyunᵘ, m. firewood, ii, 12; xi, 7; xii, 20, 1, 4 (bis); sg. dat. *zinis*, xii, 21, 2, 4.

ziyāphath, f. a feast, a dinner-party, x, 4, 11; a dish of food brought as a present, a present of dainty food, x, 5 (bis), 10; with suff. of indef. art. *ziyāphathā*, x, 5.

zyuṭhᵘ, adj. old, elder, eldest; m. the head or superior of a guild of artizans, v, 1; m. sg. dat. *ziṭhis-hihis*, to the elder (of two brothers) (cf. *hyuhᵘ*), viii, 5; f. sg. nom. *zĕṭhü*, the eldest (sister), xii, 6.

zyūṭhᵘ, adj. long; m. pl. nom. *zīṭhⁱ atha dārànⁱ*, to stretch out the arms, vii, 25.

APPENDIX I

INDEX OF WORDS IN SIR AUREL STEIN'S TEXT, SHOWING THE CORRESPONDING WORDS IN GŌVINDA KAULA'S TEXT

Figures between marks of parenthesis indicate the number of times, when there are more than one, that a word occurs in the passage to which reference is made. The word "caret" *indicates that the word referred to does not occur in Gōvinda Kaula's text. The order of words is the same as that employed in the Vocabulary.*

ạ (*ĕ*), x, 4.
ạ (*i*), xi, 4.
ai (*ay*), x, 3; xii, 4.
ai (*ạy*), viii, 11.
ại (*ạy*), viii, 6, 8.
āi̯ (*āy*), v, 9.
au (caret), vii, 13.
āu̯ (*āv*), i, 8; ii, 3, 12; iii, 1, 9; v, 1, 4, 9, 10; vi, 16 (2); viii, 3, 6 (3), 7, 8, 9, 10, 1 (2), 3; x, 6, 7, 12; xi, 20; xii, 3, 4 (3), 5 (5), 7 (2), 9, 10, 1, 2, 3 (3), 4, 20, 3, 4.
i (*ĕ*), vi, 17; x, 4 (2).
i (*i*), x, 13; xii, 10, 5, 7, 9 (3).
o (*ō*), vii, 26.
āb (*āb*), v, 4 (4); viii, 7 (2).
ābᵊ (*āba*), viii, 7 (2); x, 5.
ibrāhim (*yibrāhim*), iv, 6.
ābas (*ābas*), viii, 7.
ābtạr (*abtar*), vi, 12.
ạch (*achĕ*), xii, 22.
achạn (*achĕn*), v, 11.
aḍ (*aḍa*), vii, 20.
adᵊ (*ada*), viii, 10.
adạ (*ada*), v, 6, 9 (2); viii, 3, 10, 1, 3; x, 2, 7; xii, 3, 4.
adᵉ (*ada*), iii, 1.
ade (*ada*), v, 8.
āda (*ādā*), x, 8; xii, 4, 9, 11, 2.
å̄dạ (*ōra*), xii, 12.
īdgāh (*yīdⁱkāh*), vi, 16 (2).
ạdālat (*adālütsᵘ*), v, 9.
adạl (*adᵃla*), i, 3.
ādam (*ādam*), iv, 2, 3; vii, 6, 7.
ādᵊmas (*ādamas*), vii, 6.
īdam (*yīdam*), vii, 6.
afsạrạs (*apsaras*), x, 12.
age (*āgē*), xi, 4.
āga (*āgāh*), ii, 9.
agar (*agar*), viii, 13.
āgur (*āgur*), viii, 7.
āgạs (*āgas*), viii, 6, 8, 11.
āgạye (*āgayi*), v, 7.
ah (*āh*), i, 5; iv, 3.
ahᵃdai (*ahᵃday*), i, 2.
ahmạd (*ahmad*), i, 13.
ahengārạn (*āhan-gārān*), xi, 16.
ajạ (*ajĕ*), xi, 7.
ak (*akh*), ii, 1; v, 1, 9, 11; vi, 15; viii, 7, 9, 11, 4; x, 5, 7, 8; xii, 1 (3), 3 (2).
ak (caret), viii, 7.
akⁱ (*aki*), v, 1; viii, 3.
akⁱ (*ȧkⁱ*), viii, 1; x, 12; xii, 1.

ās^i (*āsi*), vii, 29, 30 ; viii, 6.
ās^i (*ös^i*), viii, 1, 4 ; xi, 5.
āsi (*āsi*), i, 2 ; viii, 7 ; x, 1, 8 (2).
āsi he (*āsihē*), ii, 4.
ạ^{i}s^i (*ȧs^i*), xii, 19.
ạ̄^{i}s^i (*āsi*), xii, 23.
ạs^i (*ös^i*), v, 9 ; x, 1.
å̄s (*ās*), vi, 16 ; viii, 7.
å̄s (*ös^i*), vi, 11 ; viii, 3 (2), 5, 11 (2) ; x, 5 ; xii, 1.
å̄s (*ös^ü*), ii, 1 ; v, 1, 10 ; vii, 7, 16 ; viii, 1 ; ix, 1 ; x, 5 (3), 7 ; xii, 4, 15, 20 (2), 5.
å̄s (*ôs^u*), i, 4, 5, 6 ; ii, 1 (2), 4, 5 (2), 7, 8, 9 (3), 10 (2), 11 (2) ; iii, 1 (2) ; v, 1 (2), 2, 7, 9 (2) ; vi, 10 (2), 4 ; vii, 8 ; viii, 1 (2), 6, 7 (2), 9 (5), 11, 3 (3) ; x, 4, 7 (2), 10, 2 (2) ; xii, 15 (2), 25 (2).
å̄s (*ôsus*), v, 2.
å̄s, see *buḍ^i å̄s*, xii, 1.
å̄s na (*ôs^{u}na*), xii, 2.
å̄s nạ (*ās-na*), vi, 16.
å̄s nạ (*ôs^{u}na*), vi, 16.
å̄s nas (*ôs^{u}nas*), v, 6.
å̄s suy (*ös^{ü}y*), vii, 16.
å̄sa (*āsa*), iii, 7.
å̄sạ (*āsa*), x, 14 ; xi, 19.
å̄s^i (*ös^i*), i, 3 ; viii, 1, 11 ; xi, 8.
å̄si (*āsiy*), xii, 11.
å̄s^i nāv (*āsh^{ĕ}nāv*), x, 6.
å̄s^u (*ösa*), viii, 7.
å̄s^u (*ôs^u*), i, 1, 2.
īsā (*yīsāh*), iv, 4.
ōs (*ôs^u*), xii, 15.
āsihe (*āsihē*), ii, 5.
ashkạ (*ạsh^{ĕ}ka*), vii, 30.
ạshik (*ạsh^{ĕ}kh*), v, 2 (2).
ạshkun (*ạsh^{ĕ}kun^u*), v, 10.
ashkanye (*ạsh^{ĕ}kañĕ*), v, 2.
āsh^i nāv (*āsh^{ĕ}nāv*), x, 1.
å̄shnāụ (*āsh^{ĕ}nāv*), x, 10.
ạshis (*ös^{ü}s*), xii, 9.
āsak (*āsakh*), i, 3.
å̄suk (*ôsukh*), viii, 2.
ōsuk (*ôsukh*), xii, 15.
ạskun (*ạsh^{ĕ}kun^u*), v, 3.
as^{i}kya (*ȧs^i kyāh*), v, 9.
asạl (*as^{a}l*), ii, 8, 11.
asl (*as^{a}l*), xii, 16.
aslā malaikum (*aslāmalaikum*), xii, 26.
āsim (*āsim*), viii, 13.
å̄sum (*ôsum*), iii, 1 ; vii, 11, 5 ; x, 14.
asmān (*asmān*), ii, 6.
asmānau (*asmānav*), iii, 8.
as^{ạ}mānạn (*asmānan*), iv, 4.
å̄smut (*ôs^{u}mot^u*), v, 1, 4.
ạs^{i}nau (*ȧs^i nau*), xi, 15.
ās^{ạ}na (*ās-na*), x, 4.
āsạn^i (*āsȧn^i*), xii, 5.
āsun (*āsun*), xii, 10 (2).
āsun (*āsun^u*), xii, 4 (2), 5, 13 (3).
å̄san (*ös^{ü}san*), xii, 15.
ās^{ạ}nas (*āsanas*), x, 1 (2), 10.
ās^{i}nas (*āsanas*), x, 6 (2).
asar (*asar*), vi, 16.
asr^ạ (*asara*), vi, 16.
å̄sis (*ösis*), x, 5.
å̄sus (*ôsus*), i, 6 ; ii, 5 ; viii, 7, 9 ; ix, 1 ; x, 14.
å̄sus (*ös^{ü}s*), iii, 1 ; vii, 10 (2) ; ix, 2 ; x, 10.
ustād (*wustād*), ii, 1.
ōstan (*ôs^{u}than*), x, 12.
å̄syu (*ös^{i}wa*), x, 12.
at (*ath*), ii, 5, 7 (2) ; iii, 9 ; v, 6 (4) ; viii, 7 (3) ; x, 3, 5 (2), 7 (5), 8, 10, 2, 3 ; xii, 2, 3, 17.
at (caret), x, 7, 8.

dit (*dith*), vi, 7 ; x, 12.
dāth, see *va*^{i}*r*^{y} *dāth*, xii, 19.
dithai (*ditay*), v, 2.
dithin (*ditin*), x, 2.
dithas (*diṭs*^{ü}*s*), viii, 7.
ditam (*ditam*), x, 5.
ditim (*ditim*), x, 12 (2).
dit^{a}*mak* (*dit*^{i}*makh*), ix, 11.
dit^{a}*nas* (*ditin*), vii, 5.
ditinas (*dit*^{i}*nas*), x, 14.
diṭs (*diṭs*^{ü}), vi, 16.
diṭs^{a} *has* (*diṭs*^{ü}*has*), x, 5.
diṭsuk (*diṭs*^{ü}*kh*), iii, 8.
diṭsan (*diṭs*^{ü}*n*), x, 7 (2).
diṭsạn (*diṭs*^{ü}*n*), x, 7.
diṭsun (*diṭs*^{ü}*n*), xii, 7, 12.
diṭsạnas (*diṭs*^{u}*nas*), v, 9 ; x, 8.
dittạ (*dita*), v, 9 ; x, 4.
ditti (*dit*^{i}), xi, 17.
dava (*dawāh*), v, 6.
davā (*dawā*), vi, 14.
davā (*dawāh*), v, 6 (3).
davạ (*dawa*), v, 4.
dāvā (*dāwāh*), v, 11.
davāhan (*dawāhan*), v, 6.
divān (*diwān*), v, 11 ; vii, 11, 4, 7, 8, 22 ; x, 14 ; xii, 4, 14, 7 (2), 23.
dv^{o}*y*^{u} (*dwā-yi*), i, 3.
daye (*dayĕ*), iv, 1.
diyạ (*day*^{i}), vii, 2.
diyu (*diyiv*), xii, 21.
dīyu (*diyiv*), x, 12.
doyau (*dŏyav*), iii, 1 ; v, 7 ; viii, 2, 3, 5 ; x, 5.
doye (*dŏyi*), viii, 7.
duy (*dŏy*), vi, 6.
dyau (*dĕv*), xii, 7.
diyehe (*diyihē*), viii, 13.
dīyūm (*diyūm*), vi, 16.
duyạmis (*dŏyimis*), viii, 6.
dyun (*dyun*^{u}), x, 6.
dyār (*dyār*), i, 9 ; x, 1, 6.
d^{y}*ut* (*dyut*^{u}), v, 9 ; x, 2.
dyut (*dyut*^{u}), viii, 11, 2.
dyūt (*ḍyūṭh*^{u}), vi, 11 (2).
ḍyūṭ (*ḍyūṭh*^{u}), vi, 15 ; x, 12.
dyuth (*dyut*^{u}), xii, 22 (2).
d^{y}*üthuk* (*dyutukh*), xii, 24.
ḍyūṭhum (*ḍyūṭhum*), vi, 15 (2).
d^{y}*üthun* (*dyutun*), xii, 25.
dyüth^{u}*nas* (*dyut*^{u}*nas*), xii, 22.
ḍyūṭhut (*ḍyūṭhuth*), vi, 15.
d^{y}*utuk* (*dyutukh*), v, 10.
d^{y}*ütuk* (*dyutukh*), xii, 17.
dyutuk (*dyutukh*), x, 5.
dyōt mai (*ḍyūṭh*^{u}*may*), xi, 1.
dyüt^{u}*mau* (*dyutum*^{a}*wa*), x, 12.
dyut^{a}*mut* (*dyut*^{u}*mot*^{u}), viii, 1.
dyutmut (*dyut*^{u}*mot*^{u}), v, 6 ; viii, 1.
dyūtmut (*ḍyūṭh*^{u}*mot*^{u}), vi, 14.
d^{y}*ütmat* (*dit*^{i}*mȧt*^{i}), x, 12.
dyüt^{a}*mut* (*dyut*^{u}*mot*^{u}), x, 12.
d^{y}*itạmạtỷ* (*dit*^{i}*mȧt*^{i}), x, 12.
d^{y}*utun* (*dyutun*), v, 4.
d^{y}*ütun* (*dyutun*), x, 5.
dyutun (*dyutun*), v, 4 ; viii, 4, 7.
dyütun (*dyutun*), x, 9, 11, 2, 3, 5 (2).
dyut^{a}*nak* (*dyut*^{u}*nakh*), x, 5.
dyutạnak (*dyut*^{u}*nakh*), ii, 7.
dyüt^{u}*nak* (*dyut*^{u}*nakh*), xii, 17.
d^{y}*üt*^{u}*nas* (*dyut*^{u}*nas*), xii, 16.
dyut^{a}*nas* (*dyut*^{u}*nas*), v, 6.
dyutạnas (*dyut*^{u}*nas*), x, 6.
dyutạnạs (*dyut*^{u}*nas*), i, 9.
dyut^{u}*nas* (*dyut*^{u}*nas*), xii, 5, 7 (2), 11.
dyüt^{u}*nas* (*dyut*^{u}*nas*), xii, 15, 6.
dyutanay (*dyutun*^{ü}*y*), ii, 7.
dyutus (*dyutus*), i, 10 ; xii, 4.
dyav^{a}*zāth* (*dĕva-zāth*), xii, 16.
diyiy (*diyiy*), xii, 14.
dāz, see *tīran dāz*, ii, 7.

laṭ^{i} (*laṭi*), viii, 7 (2).
laṭi (*laṭi*), xi, 9.
loṭ (*loṭ^{u}*), v, 7.
lu^{i}t^{i} (*lŏt^{i}*), xii, 5.
latan (*latan*), viii, 7.
lit^{a}ri (*litri*), vii, 19.
lāy (*lāy*), i, 7.
lāye (*lāyi*), iii, 9.
lôy^{a}has (*lôy^{u}has*), ii, 11.
l^{y}eją (*lĕjĕ*), xi, 10.
lāy^{a}ką (*lŏyik-ĕ*), x, 4.
lāyak (*lŏyikh*), xii, 10, 9.
lāyiki (*lŏyik-i*), xii, 19 (2).
lå̄yuk (*lôyukh*), x, 1.
l^{y}ükh (*lyukh^{u}*), xii, 15.
l^{y}ükhmut (*lyukh^{u}mot^{u}*), xii, 15, 23.
lyükhmut (*lyukh^{u}mot^{u}*), viii, 10.
l^{y}ükh^{a}nas (*lyukh^{u}nas*), xii, 15 (2).
l^{y}ükhunas (*lyukh^{u}nas*), xii, 16.
l^{y}ükhas (*lyukh^{u}has*), xii, 17.
l^{y}ükhas (*lyukhus*), xii, 17.
l^{y}ekan (*lĕkan*), viii, 11.
lā̤y^{a}mas (*lŏy^{i}maș*), v, 4.
lāyān (*lāyān*), i, 6 ; v, 4 (2).
lāyin (*lāyȧn^{i}*), v, 3.
lāyin (*lŏyin*), v, 4.
lāyine (*lāyĕni*), ix, 8.
lā̤yin (*lŏy^{u}n*), viii, 6.
lā̤yun (*lôyun*), iii, 1, 2.
lå̄yun (*lôyun*), i, 8.
lā̤yinam (*lŏy^{u}nam*), v, 9.
lāyānas (*lāyānas*), v, 5.
lā̤y^{a}nas (*lôy^{u}nas*), viii, 10.
lā̤^{i}yinas (*lŏy^{ü}nas*), iii, 6.
lāyus (*lāyus*), iii, 5.
lazak (*lazakh*), viii, 4, 12.
lazan (*lazan*), v, 7.
lazun (*lüz^{ü}n*), x, 3.
laz^{a}nas (*lüz^{u}nas*), x, 3.
laząnas (*lüz^{ü}nas*), x, 3.
ma (*mā*), viii, 10 ; x, 5, 12 ; xii, 23.
ma, see *maṭ^{i}ma*, v, 9.
mā (*mā*), i, 2 ; v, 2, 8 ; vii, 20 ; viii, 9, 13 (2).
mā (*na*), viii, 7.
mą (*ma*), xii, 7.
mą (*mĕ*), v, 9 ; viii, 3 ; x, 8.
mą, see *gai mą*, vii, 12.
mai (*may*), v, 2.
mai, see *dyōt mai*, xi, 1.
me (*mĕ*), i, 7 ; ii, 2 (2) ; v, 8, 11 ; vi, 15 ; vii, 11, 3, 5 ; viii, 5, 11 (2) ; x, 1, 3 (3), 12 (4), 4 ; xii, 5.
mebar (*mĕ bȧr^{i}*), ix, 11.
mubārak (*mŏbārakh*), x, 8.
mãch tulari (*mãch-t^{a}l^{a}ri*), ix, 6.
mãch tulạr (*mãch-t^{a}l^{ü}r^{ü}*), ix, 1 (3), 3, 4.
mãch tulạri (*mãch-t^{a}l^{a}ri*), ix, 1.
macāmą (*macāma*), ii, 3.
mad^{a} (*mad*), vii, 15.
mōd (*mūd^{u}*), ii, 3.
mōḍ (*môr^{u}*), vi, 11.
mudā (*mŏdā*), vi, 7.
muḍ (*moḍ^{u}*), ii, 5, 9.
muḍ (*mor^{u}*), ii, 10 (2), 1.
mūḍ (*mūd^{u}*), ii, 6.
mādān (*mŏdān*), xi, 3.
ma^{i}dān (*mŏdān*), x, 1.
maidān (*mŏdān*), x, 1 (3).
maidāną (*mŏdānā*), x, 5.
maidānas (*mŏdānas*), viii, 9; x, 1.
maidānạs (*mŏdānas*), iii, 1.
mā̤^{i}dānas (*mŏdānas*), xii, 20.
mudur (*mŏdur^{u}*), vii, 31.
mudr^{y}au (*mŏdaryiv*), ix, 7.
moḍis (*maḍis*), ii, 5.
mahabat (*mahabata*), x, 4.
mah kam (*mahkam*), xi, 9.
mahkam (*mahkam*), iv, 6.
mahalą (*mahala*), xii, 19.
mah^{a}lạkhān (*mahalakhān*), viii, 3.

mom^{a}tis (mumatis), xii, 20.
momuts (mumüts^{ü}), viii, 1.
momut^{y} (mumàt^{i}), viii, 1 (2).
mane (mani), vi, 6.
māne (mānĕ), vii, 27, 8.
mā^{i}ni (mānĕ), iii, 5.
mang (mang), xii, 5, 10, 1.
mangạ (manga), iii, 6.
mangai (mangay), xii, 7.
mangạ has (mangahas), xii, 19.
mang^{a}lạj (mang lüj^{ü}), xi, 16.
mangum (mangum), xii, 18.
ming^{e} mạr (miñĕ-mür^{u}), ii, 8.
mangān (mangān), xi, 14; xii, 4, 5, 11, 4.
mangun (mangun^{u}), xii, 13, 8 (2).
mangạ nāv^{i}hai (manganöv^{i}hay), xi, 8.
mañge nåvun (manganôwun), vi, 16.
ming^{ye} mạri (miñĕ-marĕ), ii, 9.
ming^{ye} mạri (miñĕ-mari), ii, 9.
mē^{i}nis (myönis), xii, 20 (2).
manōsh (manōsh), xii, 15 (2).
manoshas (manōshĕs), xii, 15.
māntsạ (mõtsa), xii, 15.
mā^{i}nye (mānĕ), iii, 4.
mānye (mānĕ), vi, 14.
mēn^{y} (myön^{i}), vii, 20.
mạ^{i}n^{y}g^{a}zạs (màng^{i}zĕs), xii, 18.
manz (manz), ii, 1 (3), 4, 5 (3), 6 (2), 7 (2), 8 (2), 9, 10 (2), 1 (2); iii, 1, 4, 5, 7 (2), 9; v, 4 (3), 5 (2), 6, 9 (3), 11; vi, 7; viii, 1, 9, 12; ix, 1; x, 3, 7 (5), 8 (2), 14; xii, 2 (3), 3 (2), 6, 7 (2), 11 (3), 2 (2), 5, 8 (2), 9, 20 (2), 2, 3 (2), 4 (2).
manzạ (manza), viii, 7, 11; ix, 4; x, 7 (2), 12 (3); xii, 4 (2), 6, 7, 11, 5, 23.
månzūr (mônzur), i, 12.
mun^{a} zāt (munazāth), vii, 3.
mēñy (myöñ^{u}), iii, 2, 8, 9.
mār (mār), ix, 5.
māra, see shah māra, viii, 7.
mārạ (māra), viii, 13; x, 8.
mạr (mür^{u}), ii, 8.
marai (maray), viii, 1 (2).
māre (māra), x, 7.
mārē (mārē), v, 7.
mạri (marĕ), ii, 9.
mạri (mari), x, 7.
mạri, see ming^{ye} mạri, ii, 9.
mạ^{i}ri (mari), xii, 19.
mạ̄^{i}ri, see tsimạ̄^{i}ri, vi, 11.
mōr (môl^{u}), viii, 13.
mōr (môr^{u}), ii, 8; iii, 3 (3).
mardạ (marda), vii, 23.
murād (murād), i, 10.
murde māzạ̄^{i}ry (murdamāzör^{i}), x, 12.
margạ, see son^{a} margạ, xi, 3.
mārihe (mārihē), viii, 7.
mạrihe (mārihē), viii, 10.
marhaba (marhabāh), ii, 10.
mōrham (môr^{u}ham), iii, 3.
mār^{a}hat (mārahath), ii, 11.
marih^{y}e (marihē), viii, 7.
mạrāj (marāz-i), xi, 5.
murkhas (murkhas), viii, 11.
mār^{a}kan (mārakan), vii, 23.
marān (marān), v, 9.
mārạnạ (mārana), x, 12.
mārạni (mārani), viii, 13.
mārun (mārun^{u}), x, 5 (2), 12, 5.
mårun (môrun), viii, 10 (2).
mōrun (môrun), viii, 7; x, 7.
mārenak (māranakh), viii, 4.
mārạnas (māranas), ii, 7.
mārạs, see shah mārạs, viii, 6.
mạris (maris), ii, 6, 7 (2), 11.
mārat (mārath), ii, 11.

6; x, 5, 8, 9; xii, 4 (2), 5 (3), 10, 1 (2), 2, 3, 4, 5 (2), 6, 7, 8, 20, 2 (2), 5.

panenen (*pananĕn*), viii, 10.

paneneñy (*pananĕn*), x, 14.

panạnạs (*pananis*), viii, 9.

panạnis (*pananis*), ii, 7, 11; iii, 2, 4; v, 8, 10, 2; viii, 10; x, 5; xii, 4, 5, 10, 3, 5, 8.

panenis (*pananis*), x, 12, 4.

panạn^{y}e (*panañĕ*), v, 10.

panen^{y} (*panüñ^{ü}*), viii, 1, 11.

paneñ^{y}e (*panañi*), v, 5; x, 12.

paneñy (*panȧn^{i}*), x, 14; xi, 10.

paneñy (*panüñ^{u}*), x, 1, 3 (2), 6, 8, 13; xii, 14, 25.

paneñye (*panañĕ*), v, 4, 12; x, 3; xii, 4.

paneñye (*panañē*), vi, 6.

paneñye (*panañi*), x, 13.

paniñy (*panüñ^{ü}*), x, 10.

panenuy (*panunuy*), x, 1.

panunuy (*panunuy*), vii, 21 (2).

panen^{y}en (*pananĕn*), viii, 13.

pānas (*pānas*), v, 9 (2); vi, 4; vii, 24, 5; x, 6; xii, 5, 25.

pānạs (*pānas*), ii, 5; iii, 8; vii, 1, 15 (2); viii, 3, 8; xii, 12, 25.

pānes (*pānas*), v, 9; x, 1.

pāne suy (*pānas^{ü}y*), vii, 3.

pānts (*pānts*), x, 1 (5), 2 (6), 6, 14.

pā̊ntsim (*pöntsim^{u}*), x, 6.

pāntsen (*pāntsan*), x, 1, 6.

pānts^{y}ūm (*pöntsyum^{u}*), x, 1.

pạnts^{y}um (*pöntsim^{ü}*), x, 6.

pane vạ̄^{i}n^{i} (*pānawöñ*), xii, 25.

pāne vān^{y} (*pānawöñ*), viii, 2.

pāne vāny (*pānawöñ*), viii, 1.

pānevāñy (*pānawöñ*), xi, 19.

pānevāñy (*pānawüñ*), x, 1.

pāne vāñy (*pānawöñ*), viii, 3.

pan^{y}en (*panin*), iv, 7.

pānz (*pānts*), viii, 10 (2).

papit (*papith*), ix, 9.

parạ (*para*), xii, 1 (2).

pār (*pāra*), ii, 3, 5.

pār, see *zārạ pār*, x, 5 (2).

pạ^{i}r^{i} (*parī*), xii, 25.

pạ^{i}ri (*parī*), xii, 8, 11 (2), 4, 20.

pạ̄^{i}r^{i}, see *tso pạ̄^{i}r^{i}*, xii, 24.

pạ̄^{i}ri, see *so pạ̄^{i}ri*, xii, 21.

pīrau (*pīrav*), v, 8.

pūr (*pūr^{u}*), v, 2.

parda (*pardā*), vi, 4.

parda (*phardā*), vi, 11.

pargan (*pargan*), xi, 5.

paran (*paran*), ix, 1.

parān (*parān*), vi, 17; vii, 4; viii, 4.

pārạn (*pör^{ü}n*), v, 10.

pīran (*pīran*), vi, 13.

pōrun (*pūrun*), x, 2.

purun (*pūrun*), x, 9.

prang (*prang*), xii, 18.

prān^{y} (*prön^{i}*), viii, 5.

prāñy (*prön^{i}*), vi, 11.

prārān (*prārān*), v, 6, 11.

prạ̄^{i}ryau (*prāryāv*), ii, 10.

prat (*prath*), viii, 1 (2).

pạ̄^{i}rit (*pörith*), iii, 7.

pạ̄^{i}rit (*pürith*), xi, 9.

par tav^{a} (*partawa*), xii, 15.

prütsun (*pryutshun*), xii, 1.

pā̊ravī (*pöravī*), i, 1.

parvardigār (*parwardigār*), i, 11.

parvahab (*par wahab*), vi, 17.

pạ^{i}riye (*par^{i}yi*), xii, 15.

pạ̄^{i}riye (*par^{i}yĕ*), iii, 7, 8.

pār^{y}ehna (*pāri-hanā*), xii, 2.

parzạ nā̊u̯ (*parzanôw^{u}*), xii, 2.

parzạ nā̊u̯ (*parzanôw^{u}*), x, 5.

parzạ nā̊u̯ muts (*parzanöv^{ü}-müts^{ü}*), x, 5.

saudāgār (*sōdāgār*), v, 11.
saudāgaṛa (*sōdāgara*), iii, 1.
sodāgaṛ (*sōdāgār*), viii, 9.
sōdāgaṛ (caret), viii, 9.
sōdāgār (*sōdāgār*), v, 11; viii, 9, 10 (2).
sōdāgār^{a} (*sōdāgārā*), viii, 9.
sōdāgāṛa (*sōdāgārā*), viii, 9.
sōdāgaṛan (*sōdāgāran*), viii, 10.
sōdāgāṛan (*sōdāgāran*), viii, 9 (2).
saudāgāṛas (*sōdāgaras*), iii, 2.
saudāgāṛas (*sōdāgāras*), viii, 9.
sōdāgāṛas (*sōdāgāras*), viii, 10.
saudāgāṛasund (*sōdāgāra-sond*^{u}), iii, 1.
sōdahas (*sōdāhas*), v, 10.
sōdahaṣ (*sōdāhas*), iii, 1.
sudaṛ balai (*sōdurabalaỵ*), vii, 31.
sāf, see *yin sāf*, viii, 4.
safar (*saphar*), xii, 25.
safarun (*sapharun*^{u}), xi, 13.
saf^{a}*ras* (*sapharas*), x, 1.
safaras (*sapharas*), x, 6.
she (*shĕh*), xii, 6, 7.
sāhib (*sōhib*), vii, 2, 3; xi, 20.
sāhib^{i} (*sōhib-ĕ*), ii, 9.
sāhibi (*sōhib-i*), x, 13.
sāhībō (*sōhibō*), ix, 3.
shōbān (*shūbān*), vii, 5, 10.
shūbān (*shūbān*), ii, 4, 5.
sāhiban (*sōhiban*), vii, 5.
sāhib^{a}*sund* (*sōhiba-sond*^{u}), iv, 4, 5.
shech^{v} (*shĕch*^{i}), x, 3 (3).
shod (*shod*^{u}), ii, 10.
shāhī (*shāh-i*), vi, 1.
shāhī (*shōhī*), x, 4 (2).
shạhij (*shĕh*^{u}*j*^{u}), v, 6 (2).
shuhul (*shĕhul*^{u}), i, 11.
shahmār (*shĕhmār*), viii, 6 (2).
shah māra (*shĕhmārā*), viii, 7.
shahmār^{a} (*shĕhmāra*), viii, 6.
shahmāṛa (*shĕhmāra*), viii, 13 (2).
shạhmār (*shĕhmār*), viii, 13 (2).
shah māṛas (*shĕhmāras*), viii, 6.
shạhmāṛas (*shĕhmāras*), viii, 13.
shạhaṇ (*shĕhan*), i, 7.
shāhạnshāh (*shĕhan-shāh*), i, 1.
shah^{a}*ra* (*shĕhara*), viii, 11.
shah^{a}*ṛa* (*shĕhara*), viii, 4.
shahar (*shĕhar*), ii, 1; x, 9.
shehra (*shĕharāh*), v, 1.
shehri (*shĕhar-ĕ*), ii, 1.
sheheṛa (*shĕhara*), viii, 11.
sheharạkis (*shĕharakis*), xii, 3.
shahras (*shĕharas*), xii, 2.
shah^{a}*ras* (*shĕharas*), x, 3 (2), 5 (2), 12.
shahạras (*shĕharas*), x, 10.
sheh^{a}*ras* (*shĕharas*), x, 14.
shehạras (*shĕharas*), v, 9, 11; x, 5.
shahtsa (*shĕkhtsā*), x, 1.
sh^{a}*hzādạ* (*shāhzāda*), viii, 5.
shahzādạ (*shāhzāda*), viii, 11 (2), 3.
shahzādạs (*shāhzādas*), viii, 13.
shak (*shĕkh*), v, 8.
shāk^{a} (*shākh*), vii, 10.
shōk (*shĕkh*), xii, 15.
shakhtsạn (*shĕkhtsan*), x, 2, 6.
shakhtsas (*shĕkhtsas*), x, 2 (2).
shakạl (*shĕkal*), x, 7.
shikma (*shikama*), x, 7.
shik^{a}*mạ* (*shikama*), x, 7.
shikmas (*shikamas*), x, 7 (2).
shikāṛas (*shikāras*), ii, 4, 8; viii, 7.
shikasta (*shikasta*), v, 5.
shōlan (*shōlān*), vi, 6.
shamā (*shĕmāh*), vi, 6; x, 7 (2).
shạmā (*shĕmāh*), viii, 13.
shāman (*shāman*), v, 5.
shumār (*shumār*) xi, 16; xii, 20, 4.

tam^{i} (*tami*), ii, 7 ; iii, 9 ; v, 5 ; x, 12 (2), 4 ; xii, 4.
tam^{i} (*tamiy*), x, 14.
tami (*tami*), viii, 9 ; x, 10 (3), 2 ; xii, 6.
tami (*tamiy*), xii, 6.
tạm^{i} (*tami*), iii, 5, 8.
tạm^{i} (*tȧm*^{i}), i, 3 ; ii, 1 ; iv, 3, 4, 5, 6 ; vii, 13 ; x, 3, 12.
tạm^{i} (*tȧmiy*), iii, 1.
ta^{i}*m*^{i} (*tamiy*), xii, 14.
ta^{i}*mi* (*tami*), xii, 16.
ta^{i}*mi* (*tamiy*), xii, 15.
tạ^{i}*mi* (*tami*), xii, 14.
tim (*tim*), v, 4 (2), 8 ; viii, 3, 4, 11, 3 ; x, 12 (4) ; xi, 5 ; xii, 16 (3).
tim^{ạ} (*tima*), xi, 19 ; xii, 19.
timạ (*tima*), viii, 11.
timai (*timay*), x, 14.
timai (*timạy*), v, 5, 9 ; viii, 4.
timau (*timau*), vi, 11 ; xii, 7.
timau (*timav*), x, 12.
tim^{i} (*tim*), viii, 3.
tōm, see *vuch tōm*, vii, 24.
tum (*tum*), xi, 4.
tim hai (*tim-hay*), ix, 8, 9.
tim hay (*tim-hay*), ix, 10.
tam^{i} *kuy* (*tamyukuy*), vii, 12.
timan (*timan*), viii, 1 ; xi, 6, 8 ; xii, 6 (2), 7, 16, 7.
timạn (*timan*), x, 6.
tim^{ạ} *nai* (*timan*^{ü}*y*), xii, 1.
timạnai (*timan*^{ü}*y*), viii, 11.
tạmis (*tamis*), ii, 7 ; iii, 9 ; viii, 9 (2) ; xii, 10.
ta^{i}*mis* (*tamis*), xii, 19.
tamāshạs (*tamāshĕs*), iii, 7.
tamis kuri (*tamaskhurī*), x, 5.
tạm^{i}*sandi* (*tȧm*^{i}*-sandi*), vii, 6.
ta^{i}*misạnzüy* (*tȧm*^{i}*-sünz*^{ü}), xii, 15.
tạm^{i}*süy* (*tamis*^{ü}*y*), ii, 1.
tạm^{i} *süy* (*tamis*^{ü}*y*), viii, 9 (2) ; xii, 1.
tāmat (*tāmath*), xi, 20.
tim^{y} (*tim*), viii, 4.
tān (*tān*), viii, 7.
tān, see *nạyis tān*, vii, 27, 8.
tān, see *nạyis tān nạch*, vii, 29.
tūnī, see *khå tūnī*, xii, 22.
tānuk, see *nạyis tānuk*, vii, 26.
tanā nai (*tanānai*), v, 12.
tannana (*tan*^{a}*nana*), v, 12.
tānnạnạ (*tānana*), v, 12.
tīnanān (*tiy nanān*), vii, 1.
tānạs, see *nạyis tānạs*, vii, 26.
tān^{y}, see *nạyis tān*^{y}, vii, 26.
tāny, see *kustāny*, v, 4.
tāny^{e} (*tāñ*), xi, 20.
tāñy (*tāñ*), v, 6 ; viii, 10 ; x, 4, 6, 7, 8 ; xii, 1, 6, 20.
tāñy, see *yutāñy*, v, 7 ; *yu tāñy*, v, 10.
tap (*tab*), v, 3, 10.
tap (*thaph*), iii, 4, 8 (2) ; v, 6, 9 (3) ; vi, 9 ; viii, 7 (2), 9.
tāp (*tāph*), i, 11.
trāu̯ (*trāv*), iii, 4 ; v, 9.
tre (*trĕh*), xii, 19 (3), 24.
tre (*trih*), x, 1, 5, 12 (2) ; xii, 6, 11.
tạr (*thür*^{ü}), v, 4.
tạr (*tür*^{ü}), x, 5 (2), 12.
tārē (*tārē*), v, 7.
tor (*thüḍ*^{u}), v, 4.
tōr^{ạ} (*tōra*), i, 8.
tōrạ (*tōra*), i, 6 ; viii, 11 ; xii, 1.
tōre (*tōra*), v, 4, 9.
tōr^{i} (*tōr*), x, 3.
tōr^{i} (*tūr*^{i}), x, 3.
tō^{i}*ri* (*tōri*), vii, 18.
tūrạ (*tōra*), iv, 5.
tūri (*tūr*^{i}), vii, 20.
tür (*thür*^{ü}), ii, 3.

vupha dāirī (*wŏphādörī*), ii, 2, 3, 4 (3).
vāphīr (*wöphīr*), vi, 14.
vupar (*wŏpar*), v, 4.
vāre (*wāra*), vii, 24.
vāre kāre (*wāra-kāra*), x, 8.
vāri (*wārĕ*), xi, 13.
va^{i}*ri* (*warihy*), xii, 20.
vir (*vir*), v, 7.
vir^{i}*d* (*vir*^{i}*d*), ii, 3, 4.
vurdī (*wurdī*), vi, 16.
vurudz (*wŏrüz*^{u}), viii, 1, 11.
vur māj (*wŏramöj*^{u}), viii, 1.
vur^{a}*mōj* (*wŏramöj*^{u}), viii, 11.
vura māj^{i} (*wŏramājĕ*), viii, 11.
vura n^{y}*ech*^{a} *vin* (*wŏranĕcivĕn*), viii, 3.
vartāvān (*wartāwān*), xi, 7.
vār^{a}*vis* (*wör*^{i}*vis*), x, 3.
vārya (*wārayāh*), viii, 2.
vārya (*wārayāh*), viii, 2.
va^{i}*r*^{y} *dāth* (*wöridāth*), xii, 19.
vāryahas (*wārayāhas*), iii, 1.
vesī (*vĕsī*), ix, 1.
vis (*vĕs*), xii, 14.
vāshe, see *vāle vāshe*, v, 2.
vōsh (*wōsh*), i, 5.
vasan^{i} (*wasüñ*^{ü}), ix, 6.
vasani (*wasani*), viii, 6.
vasān (*wasān*), v, 7 ; viii, 13.
vast (*wasth*), v, 1.
vasit (*wasith*), ii, 3, 6.
vāstu, see *bē vāstu*, v, 11.
vustad (*wustād*), vii, 26.
vustād (*wustād*), ii, 5, 9, 10, 2 ; iii, 2, 4, 5, 7, 9 ; v, 1, 4, 5, 6, 7, 8, 9, 11, 2 ; vi, 16 ; vii, 24 ; viii, 1, 10, 2 ; ix, 1 ; x, 1, 2, 3, 10, 3 ; xii, 4, 8, 9, 20, 2, 5, 6.
vustāda (*wustādāh*), i, 13.
vas^{y}*u* (*wasiv*), vi, 16.
vasyu (*wasiv*), viii, 4.
visyāi (*vis*^{i}*yiy*), ix, 11.
vasīy (*wasiy*), xii, 6.
vasyat (*was yith*), iii, 9.
vasyat (*was yith*), iii, 5.
va^{i}*s*^{i} *zina* (*wâs*^{i}*zi-na*), xii, 11.
vat (*wath*), ii, 1 ; v, 9.
vat^{i} (*wati*), v, 7 ; vii, 17 (2) ; x, 1, 4.
vat^{i} (*wâth*^{i}), x, 5.
vāte (*wāta*), xii, 24.
vāt^{i} (*wāti*), viii, 3, 6, 11 (2).
vāt^{i} (*wöt*^{i}), v, 9 ; viii, 5 ; x, 2.
vāt^{i} (*wöt*^{i}), iii, 1 ; xii, 2.
vāt (*wôt*^{u}), xii, 18.
vāt^{i} (*wöt*^{i}), v, 11.
va^{i}*t*^{i} (*wati*), ii, 2.
va^{i}*ti* (*wati*), xii, 14, 5.
vā^{i}*t*^{i} (*wāti*), xii, 15.
vā^{i}*t*^{i} (*wöt*^{i}), x, 4 ; xii, 8.
vā^{i}*t*^{i} (*wöt*^{i}), xii, 18.
vōt (*wôt*^{u}), ii, 8 ; iii, 1 (2), 3, 4 ; v, 1, 4 (2), 6 ; viii, 4, 7, 9, 10, 1 (2) ; x, 4 (2), 5 (2), 6, 7 (2), 9, 11, 4 (2) ; xii, 1, 5 (2), 10 (2), 1, 2 (2), 3, 9 (2), 20, 2, 5 (2).
vot^{i} (*wâth*^{i}), vi, 16.
vot^{i} (*wŏth*^{u}), xii, 3.
vōt^{i} (*wôt*^{u}), viii, 7 ; x, 3 ; xii, 4, 5.
vut (*woth*^{u}), iii, 9.
vut (*wŏth*), iii, 8 (2).
vut (*wŏth*^{u}), ii, 5, 6 ; v, 9 ; vi, 12, 3.
vut (*wŏth*), iii, 4.
vāt (*wāth*), x, 12 (2).
vōt (*wôth*^{u}), xii, 14.
vut (*wŏth*), ii, 9 (2).
vath (*wath*), xii, 14.
voth (*wŏth*^{u}), xii, 23.
vōth (*wôt*^{u}), xii, 15, 17.

APPENDIX II

INDEX OF WORDS IN GŌVINDA KAULA'S TEXT, ARRANGED IN THE ORDER OF FINAL LETTERS, SHOWING THE CORRESPONDING WORDS IN SIR AUREL STEIN'S TEXT.

KAULA	STEIN
Words ending in *a*	
āba	*āb^{ạ}.*
dŏba	*dob^{ạ}.*
zŏmba	*zumbạ.*
söba	*sābạ.*
ada	*ad^{ạ}, adạ, ade, ad^{e}.*
aḍa	*aḍ.*
dŏda	*dud^{ạ}, dudạ, dod^{ạ}.*
gāḍa	*gāḍạ, gå̄ḍạ.*
gŏḍa	*guḍ^{a}, guḍ^{ạ}, guḍa, guḍe.*
banda	*bande.*
cĕnda	*chandạ.*
danḍa	*danḍ, danḍa.*
shānda	*shāndạ.*
jĕnḍa	*jande.*
zinda	*zindạ.*
pöda	*pādạ, pạ̄d^{ạ}, pạ̄da, pạ̄dạ, pạ̄^{i}dạ, på̄da.*
har^{a}da	*harde.*
marda	*mardạ.*
sarda	*sarde.*
wōḍa	*vōḍạ.*
zāda	*zādạ, zāde.*
shāhzāda	*shahzādạ, sh^{a}hzādạ.*
pātashāhzāda	*pādshah zādạ, pādshāh zādạ.*
rajĕzāda	*rājạ zādạ.*

KAULA	STEIN
dēga	*dēgạ.*
nāga	*nāge.*
hanga-ta-manga	*hangạt^{ạ} mangạ.*
ha	*ha.*
bĕha	*behe.*
dŏha	*doh, doha, dohạ, doh^{o}, doho.*
wuchaha	*vuch^{ạ} ha.*
pātashāha	*pādshah^{ạ}, pādshāh, pādshāhạ, pād^{ạ}shāhạ.*
pātashĕha	*pādshaha, pādshahạ, pādshāh^{ạ}, pād^{ạ}shahạ, pādshahạs.*
kŏha	*koh^{ạ}.*
sapadakha	*sap^{a}dak^{ạ}.*
chukha	*chukạ.*
shākha	*shāk^{ạ}.*
mŏkha	*mukhạ, mukhe.*
nakha	*nakh^{ạ}.*
pakha	*pakạ.*
rōzakha	*rōz kạ.*
yūsūpha	*yūsūf^{ạ}.*
brŭha	*broho.*
atha	*athạ, atho, atạ.*
bātha	*bāṭhạ.*
katha	*kathạ, kathe, katạ.*

KAULA	STEIN
kĕtha	kh^{y}ạthạ, k^{y}eta, k^{y}etạ, k^{y}ita, kyatạ.
bōnṭha	bōnt^{a}, bōntạ.
pĕṭha	p^{y}eṭh, p^{y}eṭhạ, p^{y}eṭhạ, peṭạ, pyeṭe.
yĕtha	yithạ.
wūṭha	vūntạ.
titsha	titsạ.
panja	panje, pañje.
ạsh^{e}ka	ashkạ.
tŏrka	turke.
ṭŏka	tok^{a}.
bāla	bāl^{a}, bālạ.
ad^{a}la	aḍạl.
bagala	bag^{a}lạ.
hala	hal^{a}.
chĕla	chale.
mahala	mahalạ.
phala	phal^{a}.
tsāṭahāla	tsāt^{a}hāl^{a}.
kala	kal^{a}, kale, kalạ.
cakla	chaklạ.
lāla	lālạ.
jumala	jumạlạ.
nāla	nāl^{a}, nālạ.
musla	muslạ, mus^{a}lạ.
tala	tala.
wŏla	volo, vulạ.
hawāla	havāla, havālạ, havāle, havālē.
yĕla	yelạ, yele, yil^{a}, yile.
pyāla	pyālạ.
zāla	zālạ.
ma	mạ.
macāma	macāmạ.
nagma	nagmạ.
khĕma	kh^{y}ema.
muhima	muhimma.

KAULA	STEIN
cĕshma	ceshmạ.
jāma	zhāmạ.
shikama	shikma, shik^{a}mạ.
kalama	kalạma.
nŏma	nomạ.
pāma	pāmạ.
tima	tim^{a}, timạ.
yima	yima, yim^{a}, yimạ
zima	zima, zimạ.
na	mā, na, nạ, ne.
ana	anạ.
ŏna	ānạ, âne.
bŏna	bun^{a}.
nādāna	nā dānạ.
landana	landạnạ.
tog^{u}-na	tōg^{u}nạ.
chĕna	chạ nạ, che na, che nạ, che ne, chanạ, chenạ, ch^{y}enạ.
chuna	chu na, chu nạ.
wŏthihē-na	vutehenạ.
khāna	khān.
chukhna	chuk nạ.
kashĕna	kash na.
nishāna	nishānạ.
gatshi-na	gats^{a}nạ.
kana	kanạ, kane.
kina	kinạ, k^{y}in na, k^{y}inna.
kōna	kōne.
wālana	valenạ.
yĕli na	yelinạ.
gatshĕm-na	lagimnạ.
yim na	yimnạ.
nuna	nuna.
banana	banạnạ.
k^{a}nana	kạnanạ.
tan^{a}nana	tannana.
tānana	tānnạnạ.
zanāna	zanānạ, zạnānạ.

KAULA	STEIN
pāna	*pān^{a}, pānạ, pāne.*
mārana	*mārạnạ.*
ôs^{u}na	*ā̊s na.*
ās-na	*ās^{a}nạ.*
sīna	*sīn^{a}.*
sŏna	*sune.*
chĕsna	*chesna, chạs nạ, che sa.*
kă̄h chus-na	*kahchus na.*
kür^{ü}sna	*kạrus nạ.*
tas na	*tasnạ.*
yĕsa na	*yạsinạ.*
khôtūna	*khātūnạ, khā̊tūn.*
rạt^{a}na	*rothunạ, roṭhunạ, rotunạ, rutun^{a}, rutunạ.*
wana	*vanạ, vane.*
chĕwana	*ch^{v}auvna.*
rawāna	*revānạ.*
āyĕ-na	*āyinạ.*
yina	*yinạ.*
zāna	*zānạ.*
bōzana	*bōz^{a}nạ, bōzạnạ, bōz^{a}ne.*
kår^{i}zi-na	*kar^{i}zạnạ, kạ^{i}r^{i} zinạ.*
rōzana	*rōzạnạ*
wås^{i}zi-na	*vạ^{i}s^{i} zinạ.*
tshŏpa	*tsop^{a}*
āmpa	*ā̊mpa.*
ōra	*ā̊ḍạ, ā̊r, ā̊rạ, ā̊re, ā̊^{u}re, vōḍạ.*
gara	*gar, gar^{a}, garạ.*
sōdāgara	*saudāgạrạ.*
hihara	*h^{y}ạhạrạ.*
shĕhara	*shah^{a}ra, shah^{a}rạ, sheherạ.*
khāra	*kārạ, kāre.*
mŏhara	*mohrạ, moh^{a}rạ, moh^{a}rạ.*
pahara	*paharạ.*

KAULA	STEIN
kara	*kare.*
kāra	*kāre.*
phakīra	*fakīrạ.*
wāra-kāra	*vāre kāre.*
ṭuk^{a}ra	*tukrạ.*
māra	*mārạ, māre.*
shĕhmāra	*shahmār^{a}, shahmārạ.*
nūra	*nūr^{a}.*
para	*parạ.*
pāra	*pār.*
sara	*sar, sar^{a}, sare, serạ.*
sūra	*sūrạ.*
asara	*asr^{a}.*
tōra	*tōḍ^{a}, tōr^{a}, tōrạ, tōre, tūrạ.*
wāra	*vāre.*
yāra	*yār, yār^{a}, yārạ.*
yōra	*yōrạ.*
zāra	*zār^{a}, zārạ.*
wazīra	*vazīr^{a}, vazīrạ.*
sa	*sa, sạ, se.*
ăsa	*āse, ā̊sa, ā̊sạ.*
ösa	*ā̊s^{u}.*
di-sa	*disạ.*
gāsa	*gāsạ, gāse, gāsu.*
hasa	*ha se, h^{a}sạ, hasa, hasạ, hase.*
chĕsa	*chạsạ.*
bŏh hasa	*boh^{a}sạ, boha se.*
ts^{a}h hasa	*tsahasạ.*
khāsa	*khās, khās^{a}.*
kusa	*kusạ.*
dilāsa	*dīlāsạ.*
an sa	*ansạ.*
nin sa	*ninsạ.*
tsaṭanasa	*tsaṭan^{a}sạ.*
wan-sa	*vanse, van^{a}sạ.*
yĕsa	*yasạ, yesạ.*
ta	*t^{a}, ta, tạ, te.*

KAULA	STEIN
aṭa	aṭa.
bata	bat^{a}, batạ, baṭṭạ.
bŏṭa	buṭṭạ.
mahabata	mahabat.
dita	dittạ.
gāṭa	gāṭạ.
hata	hatạ.
wuchta	vuch tạ.
khŏta	kutạ, khotạ, khuṭạ.
nŏkhta	nukhtạ.
daskhata	daskatạ.
raṭhta	rath tạ.
tshĕta	tsetạ.
tshōṭa	tsōṭ^{a}.
gatshta	gats tạ.
wakta	vaktạ.
tshunta	tsunthạ.
wanta	vantạ, vante.
niyĕn ta	niyantạ.
zyun^{u} ta	z^{y}ünte.
pata	pat^{a}, patạ.
pata-pata	patạ-patạ
karta	kartạ, karte, kar the.
sāta	sāt^{a}, sāthạ.
sō̃ta	sōntạ.
basta	bastạ.
shikasta	shikasta.
bēwāsta	bē vāstu.
tōta	tōta, tōtạ, tōt^{u}, tōtu.
tsĕ ta	ts^{y}eta.
chiv ta	ch^{y}ūtạ.
thāvta	thāu̯ tạ.
wāta	vāte.
katsa	katse.
kātsa	kāts^{a}.
mō̃tsa	māntsạ.
hĕtsamatsa	hetsạmatsạ.
wa	vu.

KAULA	STEIN
dawa	davạ.
chĕwa	ch^{y}au.
chiwa	chu.
chuwa	chu.
kuwa	kuv^{a}.
jalwa	jal^{a}va.
tālawa	tāl^{a} va.
mĕwa	m^{y}eva.
wanamōwa	vanemau, vanemō^{u}, vanemo^{v}.
wañĕmōwa	vañye mōv.
dopum^{a}wa	dop^{u}mau.
dyutum^{a}wa	dyüt^{u}mau.
yimawa	yimau.
wañĕwa	van^{y}au.
kor^{u}wa	kuru, kurū.
kür^{ü}wa	kạru.
māriwa	mạ̄^{i}ryu.
ös^{i}wa	åsyu.
phüṭ^{ü}wa	phutu.
roṭ^{u}wa	rutu.
partawa	par tav^{a}.
nēza	n^{y}ạ̄zạ.
hanza	hanzạ, hạnza, hạnzạ.
tihanza	tạ hanzạ, ti hạnzạ.
manza	manzạ.
rēza	rēzạ.
garza	gar ze.
darwāza	darvāza, dạrvāzạ.

Words ending in ā

KAULA	STEIN
bā	bā.
ādā	āda.
khŏdā	kudā, kūdā, khudā.
bā-khŏdā	bā-khudā.
mŏdā	mudā.
pardā	parda.

KAULA	STEIN
phardā	*parda.*
sōdā	*sōdā.*
hā	*hā.*
bēbahā	*bē bahā, bēb^{a}hā, bēbahā.*
dŏhā	*doha.*
pātashĕhā	*pādshahạ.*
zalīkhā	*zalīkhā, zulīkhā.*
bē-wŏphā	*bēvophā.*
srĕhā	*sreha.*
ziyāphathā	*ziāfat.*
sāthā	*sātha, sāṭạ.*
hātshā	*hā tsā.*
kālā	*kāla.*
dalīlā	*dalila, dalīla, dalīlạ.*
bismillā	*bismilla.*
guṭ^{i}lā	*guṭ^{i}lā.*
lāyilā	*lā illāh.*
z^{a}lā	*zilla.*
mā	*ma, mā.*
hakīmā	*hakīma.*
samā	*samā.*
tsĕ mā	*tsima.*
nā	*na, nā.*
mödānā	*maidānạ.*
wadanā	*vade nā.*
hanā	*h^{a}nā, hana, hạna, hạnā, hạnạ, hna.*
dŏba-hanā	*dob^{a}hạnạ.*
khĕkh-nā	*k^{y}eknā.*
yikh-nā	*yihna.*
ratshi-hanā	*ratseh^{a}na, ratse h^{a}na.*
khashĕna-hanā	*khash^{a}nạ h^{a}nā.*
pāri-hanā	*pār^{y}ehna.*
tagĕm-nā	*tagimna.*
bani-nā	*banina.*
zāna-nā	*zānenā.*
zanānā	*zạnānạ.*

KAULA	STEIN
khôtūnā	*khâtūnạ, kōtūna.*
āy-nā	*āyna.*
thūñ^{u}ā	*thanyā.*
sōdāgārā	*sōdāgār^{a}, sōdāgārạ.*
phakīrā	*fakirạ.*
shĕhmārā	*shah māra.*
shĕkhtsā	*shahtsa.*
dawā	*davā.*
chwā	*cha.*
yā	*ya, yā.*
chyā	*cha, chā, che, ch^{y}ā.*
kyā	*kya, kyā.* Cf. *kyāh.*
balāyā	*balāyạ.*
pazyā	*pazyā.*

Words ending in *ai*

kŏhai	*kohạy.*
yihai	*yi hoi.*
tanānai	*tanā nai.*

Words ending in *au*

bargau	*burgau.*
hau	*ho.*
kathau	*kathau.*
lālau	*lālau.*
krālau	*krālau.*
talau	*talau.*
mārawātalau	*mārạvātạlau, mārạvāt^{a}lau.*
timau	*timau.*
yimau	*yimau.* Cf. *yimav.*
nau	*nau.*
gānau	*gānau.*
nigīnau	*nigīnau.*
ȧs^{i} nau	*ạs^{i}nau.*
rost^{u} nau	*rust^{a}nau.*
tsūrau	*tsūrau.* Cf. *tsūrav.*

KAULA	STEIN
wazīrau	*vazirau, vazīrau.*
bātsau	*bātsau.*
dŏyau	*doyau.*
ködyau	*kạ̄^{i}dyau, kạ̄dyau.*
sandyau	*sandyau.*
bāranyau	*bār^{ạ}nyau.*
guryau	*gur^{y}au.*

Words ending in *ĕ*

KAULA	STEIN
ĕ	*ạ, i.*
söhib-ĕ	*sāhib^{i}.*
bacĕ	*bache.*
jĕnatacĕ	*janạtạch.*
tsöcĕ	*su cho, suche, tsuche.*
zacĕ	*zache.*
kōḍĕ	*kūḍ^{y}e.* Cf. *kōrĕ.*
zadĕ	*zade.*
achĕ	*ạch.*
bŏchĕ	*boche.*
lachĕ	*lache*
törīph-ĕ	*tạ̄^{i}rīf-i.*
tsārihĕ	*tsārihe.*
bāshĕ	*bāshe.*
khāba-nishĕ	*kāb^{ạ}nish.*
nishĕ	*nish, nishi.*
pēsh-ĕ	*pēshe.*
pōshĕ	*posha, pōsh^{ạ}, pōshe.*
tŏhĕ	*tohi, toh^{y}i.*
ajĕ	*ajạ.*
bujĕ	*buje.*
gĕjĕ	*g^{y}ajạ.*
lĕjĕ	*l^{y}ejạ.*
mājĕ	*māje, māj^{i}, māji.*
dŏda-mājĕ	*dod^{ạ}māj^{i}.*
wŏramājĕ	*vurạ māj^{i}.*
wölinjĕ	*vālinjạ, vālinje, vāliñjạ, vāliñje, vāliñj^{i}.*

KAULA	STEIN
kranjĕ	*krañj^{e}.*
rājĕ	*rājạ, rāje.*
wāt^{a}jĕ	*vātüjạ.*
löyik-ĕ	*lāy^{ạ}kạ.*
mĕ	*mạ, me, m^{y}e, mye.*
sak^{a}th mĕ	*sakhme.*
pyōm mĕ	*pyōm^{i}.*
kar mĕ	*karme.*
kor^{u} mĕ	*kurme.*
bĕñĕ	*bạñye, beñye.*
wŏdañĕ	*vud^{ạ}nye, vudanye, vud^{ạ}ñye, vudañye.*
gañĕ	*gan^{y}i, gañye.*
kañĕ	*kanye, kañye.*
ạsh^{ĕ}kañĕ	*ashkanye.*
mānĕ	*māne, mā^{i}ni, mānye, mā^{i}nye.*
panañĕ	*panạni, panạn^{y}e, paneñye.*
bög^{a}rañĕ	*bāg^{a}ranye.*
wuñĕ	*vuñye.*
cyāñĕ	*chān^{y}e, ch^{y}āñye.*
zañĕ	*za^{i}n^{y}e, zañye.*
dārĕ	*dạ̄^{i}ri.*
shĕhar-ĕ	*shehri.*
karĕ	*ka^{i}ri.*
kōrĕ	*kōḍ^{i}, kūḍis, kōḍ^{y}e, kōḍ^{y}i, kūḍ^{y}e, kōḍye, kōr^{y}e, kōr^{y}i.* Cf. *kōḍĕ.*
marĕ	*mạri.*
miñĕ-marĕ	*ming^{ye} mạri.*
wārĕ	*vāri.*
asĕ	*as^{i}, asi.*
khal^{a}t-ĕ	*kal^{ạ}ti.*

KAULA	STEIN
tsĕ	*tsa̤, tse, tsᵛe, tsye.*
āyĕ	*āya̤, āye, āyi, āyī.*
bāyĕ	*bai, bāyᵉ, baye.*
biyĕ	*ba̤yⁱ, bey, beye.*
pūtashāhbāyĕ	*pādshah bāye.*
gūrⁱ-bāyĕ	*gūr bāye.*
grīstⁱ-bāyĕ	*grēstᵃ bāye, grēsta̤ bāye.*
dayĕ	*daye.*
khŏdāyĕ	*kudāye.*
gayĕ	*gayᵉ, gaye, ga̤yᵉ.*
tagiyĕ	*tagᵛe, tagⁱye.*
gatshiyĕ	*gatsiye.*
jāyĕ	*jai, jāya̤, jāyᵉ, jāye.*
mŏyĕ	*moye.*
nayĕ	*naye.*
niyĕ	*niy, niyᵉ, niye.*
rŏpayĕ	*rupia, rupⁱya̤.*
rāyĕ	*rai.*
barāyĕ	*ba rai.*
drāyĕ	*drāye.*
grāyĕ	*grāye.*
phakīriyĕ	*fakīri.*
parⁱyĕ	*pa̤ⁱriye.*
hamsāyĕ	*hamsai, ham sāye.*
gadöyiyĕ	*gadoi yiye.*
ṭuvyēyĕ	*tuvⁱy.*
kĕnzĕ	*kyenzi.*
sanzĕ	*sanzi, sa̤nzi.*
pātashāha-sanzĕ	*pādshāhasa̤nzi.*
pātashĕha-sanzĕ	*pādshaha̤ sanzi, pādshaha̤ sa̤nzi, pādshaha̤s sa̤nzi.*

Words ending in *ē*

āgē	*age.*
pīchē	*pīche.*
wuchihē	*vuchᵃhe.*
wanihē	*vana̤he.*
karihē	*karehe, kaⁱrihe, kari hᵛe.*
marihē	*marihᵛe.*
mārihē	*ma̤rihe, mārihe.*
āsihē	*āsi he, āsihe.*
cĕyihē	*chᵛaye hᵛe.*
diyihē	*diyehe.*
bālē	*bālᵛē.*
nālē	*nāle.*
gŏpālē	*gupālᵛē.*
panañē	*paneñye.*
gārē	*gārᵛē.*
mārē	*mārē.*
tārē	*tārē.*
dukhtar-ē	*dukhtarē.*
kŏng-wārē	*kuṅgᵃvārᵛē.*
gayē	*gayᵉ.*

Words ending in ⁱ

sumbⁱ	*sumb.*
bŏdⁱ	*budⁱ.*
hata-bŏdⁱ	*hata̤ budⁱ.*
kådⁱ	*kaⁱrᵛ.*
ködⁱ	*ka̤ⁱd, ka̤ⁱdⁱ, kūdⁱ.*
gåndⁱ	*gandⁱ, ga̤ndi.*
håndⁱ	*ha̤ndⁱ.*
såndⁱ	*sandⁱ, sandi, sa̤nd.*
sŏna-såndⁱ	*sunasandⁱ, suna̤sandⁱ, suna̤sandi.*
sŏnara-såndⁱ	*suna̤rsandi.*
rūdⁱ	*rōdⁱ.*
bögⁱ	*ba̤ⁱgⁱ.*
lågⁱ	*lagⁱ, la̤gⁱ.*
shĕchⁱ	*shechᵛ.*
wuchⁱ	*vuch.*
dŏhⁱ	*duhᵛ.*
hihⁱ	*hi.*

KAULA	STEIN
kĕh^{i}	*kạd.*
hŏkh^{i}	*huk*^{i}.
wŏtamukh^{i}	*vutamak*^{i}.
kȧsh^{i}	*kash*^{a}.
ath^{i}	*at*^{i}, *ạt*^{i}, *a*^{i}*t*^{i}, *ạ*^{i}*t*^{i}, *at*^{v}, *a*^{i}*t*^{v}.
ȧth^{i}	*ạt*^{i}.
tŏh^{i}	*toh*^{i}, *tuh, tuh*^{i}, *tuh*^{v}.
bīṭh^{i}	*bēth*^{v}, *b*^{v}*ēth*^{i}, *bạṭ*^{i}.
ciṭh^{i}	*chit.*
kuṭh^{i}	*kuṭ*^{i}.
pĕṭh^{i}	*p*^{v}*eṭh, pyet.*
pöṭh^{i}	*pạ̄*^{i}*th*^{i}, *pạ̄*^{i}*ṭh*^{i}, *pạ̄*^{i}*ṭ*^{i}, *pạ̄*^{i}*th*^{v}, *pạ̄*^{i}*ṭh*^{v}, *pạ̄*^{i}*ty*, *pạ̄*^{i}*t*^{v}.
tath^{i}	*tat, tạt*^{i}, *ta*^{i}*t*^{i}, *tạ*^{i}*t*^{i}, *ta*^{i}*ṭ*^{v}.
wȧth^{i}	*vat*^{i}, *vot*^{i}, *vat*^{v}.
zīṭh^{i}	*zīṭ*^{i}.
wāt^{a}*j*^{i}	*vātạj.*
ȧk^{i}	*ak*^{i}.
harȧk^{i}	*harik.*
rātȧk^{i}	*rātik.*
thövik^{i}	*thāvik.*
nyövik^{i}	*n*^{v}*āvik.*
gȧl^{i}	*gạ*^{i}*l*^{i}.
gul^{i}	*gul*^{i}.
hĕl^{i}	*hil.*
ṭahȧl^{i}	*tạhạl, tạhạl*^{i}, *tạhạl*^{v}.
möl^{i}	*mạ*^{i}*l.*
nöl^{i}	*nāl, nāl*^{i}, *nāl*^{v}, *nạ̄*^{i}*l*^{v}.
gŏpöl^{i}	*gupāl*^{i}.
tȧl^{i}	*tạ*^{i}*l*^{i}.
tul^{i}	*ṭu*^{i}*l*^{v}.
gāṭ^{a}*l*^{i}	*gātily.*
wātȧl^{i}	*vātạl*^{i}.

KAULA	STEIN
tsȧl^{i}	*tsạl*^{v}.
ȧm^{i}	*am*^{i}, *ạm*^{i}, *a*^{i}*m*^{i}, *ạ*^{i}*m*^{i}, *ạm*^{v}.
öm^{i}	*ạ̄*^{i}*mi.*
kȧm^{i}	*kạm*^{i}.
tröm^{i}	*trā̤m, trạ̄m*^{v}.
tsūrim^{i}	*tsorim.*
tȧm^{i}	*tạm*^{i}.
yĕm^{i}	*yim.*
yim^{i}	*yim, yem*^{i}.
din^{i}	*din*^{i}, *din*^{v}.
bāgȧn^{i}	*bāgen*^{i}.
hūn^{i}	*hūn, hūnạ, hōni.*
kȧn^{i}	*kan*^{i}, *kạn*^{i}, *kạn*^{v}.
lön^{i}	*lạ̄*^{i}*ni.*
ḍulȧn^{i}	*duleñy.*
panȧn^{i}	*pan, panen, paneñy.*
bārȧn^{i}	*bārạn.*
prön^{i}	*prāñy, prān*^{v}.
āsȧn^{i}	*āsạn*^{i}.
tsaṭȧn^{i}	*tsaten*^{i}.
wȧn^{i}	*vạn*^{v}.
sọmb^{a}*rāwȧn*^{i}	*somb*^{a}*rāva*^{i}*n*^{i}.
lāyȧn^{i}	*lāyin.*
myön^{i}	*mēn*^{v}, *myẽ, m*^{v}*ēn.*
zȧn^{i}	*zan*^{i}.
dazön^{i}	*dazān*^{i}.
tsȧp^{i}	*tsạp*^{v}.
bȧr^{i}	*bar, bari.*
mĕ bȧr^{i}	*mebar.*
dör^{i}	*dạ̄r.*
gȧr^{i}	*gar*^{i}.
gur^{i}	*gur, gur*^{i}.
gūr^{i}	*gūr.*
phir^{i}	*phīr*^{i}.
hȧr^{i} *hȧr*^{i}	*hạri hạri.*
shur^{i}	*shūri.*
köshir^{i}	*kāshir*^{i}.
kȧr^{i}	*kạr, kạ*^{i}*r*^{i}.

KAULA	STEIN
kūr^{i}	*kūḍ^{i}.*
mör^{i}	*mạ̄^{i}r^{y}.*
apör^{i}	*apạ̄^{i}r, apạ̄^{i}r^{i}.*
tsŏpör^{i}	*so pạ̄^{i}ri, tso pạ̄^{i}r^{i}.*
yipör^{i}	*yipạ̄^{i}r^{i}.*
tūr^{i}	*tōr^{i}, tūri.*
tsīr^{i}	*tsīr^{y}.*
paṭhwör^{i}	*paṭ^{a}vār^{i}.*
yūr^{i}	*yūr^{i}, yūr^{y}, yūr^{i}, yūry.*
murdamāzör^{i}	*murde māzạ̄^{i}ry.*
ȧs^{i}	*as^{i}, ạs^{i}, ạ^{i}s^{i}.*
ös^{i}	*ās^{i}, ạ̄s^{i}, å̄s, å̄s^{i}.*
ạt^{i}	*at^{i}, a^{i}ti, ạt^{y}.*
dit^{i}	*ditti.*
langūṭ^{i}	*longū^{i}ṭh^{i}.*
khȧt^{i}	*khat^{i}, kạ^{i}t^{y}.*
kit^{i}	*kit, kit^{i}.*
kṻt^{i}	*kạ̄t^{i}.*
lŏk^{a}ṭ^{i}	*lokat.*
lŏt^{i}	*lu^{i}t^{i}.*
mȧt^{i}	*mat^{i}.*
gȧnḍ^{i}mȧt^{i}	*gand^{a}maty^{i}.*
gamȧt^{i}	*gamat^{i}, gạmạt^{y}, gamut^{y}.*
lȧg^{i}mȧt^{i}	*lạg^{i}mat^{i}.*
lög^{i}mȧt^{i}	*lạ̄gimat^{y}.*
mumȧt^{i}	*momut^{y}.*
ȧn^{i}mȧt^{i}	*ani mot^{i}.*
dit^{i}mȧt^{i}	*d^{y}ütmat, d^{y}itạmaty.*
thöv^{i}mȧt^{i}	*thạ̄ymak.*
rȧṭ^{i}	*rạṭ^{i}, rạ^{i}ṭ^{y}.*
mŏtasṻt^{i}	*mut^{a}sạ̄^{i}th^{i}.*
tȧt^{i}	*tat^{i}, tạt^{i}.*
yĕtȧt^{i}	*ye tạ^{i}ṭ^{i}.*
wöt^{i}	*vāt^{i}, vạ̄t^{i}, vå̄t^{i}, vā^{i}t^{i}, vạ̄^{i}t^{i}.*
yit^{i}	*yi, yet^{i}, yạ^{i}t^{y}, ye^{i}ty.*
nĕciv^{i}	*nechiv.*

KAULA	STEIN
pŏlādȧv^{i}	*polādev^{y}.*
mahaniv^{i}	*mahñyiu̯.*
kañiv^{i}	*kañyev^{i}.*
shĕstrȧv^{i}	*shastrev^{i}.*
biy^{i}	*bēy.*
böy^{i}	*bạ̄i, bạ̄y.*
day^{i}	*diyạ.*
laḍöy^{i}	*laḍāi.*
gawöy^{i}	*gavạ̄i.*
hā hȧz^{i}	*yāhaz^{i}.*
rīnz^{i}	*rạ̄nz, rēnz, rīnz.*
pȧz^{i}	*pạz, pạz^{i}.*
rūz^{i}	*rōz, rōz^{i}.*

Words ending in *i*

i	*ạ, i.*
zūnaḍabi	*zün^{a} dabi.*
söhib-i	*sāhibi.*
dādi	*dạ̄^{i}de.*
wŏlād-i	*vulādi.*
mahmōd-i	*mahmūd^{i}.*
handi	*handi, hạndi.*
dŏn-handi	*don hạndi.*
gŏḍañicĕ-handi	*guḍe nyechi hạndi.*
kōndi	*kōndạ.*
sandi	*sandi, sạndi.*
pātashĕha-sandi	*pādshahạsạndi.*
möl^{i}-sandi	*mạ̄^{i}l^{i}sandi.*
ȧm^{i}-sandi	*ạmisạndi.*
tȧm^{i}-sandi	*tạm^{i}sandi.*
wazīra-sandi	*vazīrạsạndi.*
sapadi	*sapạd^{i}.*
wŏḍi	*vōḍ^{y}e, vuḍ^{y}e, voḍye.*
yād-i	*yādi.*
sŏnamargi	*son^{a}margạ.*
bĕhi	*behe.*
bŏchi	*bo che.*
nĕchi	*n^{y}eche, nyeche.*
phahi	*phahi.*

KAULA	STEIN
shāh-i	shāhī.
kōh-i	koh^{v}e.
hakh-i	ha^{i}khi.
rakhi	rakhi, rakh^{v}e.
tsakhi	tsakh^{i}, tsakh^{v}e.
bår^{i}shi	barshạ.
wālawāshi	vāle vāshe.
athi	a^{i}th^{i}, a^{i}thi, at^{i}.
öthi	åth^{i}.
wöthi	vuthi.
gatshi	gatsạ, gatse, gatsē, gatsi.
mĕ gatshi	m^{v}egatse.
matshi	matsạ, mats^{v}e.
ratshi	rats^{a} hạn.
māji	māje, māji, mạ̄j, mā^{i}ji.
dŏda-māji	dod^{ə}mạ̄j.
krāji	krāje.
aki	ak^{i}, aki.
bal^{i}ki	balki.
löyik-i	lạ̄^{i}ki, lāyiki.
ḍōli	doili.
gali	ga^{i}li.
dökhil-i	dākh^{i}li.
kŏli	kul^{v}e, kulye.
kuli	kul^{i}.
mŏkali	mokli, mukli.
rumāli	rumāli.
sōli	sulli.
suli	sulạ.
tĕli	telạ, teli, til^{i}.
rāt^{a}li	rāt^{ə}li.
yĕli	yeli, yel^{i}.
ami	am^{i}, ami, ạm^{i}, ạmi, a^{i}m^{i}, a^{i}mi, ạ^{i}m^{i}, ạ^{i}mi, ạmis.
kami	kami.
hukm-i	huk^{u}mạ.
salāmi	salāmi.

KAULA	STEIN
nami	nam^{i}.
tami	tam^{i}, tami, tạm^{i}, ta^{i}mi, tạ^{i}mi.
patimi	pat^{v}ạmi.
yĕmi	yam^{i}, ye^{i}mi.
yimi	yạmi, yemi.
trĕyimi	treyimi.
bani	banạ, bani.
dini	dinạ.
dīn-i	dīn^{i}.
hani	hani.
dachini	dach^{i}nạ.
wuchani	vuch^{i} ne.
khĕni	khyeni.
khŏni	kun^{v}ạ.
kani	kane, kan^{i}, kani, kạn^{i}, ka^{i}ni, kạ^{i}n^{v}.
kuni-kani	kun^{i}kạ^{i}n^{v}.
kuni	kunạ, kuni, kun^{i}.
phŏlani	pholen^{i}, phuleni, phulen^{i}.
tōlani	tōlạni.
mani	mane.
zamīni	zemīni.
anani	anạni.
k^{a}nani	kanạni.
panani	panạne, panạn^{i}, panạni, paneni.
wanani	vaneni.
zanāni	zạnạnạ, zạnānạ
wötharani	vutherạni.
karani	karnạ, kar^{ə}ni, karạni, karạ^{i}ni.
mārani	mārạni.
nērani	nạ̄^{i}rini.
kāsani	kās^{ə}ni, khāsạni.
wasani	vasạni

KAULA	STEIN
khôtūni	*khātūni, khātūnī, khåtūni, khå tūnī, khåtūnī.*
sultān-i	*sultān^{i}.*
atsani	*atsạni.*
wātani	*vātạne.*
wani	*vane.*
yini	*yini.*
lāyĕni	*lāyine.*
myāni	*myāni.*
zāni	*zānạ, zāne.*
zēni	*za^{i}ni, z^{y}ạ̄ni.*
rōzani	*rōzạn^{i}.*
bĕñi	*beñye.*
kañi	*kanye, kañye.*
mål^{i}kāñi	*malkānye.*
panañi	*paneñ^{y}e, paneñye.*
tilawāñi	*tilavāñye.*
dapi	*dapi, dạpi.*
thapi	*tha^{i}pi.*
bāri	*bā^{i}ri.*
kabari	*kab^{ə}rạ.*
dāri	*dā^{i}ri, dạ̄^{i}ri.*
dūri	*dūri.*
dadari	*dad^{ə}ri.*
gari	*gar^{i}, ga^{i}ri.*
guri	*gur^{i}.*
makh^{a}r-i	*makhri.*
shĕmshēri	*shamshēr^{i}, shamsēri, samshēri.*
kari	*ka^{i}re, ka^{i}rē, ka^{i}ri, kạ^{i}ri.*
kōri	*kōd^{ye}, koḍ^{y}e, kōḍ^{ye}, kōḍ^{y}i, kōr^{y}e.*
phikiri	*phikri.*

KAULA	STEIN
lashkari	*lashkạrạ, lashkạr^{i}, lashkạ^{i}ri, khal^{a}kan.*
lari	*lạ̄^{i}r^{i}.*
t^{a}l^{a}ri	*tulạri.*
māch-t^{a}l^{a}ri	*māch-tulari, māch-tulạri, māsh-tulạri.*
mari	*mạri, mạ^{i}ri.*
miñĕ-mari	*ming^{ye} mạri.*
tōri	*tō^{i}ri.*
litri	*lit^{a}ri.*
tsūri	*tsūri, tsu^{i}r^{i}, tsū^{i}r^{i}, tsū^{i}ri.*
kŏng-wāri	*kuṅg^{a}vār^{i}.*
nazari	*naz^{a}ri, naz^{ə}ri.*
āsi	*ās^{i}, āsi, ā^{i}s^{i}.*
kaīsi	*ka^{i}sī, kạ̄^{i}si.*
kŏsi	*kāsi.*
lasi	*lasạ.*
waīsi	*vạ̄^{i}nsi.*
ti	*ti, t^{y}e, t^{y}i.*
ati	*at^{i}, ạt^{i}, a^{i}ti, at^{y}e.*
bŏti	*bɔt^{ye}.*
kāh ti	*kahti.*
pĕṭh^{i} ti	*p^{y}eti.*
kati	*kat^{i}, kati, ka^{i}ti, kạ^{i}ti, kat^{y}e, kat^{y}i, katye.*
laṭi	*laṭ^{i}, laṭi.*
tål^{i} ti	*tạ̄^{i}lti.*
maṭi	*maṭ^{i}.*
mĕ-ti	*mạṭ^{i}, m^{y}eti.*
hĕkmat-i	*hekạmati.*
drāti	*drātis.*
hazrat-i	*hazrat, hazrạt^{i}, hazrạ^{i}t^{i}, hazret, hazret^{i}, hāzret.*

KAULA	STEIN
suti	*sut^{i}.*
tati	*tat^{i}, ta^{i}ti, ta^{i}ṭ^{i}, tat^{y}.*
ti-ti	*titi.*
tō-ti	*tōt^{y}i.*
ts^{a}-ti	*tsạti.*
wati	*vat^{i}, va^{i}t^{i}, va^{i}ti, vat^{y}e.*
wāti	*vāt^{i}, vā^{i}t^{i}, vāt^{ye}.*
yĕti	*yạt^{i}, yet^{i}.*
yi-ti	*yi ti.*
yiti	*yeti, yit^{i}.*
hāvi	*hā̤vi.*
shĕstravi	*shast^{ạ}rvi, shīt^{ạ}rạvi.*
bāyi	*bāyạ, bāye.*
grīst^{i}-bāyi	*grēst bāye, grēst^{ạ} bāye.*
dŏyi	*doye.*
āgayi	*āgạye.*
khĕyi	*kheye.*
lāyi	*lāye.*
salayi	*salạyạ.*
cārpāyi	*palangas.*
par^{i}yi	*pạ^{i}riye.*
dwā-yi	*dv^{o}y^{u}.*
hawā-yi	*havāye.*
yiyi	*yiye.*
zi	*ze.*
dizi	*dīzi.*
bĕh^{i}zi	*bih zi.*
khĕzi	*khyēzi.*
tshån^{i}zi	*tsạn^{ạ}zi.*
sanzi	*sanzi, sạnzi.*
pātashāha-sanzi	*pādshahasạnzi.*
pātashĕha-sanzi	*pādshahạ sanzi, pādshahạ sạnzi*
åm^{i}-sanzi	*a^{i}misạnzi.*
sŏnara-sanzi	*sunạr sanzi, sunạrsạnzạ.*
yāra-sanzi	*yārisạnzi.*

KAULA	STEIN
rōzi	*rōzi.*
kår^{i}zi	*kạ^{i}rzi.*
marāz-i	*mạrāj.*
wås^{i}zi	*vạz^{i}zạ.*
vizi	*vizē.*
pöv^{i}zi	*pạ^{i}vzi.*
kyāzi	*kyāzi, kyā ze, kyā zi, kyā^{i}z^{i}.*
ti-kyāzi	*ti kyā zi.*
azīz-i	*azīza, azīzạ.*

Words ending in ī

KAULA	STEIN
wurdī	*vurdī.*
saragī	*sargi, sargī, sargēh.*
shöhī	*shāhī.*
pātashöhī	*pādshāhi, pādshāhī, pād^{ạ}shāhī.*
jūshī	*jōshī.*
hab-jūshī	*habjōshī.*
wŏbālī	*vu bạ^{i}lī.*
ḍōlī	*dạ^{i}li.*
tasalī	*tas^{ạ}li.*
miskīnī	*miskīnī.*
wŏphādörī	*vuph dạ^{i}ri, vupha dạ^{i}ri, vuphā dạ^{i}rī, vupha dạirī.*
tamaskhurī	*tamis kuri.*
phakīrī	*fakīrī.*
nōkarī	*naukrī, nōk^{ạ}rī.*
parī	*pạ^{i}r^{i}, pạ^{i}ri.*
huzūrī	*hazūri.*
wazīrī	*vazīrī.*
vĕsī	*vesī.*
tī	*tih.*
baltī	*balti.*
masnavī	*masnavī.*
gaznavī	*gaznavī.*
pöravī	*pâravī.*

KAULA	STEIN
yī	*yi.*
judöyī	*zhudāī.*
wŏphöyī	*vuphāī.*
bē-wŏphöyī	*bēvophāī.*
bēwŏphöyī	*bē vuphāī.*
gum-röyī	*gum^{a}rå̄ yiy.*

Word ending in *ŏ*

kĕ-hŏ	*k^{y}ạho, kyạho.*

Words ending in *ō*

ō	*o.*
söhibō	*sāhībō.*
hō	*hō.*
khös^{i} hō	*khạsihō.*
ākhō	*ākhu.*
tsākhō	*tsākhu.*
kathō	*kathu.*
phakīrō	*fakīrō.*
wazīrō	*vaziro.*
hatō	*hatō.*
jāwō	*jāo.*
khŏdāyō	*kodāyu.*
khyō	*kh^{y}au.*
atsayō	*atsayo.*
arz ō	*arzo.*

Words ending in *ö*

lagahö	*lagaha.*
chalahö	*chạlạha.*
dimahö	*dim^{a} ha.*
yimahö	*yimạha.*
yith tshunahö	*yetsanạ ha.*
karahö	*kare ha, karạha.*
bāwahö	*bāvạ ha.*
hāwahö	*hāv^{a} ha.*

Words ending in ^{u}

amôb^{u}	*amōb.*
sumb^{u}	*sumb.*
rĕtas sumb^{u}	*ritasumb.*

KAULA	STEIN
boḍ^{u}	*buḍ.*
dod^{u}	*dud.*
dôd^{u}	*då̄d, dōd.*
shod^{u}	*shod.*
thod^{u}	*thud.*
koḍ^{u}	*kur.*
moḍ^{u}	*muḍ.*
mūd^{u}	*mōd, mūḍ.*
gŏnd^{u}	*gund.*
hond^{u}	*hund.*
pātashöhī-hond^{u}	*pādshāhīhund.*
kathi-hond^{u}	*kat^{y}ehund.*
mājĕ-hond^{u}	*māje hund.*
lālan-hond^{u}	*lālan hund.*
tihond^{u}	*tihund.*
tuhond^{u}	*tuhund.*
konḍ^{u}	*kund.*
sond^{u}	*sund.*
asond^{u}	*am^{i} sund.*
söhiba-sond^{u}	*sāhib^{a}sund.*
pātashāha-sond^{u}	*pādshāh^{a}sund.*
pātashĕha-sond^{u}	*pādshahạ sund, pādshahạsund.*
shĕnāka-sond^{u}	*shinākạsund.*
möl^{i}-sond^{u}	*mạ^{i}l^{i}sund.*
ȧm^{i}-sond^{u}	*ạm^{i}sund, ạmisund, ạ^{i}mi sund.*
gŏlāma-sond^{u}	*gulāmạsund.*
sōdāgāra-sond^{u}	*saudāgārạsund.*
phakīra-sond^{u}	*fakīrạsund.*
sŏnara-sond^{u}	*sunạrsund.*
yāra-sond^{u}	*yārạsund.*
khŏdāyĕ-sond^{u}	*khudāyesund.*
sapod^{u}	*sapud.*
rūd^{u}	*rūd.*
syod^{u}	*syud, s^{y}ud.*
log^{u}	*log, lug.*
lôg^{u}	*lōg.*
shŏng^{u}	*shung.*
tog^{u}	*tug.*

KAULA	STEIN
wuch^{u}	*vuch.*
lyukh^{u}	*l^{y}ükh.*
rosh^{u}	*rush.*
buth^{u}	*but.*
khoth^{u}	*khut.*
ṭhôṭh^{u}	*ṭōṭ.* Cf. *ṭôṭh^{u}.*
kuṭh^{u}	*kuṭ.*
moṭh^{u}	*muṭ.*
ṭôṭh^{u}	*ṭōṭ.* Cf. *ṭhôṭh^{u}.*
woth^{u}	*vut, vuth.*
wọ̆th^{u}	*vot^{i}, vut, voth, vuth.*
yuth^{u}	*yūth.*
byūṭh^{u}	*byūt, byūṭ, byōth, byōṭh, byūṭh.*
ḍyūṭh^{u}	*dyūt, ḍyuṭ, ḍyūṭh^{u}, vuch.*
kyuth^{u}	*kyut.*
myūṭh^{u}	*myūt.*
zyuṭh^{u}	*zyuṭ.*
gotsh^{u}	*gōts, guts.*
hyuh^{u}	*h^{y}u, hyu.*
khābuk^{u}	*kābuk.*
bāguk^{u}	*bāguk^{u}.*
dŏhuk^{u}	*dohuk.*
watharanuk^{u}	*vat^{a}ranuk.*
nayistānuk^{u}	*nạyis tānuk.*
wanuk^{u}	*vanuk.*
jĕnatuk^{u}	*jan^{a}tuk, jan^{a} tukh.*
amyuk^{u}	*am^{i} kuy, ạm^{y}uk, ạmyuk, a^{i}m^{y}uk.*
kamyuk^{u}	*kam^{y}ük.*
gŏḍanyuk^{u}	*guḍeñyuk.*
hatsyuk^{u}	*hats^{y}uk.*
ôl^{u}	*å̄l.*
phol^{u}	*phul.*
phọ̆l^{u}	*phul.*
shĕhul^{u}	*shuhul.*

KAULA	STEIN
kôl^{u}	*kōl.*
môl^{u}	*mōl, mōr.*
buñul^{u}	*buñyül.*
tul^{u}	*tul.*
tsol^{u}	*tsul.*
yĕñĕwôl^{u}	*yeñyi vå̄l, yeñyivōl, yeñy^{i}vōl.*
zôl^{u}	*zōl.*
kyom^{u}	*kyum.*
trĕyum^{u}	*treyimi.*
pöntsyum^{u}	*pānts^{y}ūm.*
kaḍun^{u}	*kạḍun.*
ladun^{u}	*ladun.*
mangun^{u}	*mangun.*
hūn^{u}	*hūn.*
ḍēshun^{u}	*dēshun.*
tshon^{u}	*tsun.*
gatshun^{u}	*gatsun.*
ạsh^{e}kun^{u}	*ạshkun, ạskun.*
galun^{u}	*galun.*
tulun^{u}	*tulun.*
anun^{u}	*anun.*
khanun^{u}	*khanun.*
panun^{u}	*panen, panun.*
dapun^{u}	*dopun.*
sọ̆mb^{a}run^{u}	*somb^{a}run.*
sapharun^{u}	*safarun.*
watharun^{u}	*vat^{a}run.*
karun^{u}	*karun.*
mārun^{u}	*mārun.*
sôn^{u}	*sōn.*
sọ̆n^{u}	*sun.*
āsun^{u}	*āsun.*
khasun^{u}	*khasun.*
bikarmājĕtun^{u}	*vikarmājitun.*
tsaṭun^{u}	*tsatun.*
wātun^{u}	*vātun.*
atsun^{u}	*atsun.*
won^{u}	*vun.*
nērawun^{u}	*nēravun.*

KAULA	STEIN
trāwun^{u}	*trå̄vun.*
kāsawun^{u}	*kās^{u}vun.*
yun^{u}	*h^{y}ün, yün.*
byon^{u}	*b^{y}ün, b'yun.*
cyon^{u}	*chun, ch^{y}un.*
cyôn^{u}	*chōn, chōn^{y}, chōny, ch^{y}ōn.*
dyun^{u}	*dyun.*
hyon^{u}	*h^{y}un.*
khyon^{u}	*khyun.*
myôn^{u}	*myå̂n, myōn.*
zyun^{u}	*zün, z^{y}ün, zyün.*
zon^{u}	*zun.*
bōzun^{u}	*bōzun.*
sōzun^{u}	*sōzun.*
gusôñ^{u}	*gosōny.*
dop^{u}	*dop, dop^{u}, dup, dup^{a}.*
bôr^{u}	*bōr.*
mŏdur^{u}	*mudur.*
gur^{u}	*gur.*
gūr^{u}	*gūr.*
phor^{u}	*phurtas.*
kor^{u}	*kuḍ, kạr, kur, kur^{i}.*
mor^{u}	*muḍ.*
môr^{u}	*mōḍ, mōr.*
pūr^{u}	*pūr.*
tsŏpôr^{u}	*tsopōr.*
khôwur^{u}	*khå̂vur.*
hyor^{u}	*h^{y}ur, hyür.*
phyūr^{u}	*p^{y}ūr.*
ôs^{u}	*ās, ås, å̂s^{u}, ōs.*
bus^{u}	*bus.*
ot^{u}	*at^{i}, ot, ut, ạth, uth.*
hot^{u}	*hut.*
hoṭ^{u}	*hot.*
khot^{u}	*khot^{u}, khut, khuṭ, khuṭh, kut.*

KAULA	STEIN
khŏṭ^{u}	*khuṭ.*
kot^{u}	*koṭ.*
koṭ^{u}	*khuṭh.*
kūt^{u}	*kūt.*
loṭ^{u}	*loṭ.*
āmot^{u}	*āmut.*
rūd^{u}mot^{u}	*rōd^{a}mut, rūd^{a}mut.*
gamot^{u}	*gommut, gōmus, gomut.*
gŏmot^{u}	*gạmut, gomut.*
lôg^{u}mot^{u}	*lå̂g^{u} mut.*
ḍyūṭh^{u}mot^{u}	*dyūtmut.*
lyukh^{u}mot^{u}	*l^{y}ükhmut, lyükhmut.*
gôl^{u}mot^{u}	*gå̂lmut.*
mumot^{u}	*momut.*
on^{u}mot^{u}	*on muth.*
pĕmot^{u}	*p^{y}ümut, pyạmut, pyümut.*
kor^{u}mot^{u}	*kurmut.*
ôs^{u}mot^{u}	*å̂smut.*
roṭ^{u}mot^{u}	*ruṭmut.*
rôṭ^{u}mot^{u}	*roṭ^{a}mut.*
wôt^{u}mot^{u}	*vot^{u}mut, vōt^{u}muth.*
dyut^{u}mot^{u}	*dyutmut, dyut^{a}mut, dyüt^{a}mut.*
thow^{u}mot^{u}	*thāu̯ mut.*
thôw^{u}mot^{u}	*thāu̯mut, thåu̯mut.*
lāḍyōmot^{u}	*lāḍ^{y}ōmut.*
nyūmot^{u}	*nyumut.*
noṭ^{u}	*nut.*
pot^{u}	*phot, phut, put, puth.*
roṭ^{u}	*rōt, rut.*
drôt^{u}	*drōt.*
troṭ^{u}	*truṭ.*
host^{u}	*host, host^{u}.*

KAULA	STEIN
gryūst^{u}	*grost.*
tot^{u}	*thuth, tot, tut.*
tsoṭ^{u}	*tsōt.*
wôt^{u}	*vā̊t, vōt, vōt*^{i}*, vōṭ, voth.*
yūt^{u}	*yūt.*
dyut^{u}	*d*^{v}*ut, dyut, dyuth.*
kyut^{u}	*kh*^{v}*ut, khyuth, k*^{v}*ut, kyut, kyuth.*
tshyoṭ^{u}	*tsuṭ, ts*^{v}*ut, ts*^{v}*uṭ.*
tyūt^{u}	*tyṻt.*
hots^{u}	*hots, huts.*
bôw^{u}	*bōu̯.*
thôw^{u}	*thā̊u̯.*
lôw^{u}	*lāu̯.*
mŏkalôw^{u}	*moklau.*
nôw^{u}	*nā̊u̯, nōu̯.*
parzanôw^{u}	*parzạ nāu̯, parzạ nā̊u̯.*
sọmb^{a}*rôw*^{u}	*somb*^{a}*rau, somb*^{a} *rau.*
tsamruw^{u}	*tsam ru, tsam*^{a}*ru.*
trôw^{u}	*trōv.*
shĕstruw^{u}	*shast*^{a}*ro.*
nĕcyuv^{u}	*n*^{v}*echu.*
mahanyuv^{u}	*mahñyu.*
bôy^{u}	*boy, bōy.*
būz^{u}	*bōz.*
poz^{u}	*puz.*
apoz^{u}	*apuz.*

Words ending in ^{ü}

KAULA	STEIN
dŏhüc^{ü}	*dohuch.*
nayistānüc^{ü}	*nạyis tān nạch.*
azic^{ü}	*azich.*
buḍ^{ü}	*buḍ.*
thüḍ^{ü}	*tạḍ, tor.* Cf. *thür*^{ü}.
kūḍ^{ü}	*kūḍ.* See also *kūr*^{ü}.
krünḍ^{ü}	*k*^{a}*rạnd.*
tsünḍ^{ü}	*tsunḍ.*
wuch^{ü}	*vuch.*
bōlbösh^{ü}	*bōlbā̊sh.*
hish^{ü}	*hish.*
zĕṭh^{ü}	*ziṭh.*
wŏ̈tsh^{ü}	*vuts.*
wütsh^{ü}	*vuts.*
dŏmbij^{ü}	*dumbij.*
düj^{ü}	*dạje.*
shĕh^{ü}*j*^{ü}	*shạhij.*
lüj^{ü}	*lạj.*
mang lüj^{ü}	*mang*^{a}*lạj.*
mōj^{ü}	*māj, mōj.*
dŏda-mōj^{ü}	*dod*^{a}*māj.*
wŏramōj^{ü}	*vur māj, vur*^{a}*mōj.*
wölinj^{ü}	*vālĭnje.*
tuj^{ü}	*tuj.*
gāṭ^{ü}*j*^{ü}	*gātij.*
tsüj^{ü}	*tsạj, tsạ*^{i}*jy.*
wöj^{ü}	*vāj, vāj, vāj*^{v}.
köm^{ü}	*kā̊m, kā̊ma, kōm.*
tröm^{ü}	*trōm.*
satim^{ü}	*sạtim*^{v}.
pöntsim^{ü}	*pā̊ntsim, pā̤nts*^{v}*um.*
trĕyim^{ü}	*triyim.*
dön^{ü}	*dān.*
zabōñ^{ü}	*zạbāñy.*
diñ^{ü}	*diñy.*
chōñ^{ü}	*chān*^{v}.
küñ^{ü}	*kan.*
wālüñ^{ü}	*vālạñy.*
nüñ^{ü}	*nañyi.*
anüñ^{ü}	*anạn*^{v}*, aneñy.*
tshunüñ^{ü}	*tsạneñy.*
panüñ^{ü}	*panen, panen*^{i}*, panen*^{v}*, paneñy, paniñy.*

KAULA	STEIN
karüñ$^{\ddot{u}}$	*karin*^{y}, *kareñy*, *kariny*.
söñ$^{\ddot{u}}$	*sāñ*^{y}, *sạ*^{i}*ñy*.
wasüñ$^{\ddot{u}}$	*vasan*^{i}.
bikarmājĕtüñ$^{\ddot{u}}$	*vikarmājiteñy*.
mōtüñ$^{\ddot{u}}$	*mōteny*.
bacāwüñ$^{\ddot{u}}$	*bachāviny*.
pakawüñ$^{\ddot{u}}$	*pak*^{a}*vañy*.
mŏkalāwüñ$^{\ddot{u}}$	*mokalāvañy*.
yiñ$^{\ddot{u}}$	*yiny*.
cyöñ$^{\ddot{u}}$	*ch*^{i}*ān*, *ch*^{y}*ān*^{i}, *ch*^{y}*ạn*^{y}.
chyöñ$^{\ddot{u}}$	*chāny*.
myöñ$^{\ddot{u}}$	*myĕ*, *mēñy*, *m*^{y}*ēn*, *myēn*, *m*^{y}*ēñy*.
züñ$^{\ddot{u}}$	*zạny*, *za*^{i}*n*^{y}.
ör$^{\ddot{u}}$	*å̄r*.
thür$^{\ddot{u}}$	*tạr*, *tür*. Cf. *thüḍ*$^{\ddot{u}}$.
ạth$^{\ddot{u}}$*r*$^{\ddot{u}}$	*ạtạr*.
ḳūr$^{\ddot{u}}$	*ḳūd*, *kūr*, *khūḍ*. See also *ḳūḍ*$^{\ddot{u}}$.
kür$^{\ddot{u}}$	*kạr*, *kạ*^{i}*r*^{i}.
phikir$^{\ddot{u}}$	*fik*^{ə}*r*, *phikir*.
t^{a}*l*$^{\ddot{u}}$*r*$^{\ddot{u}}$	*tulạr*.
'*māch-t*^{a}*l*^{u}*r*$^{\ddot{u}}$	*māch tulạr*.
mür$^{\ddot{u}}$	*mạr*.
miñĕ-mür$^{\ddot{u}}$	*ming*^{e} *mạr*.
nür$^{\ddot{u}}$	*nur*.
tür$^{\ddot{u}}$	*tạr*.
tsūr$^{\ddot{u}}$	*tsūr*.
zīr$^{\ddot{u}}$	*zēr*, *z*^{y}*ēr*.
ös$^{\ddot{u}}$	*å̄s*.
phüṭ$^{\ddot{u}}$	*phut*.
rüṭ$^{\ddot{u}}$	*rạt*.
böts$^{\ddot{u}}$	*bạts*, *bå̄ts*.
dits$^{\ddot{u}}$	*dits*.
khüts$^{\ddot{u}}$	*khats*, *kạts*.
kits$^{\ddot{u}}$	*kits*.
köts$^{\ddot{u}}$	*kå̄ts*.
adālüts$^{\ddot{u}}$	*ạdālat*.

KAULA	STEIN
āmüts$^{\ddot{u}}$	*āmuts*.
gamüts$^{\ddot{u}}$	*gamuts*.
tsüj$^{\ddot{u}}$*müts*$^{\ddot{u}}$	*tsajmạts*, *tsajạmạts*.
hĕkmüts$^{\ddot{u}}$	*hekạmats*.
mumüts$^{\ddot{u}}$	*momuts*.
tshuñ$^{\ddot{u}}$*müts*$^{\ddot{u}}$	*tsuñye muts*.
wüñ$^{\ddot{u}}$*müts*$^{\ddot{u}}$	*vun*^{y}*muts*.
pĕmüts$^{\ddot{u}}$	*p*^{y}*imats*.
kür$^{\ddot{u}}$*müts*$^{\ddot{u}}$	*kạrmuts*, *kurmuts*.
parzanöv$^{\ddot{u}}$*müts*$^{\ddot{u}}$	*parzạ nå̄ụ̂ muts*.
tröv$^{\ddot{u}}$*müts*$^{\ddot{u}}$	*trau mûts*.
röts$^{\ddot{u}}$	*rå̄ts*.
wöts$^{\ddot{u}}$	*vạts*, *våts*.
yüts$^{\ddot{u}}$	*yits*^{ə}.
gōv$^{\ddot{u}}$	*gau*, *gaụ̂*, *gāụ̂*.
shĕstrüv$^{\ddot{u}}$	*shast*^{ə}*ro*.
būz$^{\ddot{u}}$	*bōz*.
hünz$^{\ddot{u}}$	*hạnz*, *hunz*.
gurĕn-hünz$^{\ddot{u}}$	*gur*^{y}*en-hạnz*.
yihünz$^{\ddot{u}}$	*yihas*.
sünz$^{\ddot{u}}$	*sạnz*, *sunz*, *sạnzüy*, *sünz*.
khāwanda-sünz$^{\ddot{u}}$	*kāvandạsunz*.
pātashāha-sünz$^{\ddot{u}}$	*pādshāh sạnz*, *pādshāhasạnz*.
pātashĕha-sünz$^{\ddot{u}}$	*pādshahạsạnz*, *pādshahạsunz*.
rājĕ-sünz$^{\ddot{u}}$	*rājạsạnz*, *rājạsunz*.
möl^{i}*-sünz*$^{\ddot{u}}$	*mạ*^{i}*l*^{i}*-sunz*, *mạ*^{i}*lisạnz*, *mạ*^{i}*lisunz*.
ȧm^{i}*-sünz*$^{\ddot{u}}$	*ạmisạnz*, *ạmisunz*.
gŏlāma-sünz$^{\ddot{u}}$	*gulāmạsạnz*.
tȧm^{i}*-sünz*$^{\ddot{u}}$	*ta*^{i}*misạnzüy*.
sŏna-sünz$^{\ddot{u}}$	*sunạsanz*.
phakīra-sünz$^{\ddot{u}}$	*fakīrạsạnz*, *fakīrạsunz*.

KAULA	STEIN
sŏnara-sünz^{ü}	*sunar sanz, sunarsanz.*
wŏrüz^{ü}	*vurudz.*
wuz^{ü}	*daj.*
nāyĕz^{ü}	*nāyiz.*

Words ending in *u*

KAULA	STEIN
gatshu	*gatsu.*
nu	*nu.*

Word ending in *ū*

KAULA	STEIN
saniyāsū	*sanyās^{a}.*

Words ending in *b*

KAULA	STEIN
āb	*āb.*
sabab	*sabab.*
dab	*dab.*
dŏb	*dob.*
göb	*gāb.*
khāb	*kāb, kāv.*
khūb	*khūb.*
söhib	*sāhib.*
wahab	*vahab.*
par wahab	*parvahab.*
mōjub	*mōjūb.*
phamb	*phamb, pamb.*
söb	*såb.*
tab	*tap.*
kitāb	*kitāb.*
jĕwāb	*javāb.*
sawāb	*savāb.*

Word ending in *c*

KAULA	STEIN
khar^{a}c	*kharj.*

Words ending in *d* or *ḍ*

KAULA	STEIN
had	*had^{a}.*
khŏḍ	*khoḍ.*
köd	*kād, kạd, kåd, kạ^{i}d.*
kākad	*kākad, kakạd.*
lad	*laḍ.*
jĕl^{a}d	*jal^{a}d.*
mad	*mad^{a}.*
hamud	*hamud.*
ahmad	*ahmạd.*
mahmad	*mahamad, muhammad.*
nād	*nād.*
and	*and.*
band	*band.*
ganḍ	*gand.*
shānd	*shānd.*
yārkand	*yārkand.*
pasand	*pasand, pasạnd*
khāwand	*khāvand, kāvand.*
dard	*dard.*
murād	*murād.*
vir^{i}d	*vir^{i}d.*
rasad	*rasat.*
wustād	*ustād, vustad, vustād.*
waḍ	*vaḍ.*
yād	*yād.*
nöyid	*nāyid.*
phår^{i}yād	*pharyād, pheryād.*
zad	*zad.*
zid	*zid.*
muhimzad	*mohim zad.*

Words ending in *g*

KAULA	STEIN
bāg	*bāg.*
bā̃g	*bāng.*
lāg	*lāg.*
mōv lāg	*maulāk.*
nāg	*nāg.*
palang	*palang, palạng, palaṅg.*
mang	*mang.*
prang	*prang.*
wutsha-prang	*vuts^{a}prang.*

KAULA	STEIN
zang	*zang.*
drāg	*drāg.*
yĕg	*yeg.*

Words ending in *h*

KAULA	STEIN
āh	*ah.*
bĕh	*be.*
bŏh	*bo, bu.*
marhabāh	*marhaba.*
subuh	*subu.*
hĕch	*hech.*
wuch	*vuch.*
dah	*da.*
dŏh	*do, doh.*
d^{ü}*h*	*dü.*
judāh	*zhudā.*
aj^{a}*dāh*	*ạzhda.*
sadāh	*sadau.*
wustādāh	*vustādạ.*
alvidāh	*al vida.*
yĕḍāh	*yerā.*
gāh	*ga, gā, gah.*
āgāh	*āga.*
bĕgāh	*begā.*
pagāh	*pag*^{a}*, pagā.*
hargāh	*har ga, har gā, hargā.*
shōra-gāh	*shōrạ ga, shōrạgā.*
hĕh	*h*^{v}*e.*
shūbihĕh	*shuybehe, shūybihe.*
chĕh	*shạ, che, chu.*
chih	*che, chi, chu, ch*^{v}*ạ.*
chīh	*chī.*
chuh	*che, chu, chuh.*
pātashĕhāh	*pādshāh.*
khĕh	*k*^{v}*e.*
akhāh	*akha.*
dādkhāh	*dād kha.*
shĕh	*she.*
shĕhan-shāh	*shāhạnshāh.*
pātashāh	*pādshah, pādshāh, pād*^{a}*shāh.*
pātashĕh	*pādshah, pādshāh, pād*^{a}*shāh.*
kuṭh^{u}*āh*	*kuṭha.*
rāthāh	*rātha.*
sāthāh	*sātha.*
sĕṭhāh	*setā, seṭā, sethā, seṭhā.*
kĕntshāh	*kh*^{v}*ē, kh*^{v}*ē tsa, khyē, khyē tsa, khyētsa, kēñ*^{v}*tsa, keñ*^{v}*tsā, kētsā, k*^{v}*ēntsa, k*^{v}*ētsa, k*^{v}*ētsā, k*^{v}*ẽ̄tsa, k*^{v}*ẽ̄tsā, kyē tsa, kyētsa.*
jāh	*ja, jā.*
akh	*ak, akh.*
ākh	*āk.*
kāh	*ka.*
kãh	*kah.*
kĕh	*khyē, k*^{v}*e, k*^{v}*ē, kyạ̄, kyē.*
kih	*kih.*
bēkh	*b*^{v}*ēk, byēk.*
labakh	*labak.*
sabakh	*sabak.*
dikh	*dik.*
kạḍikh	*kạ*^{i}*dik, karik, ka*^{i}*rik.*
küḍ^{u}*kh*	*kạduk.*
koḍukh	*kuruk.*
bandūkh	*bạndūk.*
sapadakh	*sapadạk.*
yīd^{i}*kāh*	*īdgāh.*
nazdīkh	*nazdīk.*

KAULA	STEIN
gōkh	*gåk.*
lagakh	*lagak.*
lagĕkh	*lagik.*
chĕkh	*chak, chek.*
chikh	*chuk.*
chukh	*chuk, chukạ.*
wuchakh	*vuchak.*
wuchikh	*vuchuk.*
wuchukh	*vuchuk, vucuk.*
wuchᵘ̈kh	*vuchuk.*
wuchⁱhakh	*vuch hak.*
katikō chukh	*kati kōchuk.*
khĕkh	*kyek.*
samokhukh	*samᵊ kukh.*
dimahakh	*dimᵊ hak.*
phakh	*phak.*
dopᵘhakh	*dop hak, dophak.*
karahakh	*karᵊ hak.*
korᵘhakh	*kur hak.*
karuhukh	*karᵘ huk.*
shĕkh	*shak, shōk.*
ạshᵉkh	*ạshik.*
pŏshākh	*poshāk.*
müṭhᵘkh	*motuk.*
wonᵘthakh	*vunthak.*
gatshakh	*gatsak.*
dȧpⁱzihĕkh	*dabzạ hek, dabzi hek.*
likh	*lekh.*
lōkh	*lōk.*
tasalī kĕh	*taslīkạ.*
tulukh	*tuluk.*
wŏlikh	*vālik.*
zôlukh	*zạluk, zåluk.*
makh	*mak.*
ditⁱmakh	*ditᵊmak.*
dapyāmakh	*dapᵛāmak.*
ankāh	*anka, ankā.*
ȧnikh	*anik, ạnik.*
anukh	*anuk.*
onukh	*ạnuk, unuk.*

KAULA	STEIN
chunakh	*chu nak.*
tshunukh	*tsunuk.*
shĕnākh	*shināk.*
dopᵘnakh	*dopᵘ nak, dopᵘnak, dopu nak, dopunak.*
kȧrⁱnakh	*kạⁱrinak.*
korᵘnakh	*kurnak.*
māranakh	*mārenak.*
rüṭᵘnakh	*rutᵊnak.*
dyutᵘnakh	*dyutᵊnak, dyutạnak, dyütᵘnak.*
tsônukh	*tsånuk.*
hôwᵘnakh	*håụ nak.*
thôwᵘnakh	*thåvnak.*
zānakh	*zānak.*
üñᵘkh	*ạñyik.*
kaññĕkh	*kanyek.*
wañĕnakh	*vañye nak.*
pākh	*pāk.*
dopukh	*dopuk.*
rakh	*rakh.*
bürᵘkh	*barᵊk, barạk.*
mŏbārakh	*mubārak.*
drākh	*drāk.*
shrākh	*shrāk.*
shĕrīkh	*sherīk.*
krēkh	*krạk, krēk, krēkh.*
karakh	*karak.*
karĕkh	*kạⁱrik, kaⁱrikh.*
kȧrikh	*kạrik.*
korukh	*kạruk, koruk, kuruk.*
kürᵘkh	*kạruk.*
porukh	*paḍuk.*
phuṭᵒrukh	*phutᵊruk.*
āsakh	*āsak.*
ôsukh	*åsuk, ōsuk.*

KAULA	STEIN
khasakh	*khasak.*
mushtākh	*mushtāk.*
wātakh	*vātak.*
dyutukh	*d^{v}üthuk,*
	d^{v}utuk,
	d^{v}ütuk,
	dyutuk.
hyotukh	*h^{v}ütuk.*
dits^{ü}kh	*ditsuk.*
thövikh	*thạvik.*
thöv^{ü}kh,	*thåvuk.*
milüv^{ü}kh	*mil^{e}vuk.*
trôwukh	*tråvuk.*
yĕkh	*yek.*
āyĕkh	*āyak.*
byākh	*b^{v}ēk, byāk.*
byēkh	*b^{v}ēk.*
bacyōkh	*bachōk.*
löyikh	*lāyak.*
lôyukh	*lâyuk.*
nyūkh	*nyūk.*
anyūkh	*ạnyūk.*
niyĕkh	*niyak.*
pĕyĕkh	*p^{v}eyak.*
h^{a}rēyĕkh	*h^{a}rēyek.*
karyūkh	*kạrūk.*
möryūkh	*mār^{v}ūk,*
	mā^{i}ryūk.
bōzakh	*bōzak.*
dizikh	*dīz^{v}ek.*
lazakh	*lazak.*
nīzīkh	*n^{v}ạzīk, n^{v}ēzik,*
	n^{v}ēzīk, nazdīk,
	nēzīk.
dȧp^{i}zĕkh	*dạbzik.*
sapüz^{ü}kh	*sap^{a}zạk.*
ạlāh	*ạlla, allạh.*
bulbulāh	*bulbula.*
luh-luh	*lolo, lōlō.*
kālāh	*kāla.*
salāh	*salā.*
sölāh	*sālạ.*
zālāh	*zālạ, zālā.*
shĕmāh	*shamā, shạmā.*
köm^{ü}āh	*kāma.*
tamāh	*tamā.*
mạti māh	*mạt^{i}ma.*
wumāh	*vuma.*
nōh	*nu.*
bīnāh	*bīnā.*
dānāh	*dānạ.*
gŏnāh	*guna* .
wuchunāh	*vuchuna.*
zanānāh	*zạnānạ.*
vig^{i}ñāh	*vigñya.*
daph	*dap.*
thaph	*tap, thap, thaph.*
shāph	*shāp.*
kuluph	*kulup.*
sar^{a}ph	*sạrp.*
yinsāph	*insāf, yin sāf.*
yūsūph	*yūsūf, yūsuf.*
tāph	*tāp.*
rāh	*ra.*
brōh	*brō.*
brūh	*broh.*
khabarāh	*kabara.*
brūh-brūh	*bro-bro.*
shĕharāh	*shehra.*
phakīrāh	*fakīra.*
phikirāh	*fik^{a}ra.*
trĕh	*tre.*
trih	*tre.*
vyūr^{u}āh	*yūra.*
nazarāh	*nazar.*
sŏh	*sạ, su.*
suh	*so, su.*
gāsh	*gāsh.*
hōsh	*hōsh.*
khash	*kash, pash.*
khŏsh	*khush, k͟hush.*
phāsh	*phāsh.*

KAULA	STEIN
yih suh	*yisu.*
nāsh	*nāsh.*
nish	*nish.*
öl^{i}-nāsh	*āl^{i}nāsh.*
manōsh	*manōsh.*
mĕ-nish	*m^{v}enish.*
pēsh	*pēsh.*
pharōsh	*pharōsh.*
trēsh	*trạ̄s, trēsh.*
wōsh	*vōsh.*
gwāsh	*ghāsh, gāsh.*
ta wōsh	*tavōsh.*
yīsāh	*īsā.*
bakh^{a}cōyish	*bakcāyish, bakhshāyish.*
ath	*at, at^{i}, ạt, ạt^{i}, ạ^{i}t^{i}, ath.*
öṭh	*åth.*
tih	*ti.*
böj^{i}-bath	*bå̄j^{e}vat.*
dith	*dit.*
kaḍith	*ka^{i}rit, kạ^{i}rit, ka^{i}rith.*
ganḍith	*ganḍit.*
wöridāth	*va^{i}r^{v} dāth.*
gath	*gat.*
lögith	*lāgit.*
shŏngith	*shungit.*
hath	*hat, hạt.*
hĕth	*het, hit, hitsạn, h^{v}et, h^{v}eth, h^{v}eṭh.*
bihith	*behit, bihit, bihith.*
khath	*khath.*
tāhkhīth	*tākhīt, tākīt.*
daskhath	*daskath.*
mạslahath	*muslạ hat, muslahat.*
nahīth	*nạhit.*
ziyāphath	*ziāfat.*

KAULA	STEIN
rahath	*rahat.*
mārahath	*mār^{e}hat.*
ḍīshith	*ḍēshit.*
mashith	*mạshit.*
mathith	*matit.*
wŏthith	*vuthit, vutit.*
ḍyūṭhuth	*ḍyūṭhut.*
kath	*kat, kath.*
kĕth	*k^{v}et, kyet, kh^{v}ạth, khyạth.*
akith	*ạ^{i}kith.*
kōtāh	*kōta.*
nŏktāh	*nukhta.*
sak^{a}th	*sak.*
pölith	*pạ̄^{i}lith.*
tulith	*tulit.*
wölith	*vålit.*
zölith	*zālit.*
math	*mat.*
yimāmath	*yimāmat.*
tāmath	*tāmat.*
yāmath	*yāmat.*
khazmath	*kismat.*
khizmath	*khismat.*
nūth	*n^{v}it.*
anith	*ạnit.*
bōnṭh	*bōnṭ.*
amānath	*amānat.*
brōnṭh	*brōnt.*
wanith	*vanit.*
zīnith	*z^{v}ēnith.*
wüñ^{ü}th	*vañyit.*
path	*pat, path.*
pĕṭh	*p^{v}et, p^{v}eṭ, pyet, pyeṭ, p^{v}eth, p^{v}eṭh.*
bāpath	*bāpat.*
hāpath	*hāpat.*
hāputh	*hāput.*
papith	*papit.*

KAULA	STEIN	KAULA	STEIN
rāth	*rāt, rāth.*	*wasith*	*vasit.*
rĕth	*rit, r^{v}eth.*	*söyīsth*	*sạ̄yist.*
raṭh	*rat.*	*tath*	*tat, tath, tạt^{v}.*
barith	*barit.*	*khaṭith*	*kạ^{i}ṭith.*
sọmb^{a}rith	*sumbrit.*	*raṭith*	*rạṭit, rạṭịt.*
khörāth	*khārāt.*	*mŏkh raṭith*	*mokrạṭịt.*
phirith	*phirit.*	*tsaṭith*	*tsạ^{i}ṭith.*
phīrith	*phērit, phīrit, phērith, phe^{i}rith.*	*wötith*	*vå̄tit, vạ̄^{i}tith.*
shīrith	*shērit.*	*daböviṭh*	*dạbāvit.*
watharith	*vatạ^{i}rith.*	*wath*	*vat, vath.*
karĕth	*ka^{i}rit.*	*wāṭh*	*vāṭ.*
karith	*karit, kạrit, ka^{i}rit, kạ^{i}rit, ka^{i}rith, kạ^{i}rith.*	*wŏth*	*vut.*
koruth	*kạrut, kurut.*	*wŏṭh*	*vut, vuṭ.*
marith	*mạrit.*	*hôwuth*	*hå̄vut.*
mārath	*mārat.*	*thāwath*	*thāvat.*
mörith	*mạ̄^{i}rit.*	*thôvuth*	*thå̄vut.*
nīrith	*nērit, nē^{i}rith.*	*wŏkavith*	*vok^{a}vit.*
prath	*prat.*	*sọmb^{a}rôwuth*	*sōmb^{a}rå̄vuth.*
pörith	*pạ̄^{i}rit.*	*tröviṭh*	*trå̄vit, trạ̄^{i}vit, trạ̄^{i}vith, trå̄^{i}vith.*
pūrith	*pạ̄^{i}rit.*	*tsāv ath*	*tsāvat.*
sörith	*sā^{i}rit.*	*yĕth*	*yat.*
sūrath	*sūrath.*	*yith*	*yat, yạt, yet, yath.*
khōbsūrath	*khå̄b surat, khōbsurat, khōb sūrat, khōbsūrat, khōb-sūrath.*	*tarbyĕth*	*tạrạ byat.*
mutsarith	*muts^{a}rit.*	*mashīyĕth*	*mashīyat.*
dŏh ta rāth	*dokht^{a}rāt.*	*zuryāth*	*zur yāt.*
sath	*sạt, sath.*	*nasīyĕth*	*nasīyat.*
sāth	*sāth.*	*nås^{i}yĕth*	*na^{i}s^{i}yat, na^{i}siyat.*
rukhsath	*rukhsat, rukhsath.*	*was yith*	*vasyat, vasyạt.*
kösith	*khāsit, khạ̄^{i}sith.*	*zāth*	*zāth.*
lāl sath	*lāl^{a}sat.*	*būzith*	*bōzit.*
phursath	*fursath.*	*būzuth*	*bōzuth.*
wasth	*vast.*	*munazāth*	*mun^{a} zāt.*
		dĕva-zāth	*dyav^{a}zāth.*
		ts^{a}h	*su, tsa, tsạ, tsi, tsu.*
		atsh	*ats.*
		gatsh	*gats, gats^{i}.*

KAULA	STEIN
shōtsh	*shūts.*
shĕkhtsāh	*sakhtsa.*
kĕntsāh	*k^yētsa.*
tsōratsh	*tsōrasta.*
vih	*v^ye.*
wŏh	*voh.*
dawāh	*dava, davā.*
dāwāh	*dāvā.*
hawāh	*havā.*
bēnawāh	*bē navā.*
siwāh	*siva.*
photuwāh	*photu va.*
nĕcyuvāh	*nichuva.*
yih	*ye, yi, yim, yiy.*
yuh	*yi.*
yüh	*yi, yü.*
töbʻyāh	*tạʻbya.*
khyuh	*khyau.*
ȧthʻ kyāh	*atʻkyā.*
kyāh	*k^yạ, kya, kyā, kyah.* Cf. *kyā.*
ȧsʻ kyāh	*asʻkya.*
wārayāh	*vārya, vāryạ.*
kötyāh	*kại t^ya, kạʻt^ya, kạʻtya.*
āyĕ yih	*āyiye.*
z^ah	*zạ, ze, z^yi.*
zāh	*za.*
hānzāh	*hånzạ.*

Words ending in *j*

KAULA	STEIN
bāj	*bāj^ạ, bājạ.*
khar^aj	*kharj, khar^ạj.*
māhrāj	*mah^arāj.*

Words ending in *l*

KAULA	STEIN
bulbul	*bulbul.*
dil	*dil.*
badal	*badal.*
gāl	*gāl.*
hāl	*hāl.*
bŏdʻhāl	*bāndʻhāl.*
phal	*phal.*
tsāṭahāl	*tsat^ạhāl, tsāt^ạhāl.*
jĕl	*jal.*
kāl	*kāl.*
shĕkal	*shakạl.*
lāl	*lāl, lāl^ạ, lal.*
alīl	*alīl.*
dalīl	*dalīl.*
zalīl	*zalīl.*
māl	*māl, māl^a.*
mŏl	*mul.*
lālmāl	*lāl māl.*
nāl	*nāl.*
pal	*pal.*
as^al	*asl, asạl.*
tal	*tal, thal.*
chĕh tal	*chetal.*
putal	*puṭal.*
wātal	*vātạl.*
mārawātal	*mārạvātal.*
tshāwul	*tsāvul.*
sawāl	*savāl.*
kuṭ^awāl	*kuṭvāl, kuṭ^ạvāl.*
pyāwal	*pyāv^ạlạ.*
azal	*azal, azạl.*

Words ending in *m*

KAULA	STEIN
ām	*ām.*
dim	*dim.*
ādam	*ādam.*
kadam	*kadam, kadạm.*
mukadam	*mukadam.*
sapodum	*sapạnum.*
yīdam	*īdam.*
gōm	*gōm.*
mangum	*mangum.*
chĕm	*chạm, chem.*
chim	*chim, chum ch^yum, chyum*
chum	*chum, chum^ạ, chum^u.*

KAULA	STEIN
larĕ chim	*larichim.*
lŏhlari chim	*lō larichim.*
wuchĕm	*vuchun.*
wuchim	*vuchun*
gōham	*gōhạm.*
lagaham	*lag^{a}ham.*
tagıhĕm	*tag^{y}ehạm.*
pātashĕham	*pādshahạm, pādshạhạm, pādshahạn.*
khām	*khām, kām.*
muhim	*mohim, muhim, muh^{y}im.*
dop^{u}ham	*dop ham.*
yibrāhim	*ibrāhim.*
môr^{u}ham	*mōrham.*
khashĕm	*khashim.*
ḍyūṭhum	*ḍyūṭhum.*
kür^{ü}tham	*k^{a}r tam.*
tsĕ kür^{ü}tham	*tsik^{a}r tam.*
gatshĕm	*gats^{y}em.*
kam	*kam.*
hakīm	*hakīm.*
hukum	*hukạm, hukm, hukum.*
mahkam	*mah kam, mahkam.*
lākam	*lākam.*
aslāmalaikum	*aslā malaikum.*
wālaikum	*vālai kum.*
ālam	*ālam.*
gŏlām	*gulām.*
halam	*halam.*
salām	*salām, sạlāmạ.*
zulm	*zulm.*
nam	*nam.*
nŏm	*nom.*
lod^{u}nam	*lud^{a}nam, lud^{a}nam, ludnam.*
gatshanam	*gatse nam.*
wālanam	*vāle nam.*
tsöñ^{ü}nam	*tsāny nam.*
dapanam	*dạpạnam.*
dop^{u}nam	*dopu nam.*
dör^{i}nam	*dạ̄^{i}ri nam.*
harĕnam	*ka^{i}ri nam.*
karinam	*kạrnam.*
kor^{u}nam	*kur nam, kur^u nam.*
tör^{i}nam	*tạ̄^{i}ri nam.*
tsàṭ^{i}nam	*tset^{i}nam.*
wanum	*vanum.*
hāwanam	*hāv^{a}nam.*
hôw^{u}nam	*haunam.*
thôw^{u}nam	*thāu̯nam.*
trôw^{u}nam	*traunam, trāunam, trāu̯nam.*
löy^{ü}nam	*lạ̄yinam.*
añām	*añyām.*
arām	*arām.*
bar^{a}m	*barạm.*
garam	*garm.*
mah^{a}ram	*mạh^{a}ram.*
karĕm	*kairim.*
kàrim	*karim, ka^{i}rim*
kür^{ü}m	*kạrüm.*
yikrām	*ikrām.*
narm	*narạm.*
kasam	*kasm, khasam, kasam.*
kas^{a}m	*kas^{a}m.*
āsim	*āsim.*
ôsum	*âsum.*
tam	*tam.*
tim	*tim, tim^i, tim^y.*
tum	*tum.*
ditam	*ditam.*
ditim	*ditim.*
bĕhtam	*beh tam.*
wuch^{i}tōm	*vuch tōm.*

KAULA	STEIN
khĕtam	*k^{y}e tam.*
hāvtam	*hāvtam.*
thāvtam	*thāu̯tam, thāv tam.*
yitam	*yitam.*
bōztam	*bōz tam.*
thāwum	*thāvum, tāvum.*
dop^{u}wam	*dopūm.*
wȧwim	*vavim.*
yim	*yim.*
āyām	*āyām.*
āyĕm	*āyem.*
diyūm	*dīyūm.*
gayĕm	*gayem.*
tshā̃jyām	*tsān^{y} jām.*
anyūm	*ạñyūm.*
banyōm	*ban^{y}â̄m.*
wanyūm	*vạn^{y}ūm.*
pyōm	*pyōm.*
pĕyĕm	*peyem.*
dapyām	*dap^{y}ām.*
dȧp^{i}zĕm	*dap^{a}zim.*

Words ending in *n*

KAULA	STEIN
an	*an.*
bŏn	*bun.*
bāban	*bāban.*
shūbān	*shōbān, shūbān.*
sōhiban	*sāhiban.*
lobun	*lobun.*
sōban	*sābạn.*
biyābān	*biyā bān.*
zabān	*zabān.*
kālacĕn	*kāl^{a}chen.*
racĕn	*rachen.*
dŏn	*don.*
dādĕn	*dāden.*
gaḍān	*garān.*
goḍun	*guḍun.*
tshāḍān	*tsārān.* Cf. *tshārān.*

KAULA	STEIN
kaḍan	*karạn.*
kaḍān	*kaḍān karān.*
kaḍōn	*korōn^{y}.*
kaḍun	*karun.*
koḍun	*koḍun, kuḍun, korun, kurun.*
küd^{u}n	*kạdin, kạdun.*
lodun	*lodun, ludun.*
mödān	*mādān, ma^{i}dān, maidān.*
gȧṇḍin	*gandin.*
gonḍun	*gundun.*
sandĕn	*sạndin, sạndyan.*
pātashĕha-sandĕn	*pādshahas sạndyan.*
tasandĕn	*tasạnden.*
gardan	*gardan.*
wadān	*vadān.*
nöyidan	*nāyidan, nạ^{i}ydan.*
zādan	*zādạn.*
pātashāhzādan	*pādshāh zādạn, pādshāhzādạn.*
lagān	*lagān.*
lôgun	*lå̄gun, lōgun.*
nāgan	*nāgan.*
nigīn	*nigīn.*
mangān	*mangān.*
pargan	*pargan.*
martsawā̃gan	*martsevāngan.*
zāgān	*zāgān.*
han	*han, hạn, hen.*
bahan	*bahan.*
bĕhān	*bihān.*
subhān	*subhān.*
sub^{a}han	*suban.*
chān	*chān, ch^{y}ān.*
achĕn	*achạn.*
lich^{u}n	*lichin.*
wuchān	*vuchān.*

KAULA	STEIN
wuchin	*vuchān.*
wuch^{ü}n	*vuchạn, vuchin, vucun.*
wuchun	*vuch^{u}n, vuchun, vucun, vucun^{a}.*
wuchahan	*vucehan.*
shĕhan	*shạhạn.*
pātashāhan	*pādshahạn.*
pātashĕhan	*pād^{i}shạhạn, pādshahan, pādshạhan, pādshahạn, pādshạhạn.*
ratshi-han	*ratsạ hạn.*
khān	*khān.*
khĕn	*khyen.*
ôkhun	*ākhun, åkhun.*
köd-khān	*kạd khān.*
likhan	*likhan.*
likhān	*lekhān.*
mahalakhān	*mahalạ kān, mah^{a}lạkhān.*
lyukhun	*likhun.*
musla-han	*musl^{a}han.*
k^{a}nahan	*kạn^{a}han.*
pinhān	*pin hām.*
pahān	*pahan, pahạn.*
taraphan	*tarfan.*
yūsūphan	*yusūfan.*
kār^{i}-han	*kạ^{i}d^{i}hen.*
nāra-han	*nār^{a}hạn.*
shĕn	*shen.*
ḍēshān	*dēshān.*
nishin	*nishạn, nishin, nisạn.*
nishīn	*nishīn.*
hamnishīn	*ham nishīn.*
athan	*athan.*
bata-han	*battạhạn.*
tshĕṭh han	*tsẹthan.*
kathan	*kathen.*

KAULA	STEIN
pöṭhin	*pāthin, pạtin.*
kār^{i}than	*kạ^{i}rtạn.*
ôs^{u}than	*ōstan.*
tshun	*tsün.*
gatshan	*gatsan.*
gatshān	*gatsān, gatsun.*
pryutshun	*prütsun.*
dawāhan	*davāhan.*
mŏkalāwahun	*muk^{a}lāvạ hun.*
jān	*jān.*
dujān	*dujān.*
rājĕn	*rājạn.*
tuj^{ü}n	*tuh jin, tujen, tujy^{e}n.*
kan	*kan.*
kun	*kōna, kun.*
ō-kun	*ōkun.*
path-kun	*pat^{a} kun, patkun.*
lĕkan	*lekan, l^{y}ekan.*
lōkan	*lōkan.*
mulkan	*mulken.*
makān	*makān.*
lā-makān	*lā makān.*
shĕnākan	*shinākan.*
pakān	*pakān.*
pakun	*pakun.*
mārakan	*mār^{a}kan.*
miskīn	*miskīn.*
cālān	*chālān chālānạ.*
ningalān	*ning^{a}lān.*
hĕlĕn	*helen.*
cholun	*cholun, chulun.*
phŏlān	*pholān.*
shōlān	*shōlan.*
mŏkalan	*muklan.*
lālan	*lālạn.*
malan	*malan.*
krālan	*krālan.*
tsrālĕn	*tsrālin.*

KAULA	STEIN
tulān	*tulān.*
tulin	*tulin.*
tulun	*tulun.*
putalĕn	*puṭalin.*
wātalan	*vāt^{a}lan, vāt^{a}laṇ.*
mārawātalan	*mār^{a}vāṭalan, mār^{a}vātelan, māraṿāt^{a}lan, māre vāt^{a}lan, māre vāt^{a}laṇ, mārevāt^{a}lan, mārevāṭalan.*
tsalān	*tsalān.*
walān	*valān.*
wālān	*vālān.*
wālun	*vālun.*
wolun	*vulun.*
kuṭ^{a}wālan	*koṭvālaṇ, kuṭvālen.*
mukadaman	*mukạ daman.*
gāman	*gāman.*
shāman	*shāman.*
lamān	*lamān.*
gŏlāman	*gulāman, gulāmaṇ.*
nŏman	*noman.*
armān	*armān.*
asmān	*asmān.*
sāmān	*sāmān.*
timan	*timan, timaṇ.*
yiman	*yiman, yimaṇ.*
sulaymān	*sulaimān.*
mizmān	*mēz^{a}mān.*
nīn	*nīñy.*
anān	*anān.*
anōn	*anōn.*
anun	*anun, ạnun.*
onun	*ạnun.*
banān	*banān.*
d^{a}nān	*dōnān.*
khānan	*kānaṇ.*

KAULA	STEIN
köd-khānan	*kādkhānen.*
nishīnan	*nishīnan, nishīnaṇ.*
hamnishīnan	*ham nishīnan, ham nishīnaṇ.*
tshanān	*ts^{a}nān.*
tshunun	*tsunun.*
k^{a}nan	*kạnan.*
k^{a}nān	*kạnān.*
asmānan	*as^{a}mānaṇ.*
lōnān	*lōnān.*
nanān	*nanān.*
pananĕn	*panenen, paneneñy, panen^{y}en.*
tiy nanān	*tīnanān.*
zanānan	*zạnānan, zạnānaṇ.*
panin	*pan^{y}en.*
shētānan	*shētānaṇ.*
wanan	*vanan, vanaṇ, vanān.*
wanān	*vanān.*
wanun	*vanun.*
wonun	*vunun.*
cyānĕn	*chān^{y}en, ch^{y}āñyen.*
myānĕn	*myānen.*
zānan	*zānan.*
zanĕn	*zanen, zan^{y}en.*
zēnan	*z^{y}ēnan.*
zēnān	*zēnān.*
üñ^{ü}n	*añyēn, ạnyin.*
tshuñ^{ü}n	*tsin^{y}an, tsiñyen.*
zañĕn	*zanyen.*
pān	*pān.*
dapān	*dapān, daṗān, dopān.*
dapun	*dapun.*
dopun	*dopun.*
borun	*borun, burun.*

KAULA	STEIN
sŏmb^{a}rān	*sumb^{a}rān.*
dūran	*dūran.*
gudarun	*gud^{a}run.*
töyiphdāran	*tạ^{i}fạdāraṇ.*
kārdāran	*kārdāran.*
garan	*garaṇ.*
bög^{a}rĕn	*bāg^{a}ren.*
sōdāgāran	*sōdāgaraṇ, sōdāgāraṇ.*
āhan-gārān	*ahengāraṇ.*
harān	*harān.*
khōran	*kuraṇ.*
phērān	*phērāṇ.*
ṭhaharān	*tah^{a}rān.*
wŏtharān	*vutherān, vuthạrān^{v}.*
tshārān	*tsārān.* Cf. *tshāḍān.*
mējĕran	*mējaran.*
karān	*karān.*
karĕn	*ka^{i}rin, kạ^{i}rin.*
kårin	*kạrin, ka^{i}rin.*
karun	*karun.*
korun	*kạrun, korun, kurun.*
kür^{ü}n	*karaṇ, karun, karün, kạraṇ, kạrun, ka^{i}rin, kạ^{i}rin, korun.*
phakīran	*fakīran, fakīraṇ.*
lārān	*lāḍān, lārān.*
marān	*marān.*
môrun	*mårun, mōrun.*
naran	*naraṇ.*
nērān	*nerān, nērān.*
nērun	*nērun.*
paran	*paran.*
parān	*paḍān, parān.*
pīran	*pīran.*
porun	*pạḍun.*

KAULA	STEIN
pör^{ü}n	*pạraṇ.*
pūrun	*pōrun, purun.*
prārān	*prārāṇ.*
srān	*srān.*
sārān	*sārān.*
misaran	*misren.*
trĕn	*tren.*
tārān	*tārān.*
katarān	*kat^{e}rān.*
pĕtarun	*pitarun.*
mutsarĕn	*muts^{a}rin.*
mutsorun	*muts^{a}run.*
jānāwāran	*janavāran.*
yāran	*yāraṇ.*
yīran	*yiran.*
yīrān	*īrān.*
guzarān	*guzrān.*
wazīran	*vazīran, vazīraṇ.*
sān	*sān.*
āsun	*āsun.*
khasān	*khasān.*
kôsun	*khåsun, khōsun.*
yinsān	*insān, yinsān.*
pō̃san	*pā̃san, pā̃saṇ.*
ös^{ü}san	*åsan.*
wasān	*vasān.*
tān	*tān.*
ditin	*dithin, dit^{a}nas.*
hatan	*hatan.*
pŏkhtan	*pukhtan.*
shētān	*shētān.*
bikarmājĕtan	*vikarmājitan.*
latan	*latan.*
pōtĕn	*pōt^{y}en.*
hāpatan	*hāpaṭan.*
rĕtan	*ritan.*
roṭun	*rotun, rutun.*
baritĕn	*bart^{y}en.*
satan	*satan, saṭan.*
sötin	*saitin, sạ̄^{i}tin, sạ̄itin.*

KAULA	STEIN
mastan	*mast.*
grēstĕn	*grēstʸen.*
nayistān	*nạyis tān, nạyis tānʸ.*
tōtan	*tōtan, tōtạn.*
wātān	*vātān.*
thāvtan	*thāvᵘtan.*
dyutun	*dʸüthun, dʸutun, dʸütun, dyutun, dyütun.*
hyotun	*hʸütun, hyütun.*
tsŏn	*tsun, tsuan.*
bātsan	*bātsan, bātsạn, bātsen.*
ditsᵘn	*ditsan, ditsạn, ditsun.*
hĕtsan	*hitsan.*
hĕtsᵘn	*hitsan, hitsạn, hitsun, hʸeten.*
shĕkhtsan	*shakhtsạn.*
pāntsan	*pāntsen.*
wan	*van.*
wān	*vān.*
bôwun	*bå̄vun.*
cĕwān	*chʸavān.*
nĕcivĕn	*nechᵃvin, nechevin.*
wŏranĕcivĕn	*vurạ nʸechᵃ vin.*
diwān	*divān.*
gōvᵘn	*gå̄vun.*
bāgwān	*bāgvān.*
hĕwān	*hʸevān.*
hôwun	*hå̄vun, hōvun.*
chāwān	*chāvān.*
chāwun	*chāvun.*
khĕwān	*khyavān, khyevān, kʸavān.*
thāwān	*thāvān.*
thôwun	*thå̄vun.*
lalawān	*lalạvān.*

KAULA	STEIN
banôwun	*banå̄vun.*
manganôwun	*maṅge nå̄vun.*
ḍakhanāwān	*dakhe nāvān.*
pakanāwān	*pakᵃnāvān.*
khananôwun	*khanenå̄vun.*
tshananövin	*tsạnạnāvin.*
garanāwān	*garạ nāvān.*
karanôwun	*karanå̄vun.*
karanövᵘn	*kar naviñy.*
wātanāwan	*vātᵃnāvan.*
wātanôwun	*vāte nō vun, vātᵃnå̄vun, vatạnå̄vun.*
wātanöwᵘn	*vå̄tạnāvun.*
wāna-wān	*vānᵃvān.*
parzanāwān	*parzenāvān.*
parzanôwun	*parze nå̄ vun, parze nå̄ụ vun.*
pāwun	*pāvun.*
pĕwān	*pʸevān, pʸivān.*
riwān	*rivān.*
trāwān	*trāvān.*
trôwun	*trāvun, trạvun, trå̄vun.*
trövᵘn	*trạvun.*
nôtuwān	*nōtᵘvān.*
wartāwān	*vartāvān.*
yiwān	*yivān.*
bāyĕn	*bāyen.*
biyĕn	*beyen.*
cĕyĕn	*chayen.*
khŏdāyĕn	*khudāyen.*
pātashöhiyĕn	*pādshahiyạn.*
khyōn	*khyå̄n, kyō̃n.*
tujyān	*tu jān.*
lāyān	*lāyān.*
löyin	*lāyin.*
löyᵘn	*lạyin.*
lôyun	*lạyun, lå̄yun.*
khālyūn	*khạ̄ⁱlyūn.*
wālyūn	*vālyūn.*

KAULA	STEIN
nyūn	*nyūn.*
niyūn	*nīyūn.*
pĕyin	*p^{y}iyen.*
möryūn	*mạ̄^{i}ryūn.*
phuṭ^{a}ryūn	*phuṭạ r^{y}ūn.*
zan	*zan.*
zān	*zān.*
zīn	*zīn.*
bōzan	*bōzan.*
bōzān	*bozān, bōzān.*
bōzun	*bōzun.*
būzun	*bōzun.*
dazān	*dazān.*
tirandāzan	*tīran dāzạn.*
lazan	*lazan.*
lüz^{ü}n	*lazun.*
nāzan	*nāzan.*
rōzan	*rōzan.*
rōzān	*rōzān.*
sūzun	*sōzun.*
thöv^{i}zĕn	*thạ̄ivzin.*

Words ending in *ñ*

KAULA	STEIN
āñ	*āñy.*
gŏḍañ	*guḍa^{i}ny, guḍeny, guḍeñy.*
kangañ	*kangạñ^{v}.*
kañ	*kan^{i}.*
kiñ	*kan^{i}.*
kākañ	*kākin^{v}.*
tāñ	*tāny^{e}, tāñy.*
kus-tāñ	*kustāny.*
ot^{u}-tāñ	*ottāñy, ot^{u}tāñy.*
yot^{u}-tāñ	*yuttāñy.*
yut^{u}-tāñ	*yutāñy.*
yotāñ	*yu tāñy.*
yutāñ	*yutāñy.*
wŏñ	*vu, vuny.*
wuñ	*vo, vu, vū, vun, vony, vun^{v}, vuny, voñy, vuñy.*
pānawöñ	*pane vạ̄^{i}n^{i}, pāne vān^{y}, pāne vāñy, pānevāñy, pane vāny.*
pānawüñ	*pānevāñy.*
katawañ	*katạ vạny.*
yāñ	*yāñy.*

Words ending in *r*

KAULA	STEIN
ār	*ār.*
bar	*bar.*
bār	*bār.*
gabar	*gab^{a}r, gabạr.*
khabar	*kabar, khab^{a}r, khabar, khabạr.*
bē-khabar	*bē khabar.*
ayālbār	*ayāl bār.*
nĕbar	*nebar, nebạr.*
barābar	*barābạr.*
darbār	*dạrbār.*
söbir	*sābir.*
töbīr	*tạ̄^{i}bīr.*
zabar	*zabar, zab^{a}r, zabạr.*
dar	*dar, dạr.*
dūr	*dūr.*
bĕdār	*bedār, bēdār.*
dīdār	*dīdār.*
bạh^{a}dūr	*bah^{a}dūr, bạh^{a}dūr.*
andar	*andar.*
bĕbi andar	*bebind^{a}r,*
nĕnd^{a}r	*nindạr.*
gar	*gar.*
gār	*gār.*
gör	*gār, gạ̄^{i}ri.*
agar	*agar.*
āgur	*āgur.*
parwardigār	*parvardigār.*
sōdāgar	*saudāgạr.*

KAULA	STEIN
sōdāgār	*saudāgar, saudāgār, sōdāgār, sodāgạr.*
lāgar	*lāgar.*
nān-gār	*nān gār.*
yĕngar	*yingar.*
zargar	*zargạr.*
bōz^{i}gār	*bāzi gār.*
har	*har.*
bahār	*bahār.*
shĕhar	*shahar.*
mashhūr	*maushūr.*
khar	*khar, kar.*
khŏr	*khur.*
khōr	*kār.*
mŏhar	*mohạr, mohur.*
pahar	*pahar, pahạr.*
kuphār	*kuphār.*
saphar	*safar.*
wöphīr	*vāphīr.*
shĕmshēr	*shamshēr.*
nēth^{a}r	*nēth^{a}r, n^{y}ētar.*
pathar	*pathar, patar, patạr.*
zahar	*zahạr, zehar.*
mējĕr	*mējạr.*
kar	*kar, kạr.*
kār	*kār.*
kōr	*kōr.*
bakār	*bakār.*
phakīr	*fakīr.*
lashkar	*lashkar.*
pēshkār	*pēshkār.*
kukar	*kukạr.*
nakār	*nakār.*
nōkar	*naukar, nāūkar.*
lār	*lār.*
mār	*mār.*
amār	*amār.*
bĕmār	*bimār, bīmār.*

KAULA	STEIN
khumār	*kumār.*
shĕhmār	*shahmār, shạhmār.*
shumār	*shumār.*
bĕ-shumār	*bē shumār, bēshumār.*
kashmīr	*kashmīr.*
nār	*nār.*
nēr	*nēr.*
sŏnar	*sunạr.*
zārapār	*zār^{a}pār, zārạ pār.*
wŏpar	*vupar.*
sar	*sar.*
asar	*asar.*
sār	*sār.*
sēr	*sēr.*
sīr	*sīr.*
sūr	*sūr.*
sangsār	*sang sār.*
takhsīr	*tahsīr.*
kusūr	*kosūr.*
misar	*misạr.*
samsār	*samsār.*
tōr	*tōr^{i}.*
abtar	*ābtạr.*
khötir	*khātir.*
tsēr	*tsēr.*
tsōr	*tsōr.*
tsūr	*tsūr.*
vir	*vir.*
bāwar	*bāvar.*
wumĕdwār	*vumedvār.*
jānāwār	*jān^{a}vār, jānạvār.*
sawār	*savār.*
baktāwār	*bakhtāvār.*
zōrāwār	*zōrāvār.*
yār	*yār, yār^{a}.*
yōr	*yōr.*
dyār	*dyār.*

KAULA	STEIN
hushyār	*hushār.*
tayār	*taiyār.*
zār	*zār.*
zōr	*zōr.*
bāzar	*bāzar.*
nazar	*naz^{a}r, nazar, nazạr.*
mônzur	*mā̊nzūr.*
wazīr	*vazīr.*

Words ending in *s*

KAULA	STEIN
ās	*ās, ā̊s.*
ābas	*ābas.*
dŏbas	*dobas.*
khābas	*kābus.*
söbas	*sābạs.*
dis	*disạ.*
badis	*bạdịs.*
dödis	*dạ^{i}dis.*
khŏḍas	*khuḍas.*
ködis	*kạ^{i}dis.*
kākadas	*kākadas.*
maḍis	*moḍis.*
andas	*andas.*
cĕndas	*chandạs.*
handis	*hạndis.*
sandis	*sandis, sạndis.*
pātashĕha-sandis	*pādshah^{a}sạndis.*
khāwandas	*khāv^{a}ndas, khāvạndas, kāvandas, kāvandạs, kāvạndas.*
zādas	*zādas, zādạs.*
shāhzādas	*shahzādạs.*
pātashāhzādas	*pādshāh zādạs.*
gōs	*gā̊s, gōs.*
gös	*gās, gạ̄s, gā̊s.*
āgas	*āgạ̄s.*
bāgas	*bāgas, bāgạs.*
nāgas	*nāgas, nāgạs.*
palangas	*palangas, palạngas, palaṅgas.*
tēgas	*t^{y}ēgas.*
togus	*togus.*
hĕs	*hạs.*
sub^{a}has	*subhas.*
chĕs	*chạs, ches.*
chis	*chạs, chis, chus.*
chus	*chus.*
yih chus	*yichus.*
yim chis	*yimchis.*
wŏñ chus	*vuchus.*
khŏra chĕs	*khurachạs.*
wuchus	*vuchus.*
dŏhas	*dohas.*
ạj^{a}dāhas	*ạzhdạhas.*
sōdāhas	*sōdahas, sōdahạs.*
mangahas	*mangạ has.*
hihis	*hihis.*
lyukh^{u}has	*l^{y}ükhas.*
pātashāhas	*pādshahạs, pādshāhạs.*
pātashĕhas	*pādshahas, pādshahạs, pādshāhạs, pādshạhas, pādshahis, pād^{i}shạhạs.*
khas	*khas.*
murkhas	*murkhas.*
lyukhus	*l^{y}ükhas.*
on^{u}has	*ạnhas.*
tshun^{u}has	*tsun has.*
añĕhas	*añye has.*
dop^{u}has	*dop has, dophas, duphas, dop^{u}has.*
yūsūphas	*yusūfas, yūsufas.*
kor^{u}has	*kurhas, kur has.*

KAULA	STEIN
phuṭ^{o}r^{u}has	phuṭ^{ə}rhas.
tamāshĕs	tamāshạs.
manōshĕs	manoshas.
athas	athas, atas.
baṭhis	ba^{i}ṭhis.
kuṭhis	kuṭhis, kuṭis, kuṭis.
üñ^{ü}thas	añythas.
kor^{u}thas	kur thas.
môr^{u}thas	mōr thas.
wọ̈thus	vothus, vuthus, votus.
byūṭhus	b^{y}uthus.
ziṭhis	z^{y}ithis.
diṭs^{ü}has	diṭs^{ə} has.
gaṭshĕs	gaṭsạs, gaṭses, gaṭs^{y}es, gaṭsyes.
wọ̈ṭsh^{ü}s	vuṭsạs, vuṭsus.
wüṭsh^{ü}s	vaṭsās.
trôw^{u}has	trāụ has, trâvhas.
lôy^{u}has	lōy^{ə}has.
nyūhas	nyū has.
dun^{i}yāhas	duny^{i}has, du^{i}n^{i}has.
wārayāhas	vāryahạs.
lüj^{ü}s	lajis.
rājĕs	rājas, rājạs.
kās	kās.
kus	kus.
akis	akis, ạkis.
kŏmbakas	khumba khas.
sabakas	sabakas, sabạkas.
ḍākas	ḍākas.
pŏshākas	poshākas, pushākas.
malikas	mal^{i}kas.
shĕnākas	shinākas.
carkas	char kas, charkas.
shĕharakis	sheharạkis.

KAULA	STEIN
ṭōkis	ṭạ^{i}kis, ṭạkis.
yitikis	yeti kis.
dōzakas	dōzakas.
ölis	å̄lis.
yiblīs	yib^{ə}līs.
dilas	dilas.
khalas	kalạs.
khalās	khalās.
lālas	lālas.
mölis	mạ^{i}lis, mạ^{i}lyis.
nālas	nālas.
palas	palas.
pyālas	pyālạs.
sālas	sālas.
sölas	sālạs, så̄lạs.
muslas	mus^{ə}las.
paharawölis	pah^{ə}rạ vālis.
zālas	zālas, zālạs.
mas	mas.
amis	amis, ạmis, ạmis suy, a^{i}mis, ạ^{i}mis.
ādamas	ād^{ə}mas.
pĕmōs	p^{y}imōs.
shikamas	shikmas.
gŏlāmas	gulāmạs.
halamas	hal^{ə} mas, hal^{ə}mas, halamas.
nĕmis	nạmis, n^{y}emis.
arāmas	arāmas.
ṭsūrimis	ṭsūrimis.
tamis	tạm^{i} suy, tạmis, ta^{i}mis.
satimis	satyạmis.
yimis	yạmis, yemis.
dŏyimis	duyạmis.
löy^{i}mas	lạ̄y^{ə}mas.
trĕyimis	treyimis.
badanas	badanạs, badạnas.

KAULA	STEIN
kȧḍ^{i}nas	*kaṛ^{y}inas.*
koḍ^{u}nas	*kuraṇas.*
mödānas	*maidānas,*
	maidāṇas,
	mạ̄^{i}dānas.
nādānas	*nā dānas.*
gonḍ^{u}nas	*gund^{a}nas.*
gānas	*gānas, gāṇas.*
hūnis	*hūnis.*
sub^{a}hanas	*subahanas.*
chānas	*ch^{y}āṇas.*
khānas	*khānas, kānas.*
lyukh^{u}nas	*l^{y}ükh^{a}nas,*
	l^{y}ükhunas.
göj^{ü}nas	*gạ̄j^{a}nas.*
khöj^{ü}nas	*khạ̄j^{i}nas.*
kanas	*kanas.*
khôl^{u}nas	*kōlnas.*
tul^{i}nas	*tulinas.*
tul^{u}nas	*tul^{u}nas.*
dāmānas	*dāmānas.*
tshun^{u}nas	*tsun^{a}nas,*
	tsununas,
	tsunuṇas.
pananis	*panaṇas,*
	panaṇis,
	panenis.
won^{u}nas	*vununas.*
pānas	*pānai, pānas,*
	pāṇas, pānes.
dop^{u}nas	*dop^{u} nas,*
	dop^{u}nas,
	dop^{u}ṇas,
	dopunas,
	dopuṇas.
trop^{u}nas	*trop^{u}nas,*
	trup^{a}nas.
karĕnas	*ka^{i}rinas.*
kȧr^{i}nas	*karinas.*
kor^{u}nas	*kur^{a}nas,*
	kuraṇas,
	kurnas,
	kür^{a}nas.

KAULA	STEIN
kür^{ü}nas	*kaṛ nas, kar^{a}nas,*
	kaṛ^{a}nas,
	kaṛ^{a}nas,
	kaṛ^{a}ṇas,
	kaṛnas,
	kur^{a}nas,
	kür^{a}nas.
māranas	*māraṇas.*
srānas	*srānas.*
āsanas	*ās^{a}nas, ās^{i}nas.*
ôs^{u}nas	*å̄s nas.*
kôs^{u}nas	*khå̄s^{a}nas.*
bŏṭanis	*buṭṭaṇis.*
dit^{i}nas	*ditinas.*
nayistānas	*naẏis tāṇas.*
tsaṭanas	*tsatanas.*
dyut^{u}nas	*dyüth^{u}nas,*
	d^{y}üt^{u}nas,
	dyuṭ^{a}nas,
	dyutaṇas,
	dyutaṇaṣ,
	dyut^{u}nas,
	dyüt^{u}nas.
ditsünas	*ditsaṇas.*
hĕtsanas	*hitsaṇas.*
hĕ̆ts^{ü}nas	*hitsanas.*
wanas	*vanas.*
wonus	*vonus.*
thȧv^{i}nas	*thāu̯ nas.*
thow^{u}nas	*thōu̯nas.*
thôw^{u}nas	*thāu̯nas,*
	thå̄u̯ nas.
thüv^{ü}nas	*thāu̯nas,*
	thå̄u̯ nas.
mŏkalôw^{u}nas	*muk^{a}lå̄u̯ nas.*
cyönis	*ch^{y}ānis.*
lāyānas	*lāyānas.*
lôy^{u}nas	*lạ̄y^{a}nas.*
löy^{ü}nas	*lạ̄^{i}yinas.*

KAULA	STEIN
myönis	*mē^{i}nis, m^{y}ēnis, m^{y}ē^{i}nis.*
zinis	*zinas, zinis.*
būz^{u}nas	*bōzus.*
görzānas	*gārzānas.*
lüz^{ü}nas	*laz^{a}nas, lazạnas.*
sapañĕs	*sap^{a}ñyes.*
dapas	*dapas.*
dapus	*dapus.*
dopus	*dopus, dopusạ.*
drās	*drās.*
ḍēras	*ḍēras, ḍērạs.*
garas	*garạs.*
guris	*guris.*
sōdāgaras	*saudāgārạs.*
sōdāgāras	*saudāgārạs, sōdāgārạs.*
grīst^{i}-garas	*grēst garạs, grēstạ garạs.*
shĕharas	*shahras, shah^{a}ras, shahạras, sheh^{a}ras, shehạras.*
kharas	*kharas.*
khöris	*khāris.*
sapharas	*saf^{a}ras, safạras.*
mējĕras	*mējạras, mējeras.*
karas	*karạs.*
karis	*ka^{i}ris.*
karōs	*karōs.*
karus	*karus.*
korus	*kurus.*
kür^{ü}s	*kạris.*
phakīras	*fakiras, fakīras, fakīrạs.*
shikāras	*shikārạs.*
löris	*lāris.*
maris	*mạris.*

KAULA	STEIN
shĕhmāras	*shah mārạs, shạhmārạs.*
nāras	*nārạs.*
sŏnaras	*sunạras.*
sīras	*sīras, sīrạs.*
sūras	*sūras.*
samsāras	*samsāras.*
apsaras	*afsạrạs.*
yāras	*yāras, yārạs.*
phyūrus	*ph^{y}ūrus. p^{y}ūrus.*
wazīras	*vazīras, vazīrạs.*
ôsus	*ā̊s, ā̊sus.*
ösis	*åsis.*
ös^{ü}s	*ạshis, ā̊sus.*
dāsas	*dāsas.*
kôsus	*khōsus.*
saniyāsas	*sạnyāsas.*
tas	*tas.*
hatas	*hathas, hatạs.*
hatis	*hatis.*
khätis	*kạtis.*
matis	*mạtis.*
mumatis	*mom^{a}tis.*
natis	*nạtis.*
jĕnatas	*jan^{a} tas, jan^{a}tas, janatas.*
hāpatas	*hāpạtas.*
rātas	*rātas, rātạs.*
rĕtas	*ritas.*
kär^{i}tōs	*kạr^{i} tōs.*
tratis	*trạtis.*
tōtas	*tōtas, tōtạs.*
khot^{u} tas	*khutas.*
nata tas	*natatas.*
tsātas	*tsatạs.*
wôtus	*vōtus.*
dyutus	*dyutus.*
hyotus	*h^{y}ütus.*
dits^{ü}s	*dithas.*

KAULA	STEIN
naphtsas	*naptsas.*
wöts^{ü}s	*vạ̄tsus, vå̄tsus.*
tsās	*p^{y}ēz.*
shĕkhtsas	*shakhtsas.*
rātsas	*rātsạs.*
vĕs	*vis.*
nĕcivis	*n^{y}ech^{a}vis.*
hôwus	*hå̄vus.*
thāwus	*thāvus.*
parzanôwus	*parzạnāvus.*
wör^{i}vis	*vạ̄r^{a}vis.*
yĕs	*yas.*
yus	*yis, yus, yüs.*
āyĕs	*āyạs, āyes.*
biyis	*beyes, beyis, biyạs.*
böyis	*bạ̄yis.*
buḍyōs	*buḍ^{i} å̄s.*
khŏdāyĕs	*khudāyạs.*
gayĕs	*gayạs.*
lāyus	*lāyus.*
saniyās	*sạnnyās, sạnyās, sanyās.*
pyōs	*p^{y}ōs, pyå̄s, pyōs.*
pĕyĕs	*p^{y}eyes.*
rŏpayĕs	*rupias, rupiạs.*
drāyĕs	*drạ̄yas.*
lāḍyēyĕs	*lāḍēyes.*
tsajyēyĕs	*tsajēs.*
suy yĕs	*suyyas.*
suy yus	*suyyus.*
gånḍ^{i}zĕs	*ganḍ^{i} zyes.*
måṅg^{i}zĕs	*mạ^{i}n^{y}g^{a}zạs.*
māzas	*māzas.*
pözas	*pạ̄zus.*
wuz^{ü}s	*dạjis.*

Words ending in *t* or *ṭ*

KAULA	STEIN
mast	*mast.*
rapaṭ	*rapạṭ.*
phōrsaṭ	*fōrsat.*

Word ending in *ts*

KAULA	STEIN
pānts	*pānts, pānz.*

Words ending in *v*

KAULA	STEIN
āv	*āv, āu̯.*
dĕv	*dyau.*
gav	*gau, gau̯, gāu, gāu̯.*
sår^{i}gav	*sạr^{i}gau.*
hav	*hau.*
hāv	*hāu̯.*
bĕhiv	*bihu.*
khĕv	*khyāu.*
thāv	*thāu̯.*
gatshav	*gatsau.*
gatshiv	*gats^{y}u, gatsyu.*
jāv	*jāo.*
malakav	*mal^{i}kau.*
pakiv	*pakyu.*
ālav	*ālau.*
pŏlāv	*polāu̯, pulāu̯.*
tsaliv	*tsalau, tsal^{y}u, tsạl^{y}u.*
wālav	*vālau.*
dimav	*dimau.*
nimav	*n^{y}emau.*
nŏmav	*nomau.*
karĕmav	*karimau.*
timav	*timau, yimau.*
yimav	*yimau.* Cf. *yimau.*
yimōv	*yimau.*
nāv	*nāu̯, nāv.*
nĕv	*nyu.*
baniv	*bañyau.*
āsh^{i}nāv	*å̄shnāu̯, āsh^{i}nāv, å̄s^{i} nāv.*
asmānav	*asmānau.*
zamīnav	*zemīnau.*
waniv	*vạnyu, vañyu.*

KAULA	STEIN
zanĕv	zạ^{i}nyau.
zānav	zānau.
pĕv	pyau.
bārav	bārau.
drāv	drāu̯.
gudariv	gud^{a}ryau.
khabardārav	kabar dārau, kabardārau, khabạr dārau, khābạrdārau.
khārav	kārau.
shērav	shērau.
tshārav	tsārau.
khrāv	krāu̯.
karav	karau.
kariv	ka^{i}r^{y}u.
phakīrav	fakīrau.
nērav	nērau.
nīriv	nēru, nēr^{y}ū, nēryū, nē^{i}ryu.
pīrav	pīrau.
trāv	trāu̯.
tsōrav	tsorau, tsōrau.
tsūrav	tsūrau. Cf. tsūrau.
wasiv	vas^{y}u, vasyu.
tāv	thāu̯.
vuch^{i}tav	vuch tuv̯.
wȧn^{i}tav	van^{i}tō, vạn^{i} tōv̯.
satav	satau.
tsāv	tsāu̯, tsāv.
wātsāv	vātsau.
thȧv^{i}tav	tạivtau.
trȫv^{i}tav	trạv^{i}toh.
būz^{i}tav	bōz tuv̯.
rūz^{i}tav	rōz^{i} tuv̯.
thȫviv	thạ̄^{i}vyu.
nawav	navau.
phaharawāv	pahre vāv.
diyiv	diyu, dīyu.
dŏyav	doyau.

KAULA	STEIN
lāḍyāv	lạ̄^{i}ḍyau.
gayāv	gayau.
khyauv	khyau.
khĕyĕv	kheyau.
tujyāv	tu jāu̯.
ṭahalyav	ṭạhạlyau.
mŏkalyāv	muk^{a}lyau.
namyōv	nam^{y}au.
nyūv	nyū.
banyāv	banyāu̯.
banyōv	banāu.
pyauv	pyau.
dapyāv	dapyau.
mŏdaryiv	mudr^{y}au.
h^{a}ryōv	h^{a}r^{y}au.
lāryāv	lạ̄^{i}ryau.
prāryāv	prạ̄^{i}ryau.
trȫvyuv	trạ̄vyu.
zuv	zu.
bāzav	bāzau.
nazarbāzav	naz^{a}r bāzau, nazạr bāzau.

Words ending in *y*

KAULA	STEIN
ay	ai.
āy	āi̯, āy.
ạy	ai, ại.
ôy	ạ̄y, å̄y.
bāy	bai, bāi, bāy.
bŏy	buy.
grīst^{i}-bāy	grēst bāy, grēst^{a} bāy.
dŏy	duy.
buday	budai.
ah^{a}day	ah^{a}dai.
khŏdāy	khudā, khudai.
dȫd^{i}laday	dạ̄^{i}d^{ye} ladai.
zinday	zindai.
wāday	vādai.
jyāday	zhāday.
pyāday	pyāday.

KAULA	STEIN
gay	*gai, goi.*
dagāy	*dagāi, dagāye, dagạ̄y.*
mangay	*mangai.*
tagiy	*tagi, tạgi.*
hay	*hai.*
hāy	*hāy.*
chĕy	*chai, che, chi, chạy, chạ̄y, chiy.*
chiy	*chi, chiy, chüy.*
chuy	*chi, chī, chu, chi^{v}, chiy, cüy.*
hargāh-ay	*hargạ hạy.*
khĕy	*kh^{v}aiy.*
tim-hay	*tim hai, tim hay.*
ȧn^{i}hay	*ạn^{v}hai.*
kor^{u}hay	*kur hai.*
kür^{ü}hay	*kạrhai.*
warihy	*vạ^{i}ri.*
mot^{u} hay	*muthai.*
tithạy	*tithai.*
tithiy	*tīth^{i}.*
wŏthiy	*vu^{i}thī.*
yithay	*ithai.*
yuthuy	*h^{v}üthuy, yüthuy.*
tyuthuy	*tithuy, tüthuy, t^{v}uthuy, tyutuy.*
gatshiy	*gatse, gatsi^{v}, gatsiy.*
wütsh^{ü}y	*vatsạ̄yạs.*
manganöv^{i}hay	*mangạ nāv^{i}hai.*
yihōy	*yạhoi.*
yihuy	*yohoi, yi hạ̄y, yohạ̄y, yühoi.*
yŏhay	*yohoi.*
yuhay	*yohoi.*
yuhuy	*yühạy.*
jāy	*jāi, jāy.*
mājiy	*mā^{i}ji, mạ̄^{i}jiy.*
rājy	*rāj.*
kiy	*k^{v}ēy, kyēy.*
okuy	*akoy.*
ük^{ü}y	*akạy.*
hargāh-kiy	*har^{a}gāk^{v}ēy.*
gŏḍañukuy	*guḍ nyukuy.*
tamyukuy	*tam^{i} kuy.*
lāy	*lāy.*
balāy	*balai.*
balạy	*balai.*
sŏdurabalạy	*sudạr balai.*
jĕlŏy	*yalạ vai.*
kŏlay	*kulai.*
mŏkȧliy	*moklai.*
salay	*salai.*
hawāla-y	*havālạ^{v}.*
may	*mai.*
amiy	*ami.*
ȧmiy	*am^{i}.*
dimay	*dimai.*
dimōy	*dimoı.*
log^{u}m^{ü}y	*log^{a}mai.*
hĕmay	*himai.*
ladaham-ay	*lade hamai.*
khĕmay	*k^{v}emai, k^{v}emāy.*
ḍyūth^{u}may	*dyōt mai.*
dālomuy	*dāle muy.*
wȧn^{i}may	*van^{u}mai.*
won^{u}may	*vunmai.*
bög^{a}rēmay	*bāge rēmai.*
tamiy	*tam^{i}, tami, ta^{i}m^{i}, ta^{i}mi.*
tȧmiy	*tạm^{i}.*
timay	*timai.*
timạy	*timai.*
yimay	*yimai.*
yimōy	*yimōy.*
gay^{ĕ}mạy	*gai mạ.*

KAULA	STEIN
nay	nai, nāi, nay, nāye.
niy	niy.
bŏ-nay	bunai.
yith-nay	yit^{a}nai.
gatshanay	gats^{a}nai.
kunuy	kunuy.
pakanay	pakenai.
wālanay	vāle nai.
timan^{ü}y	tim^{a} nai, timạnai.
yiman^{ü}y	yim^{a}nuy, yimạniy.
ananay	anạnai.
kananạy	kanạnuy.
nonuy	nunnuy.
panunuy	panenuy, panunuy.
zalānay	zạnānai.
zanānay	zạnānai.
pānay	pānai.
dapanay	dap^{a}nai.
dop^{u}nay	dop^{u}nai.
kor^{u}nay	kur nay^{i}.
sa nay	sạnai.
sônuy	sōnuy.
kāsunuy	kās^{a}nuy.
zāsanuy	zās^{a}nuy.
dyutun^{ü}y	dyutanay.
wanay	vanai, vanāi.
waniy	vanē.
hôw^{u}nay	haūnai, hâunai.
wālawunuy	vāle vunuy.
trôw^{u}nay	trå̄u nai, trå̄unai.
wātawunuy	vāt^{a} vunuy.
atsawunuy	ats^{a}vunuy.
yinay	yinai.
byonuy	b^{v}ünuy.
cyônuy	chōnuy.
myônuy	myō nuy.

KAULA	STEIN
añĕy	añyai.
gŏḍañiy	guḍen^{v}i, guḍeñy, guḍeñyi, guḍeñyī.
kuñ^{ü}y	ku^{i}niy.
otāñy	ạtāñy.
wuñ^{ü}y	vun^{v}ai.
myöñ^{ü}y	myeñyīy.
pay	pai.
pāy	pāy.
dapay	dapai, dapāi.
dapiy	dạ^{i}p^{i}y.
dopuy	dopuy.
rāy	rāy.
baray	bare^{v}.
drāy	drāy, drạy.
driy	driy.
bĕbi andar^{ü}y	bebindạ^{i}r^{i}.
grāy	grāy.
karay	karai, kare^{v}.
koruy	kuruy.
kōriy	kūḍ^{v}i.
maray	marai.
tsĕ māriy	tsimạ̄^{i}ri.
susarāray	sus^{a} rārai.
sôruy	sạruy, så̄ruy, sō^{i}ri, soirạ.
söriy	sạ̄^{i}rē, sạ̄^{i}ri.
mutsaray	muts^{a}rai.
say	sạ̄i, sạy, sạ̄y, sai.
sŏy	sai.
suy	su, suy.
āsiy	å̄si.
ös^{ü}y	å̄s suy.
gōsay	gōsai.
khasiy	khasī.
chĕsay	che sai, chesai.
chusay	chusai.
kusuy	kusuy.
musāy	musāi.

KAULA	STEIN
amis^{ü}y	*am^{i} suy, ami süy, ạm^{i} sạy, ạm^{i} süy, ạmi suy, a^{i}mi suy.*
tamis^{ü}y	*tạm^{i} süy, tạm^{i}süy.*
pānas^{ü}y	*pāne suy.*
wasiy	*vasīy.*
tay	*tai, tạ̄i, tạ̄y.*
tiy	*ti, tī, t^{v}ey.*
atiy	*at^{i}, atih.*
ȧtiy	*ạt^{i}.*
otuy	*ạtuy, otuy.*
ditay	*dithai.*
hatay	*hatai.*
mŏktay	*muht^{av}.*
patay	*patai.*
sātay	*sāthai.*
söty	*sạ̄it, sā^{i}th, sạ̄^{i}th, sạ̄^{i}th^{i}, sạ̄^{i}th^{v}, sạ̄t^{v}.*
sötiy	*sạ̄^{i}th^{i}, sạ̄^{i}thi, sạ̄^{i}thī.*
tatiy	*tat^{i}.*
ataty	*atạt^{v}.*
yitay	*yi tai.*
yutuy	*yütuy.*
ts^{a}y	*tsüy.*
tsāy	*tsāi̯.*
hāway	*hāvai.*
chiway	*chu vai, chu voi.*
thāway	*thāvai.*
yimav^{ü}y	*yim^{a} vuy.*
dŏnaway	*don^{a} vai, don^{u}vai, donovai, dunuvai.*
trĕnaway	*trin^{a} vai.*
trāviy	*trạ̄viy.*
trôwuy	*trå̄vuy.*
yiy	*yi, yih, yi^{v}, yey, yiy.*
yīy	*yiy.*
diyiy	*diyiy.*
chĕyĕy	*chiyai.*
wanayĕy	*vanạ yey.*
sakharyēy	*sakhr^{v}ai.*
kūr^{i}yĕy	*kūḍye.*
vis^{i}yiy	*visyạ̄i.*
yiyiy	*yeyiy, yiyiy, p^{v}eyiy.*
pozuy	*puzuy.*

Words ending in *z*

KAULA	STEIN
az	*az.*
bōz	*bōz.*
bandūkbāz	*bạndūk bāz.*
cīz	*chīz.*
tīrandāz	*tīran dāz.*
kākaz	*kākad.*
māz	*māz.*
kunz	*kunz.*
manz	*manz.*
shranz	*shrānz.*
pöz	*pạ̄z.*
raz	*raz.*
wāz	*vāz.*
özīz	*âzīz.*

ADDENDA ET CORRIGENDA

PAGE

xxix, last line of text. For "Wahāb", read "Wahb".

110, l 11. Read **gör-zānas.**

151, l. 15. Read **dukhtar-ĕ-khāsa.**

271, l. 17. For **thôwun,** read **thöv^{ü}n.**

308, l. 25. Read *grēstĕn.*

313, l. 5. For "viii, 4, 10, 1", read "viii, 4, 10", and in line 10, for "v, 4.", read "v, 4; viii, 11".

449, col. b, l. 19. For *kạ̄ⁱ tʸa,* read *kạ̄i tʸa.*

450, col. b, l. 6. For *khētam,* read *khĕtam.*

466, col. b, l. 17 from foot. For *shākh,* read *shākha.*